The Encyclopedia of Duke Basketball

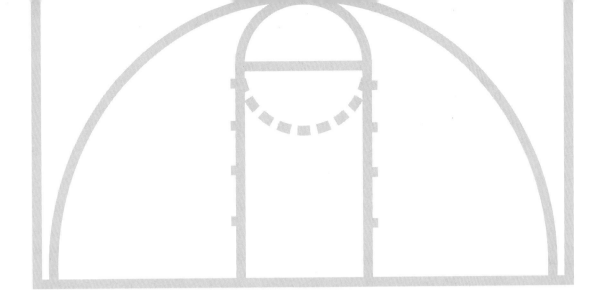

The Encyclopedia of
DUKE
BASKETBALL

John Roth

WITH PHOTOGRAPHS BY NED HINSHAW

DUKE UNIVERSITY PRESS | DURHAM AND LONDON | 2006

© 2006 Duke University Press

All rights reserved.

Printed in the United States of America on acid-free paper ∞

Designed by April Leidig-Higgins
Typeset in Minion by Copperline Book Services, Inc.

Library of Congress Cataloging-in-Publication Data appear on the last printed page of this book.

For Daniel, Kathryn, and Justin — My three favorite players of all time

Contents

Preface

"There will probably never be another season as the past one in respect to the amount and quality of basketball material."

"The fans who were able to crowd into the gym were repaid with as thrilling a game as it is possible for two championship contenders [to] stage."

As one of the winningest ventures in intercollegiate history, basketball at Duke University has engendered its share of hyperbole for over a century. Fans and observers of any number of Blue Devil contingents have felt as though they were witnessing the actions of the school's best team ever, from the Southern Conference heyday of Eddie Cameron and the 1960s power squads of coach Vic Bubas through the numerous championship and Final Four clubs of Mike Krzyzewski. Likewise, spectators have filed out of Cameron Indoor Stadium on countless occasions certain that they had just viewed the most thrilling contest possible, from conquests of Jerry West's top-ranked West Virginia and Adolph Rupp's Kentucky teams in the 1950s to a triple-overtime classic versus North Carolina in the 1960s and an assortment of nationally televised showdowns with the Tar Heels, Michigan, and other rivals in more recent decades.

The first quotation above could have been written about the Blue Devils of 1966, 1986, 1992, 1999, or 2001. It actually appeared in the *Chanticleer*, the university's yearbook, in 1912, while the institution was still known as Trinity College. The program was only seven years old, but sufficiently mature for student journalists to gush over a 6–1 record by their Methodists. The second quotation appeared in the *Durham Morning Herald* long before the idea of Cameron Indoor Stadium had even been conceived. It was occasioned by a 36–32 comeback victory over UNC in 1933 that left the 5,000 fans who packed into Card Gym breathless.

Personal involvement may not be a prerequisite to gaining enjoyment or fulfillment from following Duke basketball or any other sporting endeavor, but for the thousands of fans who live and die with the program, that individual investment undoubtedly colors their perception of reality. There is a natural egocentric tendency to believe that the games, players, teams, and seasons we have experienced personally matter the most, regardless of any empirical evidence to the contrary. Danny Ferry's 58-point night at Miami sits atop the school scoring chart, but anyone who saw Dick Groat's senior game in 1952, Art Heyman's home finale in 1963, Tate Armstrong's courageous effort at Virginia in 1977, Christian Laettner's performance against Kentucky in 1992, or J. J. Redick's against Texas in 2006 may well have felt like a witness to the best Duke performance ever.

In putting together this encyclopedia covering a century's worth of Duke basketball, I have attempted to limit the hyperbole while respecting and appreciating all eras of program history, not just the segments with which I am most familiar. Thus there are few proclamations that a particular individual, event, or accomplishment was Duke's all-time best or worst. Truly élite performers and landmark accomplishments are typically described as "one of the best" or "among the best." For the most part, information is presented in the context of the time in which it occurred, with the intrinsic supposition that an upset victory over the national powerhouse Loyola of Chicago by the 1930 team was no more or less worthy of coverage than an upset at powerful Oklahoma in 1991, each rating as a significant achievement in its day.

My own involvement with Duke basketball began in 1976–77, when I matriculated as a freshman. The school had not yet been labeled a "hot college" by the *New York Times*, so you didn't have to score 1600 on the SAT to get in or own a Fortune 500 company to pay the tuition. I attended high school in Durham, but I had never been to a Duke basketball game before my enrollment, even though tickets were neither expensive nor scarce. Students didn't have to comply with a myriad of "tenting" regulations to get choice seats back then; we just lined up on game day, and that line often snaked around the tennis courts to the blinking traffic light on Towerview.

Student passion for basketball was at least as intense as it is today, a higher percentage of the undergraduate population attended regularly, and nobody showed up to mug for TV because there just weren't a lot of games televised. Many of the cameras that were there were under strict orders *not* to show the irreverent students.

The first player to capture my attention was Tate Armstrong, who had a shot with unlimited range and a knack for winning games in the closing seconds. He had been an Olympian for UNC's coach Dean Smith the previous summer and appeared destined to lead the Blue Devils out of mediocrity when he and the team got off to an 11–3 start. I had never heard of a navicular bone before, but unfortunately Armstrong broke his early in an overtime victory at Virginia and was lost for the year. Being deprived of his 22 points a game proved too much to overcome, and Duke sank to 3–10 the rest of the way. But the next year marked the arrival of freshmen Gene Banks and Kenny Dennard, who combined with captain Jim Spanarkel and the team's big man Mike Gminski to spark the revival of the program. The 1978 team was allowed to percolate at its own pace, without much of the fanfare and scrutiny that have since become commonplace. Their chemistry was infectious, and their inspiring march to the Final Four in St. Louis made for a delirious three weeks on campus.

I worked at the student radio station my first couple of years on campus, then was hired by Tom Mickle as a student assistant in the sports information office for my junior and senior seasons. I'm not sure how productive I was; one of my assignments was to clip Duke-related stories out of the local newspapers and file articles from the out-of-town press. It took awhile, because I was fascinated by the coverage and tempted to read nearly every word. A few years after college Mickle hired me again, as an assistant sports information director. I then took his place as sports information director when he was promoted in the fall of 1985 — just in time for a season of on-the-job training with Mike Krzyzewski's first great club, another delirious winter on campus. Being a member of the support staff for Krzyzewski's first four teams to reach the Final Four was an incredible experience that made me appreciate the kind of consistent commitment that is necessary to succeed at the highest level.

After the 1990 season I joined Johnny Moore at Moore Productions. We created the *Blue Devil Weekly* newspaper just in time to cover the 1992 repeat national championship team. I was added to the Duke Radio Network crew for the 1999 season, enabling me to cover every moment of one of the most gifted teams in school history and the first perfect 19–0 campaign in ACC history. In fact, Duke won the ACC Tournament in each of my first five years on the radio team and went to the Final Four three times in my first six seasons on radio. I considered it a blessing and a privilege to closely observe the development of those players, teams, and seasons alongside a Duke treasure, the veteran voice of the Blue Devils, Bob Harris, and the sideline analyst Matthew Laurance.

Concurrently with my coverage of men's basketball, I started following the women's program almost from its inception. Duke began operating a varsity-level women's team during my undergraduate years. I was on the stats crew the night Barb Krause pulled down 24 rebounds, now the oldest individual mark in the school record book, and filled out the box score the following year when the Blue Devils beat North Carolina for the first time. I worked closely with the program while in the sports information department, covered it thoroughly from the inception of *Blue Devil Weekly,* and broadcast several games on radio during Gail Goestenkors's early years. I will never forget joining Brian Hall for the call of the 1995 four-overtime NCAA Tournament game at Tuscaloosa, doing the 1998 NCAA West Regional from Oakland, or teaming with Steve Barnes for games against the traditional powers Vanderbilt and Tennessee early in the team's first Final Four season of 1999.

That's a brief overview of the background I brought to this task of creating a comprehensive reference book on the history of Duke basketball. With over 100 years of men's basketball on the books, information on that program dominates the pages. But the 30-year-old women's program, which has reached élite status in the last decade, has also been covered, with profiles of top players and coaches, reviews of significant games, and a listing of school records along with those of the men.

This encyclopedia could not have been written without the encouragement and inspiration of many people. I would like to thank the entire staff of Duke University

Press for their enthusiastic and assiduous efforts on my behalf, and especially Reynolds Smith, who came up with the game plan; editor Fred Kameny, whose thoroughness amazed me; plus Emily Young, Deborah Wong, and their associates in marketing and production. I greatly appreciate the support of my long-time colleague and friend Johnny Moore in this and countless other endeavors over the years. The diligent staff at Duke University Archives—Tim Pyatt, Tom Harkins, Nancy Thacker, and archivist emeritus Bill King—provided invaluable assistance. Assists are also due Robert Tewksbury for his indispensable proofreading, Curtis Snyder for his statistical research, and Barry Jacobs for his early encouragement. I feel fortunate to have met and listened to many a tale by the legendary sports information director Ted Mann while he was still with us, and was ever grateful for his trove of meticulous notes and files while researching the first half-century of program history. Thanks also to all the Duke publicists of recent vintage, including former director Mike Cragg, my friend Mike Sobb, and the current staff headed by Jon Jackson, as well as to the insightful *Blue Devil Weekly* columnists Bill Brill and Jim Sumner. And a word of gratitude to a talented photographer, Ned Hinshaw, who contributed most of the images included from the mid-1970s on, plus the staff of Duke University Photography past and present, in particular Thad Sparks, Jim Wallace, Les Todd, Ron Ferrell, Jeff Camarati, Bruce Feeley, Jon Gardiner, and Chris Hildreth.

Finally, a note on what is included in this encyclopedia. A time line of major events and milestones serves as the opener, along with my selections for a five-player all-star team of Duke players from each decade. A chronological review of significant games in men's and women's basketball history, with scoring summaries, follows the time line, while a record book featuring a capsule of each year, honors, and statistical data wraps it up. In between, the bulk of the book, are alphabetical entries on every Duke head coach and assistant, every letterman, all players who have appeared in a game since the beginning of the Atlantic Coast Conference, every coach and captain from the Trinity College era, and selected rival players, coaches, and teams, including all members of the Basketball Hall of Fame to compete against Duke. The top figures in Duke women's basketball history also are covered, with entries on all head coaches and several assistants, and key players such as All-Americas, all-conference performers, record-holders, and other difference-makers.

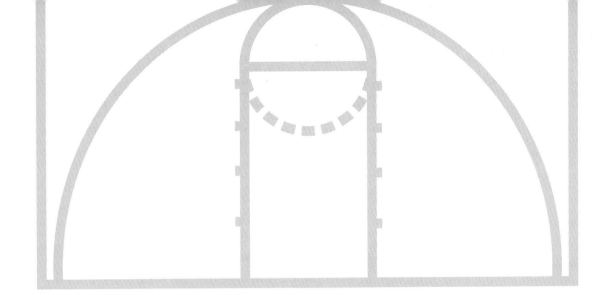

Dateline Duke

1906–1924: Basketball at Trinity College

1906

March 2. Trinity plays its first intercollegiate basketball game, dropping a 24–10 decision to Wake Forest at Angier B. Duke Gymnasium.

1908

Feb. 18. Sophomore William B. Lilly, 24-year-old captain of the Trinity basketball team, dies of pneumonia at Watts Hospital, stunning the campus community.

1912

Trinity enjoys its best season under the program's founder W. W. "Cap" Card, going 6–0 until falling to N.C. State in Card's last game on the sideline. Card had coached the team for seven years with no pay; his full-time job is director of physical education at the Trinity gym.

1913

J. E. "Big Jennie" Brinn, a former Trinity player, is hired as the first official basketball coach in school history; his biggest win comes by a 16–15 count over Trinity's nemesis Wake Forest — making Trinity the first North Carolina school to win a game at Wake.

1914

Trinity closes its season with a 33–25 victory at N.C. State, the first overtime game in school history.

1917

Under the guidance of coach Chick Doak and fueled by the play of captain Linville "Hip" Martin, Trinity posts its first 20-win season and claims the state championship.

1919

Feb. 11. A 22–19 victory over N.C. State is the highlight contest of a season in which Trinity does not have an official head coach. Sophomore starting forward Henry Cole doubles as team captain and coach.

1920

Jan. 24. Trinity welcomes North Carolina to campus for the first-ever basketball game between the archrival institutions and drops a 36–25 decision.

March 1. Before 1,000 fans in Chapel Hill, Trinity posts its first victory over North Carolina, 19–18, in a game that was rescheduled from February 20 because of an influenza outbreak on the Trinity campus.

March 12. Down by a point with two minutes left, Trinity gets a halfcourt basket from George "Brick" Starling to secure a victory over N.C. State in the state championship game at Raleigh.

1921

March 5. Trinity meets North Carolina for the state championship at Raleigh Auditorium and suffers a 55–18 defeat. Trinity coach Floyd Egan misses the contest, confined to his bed with influenza, while most of his players have been sick for several days before the game.

1922

March 7. The crowd arrives an hour early and packs Trinity's Angier Duke Gym for the season finale with North Carolina, but the home-court advantage is not enough to prevent a narrow UNC win.

Sept. 11. Excavation work begins at the site for Trinity's proposed new gymnasium.

Oct. 4. The *Trinity Chronicle*, in a football headline on the front page, begins referring to the school's sports teams as the Blue Devils. A campus contest to pick a mascot the previous year had returned inconclusive results.

1923

March 12. Everett Spikes pours in 20 points and captain Jimmy Simpson adds 16 as Trinity defeats Guilford in the last game played in Angier Duke Gym.

1924

Jan. 7. Trinity plays its first game in the new Alumni Memorial Gymnasium, defeating Mercer 29 – 25.

Dec. 11. The tobacco industrialist James B. Duke creates a $40 million charitable trust fund, a portion of which leads to the founding of Duke University from Trinity College.

Team of Trinity College

Paul Kiker	F	1907 – 11
H. G. "Bull" Hedrick	G	1909 – 12
Claude Brinn	G	1911 – 13
Linville "Hip" Martin	G	1916 – 20
Ed Bullock	F	1923 – 26

Cap Card founded the basketball program at Trinity and coached for seven years.

1925–1939: Formative Years under Eddie Cameron

1926

Sept. 25. After a year of seasoning as the football coach at Greenbriar Military Academy, 24-year-old Eddie Cameron coaches his first athletic contest at Duke — a 21 – 7 victory by the freshman football team over Apprentice. Cameron also serves as freshman basketball coach during his first two years in Durham.

1928

Dec. 15. Duke officially becomes the 23rd member of the Southern Conference, the league it would call home for 25 years.

1929

Jan. 8. Duke loses to Georgetown 48 – 33 in Eddie Cameron's début contest as head basketball coach.

Feb. 2. Cameron's first team defeats North Carolina 36 – 20, ending a 16-game losing streak against UNC. The Blue Devils' last win in the series had come as Trinity College in 1921.

March 5. Duke, seeded No. 10, loses to N.C. State in the Southern Conference Tournament championship game at Atlanta to cap off its first season in the league, after winning three close games to reach the final. Atlanta journalists declare Duke guard Bill Werber one of the outstanding players in the history of the tournament. Werber, also a baseball star, becomes Duke's first All-America in the following season.

1930

Dec. 19. Duke begins the 1930 – 31 season by falling to Villanova 22 – 21 in the first varsity basketball game played on the newly opened West Campus, at the facility later known as Card Gym.

1933

Jan. 31. About 5,000 fans fill every inch of Duke's home gym for a battle with North Carolina, setting a state attendance record. Several hundred are turned away and miss a 36 – 32 Duke victory in which the Blue Devils rally from a 31 – 25 deficit by outscoring the Tar Heels 11 – 1 down the stretch. Jim Thompson leads the way with 14 points as Duke takes the lead in the Big Five race.

1934

March 3. After knocking off Washington & Lee twice during the regular season, Duke suffers a last-second loss to coach Eddie Cameron's alma mater in the championship game of the Southern Conference Tournament.

1938

March 6. Having upset top-seeded North Carolina in the regular-season finale and No. 2 N.C. State in the opening round of the Southern Conference Tournament, Duke's "never a dull moment boys" clip Clemson 40 – 30 to claim the program's first league championship.

1939

April. Construction begins on Duke's new indoor stadium. The project was conceived in 1935 but takes only nine months to complete once construction gets under way.

Dec. 16. The last varsity game at Duke Gymnasium is a 59 – 28 destruction of Hampden-Sydney in which Glenn Price and Clyde Allen share scoring honors with 12 points apiece.

Team of the Late 1920s

Bill Werber	G	1928 – 30
Roland "Boley" Farley	G	1928 – 30
Harry Councilor	F	1928 – 30
Joe Croson	C	1929 – 31
Coke Candler	G	1927 – 29

Team of the 1930s

Jim Thompson	F	1932 – 34
Herb Thompson	G	1932 – 34
Ken Podger	G	1935 – 37
Russell Bergman	F	1937 – 39
Ed Swindell	G	1937 – 39

Two-sport star Bill Werber became Duke's first All-America in 1930.

1940–1949: New Stadium, New Success

1940

Jan. 6. Duke dedicates its new Indoor Stadium, the East Coast's largest arena south of Philadelphia, with a 36–27 victory over Princeton in front of an audience of 8,000 that includes numerous local dignitaries and former Blue Devil players.

1941

Feb. 20. Cedric Loftis, Garland Loftis, and Bob Gantt combine for 45 points as the Blue Imps freshman team defeats North Carolina 57–42 to complete an 11–2 season. Gantt and the Loftis brothers, who had helped Durham High School to 69 consecutive wins before they matriculated to Duke, are the three top scorers for the 1941 freshmen team.

1942

March 7. Eddie Cameron coaches his final basketball game, guiding Duke to a 45–34 victory over N.C. State in the Southern Conference Tournament championship contest to finish the season with a 22–2 record.

Dec. 17. Gerry Gerard launches his Duke basketball coaching career with a narrow loss to Carolina Pre-Flight, but goes on to win 20 games in his initial season. With Cameron taking over the football coaching and athletics director duties because of Wallace Wade's departure for the war, soccer coach and intramural director Gerard had been tabbed to run the basketball program.

1943

Feb. 26. Duke Indoor Stadium is the site of a unique Big Five doubleheader. N.C. State defeats Wake Forest in the opener, while the Blue Devils top North Carolina 43–24 in the second game. (Davidson is considered the other member of the state's Big Five schools.)

March 6. Gerard's first team loses to George Washington in the Southern Conference Tournament final, but the Blue Devils' Gordon Carver, another Durham High product, finishes as the tourney's leading scorer with 40 points.

1944

Feb. 26. During the peak of the war, Duke defeats North Carolina by 17 points to win the Southern Conference Tournament. Tennessee transfer Bill Wright leads the way with 15 points. Facing a schedule loaded with military teams, Duke had gone 10–13 during the regular season, with two losses to UNC.

1946

Feb. 16. Duke Indoor Stadium enjoys its first official sellout crowd of 8,800 for a 54–44 loss to North Carolina. Sold out weeks in advance, the game is played before the largest crowd to attend a college basketball game south of Philadelphia's Convention Hall. Aside from being a factor in the Southern Conference race, the game features the return of former Durham High hero Horace "Bones" McKinney to his hometown. McKinney paces the Tar Heel win with 21 points.

March 2. Playing in the championship game for the seventh straight year, Duke rides high-scoring forward Ed Koffenberger to a 49–30 victory over Wake Forest for the Blue Devils' fifth (and final) Southern Conference crown.

Nov. 1. The Basketball Association of America, which will later evolve into the NBA, launches its first season. The roster for the Washington Capitols (coached by Red Auerbach) includes Bob Gantt, a 6–4 center from Duke, making him the Blue Devils' first NBA player. He sees action in 23 games in his only year in the league.

1947

Feb. 4. Facing Washington & Lee at Lynchburg, Va., Ed Koffenberger becomes the first Duke player to record 30 points in a game, hitting 13 field goals and four free throws in a 71–57 victory.

March 6. The Southern Conference Tournament begins a four-year run at Duke Indoor Stadium. The event was moved from its traditional home at tiny Raleigh Memorial Auditorium because over 10,000 advance ticket orders were received, mostly the result of increased interest in coach Everett Case's flashy Wolfpack. The Blue

Devils lose the opener by two points to South Carolina. N.C. State will go on to edge UNC for the title.

1948

March 6. Playing in the Southern Conference Tournament final on its home floor, Duke falls to national scoring leader N.C. State, 58 – 50. The Blue Devils, in seventh place, had won three games in three days to make the championship contest.

Sept. 3. W. W. "Cap" Card, the father of basketball at Trinity College, dies of a heart attack at the age of 74.

Team of the 1940s

Ed Koffenberger	F	1945 – 47
Corren Youmans	F	1948 – 50
Gordon Carver	F	1943 – 45
Bill Mock	F	1940 – 41
Bob Gantt	C	1942 – 44

Above: Duke defeated Princeton in the first game at the Indoor Stadium.

Right: Ed Koffenberger was the first Blue Devil to score 30 points in one game.

1950

March 4. In remission after off-season cancer surgery, coach Gerry Gerard directs a 13–13 Duke team to the Southern Conference Tournament final before falling to eighth-ranked N.C. State.

Nov. 9. Less than a month away from the season opener, Gerard is granted a leave of absence because of his failing health. Athletics director Eddie Cameron announces that Harold Bradley has been hired away from Hartwick College to replace Gerard on the Duke bench.

Dec. 30. Trailing Tulane by 32 points in the first half and by 29 at halftime, Duke stages an NCAA-record comeback to win 74–72 at the Dixie Classic in Raleigh.

1951

Jan. 17. Gerry Gerard dies at the age of 47 after a two-year battle with cancer.

Feb. 17. Duke loses its national television début 85–60 at Navy. It is the Blue Devils' third game in four days and fifth in a week, all but one coming on the road.

Feb. 23. With 29 points against North Carolina, Dick Groat becomes the first 1,000-point career scorer in Duke history and breaks the national single-season scoring record of 740 points held by William & Mary's Chet Giermak. The record breaker comes with 12:45 remaining in the second half. Groat will extend the record to 831 points by the end of the year.

March 3. Before 12,250 fans — the largest crowd ever to watch a Southern Conference Tournament game — N.C. State edges Duke to win its fifth straight league title. Groat scores 31 points in the final and finishes with 85 for the tourney to break Sammy Ranzino's event scoring mark of 69 points.

Dec. 1. Duke's season-opening rout of Temple marks the first racially integrated basketball game in Indoor Stadium history, when Temple sophomore Samuel Sylvester becomes the first African American player to appear in an official game at the facility. He starts and scores 5 points.

Dec. 11. Duke makes its first appearance in an Asso- ciated Press national college basketball poll, checking in at No. 12 in the opening poll of the season. The AP began conducting the national poll in January 1949.

Dec. 15. Duke reaches the 100-point mark for the first time ever in defeating VMI 102–45.

1952

Feb. 29. Duke's single-game scoring and rebounding records are set in the same game when Dick Groat posts 48 points against North Carolina while teammate Bernie Janicki grabs 31 rebounds. Groat's record will stand for over 36 years; Janicki's has yet to be topped.

May 1. Groat, also a varsity baseball star and now a senior, becomes the first Duke athlete to have his basketball jersey number 10 retired when the university honors him at a baseball game with North Carolina, which the Blue Devils win 10–2.

1953

Dec. 28–30. Led by Rudy D'Emilio, Duke whips Oregon State, Wake Forest, and Navy to win the Dixie Classic for the first and only time in school history. D'Emilio tops the Blue Devils in scoring in all three games, netting 24 points in the final against Navy.

May 8. The Atlantic Coast Conference is founded at Sedgefield Inn near Greensboro, with Duke as one of the seven charter members.

1954

Jan. 2. Duke blasts Wake Forest 86–64 in its first regular-season game in the Atlantic Coast Conference.

March 4–6. With session tickets selling for $9 and $6, the ACC conducts its first post-season tournament at Reynolds Coliseum in Raleigh. The league grosses $70,252 at the inaugural event, with only the Friday semifinals selling out. Duke defeats Virginia before falling to eventual champ N.C. State in the semis.

1955

March 8. Villanova defeats Duke 74–73 in a triple-header at Madison Square Garden in New York in the Blue Devils' first NCAA Tournament appearance. Duke, the ACC tourney runner-up, made the trip because champion N.C. State was on probation.

1957

Feb. 9. Duke faces a No. 1 team (in the AP poll) for the first time ever, and despite a late rally absorbs a 75–73 loss at Woollen Gym to undefeated and eventual national champion North Carolina.

1958

Jan. 27. Duke enjoys its first win over a No. 1 opponent, knocking off West Virginia 72–68 at Duke Indoor Stadium.

1959

March 23. Coach Harold Bradley resigns after nine years as Duke's head coach to accept the coaching position at Texas.

May 5. Former N.C. State player and assistant coach Vic Bubas is introduced as the new head coach at Duke.

May. The University of North Carolina signs New York prep star Art Heyman, but by the end of the month Heyman (at his father's urging) changes his mind and is bound for Duke.

Team of the 1950s

Dick Groat	G	1950–52
Rudy D'Emilio	G	1952–54
Joe Belmont	G	1953–56
Ronnie Mayer	F	1953–56
Bernie Janicki	F	1952–54

1960–1969: Vic Bubas Raises the Stakes

1960

March 5. Doug Kistler is named most valuable player as Duke defeats Wake Forest 63–59 to win the ACC Tournament championship for the first time. Vic Bubas becomes the first coach to win the event in his initial year in the league.

1961

Feb. 14. ACC commissioner Jim Weaver suspends Duke's Art Heyman and UNC's Larry Brown and Donnie Walsh for the remainder of the conference season for their roles in a wild fight that marred the end of the schools' game on February 4.

Sept. 5. Bill Bradley, one of the top prep players in the nation, notifies Duke officials that he will be enrolling at Princeton, just days before the start of the fall semester. Bradley had announced at his high school graduation in June that he was coming to Duke.

1963

Feb. 23. Heyman, Duke's first ACC player of the year, saves his best for last by scoring 40 points and grabbing 24 rebounds in his final home game, a victory over North Carolina.

March 2. Duke defeats Wake Forest in the ACC Tournament final to cap off the school's first perfect year in the conference. The Blue Devils went 14–0 during the league's regular season and won their three tournament games by an average margin of 15.7 points.

March 22. After winning the East Regional in College Park, Md., Duke appears in the NCAA Final Four for the first time and falls to Loyola of Chicago in a national semifinal at Louisville. Heyman is named outstanding player of the Final Four even though Duke doesn't make the final game.

April 30. The New York Knicks make Heyman the No. 1 pick of the NBA draft. Heyman becomes the first ACC player to go first in the draft since it began in 1947.

1964

March 21. In Kansas City for its first appearance in the NCAA championship game, Duke loses 98–83 to undefeated UCLA as the Bruins begin a run of nine national titles over the next 10 years.

March 30. Duke basketball appears on the cover of *Sports Illustrated* for the first time, with a black-and-white photograph from the NCAA final of Jeff Mullins and UCLA's Walt Hazzard.

Oct. 22. Mullins, Duke's first basketball Olympian, scores 14 points to help the United States crush Puerto Rico in the Olympic semifinals at Tokyo and earn a berth in the gold-medal game against the Soviet Union. The Americans then go on to beat the Soviets for the 46th straight victory by a U.S. team in Olympic competition.

1965

April 1. Newspapers across North Carolina report that all-state basketball player C. B. Claiborne, the top-ranked student in the senior class at Langston High School in Danville, Va., will attend Duke on a national academic achievement scholarship and could become the Blue Devils' first African American athlete.

Dec. 14. After defeating top-ranked UCLA on successive nights, Duke moves to the top of the Associated Press national poll for the first time in school history.

1966

March 18. At the Final Four in College Park, Md., No. 1 Kentucky edges No. 2 Duke 83–79 in the national semifinals, the Blue Devils' first appearance in a 1-versus-2 matchup.

Dec. 29. Bob Verga sets a Greensboro Coliseum scoring record with 41 points on 16-of-29 shooting, but the Blue Devils are nipped 83–82 by Ohio State. It is Duke's first loss at the facility: the Devils had been 9–0 there since the building opened in 1961.

1967

March 13. With only the ACC champion eligible for the NCAA Tournament, Duke becomes the first conference school since the formation of the ACC to appear in the NIT. The Blue Devils lose a first-round game to Southern Illinois.

1968

Feb. 28. With 18 rebounds against N.C. State, Mike Lewis becomes the first player in Duke history to accumulate at least 1,000 career rebounds.

May 12. Don Blackman, a prep standout in New York, becomes the first African American basketball player to receive an athletic scholarship from Duke.

Dec. 11. In a hotel room in Charlottesville, Va., Vic Bubas tells assistant coaches Chuck Daly and Hubie Brown that he will step down from coaching at the end of the 1968–69 season. The news doesn't become public until the appearance of a front-page story in the *Durham Morning Herald* two months later, on February 13.

1969

March 1. With outgoing senior Steve Vandenberg pumping in a career-best 33 points, Duke upsets second-ranked North Carolina in Bubas's final home game on a snowy afternoon that holds attendance slightly below capacity. Later that night, the Indoor Stadium plays host to a concert by Janis Joplin.

March 8. With a nine-point lead at halftime, the Blue Devils appear on the verge of giving Bubas another championship in his final ACC Tournament—before UNC's Charlie Scott gets hot in the second half and finishes with 40 points in a Tar Heel victory.

March 12. West Virginia coach Bucky Waters, a former assistant to Bubas, is named Duke's head coach.

Team of the 1960s

Art Heyman	F	1961–63
Jeff Mullins	F-G	1962–64
Bob Verga	G	1965–67
Jack Marin	F	1964–66
Mike Lewis	C	1966–68

Left: Doug Kistler was the MVP of the 1960 ACC Tournament.

Above: 1966 starters Mike Lewis, Bob Riedy, Jack Marin, Steve Vacendak, and Bob Verga take aim at the East Regional after winning the ACC championship.

1970–1979: Turbulence and Transition

1970

Feb. 5. After a 14-month study of Duke athletics, the university's Academic Council backs off from earlier recommendations that the school withdraw from the Atlantic Coast Conference and base all of its athletic scholarships on need only. A month before, an ad hoc committee of the Academic Council had made both those proposals to deemphasize athletics and drastically curb spending by the athletics department. Athletics director Eddie Cameron calls the reversal a vote of confidence for his department. Before the next academic year begins, Cameron appoints baseball coach Tom Butters to head fund raising for athletic scholarships.

1971

March 25. At the semifinals of the NIT, Duke loses to North Carolina 73–67 in the fourth meeting of the season between the two rivals.

1972

Jan. 22. Duke renames its Indoor Stadium in honor of retiring athletics director and legendary coach Eddie Cameron. The Blue Devils celebrate the occasion by upsetting third-ranked North Carolina on a late basket by senior guard Rob West.

Feb. 1. With Cameron's retirement pending, Duke names former football player and recruiter Carl James as acting athletics director.

Feb. 12. Junior guard Richie O'Connor, one of the Blue Devils' top scorers with over 600 points in two years, suddenly quits the team and drives home to New Jersey the same day the Devils are defeating William & Mary. O'Connor is one of seven recruited players to leave the program in coach Bucky Waters's first three years (along with Don Blackman, Jeff Dawson, Dave Elmer, Jim Fitzsimmons, Sam May, and Ron Righter).

Aug. 18. The NCAA announces a one-year probation for the Duke basketball program because of recruiting violations in the spring of 1971 during the university's courtship of high school star David Thompson.

1973

March 8. A defeat to Virginia in the ACC Tournament gives Duke a five-game losing streak to end its season, leaving the Blue Devils with a 12–14 record, their first losing mark since 1939.

Sept. 12. Bucky Waters announces that he is stepping down from his position as head coach to take an administrative post with the Duke Medical Center.

Oct. 18. With pre-season practice already under way, Neill McGeachy, Waters's top assistant, is named Duke's head coach. Only a day before the announcement, Adolph Rupp, the 72-year-old former Kentucky coach, was considering taking the job for one year while athletics director Carl James searched for a permanent replacement for Waters.

1974

Feb. 13. Duke defeats Virginia 88–78 to post the 1,000th basketball victory in school history.

March 2. At a morning meeting, Duke's Athletic Council decides not to extend McGeachy's one-year contract as head coach. During the afternoon in Chapel Hill, McGeachy's team is victimized by one of the most memorable comebacks in ACC history. Underdog Duke leads by eight points with 17 seconds remaining in regulation, but fourth-ranked North Carolina forces overtime and wins 96–92.

March 28. Bill Foster accepts the head coaching position at Duke after leading his Utah team to the NIT championship game and a 22–8 record.

1975

April 19. Former coach Eddie Cameron and former basketball All-Americas Dick Groat and Bill Werber are among the six charter inductees in the Duke Sports Hall of Fame, along with the football legends Wallace Wade, Ace Parker, and George McAfee.

May 25. The Golden State Warriors defeat Washington 96–95 to complete a sweep of the NBA Finals, making Jeff Mullins of the Warriors the first former Blue Devil to play on an NBA championship team.

Dec. 3. Playing its first game following the merger of women's physical education with men's intercollegiate athletics at Duke, the women's basketball team drops a 65 – 45 decision to St. Augustine's. The team loses all 14 of its games in 1975 – 76, but this season marks the first time that varsity letters are awarded to women's basketball players. The five letter winners are Betsy Bergeron, Joy James, Laurie Koffenberger, Laurie Layman, and Patty Walsh.

1976

July. Two Duke players compete in the Summer Olympics in Montreal: guard Tate Armstrong for coach Dean Smith's gold-medal USA team and center Cameron Hall for his native Canada.

1977

Jan. 17. Duke ends a painful 27-game road losing streak in the ACC with an overtime victory at Virginia fueled by the heroics of senior Tate Armstrong, playing with a broken wrist.

Feb. 7. Philadelphia's Gene Banks, one of the most coveted high school players in the country, casts his lot with Duke coach Bill Foster. After reportedly having second thoughts, Banks reaffirms his decision on March 15 and becomes the school's first prominent black signee.

April 27. Athletics director Carl James and women's coordinator of athletics Lorraine Woodyard jointly announce the hiring of Debbie Leonard, 25-year-old assistant coach at UNC Greensboro, as Duke's varsity women's basketball coach.

1978

Jan. 14. An emotional home win over second-ranked North Carolina improves Duke's record to 12 – 3 and returns the Blue Devils to the national polls for the first time since 1971.

March 4. In the first ACC championship game to be shown live on national television, Duke tops Wake Forest 85 – 77 to claim the school's first conference crown since 1966.

March 25 – 27. Duke defeats Notre Dame in the national semifinals, then loses to Kentucky in the NCAA championship game in the Blue Devils' first trip to the Final Four since 1966.

Nov. 19. For the first time in school history, Duke is ranked No. 1 in the Associated Press national pre-season poll, receiving 38 of a possible 48 first-place votes.

Nov. 30. The Duke women register their first-ever ACC victory with a 65 – 52 decision at Wake Forest. After posting a 3 – 45 record over their first three varsity years, the Devils own a 2 – 0 start to the 1978 – 79 season after the win over the Deacons. They go on to a record of 11 – 11.

1979

March 11. On the day remembered as Black Sunday in ACC circles, Duke loses to St. John's and North Carolina loses to Penn in an NCAA Tournament doubleheader at Reynolds Coliseum in Raleigh. Jim Spanarkel, scoring 16 points in his last game, becomes the Blue Devils' first 2,000-point career scorer.

Nov. 17. Third-ranked Duke edges second-ranked Kentucky in overtime in the first season-opening Hall of Fame Tipoff Classic, held in Springfield, Mass.

Team of the 1970s

Mike Gminski	C	1977 – 80
Jim Spanarkel	G	1976 – 79
Gene Banks	F	1978 – 81
Randy Denton	C	1969 – 71
Tate Armstrong	G	1974 – 77

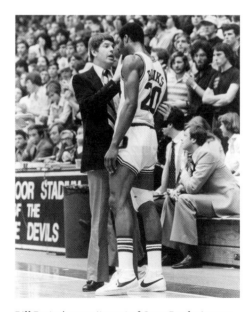

Bill Foster's recruitment of Gene Banks in 1977 helped the Blue Devils return to national glory.

1980–1989: The Mike Krzyzewski Era Begins

1980

Jan. 23. Lisa Warren scores 16 points and Barb Krause totals 11 with 14 rebounds as the Duke women upset Virginia 65–63 before a crowd of about 4,000 fans at Cameron, the Blue Devils' largest home audience to date. The contest is played as the opener of a doubleheader with the Duke and Virginia men.

Feb. 20. Duke surprises senior center Mike Gminski by retiring his No. 43 jersey in a special ceremony before the start of his final home game, marking just the second jersey retirement in school history. Gminski will graduate as the school's all-time leader in points and rebounds.

March 1. Duke defeats regular-season champion Maryland to win the ACC Tournament as the sixth seed.

March 3. Two days after guiding Duke to the ACC title, coach Bill Foster is named head coach at South Carolina. Foster had said he would remain at Duke through the NCAA Tournament, where his team upset Kentucky in Lexington before falling to Purdue in a regional championship contest.

March 18. Army coach and alumnus Mike Krzyzewski is named to replace Foster at Duke.

1982

April 14. Duke signs high school All-America Mark Alarie, completing a landmark recruiting class that includes Johnny Dawkins, Jay Bilas, David Henderson, Weldon Williams, and Bill Jackman.

1983

March 11. With four freshmen in the starting lineup, Duke ends a second straight 17-loss season with a crushing 43-point loss to Virginia in the ACC Tournament, the largest margin of defeat ever in the event.

1984

Jan. 17. In response to some tasteless incidents at Cameron Indoor Stadium, university president Terry Sanford sends every Duke student a letter encouraging better behavior at home basketball games. The page is headed "Avuncular Letter" and is signed "Uncle Terry." Once asked by William King, now university archivist emeritus, who actually wrote the letter, Sanford replied, "I did. I wrote it before breakfast one morning and asked [my wife] Margaret Rose to review it."

Jan. 25. Athletics director Tom Butters announces that he is extending the contract of coach Mike Krzyzewski despite his record of 52–51 midway through his fourth season.

March 10. Duke upsets top-ranked and heavily favored North Carolina in the semifinals of the ACC Tournament to earn its first championship game appearance under Krzyzewski.

March 18. Duke loses to Washington 80–78 in its first NCAA Tournament appearance under Krzyzewski.

1985

March 1. The Duke women win an ACC Tournament game for the first time, defeating Clemson 81–76. That ends a string of seven straight years in which the Devils absorbed a first-round loss.

April 2. Danny Ferry, national high school player of the year, ends an intense and highly publicized recruiting battle between Duke and North Carolina by choosing the Blue Devils.

1986

Feb. 6. Johnny Dawkins, in a game against Virginia, becomes the first modern Duke player to reach the 500 mark in career assists. Backcourt mate Tommy Amaker reaches 500 two games later on February 11 against Stetson.

Feb. 22. Dawkins has his jersey No. 24 retired by Duke president H. Keith H. Brodie before a nationally televised game with Oklahoma.

March 2. Duke defeats North Carolina in Cameron Indoor Stadium to wrap up its first ACC regular-season championship since 1979.

March 9. Duke defeats Georgia Tech to win its first ACC Tournament championship under Krzyzewski.

March 11. For the first time in school history, Duke is ranked No. 1 in the final Associated Press national poll of the season.

March 20. Duke's women make their first post-season appearance with a victory over West Texas State in the Women's NIT. The Blue Devils finish with a 21–9 record, the first time the program reaches the 20-victory plateau.

March 31. Duke concludes its first Final Four appearance under Krzyzewski with a loss to Louisville in the NCAA championship game, finishing the season with a 37–3 record. The Blue Devils' victory total sets a record (later tied) for most wins in NCAA history.

April 3. Dawkins is presented with the Naismith Award, making him Duke's first national player of the year since Art Heyman in 1963.

July 5–20. Rising senior guard Tommy Amaker becomes the first Duke player to compete for the United States in the FIBA World Championship, helping the Americans to a gold medal in Madrid.

1987

March 11. The Duke women make their first appearance ever in the NCAA Tournament, defeating Manhattan 70–55 in a first-round game at Cameron Indoor Stadium. The program's first ACC player of the year, Chris Moreland, scores 25 points while Katie Meier has a triple-double.

1988

March 5. Women's star Chris Moreland appears in her final Duke game, with 16 points and 11 rebounds in an ACC tourney loss to Clemson. Moreland concludes her career as the top scorer and rebounder in program history. Her scoring mark will eventually be topped by Alana Beard (2001–04).

March 13. Duke defeats North Carolina in the ACC Tournament final, its third victory of the season over the Tar Heels.

March 26. Behind the defense of forward Billy King, Duke tops No. 1 Temple 63–53 to reach the Final Four for the second time in three years.

Nov. 25. Legendary Duke basketball coach, administrator, and stadium namesake Eddie Cameron dies at the age of 86.

Dec. 10. Danny Ferry scores a school and ACC record 58 points in a 117–102 win at Miami, while Sue Harnett

sets the Duke women's scoring mark on the same day with 37 points at Virginia Commonwealth.

1989

Feb. 18. Ferry has his jersey No. 35 retired before a home victory over Kansas.

March 26. Duke upsets second-ranked Georgetown to earn a spot in the Final Four.

Team of the 1980s

Johnny Dawkins	G	1983–86
Danny Ferry	F-C	1986–89
Mark Alarie	F	1983–86
Tommy Amaker	G	1984–87
David Henderson	F	1983–86

Above: Johnny Dawkins had his jersey retired and won the Naismith Award in 1986.

Left: Chris Moreland (left) was Duke's first ACC women's player of the year in 1987, one season after Debbie Leonard (right) was named the Devils' first ACC coach of the year.

1990–1999: Back-to-Back National Titles, and the Rise of Women's Basketball

1990

March 4. Duke retires the jersey No. 25 of former star Art Heyman, the 1963 national player of the year.

March 24. Christian Laettner's buzzer-beater gives Duke a 79–78 overtime upset of third-ranked Connecticut and sends Duke to the Final Four for the third year in a row.

April 2. UNLV roasts Duke 103–73 in the national championship game at Denver, the largest margin of defeat ever in an NCAA final.

1991

March 30. Spurred by a late three-point shot from Bobby Hurley, Duke upsets defending NCAA champion and undefeated UNLV 79–77 in the national semifinals at Indianapolis.

April 1. A 72–65 victory over Kansas gives Duke its first NCAA basketball championship.

April 22. President George H. W. Bush welcomes the Duke basketball team to the White House to congratulate the Blue Devils on their national title.

1992

Feb. 26. Christian Laettner scores 32 points in a win over Virginia on the night his jersey No. 32 is retired by Duke.

March 28. In one of the greatest NCAA Tournament games ever played, Laettner's basket at the buzzer gives Duke a 104–103 overtime victory over Kentucky to send the Blue Devils to a fifth straight Final Four.

April 6. Duke becomes the first school since UCLA (1972–73) to win back-to-back NCAA titles when it defeats Michigan 71–51 at the Final Four in Minneapolis.

May 18. Duke taps Purdue assistant coach Gail Goestenkors to lead its women's program after the departure of Debbie Leonard, who had coached the Blue Devils for 15 years.

June 21. The U.S. Olympic "Dream Team," featuring lone collegian Christian Laettner and assistant coach Mike Krzyzewski, begins training camp in La Jolla, Calif. The eventual gold medalists of the Barcelona Summer Games scrimmage against a developmental squad featuring Duke players Grant Hill and Bobby Hurley.

1993

Feb. 21. Hurley totals 15 assists against N.C. State, becoming the first Duke player to top the 1,000 mark in career assists.

Feb. 28. Hurley scores 19 points and dishes 15 assists in a victory over UCLA, on the day his jersey No. 11 is retired to the Cameron Indoor Stadium rafters. In Duke's next game, on March 3, he will break the official NCAA career assists record.

1994

Feb. 3. The first-ever Duke–North Carolina game in which the two rivals are ranked Nos. 1 and 2 in the country ends with the Tar Heels on top 89–78. The contest is the first college basketball game broadcast live by ESPN2.

Feb. 27. Duke retires the No. 33 jersey of senior standout Grant Hill before a game against Temple.

Dec. 6. Jeff Mullins, the ACC athlete of the year in 1964 and a U.S. Olympian, returns to campus to see his jersey No. 44 retired by the university.

1995

Jan. 6. Duke embarks on a road trip to Georgia Tech without head coach Mike Krzyzewski, who is hospitalized for exhaustion and back pain.

Jan. 22. Krzyzewski meets with his players for the first time since his departure and tells them he will not return to the sidelines for the remainder of the season.

Feb. 12. Duke alumnus Grant Hill of the Detroit Pistons starts and scores 10 points for the Eastern Conference in the NBA All-Star Game in Phoenix. With 1,289,585 votes in fan balloting, Hill is the first rookie ever to finish as the leading vote getter for the All-Star Game.

March 5. The Duke women play in the ACC championship game for the first time, falling to 12th-ranked North Carolina 95–70.

The Blue Devils visited President George H. W. Bush at the White House after winning the 1991 NCAA title.

March 6. Krzyzewski conducts a mammoth press conference in Cameron Indoor Stadium to update the media on his health and express his intention to return to coaching. Four days later, still minus Krzyzewski, Duke concludes a 13–18 season with a loss to Wake Forest in the ACC Tournament.

March 16–18. Duke returns to the NCAA women's tourney for the first time since 1987, defeating Oklahoma State in the first round before falling to No. 13 Alabama in the second round in a record four-overtime contest in Tuscaloosa, 121–120.

Dec. 2. A 95-game home winning streak against non-conference competition comes to an end when Illinois claims a 75–65 victory. Duke's last previous home defeat outside the ACC had come on January 12, 1983, to Louisville.

Dec. 10. The Duke women appear on national television for the first time when their 76–66 home victory over Seton Hall is aired by ESPN2.

1996

Aug. 3. Grant Hill becomes the fourth former Duke basketball player to earn an Olympic gold medal, during the Summer Games in Atlanta.

1997

Sept. 2. Recovering from a summer heart attack, Tom Butters announces that he will retire from his position as director of athletics by June 30, 1998. In addition to running the athletics department for twenty years and hiring basketball coach Mike Krzyzewski, Butters served on the NCAA Basketball Committee from 1989 to 1994 and was instrumental in negotiating its $1 billion TV contract with CBS.

1998

Feb. 25. President Nan Keohane names 44-year-old associate athletics director Joe Alleva to replace Butters.

Feb. 28. Duke rallies from a 17-point deficit in the second half to edge North Carolina 77–75 for Mike Krzyzewski's 500th coaching victory at Duke.

1999

March 7. Behind 29 points from William Avery and 24 from MVP Elton Brand, Duke rips North Carolina by 23 points in the ACC Tournament final to complete the first 19–0 conference season in league history.

March 22. The Duke women's team posts the most significant win in school history, knocking off three-time defending NCAA champion Tennessee 69–63 in the

Christian Laettner had his jersey retired and led Duke to a pair of NCAA crowns.

Michele VanGorp became the first Duke women's player to make the Kodak All-America team, in 1999.

NCAA East Regional at Greensboro. The victory sends the Blue Devils to their first Final Four in San Jose and makes Duke the first school since Georgia in 1983 to see the men's and women's teams qualify for the Final Four in the same year.

March 28. The Duke women play for the national championship, dropping a 62 – 45 decision to top-ranked Purdue. During Final Four weekend, Michele VanGorp is recognized as the first Kodak All-America player in Duke history.

March 29. A 32-game winning streak is halted when the Duke men fall to Connecticut 77 – 74 in the NCAA final at St. Petersburg. The Blue Devils finish with a record-tying 37 victories and outscore their opponents by almost 25 points a game.

April 14. Sophomore and national player of the year Brand holds a press conference at Duke to announce that he is leaving school to enter the NBA draft, becom-

ing the Blue Devils' first early-entry departure. Sophomore Avery and freshman Corey Maggette subsequently decide to join Brand in the draft.

June 30. Four Duke players are selected among the top fourteen picks in the NBA draft: Brand (No. 1), Trajan Langdon (11), Maggette (13), Avery (14).

Team of the 1990s

Christian Laettner	F-C	1989 – 92
Grant Hill	F-G	1991 – 94
Bobby Hurley	G	1990 – 93
Elton Brand	C	1998 – 99
Trajan Langdon	G	1995 – 99

Trajan Langdon and the Blue Devils saw a 32-game winning streak halted by Connecticut in the 1999 NCAA final.

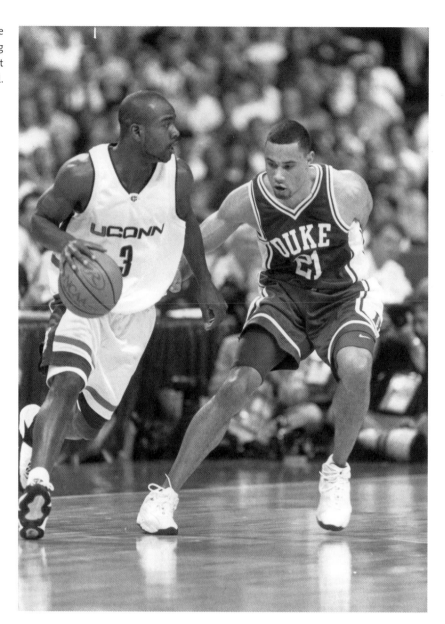

2000–2006: Another Championship and More

2000

March 6. Georgia Schweitzer and Lauren Rice score 16 points apiece and Missy West adds 14 to carry the Duke women past North Carolina 79–76 in the ACC championship game, giving the Blue Devils their first league title.

March 12. Scoring 23 points in the championship game against Maryland, Jason Williams becomes the first freshman in Duke history to be voted most valuable player of the ACC Tournament. North Carolina's Phil Ford (1975) and Jerry Stackhouse (1994) were the only other freshmen previously so honored.

April 15. The university formally dedicates its Schwartz-Butters Athletic Center, the home of the basketball program offices as well as the Duke Sports Hall of Fame.

Nov. 17. The floor in Cameron Indoor Stadium is named Coach K Court in honor of Mike Krzyzewski, who won his 500th game at Duke a few moments before the ceremony.

2001

Feb. 4. The concourse at Cameron Indoor Stadium is named to honor former coach Vic Bubas.

Feb. 21. Shane Battier, on his way to national player of the year honors, sees his jersey No. 31 retired before a contest against Georgia Tech.

March 11. A rout of North Carolina in the ACC Tournament final gives Mike Krzyzewski his 600th career victory and sixth conference championship.

April 2. Duke defeats Arizona 82–72 at the Final Four in Minneapolis to claim the school's third NCAA basketball championship.

Oct. 5. Krzyzewski is inducted into the Naismith Memorial Basketball Hall of Fame in Springfield, Mass., along with coach John Chaney and player Moses Malone. Krzyzewski, the first person from Duke to be enshrined, is presented by his former college coach, Bob Knight.

Nov. 14. Krzyzewski, Duke president Nan Keohane, and athletics director Joe Alleva appear at a press conference to announce that the university has reached agreement on a new contract that is expected to keep Krzyzewski at Duke for the remainder of his coaching career.

Sept. 21. Chris Moreland Culbertson becomes the first women's basketball player (and fifth woman overall) to be inducted into the Duke Sports Hall of Fame.

Dec. 2. Eighteen former Duke stars are inducted as charter members of the Hall of Honor, a new shrine located on the Bubas Concourse at Cameron Indoor Stadium to recognize élite men's and women's basketball players.

2002

Jan. 17. Top-ranked Duke rocks No. 3 Maryland 99–78 in a game that draws three million television viewers, ESPN's largest audience for a regular-season game.

March 11. Duke is ranked No. 1 in the final Associated Press national poll for the fourth consecutive season. No other school has ever had four consecutive No. 1 finishes in the AP poll.

June 26. Jason Williams and Mike Dunleavy become just the second pair of college teammates to be selected among the first three picks of an NBA draft. Classmate Carlos Boozer is chosen in the second round. All had one year of eligibility remaining at Duke.

Sept. 26. The ACC announces its 50th-anniversary basketball team, featuring 11 Duke honorees: Shane Battier, Elton Brand, Johnny Dawkins, Danny Ferry, Mike Gminski, Art Heyman, Grant Hill, Bobby Hurley, Christian Laettner, Jeff Mullins, and Jason Williams. All except Brand, a two-year player, have their jersey numbers retired.

Nov. 4. The Duke women are ranked No. 1 in the Associated Press pre-season poll for the first time.

2003

Feb. 1. For the first time ever, Cameron Indoor Stadium is filled to its 9,314 capacity for a women's game. Despite the partisan support, the top-ranked Blue Devils are overturned by No. 2 Connecticut, 77–65.

Left: Jason Williams helped Mike Krzyzewski claim his third national championship in 2001.

Above: Duke met Tennessee in the 2003 Final Four in Atlanta, the third Final Four trip in five years for the Blue Devil women.

Feb. 5. Jason Williams takes a break from his rookie season in the NBA to return to Duke for the annual North Carolina game, at which his jersey No. 22 is retired.

March 16. With freshman J. J. Redick exploding for 30 points, Duke rallies to defeat N.C. State in the ACC Tournament final and claim an unprecedented fifth straight league championship.

March 31. The Duke women post an NCAA regional triumph over Texas Tech to advance to the Final Four for the second straight year and the third time in five seasons.

2004

Jan. 3. A three-pointer by Jessica Foley at the final buzzer lifts the Duke women past Connecticut 68–67, ending the Huskies' 69-game home winning streak and 76-game regular-season streak.

Jan. 24. Alana Beard becomes the first Duke women's player to have her jersey (20) retired, in a special ceremony before the Blue Devils' nationally televised home defeat to Tennessee.

March 8. Beard completes her career a perfect 4 of 4 in

ACC championship games as the Blue Devil women beat North Carolina by 16 points, marking an unmatched fifth consecutive league championship for the Duke program.

March 21. The Duke women defeat Northwestern State in the NCAA Tournament to give coach Gail Goestenkors her 300th career victory, a mark she achieved faster than any coach in ACC history (387 games).

March 26. A 10-point win over Illinois in an NCAA regional semifinal game makes the Duke men 30-game winners for the eighth time in school history, more than any other school.

March 28. Luol Deng becomes the first Duke freshman to earn NCAA regional MVP honors by helping the Blue Devils defeat Xavier 66–63 to secure the school's 14th Final Four appearance, 10th under Krzyzewski.

Aug. 30. The United States defeats Australia 74–63 to capture the gold medal in women's basketball at the Olympics in Athens. Duke coach Gail Goestenkors is an assistant coach for the U.S. squad.

Dec. 12. Mike Krzyzewski becomes the second-youngest coach in NCAA history to win 700 games as the

Above: Gail Goestenkors coached the Blue Devil women to five straight ACC Tournament titles, 2000–2004.

Right: Freshman Luol Deng was selected MVP of the 2004 NCAA regional while helping Duke return to the Final Four.

Blue Devils defeat Toledo. Team captains Daniel Ewing and J. J. Redick present him with a game ball in a ceremony after the contest. The win comes in Krzyzewski's 940th game.

2005

Jan. 5. Duke celebrates its 100th year of basketball and its 65th season at Cameron Indoor Stadium with a win over Princeton. Dozens of former players and coaches attend events before and after the game to mark the occasion. During the game the Blue Devils wear uniforms reminiscent of past styles.

March 12. J. J. Redick hits 11 of 16 shots and scores 35 points to help Duke edge N.C. State in the semifinals of the ACC Tournament. Redick's point total matches Bob Verga's in 1967 versus Virginia for the top-scoring game by a Duke player in tourney history and propels the Blue Devils into their eighth straight championship

game. The next day Redick scores 26 points to lead his team past Georgia Tech for the school's sixth ACC title in seven years.

May 17 – 19. On three consecutive days Duke receives verbal commitments from three rising high school seniors considered among the top recruits in the country: Jon Scheyer, Gerald Henderson, and Brian Zoubek.

Oct. 26. Mike Krzyzewski accepts a three-year appointment from USA Basketball to coach its senior national team in major international competition, beginning with the 2006 World Championship in Japan. Krzyzewski will guide the 2008 Olympic Team in Beijing, provided that the United States qualifies for the event.

2006

Feb. 19. With 4:15 to play against Miami, J. J. Redick hits a three-pointer to become the all-time scoring leader in Duke history. Former record holder Johnny Dawkins, now an associate head coach, presents him with a game ball afterward. On the same day, 900 miles to the south, Monique Currie helps the Duke women defeat Miami 99–93 in double overtime by delivering a new school record of 43 points. She scores 15 of her 43 in the second overtime.

Feb. 25. Despite scoring a season low of 11 points, Redick hits a pair of free throws with 1:28 to play against Temple to break Dickie Hemric's 51-year-old ACC career scoring record.

March 12. Reaching the ACC Tournament final for the ninth straight season, Duke edges league newcomer Boston College 78–76 to claim its seventh league championship in eight years. The Blue Devils ride seven three-pointers from Redick — two in the last two minutes — as he becomes just the fourth player in ACC history to win the tourney MVP award twice.

March 28. Playing in their fifth consecutive NCAA regional final, the Duke women edge Connecticut 63–61 in overtime to earn their fourth trip to the Final Four. The game is played in Bridgeport, Conn., before a sold-out audience of mostly UConn supporters.

April 2–4. The ACC becomes the first conference to send more than two schools to the Women's Final Four. After Maryland defeats North Carolina and Duke defeats LSU in the semifinals, the Terps edge the Blue Devils in overtime for the crown. It is Duke's second appearance in the national championship game and Maryland's first title.

April 12. J. J. Redick receives the 76th Sullivan Award as the outstanding amateur athlete in the United States for 2005. Redick becomes the first Duke athlete to receive the honor and just the third men's basketball player, joining Bill Walton (1973) and Bill Bradley (1965). Older than college football's revered Heisman Trophy, the Sullivan Award has been presented annually by the Amateur Athletic Union (AAU) since 1930 as a tribute to its founder, James E. Sullivan.

Team of 2000–2006

Shane Battier	F	1998–2001
Jason Williams	G	2000–02
Chris Duhon	G	2001–04
J. J. Redick	G	2003–06
Shelden Williams	C	2003–06

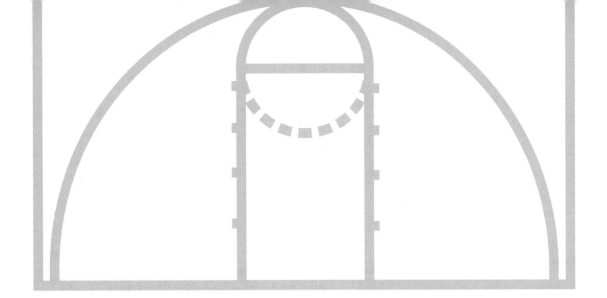

Games of the Century

101 Significant Games from the First 101 Years of Duke Basketball

The First Game

March 2, 1906

Durham — The first century of basketball at Duke began in the spring of 1906 when the institution was still known as Trinity College. Former baseball standout Cap Card, back at his alma mater as director of physical education, succeeded in organizing the first basketball team in the fall of 1905 and arranged a game with Wake Forest for the spring. Wake took the train to Durham for the contest, which it won 24 – 10 in the second official intercollegiate contest played in the state of North Carolina. Wake Forest had defeated Guilford on February 6, 1906.

Trinity's first team was small by modern standards, averaging barely 5 foot 9. It consisted of sixteen undergraduates and grad students, only six of whom played in the first game. Wake Forest was a more experienced club and jumped out to an 18 – 3 halftime lead. Trinity then outscored Wake 7 – 6 in the second half. The turnaround probably wasn't due entirely to the coaches, as Card was the umpire for the contest while Wake coach Richard Crozier was the referee, according to the custom of the day.

The game was played at Angier B. Duke Gym, later known as the Ark, on what is now Duke's East Campus. A balcony surrounding the floor enabled several hundred standing fans to observe the action below. The game was played at 8:00 p.m., a tipoff time that necessitated two days of missed classes for the visiting team. Wake took a train through Raleigh the following morning for its trip back to campus.

Trinity and Wake played again two weeks after the first game, and Wake won again. Living participants from both teams in that initial contest were invited to a golden anniversary recognition at the Duke-Wake game in Durham in 1957.

Trinity (10). Greever 2, Claywell 4, Stem 4, Pugh, White, Grant

Wake Forest (24). Couch 14, Ward, Elliott 6, Beverly 2, Gore, Turner 2

Pulsating State Championship

March 12, 1920

Raleigh — Trinity College claimed its second straight state championship with a 25 – 24 decision over the State College Techs (later to become N.C. State). Played before the largest crowd of the season and spiced by an appearance from the State band, the game was intense and closely fought throughout.

Hip Martin carried the Trinity team with 15 points, over half the team's total. The best player on both ends of the floor, Martin showcased his speed, passing ability, and defensive talents, which limited his State counterpart to just a pair of field goals.

Duke's winning basket came from one of its substitutes, Brick Starling. As State led 24 – 23 with about two minutes left, Starling hit a shot from the middle of the court to provide a pulsating finish.

Trinity (25). Ferrell 6, Cole 2, Richardson, Hathaway, Martin 15, Starling 2

State College (24). Deal 4, Ripple 2, Groome 8, Cline 10, Park, Williams

Just Getting Started

Jan. 26, 1921

Durham — Trinity College had broken off athletic relations with North Carolina in 1898, reportedly because the Trinity administration did not approve of the emphasis that UNC placed on sports. Relations resumed in 1918 and the institutions finally met each other in basketball for the first time in 1920, each winning on the other's home floor.

North Carolina was considered the superior team in 1921 and blew out the Methodists (as Trinity teams were often called at the time) in a February meeting in Chapel Hill. But the January game in Durham marked a significant upset for Trinity by a narrow 25 – 22 margin.

Jimmy Simpson, also known for his football exploits,

led Trinity with 16 points and made a major difference in the second half when he hit three straight field goals to turn the tide. Under the rules of the day, each team had a designated shooter to take all free-throw attempts. When Trinity's shooter missed four of his first five attempts, Simpson took over those duties and hit six of nine in the second half, further contributing to the victory.

The basketball rivalry with North Carolina was just getting started, but this would be the last series win for Trinity/Duke until 1929.

Trinity (25). Simpson 16, Moore 2, Richardson 4, Hathaway 2, Crute 1, Brady, Pennington
North Carolina (22). Carmichael 18, McDonald 2, Erwin, Shepherd 2, Hanby, Morris

It's About Time

Feb. 2, 1929

Durham — Duke ended an eight-year, 16-game losing streak to North Carolina with a 36 – 20 victory. The Blue Devils had not defeated the White Phantoms since a triumph by Trinity College in 1921.

Center Joe Croson, playing in his second varsity game, set the tone for the Devils by scoring 15 points and winning most of the tipoffs to help his team maintain possession of the ball. Duke's man-to-man defense prevented UNC from getting many open shots, particularly in a first half that saw the Devils claim an 18 – 8 halftime margin. Boley Farley guarded UNC's best scorer and held him to one field goal. The Phantoms endured game-long shooting woes, leading one newspaper to comment that "they couldn't hit the Washington Duke Hotel with a shotgun."

Duke (36). Candler 8, Rogers 3, Croson 15, Werber 6, Farley, Councilor 2, Folk 2
North Carolina (20). Hackney 7, Cathey 4, Harper, Marpet 1, Brown 4, Price, Satterfield 4

Maiden Voyage

March 4, 1929

Atlanta — Competing in the Southern Conference for the first time, Duke was one of 16 schools in the 23-team league to earn a spot in the conference tournament. Upon Duke's arrival in Atlanta, the local newspapers referred to the Blue Devils as the "baby members" of the conference, but Duke made journalists, opponents, and fans stand up and take notice with an inspiring effort.

The Blue Devils upset Alabama and North Carolina in their first two games to earn a semifinal date with Georgia. The Bulldogs were favored and took an early lead, but Duke rallied behind guard Bill Werber and center Joe Croson. After Georgia tied the score at 37, Duke scored the last six points on strong moves by Croson, Werber, and Harry Councilor to claim a 43 – 37 victory and a spot in the championship game.

N.C. State topped the Blue Devils in the final, but the conference "baby" had showed it could compete with the best. Fans back home celebrated the success of coach Eddie Cameron's first team and gave it a rousing reception at the railroad tracks near the main entrance to campus. And one of Duke's first true basketball legends was born as well, with Werber hailed as the hero of the tournament, his exploits praised by the *Alumni Register*: "His spectacular running, one-handed shots time after time brought the galleries to their feet, and his guarding was plaster tight."

Duke (43). Jankoski, Councilor 4, Croson 14, Farley 6, Werber 16, Rogers 3, Candler, Thorne
Georgia (37). Palmer 10, Harris 6, Sancord 13, Anderson 5, Martin 3

Early Landmark Victory

Feb. 13, 1930

Durham — Loyola of Chicago fielded one of the strongest teams in the nation and had won 34 of its last 37 games when it reached the Triangle for back-to-back games with North Carolina and Duke. But after edging UNC 26 – 25, Loyola became the victim of one of the early major victories in Duke basketball history as the Blue Devils took a 30 – 27 decision from their high-profile guests.

Loyola center Charlie Murphy was clearly the top player on the floor, but Duke center Joe Croson hit a shot with seven minutes to go that tied the score, then made a few more big baskets down the stretch, as Duke proved

Phil Weaver and brothers Jim and Herb Thompson paced the Blue Devils to the Southern Conference final in 1933..

that it could play with the best. The win was No. 8 in a 15-game winning streak for Eddie Cameron's first great team, a streak that didn't end until a loss in the conference tournament final shut the lid on an 18 – 2 season.

Duke (30). Rogers 4, Councilor 8, Croson 13, Werber 5, Farley, Shaw, Garber

Loyola (27). Waesco 5, Smith 1, Murphy 18, Sextro, Butzen 1, Schulmann 2, Durburg, Finn

Tournament Tough

Feb. 25, 1933

Raleigh — Duke reached the final of the Southern Conference Tournament for the fourth time in its five-year history in the league by whipping coach Eddie Cameron's alma mater, Washington & Lee, 41 – 32 in the semifinals.

The Generals had upset N.C. State in the first round but were no match for the Blue Devils, who spread the wealth while conserving some strength for the title game with South Carolina. Forward Wendell Horne was the star of the day for Duke and helped his team open up a 20 – 12 halftime lead. The Thompson brothers, Herb and Jim, scored the first two baskets of the second half to ignite an 8 – 0 run, and the Generals couldn't catch up. Duke couldn't continue its momentum another day, however, as South Carolina took the championship contest.

Duke celebrated its second Southern Conference title in 1941.

Duke (41). Horne 13, Hayes 8, J. Thompson 7,
H. Thompson 8, Weaver 5
Washington & Lee (32). Sawyers 6, Amith 8,
Fitzwilson 5, Holbrook 9, Henthorne, Fields 4

Duke (40). Swindell 14, Edwards 12, Bergman 8,
Hoffman 2, Minor 2, O'Mara 2
Clemson (30). McFadden 13, Cheves 7, Kitchens 6,
Flathman 3, Bryce 1

Never a Dull Moment

March 6, 1938

Raleigh — One of Duke's most unpredictable teams claimed the school's first league championship with a 40 – 30 victory over Clemson in the Southern Conference Tournament final.

Tabbed the "never a dull moment boys," this squad posted rollercoaster results all season. An upset of North Carolina (13 – 3 in the league) in the regular-season finale got the Blue Devils into the tournament with an overall record of 12 – 9. From there they also upset N.C. State and rallied late to edge Maryland on a basket by Fred "Mouse" Edwards to make their first trip to the finals since 1934.

Though not much was expected of this colorful team during the year, it delivered the championship with a strong final half, using an 8 – 0 run out of intermission to subdue the Tigers. Edwards, Ed Swindell, and Russ Bergman combined for 34 of the 40 points.

Opening of the Stadium

Jan. 6, 1940

Durham — The largest crowd to witness a southern basketball game congregated for the Duke-Princeton contest in 1940 that was the dedication event for the Blue Devils' new arena, Duke Indoor Stadium, the biggest basketball gym south of Philadelphia.

The audience of 8,000 was plunged into darkness a few minutes before the Saturday night tipoff when a faulty fuse caused a 10-minute blackout. When the lights came back on, Duke and Princeton engaged in an even battle that stood 16 – 16 at halftime.

It was still a two-point contest at 27 – 25 with four minutes to go when coach Eddie Cameron sent his resting regulars Glenn Price and Chuck Holley back into the game. Price, who had scored the first five points in the new facility, dropped in a pair of quick baskets to ignite a 9 – 2 finish that left the Blue Devils with a 36 – 27 victory, the first of many on this storied court.

Duke (36). Price 13, Parsons 4, Holley 6, Valasek 2,
  Connelly 4, Spuhler 5, Mock 1, Allen 1
Princeton (27). Meyerholz 7, Winston 4, Carmichael
  2, Bradenbough, Peters 9, Jordan, Busse, Bartlett 1,
  Stewart 4, Lloyd

Lightning Strikes Twice

Feb. 20 – 27, 1941

North Carolina was the class of the Southern Conference in 1941, owning a 14 – 0 league record heading into the regular-season finale at Duke. But the inspired Blue Devils grabbed a 35 – 33 upset in Durham and then repeated the feat a week later in Raleigh with a 38 – 37 victory in the first round of the tournament.

Hap Spuhler was Duke's offensive star in the first game with 14 points, while Bill Mock scored the winning basket with 2:09 to play. Duke froze the ball for most of the last two minutes, attempting just one field goal but getting the offensive rebound to keep possession. When the game ended, Duke students in the boisterous crowd of 4,702 streamed on to the floor and carried the players off on their shoulders.

The tournament game a week later proved just as exciting, with no more than three points separating the two rivals at any time during the second half. Duke's double-teaming defense on UNC center George Glamack, the nation's leading scorer, played a critical role as center Chuck Holley and guard Cy Valasek combined to keep the ball out of his hands. That pair also scored 10 points apiece to lead the offense, while Spuhler scored the winning points with about 2:30 to play.

After eliminating the defending champs, Duke then knocked out William & Mary and defeated South Carolina for the title.

Duke (35). Rothbaum 5, Mock 7, Holley 5, Valasek 2,
  Shokes 2, Spuhler 14, Connelly
North Carolina (33). Rose 7, Pessar 4, Glamack 17,
  Howard 3, Gersten, Severin 2, Smith, Suggs, Shytle

Duke (38). Rothbaum 6, Mock 4, Holley 10, Valasek 10,
  Shokes 2, Spuhler 6, Connelly
North Carolina (37). Rose 14, Pessar 4, Glamack 10,
  Howard 9, Gersten, Severin, Suggs

Fitting Finale, Part I

Feb. 27, 1942

Durham — Eddie Cameron's last Duke team completed a season sweep of North Carolina with one of the most exciting triumphs in the early years of the series. The Blue Devils pulled out a 41 – 40 overtime decision in the final game coached by Cameron at the building that would one day carry his name.

Though close throughout, the game appeared to belong to UNC with 30 seconds left, as the Heels had the ball and a 38 – 36 lead. But Duke took advantage of a turnover by Carolina when center Bob Gantt tapped in a rebound to tie the score. After the Devils' Garland Loftis missed a free throw with 14 seconds left, the contest was headed to overtime.

In the extra session, Loftis put Duke ahead when he hit a free throw with about three minutes to play. Twenty seconds later, Hap Spuhler gave Duke a 41 – 38 lead. Carolina hit a shot from near midcourt to close the scoring, as the Devils finished with a conference record of 15 – 1.

Duke (41). Spuhler 8, Rothbaum 6, Gantt 10, C. Loftis 7,
  G. Loftis 5, Allen 4, Stark, McCahan 1
North Carolina (40). Smith 7, Paine 5, Rose 12,
  Gersten 2, Hayworth 5, Wilson 7, Suggs 2

Fitting Finale, Part II

March 7, 1942

Raleigh — Top-seeded Duke successfully defended its 1941 Southern Conference crown by rolling through the field for a second straight title. The Blue Devils defeated the Red Terrors of N.C. State 45 – 34 in the championship contest, which was coach Eddie Cameron's last game, though no one knew it at the time.

Duke broke away from its 20 – 19 halftime lead with a 9 – 0 run to start the second half, as Cedric Loftis hit the first four points and Clyde Allen the next five. The run was extended to 14 – 3 as Cameron showed off the strength and depth of his roster by continuing to send fresh players into the game. The fast-breaking Devils eventually built up a 45 – 29 margin on the tired State team with three minutes remaining. State center Bones McKinney, a doubtful starter because of a stomach ache, led all scorers with 11 points but was held to one field goal in the second half.

The victory put the finishing touch on a 22 – 2 ledger for Cameron. Before another season came around, Cameron took over the Duke football team and the athletics directorship in the wake of Wallace Wade's departure for the war.

Duke (45). Spuhler 4, Rothbaum 6, Allen 10, McCahan 6, Stark 2, Gantt 2, Seward 2, G. Loftis 7, C. Loftis 6
N.C. State (34). Mock 10, Stevens 4, McKinney 11, Carvalho, Tabscott 5, Ball 3, Strayhorn 1, Almond

Upset in the Final

Feb. 26, 1944

Raleigh — Duke won the Southern Conference Tournament for the third time in four years by upsetting North Carolina 44 – 27 in the championship game.

This was the fourth meeting of the year between Duke and Carolina and evened the season series at 2 – 2. UNC's only conference loss during the regular season had been to the Blue Devils, who entered the tournament with a record of 10 – 13 after facing a schedule loaded with military teams.

Duke beat William & Mary and N.C. State to reach the final and then pulled off "as stunning an upset as ever seen in the Southern Conference," according to one newspaper. After a tight opening 14 minutes, Duke took a 27 – 17 halftime lead and limited UNC to just 10 points in the second half. Gordon Carver earned unanimous all-tournament recognition for his starring role with the Blue Devils, who gave coach Gerry Gerard his first title.

Duke (44). Carver 11, Hartley 8, Balitsaris, Wright 15, Hyde, Harner 7, Bailey 3, Turner, Gilbert, Metzler
North Carolina (27). Mock 7, Poole, Box 12, Donnan, Dewell 4, Altemose, Fitch 1, Creticos 2, Anderson, Hayworth 1

The Wright Stuff

Jan. 29, 1946

Durham — The Kittyhawks of Wright Field in Ohio had one of the top postwar amateur teams in America and were ranked No. 1 nationally by the Dunkle index when they came to Durham in January 1946. The service team of veteran All-Americas from various schools, put together and initially coached by Chuck Taylor, had lost only one game when it arrived in Durham, that to the professional world champion Ft. Wayne Zollners.

Taylor, no longer affiliated with the Hawks but working for Converse Rubber, was on hand to watch his old club take on a Duke team that owned a 12 – 4 record after dropping consecutive games at Maryland and Navy. The Blue Devils ended their losing streak and became the first college team to beat Wright Field, pulling off a 44 – 43 upset.

Dick Whiting and Ed Koffenberger hit key shots down the stretch, and Whiting tied the score at 40 with four minutes left. John Seward put Duke on top 42 – 41 in the closing minutes when the definitive play took place. The Hawks' Bruce Hale was whistled for a foul on Koffenberger, protested the call with abusive language, and was assessed a technical. Koffenberger made both free throws for a 44 – 41 lead with 1:15 to go, then Duke inbounded the ball and froze it until Wright Field picked up a late steal and scored with five seconds left to cut the final margin to one point.

Duke (44). Ausbon 6, Seward 10, Koffenberger 12, Gordon 2, Whiting 14, Robinson, Cheek, Roellke
Wright Field (43). Hale 12, Eddleman 11, Mahnken 11, Hansen 7, Negratti 2, Witry

Title Time Again

March 2, 1946

Raleigh — Duke reached the Southern Conference final for the seventh straight year and claimed its fourth championship of the 1940s with a 49 – 30 rout of Wake Forest in the title game.

A rather diminutive team whose tallest starter was Ed Koffenberger at 6 – 2, the Blue Devils were just a step behind UNC as the class of the league. Carolina's lone conference loss in 14 games had been an overtime upset by Duke in January, while the Blue Devils' only two league defeats included a 10-point loss to UNC in Durham.

A tournament showdown never materialized, though, as Wake Forest upset Carolina in the semis, putting the

Deacons in the final for the first time in 118 years of school history. One newspaper predicted that Wake would be going after its biggest victory ever when it met Duke, but the Blue Devils pulled away early after beating N.C. State and Virginia Tech by identical 44 – 38 scores in the first two days of the tournament.

Koffenberger finished as the event's leading scorer with 40 points in three games as Duke claimed what would prove to be its final Southern Conference crown.

Duke (49). Seward 9, Ausbon 11, Koffenberger 11, Gordon 6, Robinson 2, Whiting 10, Cordell, Cheek, Corrington, Gray

Wake Forest (30). Veitch 4, Williams 11, Mayberry, Walters 5, Hinerman 8, Lougee 2, Ognovich

Frenzied Finish at the Garden

Jan. 9, 1947

New York — Duke and New York University teamed up for the second double-overtime game in the 13-year history of the old Madison Square Garden, with the hometown Violets surviving for a 64 – 61 decision before a crowd of 18,034.

Coach Gerry Gerard's Blue Devils, playing a brutal schedule that had them on the road for nine of their first 11 games, suffered just their second defeat but battled to the end. Senior Ed Koffenberger, who played the entire 50 minutes, sent the game into the first overtime when he scored on a drive with 10 seconds left, was fouled, and completed the three-point opportunity to tie the score.

NYU got a layup with 30 seconds left in the first OT to take a 57 – 55 advantage, but Duke's Garland Loftis knocked in a rebound to tie the game again and force another five minutes. Playing without front-liners John Seward and Ben Collins, who fouled out, the depleted Devils fell behind 62 – 57 and could not overcome NYU's delay-game tactics in the closing minutes.

Duke completed a long road trip two days later with a win at Temple and went on to post a regular-season record of 19 – 7.

Duke (61). Seward 5, Koffenberger 17, Collins 11, Loftis 14, Gordon 8, Ausbon 2, Youmans 3, Wallingford, Sapp 1, Rothbaum

NYU (64). Forman 13, Goldstein 5, Schayes 3, Tanenbaum 12, Lumpp 17, Wells, Debonis 7, Roth, Kelly 4, Dolhon 3

All-Time Best Comeback

Dec. 30, 1950

Raleigh — Duke staged the most prolific comeback in NCAA basketball history when it rallied to edge Tulane 74 – 72 in the third-place game of the second annual Dixie Classic.

The first half was all Tulane. The Green Wave broke open a 22 – 19 game by holding the Blue Devils scoreless for seven minutes during a 22 – 0 run. They maintained a blistering pace and led by as many as 32 points before settling for a 56 – 27 halftime margin.

The second half, however, was all Duke. More specifically, it was all Dick Groat, the 6 – 0 guard who poured in 24 of his game-high 32 points to pace the rally, outscoring the entire Green Wave team after intermission.

Even with Groat and captain Scotty York stirring the Blue Devils, Tulane still led by 20 at 72 – 52 with eight minutes left. But the Green Wave did not score again. Groat had 12 points in the last four minutes alone and tied the score with a push shot at the one-minute mark. Center Dayton Allen then added the winning goal to give Duke new NCAA records for biggest deficit overcome to win a game and biggest halftime deficit overcome.

Duke (74). Fleming 3, Deimling 8, Allen 11, Groat 32, York 14, Engberg 4, Crowder, Kulpan 2, Johnson

Tulane (72). Payton 9, Reed 22, Holt 15, Wilhelm 12, Pederson 7, Hullenger 3, Carlin, Hubbard 4, Wick

Gerry Gerard Night

Dec. 3, 1951

Durham — Duke whipped North Carolina 77 – 59 in an early-season nonconference game that marked Gerry Gerard Night at the Indoor Stadium. The contest was organized as a tribute to the former Duke head coach, who had died of cancer earlier in the year. The proceeds went to an educational fund for Gerard's two daughters, who at halftime were presented with a color portrait of their late father.

The game itself was close early. With Dick Groat

experiencing one of his worst shooting halves, only 1 of 8 from the floor, sophomores Bernie Janicki and Rudy D'Emilio carried much of the load. Center Dick Crowder put Duke ahead 24 – 23 with five minutes left in the first half, the Devils advanced that lead to 34 – 25 by the break, and the Tar Heels could never get back in the game. Groat shared scoring honors but got most of his points late, after the game was all but decided.

Duke (77). Fleming 4, Janicki 16, Glasow 11, Groat 16, D'Emilio 12, Latimer 1, Deimling 4, Crowder 4, Lacy 2, Johnson 3, Shabel 4

North Carolina (59). Wallace 14, Grimaldi 9, Likins 6, Deasy 12, Phillips 7, Gaines 4, Lifson 5, Schwarz 2, Smith, Taylor

Record-Setting Day

Feb. 29, 1952

Durham — In his final home appearance, guard Dick Groat hit 19 of 37 field goals and 10 of 11 free throws for a Duke record of 48 points to pace a 94 – 64 destruction of North Carolina. The effort bested his previous school mark of 46 set four weeks earlier, as well as the Big Four mark of 47 held by N.C. State's Sam Ranzino.

Groat's parents and two sisters arrived from Pennsylvania just before tipoff to see him pump in 17 points as Duke opened up a huge halftime lead. When UNC rallied to within 58 – 50 in the second half, Groat promptly hit eight straight shots to help his team regain control. Scoring 22 points in the fourth quarter, he was removed from the game with 15 seconds left to a prolonged standing ovation from the crowd of 7,000.

Groat broke down in tears as his teammates swarmed him, and again in the locker room as he accepted congratulations from the Blue Devils and Tar Heels for the second-highest-scoring game in Southern Conference history. Before leaving the floor at the end of the game, Groat took the microphone and spoke to the crowd, a senior tradition that remained popular fifty years later.

"As captain of the team, I would like to thank you fans for your support during the season," he said. "We are sorry that we lost five games but we hope we can win the conference championship for you."

Groat's scoring record was not the only significant achievement in the contest. Sophomore forward Bernie Janicki collected an astonishing total of 31 rebounds, a single-game school record that still stands.

Duke (94). Janicki 13, Fleming 6, Crowder 7, Groat 48, D'Emilio 14, Deimling, Latimer, Glasow 2, Lacy, Johnson 4, Shabel

North Carolina (64). Lifson 16, Wallace 5, Deasy 21, Grimaldi 3, Phillips 6, Gaines, Likins 3, Schwartz 1, Redding, Taylor 9

What a Thriller

Feb. 12, 1953

Wake Forest — Down by 16 points in the first half and by 11 with five minutes to play, Duke finished strong to claim an exhilarating 101 – 99 overtime victory over Wake Forest. Wake star Dickie Hemric broke his own school record with 44 points, but he fouled out with 3:48 to play and the Deacons clinging to a seven-point lead. Led by Joe Belmont and Rudy Lacy, Duke outscored Wake 9 – 1 over the final 2:50 to tie the score. Bill Reigel, in the midst of his career game of 38 points, hit two free throws with 59 seconds left to cap the comeback and force the overtime.

Duke shot ahead in the extra period, but this time Wake came back to tie with 25 seconds remaining. Junior guard Rudy D'Emilio got the ball for Duke, held it at midcourt until the nine-second mark, and then made the decisive move. As a Wake defender rushed him, D'Emilio used a fake to get free and drove inside for a left-handed layup to win the game before a standing-room-only crowd of 2,500 at Gore Gym.

Duke (101). Janicki 11, Reigel 38, Mayer 2, Belmont 8, D'Emilio 19, Lacy 12, Lamley, Driesell, Shabel 5, Decker 6, Turner

Wake Forest (99). Williams 21, George 3, Hemric 44, Lyles 10, DePorter 8, Lipstas 7, Davis 2, Koch, McRae 4, DeVos

Action-Packed

Feb. 9, 1954

Raleigh — From the late 1940s through the late 1950s, Everett Case's N.C. State program enjoyed a mastery of

Backcourt aces Joe Belmont and Rudy D'Emilio keyed a three-game winning streak against N.C. State from 1953 to 1954.

its backyard rival Duke. But the Blue Devils staged a three-game winning streak over the Wolfpack between 1953 and 1954, capped by a tense 90 – 89 decision at raucous Reynolds Coliseum.

State held an 89 – 86 lead after converting a pair of free throws with 34 seconds remaining. Rudy Lacy hit two free throws for Duke seven seconds later to make it an 89 – 88 game. State then lost possession and the Blue Devils hustled down the floor, sending the ball into Lacy for a hook shot. He missed, but Don Tobin, a 6 – 5 sophomore reserve, caught the rebound just inside the foul circle and fired it back toward the goal while he was still in the air. It banked in with 13 seconds left to give Duke the lead. State was unable to get off another shot, and Tobin left the floor a hero after playing a total of three minutes on the night. Coach Harold Bradley had just inserted him back in the lineup during Lacy's free throws with 27 seconds left.

It marked the third straight narrow win for Duke over State. The Devils had won 87 – 85 a month earlier and 84 – 82 the previous year in Raleigh.

Duke (90). Janicki 25, Decker 4, Mayer 16, Belmont 19, D'Emilio 10, Lacy 2, Tobin 2, Doherty 5, Morgan 7, Driesell, Turner

N.C. State (89). Tyler 18, Thompson 7, Shavlik 31, Molodet 22, Bell, Dinardo 5, Dwyer, Gotkin 2, Scheffel 2, Applebaum 2

Oh My, Mayer

Feb. 9, 1955

Wake Forest — Duke's first NCAA Tournament team picked up a major road win when it edged Wake Forest 75 – 73 in a truculent midseason ACC battle.

Forward Ronnie Mayer led Duke in scoring with 19 points and made virtually all the key plays down the stretch. With Wake trying to freeze the ball in the final three minutes to salt away a victory, Mayer came up with two steals and converted them into four points to tie the score, the last coming on free throws with 1:15 to go.

When Duke regained possession shortly thereafter, it was Mayer who collected a rebound on a missed Blue Devil shot and scored on the putback with 18 seconds left, to put his team ahead for the first time all game. Then he rebounded a miss by Wake Forest with six seconds left and passed it out to Joe Belmont to run out the clock, as the Blue Devils moved into a tie for first in the ACC.

Duke (75). Mayer 19, Lakata 7, Morgan 14, Belmont 14, Turner 4, Lamley 13, Doherty 4, Thuemmel

Wake Forest (73). Davis 18, George 20, Hemric 22, Murdock 9, Wiggins 4, Gilley

Late Eruption

Dec. 18, 1956

Durham — Legendary coach Adolph Rupp brought his seventh-ranked Kentucky team to the Indoor Stadium and saw it build up a 15-point lead on the Blue Devils, who were playing their home opener after five road games. But Duke made several big plays in the closing minutes to claim an 85 – 84 victory, the most impressive of four wins against top 10 teams for a squad that finished with a 13 – 11 record.

Kentucky made 15 of its first 23 shots to take an early

30–15 lead. The Wildcats still led 53–40 early in the second half, and despite several Duke runs remained on top by 84–75 with 2:15 to play. But Duke's full-court press, led by Bucky Allen, Bobby Joe Harris, and Bob Vernon, began forcing turnovers and turning them into points, producing a 10–0 run to finish the game. Four times in the last 50 seconds Duke scored after stealing the ball or prompting a mistake by Kentucky.

Harris made two steals in the last 30 seconds and passed ahead to Allen after the second one for a layup that put Duke on top for the first time at 85–84. Kentucky missed a late free throw that could have tied the game, and the Devils dribbled out the clock before their student fans swarmed the court to celebrate.

Duke (85). Robertson, Miller 4, Newcome 21, Vernon 7, Harris 10, Allen 20, Clement 14, Schmidt 9

Kentucky (84). Cox 22, Mills 11, Crigler 9, Beck 6, Hatton 22, Calvert 14, Smith

Beating the Best

Jan. 27, 1958

Durham — Unranked with a 6–5 record, Duke pulled off one of the season's biggest upsets by clipping previously undefeated and top-ranked West Virginia 72–68 before a surprised home crowd of 7,800.

The Mountaineers featured sophomore star Jerry West as well as 6–10 center Lloyd Sharrar and had ended UNC's 37-game winning streak a month earlier in the Kentucky Invitational. But Duke grabbed a 10-point lead in the first eight minutes and didn't flinch when West Virginia rallied to go on top in the second half.

Jim Newcome had 20 points and 14 rebounds to pace Duke's efforts, while coach Harold Bradley used a three-guard lineup of Bucky Allen, Bob Vernon, and Bobby Joe Harris to control most of the game. This marked the first time that Duke defeated a team ranked No. 1 in the Associated Press college poll.

Duke (72). Robertson, Schmidt 12, Newcome 20, Vernon 18, Harris 10, Allen 12, Bateman

West Virginia (68). Smith 24, West 20, Akers 2, Sharrar 9, Gardner 4, Vincent 7, Retton 2

Sign of Things to Come

March 5, 1960

Raleigh — A 63–59 victory over 18th-ranked Wake Forest gave Duke its first-ever ACC Tournament championship, under the unlikeliest of circumstances. The Blue Devils had been swamped three times during the regular season by their semifinal opponent North Carolina and twice more by their final foe Wake Forest. But they edged both in tight tourney games for the first installment of what would turn out to be much postseason success enjoyed by new coach Vic Bubas.

Employing a corps of veteran players inherited from former coach Harold Bradley, Bubas saw his squad upset No. 6 Utah early in the year before closing with just a 3–6 record in February. But with Doug Kistler pumping in 26 points and Howard Hurt adding 21, the Devils got by South Carolina in the first round of the ACC, then upset UNC by two on the strength of 30 points from Carroll Youngkin.

Kistler (22 points) and captain Hurt (14) again led the way in the final over Wake, with Kistler taking MVP honors. The team kept its momentum going through two rounds of the NCAA Tournament, a sign of what awaited the program under Bubas's leadership.

Duke (63). Kistler 22, Hurt 14, Youngkin 10, Frye 12, Mullen 5, Cantwell, Mewhort

Wake Forest (59). Budd 10, Ritchie 6, Packer 5, Steele, Chappell 19, Wiggins 9, Hart 6, Forte 4, Cullen

Fight to the Finish

Feb. 4, 1961

Durham — The most notorious brawl in ACC basketball history occurred just seconds before the conclusion of the 1961 Duke-UNC contest at the Indoor Stadium. Fourth-ranked Duke topped the fifth-ranked Tar Heels 81–77 for one of the most important wins of the year, but the result was overshadowed by last-minute fisticuffs.

Art Heyman all but insured the win for Duke by sinking a pair of free throws with 15 seconds left, giving him 36 points and his team a five-point lead. The Tar Heels had led at the half, but Heyman took over with 24 of his points after intermission, finishing 11 of 13 from the field and 14 of 17 from the foul line.

A few seconds after his last free throws, Heyman fouled unc's Larry Brown right in front of the Tar Heel bench and the scene exploded. Brown threw two punches; Heyman retaliated in self-defense and was immediately pummeled by eight Tar Heels, igniting a wild free-for-all.

Duke improved to 16 – 1 and moved up to No. 3 in the national polls, but ten days after the incident the acc suspended Heyman, Brown, and unc's Donnie Walsh for the rest of the regular-season conference games. That severely disrupted Duke's chemistry, as it dropped three conference road games in the final two weeks and was blasted by Wake Forest in the tournament final.

Duke (81). Heyman 36, Kistler 4, Youngkin 18, Hurt 10, Frye 10, Schmidt 2, Mewhort 1
North Carolina (77). Moe 11, Hudock 18, Kepley 16, Larese 17, Poteet 5, Walsh, Brown 8, Krause 2

What Might Have Been

Dec. 28, 1962

Durham — When high school recruit Bill Bradley announced in 1961 that he was coming to Duke, Blue Devil fans were salivating over a potential future lineup featuring Bradley, Art Heyman, and Jeff Mullins, three of the best college players in the nation.

Bradley later changed his mind and went to Princeton, but local Duke fans did get to see all three stars on the same floor when the Tigers came to Durham for a game early in the 1962 – 63 season.

Heyman, a senior ranked sixth in the nation in scoring, poured in 27 points while Mullins, a junior, added 28. Duke threw a box-and-one defense at Bradley, a sophomore who scored 24 points, just a touch below his 24.8 average.

Duke built up a 14-point halftime lead and had to fight off a late Tiger rally to win 85 – 74. The victory broke a two-game losing streak for Duke and gave Princeton its first defeat of the year.

Duke (85). Heyman 27, Mullins 28, Buckley 9, Schmidt 11, Ferguson, Herbster, Harrison 6, Tison 2, Kitching 2

Princeton (74). Bradley 24, Haarlow 13, Niemann 4, Hyland 12, Kingston 3, Chandler, Howard 13, Hunter 5

Mastering the Mentor

Feb. 9, 1963

Raleigh — Coach Vic Bubas considered it one of his team's worst-played games of the season, but there was historical significance to the Blue Devils' 56 – 55 victory over N.C. State.

The win was Bubas's first over the Wolfpack at Reynolds Coliseum, on the campus where he played as a collegian and coached with the legendary Everett Case. It also enabled him to even his record at 4 – 4 against his mentor.

Jeff Mullins gave Duke the lead with 2:11 to play and State held for a final shot, which it missed with four seconds left. This was the closest that Duke came to losing during a 14 – 0 acc regular season.

Duke (56). Heyman 17, Mullins 21, Buckley 7, Schmidt 5, Harrison 2, Ferguson, Tison 4, Herbster
N.C. State (55). Robloff 6, Key 7, Sinnock 8, Greiner 3, Auksel 15, Speaks 5, Whitfield 11

King Arthur's Court

Feb. 23, 1963

Durham — For three straight seasons, Art Heyman was a unanimous selection for the All-acc team. As a senior his biggest personal rival was unc sophomore Billy Cunningham, also a unanimous All-acc pick. Heyman had his best game against Cunningham during his final appearance at the Indoor Stadium, a 106 – 93 clubbing of the Tar Heels on an unforgettable Senior Day.

After a close first half, Duke conducted a unique halftime ceremony in which Heyman stayed on the floor and was recognized for his many career achievements. Then he and his teammates proceeded to blast North Carolina in the second half. While Cunningham totaled 31 points and 16 rebounds for the Heels, Heyman shone even brighter by finishing with career highs of 40 points and 24 rebounds. Jeff Mullins and Jay Buckley contributed double-doubles in support of Heyman.

Coach Vic Bubas removed Heyman from the contest with 22 seconds left, to an ovation that lasted three minutes.

Duke (106). Heyman 40, Mullins 22, Buckley 18, Schmidt 12, Harrison 7, Ferguson 4, Tison 2, Herbster 1

North Carolina (93). Cunningham 31, Shaffer 4, McSweeney 4, Brown 27, Poteet 18, Cooke 7, Respess 2, Drause, Callahan

Perfect Ending

March 2, 1963

Raleigh—Duke was rarely challenged during the 1963 basketball season, a pattern that extended to the ACC Tournament when the Blue Devils defeated Wake Forest 68–57 to complete a perfect league campaign.

Ranked among the national top five most of the year, Duke had only a handful of close calls during a February road swing before finishing 14–0 in conference play, its first undefeated league season. The Devils then swept through the tournament with three wins by an average margin of over 15 points to claim the title. North Carolina's national championship club of 1957 was the only other ACC team at that point in history that had gone a spotless 17–0 in the ACC.

Art Heyman and Jeff Mullins each averaged over 20 points a game in the regular season and the tournament, with Heyman taking honors for league player of the year and tourney MVP.

Duke (68). Heyman 24, Mullins 20, Buckley 8, Schmidt 7, Harrison, Herbster 3, Tison 6

Wake Forest (57). Hassell 11, Woollard 11, Wiedeman 18, Christie 4, Carmichael 6, Watts 3, Martin, Koehler 4, Zawacki

Formidable Foe

Feb. 15, 1964

Durham—One of the showcase games of the 1964 season pitted No. 4 Davidson of the Southern Conference versus No. 5 Duke of the ACC. The Blue Devils were 16–3, the Wildcats 19–2. Each team had its share of stars, and the Wildcats were coached by a rising Duke alumnus, Lefty Driesell.

Jeff Mullins, Vic Bubas, and Art Heyman enjoyed Duke's first undefeated ACC season in 1963.

Jeff Mullins hit 12 of 28 shots for 29 points to carry the Blue Devils to an 82–75 victory, the school's 25th straight on its home court. Davidson got 28 points and 10 boards from Fred Hetzel, a former Duke recruiting target who had led the Wildcats to an upset of the Devils the previous year. But Duke won the rebounding battle and had more depth; starting center Jay Buckley had 17 points and 16 rebounds, while Duke's two "subs" were the future Hall of Famers Jack Marin and Steve Vacendak. Marin posted a double-double with 11 points and 10 rebounds.

Duke (82). Mullins 29, Tison 5, Buckley 17, Harrison 10, Ferguson 6, Marin 11, Vacendak 4

Davidson (75). Holland 18, Davidson 8, Hetzel 28, Snyder 16, Teague 1, Beerman 0, Marcon 2, Stone 2

Sweet Revenge

March 7, 1964

Raleigh—Duke's only ACC defeat in 1964 was by a scant one-point margin at Wake Forest, a February upset that ended the Blue Devils' 28-game league winning streak.

Duke got its revenge in the championship game of the ACC Tournament, routing the Deacons 80–59 as four starters scored in double figures. Duke pulled away from a nine-point halftime edge with a dominating performance.

Jay Buckley scored 59 points and Jeff Mullins 58 during the Devils' three tournament blowouts to head the all-tourney team, with Mullins claiming MVP honors.

"Duke has a great team and I wish them the best of everything in the NCAA playoffs. I hope they can keep the peak they have now," said Wake coach Bones McKinney, whose team was in its fifth straight ACC final.

Duke (80). Mullins 24, Tison 15, Buckley 18, Harrison 14, Ferguson 4, Marin, Herbster 3, Kitching 2, Mann, Harscher, Cox

Wake Forest (59). Hassell 12, Leonard 15, Christie 13, Carmichael 2, Watts 10, Herring 2, Anderson, Brooks 5, Lozier

Mullins's Signature Game

March 13, 1964

Raleigh — A week after leading Duke to the ACC title, senior All-America Jeff Mullins was back in Reynolds Coliseum for the NCAA Eastern Regional and vaulted his Blue Devils past Villanova, 87–73.

Mullins threw his best career game at the Wildcats, scoring 43 points that accounted for almost half his team's total in its conquest of a squad ranked No. 7 in the nation. Mullins hit 19 of 28 from the field and grabbed 12 rebounds. The most spectacular of his many noteworthy plays was just before halftime, when he hit a halfcourt shot at the buzzer to give the Devils a 49–33 lead.

Mullins had 28 points in the first half and hit Duke's first three shots of the second half, before cooling off and going scoreless for nine minutes while the Wildcats roared back. But then Mullins hit three in a row and the Devils put together a 13–1 run in the closing minutes to resume command.

Mullins also turned in a solid defensive performance, holding Villanova's high-scoring Richie Moore to 4-of-12 shooting for eight points.

Duke (87). Mullins 43, Tison 13, Buckley 9, Harrison 2, Ferguson, Vacendak 8, Marin 8, Herbster 4

Villanova (73). Melchionni 18, Jones 18, Moore 8, Washington 8, Sallee 6, Erickson 10, Schaffer 5, Leftwich

Payback Time

March 20, 1964

Kansas City — When they met in Ann Arbor in December, No. 3 Michigan humbled No. 5 Duke 83–67, a rare lopsided defeat for a program that had spent most of four years ranked in the national top 10. When the two schools met in the Final Four at season's end, the Blue Devils avenged that loss with a satisfying 91–80 triumph that sent them into their first national championship game.

Seniors Jay Buckley and Jeff Mullins were sensational for the No. 3 Devils against the No. 2 Wolverines. Buckley hit 11 of 16 shots for 25 points and grabbed 14 rebounds, while Mullins scored 21 points with eight rebounds. All five starters scored in double figures, with point guard Denny Ferguson running the Devils' fast-paced attack while Hack Tison complemented Buckley inside with 12 points and 13 boards.

Rebounding made a major difference. Duke had been creamed on the boards in Ann Arbor, 62–35, but forged a 41–41 deadlock in the Final Four game.

Cazzie Russell and Bill Buntin combined for 50 of Michigan's points, and both fouled out in the final minute after Duke had all but assured itself a spot in the NCAA final, where it lost to UCLA.

Duke (91). Mullins 21, Tison 12, Buckley 25, Harrison 14, Ferguson 12, Marin 2, Vacendak 5, Herbster

Michigan (80). Buntin 19, Cantrell 12, Russell 31, Tregoning 8, Darden 5, Myers 4, Pomey 1, Herner

Statement Games

Feb. 3–9, 1965

Sixth-ranked Duke faced N.C. State twice in one week and won both games thanks to the heroics of Jack Marin.

First came an 84–74 decision at Reynolds Coliseum, in which the Blue Devils took over first place in the ACC. Marin, averaging just under 17 points a game, hit 14 of 17 from the field and finished with 32 points along with 11 rebounds. His biggest basket came with about five minutes left after State had drawn to within three at 70–67. A jumper by Marin at that point sent Duke on its winning run and handed the Wolfpack its first defeat after 11 straight wins under new coach Press Maravich.

"We didn't figure on Marin being that hot," Maravich noted. "We'd have won without him in there. He was out of this world."

The next week Duke defeated the Pack in Durham 78 – 67 in overtime. Marin hit 12 of 18 shots for 27 points and added 10 rebounds. After a 65 – 65 stalemate in regulation, Marin hit a rebound basket early in overtime to trigger a 13 – 2 onslaught over the extra five minutes. State was playing without starter Pete Coker, who had a virus.

"It's tough to play a team when it holds the ball," Duke coach Vic Bubas said. "It was our second straight bruising ball game with them and we're very happy to win this one."

At halftime, recently retired N.C. State coach Everett Case was honored for his legendary career, with gifts from the Duke athletics department and the Blue Devil Club of Durham.

Duke (84). Marin 32, Vacendak 15, Tison 11, Ferguson 3, Verga 15, Riedy 4, Herbster 4

N.C. State (74). Matlocks 13, Lakins 19, Moffitt 4, Moore 16, Coker 15, Biedenbach 7, Hodgdon, Gealy

Duke (78). Marin 27, Vacendak 5, Tison 21, Ferguson 4, Verga 18, Riedy 1, Herbster 2

N.C. State (67). Matlocks 16, Lakins 30, Moffitt 8, Moore, Biedenbach 10, Hodgdon 2, Gealy, Worsley, Blondeau 1, Taylor

A Cavalcade of Points

Feb. 11, 1965

Durham — The most overwhelming offensive display in school history led to a total destruction of the Virginia Cavaliers, as Duke posted a 136 – 72 victory. It marked the highest-scoring Duke output ever and the Blue Devils' largest victory margin (64 points) in an ACC game.

The game was the last at home for the season, so coach Vic Bubas started four seniors: regulars Hack Tison and Denny Ferguson, with reserves Ron Herbster and Brent Kitching. They got the Devils off to an 11 – 0 start before regulars Jack Marin and Steve Vacendak even entered the contest. Duke blew out to a 33 – 11 lead in the first 10 minutes.

All 14 Duke players scored, with Marin topping the

charts at 25 points. No starter played more than 25 minutes. The Devils made 55 field goals, a school record, and hit 59 percent from the floor.

"This is the type of game you dream about your team playing," Bubas said. "Once in a blue moon everything you touch turns to gold, and that was the kind of night we had."

There were two interesting sidebars to the Devils' record-shattering performance. Before the game, the crowd stood for a moment of silence to honor the memory of veteran Duke trainer and track coach Bob Chambers, who had died earlier that day. Then at halftime, Bubas accepted a trophy from the Kappa Sigma fraternity that would be presented each year to the basketball reserve contributing the most to team morale. The award was named for Ted Mann Jr., who would have been a senior on the 1965 team. He had died in a swimming accident on Labor Day.

Duke (136). Kitching 7, Herbster 7, Tison 19, Ferguson 13, Verga 18, Marin 25, Vacendak 12, Riedy 14, Allen 2, Liccardo 4, McKaig 2, Zimmer 4, McBride 7, Fitts 2

Virginia (72). Connelly 27, Caldwell 13, Davis 6, Meyer 6, Metzger, Sanders 17, Goble 3, Wilcox, Wafle

Bad to the Bruins

Dec. 10 – 11, 1965

Two-time defending national champion UCLA left Los Angeles with an undefeated record and the No. 1 national ranking. But the Bruins were humbled on back-to-back dates with Duke. They dropped an 82 – 66 decision in Durham on Friday night, and then fell by 94 – 75 on the following night before a sellout crowd at the old Charlotte Coliseum.

Irreverent Duke students yelled, "Who's he?" when the Bruins were introduced before the game. The Blue Devil players also refused to be intimidated, repeatedly attacking and breaking coach John Wooden's famed full-court zone press to score. Though Duke didn't enjoy its best shooting night in the Durham game (38 percent), it completely dominated the boards by a 58 – 34 margin, with Mike Lewis claiming 21 rebounds and Bob Riedy 18.

Duke had such a commanding lead that Wooden pulled his starters with 11 minutes to play.

Duke's shooting touch was on display the next night in Charlotte, as the Devils hit 58 percent from the floor. Jack Marin connected on 10 of 15 field goals and Bob Verga hit 10 of 14 to lead the way. A long shot by Verga early in the second half helped Duke to take command, while strong offensive rebounding again played a role. Duke's lead ballooned to as much as 28 points at 80–52.

The two triumphs ended a 17-game winning streak by UCLA and shot Duke up to No. 1 in the polls, a ranking that the Devils held until a loss in February to West Virginia.

Duke (82). Marin 20, Riedy 3, Lewis 16, Vacendak 14, Verga 16, Wendelin, Chapman 9, Liccardo 4, Allen, McKaig

UCLA (66). Lacey 2, McIntosh 9, Lynn 19, Warren 13, Washington 6, Saffer 2, Saner 2, Judd 2, Hoffman 1, Sutherland 2, Chamber 2, Chrisman 2

Duke (94). Marin 23, Riedy 14, Lewis 8, Vacendak 10, Verga 22, Wendelin 6, Chapman 9, Liccardo 2, McKaig

UCLA (75). Lacey 13, McIntosh 10, Lynn 14, Warren 17, Washington 2, Saffer 12, Saner 2, Judd, Hoffman 2

Overtime Sensation

Dec. 21, 1965

Detroit — One of the Blue Devils' most exciting wins of the 1960s came on this visit to Cobo Arena, where No. 1 Duke edged No. 3 Michigan 100–93 in overtime.

Jack Marin and Cazzie Russell enjoyed matching 30-point games. But the Blue Devils had more balance in bouncing back from a 14-point deficit. A pair of steals and baskets by Bob Verga gave Duke a one-point lead with nine seconds left in regulation, and Steve Vacendak added a free throw to make it 85–83. But the Wolverines tied the score with a rebound basket to force overtime. Verga then hit nine of his 27 points in the extra session to point Duke toward victory.

"I had a lot of questions about this team until tonight," coach Vic Bubas said. "They won what I believe was the greatest comeback any Duke team of mine has ever had."

Duke (100). Marin 30, Riedy 12, Lewis 14, Vacendak 11, Verga 27, Chapman 6, Liccardo, Wendelin

Michigan (93). Russell 30, Darden 2, Dill 12, Thompson 13, Clawson 20, Myers 14, Bankey 2

Four Corners Foiled

March 4, 1966

Raleigh — North Carolina coach Dean Smith employed his "four corners" delay strategy for the first time in an attempt to slow down a Duke team that had beaten his Heels by double digits twice during the regular season. UNC opened up a five-point lead in this ACC Tournament semifinal, but the Blue Devils rallied for a 21–20 victory. A basket by Steve Vacendak with 2:09 left tied the score, and Mike Lewis made the second of two free throws with four seconds left for the win.

"I knew I was a pretty good foul shooter. I was pretty sure I could make one of two," Lewis recalled later. "Then I choked on the first one and the rim got a little smaller."

Duke knocked off N.C. State on the Wolfpack's home floor the following day for its third ACC title in four years.

Duke (21). Marin 5, Riedy 2, Lewis 4, Vacendak 6, Verga 4, Liccardo, Wendelin

North Carolina (20). Yokley 6, Lewis 5, Bennett 5, Gauntlett 1, Miller 3

Clash of the Titans

March 18, 1966

College Park, Md — Duke's best shot at a national title during the Vic Bubas era ended with an 83–79 loss to Kentucky in a superbly played NCAA semifinal between the top two teams in the country.

Each team, unfortunately, had to play with one of its best not at full strength. Duke's Bob Verga had been hospitalized all week with strep throat and was able to hit just two shots for four points. Kentucky's Larry Conley was stricken by the flu but was still able to inspire his team with 10 points.

Jack Marin, who had a deadly left-handed shot, compensated somewhat for Verga's offense with a brilliant

29-point game on 11-of-18 shooting. He had two free throws late to keep Duke alive after the Wildcats had claimed a 77 – 71 lead. But for the most part the game was even throughout, with four free throws by Kentucky reserve Cliff Berger making the difference in the final 45 seconds.

After surviving the strong challenge from No. 2 Duke, Rupp's Runts saw their 23-game winning streak come to an end the next night with an upset loss in the national title game against Texas Western, the first team with an all-black starting five to win an NCAA championship.

Duke (79). Marin 29, Riedy 6, Lewis 21, Vacendak 17, Verga 4, Wendelin 2, Liccardo, Barone
Kentucky (83). Conley 10, Riley 19, Jaracz 8, Dampier 23, Kron 12, Tallent 4, Berger 7, Gamble

Very Verga

Feb. 21, 1967

Durham — With Mike Lewis dominating inside and Bob Verga hitting from outside, Duke crunched Wake Forest 97 – 84 on another memorable Senior Day at the Indoor Stadium.

Coach Vic Bubas started seniors Verga, Bob Riedy, Jim Liccardo, and Stuart McKaig. They helped Duke open up an early 10-point lead before Wake rallied to pull ahead by 43 – 39 at halftime.

But Verga was not about to lose his last home game. He fired in 12 of 28 shots and notched the sixth 30-point game of his career before leaving to a standing ovation with 52 seconds left. Riedy, removed from the game just before Verga, also had a satisfying swan song with 20 points and nine rebounds.

But Lewis's work around the basket was equally important. His 24 rebounds helped trigger the fast break, and his 28 points included 12 field goals deep in the paint.

Duke (97). Riedy 20, Liccardo 7, Lewis 28, McKaig 1, Verga 30, Wendelin 3, Golden 2, Vandenberg 2, Kolodziej 2, Barone 2, Chapman, Kennedy
Wake Forest (84). Scott 7, Boshort 6, Stroupe 20, Montgomery 15, Long 23, Randall 6, Wills 2, Crinkley 2, Broadway 2, Snyder 1, Whitaker

Fabulous Fred

March 2, 1968

Durham — Fred Lind had scored only 12 points all year, but his work off the bench in the Duke-Carolina game in 1968 turned him into a legendary figure in Blue Devil basketball history.

A 6 – 7 junior forward, Lind hadn't seen a minute of action against UNC since scoring 20 points on the Tar Heel junior varsity his freshman year. But with star center Mike Lewis plagued by foul trouble, coach Vic Bubas called Lind's number and saw his reserve make play after play in an 87 – 86 triple-overtime thriller that some regard as the most exciting Duke-Carolina game ever staged at the Indoor Stadium.

Lind played 31 minutes, scored 16 points, and had nine rebounds. When Lewis fouled out with 3:54 to go, Lind went the rest of the way. He hit a pair of foul shots at the end of regulation to force overtime, and knocked down an 18-footer with seven seconds left in the first OT to force the second one. He came up with several key rebounds in the second OT. In the final five minutes he nailed a hook shot, blocked a shot by the Tar Heels, and grabbed another critical rebound — all to the delight of his fellow students, who carried him on their shoulders when he was the last to emerge from the locker room.

Duke (87). Kennedy 14, Vandenberg 13, Lewis 18, Golden 13, Wendelin 8, Lind 16, Barone 5, Claiborne, Kolodziej, Teer
North Carolina (86). Miller 15, Scott 14, Clark 15, Bunting 14, Grubar 17, Brown 9, Fogler 2

Refrigerator Bowl

March 8, 1968

Charlotte — Sixth-ranked Duke was denied a sixth straight berth in the ACC championship game when N.C. State pulled off a 12 – 10 upset in one of the most famous slowdown games in league history.

Clemson had used a deliberate style in a narrow 43 – 40 loss to Duke in the tournament opener; State coach Norm Sloan chose the same strategy in the semifinals and made it work. After a 4 – 2 first half, Duke opened up an 8 – 6 lead with 16:15 left in the game. The Wolfpack then held the ball, refusing to shoot for almost

14 minutes, until Eddie Biedenbach hit a jumper with 2:29 to go to tie the score at 8–8.

Dave Golden scored on a free throw with 43 seconds left to put Duke back on top 9–8, but State scored off a missed free throw with 36 seconds remaining to take the lead for good at 10–9. The Pack hit two more foul shots in the last 16 seconds to seal it. Duke didn't help itself with a traveling violation, a double dribble, and a missed free throw in the last 45 seconds.

"This is about as exciting as artificial insemination," announcer Bill Currie remarked on the standstill pace during his broadcast. It was a lot more exciting for State than Duke, before the Wolfpack was trounced by UNC in the championship game.

Duke (10). Kennedy 2, Lind, Lewis 4, Golden 2, Wendelin, Vandenberg 1, Barone 1, Kolodziej

N.C. State (12). Braucher 3, Williford 3, Biedenbach 4, Serdich, Kretzer 2, Isley

Bubas Says Goodbye

March 1, 1969

Durham — An unheralded Duke team with a 12–12 record pulled off a major upset, defeating second-ranked North Carolina 87–81 in coach Vic Bubas's last game at the Indoor Stadium.

Senior Steve Vandenberg, relegated to reserve duty for much of his final year, had a Senior Day to remember with a career high of 33 points. He made 10 of 14 field goals and 13 of 13 foul shots while also claiming 12 rebounds. He had plenty of help from four other seniors, as Fred Lind, Dave Golden, C. B. Claiborne, and Warren Chapman all had Duke at an emotional peak.

Duke was able to ride that momentum to the ACC Tournament, where it reached the championship game and had a nine-point halftime lead on UNC until Charlie Scott erupted to save the Tar Heels.

Duke (87). Vandenberg 33, Lind 18, Denton 6, Golden 10, DeVenzio 13, Chapman 5, Claiborne 2

North Carolina (81). Bunting 15, Scott 22, Clark 11, Grubar 16, Fogler 6, Dedmon 10, Delany 1, Brown, Tuttle

Dedication Day

Jan. 22, 1972

Durham — On the day Duke renamed its stadium in honor of retiring athletics director Eddie Cameron, the Blue Devils enjoyed one of their most dramatic and exciting finishes to beat North Carolina 76–74.

The Tar Heels were ranked No. 3 in the nation while the Devils owned a record of 7–6. But that meant nothing in this rivalry, especially when senior Rob West hit a free throw in the final minute to put Duke on top 74–72. The Heels tied the score, but Duke got the ball with 13 seconds left.

After a timeout, the Devils inbounded the ball with eight seconds remaining. West took it at midcourt, proceeded to the top of the key, and launched the shot heard 'round the world. It dropped through with three seconds to play. When a last-gasp jumper by UNC bounced off the rim, Duke owned a home-court win over its biggest rival for the fifth straight season.

"I can still remember sitting in the locker room after the game with the net around my neck," West said over thirty years later. "What a great way to win the Duke-Carolina game."

Duke (76). O'Connor 24, Redding 24, Shaw 6, Melchionni 12, West 10, Burdette, Yarbrough

North Carolina (74). Chamberlain 11, Wuycik 23, McAdoo 3, Karl 14, Previs 4, Johnston 8, Jones 5, Huband 3, Corson 3, O'Donnell, Hite, Chambers

Mongoose Tames Terps

Feb. 3, 1973

Durham — Wins by the home team are not normally considered upsets in Cameron Indoor Stadium, but with the Blue Devils struggling at 8–9 and Maryland ranked No. 3 in the country, the Terps were clearly favored in this game.

Senior playmaker Gary Melchionni played the best game of his career in driving Duke to an 85–81 upset over a Maryland team that featured John Lucas, Len Elmore, and Tom McMillen. Melchionni hit 17 of 25 from the floor — 12 of 14 in the second half alone — for 39 points. Late in the game, when coach Bucky Waters called for his deliberate offense, the "mongoose," Mel-

Eddie Cameron accepted a game ball from Robby West after a last-second victory over UNC on stadium dedication day in 1972.

chionni ran it to perfection. With the defense spread, Melchionni penetrated for five baskets that enabled the Devils to take a 15-point lead with two minutes left.

This team dropped its last five games to post Duke's first losing record since 1939, but it enjoyed one shining moment in slaying one of Lefty Driesell's best teams.

Duke (85). Redding 6, Kramer 12, Fleischer 12, Melchionni 39, Billerman 8, Shaw 4, Hodge 4, Burdette

Maryland (81). McMillen 26, O'Brien 12, Elmore 3, Bodell 8, Lucas 16, O. Brown 2, Roy 7, Porac, D. Brown 5, Howard, White 2

And Then Along Came Jones

Jan. 19, 1974

Durham — On the same afternoon that Notre Dame ended UCLA's 88-game winning streak, a mediocre Duke team almost upset fifth-ranked North Carolina.

With point guard Kevin Billerman playing one of his best games — 8-of-9 shooting for 22 points — Duke opened up several six-point leads in the second half.

After Billerman fouled out on a charge with 2:37 to play, UNC hit a free throw to tie the score at 71. Duke tried to stall but committed a turnover with 1:08 left, prompting UNC to hold the ball for a last shot.

Walter Davis missed the attempt and Bill Suk rebounded for Duke with six seconds left. Duke called a timeout with four seconds to go and had only to get the ball in play to reach overtime. But Paul Fox's inbounds pass was intercepted by Bobby Jones, who raced toward the basket and hit a layup at the buzzer for a 73–71 victory by the Tar Heels.

"My whole life flashed before my eyes in that last four seconds," Duke coach Neill McGeachy said.

Duke (71). Redding 17, Suk 4, Fleischer 4, Fox 4, Billerman 22, Hodge 16, Burch 4, Armstrong, Kramer

North Carolina (73). Jones 19, Harrison 4, Stahl 8, O'Donnell 5, Elston 10, Davis 16, Kupchak 9, Hite 2, LaGarde, Chambers, Bell, Hoffman, Kuester

What Happened?

March 2, 1974

Chapel Hill — Duke absorbed its second devastating defeat of the year to North Carolina, on an afternoon when the Tar Heels provided the ACC with a comeback that would set the standard for future generations.

Duke led the fourth-ranked Tar Heels 86–78 when Bobby Jones went to the foul line with 17 seconds left. He hit two to make it 86–80. Then Walter Davis stole an inbounds pass and John Kuester hit a layup to make it 86–82 with 13 seconds left. Davis stole another inbounds pass but missed his shot — and Bobby Jones scored on the rebound to make it 86–84 with six seconds left.

Duke finally got the ball in play and Pete Kramer was fouled. He missed his shot at 0:04, and UNC called time at 0:03. Mitch Kupchak threw the ball up to Davis at midcourt, and Davis took two dribbles before launching a 30-footer that sent the game into overtime.

Davis also scored on a drive with 48 seconds left in OT to put UNC ahead to stay; the Tar Heels won 96–92. It was an ACC classic that featured 27 lead changes and 17 ties but has always been remembered most for that rally — eight points in 17 seconds.

Duke (92). Redding 18, Kramer 15, Fleischer 17, Armstrong 12, Billerman 8, Hodge 20, Fox 2, Suk, Chili

North Carolina (96). Jones 24, Hite 2, Stahl 7, O'Donnell 2, Elston 10, Davis 31, Harrison 8, Kupchak 5, Hoffman 4, Kuester 3, LaGarde, Chambers, Bell

Breakthrough

Feb. 21, 1976

Durham — When seventh-ranked Maryland visited Duke late in February, the Blue Devils owned a 12 – 11 record, with eight of the losses coming by six points or fewer. Duke finally got a close game to finish in its favor with a 69 – 67 upset of the Terps.

Duke's zone defense limited the driving ability of Maryland guard John Lucas, while its big men George Moses (17 rebounds) and Terry Chili controlled the boards. Forward Mark Crow hit 19 points to lead the way, while Chili had two clinching free throws in the closing seconds to secure the win.

Victory-starved students rushed the floor and cut down the nets, which coach Bill Foster carried to his postgame press conference. Unfortunately, Duke's hard luck did not end with the breakthrough win. The Devils lost their last three games, one by 90 – 89 and another by 80 – 78.

Duke (69). Hodge 13, Crow 19, Moses 7, Spanarkel 4, Armstrong 16, Fox 3, Chili 7, Young, Morrison

Maryland (67). Sheppard 18, Howard 7, Boston 6, Davis 10, Lucas 18, Newsome 2, Patton 4, Magid 2

Blue Badge of Courage

Jan. 17, 1977

Charlottesville, Va. — A long and painful 27-game ACC road losing streak came to a merciful end when the Blue Devils claimed an 82 – 74 victory at Virginia. The cost of the victory, though, was high.

Senior guard Tate Armstrong, a USA Olympian the previous summer, fell and broke his wrist early in the contest but refused to come out. He went on to hit 14 of 24 from the field for 33 of the most courageous points

ever scored by a Blue Devil. Mike Gminski chipped in with 20 points and Jim Spanarkel hit 11 of 12 from the foul line, as the Devils finally won a conference road game and improved their record to 11 – 3.

Armstrong, however, was done for the year. Without their most potent offensive weapon, the Devils won just three of the remaining thirteen games.

Duke (82). Morrison 2, Spanarkel 19, Gminski 20, Gray 4, Armstrong 33, Hall 4, Goetsch

Virginia (74). Iavaroni 14, Owens 12, Castellan 11, Stokes, Langloh 12, Napper 15, Fulton 4, Koesters 6, Newlen, Briscoe

Catharsis at Cameron

Jan. 14, 1978

Durham. — After its home win over UNC in 1972 Duke went into a dry spell against the Tar Heels, with just one victory in its next 17 encounters. There were also two coaching changes and three losing seasons during that time, so it goes without saying that some frustration had built up on the part of the team and its fans.

Duke's hopes that the 1978 season would provide a change in fortunes were bolstered with an impressive 92 – 84 victory in January over No. 2 North Carolina. Sparked by 29 points and 10 rebounds from center Mike Gminski, an inside attack dubbed the "Duke Power Company" set the tone for a most satisfying victory. Duke shot over 65 percent from the field and overcame a 29-point performance by the Tar Heels' guard Phil Ford.

When the clock expired on a streak of eight consecutive losses to the Heels, the fans stormed the floor and the national pollsters took notice by voting Duke back into the top 20 for the first time in seven years.

Duke (92). Banks 15, Dennard 7, Gminski 29, Spanarkel 23, Harrell 4, Bender 11, Goetsch 3, Suddath

North Carolina (84). Bradley 2, O'Koren 19, Wolf 7, Ford 29, Zaliagiris 12, Wood 10, Crompton 5, Virgil, Colescott, Doughton

Back to the Penthouse

March 4, 1978

Greensboro — A year after finishing at the bottom of the ACC, Duke won its first conference championship in over a decade with an 85 – 77 victory against Wake Forest, the first ACC Tournament final to be broadcast live on national television.

Duke had lost in the first round of the tournament for five straight years, so no one in the program had ever experienced a win in the event. But a 22-point game by Kenny Dennard helped Duke get past Clemson in the opener, and a strong inside attack made the difference in a semifinal win over Maryland, putting the Devils in the championship contest.

Wake Forest stormed to the first-half lead, but Duke took control of the backboards in the second half, with Gene Banks and Mike Gminski combining for 34 of their team's 48 points. For the game they totaled 47 points and 26 boards as Duke earned its first automatic bid to the NCAA Tournament since 1966. Captain Jim Spanarkel, with games of 12, 21, and 20 points, took home the tourney MVP award.

Duke (85). Banks 22, Dennard 6, Gminski 25, Spanarkel 20, Harrell 6, Bender 2, Suddath 4, Goetsch

Wake Forest (77). Dale 4, Griffin 25, McDonald 22, Johnson 14, Harrison 6, Thurman, Morris 2, Ellis, Hendler, Singleton 4

Rejection, Quakers

March 17, 1978

Providence — Playing Ivy League champion Penn in the Sweet 16 of the NCAA Tournament, seventh-ranked Duke escaped with an 84 – 80 victory to move on to the championship game of the Eastern Regional.

A 13 – 0 run in the second half seemingly put the Quakers in control, as their spread offense was opening up Duke's zone for drives inside. But then center Mike Gminski stepped in and blocked three straight layup attempts, and Duke turned all three rejections into points during a decisive, seven-minute 18 – 2 spurt.

While Gene Banks and Jim Spanarkel scored 21 points apiece, Gminski delivered 10 rebounds and seven blocks to move Duke within one game of the Final Four.

Duke (84). Banks 21, Dennard 8, Gminski 14, Spanarkel 21, Harrell 6, Bender 8, Gray, Morrison 2, Suddath 2, Goetsch 2

Penn (80). McDonald 10, Price 17, White 6, Willis 16, Greene 6, Crowley 12, Salters, Smith 13

Spirit of St. Louis

March 25, 1978

St. Louis — A youthful Cinderella Duke team playing in the school's first Final Four in twelve years knocked off a strong and talented Notre Dame club 90 – 86 to earn a berth in the national championship game.

A strong showing by sophomore Mike Gminski helped neutralize the Irish's inside attack. Gminski hit 13 of 17 shots for 29 points as Duke built up a 14-point lead. Gene Banks also stood out with 22 points and 12 rebounds, while Jim Spanarkel sparkled at the foul line, going 12 for 12 to finish with 20 points.

Duke had an 80 – 66 advantage with just under four minutes to play and had to survive a battery of long-range shots by the Fighting Irish, who closed to within two at 88 – 86. Duck Williams launched a 20-footer that would have tied the score, but it was short and Spanarkel tapped the rebound to guard John Harrell with nine seconds left. Harrell was fouled and hit both pressure free throws to seal the landmark win. It was the last victory of the year, as a 41-point night by Jack Givens carried triumphant Kentucky in the national final.

Duke (90). Banks 22, Dennard 7, Gminski 29, Spanarkel 20, Harrell 6, Bender 2, Goetsch 2, Suddath 2

Notre Dame (86). Tripucka 12, Batton 10, Flowers 10, Branning 8, Williams 16, Laimbeer 7, Hanzlik 8, Jackson 11, Wilcox 4

Air Ball!

Feb. 24, 1979

Durham — In perhaps the most unusual game in the history of Cameron Indoor Stadium, Duke topped North Carolina 47 – 40 to claim a share of the ACC regular-season championship.

The first half couldn't have been stranger. After Duke scored first to take a 2 – 0 lead, UNC opted to hold the ball.

Mike Gminski, Gene Banks, and Co. stirred fan enthusiasm with their march to the 1978 Final Four.

While the Blue Devils sat back in their customary zone defense, the Tar Heels—ranked fourth in the country—played keep-away for 11 straight minutes before attempting a shot. They also committed a few turnovers, and by halftime Duke owned a 7–0 lead. UNC had just two field-goal attempts in the half, and neither touched the rim. The first, by center Rich Yonakor, prompted the now-famous "Airball" chant by the Duke students.

The Tar Heels abandoned their stall strategy in the second half, which was played at a normal pace. In fact, it was an even 40–40 game over the last 20 minutes. Duke's seven first-half points made the difference, enabling beloved captain Jim Spanarkel and his classmates to go home happy on Senior Day.

Duke (47). Taylor 2, Dennard 5, Gminski 9, Spanarkel 17, Bender 5, Banks 5, Harrell 2, Gray 2, Goetsch

North Carolina (40). Wood 12, O'Koren 6, Budko, Bradley 2, Colescott 4, Virgil 8, Doughton 6, Wolf 2, Yonakor, Black, Wiel

Black Sunday

March 11, 1979

Raleigh—Duke and North Carolina split four meetings during the 1979 season, and there could have been five. The NCAA bracketed both teams in the East Region,

making the Tar Heels the No. 1 seed and the Blue Devils No. 2, with the possibility that they would have to meet for the right to go to the Final Four.

Both teams had first-round byes and were slated for second-round action in a doubleheader at Reynolds Coliseum. But neither powerhouse was able to uphold its seeding, as Penn tripped up UNC 72–71 before St. John's eliminated Duke 80–78 on a day that became known as Black Sunday in ACC basketball lore.

Jim Spanarkel became Duke's all-time scoring leader during the game and Gene Banks was all over the floor for 24 points and 10 rebounds. But the Devils missed two starters—point guard Bob Bender had suffered appendicitis during the ACC tourney and forward Kenny Dennard had been injured playing a pickup game earlier in the week—while center Mike Gminski played with a stomach illness. Guard John Harrell also had to miss much of the second half when he was poked in the eye.

Even with all those problems, Duke had a late lead. Reggie Carter's short bank shot with three seconds left gave St. John's its winning margin.

Duke (78). Taylor 6, Banks 24, Gminski 16, Spanarkel 16, Harrell 7, Suddath 7, Goetsch 2, Morrison, Gray

St. John's (80). Plair 11, Gilroy 4, McKoy 18, Rencher 6, Carter 21, Wright 8, Thomas 12

Productive Retirement

Feb. 20, 1980

Durham — After retiring the jersey of two-sport All-America Dick Groat in 1952, Duke went almost thirty years before opting to retire another. As the program's all-time scoring and rebounding leader, and a multiple All-America and Academic All-America, Mike Gminski was the perfect candidate for the ultimate honor. But when Duke decided to hang up Gminski's No. 43 at his final home game, the school didn't inform the honoree ahead of time. The surprising pre-game ceremony, combined with the finality of Senior Night, left Gminski an emotional wreck as the contest with Clemson got under way.

It didn't take the big guy long to warm to the occasion, however. "The first basket cleared my head," he said. He went on to score 29 points and grab 19 rebounds in an 87 – 82 overtime victory. The Devils had lost at Clemson in overtime by the same score earlier in the year, when they were 12 – 0 and ranked No. 1 in the country.

Duke (87). Banks 24, Dennard 6, Gminski 29, Taylor 11, Bender 2, Williams 7, Emma 8, Suddath
Clemson (82). Wyatt 4, Gilliam 4, Nance 15, Conrad 6, Williams 27, Dobbs 9, Campbell 9, Wiggins 8, McKinstry

Bucking the Bracket

March 1, 1980

Greensboro — Almost no one saw this coming. After the Blue Devils began the year as the nation's No. 1 team, a February slump and rumors of coach Bill Foster's departure for South Carolina helped conspire to drop Duke to .500 in the ACC. The Devils entered the ACC tourney unranked as the sixth seed, coming off a 25-point loss at UNC.

But a rejuvenated, determined team took the floor at Greensboro and whipped through the top three seeds, all nationally ranked, to win the tournament for the second time in three years. The championship came with a 73 – 72 decision over seventh-ranked Maryland, the regular-season champ, before a crowd of just 10,392 that was held down by a snowstorm. Gene Banks, in a strong bid for tourney MVP honors, played his third straight sensational game with 21 points while bottling up the eventual MVP Albert King as Duke rallied at the end.

Duke hit 15 of 19 from the floor in the second half. Mike Gminski got the game-winner on a second chance in the final seconds, while Kenny Dennard's blockout on Buck Williams kept the Terps from tapping in a winner as time expired.

Duke (73). Banks 21, Dennard 6, Gminski 13, Taylor 19, Bender 4, Engelland 4, Emma 2, Suddath, Tissaw 2, Williams 2
Maryland (72). Graham 17, King 27, Williams 14, Jackson, Manning 14, Morley, Baldwin

Stunner in Lexington

March 13, 1980

Lexington, Ky. — To start the 1979 – 80 season, Duke, ranked No. 3, and Kentucky, No. 2, met in Springfield, Mass., in the first Hall of Fame Tip-Off Classic. The Devils topped the Wildcats in overtime, but the Wildcats were favored to win the rematch when the two hooked up in the NCAA regional semifinals at Kentucky's Rupp Arena.

Duke got off to a fast start, grabbing a 37 – 23 halftime lead. A Duke press confounded the Cats, as did the play of Vince Taylor, a Lexington native enjoying a homecoming game. Taylor scored most of his 15 points in the first half but also made a strong defensive play at the end of the game, after Kentucky had come charging back into contention.

After a timeout with nine seconds left in a one-point battle, Wildcats star Kyle Macy tried to shoot an 18-footer over the Duke zone, but Taylor got in his face and distracted the shot, enabling the Devils to claim a 55 – 54 win. Duke made only 5 of 13 shots from the floor in the second half and hit less than 50 percent from the foul line, but it enjoyed one of its most significant NCAA wins to advance to the regional championship contest against Purdue.

Duke (55). Banks 11, Dennard 6, Gminski 17, Taylor 15, Bender 4, Tissaw 2, Engelland, Emma, Suddath, Williams
Kentucky (54). Cowan 26, Williams 6, Bowie 2, Macy 6, Minniefield 6, Shidler 2, Hord 4, Hurt 2, Heitz, Verderber

Storybook Ending

Feb. 28, 1981

Durham — One of Duke's most charismatic players enjoyed a storybook finish to his home career when the Blue Devils edged North Carolina 66 – 65 in overtime in the regular-season finale of coach Mike Krzyzewski's first year.

Gene Banks's arrival at Duke four years prior had prompted 5,000 fans to show up for his first practice and prompted a sellout of season tickets for the first time in years. After helping the program to two ACC titles and three NCAA berths in his first three years, Banks marked his senior introduction at Cameron by throwing roses to the crowd.

The Tar Heels, ranked No. 11, were on the verge of spoiling his day when they took a 58 – 56 lead with two seconds left. But the script called for one of the most dramatic finishes in stadium history. First, senior Kenny Dennard threw the inbounds pass to Chip Engelland at midcourt, and Engelland immediately called a time-out with one second left. Dennard then threw a second straight perfect pass, this time to Banks near the top of the key. Banks's shot barely eluded oncoming UNC center Sam Perkins and fell through to send the game into overtime.

Banks then scored six of Duke's eight points in the extra session, the final two with 12 seconds left to seal the outcome. "You couldn't have gotten a better ending," said Banks, "even if you'd gotten Shakespeare to write it."

Duke (66). Banks 25, Dennard 16, Linney, Taylor 14, Emma 4, Tissaw 7, Engelland, Williams, Suddath
North Carolina (65). Wood 16, Doherty 4, Perkins 24, Pepper 8, Black 12, Braddock 1, Brust, Barlow, Kenny

Invincible

Feb. 24, 1982

Durham — A season devoid of highlights had one magical moment near the end. On Senior Night at Cameron, veteran guard Vince Taylor simply refused to lose. He connected on 16 of 25 shots from the field for a career high of 35 points as the Blue Devils defeated Clemson 73 – 72 in triple overtime.

Taylor led the ACC in scoring in his senior year and was an all-conference selection, but this was his team's only win in its last seven games as the Devils struggled through a 10 – 17 campaign.

Duke (73). Wendt, Tissaw 4, Anderson 11, Taylor 35, Engelland 16, Emma 4, McNeely 2, Meagher 1
Clemson (72). Eppley 8, Hamilton 21, Wyatt 13, Gilliam 16, Shaffer 8, Ross 6, Bynum, Dodds

Surprise, Surprise

March 10, 1984

Greensboro — After twice coming up tantalizingly short of its nemesis UNC during the regular season, Duke pulled off one of the all-time ACC Tournament shockers by upsetting the Tar Heels 77 – 75 in the semifinals.

North Carolina, with one of its better teams, was ranked No. 1 in the nation, had gone 14 – 0 in the league to finish five games ahead of second-place Maryland, and had lost just one contest all year. It was considered a foregone conclusion that the Tar Heels would be cutting down nets when the tourney ended.

But Duke, a double-overtime loser at Chapel Hill the week before, came through with a game that helped transform the program. Playing suffocating post defense on the Tar Heels' vaunted inside attack, Duke was able to maintain a lead or stay within striking distance the entire afternoon.

Johnny Dawkins gave Duke a 69 – 67 lead late in the contest, and David Henderson's free throws with 17 seconds left put the Devils up 77 – 73. After Michael Jordan scored for UNC and Henderson missed a free throw, the Heels had a chance to force overtime. But Matt Doherty's inbounds pass went out of bounds and Duke moved on to the final.

"That was the coming of age for all of us," Mark Alarie said later of this sophomore-laden team.

Duke (77). Meagher 6, Alarie 21, Bilas 10, Dawkins 16, Amaker 6, Henderson 14, McNeely 4
North Carolina (75). Doherty 20, Perkins 9, Wolf 6, Jordan 22, Smith 6, Daugherty 8, Hale 4, Popson

Long Time Coming

Jan. 19, 1985

Chapel Hill—When North Carolina moved into Carmichael Auditorium for the 1965–66 season, rival Duke was ranked No. 1 in the country and didn't think twice about posting an 11-point victory in the enemy's new territory.

But then the Blue Devils went on an 18-year losing streak in Blue Heaven, not winning again until their final appearance in Carmichael in 1985, when they enjoyed a rousing 93–77 triumph.

The streak-ender did not come under ideal circumstances. After a 12–0 start, Duke was coming off back-to-back overtime losses and had only one day of preparation between a game with Wake and its visit to No. 6 UNC.

But just about everyone in Duke blue shook off the frustrations of a long week. Johnny Dawkins had one of his best games with 34 points, eight rebounds, four assists, and four steals in a complete 40-minute performance. Jay Bilas had a double-double with 17 points and 11 rebounds, helping the Devils enjoy a double-digit rebounding margin. Tommy Amaker teamed with Dawkins to set a defensive tone in the backcourt, while the two together had just one turnover on offense. Mark Alarie scored 19, Dan Meagher had 10 rebounds, and the Devils cleaned up at the foul line, hitting 35 of 46 attempts.

UNC posted a record of 169–20 at Carmichael before moving on to the Smith Center. Duke accounted for just two of those defeats, but this was a special one.

Duke (93). Meagher 7, Alarie 19, Bilas 17, Dawkins 34, Amaker 6, Henderson 10, King, Williams, Nessley
North Carolina (77). Peterson 4, Popson 5, Daugherty 18, Hale 12, K. Smith 14, Martin 16, R. Smith 8, Roper, Morris

Auspicious Beginning

Dec. 1, 1985

New York—One of Duke's greatest seasons had to start somewhere, and this one began with the Blue Devils claiming the championship of the Preseason NIT. After surviving a one-point game with St. John's at Madison Square Garden, the Devils edged Kansas 92–86 for their first title of the year.

David Henderson was the clear-cut choice for MVP after he hit 12 of 14 from the field for 30 points. Classmates Johnny Dawkins and Mark Alarie also reached the 20-point mark, while junior point guard Tommy Amaker dealt nine assists. The Devils outrebounded the Jayhawks and made nearly every free throw (22 of 25) to offset a Kansas team that shot almost 60 percent from the floor.

Duke won the title without one of its senior starters, Jay Bilas, who missed the first several games recovering from an injury. Freshman Danny Ferry took his place in the lineup.

Duke (92). Henderson 30, Alarie 21, Ferry 4, Dawkins 20, Amaker 9, King 6, Williams 2, Strickland, Snyder
Kansas (86). Hunter 8, Dreiling 8, Manning 24, Kellogg 20, Thompson 22, Marshall 4, Turgeon, Johnson, Piper

Weekend in the Clutch

Feb. 14, 1986

Durham—Even before it won the ACC title and reached the Final Four, the 1986 Duke basketball team began capturing attention across the country when it appeared on national network television for four straight weekends to close the regular season. The most compelling of those contests was a 75–74 win over Notre Dame in which the Blue Devils' best offensive player made the decisive defensive play.

On Saturday night before the Fighting Irish came calling on Sunday, Duke was busy in Raleigh battling its ACC foe N.C. State in a non-televised game. The Blue Devils pulled out the win at the end, 72–70, thanks to a pair of free throws by Johnny Dawkins. Dawkins was in the spotlight again less than twenty-four hours later. Duke was up by eight points on the Irish with 2:18 to play, but a 9–2 Notre Dame run made it a one-point game with 13 seconds left. When Duke missed a free throw, the Irish had a chance to play for a final shot and an upset victory.

Coach Digger Phelps wanted the ball in point guard

David Rivers's hands to orchestrate the final play. Despite excellent defense from Tommy Amaker and Billy King all afternoon, Rivers had 20 points and no doubt could make something happen with a drive or dish. Amaker had fouled out, so Duke coach Mike Krzyzewski told Dawkins to blanket Rivers on the last play. Rivers tried to slash toward the lane for a shot with the clock about to expire, and Dawkins got his left hand cleanly on the ball for a block that saved the game.

Duke (75). Henderson 12, Alarie 22, Bilas 3,
    Dawkins 18, Amaker 2, King 8, Ferry 10, Snyder
Notre Dame (74). Royal 10, Barlow 21, Kempton 2,
    Hicks, Rivers 20, Price 8, Dolan 11, Stevenson 2

No Other Option

March 2, 1986

Durham — Mike Krzyzewski's special class of 1986 went out in style, topping North Carolina 82–74 in the home finale to secure the school's first outright ACC regular-season crown in twenty years.

Seniors Mark Alarie, Jay Bilas, Johnny Dawkins, David Henderson, and Weldon Williams put the finishing touch on an outstanding regular season that concluded with a 12–2 ACC record. It wasn't the Blue Devils' best performance of the year, but maybe their most important.

"I remember feeling as much pressure for that game as any game that I've ever played in, including the national championship game," Alarie said later. "I could not see losing that game to those guys and having that blemish . . . We were going to win that game no matter what."

Alarie had a key dunk late in the game and David Henderson scored on a backdoor play as Duke held off a Tar Heel charge to finish the regular season 29–2, setting the stage for its first ACC tourney title and Final Four run under Krzyzewski.

Duke (82). Henderson 27, Alarie 16, Bilas, Dawkins 21,
    Amaker 14, Ferry 2, Williams 2, King, Snyder,
    Strickland
North Carolina (74). Wolf 12, Hunter 10,
    Daugherty 24, Lebo 18, K. Smith 4, R. Smith 2,
    Popson 2, Madden 2, Bucknall, Daye

Krzyzewski's First Ring

March 9, 1986

Greensboro — Maturing under a young coach at about the same time and pace as the Blue Devils, Georgia Tech was one of Duke's biggest rivals during the mid-1980s. The Yellow Jackets handed the Devils one of their two regular-season defeats in 1986, but Duke avenged that with a 68–67 victory in the ACC Tournament championship game.

Each team took its turn with the lead, and the last couple of minutes boiled down to back-and-forth big plays. Mark Alarie scored down low with 44 seconds left to give Duke a 66–65 advantage, and Johnny Dawkins added two late free throws to secure the victory. In the battle of premier senior guards, Dawkins outscored Mark Price 20–16 and teamed with Tommy Amaker to prevent Price from trying a go-ahead shot in the closing seconds. Dawkins, with a 20.0 tourney average, picked up the MVP trophy as Duke earned its first conference crown of the Krzyzewski era.

Duke (68). Henderson 10, Alarie 17, Bilas 2,
    Dawkins 20, Amaker 8, Snyder, Ferry 6, King 5
Georgia Tech (67). Hammonds 14, Ferrell 16, Salley 13,
    Price 16, Dalrymple 6, Neal 2, Ford, Sherrod

On to the Final

March 29, 1986

Dallas — The Blue Devils defeated Kansas in December for the Preseason NIT championship and saw the Jayhawks standing in the way of a national championship when they reached their first Final Four under Mike Krzyzewski. Duke defeated coach Larry Brown's club for the second time, 71–67, to earn a date with Louisville in the NCAA title contest.

Duke trailed the Jayhawks by four points with just over four minutes left, but finished the game with a 10–2 run. While Dawkins enjoyed a typically productive performance with 24 points on 11-of-17 shooting, two of the biggest plays late came from freshman Danny Ferry. With the score tied in the last minute, Ferry picked up a loose ball after a missed shot and scored to put Duke on top 69–67. Then with 11 seconds left he drew a charging foul on Ron Kellogg. He missed his foul shot, but the Jayhawks couldn't get off a solid attempt at the other end. A pair of free throws by Tommy Amaker with one second left provided the final margin.

Mark Alarie didn't have one of his better offensive games with 4-of-13 shooting, but he was a key figure nonetheless. He totaled eight rebounds and four steals and played excellent defense on Danny Manning, who fouled out with only four points. Manning had scored 24 in the NIT meeting.

Duke (71). Henderson 13, Alarie 12, Bilas 7, Dawkins 24, Amaker 7, Strickland, Ferry 8, King

Kansas (67). Manning 4, Kellogg 22, Dreiling 6, Hunter 5, Thompson 13, Turgeon 2, Marshall 13, Piper 2

Dripping with Intensity

March 13, 1988

Greensboro — Duke won its second ACC Tournament in three years with a 65 – 61 victory over North Carolina that ranked as one of the most hotly contested league games in the conference's first 50 years.

During the regular season Duke had edged UNC in Chapel Hill by one point when Robert Brickey blocked the Tar Heels' buzzer shot, and it crushed the Heels by 15 on Senior Day. The tournament encounter was hard-fought throughout, with Duke's trademark man-to-man defense making a major difference down the stretch. The Devils held UNC to 1-of-12 shooting over the final 11-plus minutes, yet still the contest was in doubt to the end.

Tournament MVP Danny Ferry, with 19 points and 10 rebounds, gave the Devils a little breathing room when he scored off an offensive rebound with just under 90 seconds to play. With Duke up 63 – 61, Carolina had a chance to tie the game on a fast break but couldn't convert. Quin Snyder then knocked in a pair of clinching free throws with four seconds remaining.

When the clock expired, Duke owned a "triple crown" season over UNC for the first time since 1966.

Duke (65). Ferry 19, King, Brickey 7, Strickland 11, Snyder 11, Smith 12, Henderson 5, Koubek, Abdelnaby, Cook, Burgin, Buckley

North Carolina (61). Bucknall 4, Reid 7, Williams 8, Madden 13, Lebo 16, Smith 7, Fox 4, Rice 2, Chilcutt, Denny, Hyatt, Elstun, May, Jenkins

Defensive Masterpiece

March 26, 1988

East Rutherford, N.J. — Senior Billy King's signature defensive performance came in February 1988 when he hounded Notre Dame guard David Rivers into a 3-of-17 shooting day with four turnovers during a nationally televised contest at Cameron. King was just as good, however, in the Blue Devils' biggest game — a matchup with Temple, ranked No. 1 and top-seeded, in the championship contest of the NCAA East Region.

With a spot in the Final Four on the line, King led the Blue Devils to a 63 – 53 decision over the Owls even though he scored just four points and had three rebounds. Selected the national defensive player of the year, King spearheaded Duke's effort with his work against Temple freshman and scoring star Mark Macon. Macon played the entire 40 minutes but was able to hit just 6 of 29 field goals, only 1 of 8 from three-point range, for a total of 13 points. Temple's team followed Macon's lead, hitting just 28 percent from the field for the game in the face of Duke's aggressive defense.

With Kevin Strickland scoring 21 points and Danny Ferry 20, Duke was able to overcome a three-point halftime deficit and advance to the Final Four.

Duke (63). Ferry 20, King 4, Brickey 3, Strickland 21, Snyder 9, Koubek 2, Abdelnaby 2, Henderson 2

Temple (53). Vreeswyk 6, Rivas 4, Evans 12, Perry 13, Macon 13, Dowdell 3, Brantley 2, Causewell

Ferry on Fire

Dec. 10, 1988

Miami — Duke's 117 – 112 victory at Miami featured the top individual scoring game in Duke and ACC history.

Senior Danny Ferry, on his way to national player of the year honors, scorched the Hurricanes for 58 points with an incredible shooting display. He hit 23 of 26 field goals and 10 of 12 free throws. Only two of his 23 field goals were from three-point range.

And Ferry was not just a scoring machine. He also had seven assists, six rebounds, two blocked shots, and three steals. "His performance has to rank with one of the most phenomenal I've ever seen," Miami coach Bill Foster said.

The performance broke Dick Groat's Duke record

of 48 points and the ACC record of 57, set by N.C. State star David Thompson. Ironically, on the same night that Ferry set his record, Sue Harnett established a new scoring record for the Duke women with 37 points against Virginia Commonwealth.

Duke (117). Ferry 58, Brickey 9, Abdelnaby 17, Henderson 8, Snyder 6, Smith 14, Koubek 5, Laettner, Buckley

Miami (102). Brown 20, Burns 24, Williams 19, Hocker 5, Richardson, Wylie 17, Presto 13, Brandon 4, Randon, Scott, Morton

Hoyas Denied

March 26, 1989

East Rutherford, N.J.—For the second year in a row, Duke knocked the beast of the East out of the NCAA Tournament with a strong performance in a regional championship game at the Meadowlands. In 1988 it was top-ranked Temple, and a year later it was second-ranked Georgetown that saw its Final Four aspirations dashed by Duke, 85–77.

Senior Danny Ferry, junior Phil Henderson, and freshman Christian Laettner all topped the 20-point mark for Duke. The Blue Devils shot over 50 percent from the field, outrebounded a squad that had Alonzo Mourning in the middle and Dikembe Mutombo coming off the bench, and got to the foul line with regularity, hitting 26 of 33. Duke's lithe guard Henderson had the play of the game when he drove into the lane and dunked in the face of Mourning.

For seniors Ferry, Quin Snyder, and John Smith, the win meant a trip to the Final Four in Seattle, making them the first Duke class to earn three career Final Four berths.

Duke (85). Ferry 21, Brickey 10, Laettner 24, Henderson 23, Snyder 4, Smith 3, Abdelnaby, Koubek

Georgetown (77). Jackson 2, Mourning 11, Bryant 2, Smith 21, Turner 4, Winston 9, Tillman 16, Jefferson 8, Edwards 2, Mutombo 2

Special Ending

March 24, 1990

East Rutherford, N.J.—Few basketball observers pegged the 1990 Blue Devils as Final Four material. Several of the players that would carry Duke to future greatness were freshmen and sophomores, and the team had been bounced from the ACC Tournament with an inglorious semifinal effort.

But No. 15 Duke earned a trip to Denver with a 79–78 overtime win against No. 3 Connecticut in the East Region final, on one of the great audibles in school history. With the Huskies ahead 78–77 and poised for their first Final Four, Duke coach Mike Krzyzewski huddled with his players to set up a last-second shot. But as the players took their places on the floor, Krzyzewski changed the play by calling out, "Special." The result certainly was, as Christian Laettner passed the ball in to Brian Davis, who gave it right back. Laettner then canned a 17-foot buzzer-beater that stunned the Huskies and kept the Blue Devils' season alive.

Duke (79). Brickey 2, Laettner 23, Abdelnaby 27, Henderson 21, Hurley 3, McCaffrey 1, Davis 2, T. Hill, Koubek

Connecticut (78). Burrell 12, Henefeld 15, Sellers 1, Smith 11, George 9, Macklin 15, Walker 9, Cyrulik 4, Depriest 2, Williams

Norman Invasion

Dec. 22, 1990

Norman, Okla.—Ninth-ranked Duke showed glimpses of its championship potential when it traveled to Oklahoma and administered a 90–85 defeat to the Sooners. Oklahoma, ranked No. 11, had won 51 straight games on its home floor at the Noble Center.

In between fall semester exams and a holiday break, the Blue Devils were dragging when inclement weather put their arrival in Norman five hours behind schedule. Guard Terry Evans then dropped five three-pointers on them as the Sooners flew out to an early 10-point lead.

But Duke battled back to within five at halftime and rode its young players to an impressive victory in the second half. Most noteworthy was the play of sophomore Thomas Hill, who scored 16 points on 7-of-10 shooting while playing tenacious defense on Oklahoma sharpshooter Brent Price (11 points, five in the second half). Hill had a devoted cheering section on hand, as his father, a former track Olympian, was working as an assistant athletics director at Oklahoma.

Duke (90). G. Hill 19, Laettner 19, Palmer 1, T. Hill 16,
  Hurley 13, Lang 11, McCaffrey 4, Davis 7
Oklahoma (85). Webster 32, Mullins 8, Holmes 10,
  Evans 17, Price 11, Sallier 2, Ware 4, Keane 1

A Win for the Ages

March 30, 1991

Indianapolis—Duke registered one of the most remarkable victories in its storied history with a 79–77 decision over UNLV in the national semifinals. The Rebels were undefeated at 34–0, ranked No. 1 in the country, and seemingly destined to win a second straight NCAA crown. They had pounded Duke by 30 points in the final in 1990 and had barely been tested in making their return run to the Final Four.

But coach Mike Krzyzewski convinced his team that the rematch didn't have to be a mismatch, and the Blue Devils bought it. They were so determined to show that they weren't just happy to be on the same court with UNLV that they opened the game with a 15–6 run. Vegas regrouped to tie the score and took a 43–41 lead at halftime, but the Blue Devils scored the first two baskets of the second half to reclaim the advantage.

Neither team would let the other take control, and with four minutes left it was a 74–71 game, Vegas on top. The Rebels increased the lead to 76–71 with 2:32 to go, but then Bobby Hurley made perhaps the biggest shot in Duke basketball history. With 2:14 to play, he nonchalantly buried a three-pointer that made it a two-point contest, and suddenly there was real game pressure on UNLV. The Rebels committed their first 45-second shot clock violation of the year, and Duke answered by taking the lead when Brian Davis, playing one of his best games, scored inside and added a free throw. Larry Johnson tied the score at 77 with a free throw, and Christian Laettner hit a pair of foul shots with 12.7 seconds left for the winning margin.

Duke (79). Koubek 2, G. Hill 11, Laettner 28, T. Hill 6,
  Hurley 12, McCaffrey 5, Lang, Davis 15, Palmer

UNLV (77). Johnson 13, Augmon 6, Ackles 7, Hunt 29,
  Anthony 19, Gray 2, Spencer 1

Champions at Last

April 1, 1991

Indianapolis—Duke finished the job it had started against UNLV, taming Kansas 72–65 to grab the first national basketball championship in school history on its ninth visit to the Final Four.

Senior Greg Koubek set the tone early by scoring his only five points in the first 90 seconds of play. Grant Hill then made the most spectacular dunk in Duke history on a fast-break pass from Bobby Hurley to put the Blue Devils ahead 7–1. The game remained close throughout, but Duke had made a statement that it was out to win a title, not bask in its upset of UNLV.

Thomas Hill's only basket of the game, a three-pointer at the halftime buzzer, gave Duke a 42–34 margin. Billy McCaffrey sparked a run midway through the second half that put Duke ahead 61–47 with 8:30 to go. Coach Roy Williams's Jayhawks edged back to within five in the final minute, but the Blue Devils made the insurance play when Brian Davis dunked off an inbounds pass from Grant Hill to close the scoring.

Christian Laettner's two-game totals of 46 points and 17 rebounds made him the Final Four MVP. His 10 boards and 12-of-12 night at the foul line were of particular importance against Kansas. The work of McCaffrey and Davis off the bench also was significant for a team that couldn't afford to be tired when the title was on the line.

Duke (72). Koubek 5, G. Hill 10, Laettner 18, T. Hill 3,
  Hurley 12, McCaffrey 16, Lang, Davis 8, Palmer
Kansas (65). Jamison 2, Maddox 4, Randall 18,
  Brown 16, Jordan 11, Richey, Woodbery 2, Tunstall 2,
  Wagner 2, Scott 6, Johanning 2

Overwhelming

March 15, 1992

Charlotte—Plagued by injuries down the stretch of a remarkable season, Duke used the ACC Tournament to bring all its pieces back together and recapture its unique

Duke obliterated rival UNC to claim the 1992 ACC hardware.

chemistry heading into the NCAA. A dominating 94–74 victory over North Carolina in the championship game showed that the Blue Devils were in sync and ready to pursue the national crown.

A torrential defense set the tone. After coach Mike Krzyzewski blasted his team during a TV timeout with 7:41 to go in the first half, the entire complexion of the game changed in Duke's favor. The most inspirational play came from Grant Hill, who soared high into the Charlotte Coliseum sky to tip away an inbounds pass, outran Pat Sullivan for the loose ball, scooped it up in front of the UNC bench, and drove in for a slam dunk that put the Devils ahead 37–30. "From then on, we were all saying, 'If he can do it, I can do it,'" Thomas Hill noted. Duke made three more hustle steals over the next two minutes and finished the half with nine and a 44–36 lead.

The Blue Devils then executed almost flawlessly in the second half, hitting 62 percent from the floor while committing just five turnovers and three personal fouls. When UNC went to a zone to deny Duke's penetration, the Devils worked the clock and nailed corner baseline jumpers on four of five possessions to open up a 17-point lead.

Christian Laettner hit five three-pointers, totaled 25 points, and added 10 rebounds. He was the obvious choice for tournament MVP, with three-game averages of 24.3 points and 10.3 rebounds. This marked the only ACC tourney crown for Laettner and his fellow senior Brian Davis, whose careers had included championship game defeats to the Tar Heels in 1989 and 1991.

Duke (94). Lang 11, Davis 12, Laettner 25, T. Hill 13, Hurley 11, G. Hill 20, Ast 2, Parks, Clark, Meek, Blakeney, Burt

North Carolina (74). Reese 9, Lynch 15, Montross 8, Davis 19, Phelps 9, Sullivan 8, Salvadori 4, Rodl 2, Williams, Wenstrom, Cherry, Burgess, Stephenson, Smith

Unforgettable

March 28, 1992

Philadelphia — It has been called the greatest game in the history of the NCAA Tournament. Duke's 104–103 overtime victory over Kentucky in the NCAA East Region final at the Spectrum sent the Blue Devils to their fifth straight Final Four and plunged Wildcat fans into despair. Charged with drama and intensity, the entire contest was fit for a time capsule. Both squads shot well over 50 percent from the floor and each answered every punch thrown by the other in a battle of glamorous heavyweights.

Grant Hill's brilliant play in a racehorse first half staked Duke to a 50–45 lead. Thomas Hill came alive in the second half and delivered two of the Devils' last three field goals in regulation on running jumpers. Bobby Hurley, who played all 45 minutes with 22 points and 10 assists, knocked down a three-pointer to tie the game in overtime — a basket that Kentucky coach Rick Pitino called a real back-breaker because it came on an offensive rebound.

But despite all those highlights, it was the final 32 seconds of overtime that turned this contest from great to greatest. First Christian Laettner made an eight-footer in traffic to put Duke up by 100 – 98. Then Jamal Mashburn drove inside, scored, was fouled, and added the free throw for a 101 – 100 UK lead. With 14 seconds left, Mashburn fouled out and Laettner hit two free throws to put Duke back up, 102 – 101.

Kentucky called a timeout with 7.8 seconds left to set up a last play, which Sean Woods converted by penetrating past Hurley for a one-handed bank shot that gave the Wildcats a 103 – 102 lead. But it wasn't quite the last play, as Hurley quickly called a timeout with 2.1 seconds remaining so that Duke could organize a final attempt. Unguarded on the throw-in, Grant Hill hurled a perfect 75-foot pass to Laettner, who caught it with his back to the basket, faked right, took one dribble to the left, and launched a 16-foot turnaround jumper that went through the rim as time expired.

Laettner finished with a perfect line in the box score: 10 of 10 from the field and 10 of 10 from the foul line for 31 points, capped off by one of the most famous March Madness shots of all time.

"For a guy who loves the game for the game itself, you hope that some day you're a part of something like this, and I was," coach Mike Krzyzewski said. "I've just been standing around trying to figure out what a lucky son of a gun I am just to be involved. How many kids from each team made great plays tonight? You can't write enough about how many good plays there were."

Duke (104). Lang 4, Davis 13, Laettner 31, T. Hill 19, Hurley 22, G. Hill 11, Parks 4, Clark

Kentucky (103). Mashburn 28, Pelphrey 16, Martinez 5, Woods 21, Farmer 9, Feldhaus 5, Brown 18, Ford, Timberlake 1, Riddick, Braddy

Back to Back

April 6, 1992

Minneapolis — Duke made history by storming past Michigan 71 – 51 in the NCAA championship game. The outcome enabled Duke to become the first school to repeat as national champs since UCLA's run in 1967 – 73.

The Final Four was a Big Ten challenge for Duke, as the Blue Devils edged Indiana 81 – 78 in the semifinals

behind 26 points from guard Bobby Hurley. His career-high six three-pointers and late clutch free throws by Marty Clark helped Duke to overcome a halftime Hoosier lead and reach its third straight final.

Hurley then had seven assists and nine points against the Wolverines and was named Final Four MVP. His Blue Devils scored on their final 12 possessions of the championship game, blowing open the contest with a 23 – 6 run in the last seven minutes. Duke had trailed 31 – 30 at halftime after hitting just 12 of 30 from the field and watching star Christian Laettner commit seven turnovers.

After hearing some harsh words in the locker room at halftime, Laettner hit two shots early in the second half and started forcing turnovers on defense as the Devils took control. As they had done against Indiana, the Blue Devils played suffocating half-court defense in allowing the Wolverines just 20 points over the final 20 minutes.

Grant Hill hit 5 of 7 shots in the last five minutes to finish with 18 points, 10 rebounds, five assists, and three steals. He caught passes from Hurley for a fast break and a late dunk to close the contest, putting the final stamp on a season in which Duke was ranked No. 1 in the country from beginning to end.

Duke (71). Lang 5, G. Hill 18, Laettner 19, T. Hill 16, Hurley 9, Parks 4, Davis, Ast, Clark, Blakeney, Burt, Meek

Michigan (51). Webber 14, Jackson, Howard 9, Rose 11, King 7, Riley 4, Voskuil 4, Pelinka 2, Hunter, Talley, Bossard, Seter, Armer

Rematch, Repeat

Dec. 5, 1992

Durham — After routing a young and brash Michigan team in the 1992 NCAA title game, the Blue Devils didn't have to wait long for the Wolverines to seek revenge. The two schools met in the second game of the 1992 – 93 season. With nine of 10 starters back from the title contest and Michigan now rated No. 1 in the country, the Saturday night event was one of the most hyped in the history of Cameron Indoor Stadium.

The Wolverines fueled the intense focus on the game with several pre-game statements declaring that it was

Thomas Hill's game-high 21 points silenced Michigan in a much-hyped 1992–93 contest.

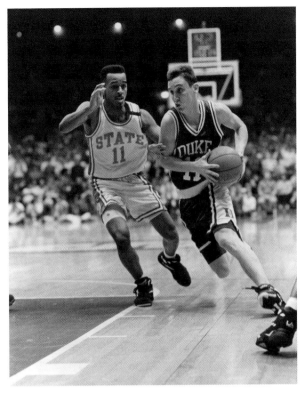

Bobby Hurley had 15 assists to pace a win over N.C. State on the day the Wolfpack paid tribute to Jim Valvano.

their turn to shine. But it was Duke's stars that shone the brightest as the Blue Devils soared for a 79–68 victory.

Senior All-America Bobby Hurley orchestrated the win, playing all 40 minutes while scoring 20 points with five assists and just one turnover. He had a three-pointer late in the second half that stemmed a rally by Michigan, and he put a punctuation mark on the late-night showcase with an uncontested layup at the buzzer that sent Duke students storming the court.

Thomas Hill and Grant Hill also played major roles, but a key was the effort of the one new starter, center Cherokee Parks, now in the lineup with the graduation of Christian Laettner. Parks scored 15 points, played solid defense on Michigan's inside forces, and set the screen on Hurley's big three-pointer.

"It feels great to beat them," Parks said. "They've been talking, it seems like since last April, about getting us this year and we just let it slide until this week when it was time to play them. When it came down to business, we just played harder."

Duke (79). Lang 1, G. Hill 15, Parks 15, T. Hill 21, Hurley 20, Meek, Clark 7
Michigan (68). Jackson 7, Webber 14, Howard 10, King 20, Rose 15, Riley, Pelinka 2, Talley, Voskuil, Fife

Crashing the Reunion

Feb. 21, 1993

Raleigh — It was one of the most emotion-drenched scenes in ACC basketball history. Reynolds Coliseum was packed to its ancient rafters with Wolfpack fans on hand to celebrate a reunion of their school's 1983 NCAA championship team as well as to pay tribute to their cancer-stricken former coach Jim Valvano.

Valvano's pregame speech energized the crowd as well as the Wolfpack, which was struggling with a record of 1–10 in the ACC. Kevin Thompson's 30 points kept the Pack in contention, and the score was tied at 71 with six minutes left. But a 20–11 run to finish the contest left Duke with a 91–82 victory for win No. 20 of the season.

Duke played without Grant Hill, who was nursing a toe injury. Thomas Hill stepped up with 20 points, Cherokee Parks delivered a double-double with 19 points and 10 rebounds, and Chris Collins nailed two three-pointers in his first start. But the biggest hero was guard Bobby Hurley, who tied his single-game Duke assists record with 15. He accounted for 11 of the Devils' final 20 points, scoring seven himself and contributing two assists to lead the late charge. "Some of his passes at the end were magical," said Mike Krzyzewski.

Duke (91). Lang 11, T. Hill 20, Parks 19, Collins 14, Hurley 13, Clark 10, Meek, Blakeney 4

N.C. State (82). Davis 6, Lewis 7, Thompson 30, McCuller 13, Marshall 16, Wilson 1, Fuller 9, Newman

Biting the Big Dog

March 26, 1994

Knoxville — In one corner stood Glenn "Big Dog" Robinson, the NCAA's leading scorer and national player of the year. In the other corner stood Grant Hill, the most versatile and best defensive player in the country. In between stood Jeff Capel, a freshman guard who made the difference in this Southeast Region final of the NCAA Tournament.

With Robinson held to 17 points below his 30.8 average and Hill sidelined by late foul trouble, Capel came up big to help his Blue Devils tame top-seeded Purdue 69–60 and advance to the Final Four for the seventh time in nine years.

Capel hit 5 of 7 shots for 13 points in the decisive second half and stepped up most when Hill went to the bench with his fourth foul at the 9:54 mark. He hit a spinning drive through the lane to beat the shot clock, delivered a behind-the-back pass that Tony Lang converted for a 58–50 lead, and then punched Duke's ticket to Charlotte with 38 seconds left when he took a breakaway feed from his backcourt mate Chris Collins and let loose with a thunderous dunk. Capel hit 7 of 12 shots for his 19 points and added seven assists, sparking a team that was upset in the ACC Tournament semifinals on to the final weekend of the season.

Duke (69). Lang 19, Hill 11, Parks 15, Capel 19, Collins 5, Clark, Meek, Brunson, Beard, Wallace, Moore, Newton

Purdue (60). Robinson 13, Martin 12, Brantley, Waddell 16, Roberts 7, Stanback 8, Dove 2, Jennings 2, Darner

Inches Short

April 4, 1994

Charlotte — When the 1994 season began, many college basketball observers figured that the most likely team from North Carolina to challenge for a Final Four berth at the Charlotte Coliseum would be the UNC Tar Heels, the defending 1993 champs. But after knocking off Florida in the semifinals and surviving a bruising second-half run by Arkansas, it was the Duke Blue Devils who were well within reach of a third NCAA crown in four years.

A clutch 22-footer by Grant Hill had the Devils in position to win it all as the season entered its final minute with the score tied. But Razorbacks guard Scotty Thurman lofted a clinching jumper that barely beat the shot clock and barely cleared the outstretched arm of defender Tony Lang. Duke's answer at the other end was off target, and second-ranked Arkansas raised its first NCAA championship trophy with a 76–72 victory, as President Bill Clinton looked on.

Duke (72). Lang 15, Hill 12, Parks 14, Collins 12, Capel 14, Clark 3, Meek 2

Arkansas (76). Biley, Williamson 23, Stewart 6, Beck 15, Thurman 15, McDaniel 7, Robinson 2, Dillard 4, Rimac, Wilson 4

A Cameron Classic

Feb. 2, 1995

Durham — It should have been no contest, with North Carolina ranked No. 2 in the nation and Duke struggling with a winless ACC mark. Instead, this apparent mismatch turned into one of the great Duke-Carolina games ever, with the Tar Heels pulling out a 102–100 decision in double overtime.

UNC hit 10 of its first 11 shots and bolted to a 17-point lead in the first 8:30 of play. Jerry Stackhouse capped

A narrow loss to Arkansas in his last game left Grant Hill just short of a third national championship.

that run with a jaw-dropping reverse dunk that seemed to signal an impending rout by the Tar Heels. A noteworthy dunk by Greg Newton fueled a 10–0 run by Duke, however, and the Blue Devils went on to build a 12-point lead midway through the second half by hitting 16 of their first 20 shots and committing no turnovers on their first 18 possessions.

Cherokee Parks hit two free throws with 19 seconds left to tie the score at 81 and send the game into overtime. North Carolina built up a nine-point lead in the extra session and had a chance to ice the game with free throws. But Serge Zwikker missed a pair with four seconds to go, leaving just enough time for Jeff Capel to cross midcourt and launch one of the most famous shots in Cameron history — a 30-footer to send the stadium into hysteria and force another OT at 95 – 95.

Points were hard to come by in the final five minutes. Jeff McInnis stole an inbounds pass and scored immediately with 52 seconds left to give UNC a four-point lead. Ricky Price hit a jumper to bring Duke to within two, and Newton picked up a UNC turnover with 13 seconds

left to give the Devils a final shot, but there was no second miracle as the Heels prevailed in the highest-scoring Duke-UNC game ever.

Duke (100). Price 16, Parks 25, Meek 11, Langdon 20, Capel 17, Collins 9, Newton 2, Wojciechowski
North Carolina (102). Calabria 11, Stackhouse 25, Wallace 25, D. Williams 24, McInnis 8, Landry 9, Zwikker, S. Williams, Geth

Road to Recovery

Jan. 18, 1996

Raleigh — One of the most significant performances of the mid-1990s came on this ACC venture to old Reynolds Coliseum on the N.C. State campus. A year after stumbling to last place in the conference with Mike Krzyzewski out of commission, the Blue Devils got off to a start of 0 – 4 in the ACC thanks to a series of narrow defeats in January. But a last-second road victory over the Wolfpack helped right the ship for this bridge season back to prominence.

Duke battled back from 10-point deficits a couple of times in the second half and got a key play from guard Chris Collins when his team was down by five late in the game. Collins dived into the scorer's table to save a ball, hustled back on to the floor, took a pass from Ricky Price, and drained a long three-pointer to draw the Devils within two at 68 – 66. "If we lose that possession there is a good chance we lose the ball game," Collins said. "That play put us in position to get the last shot."

Down 70 – 68 in the closing seconds, Krzyzewski called a play for Price to win or tie the game. But Collins had the ball, read a switch in the State defense, and launched a 25-footer instead of handing off to Price. The ball hit the front of the rim, kissed it four more times, and then finally dropped through for the winning points with 5.5 seconds left. When State missed a contested layup at the buzzer, Duke celebrated an important 71 – 70 victory.

"When it hit that front rim, I kind of held my breath," said Collins, who hit five three-pointers on the night. "I knew I shot it pretty soft and knew I would get a soft bounce, but you never know."

Duke (71). Price 8, Wallace 12, Newton 6, Collins 20, Capel 20, Domzalski, Wojciechowski 5, Brunson

N.C. State (70). Hyatt 12, Strong 11, Fuller 27, Marshall 3, Benjamin 1, M. Harrison 2, C. Harrison 8, Pinkins 6, Sutton, Wagner

The Clincher

Feb. 27, 1997

Durham — A loss in late January at Maryland left Duke with a 4–3 conference record heading into the meat of the schedule. But the Blue Devils defeated North Carolina at home in their next game to start an eight-game ACC winning streak that brought the league's regular-season title back to Durham for the first time in four years. The clincher was an 81–69 victory over Maryland in the home finale, the 700th contest in Cameron Indoor Stadium.

"Now Duke is back," senior captain Jeff Capel said after the win over the Terps. He had played on a Final Four team as a freshman in 1994 but endured a losing campaign in 1995 before helping the program return to championship form. Capel scored 18 points on 7-of-12 shooting to trigger his last home victory.

There were 12 lead changes and three ties in the first 10 minutes of the second half, and the score was knotted at 52 with 10:32 to play. Duke built a working margin over the next several minutes with a flurry of three-point shots. Steve Wojciechowski drained the first one to put Duke ahead to stay, then assisted on four others as the Devils crafted a nine-point lead with five minutes to go.

Duke (81). Capel 18, Wallace 2, Newton 6, Langdon 12, Wojciechowski 11, McLeod 10, Price 6, Carrawell 4, Chappell 10, James 2

Maryland (69). Profit 12, Booth 22, Ekezie 4, Stokes 6, Jasikevicius 7, Kovarik 2, Elliott 14, Watkins 2

Dramatic 500th

Feb. 28, 1998

Durham — Mike Krzyzewski's 500th career coaching victory couldn't have come under more dramatic and emotional circumstances. On Senior Day at Cameron Indoor Stadium, his top-ranked Blue Devils rallied from a 17-point deficit in the second half to claim a thrilling 77–75 victory over North Carolina.

Jeff Capel sparked a win over Maryland in his final home game to secure an ACC regular-season crown.

After falling behind 18–4 at the start, Duke trailed by 12 points at halftime and 64–47 with 11:39 to play. But Duke held the Tar Heels to just two field goals over that final span, both on offensive rebounds, while scoring on 15 of its last 18 possessions for a win that secured the ACC regular-season title.

Most of the rally was forged on the backs of senior Roshown McLeod and freshman Elton Brand, who relentlessly pounded inside against UNC's more vaunted post players. The Blue Devils scored 10 of their last 13 field goals in the paint and held the Tar Heels' star Antawn Jamison to just one tip-in and one free throw over the last 11 minutes. Jamison had scored 35 points against Duke in an earlier meeting.

Guard William Avery began the comeback with a pair of free throws and a drive inside. Brand, coming off the bench while recovering from a broken foot, scored eight points in three minutes to make it a seven-point game. Avery made it 70–64 with a three just inside the

Duke rallied from 17 points down to defeat UNC in 1998, giving Mike Krzyzewski his 500th victory.

six-minute mark, and McLeod finished off a 23-point performance in his home finale with six points in the last three minutes, including the game-winning drive over Jamison with 59 seconds left. McLeod also made two big defensive plays at the end by stealing a lob pass and tying up Vince Carter for a jump ball with 45 seconds left to give Duke possession.

Chris Carrawell scored only one basket, but it was the game-tying layup. And Steve Wojciechowski scored only one point, but his 11 assists and leadership were major factors in the comeback. UNC contributed to its own demise by missing four free throws in the closing seconds.

Duke (77). McLeod 23, Price, Battier 5, Langdon 17, Wojciechowski 1, Brand 16, Avery 9, Burgess 4, Carrawell 2, Chappell
North Carolina (75). Okulaja 4, Carter 14, Jamison 23, Williams 15, Cota 6, Haywood 7, Ndiaye 6

Slipped Away

March 22, 1998

St. Petersburg — Haunted by memories of Duke's last-second overtime win in the NCAA regional final in 1992, Kentucky basketball fans tasted a measure of revenge when their fifth-ranked Wildcats topped the third-ranked Blue Devils 86 – 84 in this regional championship game. The victory sent Kentucky to its third straight Final Four, where it claimed its second NCAA crown in three years.

A championship did not appear likely for first-year coach Tubby Smith, however, when a hot Trajan Langdon sparked a 17 – 0 run by Duke in the first half, putting the Blue Devils firmly in the driver's seat. Duke led by 10 at the break, maintained that margin for several minutes, and then bolted to a 71 – 54 advantage with 9:38 to go after back-to-back threes by Mike Chappell and Steve Wojciechowski and a tip-in by Chris Carrawell.

But the Wildcats scored on seven straight possessions to narrow the gap and finally completed the 17-point comeback by tying the score at 81 with 1:20 to go. Scott Padgett hit a three-pointer with 39.4 seconds left to put

Kentucky ahead to stay, as Duke missed a last-second shot to absorb its first loss in eight NCAA regional finals under Mike Krzyzewski.

Duke (84). McLeod 19, Carrawell 12, Brand 4, Langdon 18, Wojciechowski 10, Avery 4, Battier 11, Chappell 6, Burgess

Kentucky (86). Edwards 11, Padgett 12, Mohammed 8, Turner 16, Sheppard 18, Smith, Evans 14, Mills 5, Magliore 2

Nothing Could Be Finer

March 7, 1999

Charlotte — Playing without their injured senior captain Trajan Langdon, the Blue Devils stormed past North Carolina 96 – 73 to win the ACC Tournament for the 10th time in school history. The margin of victory was the most lopsided for an ACC title contest since 1968. The decision culminated a perfect conference year for Duke, which went 16 – 0 during the regular season and 3 – 0 in the tourney.

Tournament MVP Elton Brand hit 9 of 11 shots for 24 points and added 13 rebounds. Sophomore guard William Avery hit 10 of 19 shots with five three-pointers to finish with 29 points.

Duke broke open a close game with a 17 – 6 run late in the first half. The Blue Devils then scored the first 10 points of the second half to bolt out to a 59 – 35 advantage. UNC rallied to within nine points, but Brand and Avery made several key plays down the stretch to help Duke regain control.

Duke's five starters all scored in double figures and combined for all but seven of the team's points. The win was Duke's third of the year over Carolina. The previous year, UNC had beaten Duke in the ACC final and provided the only blemish on a 15 – 1 conference campaign.

Duke (96). Battier 13, Maggette 11, Brand 24, Carrawell 12, Avery 29, Simpson 4, James 3, Burgess, Domzalski, R. Caldbeck, J. Caldbeck, Bryant

North Carolina (73). Okulaja 13, Lang 12, Haywood 5, Owens 22, Cota 5, Evtimov 10, Curry 4, Bersticker 2, Capel, Williams, Frederick, Newby, Melendez

Championship Savvy

March 21, 1999

East Rutherford, N.J. — Duke displayed the offensive strength and defensive prowess that made it the nation's most dominant team in whipping Temple 85 – 64 to secure its fifth trip to the Final Four in the 1990s.

Selected the most valuable player of the East Region, Trajan Langdon ignited the Blue Devils with 23 points. His three consecutive three-point shots early in the game underpinned a 17 – 2 run that put the Blue Devils in control. Langdon had missed two ACC tourney games and one NCAA game with an injury but bounced back to hit 15 of 21 field goals and 9 of 12 threes in the two regional games at the Meadowlands.

Duke made 16 of its 23 shots in the first half against Temple and opened up a 43 – 31 margin when freshman Corey Maggette delivered a stunning offensive rebound dunk in the closing seconds. Defensively, Duke held Temple's leading offensive threat, Mark Karcher, to a 7-of-25 shooting performance that included just 3 of 15 from three-point range. Temple hit only 37 percent from the field and just 18 percent on three-pointers.

Critical to Duke's efforts was the performance of Chris Carrawell, who made play after play in penetrating the Owls' matchup zone defense. Carrawell would either dump a pass off to Elton Brand if the defense collapsed, relocate the ball back outside to a three-point shooter, or finish at the basket himself.

Duke (85). Battier 6, Carrawell 12, Brand 21, Langdon 23, Avery 13, Maggette 8, Burgess 2, James, Simpson, Domzalski

Temple (64). Karcher 19, Barnes 19, Lyde 2, Brokenborough 12, Sanchez 10, Wadley, Sanders, Rollerson 2, Reid, Barry

Hard Fall

March 29, 1999

St. Petersburg — No. 1 Duke edged No. 2 Michigan State in the NCAA semifinals but couldn't get past No. 3 Connecticut in the national championship game. The Huskies claimed their first title in their first Final Four appearance with a 77 – 74 victory that stunned one of the most complete Duke teams ever, a national juggernaut that featured four first-round NBA draft picks.

A regional championship victory over Temple at the Meadowlands sent Mike Krzyzewski to the 1999 Final Four.

MVP Richard Hamilton's 27 points paced UConn, which held a 73–69 lead just inside the two-minute mark. Senior Trajan Langdon hit a three-pointer to bring Duke within one, and after a UConn drive made it 75–72, William Avery's two free throws with 54 seconds left again had the Devils within a point at 75–74. Chris Carrawell rebounded a miss by the Huskies with 24 seconds to go, and Duke had a chance to play for the winning shot. Langdon, the Blue Devils' leader with 25 points, had the ball in his hands for his team's last two plays but couldn't score. First UConn's Ricky Moore forced him into a travel with 5.4 seconds left. Then, after a pair of free throws by UConn with 5.2 seconds left, Duke quickly inbounded to Langdon, who raced up the floor for a last-ditch three. But he lost his balance and the ball, and UConn had the championship.

The loss was Duke's first since it fell to Cincinnati in the Great Alaska Shootout title game in November, ending a 32-game winning streak that set a school record. The team's 37–2 final record matched the NCAA mark for most victories in a season, shared by Duke in 1986 and UNLV in 1987.

Duke (74). Battier 6, Carrawell 9, Brand 15, Langdon 25, Avery 11, James, Maggette 8, Burgess
Connecticut (77). Freeman 6, Hamilton 27, Voskuhl 2, Moore 13, El-Amin 12, Wane 4, Mouring 6, Saunders 4, Jones 3, Klaiber

Crash Landing

Feb. 9, 2000

Durham — A couple of historic streaks came to an end when 23rd-ranked Maryland upset third-ranked Duke 98–87 on the Blue Devils' home floor.

The loss marked the end of a record 31-game ACC winning streak and a 46-game home winning streak for the Blue Devils. Duke had not dropped a regular-season conference game since falling at UNC in 1998 or a home contest since 1997.

Shane Battier played brilliantly for Duke, with 28 points on 10-of-15 shooting. But Maryland's Juan Dixon was just a little better, hitting 14 of 19 shots for 31 points. Lonny Baxter and Terence Morris added double-doubles for the Terps. Struggling most of the night (shooting 7 of 22), Morris made two of the biggest plays when he hit back-to-back three-pointers to break open an 83–83 tie late in the game.

Duke shot 53 percent from the field but committed 20 turnovers. The loss ended the nation's longest active winning streak at 18 games.

Duke (87). Battier 28, Carrawell 14, Boozer 6, James 13, Williams 9, Dunleavy 13, Christensen 4
Maryland (98). Miller 16, Morris 20, Baxter 22, Dixon 31, Blake 7, Holden 2, Mardesich, Nicholas

Miracle Minute

Jan. 27, 2001

College Park, Md. — Second-ranked Duke was well on its way to its first ACC defeat of the year, trailing eighth-ranked Maryland by 10 points with a minute to play. But one of the most improbable rallies in school history sent the game into overtime, and Duke won 98–96 to extend its ACC-record road winning streak to 23 games.

Duke was down 46–37 at halftime and still trailed

90 – 80 with a minute to play. Sophomore Jason Williams was mired in one of his worst games with 10 turnovers, only four assists, and no three-pointers. The Maryland student section was chanting "Overrated" at the Blue Devils.

But then Williams exploded with a layup and two three-pointers in a span of 14 seconds to make it a 90 – 88 game with 41 seconds remaining. Senior Nate James made a key steal from the Terps' star Juan Dixon with 35 seconds left, and hit a pair of free throws when he was fouled on an offensive rebound to tie the score at 90. That sent the contest into overtime.

Senior Shane Battier made the extra period as memorable as the 10 – 0 finish to regulation by scoring his team's last six points and blocking Dixon's game-tying layup attempt with three seconds left to play.

Duke (98). Battier 20, Dunleavy 18, Boozer 15, James 16,
   Williams 25, Duhon 4, Christensen, Buckner
Maryland (96). Mouton 13, Morris 13, Baxter 7,
   Dixon 17, Blake 11, Nicholas 8, Miller 9, Mardesich 4,
   Holden 14, Wilcox

Reversal of Fortune

March 4, 2001

Chapel Hill — Though ranked No. 2 in the country, Duke was given little chance of defeating fourth-ranked North Carolina in the season finale after the Blue Devils lost center Carlos Boozer to a foot injury in a Senior Night defeat to Maryland. But coach Mike Krzyzewski completely reworked his lineup by inserting reserve Casey Sanders for Boozer and elevating freshman Chris Duhon to the starting backcourt. The result was a stunning 95 – 81 victory that gave Duke a share of its fifth straight ACC regular-season title, a new conference standard.

With Duhon at the point, Duke tried to move the ball more quickly up the floor and push the tempo at every opportunity. After shooting 0 for 4 in the first half, Duhon proved to be a catalyst in the second by hitting 5 of 7 shots. He had all 15 of his points after halftime, with no turnovers. Putting the ball in Duhon's hands more often also opened up the floor for his fellow guard Jason Williams, who hit seven three-pointers and to-

taled 33 points. And senior Shane Battier anchored a defense that trapped, swarmed the ball, and thoroughly disrupted UNC's plan to go inside on the Devils' depleted frontcourt.

After a close first half, Duke broke open the game by scoring 30 points in the first 8:09 of the second half to take a 15-point lead. A key moment came with Duke on top 50 – 47. UNC's Joseph Forte stole the ball from Mike Dunleavy at the top of the key and headed down the floor for an apparent fast-break dunk. But Battier caught Forte from behind and forced him to jam the ball into the front of the rim. Dunleavy grabbed the rebound and dished it to Williams, who nailed a three-point shot to extend Duke's lead to six.

Duke (95). Battier 25, Dunleavy 16, Sanders 2,
   Williams 33, Duhon 15, James 4, Love, Christensen
North Carolina (81). Brooker, Everett, Haywood 12,
   Owens 8, Curry 7, Forte 21, Capel 11, Morrison 8,
   Lang 7, Peppers 7, Boone

Final Four Rally

March 31, 2001

Minneapolis — After splitting with Maryland in the regular season and edging the Terps on a last-second tip-in at the ACC Tournament semifinals, the Blue Devils' fourth meeting with their heated rival got off to a shocking start when Maryland opened up a 22-point lead in the first half at the Final Four. But Duke responded with the biggest comeback ever in an NCAA semifinal to win 95 – 84 and earn a spot in the national championship game.

Hot-shooting Maryland led 39 – 17 with just under seven minutes to go before halftime. Duke cut the deficit to 11 points by the break, then finally claimed its first advantage at 73 – 72 with 6:52 remaining on a three-pointer by Jason Williams. Duke went on to outscore the Terps by 22 in the second half, 57 – 35.

While stalwarts Williams and Shane Battier combined for 48 points, the Blue Devils got a lift with 19 points off the bench from Carlos Boozer, who had broken his foot in their loss to the Terps on February 27. Nate James also played a crucial role on defense. After Maryland's Juan Dixon scored 16 points in the first half,

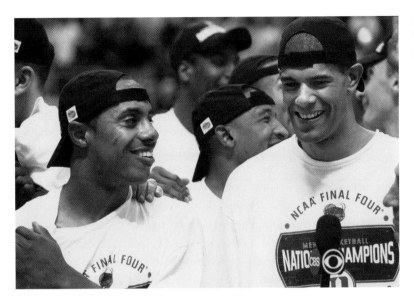

Co–national players of the year Jason Williams and Shane Battier shared a smile after the 2001 NCAA title was secured.

James took over the defense on him in the second half and limited him to three points.

Duke (95). Battier 25, Dunleavy 4, Sanders 5,
    Williams 23, Duhon 10, Boozer 19, James 9, Buckner
Maryland (84). Mouton 9, Morris 10, Baxter 10,
    Blake 13, Dixon 19, Nicholas 7, Miller 4, Mardesich 6,
    Holden 4, Wilcox 2

Third Time on Top

April 2, 2001

Minneapolis — Top-ranked Duke stopped fifth-ranked Arizona 82 – 72 to claim the Blue Devils' third NCAA title and finish the season with a 35 – 4 record.

Shane Battier, national player of the year, led the way by playing all 40 minutes while totaling 18 points, 11 rebounds, and six assists. His roommate Mike Dunleavy also had a major hand in the decision with a team-high 21 points, 18 in the second half. Dunleavy connected on a trio of three-pointers in a span of only 45 seconds to give the Devils a 50 – 39 lead before the 16-minute mark.

Arizona came back with a 9 – 0 run to close the gap, but Duke rebuilt its cushion over the next four minutes, stretching it to 61 – 51 when Dunleavy hit another three with 10:08 to go. Again Arizona answered to make it a three-point game, but then Chris Duhon delivered a drive that coach Mike Krzyzewski called the biggest basket of the game. MVP Battier followed with three spectacular shots — a putback dunk, a backhanded tip-in, and a driving, one-handed slam — before Williams hit a three with 1:44 to play to effectively seal the decision.

Duke became the first No. 1 team to win the NCAA title since UCLA in 1995, and Krzyzewski became the fourth coach to win at least three national championships, joining John Wooden (10), Adolph Rupp (4), and Bob Knight (3).

Duke (82). Battier 18, Dunleavy 21, Sanders,
    Williams 16, Duhon 9, Boozer 12, James 6
Arizona (72). Arenas 10, Wright 10, Woods 22,
    Gardner 7, Jefferson 19, Walton 4, Wessel,
    Edgerson

Ground Zero

Dec. 18, 2001

East Rutherford, N.J. — The night before taking on Kentucky in the Jimmy V Classic, Duke made a trip into New York City to visit ground zero of the September 11 terrorist attacks on the World Trade Center. The morning of the game, coach Mike Krzyzewski talked at length with his team about how much it meant to be supporting the V Foundation's fight against cancer. It all added up to a lot of extra emotion for Duke guard Jason

Williams, back in his home in New Jersey for one of the marquee games of the season.

Williams found an outlet for his emotions and poured in a career-high 38 points to help the top-ranked Devils overcome a 12-point second-half deficit and win a classic overtime duel with seventh-ranked Kentucky, 95 – 92.

The first half was back and forth, but the Wildcats held Duke scoreless for the first four minutes of the second half to take a 10-point lead. Krzyzewski removed all his starters from the game for almost three minutes, and the reserves gave the Devils a boost. With just over 10 minutes to play, Kentucky still led by eight when Krzyzewski moved Williams from the wing to point guard. Over the next six minutes he scored 17 of Duke's 19 points to bring his team back. With 1:21 left he nailed a three-pointer to give Duke a 77 – 75 lead, and with 8.8 seconds left he hit a free throw to send the game into overtime.

Heading into the extra five minutes, Williams had scored 23 of Duke's final 31 points. Mike Dunleavy took over the scoring load early in overtime with seven straight points, and Williams came back with a three-point play that gave his team the lead for good with 1:39 to play in arguably the best game of the 2001 – 02 college season.

"I had a couple of friends die in the World Trade Center and I couldn't even stand to look at the site," Williams said. "I had to go back to the bus and sit. And then talking to Coach about the fight against cancer . . . It has been a very emotional win, and I'm really glad that I came home and we won the game."

Duke (95). Jones 10, Dunleavy 21, Boozer 15, Williams 38, Duhon 2, Ewing 2, Buckner, Sanders 2, Christensen 3, Love 2
Kentucky (92). Bogans 8, Prince 17, Camara 10, Hawkins 15, Fitch 11, Daniels, Carruth 19, Chiles, Stone 1, Blevins, Hayes 2, Estill 9

Early Departure

March 21, 2002

Lexington, Ky. — Duke's hopes of securing a second straight NCAA title came to an abrupt halt at Rupp Arena when the top-seeded Blue Devils were eliminated by Indiana 74 – 73 in the South Regional semifinal.

Duke had every opportunity to storm into the quarterfinals, opening up a 17-point lead in the first half and a 13-point lead at intermission. The margin remained at double figures well into the second half before the Hoosiers rallied behind the Big Ten player of the year, Jared Jeffries, to take a one-point lead with 5:42 to go.

Duke recovered to reclaim the lead at 70 – 64 on a three-pointer by Mike Dunleavy with 2:50 to play, but then the Hoosiers scored 10 straight points to go up 74 – 70 with only 11 seconds left. The Devils made a final spurt when Jason Williams grabbed an offensive rebound, stepped back behind the three-point line, and drilled a shot with just 4.2 seconds left. He was fouled on the play by Dane Fife, a former Duke recruit, but missed the free throw that would have tied the game. Carlos Boozer grabbed Williams's rebound in position to power in for the winning points, but he was shackled by Jeffries and missed the follow-up. Duke finished with a 31 – 4 record but fell shy of a return trip to the Final Four.

Duke (73). Jones 6, Dunleavy 17, Boozer 19, Williams 15, Duhon 7, Ewing 6, Sanders 3
Indiana (74). Jeffries 24, Hornsby 2, Odle 15, Coverdale 6, Fife 3, Moye 14, Leach, Perry 2, Newton 8

Five in a Row

March 16, 2003

Greensboro — Duke's historic run of four consecutive ACC titles appeared to be over when N.C. State opened up a 55 – 40 lead with less than 12 minutes to play in the tournament championship contest. But sparked by the torrid shooting of freshman J. J. Redick, the Blue Devils rallied for an 84 – 77 victory to win the 50th ACC Tournament and an unprecedented fifth straight crown.

Redick scored 23 of his game-high 30 points in the final 10:05 of play to help Duke erase the 15-point deficit. He erupted for eight points in 90 seconds to make it a six-point game. Then he went for 15 more points in the last five minutes, including a 9-of-10 stretch at the foul line, as Duke took control and extended the lead. He finished with five three-pointers and 11 free throws.

After the game Duke's Daniel Ewing was named tournament most valuable player for scoring 62 points in three games. He had 32 in a quarterfinal win over Virginia and 19 in the semifinals against UNC. The championship provided some momentum for NCAA play to a team that had suffered two losses in the final week of the regular season.

Duke (84). Jones 18, Redick 30, Williams 9, Ewing 11, Duhon 10, Sanders 5, Dockery 3, Horvath 2, Buckner

N.C. State (77). Hodge 4, Melvin 14, Powell 26, Sherrill 11, Crawford 7, Mejia, Bennerman 2, Watkins, Roach, Collins

Good to the Last Shot

Feb. 5, 2004

Chapel Hill — Ranked No. 1 in the country and riding a 15-game winning streak, Duke nevertheless had its hands full with a 17th-ranked North Carolina team that owned a losing record in ACC play. Like so many games in the Duke-Carolina series, this one evolved into a classic that the Blue Devils won in overtime, 83 – 81.

Duke led by five points at halftime before UNC scratched back to build up a 69 – 62 lead with 5:45 to go on a fast-break dunk by Rashad McCants. Duke then buckled down on defense and held UNC scoreless for over four minutes to take a 72 – 69 lead at 1:06. After Sean May scored at 53 seconds to make it a one-point game, J. J. Redick answered with a gritty drive at 38 seconds to boost Duke's advantage back to three. Then UNC's Jawad Williams nailed his only three-pointer of the game at 18 seconds and the teams were knotted at 74, headed to overtime.

A pair of free throws by Redick gave Duke a lead of 81 – 78 with 22 seconds left, but McCants hit a clutch three-pointer with just 13 seconds on the clock to tie the score again. Rather than call a timeout to set up a final play, Duke quickly inbounded the ball to Chris Duhon, who raced the length of the floor, weaving through defenders, and made a reverse layup with 6.5 seconds left to give the Blue Devils an 83 – 81 lead. After Melvin Scott missed a three at the buzzer, all the Blue Devils swarmed Duhon in celebration of a victory that registered as Duke's 13th in its last 15 contests with the Tar Heels.

"David [Noel] thought that I was going to get back to Duhon, but Duhon, being the smart, crafty player that

he is, kept going to the basket, knowing that David and I were going to run into each other," said UNC guard Raymond Felton. "He didn't get a wide-open lay-up, but he made a tough shot."

Duke (83). Deng 17, Redick 14, Williams 22, Ewing 19, Duhon 9, Randolph 2, Dockery

North Carolina (81). Williams 7, McCants 27, May 15, Scott 5, Felton 11, Manuel 8, Noel 6, Sanders 2, Terry

Above and Beyond

Dec. 10, 2005

East Rutherford, N.J. — Top-ranked Duke and second-ranked Texas met at the Meadowlands, just the second matchup of Nos. 1 and 2 in college basketball since the turn of the century (along with the NCAA title game between Illinois and UNC in 2005). Before a sold-out house and a national television audience, the Blue Devils remained undefeated with a landslide victory, 97 – 66.

The game got out of hand in the second half when a spurt by the Longhorns trimmed Duke's lead to 47 – 42. After a pointed timeout huddle with Mike Krzyzewski, the Devils went on a 19 – 2 tear and the score never drew closer than 19 points the rest of the way. Shelden Williams anchored the inside with 23 points, while point guard Sean Dockery keyed the perimeter defense with his work against his counterpart Daniel Gibson, but the day belonged to senior J. J. Redick. He notched a career high of 41 points on 13-of-24 shooting and tied the school record with nine three-pointers. It marked the most torrential offensive output by a Duke player since Danny Ferry scored a school record 58 points 17 years earlier to the day.

"It's hard to guard J. J. — believe me, I know that. I have to face him every day in practice," noted Dockery. "It's hard especially when he is shooting like that. He showed how much he really wanted to win this game and played his heart out."

Duke (97). McRoberts 6, Williams 23, Redick 41, Paulus 8, Dockery 7, Melchionni 3, Pocius 5, Boateng, Boykin 4, Perkins

Texas (66). Tucker 14, Buckman 2, Aldridge 21, Paulino 14, Gibson 13, Williams 2, Abrams, Atchley, Lewis, Winder

Fifteen Milestone Games in Duke Women's Basketball History

Long Time Coming

Feb. 14, 1980

Durham—Duke had never beaten North Carolina in varsity competition, and most of the meetings between the two schools during the 1970s were decided by double-digit margins. But less than a week after falling to the Tar Heels by 22 points in the ACC Tournament (held then in early February), the Blue Devils recorded their first victory in the series with a 66–61 decision at Cameron Indoor Stadium.

Tara McCarthy, a junior and Duke's first scholarship recruit, was one of four players in double figures with 13 points, while forwards Barb Krause and Margo Walsh had 10 rebounds apiece. The game was far from a technical masterpiece, as Duke committed 34 turnovers and shot just 36.9 percent from the field, while UNC had 27 turnovers and shot only 29.2 percent. But the win in Duke's final home game before 500 fans was a long time coming.

"Desire was the key word for us tonight," coach Debbie Leonard said. "We wanted to win this game very badly and worked hard for it. We shot well, boxed out well, and did the things that we have to do to win games."

The game was one of four between the two schools during the 1980 season. UNC won the other three by a total of 79 points. After a meeting at Chapel Hill in December, the remaining three games were played in February at the ACC, in Cameron, and at the state AIAW tourney in Raleigh.

Duke (66). Krause 11, Matthews 12, Warren 8, McCarthy 13, Thomasson 13, Walsh 9, Rose, Monroe, Reid, Earnhardt

North Carolina (61). McGlade 19, Crawford 11, Walls 8, Shaffer 16, Berry 4, Boykin, Cermola, White 1, Jones 2, Burch, Thomas

Catharsis at Reynolds

Feb. 21, 1984

Raleigh—During Debbie Leonard's first season as Duke's coach in 1978, the Blue Devils suffered a most humbling loss to N.C. State, 125–43, in Reynolds Coliseum. The Wolfpack was emerging as a national power at the time, in the midst of nine straight 20-win seasons under their future Hall of Fame coach Kay Yow, while Duke was playing with less than a handful of scholarships.

Leonard recalled that game in 1984 when the Blue Devils finally defeated N.C. State for the first time, 74–73 in overtime at Reynolds. After Jennifer Chestnut scored the winning basket with seven seconds left, State missed a shot at the buzzer, ending nine years of futility by the Blue Devils versus the Wolfpack.

Duke led 38–30 at intermission, but Yow's team rallied, and there were several lead changes in the second half before regulation ended at 63–63. State led 73–72 with 20 seconds left when Leonard called a timeout to set up the final play. Point guard Maura Hertzog got the ball to Connie Goins, who spotted Chestnut for an open layup.

N.C. State was ranked No. 15 in the nation. The win was Duke's second in less than a week over a ranked club, coming on the heels of a 13-point victory over No. 16 North Carolina.

Duke (74). Chestnut 21, Harlow 10, Mikels 12, Hertzog 8, Goins 17, Hurd 4, Boyle 2

N.C. State (73). Kreicker 4, Page 27, Adams 5, Mulligan 6, Mayo 8, Daye 2, Trice 7, Rouse 2, Hillman 6, Falkena 4, Treadway 2

First Dance

March 11, 1987

Durham—After winning 18 games during the regular season and finishing fourth in the ACC, the Duke women were extended their first invitation to the NCAA Tournament, in the sixth year of the event. The Blue Devils were awarded a home game for the first round and pounded Manhattan 70–55 before a crowd of about 1,200 at Cameron.

The ACC player of the year, Chris Moreland, paced the Blue Devils with 25 points, while Katie Meier posted the first triple-double in program history with 16 points, 11 rebounds, and 10 assists.

Duke was sent to New Jersey for the second round and lost to Rutgers to close the year with a 19–10 mark that might have been even better: four of its ACC losses were by a total of seven points. The positive momentum continued in 1988 when Duke got off to a 12–0 start, before losing Meier to a knee injury. The program did not return to the NCAA tourney until 1995.

Duke (70). Andersen 6, Moreland 25, Sullivan 6, Hunter, Meier 16, Sonzogni 2, Harnett 14, Langhi, Christopher 1, Morgan, Kalinowski
Manhattan (55). Jack 12, Robeson 7, Harding 4, Gordon 6, O'Connor 11, Sevbold 2, Mullfinger 2, O'Flaherty 10, Sellinger, Snyder 1, Cehelsky

Special Dedication

Jan. 20, 1990

Durham — Before they began hosting an annual tournament to benefit the Ronald McDonald House, the Duke women teamed with North Carolina to raise funds for the facility by designating one of their contests each year the Ronald McDonald Challenge Game. In the fourth installment, the Blue Devils and Tar Heels were all tied up at 88 with three seconds left. Then Traci Williams inbounded the ball from underneath the Duke basket, and Leigh Morgan connected on a foul-line jumper as time expired to give the Devils a 90–88 victory.

The finish evoked memories of a game between Duke and UNC in 1986 that ended in almost identical fashion. In that one, Duke trailed by one with three seconds left, before guard Carolyn Sonzogni hit a jumper from the free-throw line as time ran out to provide a 79–78 victory.

The two dramatic endings were connected by tragedy. In the fall of 1989 Sonzogni, having graduated, was killed by a drunk driver in an auto accident in Orlando.

The 1989–90 Devils dedicated their season and the Ronald McDonald Challenge Game to her memory.

"The first thing I said when I went into the locker room was 'Carolyn Sonzogni lives,'" coach Debbie Leonard reported after the 1990 game. Morgan added about her winning shot: "It was kind of eerie. It was the same exact play, the same exact shot."

Duke played well throughout the game, starting on a 14–4 run and never trailing. When UNC tied the score at 88, it marked the only tie since 2–2. Monika Kost had one of the best games of her Duke career with 25 points and 16 rebounds, while Dana McDonald added 23 points and Katie Meier 20. Morgan played the entire 40 minutes, with seven assists and four field goals. The first three were from three-point range, while the last won the game. Leonard used only six players in the contest, played before a crowd of 2,314.

Duke (90). Williams 4, Meier 20, Kost 25, Morgan 12, McDonald 23, McKisson 6
North Carolina (88). Thompson 2, L. Kennedy 10, Williams 16, Johnson 9, Anderson 6, Oden 13, Lamb 23, Waddell 3, K. Kennedy 2, Montgomery 4

Oh, What a Night for Day

Jan. 25, 1995

Durham — With three seconds to play in a tie game between Duke and North Carolina, the Blue Devils' coach, Gail Goestenkors, drew up a play that was supposed to free forward Tyish Hall for a potential game-winning shot in the lane. The fake screen with Kira Orr worked to perfection, and Hall found herself wide open in the paint. But the inbounds passer, Jen Scanlon, couldn't see Hall because UNC had a 6–7 center obstructing her vision. Scanlon did see Ali Day pop out on the baseline and quickly fed her the ball. Day wheeled around and lofted a 10-footer with one second left on the clock. It kissed the rim five times and then dropped through the net to give Duke a 74–72 victory.

"I really didn't think it was going in after the first bounce, when it bounced about five feet up in the air," Goestenkors said. "But she is going to make that shot seven or eight times out of 10. We all know she has great touch from there."

"It was destiny for us to win," said Day, who was

Alison Day's shot at the buzzer lifted Duke over defending NCAA women's champion North Carolina in 1995.

mobbed by jubilant students from the crowd of 5,000. "It was something you dream about, hitting the last shot to beat Carolina at home."

The game was close throughout, with UNC opening up a lead of 72–68 at the 1:28 mark. Duke scored the rest of the points, first on a baseline reverse by Orr and then on a short jumper by Hall to tie.

The victory ended third-ranked North Carolina's 32-game winning streak, dating back to the 1994 season, when the Tar Heels claimed the national championship. It also ended a six-game losing streak for Duke against its biggest rival, giving seniors such as Carey Kauffman (19 points, 10 rebounds) their first career win in the series.

Duke (74). Kauffman 19, Hall 9, Day 16, Scanlon 15, Orr 6, Brandau, Blanding 4, Meiman 5
North Carolina (72). Smith 7, Lawrence 13, Gillingham 4, Gear 2, Jones 28, Jackson 6, McKee, Reid 11, Cooper 1, Suddreth

Kira in the Clutch

March 4, 1995

Rock Hill, S.C. — Duke advanced to its first ACC Tournament championship game with one of the most dramatic and improbable comebacks in the history of

the event. Down by 22 points to a Virginia team that went 16–0 during the ACC regular season, the Devils rallied for an 83–82 overtime victory behind the heroics of their sophomore point guard Kira Orr.

After going scoreless in the first half, Orr finished with 24 points and hit two buzzer-beaters to spark her team. Duke trailed by 12 with 2:08 remaining in regulation before Orr came out of nowhere with 18 points over the final two minutes plus overtime.

Virginia took a 73–70 lead on a three-pointer with only five seconds left in regulation. The Blue Devils had no timeouts remaining, so they rushed an inbounds pass to Orr, who took a few dribbles and lofted a long soft shot that tied the game as time expired.

Virginia led by one with six seconds left in overtime, and Duke again was out of timeouts. Orr took the pass and this time faced resistance from her Cavalier counterpart Tora Suber. But she kept her dribble until she approached the foul line and got off a shot just before the horn sounded. When it went through, the Devils celebrated one of their most significant triumphs to date.

"The play was, get the ball to Kira and Kira take the court. I just listened to Coach," Orr said.

"Hopefully we showed people across the country that we are a program on the rise and a program to be reckoned with," coach Gail Goestenkors said after a loss to UNC in the ACC final. "Our kids played with so much

Jennifer Scanlon (13) played all 60 minutes when the Duke women dropped a four-overtime decision at Alabama in the 1995 NCAA Tournament.

heart, so much intensity, so much hustle over this three-day period that people have to step back and say we're for real."

Duke (83). Day 17, Orr 24, Scanlon 15, Coggeshall 5,
   Meiman, Blanding 2, Kauffman 8, Hall 12, Brandau,
   Brown
Virginia (82). Gardner, Foote 9, Gausepohl 18,
   Lesoravage, Boucek 9, Palmer 20, Lofstedt 11,
   Beale 3, Suber 12, Glessner

Battle to Exhaustion

March 18, 1995

Tuscaloosa, Ala. — In a contest fit for a time capsule, Alabama outlasted Duke 121 – 120 in four overtimes to capture a second-round NCAA Tournament game at Coleman Coliseum. It was the longest game ever in the event and ended a season of dramatic finishes for the Blue Devils, who were appearing in the postseason for the first time under coach Gail Goestenkors and only the second time in school history (1987).

The game appeared to be settled several times, but on each occasion one side or the other simply refused to let its season end:

—Duke had the lead and the ball with less than 20 seconds to play in regulation when guard Kira Orr drove for a layup to clinch the victory. But she was whistled for charging, and Alabama hit a desperation three-pointer with 1.6 seconds left to force overtime.

—Orr gave Duke the lead at the end of the first overtime on a driving jumper, but she committed a foul on the defensive end and Alabama hit a pair of free throws to tie it up again.

—A wide path to the basket opened for Duke's center Ali Day in the closing seconds of the second OT, setting up a potential game-winning drive. But a defender for the Crimson Tide stuck out a hand and knocked the ball out of bounds off Day's knee.

—The teams furiously traded baskets in the third overtime before a miss by Duke at the end left the score still tied, this time at 108.

—Alabama took a quick five-point margin in the fourth overtime, but Duke made the home team squirm by scoring three field goals in the last 20 seconds.

"Each time, at the end of regulation and in the overtimes, I kept thinking we had this wrapped up, we're going to win it. Then something would happen. They wouldn't back down," said Orr.

"They were kind of reminding us of ourselves," said guard Jen Scanlon in a reverent allusion to four previous games that the Blue Devils had pulled out with late-game miracles.

Scanlon played the entire 60 minutes and three teammates played more than 50. Day matched the school record with 37 points on 14-of-20 shooting, while Orr poured in 30 points and senior Carey Kauffman added 24 points plus 14 rebounds in her final game.

Duke (120). Kauffman 24, Hall 12, Day 37, Orr 30,
   Scanlon 12, Brandau, Meiman 5, Blanding, Brown,
   Coggeshall

Alabama (121). Thompson 5, Stevenson 1, Watkins 33,
Johnson 28, Ezell 11, Smith 12, Duncan 7, Daniels 11,
Koonce 7, Monteith 6

The Way to San Jose

March 22, 1999

Greensboro — Tennessee senior Chamique Holdsclaw
had celebrated a state championship during all four years
of high school and an NCAA crown during her first three
years in college. But the best player in women's basketball was denied a perfect finish to her amateur career
when Duke upset the Lady Vols 69 – 63 in the NCAA East
Regional championship game. The victory sent the Blue
Devils to the Final Four in San Jose for the first time in
program history.

Duke found its way to San Jose by shutting down
Holdsclaw with an assortment of defenses and remaining poised when the powerful Lady Vols made their
move in the second half. Sophomore Georgia Schweitzer
scored 22 points on 7-of-11 shooting and was named
regional MVP, while guard Nicole Erickson hit for 17
points; All-America center Michele VanGorp added 13
and forward Lauren Rice worked the lane like a warrior
with nine points and eight boards.

Duke forward Peppi Browne set an aggressive tone
when she rejected Tennessee's first shot of the game.
Point guard Hilary Howard followed a few moments
later by stripping the ball from Holdsclaw on her first
drive. VanGorp sparkled on both ends of the floor late
in the first half to help the Blue Devils open up a 33 – 20
lead; Duke eventually took an 11-point advantage into
the locker room at halftime, while Holdsclaw was 0 for
10 from the field.

Tennessee outscored Duke 15 – 6 over the first eight
minutes after intermission but could never take the lead,
as the Blue Devils refused to succumb to the Vols' onslaught. Duke hit 11 of 14 free throws over the final 90
seconds to remain in control and never relented in its
defense of Holdsclaw, the all-time scoring and rebounding leader in NCAA Tournament history. She finished
with eight points on 2-of-18 shooting.

"We knew they were going to get their runs," Schweitzer said. "They are a great team and they play great
pressure defense. We felt like we really had to stay poised

Sophomore Georgia Schweitzer was voted East Regional MVP
in 1999 when Duke upset Tennessee, three-time defending
NCAA champion, to reach the Final Four for the first time.

when they made their runs and I think we did a great
job of that."

"If people consider this a huge upset, okay," said coach
Gail Goestenkors, "but I don't know if we do."

With crowds of 13,190 for the regional semifinals and
12,235 for the Duke-Tennessee final, a new attendance
record for the NCAA East Regional was established. The
game's appearance on prime-time national television
on ESPN resonated in recruiting for Duke over the next
several years.

Duke (69). Browne 6, Schweitzer 22, VanGorp 13,
Howard 2, Erickson 17, Black, Rice 9, Parent
Tennessee (63). Holdsclaw 8, Catchings 13, Snow 6,
Jolly 11, Randall 18, Clement 3, Geter 2, Butts 2

Historic Journey a Step Short

March 28, 1999

San Jose—After a seven-day tournament run that went through élite programs from Old Dominion, Tennessee, and Georgia—arguably the best stretch of basketball in program history—the Duke women came up short in their first trip to the NCAA championship game. Top-ranked Purdue defeated the Blue Devils 62–45 in the lowest-scoring title game ever.

The final was filled with irony, as Goestenkors was pitted against the school where she had been an assistant coach before coming to Duke. Her Purdue counterpart, Carolyn Peck, had been her assistant coach for a USA Basketball team two summers before. What's more, two of Duke's best players, seniors Michele VanGorp and Nicole Erickson, had started their careers at Purdue before transferring to Durham in the wake of a mass exodus from Purdue when veteran coach Lin Dunn was dismissed.

Duke's team, loaded with seniors, shot just 33 percent from the field and committed 20 turnovers while matching the lowest point total in Goestenkors's career with the Blue Devils. Ukari Figgs and Stephanie White-McCarty—former freshman teammates of VanGorp and Erickson and among the few players who stuck it out during the Purdue turmoil—continually broke down Duke's defense and contributed 30 points between them.

"I think it was nerves combined with excellent defense on Purdue's part," Goestenkors said in analyzing the defeat. "I thought going in that we were in a good place mentally because we had played so well and with such confidence. Finally, after all this time, the ability to attain our ultimate goal was right before us. Before then it had always seemed like it was a couple of steps away, so our sights were set in the near future but it was still out there. Then all of a sudden it was right there. That's the only thing I can think of that caused us to get rattled a little bit."

Duke (45). Browne 5, Schweitzer, VanGorp 15, Howard 9, Erickson 8, Parent 6, Rice 2, Black, Gingrich
Purdue (62). White-McCarty 12, Duhart 5, Cooper 13, Figgs 18, Douglas 13, Crawford, Young, Komara

Third Time the Charm

March 6, 2000

Greensboro—Playing in the ACC Tournament championship game for the third time, second-seeded Duke edged fifth-seeded North Carolina 79–76 before the largest crowd (8,090) in the event's first 23 years. The conference title was Duke's first ever, after runner-up finishes in 1995 and 1996.

Upon the team's arrival in Greensboro, coach Gail Goestenkors asked the players to reenact some of the celebratory moments that occurred on the coliseum floor the previous March, when Duke beat Tennessee in an NCAA regional final. And before her team took the court to play Carolina, the coach showed a seven-minute highlight tape from the Tennessee game. "Then after we watched it, I said, 'Okay, that's the past. We have those good feelings. Now it's time to make new memories,'" Goestenkors said.

Her Blue Devils complied. The coach called this ACC final one of the best games she'd ever been involved with because both teams played at a high level throughout. Duke displayed some of its best offensive execution in the second half to take a 64–55 lead, but UNC guard Nikki Teasley led the Tar Heels back and helped them take a 72–71 lead with 1:50 left to play.

Georgia Schweitzer drove inside and Missy West converted three free throws to put Duke back on top 76–72 with 20.9 seconds left. After MVP Teasley scored with 13 seconds left to make it a two-point game, Duke sealed it with a home-run play drawn up by Goestenkors. Lauren Rice threw a long pass down court to Schweitzer, who held back on a fast-break attempt and pretended to call a half-court play out on the wing. Freshman Michele Matyasovsky then streaked into the lane, and Schweitzer hit her for the decisive layup with 8.4 seconds left.

Duke (79). Mosch 10, Parent 6, Gingrich 11, Schweitzer 16, Rice 16, West 14, Matyasovsky 6, Brown
North Carolina (76). Allen 2, Sharp, J. Brown 15, Barksdale 12, Teasley 31, Higgins 14, Huntington, Thomas, C. Brown, Lea 2

Here to Stay

Nov. 24, 2002

Raleigh—Duke opened the 2002–03 season at the top of the national polls and played as if it had no intention of relinquishing the spot with an impressive 76–55 victory over No. 2 Tennessee in the inaugural Jimmy V Women's Basketball Classic.

The Blue Devils brushed off a slow start, claimed a five-point lead at the half, and then opened an insurmountable 53–34 margin by holding the Lady Vols without a field goal for the first seven minutes of the second period. Duke made it stand with relentless defensive pressure as Tennessee shot just 21 percent from the field in the second half and finished with 23 turnovers.

"They went after it today," said Tennessee's coach Pat Summitt. "They got every loose ball, and that says a lot about their effort and desire. They went after us and after this game, and they were very, very impressive. Duke played great team defense. They had good ball pressure, they overplayed us in the post, and we just couldn't deliver the ball. I have to credit Duke and their defense."

Junior Alana Beard stood out on the national stage with 22 points, nine rebounds, seven assists, and five steals, while freshman Lindsey Harding showed excellent composure in her first major backcourt test.

"Going into the game, there were a lot of doubters, people who didn't think we should be ranked No. 1," said junior Iciss Tillis. "That was a lot of motivation for us."

"This was a great opportunity for us to show the nation that we were ready to play, even without Monique [Currie, who was injured]," Goestenkors said. "I hope that we proved to everyone that we are here to play, and we're here to stay."

Duke (76). Tillis 17, Matyasovsky 6, Beard 22,
    Mosch 3, Krapohl 3, Harding 7, Whitley 8, Foley 3,
    Bass 7, Smith
Tennessee (55). G. Jackson 12, B. Jackson 5,
    Robinson 1, Lawson 9, Moore 5, Butts 8, Davis 2,
    Zolman 2, McDaniel 4, Ely 2, Fluker 5

Alana Beard led Duke over Tennessee in November 2002, the first matchup of No. 1 and No. 2 in Duke women's basketball history.

Hype and Circumstance

Feb. 1, 2003

Durham—Top-ranked Duke (20–0) hosted second-ranked Connecticut (19–0) in the first sellout of a women's basketball game at Cameron Indoor Stadium. The Huskies played a superb first half and opened up a 28-point lead five minutes into the second period, then withstood a late Blue Devil charge to grab a 77–65 victory.

UConn, the defending national champion with a 58-game winning streak on the line, went on runs of 10–0 to start the game and 15–0 to finish the first half, while Duke looked frazzled. Duke finally began to click with about eight minutes to play and cut the Huskies' mar-

Duke enjoyed its first home sellout for a women's basketball contest when Connecticut visited on February 1, 2003.

gin to nine points when Iciss Tillis hit a short jumper at the 4:31 mark. With the capacity crowd standing and screaming, UConn coach Geno Auriemma had to call a timeout to calm his team. "That's as loud as I have ever heard anything," he said.

Paced by Alana Beard's top competitor for national player of the year, Diana Taurasi, the Huskies handled the comeback, extended their national record winning streak, and moved to the top of the polls. The Blue Devils were left to reflect on a lesson in intensity learned from a game that helped them eventually reach the Final Four.

"In the first half, when we were down by 21 points, I never once had a doubt in my mind that we couldn't win this game," Beard said. "Then with about seven minutes to go, it was like Coach G said, she could really start to see the fire in our eyes. If we could put 40 minutes together like we did the last seven minutes of this game, I think we can be an awesome team at the end."

Duke (65). Tillis 9, Matyasovsky 3, Bass 3, Beard 26, Krapohl 3, Mosch, Harding 9, Whitley 9, Foley 3
Connecticut (77). Battle 12, Moore 9, Taurasi 17, Conlon 4, Strother 17, Crockett 13, Turner 5

Simply Amazing

Jan. 3, 2004

Hartford — Eerily reminiscent of Connecticut's victory at Cameron Indoor Stadium in 2003, this nationally televised battle from the Hartford Civic Center saw the two-time defending NCAA champions open up a 20-point advantage in the first half and dominate play for 35 minutes.

But this time Duke's late-game rally was not snuffed out. The Blue Devils outscored the Huskies 18 – 3 over the final four minutes and won the game improbably, 68 – 67, when sophomore Jessica Foley canned a three-pointer from the right wing as time expired.

"I was in position to take the last shot," Foley said. "I felt like I was open to take it, then I see No. 43 [Ann Strother] right there, coming after me. I have been in a lot of last-second shots before, but nothing can compare to this."

"It's really tough to swallow," said the Huskies' All-America guard Diana Taurasi, whose bank shot with four seconds left gave the Huskies a 67 – 65 lead. "Whenever you're up 20 and then all of a sudden you just give it away . . . it's definitely stunning."

Duke point guard Lindsey Harding answered Taurasi's last basket by dashing down the floor through traffic. When she got to the lane, she whizzed a pass out to Foley for one of the biggest threes in school history.

Duke used an all-out full-court pressing defense to make its late push. The decision ended UConn's 69-game home winning streak and 76-game regular-season winning streak.

Duke (68). Currie 17, Tillis 6, Bass 6, Harding 8, Beard 21, Foley 8, Hunter 2, Krapohl, Bales
Connecticut (67). Turner 15, Strother 12, Moore 14, Taurasi 16, Conlon 3, Valley, Battle 7, Crockett

Drive for Five

March 8, 2004

Greensboro — Top-ranked Duke reaffirmed its dominance of the ACC by whipping North Carolina 63 – 47 with one of its most authoritative defensive performances. The decision marked the Blue Devils' fifth straight conference championship and 12th consecutive victory over the Tar Heels, while improving Duke's record at Greensboro Coliseum to 16–0.

Senior Iciss Tillis earned tournament MVP honors for the second consecutive year after leading Duke in scoring for the second time in three days. She had 17 points against the Heels and previously had scored 26 on Wake Forest in the opener. Her best string was late in the first half, when the Devils built up a 30–15 lead after a technical foul by UNC against Duke star Alana Beard.

"We were playing good defense before that tech, and when they got that tech, it was so malicious it really fired us up," Tillis said. "We knew that we really had an advantage with that. When Alana came to the side, we said this was where we really needed to pull together and play our game and not get caught up in that."

UNC eventually drew to within eight points midway through the second half, but Duke responded with another run sparked by Tillis and Mistie Bass to open up a 19-point advantage. The Tar Heels finished with 19 turnovers, hit just 19 of 58 shots, and missed all of their three-pointers.

"Our team defense was the best it has been all year long, and I don't know if we have ever played defense like that for 40 minutes," coach Gail Goestenkors noted.

Her seniors—Tillis, Beard, and Vicki Krapohl—wrapped up their ACC careers by never losing a conference tournament game. They won the event in Greensboro four straight times. The finale was played before a record crowd of 11,466—a mark that was topped by a margin of 112 when UNC ended Duke's ACC streak the following year.

Duke (63). Currie 6, Tillis 17, Bass 16, Harding 7, Beard 15, Krapohl, Hunter, Bales 2, Foley, Howe, Marsh
North Carolina (47). Little 7, Atkinson 12, Sutton 13, Latta 9, Metcalf, Nelms, Bell 6, McBee, Tucker, Sell, Davis

Changing of the Guard

Dec. 2, 2004

Knoxville—Tennessee's Lady Vols have enjoyed one of the most partisan home court environments in women's college basketball since the opening of their cavern-

ous Thompson-Boling Arena in 1987. When Duke came calling for the first time, only six schools had ever beaten the Lady Vols there, for a total of just 13 losses by UT in 17 years.

Duke became the seventh visiting victor with a 59–57 decision before an audience of 11,459. The Blue Devils were still searching for a team identity in this early season matchup, after the graduation of three senior standouts and the loss of their point guard Lindsey Harding to an internal suspension. But their defense carried them to a significant outcome against the fourth-ranked Lady Vols.

Duke held Tennessee to 28 percent shooting from the floor and relied offensively on its post game, especially from Mistie Williams (14 points, 10 rebounds). Veteran Monique Currie then took over down the stretch, scoring 16 of her 20 points in the second half and six in the final 1:41 on a pair of driving jumpers, indicating that she was prepared to take on the go-to role abdicated by the graduated standouts Alana Beard and Iciss Tillis.

"We proved that we can play in any environment with anybody in the country and really battle with them. With that, we are starting to gain a lot of confidence," coach Gail Goestenkors said.

Duke (59). Williams 14, Currie 20, Bales 5, Smith 5, Foley 11, Whitley 4, Kurz, Black
Tennessee (57). Spencer 7, Ely 15, Fluker 4, Zolman 19, Moore 1, Hornbuckle 2, Jackson 8, Dosty 1, Anosike

Orange Crush

Jan. 23, 2006

Durham—The most impressive performance of Duke's 2006 Final Four season came on a Monday night at a sold-out Cameron Indoor Stadium, when ESPN2's cameras were rolling for a matchup of the top two teams in the polls. The second-ranked Blue Devils put on a defensive clinic in keeping top-ranked Tennessee almost 30 points below its season average and won in convincing fashion, 75–53.

After Tennessee grabbed an early lead, Duke shut out the Lady Vols for over four minutes to seize control and build up a seven-point margin at halftime. The Devils then enjoyed a 14–4 blitz early in the second half and a

13 – 0 run later in the period to go up by as many as 27 points in a game that most observers had thought would go down to the wire.

Point guard Lindsey Harding was Duke's catalyst with 15 points, eight steals, and four assists, but she had plenty of help as five players scored in double figures and contributed to an excellent defensive effort. Duke held Tennessee's leading scorer Shanna Zolman to an 0-for-7 shooting night and pressured its star freshman Candace Parker into seven turnovers while pressing and running for the full 40 minutes. The Lady Vols had defeated eight nationally ranked teams, and coach Pat Summitt had just won her 900th game, but it was an aggressive and confident Duke team that remained undefeated by improving to 19 – 0. "I think they had the swagger that we usually carry," said Tennessee guard Alexis Hornbuckle.

Duke followed this game with a road victory at Clemson to move to 20 – 0, matching the best start in school history. Undefeated North Carolina then visited Cameron for the Blue Devils' second nationally televised home sellout in a week. A 15 – 0 run in the first half gave Duke a 38 – 22 lead, but the Tar Heels rallied to win 74 – 70 and end the Devils' perfect record to close a historic week.

Duke (75). Williams 10, Currie 13, Bales, Harding 15, Smith 7, Black 10, A. Waner 10, Foley 8, Gay 2, E. Waner, Kurz

Tennessee (53). Spencer 11, Parker 17, Anosike 6, Zolman, Hornbuckle 10, Fluker 6, Fuller 3, Redding, Moss, Dosty

Almost Heaven

April 4, 2006

Boston — ACC rivals Duke and Maryland, the two highest-scoring teams in the country, met for the championship of the 25th NCAA Tournament, each looking for its first title in school history. The trophy seemed to be well within Duke's grasp for much of the night before Maryland rallied to force overtime and claim a 78 – 75 victory at TD Banknorth Garden.

Point guard Lindsey Harding hit 6 of 8 shots for 13 points to spark Duke to a 10-point halftime lead, and the Blue Devils were up by 13 points with just under 15 minutes to play. But the Terps gradually narrowed the gap and tied the score at the 6:15 mark. Duke took a four-point lead into the final minute of regulation before Maryland freshman Kristi Toliver hit two clutch jumpers in the final 30 seconds. Just when Duke appeared on the verge of celebrating a championship, Toliver drained a step-back three over the defensive presence of 6 – 7 center Alison Bales with 6.1 seconds left to tie the score at 70 and force overtime. "I even felt her fingertips as I was holding my follow-through," Toliver said of Bales. "So, she did a great job contesting. I just had a lot of confidence. And I knew I wanted to take the big shot so I just took it."

The stunned Blue Devils gave up just one field goal in the extra period, but the Terps hit all six of their free throws and rode the momentum of their comeback plus the confidence of having won five previous overtime games. Duke had defeated Maryland twice in the regular season while the Terps had knocked out the Blue Devils in the ACC Tournament. In the final Maryland held the lead for only 86 seconds the entire night, but that was just enough to deny Duke's championship bid. This marked just the second women's title game to be decided in overtime, along with Tennessee's win over Virginia in 1991.

Duke (75). Williams 3, Currie 22, Bales 19, Harding 16, Smith, A. Waner 5, Foley 10, Black

Maryland (78). Harper 16, Coleman 10, Langhorne 12, Toliver 16, Doron 16, Newman 4, Perry 4, Carr

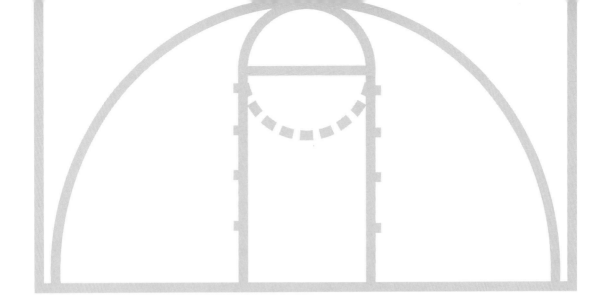

The Encyclopedia of
Duke Basketball

Abdelnaby, Alaa. Born in Cairo and raised in New Jersey, where he attended Bloomfield High School, Abdelnaby progressed from a 6–10 backup center to an NBA draft pick during his four years at Duke. He averaged eight minutes a game over his first two seasons, then developed into a part-time starter as a junior and a fixture in the lineup as a senior. Abdelnaby's totals from 1987 through 1990 included 134 games played, with 57 starts, 1,137 points for an 8.5 average, 494 rebounds, 70 blocked shots, and a career field-goal percentage of 59.9, the third-best mark in school history for players with at least 300 made field goals.

Abdelnaby enjoyed a 19-point game against Davidson in 1988, connecting on 13 of 14 at the foul line. Later in the year he had a solid postseason. In the ACC Tournament he scored 12 points in only nine minutes versus N.C. State and shot a perfect 6 for 6 in an NCAA victory over SMU. He hit 15 of 22 shots during eight postseason appearances.

Abdelnaby became more of an offensive force as a junior, usually playing behind All-America Danny Ferry. His best game was at N.C. State, when he started for an injured Ferry and hit 11 of 14 shots for 24 points. Also that year he set an ACC record when he hit 20 straight field goals over a four-game span. Duke had a 14–1 record in 1989 in games in which Abdelnaby scored at least 10 points.

Abdelnaby moved into the starting lineup full time in 1990 and helped Duke reach the national championship game with his 15.1 points and 6.6 rebounds a game. He scored in double figures in all but four games, with a career high of 32 on the road against N.C. State. One of his best games was the NCAA regional final against Connecticut. While Christian Laettner won the game with a last-second shot in overtime, Abdelnaby totaled 27 points and 14 rebounds. Abdelnaby earned third-team All-ACC honors.

Portland made Abdelnaby the 25th pick of the NBA draft, and he played in the league for parts of five years with six teams before retiring in 1995.

Abdul-Jabbar, Kareem. Before he became the all-time scoring leader in NBA history, Hall of Famer Kareem Abdul-Jabbar was the UCLA star Lew Alcindor, a three-time most valuable player of the Final Four. Alcindor faced Duke on back-to-back nights in December 1966, when he was a sophomore just getting started with the top-ranked Bruins. He led his school to a pair of overwhelming wins, with 19 points and 16 rebounds in the first game followed by 38 points and 22 rebounds in the second. He hit 24 of 30 field goals in the two games combined.

Academic All-America. Nine Duke players in the program's first 100 years were selected to the official Academic All-America team for Division I as chosen by the College Sports Information Directors of America. Four of the players were also All-Americas on the court: Shane Battier, Mike Dunleavy, Mike Gminski, Jim Spanarkel. Two, Battier and Gminski, had their jersey numbers retired. Battier was chosen the Academic All-America of the year nationwide in 2001.

The Academic All-America list includes Jay Buckley (1962, 1963), Dick DeVenzio (1971), Gary Melchionni (1972), Bob Fleischer (1974, 1975), Jim Spanarkel (1978, 1979), Mike Gminski (1978, 1979, 1980), Quin Snyder (1989), Shane Battier (2000, 2001), and Mike Dunleavy (2002). Katie Meier from the women's team earned second-team Academic All-America honors in 1988.

ACC. The Atlantic Coast Conference was born on May 8, 1953, from an alliance of seven schools that had with-

International Connections

Duke players born in other countries:

MEN

Alaa Abdelnaby	Egypt
Christian Ast	Germany
Eric Boateng	England
Luol Deng	Sudan
Cameron Hall	Canada
Dan Meagher	Canada
Greg Newton	Canada
Martynas Pocius	Lithuania

WOMEN

Jessica Foley	Australia
Juanita Hepburn	South Africa
Nazrawit Medhanie	Sweden

drawn from the Southern Conference earlier that day. Duke was one of the charter institutions, along with North Carolina, N.C. State, Wake Forest, Clemson, Maryland, and South Carolina. Among their priorities was the creation of a league in which all the members could play each other regularly, unlike in the unwieldy 17-school circuit they had left behind. Representatives from the seven schools met in Raleigh on June 14 to adopt their bylaws and choose a name. Atlantic Coast Conference, the suggestion of Duke's director of athletics, Eddie Cameron, was approved unanimously.

Conference officials met in December 1953 to admit Virginia as the eighth school, and the league stayed at that number until South Carolina withdrew in 1971. Georgia Tech was admitted in April 1978 and Florida State in July 1991 to increase membership to nine. Expansion in 2004 brought in Miami and Virginia Tech, with Boston College coming on board to make it a 12-team conference beginning with the 2005–06 academic year.

From the beginning the ACC was an all-sports conference, and its members amassed 93 NCAA team championships in the league's first 52 years. Although formed largely because of football scheduling concerns, over the years the ACC became noted nationally for its exceptional basketball success. From the inception of the NCAA's basketball tournament in 1939 through North Carolina's national title in 2005, the ACC had a better postseason record than any other conference. The Tar Heels' title was their fourth and the 10th for the conference, with Duke collecting three, N.C. State two, and Maryland one. From 1985, when the NCAA field was expanded to 64 teams, through 2005 the ACC had 21 Final Four teams in 21 years. Five times the league had two teams reach the Final Four in the same year.

A former Trinity College student and brother of two former Duke athletes, James H. Weaver was the ACC's first official full-time commissioner, from 1954 until his death in 1970. He was followed by Bob James (1971–87), the former Duke lacrosse standout Gene Corrigan (1987–97), and John Swofford, who assumed leadership in July 1997.

Duke won or shared the ACC regular-season basketball title 18 times and claimed the postseason tournament 16 times in the league's first 53 years. The Blue Devils' five consecutive tournament crowns from 1999 through 2003 were unprecedented in league annals. In regular-season play Duke finished first in the inaugural season, had a four-year run at the top in 1963–66, claimed six outright titles in the 1990s, and won or shared first place five straight times from 1997 to 2001.

Hall of Fame rivals Dean Smith (UNC) and Mike Krzyzewski dominate most of the ACC coaching records, but former Duke boss Vic Bubas set two marks during his 10-year tenure that have never been topped. He had the best winning percentage in ACC regular-season games at .768 (106–32) and the best mark in ACC Tournament play at .786 (22–6).

The ACC celebrated its 50th anniversary in 2003 with numerous activities, including the selection of a golden anniversary basketball team with 50 players. The squad included 11 former Duke stars: Shane Battier, Elton Brand, Johnny Dawkins, Danny Ferry, Mike Gminski, Art Heyman, Grant Hill, Bobby Hurley, Christian Laettner, Jeff Mullins, and Jason Williams.

Women's basketball became an official ACC sport starting with the 1978 season. Duke won its first regular-season title in 1998 and its first tournament crown in 2000. The Blue Devils claimed an unprecedented five straight ACC Tournaments from 2000 to 2004. Duke became the only league school to post consecutive undefeated regular seasons when it went 16–0 in both 2002 and 2003. North Carolina's NCAA title in 1994 marked the first by an ACC member, while Maryland added a second in 2006. Duke (1999, 2006) and Virginia (1991) also have reached the championship game. The ACC has had 12 Final Four appearances, four by the Blue Devils.

Five Duke players made the ACC's 50th anniversary women's team: Alana Beard, Katie Meier, Chris Moreland, Georgia Schweitzer, and Michele VanGorp. Beard, Moreland, and Schweitzer were among the 15 basketball players on the conference's list of the top 50 female athletes of all time.

ACC Honors. Players named to the official All-ACC team are listed within the year-by-year summaries in the Record Book section of this encyclopedia. Five Blue Devils earned the distinctive honor of making the All-ACC first team three times in their careers: Art Heyman (1961–63), Jeff Mullins (1962–64), Bob Verga (1965–67), Mike Gminski (1978–80), and Trajan Langdon (1997 – 99). In 2002 Duke became the first (and only) school to have three players named to the All-ACC first team in one year, as Jason Williams, Mike Dunleavy, and Carlos Boozer were among the top five vote-getters. In women's play, Duke's Alana Beard is the only person to earn first-team All-ACC honors four times (2001 – 04). Her classmate Iciss Tillis made the first team three times (2002 – 04).

Here is a summary of other major ACC honors bestowed upon Duke basketball players and coaches:

ACC player of the year (13 times): Art Heyman (1963), Jeff Mullins (1964), Steve Vacendak (1966), Mike Gminski (1979), Danny Ferry (1988, 1989), Christian Laettner (1992), Grant Hill (1994), Elton Brand (1999), Chris Carrawell (2000), Shane Battier (2001), J. J. Redick (2005, 2006).

ACC rookie of the year (4): Jim Spanarkel (1976), Mike Gminski (1977), Gene Banks (1978), Chris Duhon (2001).

ACC coach of the year (10): Harold Bradley (1959), Vic Bubas (1963, 1964, 1966), Bill Foster (1978), Mike Krzyzewski (1984, 1986, 1997, 1999, 2000).

ACC Tournament MVP (15): Doug Kistler (1960), Art Heyman (1963), Jeff Mullins (1964), Steve Vacendak (1966), Jim Spanarkel (1978), Johnny Dawkins (1986), Danny Ferry (1988), Christian Laettner (1992), Elton Brand (1999), Jason Williams (2000), Shane Battier (2001), Carlos Boozer (2002), Daniel Ewing (2003), J. J. Redick (2005, 2006).

ACC athlete of the year (8): Art Heyman (1963), Jeff Mullins (1964), Danny Ferry (1988, 1989), Christian Laettner (1991, 1992), Elton Brand (1999), Shane Battier (2001).

Major ACC honors received by Duke women:

ACC player of the year (7): Chris Moreland (1987), Georgia Schweitzer (2000, 2001), Alana Beard (2002, 2003, 2004), Monique Currie (2005).

ACC rookie of the year (3): Chris Moreland (1985), Katie Meier (1986), Alana Beard (2001).

ACC coach of the year (7): Debbie Leonard (1986), Gail Goestenkors (1996, 1998, 1999, 2002, 2003, 2004).

ACC Tournament MVP (4): Georgia Schweitzer (2001), Monique Currie (2002), Iciss Tillis (2003, 2004).

ACC athlete of the year (2): Alana Beard (2003, 2004).

In addition, Beard's 18 career selections as ACC player of the week top all conference players in every sport.

ACC statistics. Duke produced the ACC scoring leader ten times and the league rebounding leader five times in the first 53 years of conference history. Duke's J. J. Redick became the ACC's all-time scoring leader during his senior season of 2006.

ACC Scoring Leaders from Duke
Men

Art Heyman	1963	24.9
Bob Verga	1967	26.1
Gene Banks	1981	18.5
Vince Taylor	1982	20.3
Danny Ferry	1988	19.1
Danny Ferry	1989	22.6
Jason Williams	2001	21.6
Jason Williams	2002	21.3
J. J. Redick	2005	21.8
J. J. Redick	2006	26.8

Women

Chris Moreland	1986	23.0
Chris Moreland	1987	20.9
Alana Beard	2002	19.8
Alana Beard	2003	22.0
Alana Beard	2004	19.7

ACC Rebounding Leaders from Duke
Men

Mike Lewis	1966	11.0
Mike Lewis	1968	14.4
Mike Gminski	1978	10.0
Shelden Williams	2005	11.2
Shelden Williams	2006	10.7

Women

Barb Krause	1979	10.7
Chris Moreland	1986	11.8
Chris Moreland	1988	12.3
Tracey Christopher	1989	9.6

Career Scoring Leader at Each ACC School

School	Men's Leader	Points	Women's Leader	Points
Boston College	Troy Bell (2000–03)	2,632	Sarah Behn (1990–93)	2,523
Clemson	Elden Campbell (1987–90)	1,880	Barbara Kennedy (1979–82)	3,113
Duke	J. J. Redick (2003–06)	2,769	Alana Beard (2001–04)	2,687
Florida State	Bob Sura (1992–95)	2,130	Sue Galkantas (1981–84)	2,323
Georgia Tech	Rich Yunkus (1969–71)	2,232	Kisha Ford (1994–97)	1,955
Maryland	Juan Dixon (1999–2002)	2,269	Vicky Bullett (1986–89)	1,928
Miami	Rick Barry (1962–65)	2,298	Miria Rivera (1985–88)	2,358
North Carolina	Phil Ford (1975–78)	2,290	Tracy Reid (1995–98)	2,200
N.C. State	Rodney Monroe (1988–91)	2,551	Genia Beasley (1977–80)	2,367
Virginia	Bryant Stith (1989–92)	2,516	Dawn Staley (1989–92)	2,135
Virginia Tech	Bimbo Coles (1987–90)	2,484	Renee Dennis (1984–87)	1,791
Wake Forest	Dickie Hemric (1952–55)	2,587	Jenny Mitchell (1988–91)	1,728

ACC Tournament. The Atlantic Coast Conference wasn't the first league to conduct a postseason basketball tournament, but the ACC perfected the concept, making it the most important event of the season and the model for the many tourneys that followed. The ACC has long been recognized as one of the premier forces in college basketball, and the tournament has been its signature.

Former N.C. State coach Everett Case once said that the tournament was a banquet and every game a feast. If so, his Wolfpack was well fed in the early years, as State's Reynolds Coliseum hosted the first 13 ACC tourneys. State had a 20–8 tournament record with five titles during that run, and only once did a team from outside North Carolina win it. The Big Four programs had 23 of the possible 26 spots in the championship game during those first 13 years. It is little wonder that coaches from outside the state often lobbied to move the event to other geographic points within the league's footprint.

Part of the initial appeal, and attending pressure, was that the winner received an automatic bid to the NCAA Tournament during an era when only one team from a conference could go. Duke, in coach Vic Bubas's first year of 1960, was an upstart that knocked out the two best teams in the league to win the event for the first time. In turn, one of Duke's best teams, in 1965, was unable to compete in the NCAA because it was beaten by

N.C. State in Reynolds in the ACC final. In 1973 and 1974 Maryland was one of the top 10 teams in the country but couldn't go to the NCAA because it lost to State in a pair of epic ACC finals. The following year the NCAA permitted more than one school from a conference to receive a bid. The year after that, 1976, the ACC moved its tourney out of North Carolina for the first time, and Virginia became just the third champion from outside the Big Four.

Volumes have been written on the competitive and dramatic nature of the ACC Tournament, and the interest surrounding it. Despite various changes in the league membership and the national landscape, the tournament has always been viewed as one worth winning and cherishing. Every member of the league has always participated, with the exception of 1961 and 1991 when NCAA-ineligible teams were omitted. Even with expansion to 12 teams, there was little thought of leaving anyone out of the tournament.

"This is the essence of the ACC Tournament," former Duke playmaker Quin Snyder wrote six years after he last played in the event. "Three games in 48 hours, an endurance contest pumped with uncertainty and hopeful expectations. A prize that the best team doesn't always win. The history of these games makes room for the average team that believes in itself to walk away a

Captain Trajan Langdon clipped the nets after Duke won the 1999 ACC tourney.

champion. This is an event that embraces an underdog but also respects a regular-season favorite with the strength to prove its mettle one last time."

There hasn't been a public sale of tickets since 1966, with every event sold out in advance since then. The best-attended tourney was in 2001 at the Georgia Dome in Atlanta, when 182,525 fans watched the action, an NCAA record and an average of over 36,000 per session.

Duke has been one of the most successful teams in tournament history. Through 2006 it had appeared in 27 of the 53 championship games and won 16, the most in league history. The Blue Devils' overall tourney winning percentage at 80 – 37 was also the best.

Duke won four ACC tourneys under Vic Bubas, two under Bill Foster, and 10 under Mike Krzyzewski. Duke's five straight championships from 1999 through 2003 have not been approached during any other era,

nor has its string of nine consecutive trips to the championship game, 1998 – 2006. Duke has entered the event as the No. 1 seed 16 times and won eight of those. It has won from as low as the sixth-seeded spot in the bracket (1980).

The ACC Tournament has been held in seven arenas: Greensboro Coliseum (21 times), Reynolds Coliseum in Raleigh (13), Charlotte Coliseum (11), the Omni in Atlanta (3), Capital Centre in Landover (3), Georgia Dome in Atlanta (1), and the MCI Center in Washington (1).

The ACC women's tourney began in 1978 and has been conducted in eight locales, with the longest runs in Fayetteville, N.C. (9 times), and Greensboro (7). Duke won only two games in the first 17 years of the tournament's existence. But over the event's next 11 editions (1995 – 2005) the Blue Devils advanced to the championship game eight times and won five titles. The five crowns were secured in successive years, all at the Greensboro Coliseum.

Airball. This term, frequently used by basketball fans to describe an errant field-goal attempt that does not touch the rim or the backboard, was first used as a notorious taunt at Duke's Cameron Indoor Stadium on February 24, 1979. In the home finale against North Carolina, Duke students began chanting "Airball" after Tar Heel Rich Yonakor missed everything on a rare UNC shot in the first half. Employing a delay game offensively, the Heels came up empty the entire half. Duke led 7 – 0 after 20 minutes and went on to win 47 – 40.

Alarie, Mark. Not that a four-year roommate would be the most objective source, but the TV analyst and attorney Jay Bilas can make the case that Mark Steven Alarie's jersey should hang with the others that have been retired at Cameron Indoor Stadium. Alarie, a 6 – 8 forward from Scottsdale, Ariz., was one of the prime-time players who piloted Duke's charge back to national glory in the mid-1980s. From the humble origins of an 11 – 17 freshman year in 1983, the nucleus of Alarie, Bilas, Dawkins, and Henderson drove the Blue Devils to three subsequent NCAA bids, an ACC title, and a Final Four season of 37 – 3 in their senior year of 1986.

While Dawkins led all four of those teams in scoring, Alarie was right there every year administering

Mark Alarie started every game for four years and scored over 2,000 points.

the setup and follow-up punches to his teammate's numerous knockdown blows. Dawkins and Alarie started every single Duke game for four years, the first pair of teammates to do so. Dawkins was the team's primary offensive option, but Alarie still scored over 2,000 points and graduated as the No. 3 point man in school history, behind only Dawkins and Mike Gminski. He also grabbed over 800 rebounds and shot 55 percent from the field as one of the league's best perimeter shooters. That's enough for Bilas.

"He was quiet on the court but had an explosive competitive fire," Bilas wrote in 2004. "His jersey should have been retired along with Dawkins' back in 1986, and it should be done today. He was that good."

In his 133 games, Alarie scored 2,136 points for a 16.1 average and had 833 rebounds for a 6.3 mark. He shot just under 50 percent his freshman year but was well over that mark in each of his subsequent seasons, bran-

dishing a smooth, long-range jumper before the three-point field goal was established in college hoops. He also hit 79.7 percent of his free throws. While finishing second on the team in scoring to Dawkins every year, Alarie led the club in rebounding for three years and topped the charts in blocked shots for all four.

Alarie's best season statistically was his sophomore year, when he was able to play away from the basket more than he had done as a rookie post man. He averaged 17.5 points and 7.2 boards and earned first-team All-ACC honors. He was on the ACC second team as a junior, then back on the first team in 1986, when he also earned some All-America mention. He shared the team MVP award with Dawkins in 1984.

Reliability was one of his strengths. Alarie was always good for double-figures scoring and capable of 20 points against anyone. He was under 10 points just three times in his last two years, and in one of those games he played just the opening minute before leaving because of injury. He registered his career highs of 29 points and 16 rebounds against Clemson in 1984 and matched the scoring high with another 29-point showing against the Tigers in 1986.

Alarie especially enjoyed Duke's rivalries with Georgia Tech and UNC. He had 26, 24, and 17 points in three battles with the Yellow Jackets during his senior year, and contributed the go-ahead shot when Duke topped Tech for the ACC title. Alarie led the team in scoring and played superb post defense when the Devils upset No. 1 UNC at the ACC tourney in 1984 and scored the first points in the Smith Center when it opened in 1986. His most memorable game aside from the Final Four was his last at home against the Tar Heels, which Duke won to sew up its first ACC regular-season crown under Krzyzewski.

"I like the fact that the very last time we competed on that floor, we whipped a very good team," Alarie recalled. "When I look back, that's an important memory for me. The last time we play on that court, which is such a fantastic place to compete at and to witness a game, I'm just thrilled at that outcome."

Alarie made all the postseason tournament teams during Duke's run in 1986: ACC tourney, NCAA regionals, Final Four. He also won the Dr. Deryl Hart award as the top scholar-athlete on the club. Then it was off to the NBA. A first-round draft pick, he played his rookie season in Denver and four in Washington before three knee surgeries led to his retirement. His best year was 1990, when he appeared in every game and averaged 10.5 points.

After the NBA, Alarie earned his MBA and became an investment banker. He took a sabbatical from that profession in 1999 – 2000 for a season as an assistant coach at the U.S. Naval Academy. Then it was back to pursuing his lifelong dream of working as a financier and entrepreneur. The Duke Sports Hall of Fame inducted Alarie in 1999, and he was included in the charter class of the Duke Basketball Hall of Honor.

Albright, Doug. A 6 – 4 native of Greensboro, William Douglas Albright lettered as a reserve for three varsity seasons, 1959 – 61. He played in 30 games, with 30 points and 31 rebounds. The team enjoyed a 52 – 29 record dur-

ing his career. A Phi Beta Kappa student, he was known for his hustle and desire on the court.

Albright went to law school at American University and then launched a distinguished legal career, first as an attorney and then as a judge. He became assistant solicitor in Guilford County (N.C.) Superior Court in 1966, district attorney in 1969, resident Superior Court judge for the 18th Judicial District in 1975, and senior resident Superior Court judge in 1984. He also served as vice-president of the North Carolina Bar Association and president of the N.C. Conference of Superior Court Judges.

Albright sent four sons on to college athletic careers, two at Duke: Erik Albright was a three-year starter at second base for the baseball team, 1985 – 87, while Stuart Albright was a starting center and long snapper for the football team, 1988 – 91. Their older brother Jon played basketball at Memphis State, and their younger brother Ethan played football at North Carolina.

All-America. Duke's first basketball All-America selection was Bill Werber in 1930. All official first-, second-, and third-team All-America selections from Duke are listed within the year-by-year summaries in the Record Book section of this encyclopedia.

Allen, Bucky. A product of Durham High School and Staunton (Va.) Military Academy, Burwell A. "Bucky" Allen was a solid 6 – 2 guard for three varsity campaigns. After averaging 14.5 points for the freshman team in 1955, he lettered for the 1956 through 1958 seasons and played in 58 varsity games with 620 points and 153 rebounds.

Allen became a starter as a junior in 1957 and averaged a career-best 13.3 points. His high game that year was a 34-point outing to help the Blue Devils defeat N.C. State. He hit 20 of 23 from the free-throw stripe in that contest. The 20 made free throws set a school record that has not been broken, while the 23 attempts are the second-most by one player. Earlier that season he scored 20 points, including the game-winning layup, when the Blue Devils rallied from a 15-point deficit to edge seventh-ranked Kentucky.

Allen averaged 12.4 points as a senior, had three 20-point games including a 26-point outing against Clemson, and earned second-team All-ACC honors after helping the Blue Devils to the league's regular-season championship.

Allen, Clyde. J. Clyde Allen was the 6–2 starting center and No. 2 scorer for Duke's Southern Conference championship team in 1942, the last Blue Devil basketball team coached by Eddie Cameron. Allen, from Tarentum, Pa., scored 169 points for the team, which posted a 15–1 regular-season mark in the conference and went 22–2 overall. Allen scored a team-best 10 points in the Southern Conference championship game win over N.C. State.

Allen also lettered for the 1940 Duke team, which won the Southern Conference regular season with a 13–2 record but lost to North Carolina in the tournament final. He had five points in that game and was named to the all-tournament second team. Though not a starter, he was the No. 2 scorer on the 1940 team with 182 points, just two behind Bill Mock.

Allen totaled 351 points in two seasons as a Duke letterman, with the team posting a 41–9 record. He missed the entire 1941 campaign with a wrist injury.

Allen, Dayton. A two-year letterman, Dayton Allen, a native of McKeesport, Pa., played in 58 games during the 1950 and 1951 seasons, totaling 376 points. At 6–7, he was the tallest player on the team and had an effective hook shot. He was a second-team All-Southern Conference Tournament selection when he helped the Blue Devils reach the tourney final on their home floor in 1950. He also helped the 1951 team reach the league championship game. Both times the Devils fell to N.C. State. When Duke rallied from a 32-point deficit to defeat Tulane in the Dixie Classic, it was Allen's basket in the final minute that provided the winning points.

Allen, Phil. A frontcourt reserve during Vic Bubas's glory years, Philip Henry Allen Jr. lettered from 1964 through 1966 and scored 45 points with 19 rebounds in 27 career varsity games. A 6–4 product of Syracuse, Allen had a 26-point game for the 1963 freshman team versus N.C. State and hit 6 of 7 shots in five games during his first year on the varsity. He was 11 of 13 from the foul line for his career. Duke won two ACC titles and played in two Final Fours during his varsity career.

Alleva, Joe. Former Lehigh University football captain Joseph Alleva has presided over some of the greatest years in Duke basketball history as the university's director of athletics. A 1974 Lehigh grad, he arrived at Duke in 1976, began working in athletics in 1980, and progressed from business manager to assistant AD to associate AD under former director Tom Butters. Alleva was named the university's sixth director of athletics on February 25, 1998. The following year the basketball team began a run of five straight ACC championships while the university's athletics department finished seventh nationally in the Sears Directors Cup standings, which measured success in all sports. Three Duke teams won national championships in Alleva's first four years at the helm — men's basketball in 2001 and women's golf in 1999 and 2002. Duke enjoyed a school-record seven ACC titles in 2001.

Alleva's primary legacy as department head has been improving facilities: he oversaw the completion of the Schwartz-Butters Center that houses the basketball program, the construction of two tennis stadiums and a $22 million headquarters for the football program, and the complete renovation of the soccer-lacrosse facility. Most of that was made possible by the raising of $152 million during the university-wide Campaign for Duke, an eight-year initiative that concluded in 2003.

Duke Athletics Directors

James DeHart	1926–30
Wallace Wade	1931–42, 1946*
Eddie Cameron	1942–72*
Carl James	1972–76
Tom Butters	1977–98
Joe Alleva	1998–

*Cameron was named acting athletics director in 1942 when Wade left for military service. When Wade returned, he resumed the AD duties briefly before Cameron was named to the post full time.

Alpert, Roy. In the one varsity season when he lettered, 1932, center Roy Alpert, from Jamaica, N.Y., was the second-leading scorer for the Blue Devils with 159 points. He scored 14 points against VMI and had his season best of 15 against Florida in the Southern Conference Tournament, a game that Duke won, 33–22.

Nine retired jerseys gathered at the 1995 Legends Weekend: Groat, Heyman, Mullins, Gminski, Dawkins, Ferry, Laettner, Hurley, Hill.

Alumni Games. Annual alumni or old-timers' games became a Duke basketball staple during the mid-1980s and throughout the 1990s, held in conjunction with the varsity team's Blue-White scrimmage each October. Their success and popularity were due in large part to the work of then assistant coach Bob Bender, whose efforts welcomed players from throughout Duke history into the Krzyzewski era. There have been several unique alumni games over the years:

— One of the most spectacular events was the program's Legends Weekend in September 1995. A fundraiser for student recreation facilities, Cameron improvements, and the Schwartz-Butters Center, the event featured a Blue-White game pitting NBA Devils against other recent grads. Just about all of Duke's pros participated: their clubs might not have approved, but since a lockout was in effect at the time, no communication between franchises and players was permitted. Christian

Laettner said there was no doubt he would participate: "If you can't have fun and play in front of your old fans, why play basketball?"

The Blue team defeated the White team 110–89. Brian Davis had 24 points and Robert Brickey 20 to lead the Blues, while Phil Henderson's 25 topped the Whites. The event had several interesting sidelights, including an appearance by every player whose jersey number had been retired at that point and every head coach since 1960, a Saturday morning youth clinic with Grant Hill, and a halftime recreation of Laettner's shot against Kentucky (which he made, again). Gene Banks exhorted the crowd into a prolonged ovation for Krzyzewski, who was recovering from his health woes, and Mike Gminski pulled out a victory cigar on the bench near the end of the exhibition.

"I have a real strong conviction that we were the recipients of much more than we could ever give back to

Duke," said Bender, who was then head coach at Washington. "We were scholarship athletes, which in itself is somewhat of a fantasy world. We had the chance to play at the highest level in front of the greatest fans in the world, and we need to keep giving back—whether it's our time or our own money."

—During the summer of 2001 and again in the summer of 2002, the school staged a Duke All-Star Charity Game at Cameron Indoor Stadium. Forty-one former players returned in 2001 for the August gala, and 8,000 fans attended the contest, which featured most of Duke's active pro players at the time. The White team, paced by 24 points from Corey Maggette, 21 from Chris Collins, and 20 from Elton Brand, defeated the Blue team 145–124. Thomas Hill scored 26 points and Roshown McLeod 24 to lead the Blues. The event also featured a golf tournament and a memorabilia auction. All told, the festivities generated $120,000 in gifts to the Duke-Durham Neighborhood Partnership and the Emily Krzyzewski Family Life Center.

The 2002 game was even more offense-oriented, featuring Duke NBA players and other invited pros. The White team beat the Blues 165–157. Former Maryland player Juan Dixon had 40 points and former Wake Forest star Rodney Rogers had 31, joining with Shane Battier (29) and Mike Dunleavy (25) on the winning team. Corey Maggette had 38 to lead the Blues. The events included a celebrity roast of Coach K as well as a leadership conference in conjunction with the Fuqua School of Business. A total of $180,000 was raised for the same two community efforts.

—During the late 1960s and early 1970s, alumni of Duke and North Carolina met in an annual spring game to benefit facilities and scholarships at Durham Academy. Vic Bubas and Bones McKinney coached the teams for the inaugural event in 1965, then former Duke player Doug Kistler and former UNC player Lee Shaffer handled the coaching for the next six years.

The game usually featured the departing seniors from each school plus other grads from the pro ranks. In 1970 NBA players Jack Marin and Billy Cunningham were pitted against each other, as were Carolina Cougars (ABA) teammates Bob Verga and Larry Miller in 1971. Verga scored 39 points and Brad Evans added 27 to lead a Duke win that year, while Miller countered with 32 points and Larry Brown with 24 for the Heels.

—One of the earliest alumni efforts on record took place in 1933, when the members of Duke's 1930 team returned to campus for an exhibition against the 1933 varsity. The alumni team featured the future Hall of Famers Bill Werber, Boley Farley, and Harry Councilor; they were nipped by the younger generation, 35–33.

Alumni Memorial Gym. See Home courts.

Amaker, Tommy. Coach Mike Krzyzewski brought in one of his best freshman classes for the 1983 season, a class that would produce four 1,000-point scorers and form the backbone of the team that reached the Final Four in 1986. But Duke compiled a record of 11–17 with just three ACC victories during the heralded group's first season. The team didn't start to win until 1984, when it was joined by one of the great point guards in Duke history, Harold Tommy Amaker.

Amaker, a 6–0 native of Falls Church, Va., started all 138 games during his four years, 1984–87, setting a Duke record for career starts that was eclipsed only by Bobby Hurley's 139 starts in 1990–93. Johnny Dawkins and Mark Alarie were the only other players to start every Duke game over a four-year period. Amaker averaged almost 34 minutes of playing time over his 138 games; Duke won 108 of them, and it was not coincidental. His abilities as a playmaker blended well with the offensive talents around him, and he became the key figure in Krzyzewski's man-to-man defense with his tenacious application of ball pressure on the perimeter.

Amaker had 1,168 points, 708 assists, and 308 rebounds in his four years, each of which ended with a trip to the NCAA Tournament. He also led Duke in steals every year, finishing with 195. His seven steals in the NCAA championship game against Louisville in 1986 set a Final Four record and helped him earn All–Final Four honors despite Duke's defeat. Amaker's assists-to-turnovers ratio was just over 2:1 for his career. He led Duke in assists in each of his first three seasons, with a high of 241 in 1986. In a game against Miami that year he tied the school record for most assists in one game, 14, and at the same time passed teammate Johnny Dawkins as the all-time assists leader in school history. He held the career assists record until Hurley passed him in 1992.

Amaker's best scoring season was his senior year of 1987, when he captained a team that had been heavily

Tommy Amaker was the first recipient of the national defensive player of the year award.

depleted by graduation. He averaged 12.3 points while guiding the Blue Devils to a 24–9 record and a spot in the Sweet 16 of the NCAA Tournament. His career scoring high was in his final game, when he had 23 points against Indiana in the NCAA Tournament. Other highlights included a last-second shot to force overtime at Clemson in a game that Duke eventually won 105–103, and a superb defensive job on Wake Forest star Tyrone Bogues, holding him scoreless to pace a 20-point Blue Devil win. He was a second-team All-ACC pick, third-team All-America by the NABC, and the first recipient of the Henry Iba Corinthian Award as national defensive player of the year.

Amaker also enjoyed several USA Basketball experiences during his undergraduate career, including a role as a part-time starter for the American team that won the World Championship in 1986.

Amaker was drafted by Seattle of the NBA but was released in training camp. He returned to Duke and worked for the university administration as an intern and then enrolled at the Fuqua School of Business. While in business school in 1989 he also served as a graduate assistant coach for the Blue Devils. The next season, after Bob Bender left the staff to become head coach at Illinois State, Amaker took over as a full-time assistant, and he remained on Krzyzewski's staff through 1997, the last two years as associate head coach.

Amaker departed Duke after the 1997 season to assume his first head coaching position, at Seton Hall University. In four seasons, 1998 through 2001, Amaker compiled a 68–55 record with one NCAA Tournament bid and three trips to the NIT. His 2000 team was his best, with a 22–10 record and a trip to the Sweet 16 of the NCAA. During that year Seton Hall returned to the national polls for the first time since 1993.

Amaker then accepted a rebuilding job as head coach

at Michigan in March 2001. His first two Wolverine teams had records of 11 – 18 and 17 – 13. His third went 23 – 11 and won the NIT in 2004. His 2005 team finished fourth in the Preseason NIT but was eventually crippled by injuries, enduring a 10-game losing streak and finishing 13 – 18. His 2006 team bounced back with a 22 – 11 record and again played in the NIT final.

Amaker was inducted into the Duke Sports Hall of Fame in 2001 and was a charter inductee in the Duke Basketball Hall of Honor.

Anderson, Todd. One of Mike Krzyzewski's early recruits, Todd Harvey Anderson competed as a reserve forward and center for the majority of his four-year career, 1982 – 85. He participated in 81 games and scored 135 points with 117 rebounds. A 6 – 9 native of Golden Valley, Minn., he saw his most extensive action during the rebuilding seasons of 1981 and 1982. He earned seven starts as a rookie in 1981, with his most productive outing coming against Clemson, when he had 11 points and nine rebounds in an overtime victory. His playing time decreased during his junior and senior years as Jay Bilas, Mark Alarie, and Dan Meagher logged most of the inside minutes, but Anderson was always ready to provide depth and support. He won the Ted Mann Jr. award as the reserve contributing most to team morale in both his freshman and his senior seasons.

Angier B. Duke Gymnasium. See Home courts.

Arizona. Duke won its third NCAA championship in 2001 with an 82 – 72 victory over Arizona. That was the seventh all-time meeting between the two programs and the sixth featuring the coaching heavyweights and future Hall of Famers Mike Krzyzewski and Lute Olson. Duke won four of the seven.

The two schools met in December 1987 in the championship game of Arizona's Fiesta Bowl, with the Wildcats, ranked No. 1, edging the Blue Devils, ranked No. 9. Arizona visited Duke late in the 1990 season and absorbed a two-point loss; Duke then went back to Tucson in 1991 and came up short in an epic, two-overtime battle.

Other meetings between the two took place at neutral courts, including a 77 – 75 win by Arizona at the Meadowlands in 1989, as two national player of the year candidates, Danny Ferry (29 points, 12 rebounds) and Sean Elliott (24, 10), dueled. Former president Richard Nixon was at that game and consoled freshman Christian Laettner in the locker room after he missed some key free throws, telling him that his shooting would eventually win some games for the Blue Devils.

Arizona was top-ranked and the defending NCAA champion when Duke knocked it off in November 1997 in the final of the Maui Invitational, as senior Steve Wojciechowski won most valuable player honors while freshman William Avery sparkled with 21 points. Then came the 2001 NCAA final in Minneapolis, when Mike Dunleavy's strong second-half shooting and MVP Shane Battier's spectacular finish helped Duke to pull out a tightly contested affair.

Ark. See Home courts.

Armfield, Emsley. Trinity's team captain for 1909, and the starting center for the 1908 and 1909 campaigns, was Emsley Armfield of Monroe, N.C. During the early days of intercollegiate basketball, captains such as Armfield and team managers handled much more than on-the-court leadership. They were involved in tryouts, much of the training and organization of practice, and many of the logistics of operating the team.

Armstrong, Tate. An overtime victory over Virginia in January 1977 was the setting for one of the most courageous individual performances in Duke basketball history. In the first few minutes of play, senior guard Michel Taylor "Tate" Armstrong, a 6 – 3 native of Houston and the ACC scoring leader, fell hard on his right wrist but refused to come out of the game. Armstrong had two points at the time, but before the night was over he had played the entire 45 minutes and scored 33 to help the Blue Devils to an 82 – 74 win. The breakthrough ended a 27-game streak of ACC road losses that dated back five years.

Unfortunately for Armstrong, that was his last game in a Duke uniform. The following day it was determined that he had scored his last 31 points with a broken wrist. After leading the Blue Devils to an 11 – 3 start, his season was over. Duke went just 3 – 10 the rest of the year without him.

The son of an Air Force pilot who survived dozens of

Tate Armstrong averaged 24 points a game in 1976 and made the U.S. Olympic team.

Vietnam missions, Armstrong initially caught Duke's eye when alumnus Jack Marin recommended him after seeing him work out with an NBA teammate in Houston. Armstrong fell for the school on a recruiting trip and went on to a four-year career, 1974–77, in which he scored 1,304 points in 83 games and garnered a reputation as one of the greatest shooters in school history. He averaged 24.2 points a game as a junior and 22.7 as a senior before his wrist injury, shooting well over 50 percent from the field in both years. During one week early in his senior year, he had last-second shots to win games against Washington and Richmond, sandwiched around a 29-point effort in a narrow road win at Tennessee.

Armstrong had one of the most prolific offensive seasons in Duke history in his junior year of 1976. His 24.2 average was the highest at Duke since Bob Verga set the school record of 26.1 in 1967. It ranked second in the ACC that year to Kenny Carr's 26.6 for N.C. State. In ACC games only, Armstrong led the conference with a 28.5 average, and his mark in ACC road games was a

stunning 31.5. That season featured his best career scoring game of 42 points, versus Clemson, as well as some amazing shooting nights. Against Maryland in College Park he made 11 consecutive field goals on the way to 37 points. There was no three-point shot in effect at that time, but all 11 were from beyond 19 feet. Later, against the Terps at the ACC Tournament, Armstrong hit his first eight shots in a 33-point performance. "He's the best one-on-one player I've seen in this conference since David Thompson," said Maryland coach Lefty Driesell, a Duke alumnus. "I just held my breath every time he shot." And Armstrong was not just a shooter, as he tied the Cameron Indoor Stadium assists record with 12 in a game against Tennessee and was named the team's best defensive player for the second straight season.

The 1976 campaign marked the only season in which Armstrong saw action in every Duke game. He earned first-team All-ACC honors and became only the second player in conference history to make the ACC All-Tournament team after his school was eliminated in the first round. The summer of 1976 was noteworthy as well, as Armstrong was selected to the U.S. Olympic team that won a gold medal in Montreal. He was one of two underclassmen chosen at the guard position for the squad, which was coached by Dean Smith and featured seven ACC players. Armstrong saw limited playing time at the Summer Games but was the highest-scoring U.S. Olympian per minute played, with 16 points in 15 minutes.

Armstrong came off the bench for most of his freshman year, playing in 22 games, but provided a glimpse of his potential when he started the last five games and averaged 15.6 points. As a sophomore he played in 20 games but was bothered by a deep thigh bruise that limited his effectiveness late in the season.

After graduation Armstrong was a first-round NBA draft pick for the Chicago Bulls and played 92 games in a two-year career, averaging 10.6 minutes and 3.8 points. He was one of the charter inductees in the Duke Basketball Hall of Honor in 2001.

Ashley, Larry. Lettering for one varsity season in 1950, Larry L. Ashley, 5–9, of Greenville, S.C., totaled 51 points in 19 games during the Blue Devils' final campaign under coach Gerry Gerard. He was known for his speed and accurate set shot for the 1949 freshman team.

Associated Press Poll. The Associated Press began conducting a weekly ranking of the top basketball teams in the nation during the 1949 season. Duke's first appearance was in the 1951–52 season, when the Blue Devils were ranked No. 12 in both the preseason and final polls although they were unranked for most of the regular season. The 1966 team was the first to be ranked No. 1. Duke received a preseason No. 1 ranking in 1979, 1989, 1992, 1999, 2002, and 2006. The Blue Devils have been ranked No. 1 in the final poll seven times, in 1986, 1992, 2006, and for a record four straight years in 1999–2002. Duke was ranked No. 1 in every poll during the 1992 season. UCLA holds the record for appearing in the most consecutive AP polls, at 221. Duke had the second-longest such streak when it was ranked in its 173rd consecutive poll during the seventh week of the 2006 season. Duke's year-by-year final ranking is included in the Record Book section of this encyclopedia.

The AP women's basketball poll dates back to the 1977 season. Duke's first appearance was on January 12, 1986, when the Blue Devils were ranked No. 20. Duke first showed up in the AP preseason poll at No. 19 to begin the 1988 campaign. The 1995 season marked the school's first listing in the final poll, at No. 20, and the 1996 season was Duke's first in which the women's team was ranked every week. The Blue Devil women were ranked No. 1 for the first time in the 2003 preseason poll and were either first or second that entire year. They finished as the No. 1 team for the first time in 2004.

It should be noted that the final AP poll in men's and women's basketball is released before the NCAA Tournament. See also Number one.

Ast, Christian. Ast, a 6–8 German-born forward, came off the bench for Duke's 1991 and 1992 national championship teams, playing a total of 31 games with 44 points and 24 rebounds. He then transferred from Duke after his sophomore year and enrolled at American University, where he was a two-year fixture in the lineup. A native of Heidelberg, where his father worked as a university math professor, Ast came to the United States before his junior year of high school as part of the Fulbright Cultural Exchange program. He was recruited by Duke out of high school in Beltsville, Md., where he led his team to consecutive state championship games. Ast was somewhat of a crowd favorite during his Duke days, beginning with the final 90 seconds of a game against East Carolina early his freshman year. He came off the bench firing, hitting three late baskets for seven points.

Auerbach, Red. His official biography in the NBA Register lists him as an assistant coach at Duke in 1949–50. But Arnold Jacob "Red" Auerbach wasn't in Durham long enough to coach in a game for the Blue Devils. Hired by Eddie Cameron in the summer of 1949, Auerbach was viewed as a potential successor to head coach Gerry Gerard, who had been diagnosed with cancer. Thinking that Gerard was recovering, Auerbach left for a pro job before the 1949–50 season got under way. But he made at least one invaluable contribution to Duke basketball history during his brief tenure: he spent many a lunch hour working one on one at the Indoor Stadium with Dick Groat leading up to his sophomore season, helping to develop one of the top Blue Devil players ever.

Auerbach's legacy after leaving Duke for the NBA is well known. Voted the greatest coach in NBA history in 1980, he amassed 938 wins in 20 years, won nine NBA titles, and was inducted into the Hall of Fame in 1968. Most of his career was spent with the Boston Celtics. Boston won the NBA crown during his last eight years as its head coach, from 1959 to 1966. Auerbach remained with the club in various executive capacities, from president and general manager to vice-chairman of the board.

Ausbon, Doug. Captain of the 1948 team, Douglas H. Ausbon, a 6–1 forward from Durham, played in 84 games during his four varsity seasons, 1943 and 1946–48. He totaled 311 points, with his best average of 6.0 points a game coming his senior year. In 1946 he tied his teammate Ed Koffenberger for the scoring lead with 11 points in the Southern Conference Tournament championship game victory over Wake Forest. Duke was the tournament runner-up in Ausbon's senior year when it lost to N.C. State in the final, played at Duke Indoor Stadium. The Blue Devils enjoyed an overall record of 57–26 and a conference mark of 30–12 during Ausbon's last three years.

Avery, William. The starting point guard for Duke's Final Four team in 1999, William Avery played for two years before leaving school for the NBA. Avery appeared in 74 games, scored 877 points for an 11.9 average, and had 283 assists and 206 rebounds.

A 6–2 guard from Augusta, Ga., Avery came off the bench as a freshman in 1998 and made several game-altering contributions. Most notable were his 21 points to lead a victory over No. 1 Arizona in the Maui Invitational final, and his game-winning basket against Clemson in the ACC Tournament. He scored in double figures 15 times.

Avery then moved into the starting lineup for every game of the 1999 campaign and was a major force, averaging 14.9 points and 5.0 assists. He played more minutes than anyone else and was second on the team in steals (57) as well as three-point shots (76). Avery had a 30-point game against Cincinnati in the Great Alaska Shootout final; delivered 21 points and five assists in a home win over UNC; led all scorers with 24 points in a season-ending rout at UNC; sparkled in the ACC Tourna-

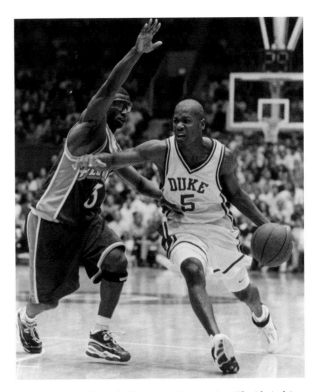

William Avery hit eight three-pointers against Florida in his sophomore year.

ment with a 29-point day in the championship game; and broke the school record for three-pointers when he hit eight against Florida, on the way to 26 points. All season long he excelled at running the offense and playing superb defense for a team that finished with a record of 37–2.

Against the advice of coach Mike Krzyzewski, Avery opted to enter the NBA draft and was the 14th pick of the first round for Minnesota. He signed a three-year guaranteed contract but played sparingly at the end of the Timberwolves' bench, averaging 2.7 points a game. After his NBA contract expired he played professionally overseas and later admitted that his career would have been better served had he remained longer in college.

Bailey, Bill. In one season at Duke, guard William F. Bailey saw action in all 26 games and scored 59 points for the 1944 Southern Conference champions. Playing mostly military teams, the Blue Devils posted a regular-season record of 10–13 but swept through the Southern Conference Tournament to claim the title. Bailey, a native of Knoxville who attended Tennessee before the war, scored three points in the championship game against North Carolina.

Baldwin, James. Hired as Trinity's director of physical training, James J. Baldwin coached the varsity basketball, football, and baseball teams. An Ivy League product and former coach at Rhode Island State and Maine, Baldwin in 1921 guided the baseball team to a record of 10 – 9 – 1 and the football team to a record of 6 – 1 – 2, and then the 1922 basketball squad to a record of 6 – 12 in his only season at the helm. He later coached the Lehigh football team and the Wake Forest basketball team for two years, 1927 – 28.

Bales, Alison. The 2005 Duke women's basketball team blocked more shots than any other team in NCAA history. Center Alison Marie Bales established an ACC record with 134 of the team's 267 blocks and finished her junior year of 2006 as the top shot blocker in school history — not to mention her role as a vital contributor to a Final Four season.

A 6 – 7 product of Dayton, Ohio, Bales ranks as the tallest women's player ever at Duke. She credits her father Charles, a 6 – 4 former football player from TCU, with helping her develop a knack for blocking shots. When they played in the driveway during her middle school and high school years, he constantly rejected her shots, which instilled in her a desire to block others.

Battling a knee injury, Bales played sparingly as a freshman in 2004 and posted 29 blocks. She enjoyed the breakout campaign in 2005, and then had 120 blocks in 2006 to increase her career total to 283 in 95 games entering her senior season. She became Duke's all-time shot blocker on January 16, 2006, in a game against Holy Cross, and in March she became the all-time leading shot blocker in the history of the NCAA Tournament, with 51. That included her career high of eight blocks in the Bridgeport Region championship game against Connecticut. Going into her final season, she was well within reach of challenging the ACC career blocked shots record of 330.

Bales averaged about seven points a game over her first three seasons but emerged as a more viable offensive weapon at the end of her junior year. She had a ca-

Gene Banks and Albert King were the nation's top two prep prospects in 1977 before heading to Duke and Maryland.

reer high of 22 points against Southern Cal in the NCAA second round and added 25 points with 21 rebounds combined against Michigan State and UConn to earn MVP honors at the Bridgeport Region. In the national championship game against Maryland in 2006, Bales had 19 points and 12 rebounds while playing all but four minutes of a game that went into overtime.

Balitsaris, George. Playing in 21 games and scoring 31 points, guard George P. Balitsaris had one basketball season at Duke during the Second World War and aided the Blue Devils' Southern Conference championship efforts in 1944. Duke had a 13 – 13 record versus opponents who were primarily military teams and finished the year strong with seven wins in the last eight games, including three straight in the league tourney. Balitsaris, a native of Pittsburgh who attended Tennessee before Duke, was scoreless in the championship contest versus UNC. He also lettered at halfback for the 1943 Duke football team.

Banks, Gene. It would be difficult to overstate the impact that Eugene Lavon "Tinkerbell" Banks had on the Duke basketball program. When he made the decision to become a Blue Devil during the winter of 1977, coach Bill Foster had the final piece of his rebuilding project. Banks was the sort of recruit Duke normally did not get: wonderfully skilled and athletic, inner-city street smart, one of the top two prospects in the country, blessed with charisma, presence, and personality. A 6–7 forward, he was already a legend in his native Philadelphia as the leader of the West Philadelphia Speedboys. His signature on a letter of intent branded Duke a contender. Hope dispelled hard-luck frustration among fans, as season tickets sold out before Banks's first game and 5,000 supporters showed up for his first practice.

Over his first three years Foster had produced a .500 record while bringing in two potential standouts in Jim Spanarkel and Mike Gminski, a crafty playmaker and a big man who were back-to-back ACC rookies of the

The Shot He'll Never Forget

Gene Banks, 1981 versus North Carolina

Coach Mike Krzyzewski's first win over North Carolina came in dramatic fashion at the end of his rookie season with the Blue Devils, and two of his seniors teamed up for the most memorable moment.

Down by two with two seconds left, Duke inbounded from underneath the UNC basket. Chip Engelland caught the ball and called timeout in the same motion, giving the Devils the ball at midcourt with one second left. Senior Kenny Dennard threw a pass to fellow senior Banks, who lofted a shot over the outstretched arm of Sam Perkins to send the game into overtime. Banks later hit the winning shot in OT as the Devils claimed a 66–65 victory.

"There's no question that had to be the highlight of my career. To go out like that was fantastic," Banks said.

"People still ask me about the shot. People still remember the shot. I can go from here to New York to Mount Airy to the backwoods of South Carolina and many Duke fans from all over the place remember that shot. That's a great connection I have with people from all over the country and it's fantastic."

year. Banks became the third straight Blue Devil to win that award in 1978, as he and classmate Kenny Dennard stepped immediately into the lineup to spark Duke's first ACC championship and trip to the Final Four in a dozen years. Banks, Gminski, and Dennard formed a frontline that could score as well as rebound, anchoring the team's 2–3 zone defense while igniting many a fast break. It didn't take long for them to be tabbed the Duke Power Company. Banks supplied 17.1 points, 8.6 rebounds, and 120 assists while shooting 52.8 percent from the field. His point total was the highest ever for a Duke freshman, before or since. He also became the first freshman to share the team MVP award, and he was named second-team All-ACC. Most important, it was clear that the enthusiasm injected by the two rookie starters had reinvigorated the entire team's chemistry.

With expectations elevated, Banks's remaining three years weren't quite so giddy. Nevertheless, he remained one of the ACC's best players and helped his team to two more NCAA bids and another ACC title before Foster departed for South Carolina after his junior year. He repeated as a second-team All-ACC selection in 1979 and 1980, and moved up to first team in 1981 when he and Dennard were the senior starters for a new-look team under Mike Krzyzewski. Banks and Dennard were the co-captains and the co-MVPs.

Banks played in 124 games over four years and scored 2,079 points, which made him the No. 2 scorer in Duke history at that time, behind only Gminski. He had 985 rebounds and 360 assists while shooting 53.1 percent from the field and 72.2 percent from the foul line. He averaged double figures in scoring every season, with career marks of 16.8 points and 7.9 boards.

Banks had the second triple-double in Duke history with 13 points, 12 rebounds, and 11 assists against Lehigh in his freshman year. His top scoring game was 32 points versus LaSalle in his sophomore year, and his best rebounding day was 18 versus N.C. State in his junior year. None of those, though, would be ranked among his best moments, and Banks was all about shining in the big moments: a pair of 22-point games in the 1978 Final Four . . . a windmill dunk over Virginia center Ralph Sampson . . . another game-winning shot to beat the Cavaliers . . . a win on Super Bowl Sunday at N.C. State . . . a tremendous defensive run in the ACC tourney in 1980 against Hawkeye Whitney, Mike O'Koren, and Albert King . . . an exquisite 40-minute performance to give Krzyzewski his first ACC win against N.C. State. The list could go on and on.

But nothing could top Banks's final home game, when he threw roses to the crowd before the contest began and then hit a shot for the ages at the buzzer to send the game with UNC into overtime. Just under five minutes later he added the winning basket on an offensive rebound, finishing with 25 points in a 66–65 victory. "I was beyond being on a high," he told the *Wilson Daily Times* 24 years afterward. "I didn't know where I was. It's the best feeling I've ever had."

Banks's 18.5 scoring average as a senior led the ACC, but his season suffered a premature end. He broke his wrist in Duke's NIT opener and had to miss the last two games, though he arrived for one in a limousine, wearing a tuxedo. Two months later the man whom some had painted as a questionable admission for Duke was one of the university's graduation speakers.

Banks, who held a press conference near the end of his junior year to announce that he wasn't leaving early for the pros, was a second-round draft pick by the San Antonio Spurs and played six years in the NBA, averaging 11.3 points. His NBA career ended when he ruptured an Achilles tendon in a charity game for inner-city youth in Philadelphia. The Chicago Bulls balked at fulfilling the remainder of his contract, but he eventually received a financial settlement.

After recovering, Banks was unable to get back in the NBA but played in several foreign leagues before turning his attention to a wide assortment of activities. He coached the women's basketball team at Bluefield State, appeared in the 1996 movie *Eddie* with Whoopi Goldberg, worked as an athletic administrator, and launched the Gene Banks Foundation. In 1994 he was enshrined in the Duke Sports Hall of Fame and in 2001 he was a charter inductee in the Duke Basketball Hall of Honor.

Barkley, Charles. An 11-time NBA all-star and one of the league's greatest rebounders despite his 6–6 size, Charles Barkley played one game at Duke as a collegian. In December 1981 his Auburn Tigers were expected to battle the Blue Devils for the Iron Duke Classic title. But both teams were upset in the first round, so they played

in the consolation game. Duke won by one point. Barkley, later named to the NBA 50th anniversary team, had four points and 11 rebounds. In 1992 he played on the Olympic team for which Mike Krzyzewski was an assistant coach.

Barone, Tony. One of the Blue Devils' most enthusiastic and aggressive players of the 1960s, Anthony Andrew Barone enjoyed two stints with the Duke program. From 1965 to 1968 he was a reserve guard under Vic Bubas, and in 1973 and 1974 an assistant coach under Bucky Waters and Neill McGeachy.

At 5–8, Barone was the smallest player recruited by Bubas, but his speed and defensive ability enabled him to contribute. After missing most of his freshman season because of illness, he played in 46 games during his three varsity seasons, scoring 69 points with 28 rebounds. His senior year was his best, when he played in 25 games and scored 60 points, with his only career double-figures contest of 14 points against Wake Forest.

After graduating in 1968 Barone entered the high school coaching ranks in his native Illinois and posted several excellent campaigns. Waters brought him back to Duke to coach the junior varsity team in 1973, and he remained on McGeachy's staff for the 1974 season. After a long stint as an assistant coach at Bradley, Barone became a college head coach at Creighton (1986–91) and then at Texas A&M (1992–98). He was named conference coach of the year at each school. He later entered the NBA ranks and worked as the Memphis Grizzlies' director of player personnel before returning to the bench as an assistant coach under Hubie Brown (another former Duke assistant).

Barrett, George. A 6–4 forward and engineering student from Wabash, Ind., George Frederick Barrett started for the 1956 freshman team and was a varsity reserve for the next three years, 1957–59. He played in 13 games with 12 points and 22 rebounds. All of his scoring came in his sophomore year, with 12 points in six games and a career best of four against Wake Forest. He did not letter that year but picked up letters in his final two campaigns.

Barry, Rick. One of the great scorers in basketball history, Hall of Famer Rick Barry led the NCAA in scoring when his Miami Hurricanes hosted Duke in December 1962. Miami upset the second-ranked Blue Devils 71–69, with Barry collecting 12 points and 12 rebounds. Duke didn't lose again that year until the Final Four.

Bateman, Larry. By the time his senior season began in the fall of 1959, Larry Neal Bateman, a 6–6 center from Greensboro, was 26 years old and married, with a two-year-old son and a newborn daughter. Bateman originally suited up for Duke as a member of the 1953 freshman team and averaged 11.0 points a game. Then he joined the Air Force, played some service ball, and returned to finish his education while lettering for the 1958, 1959, and 1960 teams. He played in 36 varsity games, with 50 points and 82 rebounds. His best campaign was in 1958, his first year back, when he came off the bench to spark a comeback win over Villanova with six points and had his career high of eight against Seton Hall in the Dixie Classic. He saw spot duty in 11 games as a senior for the ACC Tournament champs in 1960.

Battier, Shane. On paper it wasn't quite his signature performance, this semifinal game of the ACC Tournament. Forty minutes had produced 18 points, two rebounds, an assist, and no steals for junior forward Shane Courtney Battier. But Duke won to advance to the championship contest, and opposing coach Dave Odom of Wake Forest sounded afterward as if he was describing the player of the year, not just the player of the game.

"If there's been a better leader in this league than Shane Battier, I don't know how far you'd have to go back to find a young man who can lead like he can lead and still play at the very highest level," Odom said. "I don't think I've ever seen one who has as much focus and commitment and level to produce throughout 40 minutes of basketball. The kid is a great player . . . If you take Shane Battier out of that lineup, it would be devastating."

A year later Battier would be named consensus national player of the year, culminating his college career with his very best performance in the closing minutes of his last game: a spectacular putback dunk, a back-

Shane Battier capped his career by being named MVP of the 2001 Final Four.

handed tip-in, and a driving, one-handed slam. His celebratory hugs with his roommate Mike Dunleavy, which made the cover of *Sports Illustrated*, and with coach Mike Krzyzewski marked a national championship victory over Arizona. By then there were very few original remarks left to make about this All-American guy, because it had all been said before.

"Shane is the most complete player I've ever coached. He may not be the most talented player we've had here at Duke, but he's the most complete," Krzyzewski summed up. "You hear so many good things about Shane, and you think nobody could be like that. But he is. He's the real deal."

The real deal, a 6–8 forward from Birmingham, Mich., played in 146 of Duke's 148 games from 1998 through 2001, starting 120 of them. The Blue Devils posted 131 victories with Battier on the court, enabling him to match Kentucky's Wayne Turner as the winningest player in college basketball history. Against ACC foes, the Devils were 70–5 with Battier, won the regular season four times, and took the tournament three times. They finished No. 3 in the national AP poll in his freshman year and No. 1 in the remaining three.

Before he was known as a complete player, Battier cultivated a sterling reputation as a defensive fiend. That was his way of making a strong first impression, when teammates such as Trajan Langdon, Roshown McLeod, Chris Carrawell, and Elton Brand were grabbing most of the notoriety. Battier settled in by leading the Devils in blocked shots and charges taken in his freshman year. He went on to pace the team in charges every year, blocks three times, and steals twice in four years. He ended up winning national defensive player of the year honors from his sophomore through senior seasons, as much for his physical expertise as for the strong communication skills that enabled him to orchestrate the Devils' team defense.

While most star players could point to key dunks, drives, or jumpers as career highlights, Battier could be identified with memorable defensive efforts: eight blocked shots in an NCAA win over Kansas in 2000; a rejection of Juan Dixon on the last shot of the Maryland game in 2001 to assure victory in the famous Miracle Minute contest; his race from behind to catch UNC's Joe Forte and deny a fast-break slam; his block and baseline save against Arizona that Duke converted into a transition dagger in the 2001 final.

Offensively, Battier's production increased steadily over four years. He averaged 7.6 points as a freshman and 9.1 as a sophomore, before exploding to a team-best 17.4 in his junior year and 19.9 for the 2001 national champs. He just missed 2,000 points for his career, finishing with 1,984 for a 13.6 average. He hit an even 50 percent of his field goals and 77.7 percent from the foul line while gradually showing off more and more of his long-range shooting prowess—from only 24 three-point attempts as a freshman to almost 300 as a senior. He led the conference in three-point shooting percentage as a junior and set the school record with nine threes versus Princeton.

Other career totals included 887 rebounds for a 6.1 average, 266 steals, 254 blocks, 239 assists, and 246 threes. His high rebounding game was 14 against Chaminade.

Battier topped the 20-point mark just once in his first two years, but in a big way with 27 against Maryland in 1999, one of many brilliant showings versus the Terps. The next year he had three 30-point efforts, including his career high of 34 against Wake Forest and an even 30 against UNC in the regular-season finale, when he canned 11 of 18 shots with six three-pointers. Battier also had his career high of 10 assists against N.C. State in 2000.

Senior year began on a high note when Battier connected on 9 of 12 from three-point range for 29 points in the Princeton game. Several were "trailer" threes, shots that he launched just after stepping into the half-court offensive set as the trail man on fast breaks. He excelled at that nearly undefendable act. And he remained undefendable for much of the year, particularly in the biggest games. He averaged 20 points and 12 rebounds in three meetings with UNC, scored the last six points in overtime at Maryland before blocking Dixon's last shot, and pulverized Georgia Tech when he matched his career high of 34 points in Atlanta. Held to four at halftime of that game, he went through one six-minute stretch after intermission in which he scored 20 consecutive Duke points.

Battier went down swinging with 31 points in his final home game, as the Devils suffered an emotional defeat to Maryland. Then he delivered one of his best games a few days later in Chapel Hill, after Krzyzewski deployed a kamikaze defense that forced all the action into Battier in the middle of the floor. Battier had 25 points, 11 rebounds, five blocks, and four steals while the Devils pulled off a stunning 14-point win to gain a share of their fifth straight ACC regular-season crown.

That set the stage for a remarkable postseason run to the national title. Battier hit high gear in the postseason, averaging 22.5 points and 10.2 rebounds in six NCAA games, posting a double-double in all but one of them. His tournament high was 27 in an emotion-packed second-round encounter with Missouri, coached by former Blue Devil and friend Quin Snyder.

Battier capped his career as consensus national player of the year, consensus All-America, unanimous All-ACC, unanimous ACC All-Defensive, co–ACC player of the year, ACC tourney MVP, and Final Four MVP in addition to having his jersey No. 31 retired by Duke. When he picked up the Naismith trophy, he became the first person to win both the college and high school versions of that honor.

Battier was more than a complete player. He also earned Academic All-America honors and was named the national Academic All-America of the year in 2001. Thus he was able to check off all four of the goals he had written on an index card at the beginning of the year: national title, national player of the year, first team All-America, Academic All-America. Further, Battier claimed his team's top scholar-athlete award for the third straight year and was named chairman of a student basketball council that provided advice on the state of the game to the national coaches' association. Two years after graduation, the ACC named him to its 50th anniversary team.

Battier was the sixth pick of the NBA draft and got off to a solid start with the Memphis Grizzlies, making the league's all-rookie team while becoming one of the franchise's most active and popular figures in the community. After his first three years he signed a new lucrative pact with the team. He also enjoyed respect league-wide as an annual contender for the sportsmanship award.

Beal, Jay. Considered one of the best shooters and most passionate players in the program during his tenure, Jay Edwin Beal, a 5–11 guard from Wethersfield, Conn., lettered for three years from 1959 through 1961 and saw reserve action in 22 games. He scored 47 points with 15 rebounds as a varsity player. In 1958 he averaged 11.2 points for the freshman team, as all five starters scored in double figures. He also pitched for the freshman baseball team that year. After moving up to the varsity, he saw his most extensive action in his senior year, when he played in 10 games and scored 22 points while connecting on 12 of 15 free throws. His best showing was a 10-point outing in a rout of South Carolina early in 1961. Former teammates would recall his wide assortment of shots and his games of "horse" with former assistant coach Fred Shabel.

Beall, Curtis. Forward Curtis A. Beall, from Brewton, Ga., played in three regular-season games during the 1944 season and did not score a point. It was his only year on the team. He was at Georgia before his transfer to Duke during the war.

Beard, Alana. She always took the losses hard, perhaps because she had so little experience in dealing with them. Alana Beard's high school team won 144 of 150 games, including her last 53 in a row. Then at Duke, her Blue Devils won at least 30 games every year, lost only 14 times total, and went 72–4 against ACC competition. So that season-ending defeat each year in the NCAA Tournament, whether in the Sweet 16, Elite Eight, or Final Four, always hit hard and dissipated slowly for Beard.

Although she graduated without accomplishing her primary stated goal of winning a national championship, Beard, a 5–11 guard from Shreveport, La., did everything else during a four-year career that marked her as the greatest women's basketball player in Duke and ACC history. Spurred by an inextinguishable drive to win, she set new standards for excellence at her school and in her conference.

That Beard became the first female player to have her jersey number (20) retired at Duke speaks volumes for her achievements there. She played in and started 136 games from 2001 to 2004, and the Blue Devils won 123 of them, over 90 percent. She led the team in scoring each year and broke Chris Moreland's school record with 2,687 points, an average of 19.8 a game. She also finished No. 1 in career steals (404), No. 2 in assists (509), and No. 4 in rebounds (789) while hitting 52.7 percent of her field goals and 77.4 percent of her free throws.

At the conference level, Beard finished No. 2 in career points and No. 3 in steals. She became the only player in league history to make the All-ACC first team four times and win the player of the year honor three times. She was also voted to the league's all-defensive team every year and received 18 ACC player of the week citations, 11 more than anyone else in conference history.

After her junior and senior years, Beard received the Mary Garber Award as the ACC female athlete of the year. She was also named to the list of top 50 female athletes and top 50 female basketball players in league history, even though those lists were compiled after she'd played just two years.

Nationally, Beard was a three-time Kodak All-America, a three-time Associated Press All-America, and a unanimous selection to the AP team in her senior year. She became the first national player of the year from Duke in 2003 when she was presented with the Vic-

All-time women's scoring champ Alana Beard had her jersey No. 20 retired during her senior season.

tor Award, and she claimed several trophies in 2004, including the inaugural women's Wooden Award, the Wade Trophy, and awards presented by the Associated Press and the U.S. Basketball Writers.

Beard helped raise Duke's profile to a new level. The Blue Devils were ranked No. 1 during portions of her last two seasons and enjoyed final national rankings of fifth in her freshman year, followed by third, second, and first in 2004. She was the MVP of NCAA regionals in 2002 and 2003 while sparking her team to consecutive Final Fours, and she made the All–Final Four team in 2003 despite Duke's loss in the semifinals.

Beard set Duke's freshman scoring record with 33 points against Maryland in 2001 and established a new overall Duke scoring mark when she had 41 points against Virginia in 2003. Her top rebounding output of 20 came against North Carolina in the ACC Tournament

in 2003, and twice she had 11 assists in a game, one short of the school record.

The 2003 game at Virginia was far from a team masterpiece, as virtually no one played well except Beard. But it showed just how stoutly she could carry her team. She was the only Blue Devil to hit from the field in an anemic first half, and she scored 27 of Duke's 37 points in the second half. Top-ranked and undefeated, Duke trailed in the closing seconds before Beard was fouled in a scramble for a loose ball at midcourt. She hit a pair of free throws with 0.8 left on the clock to give the Devils a one-point win, scoring 41 of the team's 60 points.

"Alana is everything everybody says she is," Virginia coach Debbie Ryan said. "She's in a league by herself in comparisons with players across the country. She's the type of player that wins games for you."

Beard was not a likely candidate for Duke stardom during her high school career. She wanted to stay close to home for college and only kept the Blue Devils among her top five options at her parents' insistence. It was her parents who were also her earliest role models for the work ethic that kept her in the gym refining her game throughout high school and college. She developed her intense focus from her high school coach, Steve McDowell, at Southwood High, and she learned how to train smarter from the Duke legend Johnny Dawkins after a sophomore year in which she was simply worn out.

Beard's last Duke game was an NCAA loss to Minnesota, after which Goestenkors paid tribute to Beard and her classmates Iciss Tillis and Vicki Krapohl for changing the face of the program.

"We wanted to win a national championship for them. I feel so badly for them more than anything," she said. "They have taken this program to a new level. I told them after the game that they have set the standard of excellence for Duke women's basketball, and everyone that follows them will have to live up to the standard."

Beard was the second pick of the 2004 WNBA draft and moved immediately into the Washington Mystics lineup. She appeared in and started 64 games during her first two seasons, scoring 868 points for a 13.6 average. She made the WNBA All-Star Game in 2005.

Beard, Joey. A two-time high school All-America from Reston, Va., Joseph Edward Beard was a member of the

Duke program for a year and a half. As a freshman in 1994 he played in 16 games with 21 points and eight rebounds. A 6 – 9 forward, he had a high of eight points in a rout of N.C. State. Beard hoped for a more valuable role as a sophomore, but he came down with mononucleosis during the fall and got off to a slow start. After not seeing any action in the first few games and foreseeing a limited role the rest of the year, he decided to transfer to Boston University, where he enjoyed a solid career.

Bell, Bruce. Few Duke-related sports photographs could match the poignancy of the one that appeared on the front page of the *Chronicle* on February 23, 1978. It was taken the night before, as lone senior Bruce Bell stood under the glare of a spotlight at center court in Cameron Indoor Stadium, trying not to cry during his final introduction.

A 6 – 0 walk-on guard from Lexington, Ky., Thomas Bruce Bell played in 42 games during the 1975 through 1978 seasons, scoring 58 points with 37 assists. He played mostly on the junior varsity team as a freshman but moved up to varsity at season's end when guard Tate Armstrong was injured. He got into one game and scored two points. He led the JV team in assists as a sophomore, received a partial scholarship, and found his way into three varsity games while earning a letter.

Bell saw his most extensive varsity action as a junior, when he played in 17 games, with 29 points and 22 assists. Most of his minutes came during the second half of the year, after Armstrong was again injured. He was in the starting lineup for the last few weeks and averaged 24 minutes a game over the final seven contests. Bell was the only senior on the 1978 Final Four team, coming off the bench in 20 games while starting his Senior Night contest against Clemson. He finished with 25 points and 13 assists that season, while providing invaluable support during practice and from the sideline. A year after his Duke graduation, Bell went to law school at Kentucky and later joined his father's firm in Lexington. Bell's father Tommy was a well-known football and basketball referee.

Bell, Sammy. A three-year letterman from 1933 to 1935 and a two-year starter, Samuel Bell, a diminutive 5 – 6 forward from Charlotte, scored 225 points during

his varsity career while helping coach Eddie Cameron's teams compile records of 17 – 5, 18 – 6, and 18 – 8. Duke reached the Southern Conference Tournament final in his first two years, though he missed the end of his sophomore year with a broken hand. As a senior, Bell was team captain and had his best game with 21 points to help the Devils defeat Maryland for the first time in five years.

Belmont, Joe. Coach Harold Bradley initially placed freshman guard Joseph Elliott Belmont on his junior varsity team in 1953. But with freshmen able to compete for the varsity that season, Bradley switched him to that roster after the first two JV contests, and Belmont, a 5 – 11 playmaker from Philadelphia, quickly found a home. By the end of his rookie year he was in the starting lineup, and he remained there for four seasons, 1953 – 56, finishing his career with 1,338 points and 420 rebounds in 103 games. At that point in Duke history, Dick Groat and his teammate Ronnie Mayer were the only Blue Devils with more career points.

Belmont had a high of 17 points against William & Mary in his freshman year and established a new career high in the opening contest of his sophomore year with 21 points against Furman. It was a sign of things to come, as his scoring punch was frequently on display. When Duke won its only Dixie Classic title that season, he had 19 points in the opener against Oregon State and 21 in the final against Navy. He averaged 12.4 points for the year and saw his numbers improve steadily for the next two seasons, when he scored 15.7 and 16.9 a game and finished behind his classmate Mayer for the team lead.

Opponents found the combination of Mayer and Belmont difficult to contain in 1955 and 1956 as Duke averaged over 80 points a game each season. Mayer made the All-ACC first team in 1955 with Belmont on the second team, and Belmont was chosen for the first team in 1956 while Mayer made the second.

Belmont exploded for his first 30-point game late in 1955 with a 32-point effort in a win over North Carolina. Mayer had 28 in the same game. Belmont registered his career high the next year on a homecoming trip to play Penn at the Palestra in Philadelphia, as he poured in 37 points on the strength of a 19-of-24 day at the foul line.

Mayer, also from the Philadelphia area, had 32 points in that contest with a 16-of-22 performance at the line. Belmont's 24 foul shots set a school record that has been matched just once since (Art Heyman, 1961), and his 19 free throws made have been surpassed just once in Duke history (Bucky Allen, 1957). Frequently he made an impact even when he didn't have gaudy statistics. In a contest with North Carolina in 1956 he was held scoreless for the first 38:10 of play. But in the last 1:50 he knocked down eight free throws that iced a victory.

Belmont was a second-team ACC All-Tournament pick in 1955, when Duke made its first appearance in the young league's championship game. He scored 21 points in the semifinals against Virginia and a team high of 19 in the final loss to N.C. State. In 1956 he was the Blue Devils' most valuable player.

Belmont was chosen in the fifth round of the NBA draft by hometown Philadelphia in 1956 but never played in the league. He instead moved to Denver to play in a national industrial league. After it folded, Belmont remained in Denver and later was hired as a scout and ticket salesman for the Denver Rockets of the old ABA. When the team got off to a 9–19 start to the 1970 season, management asked him to take over the head coaching position. Led by rookie Spencer Haywood, the Rockets rolled to a 51–33 record and Belmont was chosen coach of the year. But the following season, with Haywood injured and then defecting to the NBA, the Rockets started slowly and Belmont was replaced. He later returned to basketball as an official and refereed games in the Western Athletic Conference for 25 years. In March 2005 he was inducted into the Colorado Sports Hall of Fame.

Bender, Bob. When Duke played Kentucky for the NCAA championship in 1978, Blue Devil sophomore Bob Bender, a 6–2 point guard, instantly became the answer to a tournament trivia question, as he was the first person ever to play in a national title contest for two schools. But there was nothing trivial about Bender's career contributions. He provided steady floor leadership for three NCAA Tournament and two ACC championship teams from 1978 to 1980, an era in which the Devils posted a 73–24 record and restored lost glory to the program.

A native of Quantico, Va., and a high school star under his father in Bloomington, Ill., Robert Micheal Bender

Bob Bender played in national finals for two schools, Duke and Indiana.

began his college career in another Bloomington — as a freshman under Bob Knight at Indiana University. He played in 17 games as a rookie, with 35 points and 14 assists, as the Hoosiers went undefeated and won the 1976 NCAA title. Bender saw action in the final but later called Duke to inquire about a transfer. The Blue Devils were interested, as assistant coach Ray Jones had watched him play over a dozen times in high school.

Bender had to sit out the 1977 season under the NCAA transfer rule. He became eligible to play for the Devils in January 1978, scored seven points against Lehigh in his début, and came off the bench to share point guard duties with John Harrell for the rest of the year, which culminated in his second NCAA championship game, though he was not on the winning side this time.

Bender moved into the starting lineup in his junior year and averaged 6.8 points while distributing the ball to All-Americas such as Mike Gminski, Jim Spanarkel, and Gene Banks. Duke tied for first in the ACC regular season, its best finish in over a decade. Bender scored his career high of 16 points to help Duke edge N.C. State in the tournament semifinals, but then was struck by appendicitis and had to miss the championship game with UNC as well as the NCAA opener with St. John's the following weekend. The Devils lost both. After the season, since he'd been in college for four years, he was eligible for the NBA draft and was selected by the San Diego Clippers, though he decided to return to Duke for his senior season.

As co-captain in 1980 Bender played in every game, averaged 6.4 points, and dealt a team high 159 assists. He helped the Devils win their second ACC tourney in his three years and upset Kentucky in Lexington to reach the Elite Eight of the NCAA, where his career came to an end with a loss to Purdue, one game shy of a third collegiate Final Four. Twice in his senior year he dished his career high of 10 assists, against Marquette and Providence.

Bender finished with 83 Duke appearances, 514 points, and 332 assists while shooting 51.6 percent from the field. He attended training camp with the Clippers, who still held his rights, and went briefly into private business before returning to Duke to work in the Iron Dukes fund-raising organization. In 1984 the man who was regarded as a coach on the floor during his playing days became a full-time coach for his alma mater and served Mike Krzyzewski's staff for six seasons, through 1989. Duke reached the NCAA tourney each year and played in three Final Fours.

Bender embarked on a head coaching career at Illinois State in 1990 and led his team to a Missouri Valley title and NCAA bid in his first year. His team finished first in the conference standings twice more before Washington lured him away to lead its program beginning with the 1994 season. After a couple of rebuilding years, he directed the Huskies to one NIT and two NCAA bids, with the 1998 team reaching the Sweet 16 before falling on a last-second shot to UConn. En route to the 1998 tourney appearance in Greensboro, Bender brought his team to his alma mater for a practice and a visit with Krzyzewski.

The Huskies slipped in his last couple of years, and Bender was replaced. His college coaching record was 60–57 at Illinois State and 116–142 in nine years at Washington. He next went to the NBA, joining the staff of the Philadelphia 76ers, whose president was one of his former assistants and Duke players, Billy King. After two seasons he moved on to the Atlanta Hawks in 2005.

Bennett, C. G. Charles Glenn "Cocky" Bennett, from Durham, lettered three years for the basketball team, 1926–28, and also played for the football program, for which he served as team captain. His most prominent action in basketball came early in his career. By the time he was a senior, most of the court time went to a core of sophomores led by the program's first All-America, Bill Werber.

Bergman, Russ. Dubbed the "never a dull moment boys" for their colorful antics, the 1938 Duke basketball team won the school's first conference tournament by defeating Clemson in the Southern Conference championship game. Russell "Sparky" Bergman, a native of Madison, N.J., was one of the standout performers for that club, earning second-team all-tournament honors. Bergman was a fixture in the lineup for all three years that he lettered, 1937–39, usually at a forward spot, though he started in the backcourt for the 1938 team and was known for racing up and down the floor. Bergman scored 351 career points.

Berndt, Andy. One of four walk-ons added to the 1987 Duke roster, Andrew John Berndt, a 6–6 sophomore from Chatham, N.J., played in six games during his only year on the team. He went scoreless and had three rebounds in nine minutes of action.

Big Four Tournament. As if their regular-season ACC battles were not intense enough, rivals Duke, North Carolina, N.C. State and Wake Forest got together for an early-season skirmish known as the Big Four Tournament from 1971 through 1981. Played before capacity crowds at the Greensboro Coliseum, the event featured doubleheaders on back-to-back nights, usually in December or early January, with a tournament format. The results did not count in the ACC standings. During most years, two if not three of the four schools were ranked in the national polls. In 1975 and again in 1976, both UNC and N.C. State entered the tourney ranked in the top 10, only to see unranked Wake Forest win the event and break into the poll. When Duke won in December

1978, the Blue Devils were ranked No. 1 while their victims State and Carolina were sixth and 14th. Duke had a record of 9–13 in the 11 Big Fours, with consecutive crowns during the 1978–79 and 1979–80 seasons. The most common reason given for the demise of the event was the coaches' lament that one of the four schools had to leave the weekend with two losses.

Bilas, Jay. Thanks to the ubiquitous nature of television, Jay Bilas may be the most recognized Duke alumnus on the planet, at least within the all-sports, all-the-time culture. The university has obviously produced numerous distinguished graduates in a wide range of endeavors, but who among its graduates receives more TV airtime than Bilas? As a reporter, studio personality, and college basketball game analyst for ESPN — as well as for CBS Sports during March Madness — Bilas has become one of the most familiar faces in sports broadcasting.

Which makes for an interesting contrast with his collegiate playing career, when Jay Scot Bilas, a 6–8 center from Rolling Hills, Calif., was one of the least-recognized Blue Devils. Not that David Robinson, Ralph Sampson, or any other foe needed an introduction. But in terms of being recognized for his efforts on the court, Bilas was well down the receiving line. After Johnny Dawkins, Mark Alarie, David Henderson, and Tommy Amaker were given their plaudits, maybe there was something left over for Bilas, who merely started 106 games at a time when the scope of Duke basketball was returning to a national audience.

Bilas was a member of Mike Krzyzewski's first landmark recruiting class. While Dawkins was the unstoppable scorer, Alarie the steady forward, and Henderson the tough and hungry wingman, Bilas was expected to provide many of the unsung necessities as a rebounder and post presence. During his four years, 1983–86, he played in 127 games, scored 1,062 points for an 8.4 average, and grabbed 692 rebounds. He shot 55.7 percent from the field, leading the team in that category in three seasons.

Bilas's awards were limited to a spot on the ACC All-Tournament second team in 1985 and TV player of the game honors in Duke's NCAA loss to Boston College in his junior year. But he had a hand in numerous big moments as the program progressed from 11–17 in his freshman

Jay Bilas led Duke in field-goal percentage for three of his four seasons.

year to 37–3, ACC champs, and Final Four runner-up in his senior year. He played solid post defense and had a double-double with 10 points and 11 rebounds when the Devils upset No. 1 UNC in the ACC tourney in 1984. He turned in an excellent performance with 17 points and 11 rebounds when Duke won at UNC in 1985, ending an 18-year drought at Carmichael Auditorium. His defense and 10 rebounds were clear factors when the Devils topped Robinson and Navy in the regional championship game in 1986 to earn their Final Four berth.

Bilas's career scoring high was 23 points against Loyola in 1984. He also had a 21-point outing against Georgia Tech in the 1985 ACC tourney. He reached his career rebounding high of 13 twice, against Maryland and Boston College. Bilas missed the first six games of his senior year while recovering from off-season knee surgery. Freshman Danny Ferry started in his place. Bilas was able to play the last 34 games, started 19, and had to soak his knee in ice for at least an hour after every practice to get through the season.

One of the most well-rounded and articulate Blue

Devils, Bilas didn't confine his college experience to Cameron Indoor Stadium. He was one of two student-athletes in the nation appointed to the NCAA's long-range planning committee. Exploring his interest in broad-casting, he hosted a show on campus cable, interned for ABC Sports during the 1984 Olympics, appeared on the CBS News program "Face the Nation" to discuss aca-demics and athletics, and was a favorite interview sub-ject among reporters covering the team.

His postgraduate career was just as diverse. He played professionally overseas for three years, appeared in the science fiction movie *I Come in Peace*, worked as a vol-unteer assistant coach for the Blue Devils for three years while in law school, 1990 – 92, and became a practicing attorney, based in Charlotte. He worked with Bob Har-ris on the Duke Radio Network in 1993 – 96 while also launching his TV career with Raycom/Jefferson Pilot.

In 1995 Bilas began getting ESPN assignments, and he has been under contract with the network since 1998. As an example of the pace he set while establishing his identity, Bilas in March 1996 worked the Duke-Carolina game on radio and then headed for the Mid-Continent Conference title game in Illinois, the ACC play-in game in Greensboro, and the Big Sky final in Montana in less than a week for ESPN.

Bilas was the WNBA analyst for ESPN in 1999 and the studio analyst for the NCAA women's tourney in 2000, and he soon became a regular presence on the network's various programs such as "SportsCenter," "College Hoops Tonight," and "College Gamenight." In addition, he worked some weekend games as an analyst for ABC Sports. With his quick wit and cache of humorous an-ecdotes, he has also become a popular banquet speaker and was particularly entertaining as the host of a celeb-rity charity roast of his former college coach.

Billerman, Kevin. An outstanding 6 – 2 basketball guard and football quarterback from Bricktown, N.J., Kevin John Billerman played for three head coaches during his varsity career as a backcourt standout and served the program as a two-time team captain. From 1973 to 1975 he appeared in 78 games with 793 points, 270 assists, and 174 rebounds, while scoring in double figures in each of his last two seasons.

Billerman was one of the freshman team leaders in 1972, when he averaged 15.3 points, had a 30-point out-ing against the North Carolina frosh team, and stepped into the Tar Heels' huddle one time, drawing boos at Carmichael Auditorium. He had 16 points in his varsity début under coach Bucky Waters in 1973, enjoyed a 22-point game against Harvard, and scored 17 in a win over Davidson, but he was hampered by a hip injury late in the season. As a junior under coach Neill McGeachy, he led Duke in assists with 112 and averaged 10.7 points. He also topped the ACC in free-throw shooting at 83.2 percent. Two of his best games were narrow emotional losses to UNC. He scored his high of 22 points in the home game against Carolina, but fouled out on a charg-ing call on his final basket and missed the last 2:37 of a two-point defeat. Billerman had a Duke school record of 14 assists in the regular-season finale at Chapel Hill, a game that Duke lost in overtime after leading by eight points with 17 seconds remaining in regulation.

Billerman's success against UNC continued in his se-nior year, when he posted his career high of 24 points against the Tar Heels in an overtime victory in the Big Four Tournament under his third head coach, Bill Fos-ter. Billerman captained and led the Devils in assists for a second season and had his best scoring average at 11.7.

After Duke, Billerman played for a year overseas and then entered the basketball coaching profession. He was the head boy's basketball coach at Northern Durham High School for eight years, winning 121 games, before joining former Duke star Jeff Mullins at UNC Charlotte for 10 years. Billerman was named head coach at Florida Atlantic University and coached there for four seasons, 1996 – 99. He was faced with one of the more difficult recruiting challenges in the country as the school was placed on NCAA probation for violations committed be-fore his arrival. His record there was 36 – 64.

Bing, Dave. Hall of Famer Dave Bing, named to the NBA 50th anniversary team, faced the Blue Devils in 1966 as a senior at Syracuse. With a trip to the Final Four on the line at the East Regionals in Raleigh, Duke pre-vailed by 10 points behind the efforts of All-Americas Jack Marin and Bob Verga. Bing had 10 points on 4-of-14 shooting, with eight rebounds and six turnovers. It was Bing's last college game.

Black, Payton. A member of four NCAA Tournament teams and a reserve for the first Duke women's team to reach the Final Four, Payton Black played in 127 games from 1996 to 1999. She totaled 1,312 points for a career average of 10.3 and added 541 rebounds.

A 6–4 center from Westchester, Pa., Black came off the bench to average over 10 points as a freshman. Her best year was her sophomore season of 1997, when she started 29 of Duke's 30 contests and averaged 13.7 points. She was a part-time starter in 1998 and came off the bench in 1999, when All-America Michele VanGorp handled the pivot.

During Black's career, Duke developed into a national caliber team. The Devils lost in the NCAA second round during her first two years but went to the quarterfinals in 1998 and the final in 1999, while also winning the ACC regular season each of her last two years.

Blackburn, Tom. Thomas Earl Blackburn, a 6–0 guard from Massachusetts, lettered one season for the Blue Devils, as a junior in 1955, when he appeared in 11 games and scored 11 points, with a high of four in Duke's upset of West Virginia in the Dixie Classic. He played for the junior varsity team and pitched for the freshman baseball team earlier in his career.

Blackman, Don. Duke's first high-profile African American basketball recruit, Donald Blackman, a 6–6 forward from Brooklyn, starred for the 1969 freshman team and lettered for the 1970 varsity before transferring to Rhode Island. An All-New York City selection and Scholastic Magazine prep All-America, Blackman averaged 15.9 points and 12.3 rebounds for the Duke frosh, scoring 22 points twice and grabbing 21 rebounds once. He played in 25 of Duke's 26 varsity contests under new head coach Bucky Waters in 1970, scoring 156 points with 131 rebounds. He was in double figures six times, with highs of 17 points and 11 rebounds in a home win over Maryland and 14 points in a home win over North Carolina. After the season he won the Ted Mann Jr. Award as the reserve contributing most to team morale. There were only a handful of black athletes and a few dozen black students on campus with Blackman.

Blakeney, Kenny. After playing for legendary coaches Morgan Wootten in high school and Mike Krzyzewski in college, Kenneth Lee Blakeney brought much to the table when he began his own coaching career in 1995. Fresh off his Duke graduation, he was hired by Lefty Driesell at James Madison and coached there for one season. He spent a year at LaSalle and then three years with Mike Brey at Delaware helping the Blue Hens to a pair of NCAA Tournament berths. Later he went to St. Bonaventure, then back to Delaware to assist David Henderson.

As a Duke player, Blakeney, a 6–4 guard from Washington, D.C., red-shirted during his true freshman campaign of 1991, pushing guard Bobby Hurley in practice while emulating ACC standouts such as Chris Corchiani and Kenny Anderson. Over the next four years Blakeney appeared in 93 games, accumulating 297 points, 110 assists, and 124 rebounds. A solid defensive player, Blakeney was used mostly off the bench but did earn 11 career starts, including eight in his senior year of 1995 when he averaged a career-best 5.4 points.

Blakeney faced a tough situation in the fall of 1993 when he was taking an academic underload of three courses and failed one of them. Because he didn't pass three classes, he was ruled academically ineligible by Duke for the spring 1994 semester and had to watch from afar as the Blue Devils advanced to the Final Four. He still had a worthwhile spring, however, by volunteering to help run a "Back on Track" program for Durham High School juveniles who had been caught up in the court system.

Bledsoe, Gene. Guard Eugene F. Bledsoe's brief stay with the Duke basketball team came in 1944 at the height of the Second World War, when he appeared in 17 regular-season games and scored 113 points. A native of Memphis and transfer from Mississippi State, Bledsoe was gone by the time Duke won the Southern Conference Tournament at season's end.

Blue Devil mascot. Duke's well-known Blue Devil mascot and nickname date back to the institution's days as Trinity College. Early athletic teams were usually referred to as the Blue and White or the Methodists. During the 1921–22 academic year, the *Trinity Chronicle* decided that it was time for a "catchy" name and nominated several possibilities, including Blue Devils, Blue Titans, Blue Warriors, Blue Eagles, and Royal Blazes. None of them caught on.

The following year, campus leaders at the *Archive* and the *Chanticleer* decided that the *Chronicle* should choose a nickname and start using it. Editor in chief William Lander and managing editor Mike Bradshaw opted for Blue Devils and first used it in a football headline on the front page on October 4, 1922. Although some poked fun at the name, no major opposition arose. Through continued use by the school press, Duke's teams gradually became recognized as the Blue Devils.

The origin of the nickname itself required no explanation in 1922, when the student body included numerous veterans of the First World War. The inspiration was a corps of French alpine soldiers known as the Chasseurs Alpins or Blue Devils, who wore distinctive blue uniforms with capes and berets. After researching their background, university archivist emeritus Bill King reported that units of Blue Devils toured the country helping the United States raise money for the war effort and that Irving Berlin captured their spirit in a popular song.

Boateng, Eric. A 6–10 center originally from London, Eric Yamoah Boateng was a freshman reserve on the 2006 team. He earned McDonald's and Parade All-America honors in high school at St. Andrews in Middletown, Del., and was part of a top-rated recruiting class. He scored 14 points in 20 games before deciding to transfer at the end of the season.

Boozer, Carlos. Duke's second player from the last frontier was never called the Alaskan Assassin, as his predecessor Trajan Langdon had been, but Carlos Boozer, a 6–8 power player from Juneau, was often deadly to opponents with his efficiency in the paint. Boozer was almost automatic when he got the ball on the low block, hitting 63.1 percent of his field goals over three years. That stands as the top career field-goal percentage in school history. And Boozer did it consistently, hitting at least 60 percent in each of his three years while leading the ACC in shooting in 2001 (60.4) and 2002 (66.5).

Boozer's value was rarely more evident than in a game

Carlos Boozer averaged almost 15 points a game during his three-year career.

at Virginia in 2002. Time after time, Boozer worked to get open and his teammates found him. In the first 33 minutes of play he hit 12 of 13 shots from the field and had a career high of 33 points to help the Devils build up a 15-point lead. Then, over the last seven minutes, he rarely saw the ball; Duke got outscored 21 – 1 down the stretch and Virginia claimed an upset victory.

Boozer played in 101 games from 2000 to 2002, with 93 starts. He started 47 of 48 ACC games during his tenure, missing one with a broken foot. Duke's ACC record during his career was 41 – 7 with three tourney titles, one NCAA crown, and three years as the No. 1 finisher in the Associated Press poll. Boozer contributed mightily to that record, with scoring marks of 13.0, 13.3, and 18.2. Overall he totaled 1,506 points for a 14.9 average and 724 rebounds for a 7.2 average. Along with his accuracy from the field, Boozer hit 74.1 percent of his foul shots.

Boozer was a factor from the beginning, forced into

early playing time after two big men, Elton Brand and Chris Burgess, unexpectedly left the program after the 1999 season. Boozer led Duke in rebounding in his freshman year while turning in eight 20-point games. He recorded an early high of 28 against William & Mary on 11-of-12 shooting, one of many eye-opening stat lines characteristic of his career. He hit 11 of 11 against Portland in 2001, and in three 2002 contests versus N.C. State went 9 of 13, 13 of 14, and 11 of 12.

Boozer's sophomore year was highlighted by a powerful showing in the championship game of the Preseason NIT. He had 26 points on 10-of-14 shooting to carry Duke to the title. Down the stretch of that game, he and penetrating guard Jason Williams played perfectly off each other, combining for the Devils' final 26 points in a narrow victory over Temple. Later in the year, in the home finale with Maryland, Boozer suffered the broken foot that caused him to miss his only ACC regular-season game (at UNC), as well as the ACC Tournament and the first two rounds of the NCAA. He returned to play in the regionals, not in his old role as a starter but as a reserve who adapted to the team's newfound style of play. Then he sparkled in the Final Four at Minneapolis as Duke won the national title. He scored 19 points in the semis against Maryland and contributed 12 points with 12 boards in the final against Arizona. "Carlos really put together the whole package," said his teammate Shane Battier. "He really concentrated on the defensive end, and that translated into great offense. He was much more of a complete player."

Boozer's game was even more complete in 2002. He announced at the beginning of the season that it would be his last, that he planned to turn pro afterward. He wound up joining Williams and Mike Dunleavy on the All-ACC first team, the first time that had been done by three players from one school. He was a third-team All-America selection and enjoyed one of his finest moments at the ACC Tournament when he was named MVP. In the semis against Wake Forest he had 17 points with 16 rebounds. (Earlier in the year his career rebounding high had come against the Deacs, with 18.) In the final versus N.C. State, Boozer scored 26 points as Duke won by 30, the second-largest winning margin in event history. Boozer shot 20 of 24 from the field for the three-game weekend.

Boozer also took the last shot of the season a couple of weeks later in the Sweet 16 of the NCAA tourney. His game-high 19 points against Indiana helped Duke to take control, but the Hoosiers rallied for a late lead. Williams was on the foul line for a potential game-tying free throw in the closing seconds and missed it, but Boozer rebounded. He rushed the follow shot under heavy pressure, missed, and the season was over.

Boozer mysteriously dropped to the second round of the NBA draft, meaning no lavish guaranteed contract. But he became a starter and workhorse almost immediately for the Cleveland Cavaliers, averaged double figures in scoring during his first two seasons, and ranked fifth in the NBA in rebounds with 11.4 in 2004. After that season he was named to the U.S. Olympic team and averaged 7.6 points plus 6.1 rebounds in Athens while winning a bronze medal. He also made a controversial free-agent move to Utah, where he averaged 17.8 points and 9.0 rebounds as a 51-game starter in 2005 before being sidelined by injury.

Borman, Andy. The nephew of coach Mike Krzyzewski and a grandson of the first astronaut to orbit the Moon, Andrew Marsh Borman, a 6–1 guard from Morrisville, N.C., lettered for four years as a backcourt reserve. He played in 40 games with 17 points and 12 rebounds. His career high was a six-point outing against Clemson on his 21st birthday in 2001. Borman played in 24 games from 2000 to 2002, then missed the 2003 season while coping with the death of his brother. He returned to play 16 games off the bench for the 2004 Final Four team. He also played four seasons for the Duke soccer team, 1999–2002.

Boston College. Before its acceptance in the ACC beginning in 2005, Boston College had played five games against the Blue Devils, all between 1979 and 2002. Duke won four of the five. The lone loss was in March 1985, when BC, coached by Gary Williams, upset 10th-ranked Duke 74–73 in the second round of the NCAA Tournament in Houston. The two schools traded home games in 2001 and 2002, with Duke winning both. In BC's first ACC campaign, 2006, the Eagles fell to Duke in the tournament final.

Bowman, James. A letter winner for the Southern Conference Tournament runner-up team in 1940, James Bowman, a 6 – 3 center from Harrisburg, Pa., scored six points in a reserve role. He played but did not letter in 1939, appearing in four games and scoring his lone point in the season opener. In 1938 he scored three points in three games

Boyd, Jack. Offered college scholarships in football, basketball, and baseball, John Winfield "Jack" Boyd, from Yeadon, Pa., lettered for the Blue Devils in 1958 and 1959. He appeared in 27 games, with 105 points and 47 rebounds. Boyd's career got off to a fast start with the freshman team when he scored 21 points against the varsity in the Blue-White game and was the most consistent scorer throughout the year with an average of almost 15 points a game. During his sophomore season he erupted for a team-high 16 points in a narrow double-overtime loss at Pittsburgh. He missed the first half of the 1959 season because he was not in school, but he played in the final 10 games and averaged 5.7 points. Boyd's two best outings that season were against North Carolina, with 15 points in Chapel Hill and nine in the ACC Tournament.

Boykin, Jamal. A 6 – 7 power forward from Los Angeles, Jamal Thomas Boykin was a member of Duke's top-ranked 2005 recruiting class and a freshman reserve for the 2006 team. He was the California state player of the year as a senior and made the Parade All-America team.

Boyle, Joanne. Hospitalized with a brain hemorrhage on November 28, 2001, Duke women's assistant coach Joanne Boyle faced an uncertain future. Incoherent and barely able to move, she remained in intensive care for 10 days before her medical team took a second arteriogram to pinpoint the cause of the bleeding. When the test revealed an arteriovenous malformation, Boyle underwent brain surgery on December 8 and endured months of rehabilitation to regain normal functioning.

The experience was not only life threatening but life changing. A former Blue Devil player, Boyle had been a Duke assistant coach for nine years and interviewed for some head coaching positions. Upon recovering from brain surgery, she resolved to leave the comfortable situation at her alma mater and undertake a head coaching career. She accepted a position at Richmond in the spring of 2002, guided the Spiders to records of 21 – 11, 23 – 10, and 23 – 8 with two appearances in the WNIT and one in the NCAA, and then was hired by California of the Pac-10 to revitalize its program beginning with the 2006 season. She guided the Golden Bears to an 18 – 12 record and their first NCAA bid in 13 years.

"When you are a coach, you can sometimes envision things like a recruit," Boyle said. "Is it a good fit for you? And for me this is a great fit, first because of the academics. It's a great academic school and I've only been at academic schools. And second, because of Sandy Barbour coming on board as the athletics director and being really committed. All sports do well here except basketball. Her vision is that she wants all of her sports to compete in the Pac-10, compete for national championships and she wants to put the resources behind it. I feel like it can be like the Duke of the West Coast with great academics and the resources that are being put into it."

After growing up in Pittsburgh, Boyle was in one of coach Debbie Leonard's early scholarship classes at Duke. She played in 94 games over four years, 1982 – 85, with 601 points and 227 rebounds. As a senior in 1985 she was captain of the first Blue Devil team to win an ACC Tournament game. The team finished with a 19 – 8 record, and Boyle's 75 steals that year remained a school record until Alana Beard topped the 100 mark as a freshman in 2001.

Boyle was a relative late bloomer in basketball. Her senior year was far and away her best at Duke, as she averaged 13.4 points and led the club in assists as well as steals. She then enjoyed three seasons as a professional player in Europe, twice leading a Luxembourg league in scoring. She felt the urge to coach while overseas and was hired at Duke by second-year leader Gail Goestenkors for the 1994 campaign. In nine seasons she helped coach and recruit the Devils to national prominence, with three ACC titles and two trips to the Final Four.

Bradley, Bill. Imagine the talent that Duke could have put on the floor in 1963, with Art Heyman as a senior, Jeff Mullins as a junior, and Bill Bradley as a sophomore. Or in 1965, with Bradley as a senior, joined by Jack Marin,

Coach Harold Bradley, flanked on the Duke bench by assistant Tony Drago and star guard Bucky Allen.

Bob Verga, and Steve Vacendak. Those could have been more than fantasy lineups, because in the summer of 1961 Bradley gave a verbal commitment to attend Duke. But a week before the fall semester started, coach Vic Bubas learned that Bradley had changed his mind and would enroll at Princeton instead.

Duke more than survived the loss, with a 73 – 13 record and two Final Fours during Bradley's varsity years. And Bradley took Princeton to the Final Four in his senior year, setting the event's scoring record with a 58-point game against Wichita State before embarking on his Hall of Fame NBA and political careers. But he did play one game at Duke Indoor Stadium. As a sophomore in December 1962, his Princeton team dropped a decision to the eighth-ranked Blue Devils. Bradley had 24 points and seven rebounds, but Mullins (28 points) and Heyman (27) were better.

Bradley, Harold. Taking over the reins of the Duke program less than a month before the start of the 1951 season, Harold "Hal" Bradley guided the Blue Devils to a 20-win campaign. It was the first of nine consecutive winning ledgers for the man who coached Duke through the 1950s and won 68 percent of his games with a 167 – 78 record.

Bradley coached star guard Dick Groat during his junior and senior seasons. He coached the Blue Devils' last Southern Conference team and its first ACC team. He was the first coach to take a Duke team into the NCAA Tournament, the only Duke coach to win a Dixie Classic, and the first to direct a team that finished in the final national rankings. About the only thing he never won was a conference tournament, though three times he coached the Devils to the championship game. All three attempts ended in defeat, to N.C. State on the Wolfpack's home floor.

A product of Hartwick College in upstate New York, Bradley was about to begin his fourth year as his alma mater's head coach and athletic director when Eddie Cameron hired him away to Duke, where cancer had forced coach Gerry Gerard to take a leave of absence. With Groat as the catalyst, Bradley guided the Blue Devils to records of 20 – 13 and 24 – 6 in his first two years, and a pair of trips to the Southern Conference finals. The 1952 team was the first in school history to be ranked in the final Associated Press poll, at No. 12. It won 15 straight games before losing the tournament finale. Bradley's 1954, 1956, and 1958 teams also were ranked, in 1958 finishing 10th.

Bradley, who preferred a fast-paced style of play, saw Duke post its first 100-point game in 1952 and 12 more during his tenure. His teams finished fourth in the nation in scoring in 1953 and 1954, and set a school record with an 85.2 average in 1955, which stood until Vic Bubas's 1965 team topped the 90-point mark.

Bradley coached Duke to first place in the first ACC race of 1954, and again in 1958. The Devils never finished lower than third in his six ACC seasons. His 94 – 37 record in conference games (Southern and ACC) translated to a 71.8 winning percentage, better than his overall winning percentage.

Bradley was the first Duke coach to beat a No. 1 team (West Virginia in 1958) and was successful against the Devils' top rival, with a 14 – 11 mark against UNC, including an eight-game winning streak. But he was 8 – 16 against N.C. State. The Devils lost to State three times in the 1955 season but made their first NCAA trip in place of the ineligible Wolfpack.

Bradley coached four teams that won at least 20 games. Among his best were the 1954 team that went 22 – 6 during the inaugural ACC campaign and the 1958 team that was 18 – 7. He made his best-known coaching move in 1958, when he switched to an all-senior lineup with no one taller than 6 – 6 and went on an 11-game winning streak, which included the upset of West Virginia and two wins over nationally ranked State.

Bradley's worst record was his last, a 13 – 12 mark in 1959. Ironically, that was the only year he was selected ACC coach of the year, for directing a youthful and lightly regarded contingent to third place. Most of those players helped Bubas to win the ACC the next year.

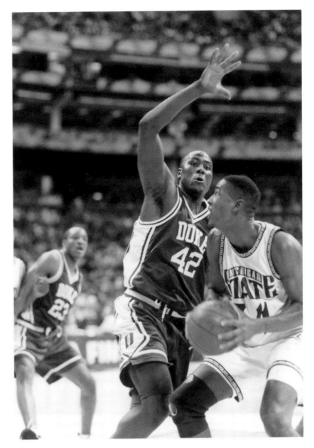

National player of the year Elton Brand powered Duke to the 1999 Final Four in his sophomore year.

Bradley left Duke for Texas, where he coached the Longhorns to three Southwest Conference titles before retiring in 1967. His overall college record: 50 – 18 at Hartwick, 167 – 78 at Duke, and 125 – 73 at Texas, for a 20-year total of 342 – 169.

Brand, Elton. When the ACC named its 50 best all-time basketball performers for the league's golden anniversary celebration of 2002 – 03, only three players with less than three years in the conference made the list. One of those was Elton Tyron Brand, a 6 – 8 power man from Peekskill, N.Y., who was the consensus national player of the year in 1999. And Brand barely had two seasons: as a freshman he suffered a broken foot that cost him most of the 1998 ACC regular season.

Brand appeared in 21 games as a rookie and all 39 in his sophomore year, when Duke went 37 – 2 and played for the national title. He scored 972 points for an average

The Game He'll Never Forget

Elton Brand, 1998 versus North Carolina

On Senior Day at Cameron in 1998, Tar Heel star Antawn Jamison scored just inside the 12-minute mark to put his club ahead 64–47. It was Jamison's 20th point of the day. But Duke rallied from 17 down to win 77–75 in a battle of the No. 1 and No. 3 teams in the country.

Part of the comeback story was Duke's ability to hold Jamison to one free throw and one tip-in over the last 11 minutes. Equally important was the Devils' attack mentality on the offensive end. Freshman Brand keyed the rally with five baskets in the paint over six possessions between the 10-minute and the 7-minute mark. It was only his third game back from a broken foot that had sidelined him for most of the ACC season, including the first UNC game in Chapel Hill.

"I had this jump hook over Jamison when he was a junior and the All-American that he was," Brand remembered. "Scoring on him and defending him and playing that game well really did a lot for my ego and for me. I will never forget that game."

The win was Coach K's 500th, and it wrapped up a 15–1 ACC season for the Blue Devils. Brand finished with 16 points off the bench.

of 16.2, and grabbed 536 rebounds for an 8.9 average. He also shot 61.2 percent from the field and blocked 113 shots.

Brand posted 19 double-doubles in 1999 and nearly averaged one, with 17.7 points and 9.8 rebounds. Both those figures ranked second in the ACC, while his 62.0 field goal percentage topped the league. As the most productive player on one of the school's most talented teams, he figured prominently in a landmark 19–0 ACC campaign during which the Blue Devils were rarely challenged. Brand was ACC player of the year, tournament MVP, and co-MVP of the team with fifth-year senior Trajan Langdon.

All that after being omitted from the starting lineup for two December games as a motivational move by coach Mike Krzyzewski. Chris Burgess started in Brand's spot for the Michigan and North Carolina A&T contests, but after Brand came off the bench to score 21 points against the Aggies (on 13-of-13 foul shooting), he was back in the lineup for good. Less than a month later

he turned in the best-scoring game of his career, with 33 points versus Virginia, as he hit 12 of 14 from the field and 9 of 10 from the line.

Brand's career rebounding high came earlier that year against Fresno State in the Great Alaska Shootout, when he had matching totals of 21 rebounds and 21 points.

After the season, with his coach's blessing, Brand became the first Duke player ever to declare for early entry to the NBA draft. His classmate William Avery and freshman Corey Maggette joined him in an unprecedented exodus. Brand was the first pick of the draft, won co-rookie of the year honors in 2000, made the All-Star Game in 2002 and 2006, and averaged 19.5 points plus 10.4 rebounds over his first six years in the league. He also played for USA Basketball in the 2002 World Championships. Brand was one of the charter inductees in the Duke Basketball Hall of Honor.

Brand, Joe. A native of Louisville, 6–1 forward Joe Brand lettered as a freshman Naval student and scored 28 points for the 1945 team that posted a 13–9 record and reached the championship game of the Southern Conference Tournament. Brand returned to play in six games and scored 14 points for the 1946 team but was not in the conference tournament.

Brey, Mike. After launching his coaching career as an assistant to the legendary Morgan Wootten at DeMatha High School, a famed basketball powerhouse in Hyattsville, Md., Mike Brey moved to the college game when he was hired by another legend-to-be, Mike Krzyzewski, to join the Duke staff. Brey spent eight seasons as a Blue Devil, from 1988 through 1995, developing a reputation as one of the top young coaches in the country while helping Duke to reach six Final Fours and win a pair of national titles.

A DeMatha alumnus, Brey played at Northwestern State and then transferred to George Washington University, graduating in 1982. In his subsequent five years as Wootten's assistant, DeMatha posted a 139–22 record. He got to know Krzyzewski and his assistants Bob Bender and Chuck Swenson during the Blue Devils' recruitment of DeMatha star Danny Ferry. When Swenson left the staff, Krzyzewski asked Brey to take his place even though he had no college experience.

Brey proved to be an ace recruiter as well as an on-the-court teacher for the Blue Devils. After the 1995 season he was hired at Delaware, where he spent five seasons as head coach and posted a 99 – 52 record with two NCAA berths. Then it was on to Notre Dame in 2001, when Matt Doherty left the Fighting Irish to go to North Carolina. Brey's first three Notre Dame teams reached the 20-win mark and went to the NCAA Tournament, an accomplishment enjoyed by no other coach in school history. Notre Dame hadn't been invited to the NCAA in the 11 seasons before Brey's arrival. Brey's 2002 season ended with a loss to Duke in the NCAA second round, while his 2003 team reached the Sweet 16 of the tournament. Through six years at Notre Dame (2001 – 06) Brey had a record of 118 – 70. His overall career record through 11 seasons as a head coach was 217 – 122, with five trips to the NCAA and four to the NIT.

Brickey, Robert. He made nearly 500 field goals during his four years in Duke blue, and just two of them were from the three-point arc. What Robert Christopher Brickey did as well as anyone was finish plays at the basket. And many of his finishes were in the form of acrobatic, high-wire slam dunks. Brickey counted 147 dunks among his 484 baskets and either owned or shared the team lead in dunks in all four of his seasons.

That Brickey stood just 6 – 5 only added to the excitement that he brought to the court. A high jumper for his high school track team in Fayetteville, N.C., Brickey was also a high jumper for Mike Krzyzewski. As a sophomore he usually jumped center to start the game, while his assortment of moves in the paint and in the air frequently had fans holding their collective breath waiting to see what he would do next. In his last two years, almost 35 percent of Brickey's field goals came on dunks (96 of 279).

From 1987 through 1990 Brickey played in 134 games with 84 starts, scored 1,299 points for a 9.7 average, and totaled 649 rebounds for a 4.8 average. He averaged scoring in double figures in each of his last three years, with a high of 11.7 as a senior. Brickey also used his jumping ability on the defensive end to block shots, leading the team in 1989 and posting 90 rejections for his career.

As a freshman Brickey earned the Ted Mann Jr. award as the reserve who contributed most to team morale. His

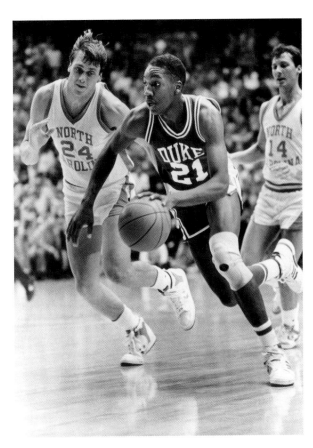

Though only 6 – 5, Robert Brickey handled the game-opening tipoffs in his sophomore year.

play against UNC in the regular-season finale made him ACC rookie of the week and earned him a start in the ACC Tournament when the regular Billy King was injured. As a sophomore Brickey produced a handful of 20-point games and again enjoyed a big moment against North Carolina. His last-second blocked shot ensured a 70 – 69 victory over the second-ranked Tar Heels, the first of three Duke wins over their rival that year. Brickey was at his best during the team's ACC Tournament championship run, when he had 16 points and 11 rebounds (with three dunks) in the semis against N.C. State. His 24 points and 24 rebounds in the tourney led him to a place on the all-tournament team.

Brickey offered more of the same as a junior, though his year ended on a down note when he was fouled and injured on a breakaway layup two minutes into the NCAA semifinals against Seton Hall. He got off to a fast start in 1990 as Duke's senior captain, topping the 20-point mark in three of the first five games. But an injury cost him eight games in the heart of the ACC schedule. By season's end he was one of the driving forces in a march to the Final Four, and his play in the national semis against Arkansas, when he had 17 points and 11 rebounds, helped push his team into the championship game.

Brickey played minor league basketball after Duke, worked in Christian ministry with the Young Life program, and later went into college coaching. He was an assistant coach at Army, SMU, and James Madison before taking over as the head coach of Shaw University in Raleigh beginning with the 2005–06 season.

Brill, Bill. Journalist Bill Brill has been a keen observer of Duke basketball since arriving at the school as a freshman in the fall of 1948, in the same class with one of the school's all-time great players, Dick Groat. Brill was a statistician for the basketball team during his undergraduate years, received his degree in 1952, and went on to an illustrious career as a sportswriter and columnist. He spent 30 years as the sports editor of the *Roanoke Times* in Virginia, during which time he was recognized as one of the most influential media figures in the Atlantic Coast Conference region. He was also known for astute commentary on national issues, including NCAA regulations and standards, and has covered more Final Fours than any other writer since 1962. After retiring from Roanoke, Brill moved to Durham and wrote briefly for the *Durham Herald-Sun*, while also becoming the lead columnist for *Blue Devil Weekly* upon its inception in 1991.

Brill was inducted into the U.S. Basketball Writers Hall of Fame and received the NCAA's Jake Wade Award for his lifetime contribution to intercollegiate athletics. He was enshrined in the Duke Sports Hall of Fame in 1996.

Brill has written several books on Duke basketball, including *Duke Basketball: An Illustrated History* (1986), *A Season Is a Lifetime* (1993, with Mike Krzyzewski), and *One Hundred Seasons: Duke Basketball, A Legacy of Achievement* (2004).

Brinn, Claude. A three-year starter from 1911 through 1913, Claudius Bertram "Little Jennie" Brinn, from Hertford, N.C., was a two-time Trinity team captain.

He teamed with his brother Joseph in 1911, captained the 1912 team, and returned as captain in 1913 when his brother was hired as the program's head coach. In 1912 Brinn scored 44 points in six games and reportedly allowed the players he guarded only one field goal all year. In the following year he moved from forward to guard and scored 31 field goals while allowing just 16.

Brinn, Joseph. A starting guard for the 1910 and 1911 Trinity teams, Joseph E. "Big Jennie" Brinn was hired as the Trinity head coach for the 1913 season. Technically he was the first person paid to coach basketball at the school; his own coach, program founder Cap Card, whose regular job was director of physical education, had not received any pay for organizing and coaching the first seven Trinity teams. Brinn, a 1911 Trinity grad from Hertford, N.C., guided his alma mater to an 11–8 record in his only coaching campaign. One of his key players was his brother Claude, who started at guard and served as team captain.

Brown, Hubie. One of the most knowledgeable basketball minds in the business spent four years percolating in the Duke basketball program. Hubert Jude Brown was hired by Vic Bubas as a 35-year-old to coach the freshman team for the 1969 season. He remained in Durham for four years, eventually becoming Bucky Waters's top assistant.

Between Bubas's departure and Waters's arrival, while Duke was without a head coach, Brown did much of the recruiting for a freshman class that posted an undefeated record in 1970. During Waters's first three years, he credited the brilliant tactician Brown with helping to develop a defense that allowed just 71 points a game. Duke posted a winning ACC record and advanced to a pair of NITs during that run.

Brown went on to greater fame after his tenure at Duke. He left the Blue Devils for an NBA assistant's job in Milwaukee, then became the head coach of the Kentucky Colonels and won an ABA title in 1975. He was head coach of the Atlanta Hawks from 1977 to 1981 and for the New York Knicks from 1983 to 1987, guiding his teams to playoff appearances in five of those 10 seasons.

Brown then spent 15 years as a basketball teacher at

coaching clinics while also working as an expert television analyst, twice earning Sports Emmy nominations. In 2000 he received the Curt Gowdy Electronic Media Award from the Basketball Hall of Fame.

Brown came out of coaching retirement to take over the Memphis Grizzlies on November 12, 2002. By the time he decided to retire again on November 25, 2004, he had coached the team to an 83 – 85 record and increased his NBA career victory total to 424, the seventh-best figure in NBA history. He was named NBA coach of the year in 2004 after guiding the franchise to its best record, 50 – 32, as well as its first playoff berth.

In 2005 Brown was enshrined in the Naismith Memorial Basketball Hall of Fame as a contributor to the game, along with college coaches Jim Boeheim, Jim Calhoun, and the late Sue Gunter, plus the great Brazilian women's star Hortencia.

Brown, Kenney. A 6 – 2 guard from Raleigh, Kenneth Bernard Brown played for the 1993 team as a walk-on, appearing in 15 games with four points and five rebounds. Brown was added to the roster after an open tryout on November 1 that attracted 72 students hoping to make the team. A sophomore, Brown had played intramural basketball the previous season while working as a manager for the women's team, for which he earned a letter. He was the only player selected from the tryout.

Brown, Ray. In his only season as a Duke letterman, Brown, a 6 – 3 native of Baltimore, scored 36 points as a reserve for the team that won the Southern Conference Tournament championship in 1941. He played mostly forward but had to man the center spot when Clyde Allen was injured. Brown scored 18 points in a backup role for the 1940 team.

Browne, Peppi. The ACC first selected an all-defensive women's team after the 2000 season. Browne, then a senior, had missed the second half of the conference season with an injury, but still she was voted to the team — a fitting tribute for the player whom coach Gail Goestenkors often referred to as the best defensive player in the country.

A 5 – 11 product of Silver Spring, Md., Browne was a fixture in the lineup for four years, 1997 – 2000. She played in 117 games and started 100, while scoring 1,132 points with 677 rebounds. She could put 20 points on the stats sheet on any given day and averaged scoring in double figures for two seasons. But where she really excelled was on defense and on the boards. Despite a significant height disadvantage, she spent most of her defensive minutes in the post, stopping bigger players or beating them for rebounds.

A classic overachiever who made her reputation on desire and intensity, Browne always wore her knee pads to work and never hesitated to take a charge or dive to the floor for a loose ball. She was emerging as one of the Blue Devils' best all-around players in her senior year, leading a team that had many holes to fill from a veteran Final Four squad the previous season.

"She is the only player in my coaching career who I've never had to yell at to give more in a practice or in a game," said Gail Goestenkors. "She's probably worth 28 – 30 points a game — the 14 she scores and the rest that she takes away from the opponent. She probably leads the world in hustle plays, too."

But as Duke was in the midst of a 43-point rout of UNC to close the first half of the conference slate, Browne suffered a knee injury while trying to finish a fast break, and her career suddenly came to an end. Duke lost its next two games but regrouped to finish 28 – 6 and win the first of five straight ACC tourneys. Based on just eight conference games, Browne was named to the All-ACC first team and the defensive team.

Browne was drafted by the WNBA after her senior year but was unable to play because of the injury.

Brunner, George. A native of West New York, N.J., Brunner, a 6 – 2 center, scored 40 points and lettered for the 1945 Duke team that won 11 of its 19 games and played for the Southern Conference title. He was scoreless in the championship game loss to North Carolina. A Naval student, he returned to play in 16 regular-season games for the 1946 team, scoring 31 points, but did not participate in the conference tournament.

Brunson, Stan. Believed to be the only athlete in NCAA history to play for Final Four teams in both men's soccer and men's basketball, Stanley Lamond Brunson, a 6 – 7 native of Newark, Del., served the Blue Devil basketball program as a reserve forward while lettering three times. Originally a soccer recruit, Brunson was a walk-on basketball player for the 1993 and 1994 seasons, then earned a basketball scholarship for 1995 and 1996. Brunson saw no game action in 1995 after suffering a knee injury on the first day of practice. But he returned from surgery to make a valuable contribution as a senior in 1996.

Brunson played in a total of 36 basketball games, scoring 17 points with 50 rebounds. By far his most productive year was 1996, when he scored 15 points and had 47 rebounds while logging 191 minutes in 21 games. He ranked eighth on the team in minutes, getting the opportunity for extended playing time when Carmen Wallace suffered an injury. One of his career highlights was at College Park, when Mike Krzyzewski chose him to make an inbounds pass with 3.6 seconds left against Maryland. Brunson was able to get the ball in play against the Terps' pressure, and his teammate Ricky Price hit a shot as time expired to give Duke a victory.

Brunson played soccer on a partial scholarship during his freshman fall of 1991 and scored two goals in 14 games. He was on Duke's NCAA semifinalist soccer team in 1992, playing in five games. After soccer season he tried out for the basketball coaches and was invited to join the squad when it returned from the Maui Invitational in late December. He appeared in eight games that year and played in seven games for the 1994 basketball team, the NCAA runner-up.

Bryan, Jay. A 6 – 8 forward from Lakewood, Colo., Jay B. Bryan was a four-year reserve, from 1982 to 1985. His career totals included 57 game appearances, with 62 points and 44 rebounds. Bryan's best year statistically was his freshman season of 1982, when he played in 21 games with two starts and posted his career high of 11 points against Virginia. Bryan improved his game but was used sparingly in 1983 and 1984, then was called on for relief work in 19 games in his senior year. Headed to law school after Duke, Bryan won the Dr. Deryl Hart award as the Devils' top scholar-athlete during his junior and senior seasons.

Bryant, D. After serving as scout team quarterback for the football program as a freshman in 1998, D. Bryant,

a 6 – 3 native of Detroit, joined the basketball team as a walk-on and contributed as a reserve for one of the Blue Devils' best seasons, 1999, when they were NCAA runner-ups. He saw action in 13 games, scoring eight points with three rebounds. Seven of his eight points were against Virginia, four in a home win and three in the ACC Tournament. Bryant played at the end of all three ACC tourney games and in the first three NCAA games. It was the only season of college basketball for the scholarship football player.

Bryant missed the 1999 football season, out of school as an academic casualty. He returned in the spring of 2000 and won the starting quarterback job during the 2000 fall campaign, which he kept through the 2001 season, passing for a total of 3,902 yards and 16 touchdowns. But Bryant was dismissed from school for academic reasons during the summer before what would have been his senior season.

Bryson, Ed. A native of Durham who was a three-sport athlete for Baylor Military Academy in Tennessee, Edwin C. Bryson played for the Duke varsity in 1956 and 1957 with 13 total appearances, four points, and eight rebounds.

Bubas, Vic. Duke's best team of the roaring sixties, in 1966, placed third in the NCAA Tournament — exactly what *Sports Illustrated* had predicted in its preseason issue. The magazine may have presented an accurate forecast, but it couldn't resist a sarcastic overview of coach Vic Bubas's operation. References to Duke's "battery of blond secretaries" answering the office phones and staff meetings "that would make a Cabinet session appear spontaneous" colored the analysis, with the declaration that all critical information would be "brought to the attention of Bubas later in the board of directors room, recorded in triplicate and carefully filed. And that is one way to run a basketball team."

In the case of Victor Albert Bubas, one of the first college coaches to run a basketball team with the vision and efficiency of a corporate CEO, the results more than validated the process. Bubas directed the Blue Devils for exactly one decade, 1960 through 1969, and there was only one coach on the planet who accomplished more during that time — UCLA's John Wooden. Bubas's teams

In his first season, Vic Bubas coached the Blue Devils past St. Joseph's and into an NCAA regional championship game.

reached the ACC championship game in eight of his 10 years and won the title four times; they made the first three Final Four trips in school history and played for the national championship once (losing to Wooden); they were ranked in the top 10 of the final AP national poll seven times; and overall they won 213 games against just 67 losses.

Bubas elevated the profile of Duke basketball from regional to national. The Blue Devils had participated in the NCAA Tournament just once before his arrival, as a replacement for N.C. State (then on probation). But Duke earned a bid in Bubas's first year and went three more times. Given that the only method of entry during that era was winning a conference championship, Bubas concentrated on ACC superiority and was wildly successful. Thirty-five years after his retirement, Bubas's overall conference record of 106 – 32 still stood as the best winning percentage in league history (76.8), as did his 22 – 6 mark in the ACC Tournament (78.6). Overall, during the middle eight years of his reign the Blue Devils won 81

percent of their games, went 76 – 5 at home, and posted a 91 – 24 mark against the ACC. From 1961 to 1967 Duke's record of 159 – 37 was the best in the nation.

Bubas was one of 135 candidates, 15 finalists, and six interviewees to replace Hal Bradley as the Duke coach. Director of athletics Eddie Cameron made the call, and it was greeted with concern in some quarters. Just imagine what it would be like, decades later, if Johnny Dawkins were hired to coach at UNC or Phil Ford at N.C. State. Bubas's appointment was no less bold a move by Cameron. Bubas had been a key recruit and floor leader for Final Four teams at N.C. State and then had worked for eight years as an assistant to a legend, Everett Case.

But he silenced any concerns by taking a .500 team to the ACC Tournament championship in his first year. During his fourth year, Duke posted its first-ever perfect league mark, going 27 – 3 overall, and Bubas gained early entry into a most select club: those who both played and coached in the Final Four. The membership list includes only six names.

Following the example set by his mentor Case, Bubas was an innovative CEO. He started a basketball camp, a weekly television show, and ladies' clinics. He added names to the backs of the jerseys, brought in a pep band and dancing girls to the Indoor Stadium, and favored a fast-paced, fan-friendly offensive attack. His recruiting, national in scope and highly organized, lured several future Duke Hall of Famers to campus, beginning with his pioneer player, Art Heyman, who had committed to UNC before Bubas was hired. And Bubas always insisted on surrounding himself with excellent assistants. Coaches Bucky Waters, Fred Shabel, Tom Carmody, Chuck Daly, and Hubie Brown all went on to head coaching positions.

Bubas's first Final Four team in 1963 was ranked No. 2 in the country but was blasted in the semifinals by No. 3 Loyola of Chicago. The next year, Duke was No. 3 when it earned a payback win over No. 2 Michigan in the semis before succumbing to top-ranked UCLA in the final. The 1965 team, an offensive juggernaut that averaged 92 points a game, might have gone just as far but was upset in the ACC semifinals by an emotional N.C. State team playing on its home floor. In 1966 Bubas's most complete team faced Kentucky in the semifinals in a matchup of No. 2 and No. 1. One of his prime offensive weapons, guard Bob Verga, was weakened from a bout of strep throat, and the Wildcats advanced.

Bubas's only mediocre team was his last one, which went 15–13, but even that one tied for third in the ACC, rose up at the end to upset No. 2 UNC in the home finale, and made it to the conference championship game before a 40-point explosion by UNC's Charlie Scott pulled the curtain on the Bubas era.

After resigning from the head coaching position at the age of 42, Bubas remained on campus for another seven years working for the university administration. Then he was hired as the first commissioner of the Sun Belt Conference and served from 1976 to 1990. During that time he spent five years on the NCAA Basketball Committee, at a time when decisions were made to expand the field to 64 teams and use domed stadiums for the Final Four.

Bubas was enshrined in the Duke Sports Hall of Fame in 1977, and the concourse at Cameron Indoor Stadium was named in his honor in 2001. In 1996 the Naismith Memorial Basketball Hall of Fame presented him with the John Bunn Award, its most prestigious honor short of enshrinement, for his great contributions to the game.

"The whole thing in coaching is getting good players, keeping good players, and not messing them up. He was a master at all three," noted Waters, his assistant and successor. "I think Vic Bubas deserves to be in the Hall of Fame for everything he contributed to college basketball. He was a coach, a conference commissioner and the chairman of the NCAA Tournament committee. He built something special at Duke, there's no question about that."

Buckheit, George. The predecessor to Eddie Cameron as head basketball coach, George Clifford Buckheit guided the Blue Devils during their first four seasons after Trinity College became Duke University. His teams combined for a 25–36 record from 1925 through 1928, with a winning record of 9–5 in his final season. He also was the assistant director of physical education, coached the track and cross-country teams, and assisted Howard Jones in guiding the football team. A Kentucky grad, Buckheit was his alma mater's head coach for five years before coming to Duke. His record there, from 1920 to 1924, was 44–27. Buckheit was a native of Beardsville, Ill., and a graduate of the University of Illinois, where he competed in football, basketball, and track.

Buckley, Clay. The senior co-captain of Duke's 1991 NCAA championship team, James Clay Buckley, a 6–10 center from Wayne, Pa., fulfilled a reserve role for four teams that reached the Final Four. He appeared in 86 games during his tenure, 1988–91, with 148 points and 88 rebounds. He hit 60 percent of his field goals. A chronic back injury limited his development and cut into his playing time.

Buckley's career high came with nine points against Harvard in 1990. He had one career start, and it was a significant one. In the lineup for his last home game versus Clemson in 1991, he battled the Tigers' standout center Dale Davis and finished with six points and six rebounds. Buckley and his four-year roommate Greg Koubek left the game in the closing minutes to a tremendous ovation after securing a perfect record of 16–0 at home. Buckley then followed with several productive minutes in the finale at UNC as his team wrapped up the regular-season crown.

In the 1960s Buckley's father Jay started at center for Duke's first two Final Four teams.

Buckley, Dan. A 5–8 guard from New York City, Buckley lettered for the 1945 team that reached the Southern Conference Tournament championship game. As an ROTC student from Jacksonville Naval Station, he scored 88 points while playing only in weekend games because of a heavy load of military studies. An excellent floor leader and defensive star of the conference tournament, Buckley was chosen to the all-tournament first team.

Buckley, Jay. As a starting big man for Duke's first two Final Four teams, Jay Lynn Buckley was an essential part of coach Vic Bubas's program in the early 1960s. A 6–10 center and a brilliant science student from Cheverly, Md., Buckley totaled 926 points and 714 rebounds as a three-year fixture in the lineup while appearing in 85 of Duke's 86 games from 1962 through 1964. After a solid sophomore year during which he developed into a starter, Buckley had superb averages of 11.2 points and 9.9 rebounds as a junior, then 13.8 points and 9.0 rebounds as a senior. Often used in a double-post arrangement with his fellow 6–10 pivotman Hack Tison, Buckley became a more physical presence as he gained weight and strength over the course of his career. He owned a proficient hook shot with either hand and made 57.1 percent of his 617 career field-goal attempts, a school record at the time for players with at least 300 made baskets. During his junior year, Buckley's field goal percentage of 59.9 ranked third in the nation and led the ACC.

One of Buckley's most spectacular games was in the national semifinals of 1964, his senior year, when he had team highs of 25 points and 14 rebounds to spark a 91–80 victory over Michigan that sent the Blue Devils to their first national championship game. Tison also had a double-double, with 12 points and 13 boards. Buckley hit 11 of 16 from the field in that game, as the Devils avenged an early-season loss to the Wolverines. Buckley then had 18 points and nine rebounds in his last game, a loss in the NCAA finals to UCLA.

Buckley led Duke in scoring six times in 1964, high-lighted by a 26-point performance in a one-point win over Wake Forest. He made the All-ACC second team in 1964 and twice was an ACC All-Tournament pick: second team in 1963 and first team in 1964, when he had 21 and 20 points in Duke's first two games to lead the Devils to the championship contest. Then in the final he put up 18 points and 18 rebounds in a wipeout of Wake Forest. After his retirement, Bubas referred to Buckley as the best defensive center of his tenure.

Also noted for his academic prowess, Buckley worked on a special grant for NASA in the summer before his senior year. He was a member of the ACC's first two ACC All-Academic basketball teams and of the national Academic All-America team in both 1963 and 1964.

Buckley was followed at Duke by his son Clay, a 6–10 center who was senior co-captain of the team that won the NCAA championship in 1991.

Buckner, Andre. Recruited to provide roster depth after a heavy departure of players in 1999, Andre Deizmond Buckner spent four years as a reserve for the Blue Devils. A 5–10 guard from Hopkinsville, Ky., Buckner played in 84 games from 2000 to 2003, with 55 points, 29 rebounds, and 27 assists. His most productive game was against Winthrop in the NCAA Tournament in 2002, when he had five points and four assists in 12 minutes. His most chronicled move, though, was in the regular-season finale in Chapel Hill in 2003, when he charged off the bench to support assistant coach Chris Collins after UNC coach Matt Doherty instigated a brief altercation late in the tense battle. All three were later reprimanded by the ACC office.

Most of Buckner's contributions came behind the scenes as a practice player, leader of the Blue squad, and vocal supporter of his teammates. He won the Ted Mann Jr. award as the reserve contributing most to team morale in his senior year. He also tried to set the stage for a post-basketball career by recording a pair of CDs of his own hip-hop and rap songs, and by launching a family entertainment business with his two brothers, Greg and Maurice. Greg played at Clemson before going on to an NBA career.

Buhowsky, Tony. After starting for the 1955 freshman team, Anthony William Carl Buhowsky, a 6–9 center from Roselle Park, N.J., lettered one year for the varsity, 1956, when he had 27 points and 33 rebounds in 15 games. Buhowsky reached double figures in one game, with 10 points against Wake Forest.

Bullock, Ed. A four-year player for the basketball and football teams as well as a track standout, Edward Junius Bullock, of Baltimore, was a fixture in the starting lineup for the last two Trinity teams (1923 – 24) and the first two Duke teams (1925 – 26). He was captain of the 1925 team.

Burbage, J. S. Trinity College's last head basketball coach, Jesse Samuel Burbage, recorded marks of 15 – 7 in 1923 and 19 – 6 in 1924. Trinity became Duke University at the start of the 1925 season. A native of Birmingham, Ala., Burbage was a four-year guard on the Auburn basketball team before graduating in 1918. He coached a Birmingham high school to the state crown in 1919 and enjoyed a successful tenure at Georgia Military Academy before coming to Trinity, where he also served as head track coach, assistant football coach, and assistant director of physical training.

Burch, Edgar. One of three freshmen on the varsity roster during coach Neill McGeachy's only Duke season of 1974, Edgar Roland Burch, a 6 – 3 guard from Pontiac, Mich., played in more games, scored more points, and secured more rebounds than either of his fellow recruits, Tate Armstrong and Mark Crow. His quick start included double-figures scoring in four of the Blue Devils' first six games, while later in the year he had 20 points against the eventual NCAA champion N.C. State (on 10-of-15 shooting) and a team-high 12 in a loss at third-ranked Notre Dame. But while Armstrong and Crow went on to productive four-year careers, Burch lasted just one season in Durham. He missed the last three regular-season games because of illness and did not return to the team the following year. His one-year statistics included 157 points and 33 rebounds in 23 games.

Burdette, Jeff. A reserve guard from Buena Park, Calif., Jeffrey Joe Burdette quarterbacked the Duke freshman team in 1971 and then lettered for three years in the var-

sity backcourt, 1972 – 74. He finished with 59 points and 66 assists in 57 games. Burdette saw his most action as a sophomore in 1972, when he had 40 points and 33 assists in 24 games, with a career high of six points against Wake Forest. A defensive ace and solid playmaker, he also performed well in running the team in a near-upset of 10th-ranked Penn.

Burger, Bud. A two-year assistant coach under Gerry Gerard, Bud Burger was head coach for the Duke freshman teams of 1946 – 47.

Burgess, Chris. Considered one of the best high school players in the country, Burgess, a 6 – 10 center from Irvine, Calif., enrolled at Duke along with a star-studded recruiting class in the fall of 1997. He stayed two years, during which time he played in 75 games, logged over 1,000 minutes, scored 367 points, and grabbed 268 rebounds. But after his sophomore year of 1999 came to an end, Burgess decided to transfer to Utah, feeling that its program would better develop him for a pro career. He completed his college eligibility there in 2002, was drafted by some minor pro leagues, and eventually played in Europe.

Burgess averaged 4.9 points during his Duke career and almost 10 points a game during an injury-plagued tenure at Utah. His decision to transfer baffled many, including Blue Devil coaches, because had he stayed he would have been the prime candidate for the starting center position in his junior year.

During Duke's Final Four season of 1999, Burgess appeared in all 39 games, starting in 13, and averaged 15.6 minutes. He was efficient around the basket, hitting over 60 percent of his field goals, and was third on the team in blocked shots, behind only Elton Brand and Shane Battier. He even went outside and hit a couple of three-point shots. One of his best games was against Fresno State in the Great Alaska Shootout, when he started in place of a flu-stricken Battier and totaled 15 points, six assists, and a career-high 16 rebounds. He had another double-double later in the year, with 11 points and 10 rebounds at DePaul, and hit 8 of 9 shots for 16 points in a rout of Michigan.

Burgin, George. After lettering for one season in high school basketball, August George Burgin, a 7–0 center from Fairfax, Va., spent three years as a reserve for the Blue Devils, 1987–89. He played in 38 games with 28 points and 17 rebounds. He made 11 of his 19 field-goal attempts.

Burgin arrived at Duke for the 1986 season but red-shirted for academic reasons; his double major in mechanical engineering and computer science required five years to complete, so he spent his first year trying to develop his lanky frame. He saw limited action off the bench in the next three seasons, totaling 28, 33, and 32 minutes. He did not use his fourth season of eligibility in 1990.

Burt, Ron. During his sophomore and junior years, Ronald Gene Burt II, a 6–0 guard and engineering student from Kansas City, played for an intramural squad known as the Dream Team, which claimed the campus championship in both years. As a senior, Burt lived a different dream. On the opening day of varsity basketball practice, he participated in a tryout with 37 other students and was invited to join the Blue Devils. Burt saw reserve action in 19 games, as Duke rolled to a 34–2 record and claimed the NCAA title in 1992. Burt contributed 10 points with eight assists and two rebounds.

Butler, Marshall. After playing freshman ball in 1925, Marshall W. Butler, of Durham, started for the Duke varsity in 1926 and 1927 and was captain of the 1927 squad.

Butters, Tom. During his 20 years as Duke's director of athletics, Tom Butters raised millions of dollars, improved facilities, insisted on excellence with integrity in his programs, and ushered a department fixated on past glories into the modern era of intercollegiate sports. But he will always be best remembered for two personnel decisions early in his tenure: hiring basketball coach Mike Krzyzewski in 1980 and extending Krzyzewski's contract in the middle of the 1984 season.

Those two moves are regarded as brilliant strokes of administrative genius — unexpected, prescient, and far-reaching. But as visionary as they appear in retrospect, they were far from universally applauded when they occurred. Krzyzewski was a young coach who'd never been to the NCAA Tournament and was coming off a 9–17 season at Army when Butters hired him on the recommendation of Bob Knight and at the urging of his associate director Steve Vacendak. This was at a time when Duke fans were heady with expectations, as their school had just competed in three straight NCAA tourneys, won two ACC titles, and appeared in a Final Four under Bill Foster.

"He was probably too young and he probably lacked the right kind of experience to come into the Atlantic Coast Conference," Butters recalled. "But I couldn't wait on him to get older or get more experience. If we were going to attract this kind of coach, then we were going to have to do it right then. In some respects, I think he would agree, he had to learn on the job basketball at this level, and he was a quick study."

Krzyzewski endured 17-loss seasons in his second and third years, and some of the team's supporters were getting restless entering his fourth season. Butters decided to extend his contract in January. The day the announcement was made, the Blue Devils lost to N.C. State to drop Krzyzewski's overall record to 52–52. But Butters was undeterred. "It had become abundantly clear that this man could not only coach, he could recruit," Butters noted. "In every way he represented Duke as I felt the university should be represented. To me it was precisely the right time to extend that contract, and it worked."

Butters's tenure at Duke spanned 30 years. A graduate of Ohio Wesleyan and a former pitcher for the Pittsburgh Pirates, he arrived in 1967 as director of special events, coached the baseball team, and created the Iron Dukes fund-raising organization. In 1977 he was tapped to replace Carl James as director of athletics, and he served in that post until his retirement in 1997. He was regarded as a superb fund raiser, no-nonsense administrator, and savvy negotiator. As a member of the NCAA Basketball Committee from 1989 to 1994, he was instrumental in the $1 billion deal struck with CBS Sports for the broadcast rights to March Madness. Closer to home, he raised millions of dollars to update many dilapidated facilities for athletes and students, initiated a scholarship endowment program that helped Duke to focus its resources in sports that could be competitive for championships, and always went to great lengths to find the right fit in personnel decisions. In 2005, 11 of the 19 head coaches on staff had been hired by Butters almost a decade or more before.

Butters was an avid golfer. Struck by a heart attack on a golf course in Baltimore during the summer of 1997, he underwent quadruple bypass surgery and announced his intention to retire shortly thereafter. In 1999 he was inducted into the Duke Sports Hall of Fame, which is located in a building named in his honor, the Schwartz-Butters Center adjacent to Cameron Indoor Stadium.

"For me it was a hard job, a wonderfully hard job, because I took seriously what this university was about and what our role in this university was," Butters said. "We always recognized here that intercollegiate athletics was only a small complementary part of what this university is, and I hope it always remains that way."

Caldbeck, Justin. A 6–3 guard from Shelburne, Vt., Justin Hiley Caldbeck was a walk-on member of the 1997 Duke team in his sophomore year and the 1999 Final Four team in his senior year. In between the two campaigns he studied abroad at the London School of Economics and averaged 25 points a game for his team. In two years at Duke he appeared in 29 games, scoring 13 points and adding 16 rebounds. His younger brother Ryan played with him on the 1999 team. In 1997 Caldbeck shared the Ted Mann Jr. award as the reserve contributing most to team morale.

Caldbeck, Ryan. After serving as a student manager for the 1998 Blue Devils, Ryan Matthew Caldbeck, a 6–3 guard from Shelburne, Vt., spent the next three seasons as a reserve walk-on player. He appeared in 33 career games, with eight points and 13 rebounds. He joined his brother Justin on the 1999 team, when Ryan was a sophomore and Justin a senior. Ryan played in 12 contests for the 1999 Final Four team while Justin appeared in 20. Ryan took the court during 13 games of the 2001 NCAA title season, including the ACC championship game.

Caldwell, Herschel. Generations of Duke athletes were touched by the coaching of Herschel Caldwell. He arrived at Duke in 1930 and remained with the athletics department through his retirement in 1971. Best remembered as an assistant football coach under five head coaches, Caldwell also influenced many young basketball players as the long-time freshman coach for Eddie Cameron.

Caldwell was hired as director of freshman athletics in 1930 and coached the freshman basketball, football, and baseball teams. Before he was elevated to varsity football assistant coach in 1946 — a role he held until his retirement — he prepped dozens of Duke basketball talents for their future success. In 1935 – 36 he recorded a remarkable feat with his freshman teams; they had achieved records of 17 – 1 in basketball, 11 – 1 in baseball, and 5 – 0 in football, for an overall mark of 33 – 2. All three teams won Big Five titles.

A former Alabama football player, Caldwell was inducted into the Duke Sports Hall of Fame in 1981 and died in 1989 at the age of 85.

Cameron Crazies. See Cameron Indoor Stadium.

Cameron, Eddie. Make no mistake, football was the king of sports at Duke when Eddie Cameron first arrived on campus in 1926, and it still reigned supreme when he hung up his basketball whistle in 1942. A football standout at Washington & Lee, Cameron coached the freshman football team as his first job at Duke. During his 14-year career as head basketball coach, he was also the football backfield coach, chief scout, and recruiter extraordinaire. That's just the way it was done in those days: most of the football assistants doubled as coaches in other sports. And for what position did Cameron eventually relinquish his basketball duties? The position of head football coach, when resident legend Wallace Wade went off to war.

But as closely aligned as Cameron always was with the university's football fortunes, he will always be regarded as the person who elevated the profile of the basketball program beyond the borders of North Carolina, brought it its first taste of greatness, and constructed the foundation from which future glories sprang.

A native of Irwin, Pa., Edmund McCullough Cameron was less than five years removed from his college graduation when he took over the basketball coaching

From 135 candidates, Eddie Cameron hired N.C. State's Vic Bubas as the Duke coach in 1959.

duties at Duke for the 1928–29 season. The program had enjoyed just one winning season in the previous four, and this was its initial foray in the Southern Conference. Relying on a core of players recruited from Washington, D.C., Cameron directed his first team to a 12–8 mark and a stunning march to the finals of the conference tournament. The next year the Devils had a 15-game winning streak, reached the finals once more, and finished 18–2. One of the early recruits, Bill Werber, was named the first basketball All-America in school history, and the die was cast. Duke would now be a player on the basketball scene.

Cameron led the program from 1929 to 1942, winning 226 games while losing only 99. He was the school's winningest coach until Mike Krzyzewski surpassed his victory total in 1990. Duke reached the Southern Conference championship game eight times under Cameron's guidance and claimed the title in 1938, 1941, and 1942. The 1938 championship, in the first year in which jump balls after every basket were eliminated, was one of the coach's most unlikely success stories. The team, nicknamed the "never a dull moment boys," was erratic all season and wouldn't have been in the tourney were it not for an upset of UNC in the regular-season finale.

Cameron's only losing season was in the following year, at 10–12. His best year was his last, as Duke went 15–1 in the conference and 22–2 overall, sweeping its Big Four rivals and rolling through the tournament. The fledgling NCAA Tournament invited only eight teams at that time, and Kentucky was the only pick from the South.

Cameron's reach and influence in basketball extended well beyond wins and losses. He significantly improved scheduling, getting the Duke name into areas such as Philadelphia, New York, and Washington. At a time when most schools began regular-season play in January, Cameron instituted an annual December trip of three or four games to get his team better prepared. And of course, he was one of the primary figures in the development of the stadium eventually named for him. Built with funds from the football team's appearance in the Rose Bowl in 1939, the arena was a revolutionary facility, the biggest and most spectacular in the South. It opened in January 1940 and Cameron coached just 32 games there before stepping down as head coach. But then and now, it would rank as one of the program's most favorable assets.

During the war Cameron coached the football program to a record of 25–11–1, its first bowl win at the Sugar Bowl in 1945, and a 5–0 mark against rival UNC. He also served as athletics director in Wade's absence, and a year after Wade returned to football Cameron was permanently installed in the AD's chair, a position he held until 1972. In this administrative capacity, Cameron provided comprehensive direction to Duke basketball, Duke athletics, and the entire Atlantic Coast Conference.

Everett Case's arrival at N.C. State in the late 1940s is rightly credited with prodding an explosion of interest in basketball in the South. But Cameron's influence should not be ignored. He was one of the founding fathers of the ACC and even came up with the name of the new league. A staunch proponent of postseason basketball, Cameron had been chairman of the Southern Conference Tournament since 1935 and continued in that role with the ACC Tournament until his retirement in 1972. His leadership behind the scenes had a direct impact on the conference's financial health and the event's ascension as a national kingpin and as the model for other leagues.

Cameron was also a strong supporter of C. D. Chesley's efforts to bring ACC basketball to television, and

Cameron Indoor Stadium was ranked the fourth-best sporting venue in the world by *Sports Illustrated*.

he used his contacts in the industry to secure many TV dates for the Blue Devils (in both basketball and football). Day to day, his alliances with his counterparts in Raleigh, Chapel Hill, and College Park helped shape conference policy.

Cameron made the Indoor Stadium available for a wide range of civic and basketball events, including a popular prep tourney, the Southern Conference tourney when it outgrew Raleigh's municipal auditorium, and even an NCAA game for Case's Wolfpack when an opponent refused to play on State's home floor. It was Cameron's persistence that brought Bill Murray to Duke to continue the football tradition that Wade had established, and his vision that put an N.C. State alumnus, Vic Bubas, in Duke blue, emphatically driving the basketball program into powerhouse territory.

Duke Indoor Stadium was named in Cameron's honor on January 22, 1972, just as he was about to retire after 46 years of service to Duke. Some consider the university's prestigious golf course another memorial to Cameron, as he came up with the idea, raised the funds,

and coddled the project to completion in the late 1950s.

Cameron was enshrined as a charter member of the Duke Sports Hall of Fame in 1975 and was also inducted in the North Carolina, Virginia, and College Football halls of fame. He died on November 25, 1988, at the age of 86.

Cameron Indoor Stadium. In March 1973, the day before Duke lost an opening-round contest in the ACC Tournament to complete its first losing season in 34 years, the outspoken television analyst Billy Packer told the Durham Sports Club what the Blue Devils needed to do to bounce back. He didn't suggest a new coach; he suggested a new gym.

"Duke has the worst gym in the ACC," Packer said. "An 18-year-old boy today is impressionable. And the Duke gym doesn't make a good impression on someone who is deciding where to play college basketball."

Most people associated with Duke basketball are glad the school didn't follow Packer's advice. Cameron Indoor Stadium remains the oldest gym in the conference

Duke's student fans have been known as the Cameron Crazies since the 1980s.

and has its drawbacks, but the home-court atmosphere and the advantage it provides on game night is one of the basketball program's most prized assets.

"I would never want to change venues," coach Mike Krzyzewski said some 30 years after Packer's quip. "To say that we would be able to take the spirit of Cameron and place it in a 16,000-seat arena across the street, I'm not sure that that's done."

The stadium opened in 1940, which made it 65 years old when Duke celebrated its first century of basketball in 2005. Every other school in the ACC had been through at least two arenas during that time, and five were using home facilities that were younger than most of the players who competed in them. But Duke was not even considering an upgrade to a bigger house. Cameron's character, charm, intimacy, tradition, and notoriety made it a unique setting for college basketball, one that *Sports Illustrated* rated as the fourth-best sporting venue worldwide of the twentieth century, behind only Yankee Stadium, Augusta National, and Michie Stadium, and ahead of classics such as Wrigley Field, Fenway Park, Roland Garros, and Lambeau Field.

Legend has it that the stadium's namesake Eddie Cameron and Wallace Wade concocted the original outline for a new arena on the back of a matchbook. When the architects' initial sketches were presented, the facil-

ity was dome-shaped and had 5,000 seats. Duke sent the designers back to the drawing board. They returned with a structure that could seat about 9,000 and would be the largest basketball facility in the country south of the Palestra in Philadelphia.

The project cost $400,000 and took less than a year to construct. The seed money came from the football team's participation in the Rose Bowl in 1939, and the debt was retired with funds from the 1945 Sugar Bowl. When 8,000 fans showed up for the christening on January 6, 1940 — a victory over Princeton — it was the largest crowd ever to see a basketball game in the South.

"The idea was to accommodate the crowd. We had already outgrown two gymnasiums," Cameron told Durham sports editor Art Chansky in 1974. "The portable bleachers bring the students closer to the court, and we could have never sold the idea to the administration without those seats. Folding them up gives us three more courts crosswise that are used for intramurals."

Cameron coached the Blue Devils during the first three years of the stadium's existence, 1940–42. It was not given his name until 30 years after he gave up the basketball post, upon his retirement in 1972 from a distinguished career as director of athletics.

From the beginning the facility encompassed much more than basketball, as it was used for graduation exercises, countless concerts, benefit performances, and rallies, and a wide assortment of activities in and out of sport. In its early years, the Indoor Stadium hosted a prominent high school basketball tourney to showcase the local powerhouse Durham High; it staged the Southern Conference Tournament for four years after the event outgrew its traditional home in Raleigh; it hosted an NCAA Tournament game for N.C. State in the 1950s; and it was the site of the first MEAC Tournament in 1972.

Considered palatial when it opened, Cameron gradually became one of the smaller arenas in big-time basketball as numerous universities turned to facilities with close to twice its capacity. Duke also did little to enhance the building for decades, which is why Packer had a point when he noted its questionable role in recruiting. But the school made some major cosmetic enhancements in the 1980s and began to celebrate its heritage with the addition of several historical displays and a new concourse after 2000. Those improvements, combined with frequent exposure on national television, helped the perception of Cameron evolve into that of a basketball shrine or landmark. It became commonplace for visitors to stop by the gym at all hours just to look inside or take a picture of this Gothic playpen with the ancient tradition and mystique.

In the field of stadium architecture, it became popular in the early 1990s to design new facilities with a retro look. There was no need for that at Duke; Cameron was the real deal.

Seating and walkways are tight and cramped, making the logistics difficult for TV and other media, and the Duke coaches no longer consider the building adequate for practice (hence the plan to develop an adjacent $15 million training center). But when public address announcer Art Chandler proclaims, "Here comes Duke" and the students start bopping up and down as the ball is tipped, the atmosphere for the ensuing two hours is unmatched in college basketball. Duke players have appreciated that environment for years. Nearly all of them can remember a time walking up to the gym before a big game where they saw their fellow students waiting outside and could feel their boost.

When former All-America Jeff Mullins returned to campus to have his jersey retired in 1994, he felt com-

pelled to mention the role of Duke's home court support to the team's exceptional winning percentage (82.5) at Cameron. "I would like to be the first to say that the next thing to be put up in Cameron should be something about the Duke fan," he noted. "I'm speaking not about the Duke fan of today that gets tremendous recognition, but primarily for the fans of the sixties, that were every bit as good, every bit as creative, had every bit as much fun, but just didn't get the national attention."

Fans weren't known as the Cameron Crazies in Mullins's day. That designation came along in the 1980s, when preening for television cameras became almost as important as cheering for the Blue Devils. But the zany, creative behavior and vociferous backing provided by the fans, particularly the students, predates even Mullins's era of the early 1960s. When N.C. State paid a visit in the 1950s, one of the students ringing the sideline jumped on to the court near the end of the game and slapped at a loose ball. A State player trying to reach the ball collided with the student, a short incident flared, and Duke was assessed a technical foul. Wolfpack assistant coach Vic Bubas pointed out the guilty student, who was removed from the gym. Eventually Duke moved its press tables courtside to provide a buffer between the floor and the students.

Many of the Cameron Crazies' antics have taken on legendary proportions. Pick an opponent, and a list of related pranks or invectives can be recited by long-time crowd watchers. Take Maryland, for example. There was the time in the 1970s when a student wearing a Bozo the Clown wig and plastic red nose jumped into the Maryland layup line right behind the red-headed Terp forward Jim O'Brien. Or the time a student put money on the floor and dared long-range shooter Brian Magid to hit a pre-game basket from that spot (he did, and slipped the bill in his shorts). Or the many times the students poked fun at Lefty Driesell, Maryland's coach and a Duke alumnus, with skin caps featuring a gas meter pointing to empty. One year, when Lefty had a cast on his leg, a few kids got casts on their own legs to aid in their mockery.

One of the more vile displays by the students came at the expense of Maryland's Herman Veal in 1984, a year after he'd been accused of some sexual improprieties. The *Washington Post* ripped the "several thousand Duke students majoring in smartass [and] chanting close to the ultimate in filth" at Veal. They cleaned up their act but didn't forget the criticism. The next time N.C. State came to town, a placard declaring, "If you can't go to college, go to State" had an addendum: "If you can't go to State, write for the *Washington Post*."

Local rivals State and UNC often provided the fodder for the Crazies' hijinks. During the 1970s and 1980s it became habitual, if highly improper, for students to throw items on the floor during pre-game introductions. Someone threw a potato on the court when Wolfpack player Spud Webb was announced. Other players who had been linked with pilfering aspirin, pizza, and underwear had those things tossed in their direction during their intros. When Chris Washburn was accused of stealing a stereo, the Blue Devil mascot wheeled a shopping cart filled with stereo components onto the floor. One time a student dressed in drag showed up on the court during the national anthem and lip-synched part of the song, mimicking State coach Norm Sloan's wife, who sang the anthem at Wolfpack home games.

The "Airball" chant was a Cameron original in 1979 when North Carolina's only two shots in a 7 – 0 first half against Duke came up empty. UNC's Steve Hale, suffering from a collapsed lung, heard "In-Hale, Ex-Hale." Tar Heel Jeff McInnis heard much worse after an altercation with reserve guard Jay Heaps late in a game in 1996. The students thundered a vulgarity, which ignited some pointed public comments from Dean Smith and a rebuttal from Krzyzewski. In 2004, with former Kansas coach Roy Williams making his first trip to Duke as UNC's head coach, several students dressed as characters from *The Wizard of Oz* set up a makeshift yellow brick road outside the opponents' locker room and let Williams know that he wasn't in Kansas anymore.

"It is almost like their gym is a big high school gym in a sense," said UNC's Raymond Felton, point guard for the Tar Heels when they won the NCAA championship in 2005. "It's great, though. The fans make you laugh, the things they do. I saw a guy in a bikini in the stands last year. It gets crazy over there, but you know, that is what the excitement is all about."

"Everybody knows that it's always tough to play there," added UNC center Sean May. "One, because it's so hot and two, because of the fans. But the fans aren't the most brutal; they're just the most clever. And they come up with some clever things. My experiences there the last two years have been fun. I like playing in a hostile environment like that."

"They're incredible," former Georgia Tech coach Bobby Cremins once told the *Atlanta Journal-Constitution*. "They're my favorite fans in the league. They do things so creative. I had a jacket with patches on the sleeves that I got from a tournament. They destroyed me."

If an opposing player has been involved in any embarrassing situation or legal transgression, chances are the Cameron Crazies will know about it and use it. For years most of their chants were totally spontaneous, and would spread throughout the crowd at the spur of the moment, precisely the right moment. Common instigators were the guys from BOG, a campus living group whose members used to sit behind the opposing bench and make life miserable for the visitors. (They were eventually disbanded as a living group and their seats turned over to buffer students.) More recently, students have taken to spreading around a tip sheet before the game featuring possible subjects or topics of scorn.

From the university's standpoint, one of the more positive aspects of the group's mentality in the twenty-first century is that they will usually listen to Krzyzewski when he asks them to cheer more for Duke and less against the opponent. As long as they keep cheering.

"Personally, I never wanted a new coliseum when I was coaching," Bubas once said. "I liked the students where they are, and you'd be surprised what an effect all the noise, the cheering, and the pep band can do to the home team during a rally."

"Cameron was a great place to play and it still is a wonderful place to play," added Jeff Mullins. "I'm so proud of Duke for preserving Cameron rather than following the trend to the mega facilities. Every time I come back it brings back fond memories."

See also Home courts; Veal Incident.

Campbell, David. A Catawba College graduate, David Campbell spent three years on the Duke basketball staff, 1969 – 71, serving primarily as the assistant coach of the freshman team. He aided Hubie Brown in 1969 and Jack Schalow from 1970 to 1971.

Candler, Coke. A versatile forward from Candler, N.C., Candler played four years of basketball, 1926–29, ran four years of track and two years of cross-country, and played one season of football. He was the captain of coach Eddie Cameron's first team in 1929 and scored 84 points. That was also Duke's first year in the Southern Conference, and the Blue Devils reached the tournament championship game.

Cantwell, John. A 5–8 guard from Shawano, Wis., John Davis Cantwell enrolled at Duke without a basketball scholarship, started for the freshman team in 1959 while averaging 10 points a game, and lettered for the varsity in 1960 and 1961. He appeared in 38 games those two years, with 114 points and 24 rebounds. He earned several starts as a sophomore playmaker in 1960, averaging 3.8 points a game, with a pair of 14-point games against N.C. State and Maryland.

A pre-med student during his basketball career, Cantwell became a noted cardiologist in Atlanta and was one of the lead physicians for the 1996 Summer Olympics there. In 1999, while he was working at the Homer Rice Center for Sports Performance at Georgia Tech, Cantwell was invited by coach Bobby Cremins to join the Yellow Jackets team for its trip to Duke. He sat on the Tech bench and watched his alma mater cruise to one of its 16 ACC victories.

Capel, Jeff. While it's tempting to remember Jeff Capel for an improbable buzzer-beater that he hit against North Carolina, there was much more substance to his four-year career. Like the way he started at point guard as a freshman in 1994 and came of age on the Blue Devils' run to the Final Four. Or his team-best scoring average for the 1996 bounce-back club. Or the way he dealt with criticism and adversity as a senior in 1997, while leading his team to a regular-season ACC title.

A 6–4 guard from Fayetteville, N.C., Selton Jeffrey Capel III played in all 129 games during his career and started 106 times. He finished with 1,601 points for a 12.4 average, with 390 rebounds and 433 assists. He averaged 29.5 minutes a game for his career and hit 220 three-pointers, a figure that ranked second only to Bobby Hurley when he graduated.

Capel's career had an odd twist in that he started

Jeff Capel started over 100 games for the Blue Devils, then followed his father into the coaching profession.

nearly every game in his first three years, then had to come off the bench for much of his senior year. The capstone of his freshman season was a trip to the Final Four, and he had a huge hand in making that happen with his performance in the regional final against Purdue. He scored 19 points with four rebounds and seven assists, and had an unforgettable spree late in the game, during which he used a spin move to drive inside for a shot, threw a behind-the-back pass to Tony Lang for an open layup, and punctuated the victory by executing a thunder dunk with 38 seconds left, on a long breakaway pass from Chris Collins.

Capel provided the shining moment of the 1995 season in a classic confrontation with UNC. Although Duke was struggling, the Devils brought their best to the table for the grudge match with the Tar Heels. Duke trailed by eight points late in overtime, but Capel closed out a furious rally when he took an outlet pass from Cherokee

Parks, crossed midcourt on two long dribbles, and let fly with a running 30-footer as time expired. It tied the score at 95 and forced a second overtime. Duke eventually lost, 102 – 100.

Capel helped the program rebound in 1996 with a team-best scoring average of 16.6 and was primed for a strong senior year in 1997 as a two-time captain. After some early struggles, Kzyzewski opted to use him off the bench. That arrangement lasted until the home game with UNC, when Capel returned to the starting lineup and scored 19 points to help Duke end a three-year losing streak in the series. He remained a starter for the rest of the year and was instrumental in several more wins, with 18 points in a road upset of second-ranked Wake Forest and 18 in his senior game against Maryland to help Duke clinch the ACC regular-season crown. He had 25 and 26 points in his last two games, in the NCAA tourney.

As the son of a successful college coach and a student of the game under Krzyzewski, perhaps it was inevitable that Capel would turn to coaching when his playing career ended. He wanted to play professionally, but a back injury and illness ended that dream. So in 2001 he became an assistant for his father at Old Dominion, then moved to Virginia Commonwealth in 2002. After the 2002 campaign, VCU elevated Capel, making him the youngest Division I head coach in the country at 27. He was an immediate success, with a 79 – 41 record for his first four campaigns. In 2004 he led the Rams to a 23 – 8 record, the regular-season and tournament championship in the Colonial Athletic Association, and a spot in the NCAA Tournament. In April 2006 he was named head coach at Oklahoma.

Capel had been expected to play against his father's team when Duke scheduled North Carolina A&T on its slate in 1995, but the elder Capel left his post with the Aggies for Old Dominion before that game took place. The following year, however, Duke and ODU were pitted against each other in the first round of the Great Alaska Shootout. Capel II had his assistant coaches present the scouting report to the Monarchs, because he didn't feel comfortable saying negative things about Capel III to his players. Capel III played 35 minutes and had 12 points, five assists, four steals, and no turnovers in the Duke win. Capel's younger brother Jason played for UNC, but the two never went head to head, as Jeff graduated two seasons before Jason arrived.

Capelli, Theodore. As a newcomer in 1930, forward Theodore Capelli, from Washington, D.C., was one of the flashier figures for the Blue Devils' undefeated freshman team. He moved up to the varsity in 1931, lettered, and scored 74 points. Capelli returned to the team in 1932 and went scoreless.

Card, Cap. Wilbur Wade Card, the man responsible for establishing the school's first basketball team, was one of Trinity College's standout baseball players at the end of the nineteenth century. In 1899 he was elected the team captain, and from then on he was known as Cap Card.

Card, from Franklinton, N.C., graduated from Trinity in 1900 and declined a pro baseball offer so that he could attend Harvard for special training in physical education. He returned to Durham in 1902 as director of physical education at his alma mater's first gym, the Angier B. Duke Gymnasium. He launched Trinity's track and field program in 1903 and introduced a handful of other sports before organizing the first basketball team, in response to a suggestion from Wake Forest coach Richard Crozier that the two institutions play a game.

Card put the first team together and trained it for three weeks, as none of the members had ever played a basketball game before. He also prepared the tiny gym to host the contest, and on March 2, 1906, the first intercollegiate basketball contest in school history took place. Card umpired the contest, while Crozier refereed. More experienced Wake won that one, as well as the rematch on its home floor a few weeks afterward.

Card organized, trained, and coached the Trinity basketball team as a volunteer for seven years, before one of his former players, Joseph E. Brinn, was hired to coach in 1912 – 13. Card, who compiled a record of 30 – 17, continued to closely follow and promote basketball, baseball, and all sports at Trinity and Duke while influencing several generations of students who came through the P.E. department. He was state chairman of the American Physical Education Association and was active at Duke until suffering a stroke in 1943. He died of a heart attack in 1948 at the age of 74. Among the pallbearers at his funeral were Wallace Wade, Eddie

Cameron, Bob Chambers, and Jack Persons, all fellow legendary Duke coaches. Ten years after his death, the school's first gym on West Campus was renamed Card Gym in his memory.

Card Gymnasium. See Home courts.

Carmichael Auditorium. Perhaps the most infamous defeat in Duke basketball history took place at Carmichael Auditorium on March 2, 1974. A heavy underdog against fourth-ranked North Carolina, the Blue Devils owned an 86–78 lead when freshman Tate Armstrong hit two free throws with 25 seconds remaining. But UNC scored eight points in the last 17 seconds, forcing overtime on a 30-footer by Walter Davis, and went on to win 96–92. The miracle comeback was reflective of Carmichael's status as a house of horrors for the Blue Devils. Duke won its first game in the facility in 1966 but then proceeded to lose in "Blue Heaven" for 18 straight seasons before pulling off an impressive victory in its last trip in 1985, behind one of Johnny Dawkins's greatest performances. Carolina had a record of 169–20 in Carmichael, taking full advantage of the loud and cozy home-floor advantage. Seating capacity was listed at 8,800 for the gym's first 10 years — the same as Cameron Indoor Stadium — before being elevated to 10,000 in 1977. The arena was named for a Durham native, William Donald Carmichael Jr., an outstanding UNC player in the 1920s and later a university administrator.

Carmody, Tom. A native of Pittsburgh, Thomas M. Carmody worked on the Duke basketball staff for three years, 1966–68, under head coach Vic Bubas. Carmody coached the Blue Imps freshman team for all three years and posted a record of 32–16. His final team, featuring Randy Denton inside and Dick DeVenzio outside, was 12–4 and averaged 90 points a game. Carmody left Duke after the 1968 campaign to become head coach at Rhode Island.

Carr, Judge. A 6–2 guard from Durham, Robert Winston "Judge" Carr Jr. was on the varsity basketball roster as a junior in 1971 and played in one game, with no points and one rebound.

Carr, Kenny. Former N.C. State standout Kenny Carr registered the highest individual scoring performance by an ACC opponent against the Blue Devils when he totaled 45 points on January 2, 1976. Carr, an Olympian in 1976, shot 18 of 26 from the field to help the Wolfpack defeat Duke at the Big Four Tournament in Greensboro. Three weeks later he hit 17 of 23 for 44 points against the Blue Devils and later in the year scored 28. For the season that was 117 points on 47-of-77 shooting. His career average against Duke was 27.1 in eight games.

Carrawell, Chris. The day before Duke was set to play North Carolina in the regular-season finale in 2000, senior Chris Carrawell was listening intently to his 130th pre-game scouting report. After talking about UNC's personnel for a few minutes, coach Mike Krzyzewski halted in midstream and changed course. "Forget about North Carolina, seedings, all that stuff," he told his team. "The most important thing about this game is that we owe it to Chris to win. He's already leaving here a winner. He deserves to win his last game, and we owe it to him to win it for him."

Before Carrawell's final game tipped off, the lights in Cameron Indoor Stadium were turned off and Carrawell was introduced to the crowd under the glare of a spotlight, as in days gone by at the old gym. He asked his mother, who was attending a game there for just the second time, to join him. The arena was stoked to a feverish, emotional apex as tipoff arrived. Then the Blue Devils did exactly what Krzyzewski had instructed — they won the game for Carrawell. Fellow veterans Shane Battier and Nate James scored 30 and 19 points, and the Blue Devils triumphed 90–76. That gave Carrawell a perfect career record at home versus UNC and, more importantly, finished off a fourth straight outright ACC regular-season championship. He was the first person in league history to win four regular-season titles.

"There couldn't be a better ending," Carrawell said. "Shane, Nate, they made sure I wouldn't lose this one. They wouldn't let me lose today."

"There'll never be another Chris. He's one of a kind, just the best," said Battier.

Carrawell didn't just idly watch his teammates. He scored 21 points, with seven rebounds, four assists, and four steals. Then he punctuated the day with a fast-break

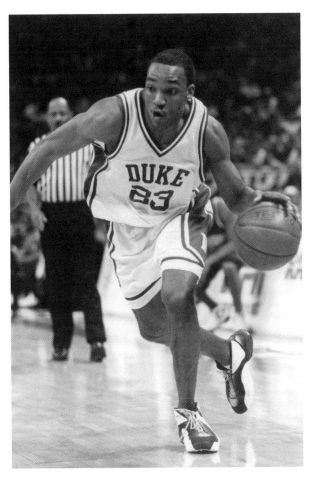

Chris Carrawell had a perfect home record versus UNC and was ACC player of the year in 2000.

slam dunk 90 seconds before the buzzer. It was a performance typical of many in his senior year, as he averaged 16.9 points and 6.1 boards in earning first-team All-America and ACC player of the year honors. When Duke capped the year with a second straight ACC Tournament crown, Carrawell had played in 66 conference victories, more than anyone else in league history. Battier topped him by finishing with 70 the next year.

Christopher Michael Carrawell played in 136 games from 1997 to 2000, with 1,455 points, 608 rebounds, and 309 assists. He captained the 2000 team with Battier and James, and shared team MVP honors with Battier. He had never scored 20 points a game entering his senior year, but he hit for 28 in the opener against Stanford and finished just behind Battier as the team scoring leader for the season. His career best of 30 points came in an overtime win versus N.C. State in which he played all

45 minutes. He had 25 points in a wild overtime win at Virginia, 109 – 100.

Carrawell's career was intriguing from the beginning. Shoulder injuries in high school left him labeled as damaged goods entering college, but Duke stuck with him. He went through several surgeries, devoted himself to rehab, and always received strong, patient support from Krzyzewski, as well as a motivational push whenever he needed it. Having grown up in inner-city St. Louis without a father, Carrawell looked to Krzyzewski as a father figure. The special relationship between the two was obvious from the beginning, as Carrawell relished any assignment he was given.

In his freshman year, one of the most telling came at Wake Forest, when the second-ranked Deacons, led by Tim Duncan, were looking for their 10th straight win over Duke. Krzyzewski opted for a smaller, quicker lineup than usual, with Carrawell, at 6 – 6, jumping center to start the game and playing some interior defense against the likes of Duncan and Loren Woods, his former high school teammate. In the first half Carrawell converged on Woods as he was receiving a pass, knocked the ball away, and set sail for a dunk that gave Duke a seven-point lead. Later, with only 1:18 left, Wake guard Tony Rutland drove inside for a layup, but Carrawell pinned the shot against the glass, enabling Duke to maintain a three-point margin. The Devils won, 73 – 68. "Chris was unbelievable throughout the entirety of the game," his teammate Trajan Langdon said. "He was giving up four or five inches and he just battled."

By the time Carrawell was a junior, he was starting every game for the powerful 1999 team that went 37 – 2 and played for the national title. His street smarts paid off most, perhaps, when the Devils defeated Temple for the right to go to the Final Four. Time after time he took the ball in his hands and penetrated into the teeth of the Owls' famous matchup zone, splitting and spreading the defense to provide open looks for Langdon, Elton Brand, and Will Avery. "That's always been my kind of game," he said. "I won't outscore you, but I know I can make plays. That's been my success this year, making plays for other guys."

Carrawell took on an even bigger role in 2000. By the time his days were through, he had been used as a spark off the bench, secondary point guard, one-on-one defender, medium-range shooter, and emotional catalyst. He closed his career with 95 starts, plus the satisfaction of knowing that he had accomplished more than anyone expected from him.

"Nobody envisioned me coming from St. Louis and doing these things," he said. "Most people thought I would be on the first train back, especially my sophomore year when that great freshman class came in. They thought I was going to come back home or transfer. It just goes to show that if you work hard, keep getting better, always stay hungry, then you have a chance to do some great things."

Carrawell's professional career included a successful stint in Australia. He was a charter inductee in the Duke Basketball Hall of Honor in 2001.

Carter, Pete. William Pete Carter, a forward from Mt. Hope, W.Va., was a reserve in 1930 and lettered for the 1931 and 1932 teams, scoring 77 points in three years. He had a high of 13 points against Catholic University in 1932.

Carver, Gordon. A Duke Sports Hall of Fame inductee from Durham, Gordon Malone Carver was one of the most versatile athletes in school history. From 1941 through 1945 he earned nine varsity letters — four in football, three in basketball, and two in track.

Carver starred for the 1943, 1944, and 1945 basketball teams, helping each to the Southern Conference final. The 1944 team won the title, with Carver scoring 11 points in the championship game. He made the all-tournament second team in 1943 (when he led the event in scoring with 40 points) and the first team the next two years. Carver was one of the top scorers for the 1943 and 1944 teams in getting 292 and 297 points, and he added 94 points in 1945 for a career total of 683 points. He finished as Duke's career scoring leader and held the mark until 1947.

Carver's 297 points in 1944 established the school's single-season scoring record, which lasted until Ed Koffenberger broke it in 1946.

Carver, a 6–1 forward, was also a back and punter on the football team. He once ripped off a 70-yard run against Virginia that was the fourth-longest in school history at the time. He also staged a couple of memo-

rable New Year's holidays as a Blue Devil. On January 1, 1944, Duke made its first-ever basketball appearance at Madison Square Garden in New York and lost an overtime game to Long Island University despite a career high of 27 points from Carver. The next year, Carver spent New Year's in New Orleans as the captain of the football team, helping the Blue Devils to beat Alabama in the Sugar Bowl. Carver's ankle-grabbing tackle on the last play of the game secured the win. The lengthy football season prevented Carver from playing in his first 1945 basketball game until January 13.

Carver earned his undergraduate degree in 1944 and played his last year while in medical school. He was presented with the Robert E. Lee Award as the outstanding student on campus and the Teague Award as the top amateur athlete in the Carolinas. Carver became a noted surgeon in Durham and was inducted into the school's Hall of Fame in 1984.

Case, Everett. Duke coach Eddie Cameron was on a recruiting trip to Indiana in the mid-1930s when he attended a clinic on fast-break basketball conducted by a high school coach, Everett Norris Case. Cameron had established himself as one of the leaders in his profession, but he recognized that there was plenty he could learn from one of the masters of the game. Case was certainly that, a renowned Indiana prep coach so immersed in the game that he'd started coaching in high school as an 18-year-old volunteer during the First World War and had written his college thesis on free-throw shooting.

Case was hired by N.C. State after he got out of the Navy in 1946, and he changed the face of college basketball in the South. He spearheaded the completion of State's Reynolds Coliseum as the region's showplace for its favorite sport, created the wildly successful Dixie Classic, and elevated the Wolfpack program to national élite status with a fast-paced, full-court style of play. Before his arrival the Southern Conference Tournament was played at Raleigh Memorial Auditorium, which seated just over 3,000. During Case's first season, N.C. State's business manager John Von Glahn received 6,000 advance ticket orders for the event in the first three days they were on sale. Glahn reportedly loaded the mail into his car and took it over to Duke to show Cameron, who was the league's basketball chairman. Mostly because of interest spawned by Case, the event was moved to Duke's 8,800-seat facility for four years, until Reynolds Coliseum took over as host in 1951.

Case coached the Wolfpack to the Southern Conference title in each of his first six years. After State broke away as a charter member of the Atlantic Coast Conference, Case directed his team to the first three ACC tourney crowns. He also generated his share of controversy, with two periods of NCAA probation for various violations. During one of those seasons, 1955, the Wolfpack won the ACC Tournament but wasn't eligible to advance to the national tourney, so Duke took that spot. It was the Blue Devils' first NCAA appearance.

Among the many players who performed under Case at State were two who later became Duke head coaches: Vic Bubas was recruited from Indiana and Bucky Waters from New Jersey to spend their college years in Raleigh. Bubas, the consummate floor leader, then worked as Case's assistant before Cameron hired him at Duke. He brought with him a fast-paced playing style as well as the vision for innovation that characterized his mentor. He ended up winning eight of the 12 times he coached head to head against Case. Bubas had helped recruit Waters, hired him as one of his Duke assistants, encouraged him to become a head coach, and saw him fill his chair after he resigned in 1969.

"Both of them thought big," Waters recalled of Case and Bubas. "They were not limited by geography or anything else. They were very intense as coaches and very positive people who lit up the people around them. You really wanted to do well for them. Case was a promoter, a producer, and Vic took that from him."

Overall Case compiled a mark of 377 – 134 at State, 28 – 18 versus Duke. He retired because of failing health two games into the 1964 – 65 season. State defeated Duke for the ACC title at Reynolds that year as he watched from a courtside press table. Larry Worsley came off the bench to score 30 points and was presented with the first Everett Case Award as tourney MVP. The players then brought Case to the floor to help them cut down the nets, one of the traditions that he brought to the area from his Indiana high school days.

When UCLA came east to play at Duke in December 1965, Bubas brought the Bruins' coach, John Wooden, to see the ailing Case and watched the two trade stories going back to their days in Indiana. Case died a few months later, just weeks after the last ACC Tournament at Reynolds, in which Duke defeated State, with Steve Vacendak earning the Case award. Case was enshrined in the Basketball Hall of Fame in 1982.

Cashman, Don. Two years in the Army interrupted the Duke career of Donald Christopher Cashman, a 6 – 4 forward from New York City. Coached in high school by former Duke player Dan Buckley, Cashman made a freshman splash in 1952 with a 13-point average and a 30-point game against the North Carolina JV team. He played in 16 games as a reserve for the 1953 varsity before spending two years in the military, where he showed off his excellent outside shot for service teams. He returned to Duke for the 1956 season and again saw reserve duty in 14 games, with a high of eight points against N.C. State. His two-year varsity career totaled 30 games, with 69 points and 60 rebounds.

Causey, Mark. As a freshman walk-on for the 2002 season, Mark Causey provided some backcourt depth for the Blue Devils. He played in 12 games, scoring 13 points and grabbing eight rebounds. Two of his four field goals were three-point shots. But Causey, a 6 – 3 guard from Gainesville, Ga., who scored over 2,000 points in high school and led his team to a state title, decided to leave Duke after one year and transferred to North Georgia College.

Chandler, Art. For many Duke fans, the official start to the Cameron Indoor Stadium game-day experience is signaled by the public address announcer's call of "Here comes Duke" when the team runs on to the floor for its final warm-up. The man who has made that call for over three decades is Dr. Arthur Chandler, a graduate of Duke Medical School and a Durham ophthalmologist since 1965. Chandler began working as the public address announcer in the fall of 1970, when athletics officials asked him if he'd like to give it a try for a preseason exhibition game against the Icelandic National Team. He's been at the microphone ever since, missing only an NIT game in 1981 because of his wedding, a Georgia Tech game because of an ice storm, and most of the 1991 NCAA championship season when he was serving in the Army

Reserve at a hospital in Saudi Arabia during Operation Desert Storm.

Chapman, Warren. Knee surgeries figured prominently in the career of Warren Arthur Chapman, a 6 – 8 center from the Houston area who originally signed with Rice before heading instead to Duke. Chapman scored 235 points and had 216 rebounds in three varsity seasons, 1966, 1967, and 1969. After scoring at a 14.4 clip for the freshman team in 1965, he was a productive reserve for the team that reached the Final Four in the following year, with 5.5 points and 3.9 rebounds per contest. He hit 56.9 percent of his field goals and turned in his career high of 16 points against Virginia. Chapman's numbers dropped dramatically after that, partly because of a serious knee injury that required surgery. He took off the entire 1968 season to recover and was limited to just 16 games as a senior in 1969.

Chappell, Mike. Four games into his college career, Mike Chappell found himself in the starting lineup at Madison Square Garden for the Preseason NIT championship game against Indiana. A year later he started 21 games for a team that went 15 – 1 in the ACC and came up one shot short of a trip to the Final Four. But the 1997 and 1998 seasons were Chappell's only ones at Duke, before he transferred back to his home state to complete his career at Michigan State.

Chappell, a 6 – 8 third-team prep All-America from Southfield, Mich., played in 68 Duke games in his freshman and sophomore years, with 23 starts. He scored 403 points and claimed 125 rebounds. An excellent long-range shooter, he hit 60 three-point field goals in two years. As a sophomore he started all but one of the first 22 games, frequently scored in double figures, and posted a career high of 18 points against Mercer. His playing time decreased, however, after a loss in February in Chapel Hill, and he scored just 43 points over the last 14 games. He decided to transfer soon after the season ended, saying he wanted to go to a program where he could be more of a focal point.

At Michigan State Chappell had to sit out the 1999 season under transfer regulations but traveled to Florida for the Spartans' Final Four date with Duke. He was back on the court the next year and saw extensive action for the Michigan State team that claimed the NCAA title in 2000.

Charlotte Coliseum. Two structures known as the Charlotte Coliseum played pivotal roles in the development of basketball as North Carolina's preeminent team sport. The first Charlotte Coliseum opened in 1955 with over 11,000 seats and assisted the NCAA's movement of its East Regional away from campus locations. Later it served the same purpose in helping to neutralize the site for the ACC Tournament. The second Charlotte Coliseum, which opened in 1988 with over 23,000 seats, brought the state its first major league franchise, the NBA's Charlotte Hornets, and provided a large enough modern setting for the NCAA and the ACC to keep the Queen City among its postseason destinations.

Duke's first contest at the old Charlotte Coliseum was a win over South Carolina in 1957. The arena brought the NCAA regionals south from Philadelphia from 1958 through 1961, and Duke appeared in one of those, with a win over St. Joseph's followed by a loss to New York University in 1960. Duke periodically scheduled regular-season games there throughout the next two decades, including a rout of top-ranked UCLA in December 1965 and a nationally televised blowout of Louisville during a snowstorm in February 1979.

The old arena hosted NCAA events well into the 1970s. Duke's run to the Final Four in 1978 began with a one-point escape from Rhode Island in Charlotte. The ACC also staged three tournaments at the old Charlotte Coliseum, 1968 – 70, as it was making its transition away from years of play on N.C. State's home floor in Raleigh. Duke was involved in one of the legendary ACC tourney games in 1968, when N.C. State used a delay game to upset the Blue Devils 12 – 10 before the advent of the shot clock. Announcer Bill Curry contributed one of the great one-liners when he called that contest "about as exciting as artificial insemination."

The expanded Greensboro Coliseum took over as the home of the ACC during the 1970s. The league didn't return to Charlotte for postseason play until 1990, when the tournament launched a five-year run in the newly minted home of the Hornets. Duke was in the final there in 1991 and 1992, before winning a pair of national titles, and again in 1999, 2000, and 2002. Overall, the second

Charlotte Coliseum hosted eight ACC Tournaments, three NCAA Tournament subregionals, two NCAA regionals, and two Final Fours (one men's, one women's). Duke won four ACC crowns there (1992, 1999, 2000, 2002), of which the most impressive effort was turned in by the 1999 club when it completed its coronation as one of the best ACC teams of all time with a perfect league season of 19 – 0.

Duke played in NCAA subregionals in Charlotte in 1997, 1999, and 2005. The Blue Devils were also involved in the NCAA finals in 1994. Not forecast as a Final Four team that year, they rode Grant Hill all the way to the national title game before losing on a last-minute jumper by Arkansas. That game marked the first trip by a sitting president of the United States to the Final Four, with Bill Clinton visiting his home state university's locker room afterward.

Duke played in the last college basketball event at the Charlotte Coliseum, and it couldn't have been a more appropriate finish. On March 20, 2005, the Blue Devils and the North Carolina Tar Heels were involved in a second-round NCAA Tournament doubleheader before a packed house of 23,207. The state's top two programs, each a No. 1 seed in the event, won their games to advance to the Sweet 16. Duke closed the curtain with a tense and narrow decision over Mississippi State.

Over 18 years at the second Charlotte Coliseum, Duke enjoyed a record of 25 – 6, with victories in its last 16 games. The building was slated for demolition after the opening of a new uptown arena for the NBA's Charlotte Bobcats in the fall of 2005.

Cheek, Herbert. A 6 – 0 guard from Durham, Cheek was a backcourt fixture for three Duke teams, 1935 – 37. Known as a defensive whiz and strong ball handler, he scored 259 career points during a time when the Blue Devils posted a record of 53 – 22. Cheek and Ken Podger were the regular guards for most of their three years together, and they were the team's top two scorers as seniors in 1937. Cheek also played baseball at Duke.

Cheek, James. A forward from Durham, James "Buck" Cheek was a starter for the team that won the Southern Conference championship in 1946. He totaled 109 points while playing 25 of the Blue Devils' 27 games. It was his only season as a letterman, but he returned as a reserve for the 1949 and 1950 teams with 24 points in 14 games.

Chestnut, Jennifer. The second player in Duke women's basketball annals to score 1,000 career points, Jennifer Chestnut starred for the Blue Devils in the early 1980s. A 6 – 1 forward from Houston, she played in 100 games from 1981 to 1984, with 74 starts. She was a lineup fixture for her last three years, leading the 1983 team in scoring at 14.0 points a game and topping the Devils in rebounding in each of her last three years. Chestnut finished with 1,023 points, following her classmate Stacy Hurd into the 1,000-point club. She also had 737 rebounds, which was the all-time school record when she graduated. Chestnut's 7.4 rebounds a game still ranks fourth all-time at Duke.

Chili, Terry. He was only a 46 percent free-throw shooter for his career, but Terry Chili's biggest moment as a Duke basketball player came at the free-throw line in a contest with Maryland in 1976. With the Blue Devils desperate to win a conference game, Chili connected on a pair of pressure-packed foul shots with four seconds left to clinch a 69 – 67 upset of the seventh-ranked Terps. It was one of only two victories that the hard-luck Devils enjoyed over the final nine games of 1976.

A 6 – 10 center from Jamestown, N.Y., Terry James Chili played in 65 games over his four seasons, 1973 – 76, scoring 264 points with 177 rebounds. He made 66.7 percent of his field goals, 108 of 162. Chili was one of the top scorers on the junior varsity team in his freshman year and also made five varsity appearances. He again split time between the varsity and JV as a sophomore, with a 19-point, 20-rebound game against the Virginia JV team and nine double-doubles for the year. As a junior in 1975 he played in 23 varsity games with a 3.8 scoring average, and in 1976 he enjoyed his best season as the team's sixth man, appearing in all 27 games with a 5.5 scoring average. His most productive varsity effort was in the opener that year, when he had 16 points and 14 rebounds against Johns Hopkins. Chili was given the Ted Mann Jr. award as the reserve contributing most to team morale in 1974 and 1975. In 1976 he was the first recipient of the Dr. Deryl Hart academic award as the team's top student athlete.

Chili wore jersey No. 43 during his Duke days and was primarily responsible for "discovering" Duke's most famous 43, Mike Gminski. Working at Maryland's summer camp before his senior year, Chili found out that Gminski intended to graduate from high school a year early. He tipped off the Duke coaches, who were able to land the young center before most other schools knew he was available.

After playing professionally in Sweden, Chili returned to his alma mater and served two years (1979–80) on Bill Foster's coaching staff, assisting with recruiting and running the junior varsity team.

Chinault, Neil. A 6–5 product of Peterstown, W.Va., Dennis Neil Chinault earned letters during his sophomore and junior seasons of 1973 and 1974. He saw limited game time with 12 appearances, scoring 10 points. He was hampered by a shoulder injury in his freshman season on the junior varsity and split his 1973 campaign between the varsity and the jv.

Christensen, Matt. When Matt Christensen was a freshman in 1996, two of his teammates were guards Chris Collins and Steve Wojciechowski. By the time Christensen graduated seven years later in 2002, Collins and Wojo were among his coaches. Few if any players in school history enjoyed a more lengthy association with the program during their playing careers than Christensen did.

A 6–10 post player from Belmont, Mass., Matthew Quinn Christensen saw limited minutes in 13 games during his rookie campaign and missed several weeks with a fractured wrist. After the school year ended he embarked on a two-year Mormon mission to Germany. Upon his return he used the 1999 season as a red-shirt year to add strength and get back into basketball condition. Then he played as an inside reserve for three years, providing veteran leadership and a physical presence during spot duty. He totaled 95 career games with three starts, 162 points, and 189 rebounds. About half (94) of his career rebounds were on the offensive end.

In Christensen's lone double-figures game he scored 11 points against Western Carolina in his freshman year. Duke won the ACC Tournament in four of his five years on the roster. One of his highlight moments was against Kentucky in the Jimmy V Classic during his senior season. With the Wildcats in control, Mike Krzyzewski removed all his starters from the game. Christensen was one of the subs, and during his five-minute stint he blocked a shot and converted a three-point play. The subs' efforts inspired the starters, who returned to the floor and led the Blue Devils to victory.

A double major in civil engineering and economics, Christensen won the team's Dr. Deryl Hart award as the top scholar athlete in 2002, as well as a coach's award for team commitment.

Chronicle. Duke's student-run campus newspaper marked its 100th year in 2005–06, just like the basketball program. The first edition of the *Trinity Chronicle* was published on December 19, 1905. A month later, on January 20, 1906, news about the formation of the school's first intercollegiate basketball team was front-page news.

The *Chronicle* was a weekly for several years before moving to a daily, Monday-to-Friday, schedule, and in the early years it was the only source of current information on the new basketball program, with detailed reporting on the varsity games as well as the popular class tournaments, a forerunner to intramural basketball.

With personnel changeover to a new group of students practically every year, the editorial tenor of the paper has run the gamut. It has been just as likely to admonish basketball fans for unacceptable behavior (in the 1950s) as to headline a Final Four story "Let's Go Big Blue, Win the NCAA." In the 1920s its leaders pushed for the adoption of Blue Devils as the nickname for the university's sports teams; in 2005 it ran to the polar extreme of such boosterism with a "What have you done for us lately?" column aimed at coach Mike Krzyzewski — the very week he was about to lead his program to its eighth straight ACC championship game and sixth title in seven years.

Perhaps the most publicized incident involving the *Chronicle* and basketball occurred late in Krzyzewski's first decade at the helm, when the paper ran a report on the team's early progress. The coach summoned several members of the sports staff to the locker room and blasted them in front of the team, igniting a wave of negative reaction in the media.

Claiborne, C. B. While driving a friend home from a Duke basketball game one night in the late 1960s, C. B.

C. B. Claiborne was Duke's first African American basketball player, 1967–69.

The History of Black Athletes at Duke

1963–64: First black undergrads admitted (5)
1965–66: First black athlete admitted (C. B. Claiborne)
1966–67: First class of black students graduated (3)
1968–69: First black scholarship athletes enrolled (Don Blackman in basketball, Ernie Jackson and C. G. Newsome in football)
1971–72: First black coach hired (basketball assistant Jim Lewis)
1976–77: First black women athletes earned letters
1979–80: First black woman received athletic scholarship (Kim Matthews in women's basketball)

	1967	1977	1987	1997	2005
Black undergraduates at Duke	28	255	249	512	672
Black football and basketball players	1	20	29	41	48

Claiborne was pulled off the road by a Durham police officer and accused of running a stop sign in his Volkswagen. When Claiborne protested that his car couldn't shift down into first gear without stopping, the officer accused him of insubordination, handcuffed him, and sent him to jail for the night.

That was not an isolated incident in the college life of Duke's first African American athlete. Claudius Barrett Claiborne, who enrolled at Duke in the fall of 1965 and went on to play three varsity seasons under coach Vic Bubas, recalled that he was not harassed by campus police, because they knew he was an athlete. But the university that admitted him in just its third class of minority undergraduate students was a very white place that frequently tested the resolve of its tiny black population.

"I felt a lot like a pioneer," Claiborne said. "That's what that experience was like. It seemed like everything I did was new."

Claiborne came to Duke from Danville, Va., where he was an all-state player and the top-ranked student academically at his all-black high school. He was one of 225 winners of a four-year college scholarship from the National Achievement Scholarship Program and planned to attend North Carolina A&T. But a Duke supporter in the Danville area got the Blue Devil coaches interested, and Claiborne's high school coach encouraged him to go to Duke, partly to break the athletic color barrier.

Claiborne played on the freshman team in 1966 and appeared in 53 varsity games from 1967 through 1969, scoring 218 points with 100 rebounds. He scored 13 points during a start against Penn State in his sophomore year and had seven double-figures games in his senior season, including the first four. His career high of 15 was against Clemson.

Claiborne's arrival made Duke the second ACC institution to integrate its varsity roster. Maryland's Billy Jones was the first African American ACC varsity player in 1966, Claiborne's year on the freshman team. North Carolina, N.C. State, and Wake Forest brought in black players during Claiborne's junior and senior seasons. From a national perspective, Claiborne enrolled at Duke during the same academic year in which the all-black Texas Western team defeated the all-white Kentucky team for the NCAA title. Duke's varsity was at the Final Four and came up four points shy of the Wildcats in the semifinals, a battle of the No. 1 and No. 2 teams in the polls.

Claiborne once said that he could not recall any overt racism within his team but experienced plenty of it from fans at road games. Teammates said that he handled it well. "C. B. was a great guy, very proud and stood his ground," teammate Steve Vandenberg remembered. "He was like Jackie Robinson in that way. He just took it. He was very stoic, very scholarly about it."

Racial tensions on campus led to a sit-in at the Allen Building during Claiborne's final semester in 1969. Several members of the Afro-American Society took over the building and threatened to destroy valuable records in the university's administrative headquarters if certain demands were not met, such as the creation of a black dorm, a black student union, and an Afro-American Studies department. Claiborne participated in the sit-in and missed a couple of days with the team, including a game at West Virginia. The other players unanimously supported his return to the team afterward. Claiborne was the only African American on the varsity roster throughout his career, though Duke's first black scholarship player, Don Blackman, was on the freshman team in Claiborne's senior season.

An engineering major, Claiborne graduated in 1969 and put his degree to work at a few industrial companies. Then he earned a masters and a PhD and became a college professor.

Clark, Dud. A 6–0 guard, D. H. Clark, from Southbridge, Mass., lettered and scored 24 points as a sophomore for the 1933 team. He had a career high of 11 points against Washington & Lee.

Clark, Marty. With less than two minutes to play in a tense NCAA semifinal, sophomore Marty Clark found himself in the glare of college basketball's brightest spot-

light. He was in the game because senior Brian Davis had suffered a severe ankle sprain. Duke led, but Indiana wasn't going down quietly. To no one's surprise, part of its strategy was to foul the young Clark and see if he could handle the pressure.

Clark, a 6–6 guard from Westchester, Ill., who'd grown up as the son of a coach, didn't flinch. He was fouled three times and canned five of his six free throws to help preserve an 81–78 victory that sent the Blue Devils to the 1992 title game. It was two minutes of play, five very important points.

Martin Matthew Wellmeier Clark was a reserve throughout his four years, 1991–94. He played in 122 games with only nine starts, but he usually made effective use of his time. He scored 647 points, with 181 rebounds and 134 assists. His last two years he received the team's Ted Mann Jr. award as the reserve who contributed most to team morale, but he contributed more than that. He came off the bench expecting to make an impact and seldom disappointed. As the sixth man in 1994, he led the team with 17 points in a three-point win at Georgia Tech, had another 17-point game in a victory over Florida State, and scored on a tip-in with three seconds left to beat Notre Dame 74–72. He also had one of his best defensive performances by stopping Cuonzo Martin late in the NCAA regional final against Purdue. He averaged 8.1 points while captaining the team along with Grant Hill and Antonio Lang. Clark played for three ACC regular-season champions and on three NCAA finalist teams.

"It embodies a lot of who I am," Clark said of his sixth-man role. "I've always been chasing something, trying to do what it takes to make the team better. I'm not in there because of any one aspect of my game. I'm in there because I can do a lot of different things pretty well. The sixth man has to be able to go in for anybody at any time, and to be able to do that you need to be good at all aspects of the game."

Clark, Robert. Robert W. Clark, of Richmond Hill, N.Y., lettered but saw little action for the team that won the Southern Conference championship in 1942.

Clay, Noble. Trinity's head coach for two seasons, 1914 and 1915, Noble L. Clay directed the young basketball program to records of 12 – 8 and 10 – 10. Clay had one of the most distinctive coaching tenures in school history. He was also the captain of the Durham YMCA team at the time and came over to Trinity on Mondays, Wednesdays, and Fridays to run practice. The coach's main duty during that era was training, because during games the two opposing coaches usually served as the official umpire and referee. Clay's game day was a little different from most on two occasions each season, when Trinity played the Durham YMCA team. As the Y captain, he was in the starting lineup at left forward and played against the team that he trained during the week. Captain Beal Siler, who started opposite his coach at forward in the two matchups between Trinity and the Y in 1914, handled more of the in-game coaching duties, as did most team captains at the time.

Clement, Hayes. After playing four sports at a prep school in New England, Donald Hayes Clement, a 6 – 7 center from New Bern, N.C., headed to Duke, where he was a reserve for the freshman team in 1955 and the varsity in 1956. Heavy personnel losses created an opportunity for Clement in 1957, and he responded by averaging 9.7 points and 7.0 rebounds in 24 games. He scored in double figures 12 times, with highs of 16 against South Carolina and Alabama and 15 on three occasions. With coach Harold Bradley employing a guard-oriented lineup for the second half of 1958, Clement saw less action as a senior. He finished his career with 291 points and 221 rebounds in 48 appearances.

Clemson. Duke's series with Clemson predates the schools' membership in the ACC and ranks as one of the most lopsided on the Blue Devil books. Through the 2006 season the two had played 124 times, with Duke winning 97. The Blue Devils' victory over Clemson in the ACC opener in 2005 marked their 18th straight win in the rivalry, and the 52nd in their 56 contests at Cameron Indoor Stadium.

Before their ACC days, the most significant Duke-Clemson game was in the Southern Conference final of 1938, with Duke winning by 10 points for the school's first conference crown. The two didn't meet in postseason play again until 1962, when the Tigers upset Duke in the ACC semifinals. It was the first of just two losses to

Clemson during the 10-year career of coach Vic Bubas. Clemson made its only appearance in the ACC finals the next day and lost to Wake Forest.

Clemson dominated the series in the mid-1970s during the career of Wayne "Tree" Rollins, who once blocked 10 shots in a game with the Devils. Perhaps the biggest Tiger win was in 1980 in Littlejohn Coliseum, when Duke's undefeated and top-ranked team fell in overtime, 87 – 82. The Devils returned the favor in their final home game that year, winning in overtime by the same score on the night that Mike Gminski had his jersey retired. Duke's home finale in 1982 also came against Clemson in a game that the Blue Devils won in three overtimes behind a virtuoso performance by outgoing senior Vince Taylor. Clemson's Vincent Hamilton played all 55 minutes that night.

One of the most exciting games between Duke and Clemson was in Littlejohn during the 1987 season, when unheralded sophomore John Smith exploded for 28 points while Tommy Amaker and Danny Ferry made several big plays down the stretch. Duke won 105 – 103 in overtime.

Duke's NCAA championship team of 1992 also won a high-scoring affair at Clemson, but barely. The Tigers led by 15 points in the second half when coach Mike Krzyzewski replaced all five of his starters. The subs stayed on the floor for over five minutes and finished their run with an 8 – 2 spurt, led by Erik Meek in one of his best games. The inspired starters returned to pull out a 98 – 97 win, with Brian Davis delivering a career high of 30 points.

Duke's 1988, 1989, and 1990 Final Four teams brought national top-10 rankings to Clemson, only to be sent home with narrow, hard-fought losses. The Blue Devils routed the Tigers in Cameron in those years, reflecting a trend in the series that Grant Hill noted several years later. "I can't figure out why they play so different," Hill said after a 25-point effort at Littlejohn his junior year. "They come into Cameron like they know they are going to lose, and then when we play them down here they are quicker and play harder."

One of the more impressive spurts in the Krzyzewski era occurred in the home finale against Clemson in 1999. With the score tied midway through the first half, outgoing senior star Trajan Langdon suffered a cut lip in a collision with a Tiger player. He had to leave the game, but the incident triggered a 26–0 blitzkrieg from his teammates. "Seeing Trajan down turned on a switch in us," said Chris Carrawell. "We went off. He took a nasty hit. This was supposed to be his day. We wanted to take care of business and blow 'em out. It was 'show no mercy.'"

Coaches' contracts. As a private university, Duke has always treated the financial terms of its employment contracts as confidential. However, some salary information has emerged over the years:

— The institution's first basketball coach, Cap Card, received no salary for the job. He was the director of physical education at Trinity College when he founded the basketball team, and he coached it as a volunteer.

— According to the late publicist Ted Mann, Eddie Cameron was paid about $7,500 a year to coach the basketball team in the 1930s. In his book *A Story of Glory,* Mann reported that the dual position of head football coach and director of athletics, which was held by Wallace Wade, was budgeted for an annual salary of $15,000 and that Cameron received half of what Wade was making.

— According to writer Bill Brill, the 1960s icon Vic Bubas confirmed that his starting salary when hired in the spring of 1959 was $8,500. Bubas has said that he did not have a formal contract, but instead operated under a yearly handshake agreement with his boss, Cameron, as his mentor Everett Case did for years at N.C. State.

— According to published university federal tax records, Mike Krzyzewski was the school's highest-paid employee six times in the nine fiscal years from 1996 through 2004. His base salary in 1995–96 was $210,000. It rose to $521,500 in 1998–99 and to $800,000 in 2002–03. His total compensation from the university has usually been substantially more than the base salary when expense allowances and contributions to benefit plans have been included. For example, he was listed as the highest-paid employee for the 2003–04 fiscal year, with a base of $800,000 and a total compensation package of nearly $1.5 million.

University officials said that 2003–04 marked the first year that a "lifetime" contract signed in 2001 figured into the university budget. Krzyzewski initially signed a five-year contract beginning with the 1981 season. During the 1984 campaign, athletics director Tom Butters tore up that agreement and extended a new five-year deal to his young coach.

In 2001, after winning his third NCAA title and earning induction in the Hall of Fame, Krzyzewski had two years remaining on a seven-year contract when he agreed to a new pact that was described as a lifetime agreement. Director of athletics Joe Alleva said that the contract would run until at least 2011, when Krzyzewski would be at the university's non-binding retirement age. Both the coach and the school described the arrangement as a two-way street, with Krzyzewski committed to remaining at Duke through the end of his coaching career and Duke committed to him.

"The decision that Coach K has made to complete his career at Duke is an amazing statement of his commitment to this university," president Nan Keohane said. "We feel deeply honored by that and determined to make sure that he will continue to flourish here and make this university flourish, which we know he can do in a way nobody else can."

About three years later, in the summer of 2004, a gauge of Krzyzewski's value in the marketplace was provided when the NBA's Los Angeles Lakers discussed with him their head coaching position, for a reported five-year term at $40 million. That's not the kind of compensation package that many universities would be capable of matching, but Duke has supported Krzyzewski's attempts to capitalize on his stature through outside corporate relationships.

Krzyzewski has pointed to the onset of endorsement deals with shoe companies as the start of skyrocketing financial packages for college coaches nationwide and says that coaches have nothing to apologize for in earning what the market will bear.

"In this country, you get paid what your market value is," he said. "It's not dissimilar with what happens with a professor on campus. This is where there's a misconception out there. There are professors who make more than others. Whether they write books, give speeches, research, they win awards. That's going on, on our campus, all the time. You should look at that on different campuses and find out what people actually make. Because a coach started doing that, it seemed like it was unusual. But it's not as unusual on a campus as you think.

"That's what our schools should be like. It should be like doing outstanding things and doing things outside of the normal box, which makes you better when you get back inside your box — as long as it's regulated under the school system and there's no underhandedness. For me, Duke has been a third party for every contract that I've signed and they have the right to terminate any contract I have."

Coach K Court. The floor at Cameron Indoor Stadium was named Coach K Court in honor of coach Mike Krzyzewski on November 17, 2000, in a special ceremony after a victory over Villanova. Dozens of Krzyzewski's friends, family members, and former players were on hand that night hoping to toast the coach's 500th win as a Blue Devil. The victory was achieved by a 98 – 85 decision in a quarterfinal contest of the Preseason NIT. Afterward, president Nan Keohane and athletics director Joe Alleva made the surprise announcement about the naming of the floor.

Cobb, Whit. A standout Durham High School and Davidson College athlete, Paul Whitlock Cobb was the freshman coach for Harold Bradley for four seasons, 1956 – 59. His records were 9 – 8, 9 – 8, 13 – 4, and 9 – 7. The 1958 team that won 13 games featured many of the players who won Duke's first ACC Tournament under their new coach Vic Bubas in 1960.

Cobb, a multi-sport star in college and the Southern Conference athlete of the year in 1950, also coached the Duke men's tennis team for four years, with a record of 35 – 31 overall and 20 – 6 in the ACC, and three second-place finishes. He was inducted into the North Carolina Sports Hall of Fame for his exploits at Davidson.

Cole, Henry. After Chick Doak's departure at the end of the 1918 season, Trinity College did not hire an official head basketball coach for the 1919 campaign. So Henry Puryear Cole of New York City, sophomore class vice-president and starting forward, doubled as the program's captain and coach, aided in the operation of the team by senior manager Frank Wannamaker. Trinity posted a record of 6 – 5 in Cole's only year as a player-coach. He contributed 60 points to the cause. Cole also started for

Trinity as a freshman under Doak in 1918. He was forced to give up basketball in 1920 because of heart trouble.

Coleman, Jack. A 6 – 5 frontcourt regular as a freshman for the 1943 varsity team that played for the Southern Conference championship, Jack L. Coleman, of Burgin, Ky., scored 115 points in his 16 games, with a high of 18 against George Washington. He was also an end on the freshman football team of 1942.

Colley, Nelson. After captaining Duke's undefeated freshman team in 1930, guard Nelson C. Colley, from Washington, D.C., lettered for the 1931 and 1932 varsity teams and scored 58 points in the two years combined. In 1932 he was an honorable mention selection for the Southern Conference All-Tournament team as Duke reached the semifinals in Atlanta.

Collins, Ben. Center Ben Collins, from Hazard, Ky., had a productive three-year varsity career, 1947 – 49. He played in 77 games and scored 672 points. He was the second-leading scorer for the 1948 and 1949 teams, behind all-star Corren Youmans. In 1948 he was named second team All-Southern Conference by the league's coaches after helping a mediocre team reach the tournament championship game. A 6 – 6 pivotman with a potent hook shot, Collins played freshman ball in 1943 and then returned after the war to finish his career. He was a senior co-captain during the 1949 season, when he had two of his best games against Davidson. He hit 10 of 16 field goals for 27 points in one meeting with the Wildcats and had 20 points in another.

Collins, Chris. Duke was about to drop to 0 – 5 in the 1996 ACC race when Chris Collins decided to improvise. The seconds were ticking off the clock in Reynolds Coliseum, the Blue Devils were losing to N.C. State, and teammate Ricky Price was cutting around Collins, expecting an exchange of the ball so that he could maneuver for a potential game-winning shot. But Collins read the defense, kept the ball, and launched a shot of his own from right in front of the Duke bench. The ball bounced around on the rim before finally settling through the net to give the Blue Devils a 71 – 70 victory. It was a most significant moment, as Duke sought to bridge the gap from its dismal 1995 campaign back to respectability. After Collins's shot the Devils won eight of their last 12 league games and returned to the NCAA Tournament.

That was just one of numerous bombs that Christopher Ryan Collins dropped on Duke opponents during his four years, 1993–96. Collins, a 6–3 guard from Northbrook, Ill., was one of the most dangerous perimeter shooters in school history, with deep range and supreme confidence in his ability to connect from anywhere. The son of the former Olympian and NBA standout Doug Collins, Chris grew up immersed in the game. When his father coached the Chicago Bulls, Collins was always around the club for practice and was a ball boy on game day. As his own game took root, he developed the ultimate shooter's mentality, the belief that his next shot was going in whether he'd missed or made several in a row.

Collins played in 120 games at Duke, with 67 starts. He scored 1,091 points with 291 assists, 243 rebounds, and 209 three-pointers. He was extremely accurate from three-point range, hitting 44.1 percent as a senior. His career mark was 38.8 percent, largely because he made only 23 percent of his shots during an injury-plagued junior season.

After averaging over 30 points a game at Glenbrook North High School, Collins enjoyed a solid rookie season in which he started five games for an injured Grant Hill and finished strong with 16 points in his first NCAA Tournament game, played against Southern Illinois at the Rosemont Horizon near his Chicago home. He started for the team that reached the Final Four in 1994 and averaged 10.0 points a game, but his junior year got off on the wrong foot, literally, when he broke a bone on the first day of practice. He went on to play in 28 games, mostly off the bench, and enjoyed a couple of high points, including a win over Illinois when the two schools met in the first college basketball game ever played at the United Center in Chicago. But a nonstop run of close games and a 13–18 record made it a year to forget.

Collins's best season by far was his senior year of 1996, when he sparked a return to respectability with his 16.3 scoring average and his leadership—all while playing with a pin in his foot because of the injury he sustained in the preceding year. Always exuberant on the court,

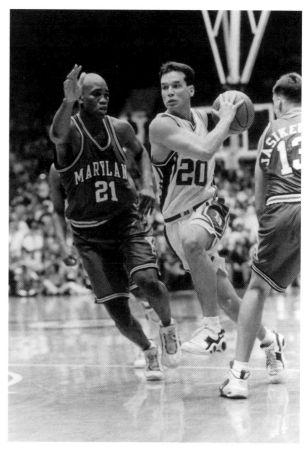

Before becoming a coach, Chris Collins was a dangerous three-point shooter for the Blue Devils.

Collins took ownership of the 1996 season and did everything he could to help restore some of the program's luster. He scored a career high of 30 points against Iowa to help Duke win the Great Alaska Shootout and had 27 early in the year at Michigan. The State shot was a highlight, as was the phone call home that night, since his father's Detroit Pistons had also won, on a shot by Grant Hill in the closing seconds.

Late in the season Collins was at his best when he scored 27 points in three consecutive games, at Florida State, UCLA, and Maryland. The FSU game featured seven three-pointers, a school record, but the game against UCLA may have been his best, as he confounded the nationally ranked Bruins with a variety of drives and jumpers in a convincing 19-point win. Collins had 18 points in 25 minutes in his home finale against UNC but had to leave the game with a foot injury that also kept him out of the ACC tourney.

Chris Duhon and Duke couldn't get past Connecticut in the 2004 Final Four.

In his book *Leading with the Heart* (2000), Krzyzewski revealed that Collins's late-season surge came after the two had a private meeting and video session, during which the coach told his senior to play with no restrictions and do anything he felt was necessary the rest of the year.

"Chris was a bridge to greatness for Duke basketball," Krzyzewski wrote. "He put passion and guts and inspiration back into our team. His heart led us into the NCAA Tournament that year and helped us win the league championship the very next season. Because, even though he had graduated, two underclassmen on Chris's team had taken particular notice of the example he set. Steve Wojciechowski and Trajan Langdon had watched and learned. And, subsequently, they were able to take the lead themselves."

A team captain with Jeff Capel, Collins was Duke's MVP in 1996 and made the All-ACC second team.

After college, Collins played a season of pro ball

in Finland before launching his coaching career. He worked first with the WNBA's Detroit Shock, then for Tommy Amaker at Seton Hall before joining the Duke staff in 2001. The Blue Devils won the national title in his first year back and returned to the Final Four in 2004. Working mostly with the perimeter players, Collins saw guard Jason Williams emerge as a national player of the year early in his career and aided in the development of another long-range shooter, J. J. Redick.

Colonna, Dave. Better known as a scholarship football player, David William Colonna was one of four walk-ons added to the 1987 basketball roster to provide depth. He played in two games, with no points or rebounds. A 6–6 native of High Point, N.C., he lettered for four years as a tight end for the football team, 1986–89, was a first-team All-ACC pick in 1988, and was invited to the East-West Shrine Game after his senior season of 1989, when Duke shared the ACC title and played in the All American Bowl. Colonna had 92 career catches and five touchdowns as an integral figure in coach Steve Spurrier's offense, and he even kicked an extra point to close out the scoring in a 41–0 rout of UNC in his final ACC game.

Connecticut. Duke squared off with the University of Connecticut eight times in its first 100 years of basketball, including five times in NCAA Tournament play and twice at the Final Four. Duke won the first four contests and UConn the next four, including both Final Four bouts.

In 1964 Duke routed UConn behind 30 points from Jeff Mullins to win the East Regional and advance to the Final Four. The Blue Devils' 1990 team also knocked off the Huskies in a regional final to make the Final Four, but in a much closer contest, as Christian Laettner's buzzer shot provided a 79–78 win in overtime. Duke beat UConn more handily the next year in the Sweet 16 on its way to the national crown.

Duke's top-ranked 1999 juggernaut, however, was thwarted by third-ranked UConn, 77–74, in the national championship game at St. Petersburg. The Blue Devils had won 32 games in a row and led the nation in scoring but had their fourth-lowest point total of the year in the final, a disappointing ending for one of the most talented and selfless teams in school history. It marked the first NCAA crown in the first Final Four appearance for the Huskies. They made it two for two in 2004, when they topped Georgia Tech for the title, after overcoming an eight-point deficit with 3:28 to play to beat Duke in the semis 79–78.

As members of the national élite, the women's programs from Duke and UConn emerged as rivals early in the twenty-first century. The schools have played six times, with the most significant contests in 2003, 2004, and 2006. Duke was ranked No. 1 and UConn No. 2 when the Huskies defeated the Blue Devils 77–65 on February 1, 2003, in the first women's basketball sellout at Cameron Indoor Stadium. The following season Duke defeated UConn 68–67 on a last-second shot by Jessica Foley, to halt the Huskies' 69-game home court winning streak, an NCAA record. Both games matched up the two best players in the country, Diana Taurasi from UConn and Alana Beard from Duke. In 2006 Duke defeated UConn to reach the Final Four.

Connelly, Tom. President of his fraternity and captain of the basketball team in 1941, Thomas Connelly was a key figure during the latter stages of Eddie Cameron's coaching career. A guard from Altoona, Pa., Connelly lettered for the 1939, 1940, and 1941 teams, scoring 87 points while also distributing the ball to other offensive threats. Duke played in two Southern Conference finals during his career, beating South Carolina for the title when he was a senior. Connelly was a junior on the 1940 team that opened Duke Indoor Stadium, scoring four points in the début win over Princeton. Connelly took the first shot in the new stadium—a missed layup in the opening seconds of play. The 1940 campaign was his highest-scoring, with 60 points.

After graduation Connelly was a Duke assistant coach in 1942 and then entered the Army in 1943, receiving a bronze star for his service in the European Theater. He returned to campus to coach the Blue Devil freshman team in 1952 and 1953 while also scouting for head coach Harold Bradley. Connelly provided color commentary on local radio broadcasts of Duke games in 1951 and joined his fellow Duke grad Add Penfield as the color man on a schedule of Big Four broadcasts for WBIG in Greensboro during the 1950s and early 1960s,

while at the same time managing his jewelry store in downtown Durham.

Cook, Bob. A 6–6 forward from Glen Rock, N.J., Robert Wilson Cook averaged a double-double for the 1973 junior varsity team (14.2 points, 11.2 rebounds) but played sparingly for the varsity across two seasons. He saw action in two games as a freshman and 14 as a sophomore in 1974, finishing his career with 18 points and 13 rebounds.

Cook, Joe. Academic difficulties contributed to the basketball demise of Cook, a 6–2 guard. Recruited out of Lincoln, Ill., where he was an all-state player as well as a football quarterback, Cook appeared in just 47 games over parts of three seasons at Duke, with career totals of 82 points, 36 rebounds, and 35 assists. Cook was a solid reserve as a freshman in 1988, revealing quality playmaking skills and tenacious defensive ability. But he played in just five games in 1989 before being ruled academically ineligible. He returned to school in 1990 and earned brief minutes in 18 games, then departed again, never to return.

Cordell, Thomas. One of 10 lettermen on the team that won the Southern Conference championship in 1946, Thomas Cordell, of Bartlesville, Okla., played in 19 games and scored 49 points. The team posted a 21–6 record and beat Wake Forest in the title game.

Corrigan, Jim. After turning down scholarship offers so that he could attend Duke as a walk-on player, James Henry Corrigan III, a 5–11 product of Winston-Salem, eventually earned a scholarship as a reserve guard for coach Bill Foster. Most of his game action in his first three years was for the junior varsity team, for which he averaged almost 25 points in 1979, when he had a 32-point outing against Lafayette. As a senior in 1980 he played in nine varsity games for a team that won the ACC championship and advanced in the NCAA Tournament. Corrigan never missed a shot for the varsity, hitting his only field goal and two free throws for four points. He also had three assists. His dedication to the program was recognized when he won the Ted Mann Jr. award in 1980 as the reserve contributing most to team morale.

Corrigan then embarked on a coaching career. He joined former Duke player Kevin Billerman's staff at Northern High School in Durham for a couple of years before returning to his prep alma mater, Bishop McGuiness. As head coach for four seasons he won 90 games and the state championship in 1987. Corrigan moved to the college ranks to serve under Chuck Swenson at William & Mary for seven years, then went to Old Dominion, where he spent his 12th year as an assistant coach in 2006.

Corrigan's father James and uncle Gene were lacrosse players at Duke in the late 1940s, with Gene going on to a distinguished career in athletic administration (including a term as ACC commissioner) and earning a spot in the Duke Sports Hall of Fame.

Councilor, Harry. A Duke Sports Hall of Famer, Harry A. "Chalky" Councilor was a mainstay during the school's transition into the Southern Conference. Councilor, a three-year starter from Washington, D.C., teamed with two other future Hall of Famers in his class, Boley Farley and Bill Werber, to help usher in a more competitive brand of basketball. The trio guided Duke to records of 9 – 5, 12 – 8, and 18 – 2 during their heyday, 1928 – 30.

Councilor scored 70 points for the 1929 team, the first coached by Eddie Cameron and the first to play in the Southern Conference. He had 127 points in 1930, when he co-captained the club with Farley. Duke stunned its new league by reaching the conference tournament finals in each of those years. Councilor was an all-tournament selection in 1930. He was inducted into the Duke Sports Hall of Fame in 1979.

Cowdrick, Tom. A 5 – 8 reserve guard from Philadelphia, Thomas W. Cowdrick lettered for the team that won the Southern Conference championship in 1941 but did not score a point. He was also a backup in 1940, and he got in one game during the 1939 campaign, scoring one point.

Cox, Fred. During the 1961 and 1963 seasons Frederick Cox, a 6 – 5 reserve from Pittsfield, Mass., played in seven varsity games. He had seven points and three rebounds. He was not in school in 1962.

Cox, Ray. The son of a former Duke football player and head tennis coach, Bob Cox, Ray Lawrence Cox was a scrappy 6 – 0 guard from Durham who lettered for three years, 1962 – 64. He played in 39 games and had 33 points with 25 rebounds. Cox was also a class officer in the engineering school, serving as president in his senior year.

Crazy Towel Guy. He used to carry a business card that claimed he was "Duke's No. 1 Fan." But Herb Neubauer became better known in Cameron Indoor Stadium as the Crazy Towel Guy. Student fans chant for him by that name a couple of times each home game, and Neubauer rises out of his seat in Section 7 to wave a white towel as everyone goes wild.

Neubauer, a native of Rockingham, N.C., and 1964 Duke grad, started bringing the towel to games to wipe away sweat in the Cameron cauldron. He began waving it to get the crowd going in the mid-1990s, and soon the routine developed into a regular occurrence at every home game.

A former mayoral candidate in Charlotte, Neubauer retired in the late 1980s at the age of 45 thanks to profitable stock in the Food Lion grocery chain. He then moved to Durham and became a fixture at Duke sports events. He endowed a scholarship on campus and has helped student groups to raise money for charity with his towels.

Croson, Joe. Considered the best big man during the early years of Duke basketball, Joe Croson, a 6 – 4 pivotman, lettered for the varsity for three seasons, 1929 – 31, and led each team in scoring. In 55 games he totaled 558 points, the school's career scoring record at the time. He averaged 10 points a game during an era when the entire team typically scored 35 to 37. His career high was a 20-point game against South Carolina in 1929.

Croson was recruited to Duke by two of his former teammates at McKinley Tech in Washington, D.C., Bill Werber and Harry Councilor. They convinced athletics director Jimmy DeHart that Croson, who was in business school in D.C., was the man the Blue Devils needed and should be offered a scholarship. Croson arrived on campus in January 1928 and stepped right into the lineup of the freshman team. He became eligible for varsity competition in 1929, the same year Eddie Cameron arrived as head coach and the same year Duke joined the Southern Conference. With the three McKinley Tech products playing almost every minute, the Blue Devils shocked the new league by reaching the championship game in each of their first two years in the circuit.

Croson scored 15 points to help Duke end a 16-game losing streak to UNC in 1929. He was Duke's only double-figures scorer in the conference final in 1929, with 12 points. The next year he totaled 13 points to aid an upset of national powerhouse Loyola of Chicago and had six of the Devils' 24 points in the conference title game. Croson made either the first or second team all-tournament squad for all three years, although Duke lost in the quarterfinals in his senior year, after Werber and Councilor had graduated.

Crow, Mark. One of Duke's most accomplished international pro players, Mark Harvey Crow, from Richmond, developed from a frontcourt reserve into a two-year starter who played in 87 varsity games during his career, 1974–77. He scored 820 points, had 346 rebounds, shot over 50 percent from the field, and hit almost 80 percent of his foul shots as a 6–8 forward.

Crow led the 1974 junior varsity team in scoring while also playing in 10 varsity contests as a freshman. He became a regular as a sophomore and blossomed as a junior when he averaged 12 points a game. He enjoyed one of his best career games in 1976, with 26 points and nine rebounds against North Carolina, hitting 13 of 17 shots. He also hit 19 points in an upset of seventh-ranked Maryland that year.

Senior co-captain of the 1977 team, Crow averaged 13.6 points and had his best rebounding season with a 6.3 average. His career rebounding high of 12 came in that year against East Carolina, while his career scoring high of 28 points (with 10 rebounds) was posted against Duquesne. He also had 20 points in a last-second win over his hometown Richmond Spiders.

Crow was the 111th pick in the NBA draft and played one season with the New Jersey Nets, 1978, before heading overseas for a long pro career, most of it spent in Italy.

Crowder, Dick. A 6–5 center-forward and all-state football player from High Point, N.C., Richard Joseph Crowder came to Duke in the fall of 1948 with three other scholarship basketball recruits, including Dick Groat, and led the Blue Imps freshmen in scoring in his first year. He then moved up to the varsity and was a regular in the lineup over the next three years, appearing in all 93 games during the 1950–52 seasons while scoring 642 points for a 6.9 average. He was also president of the senior class in 1952.

Statistically Crowder's best year was as a junior in 1951, when he averaged 8.6 points, second on the team only to Groat, and had a career high of 26 points against Washington & Lee. He averaged 6.1 points and 7.3 rebounds as a senior, the first year that Duke compiled official rebounding statistics. Duke played N.C. State in the Southern Conference championship game during all three of Crowder's varsity seasons, dropping all three meetings.

Crowder also served two years as the assistant coach of the freshman team, in 1954–55, while he was in his second and third years of divinity school.

Crowder, John. The older brother of former Duke player and coach Dick Crowder, John Crowder, a 6–2 guard and Naval trainee, lettered for one year for the basketball team. He was the second-team guard on the 1945 team that played for the Southern Conference championship, scoring 21 points for the season and giving his best performance in the conference tournament. Crowder was better known as a Duke football player, lettering at center for the 1944 and 1945 teams. In fact, his Sugar Bowl appearance delayed his arrival to the basketball squad.

Crowder, Max. See Trainers.

Crump, Vince. As a 6–6 sophomore walk-on from Durham, Vincent Fitzgerald Crump played in seven games for the 1984 Duke team, scoring one point with one rebound.

Cunningham, Billy. Hall of Famer Billy Cunningham, who starred for North Carolina from 1963 through 1965, was always ready for match-ups with Duke. He

CUNNINGHAM – CURRIE **149**

faced the Blue Devils seven times and averaged 23.6 points against them. He had 19 points with 20 rebounds in his first Duke battle, and 25 points with 16 rebounds in his last. He also had games of 31 and 28 points against Duke. Cunningham lost his first five match-ups in 1963 and 1964, when he was a unanimous All-ACC selection, but finally beat the Devils twice in 1965 when he was the league player of the year.

Currie, Monique. She provided a striking portrait of her potential in the ACC Tournament championship game as a freshman in 2002, when she poured in 30 points and grabbed 12 rebounds to help the Blue Devils whip North Carolina for the title. She'd already averaged over 14 points a game as a part-time starter and made the All-ACC second team, and now she was MVP of the ACC tourney. Monique Currie's college career was off to a flying start.

The following November there was a crash landing when Currie tore the anterior cruciate ligament in her left knee during the first minute of the opening exhibition game and was lost for the season. But after a year of recovery, Currie was back to form as an All-ACC second-teamer again in 2004, and in 2005 she firmly established herself as one of the school's and conference's all-time greats when she made the All-ACC first team, was chosen ACC player of the year, and finished as a consensus first-team All-America. Her legacy was further assured in 2006 when she made the Kodak All-America team for the second straight year and guided the Blue Devils back to the Final Four, the team's third trip in her five years. She had a team high of 22 points in the national championship game against Maryland.

Currie completed her career with 2,122 points, 874 rebounds, and 413 assists in 140 games, 127 of which she started. As a sophomore she matched her school's single-game assists record when she had 12 against Georgia Tech. During her junior year she averaged 17.5 points and emerged as the Blue Devils' go-to performer in the era after Alana Beard. Her overall numbers dipped slightly in her senior season when Duke used a deeper roster, but she also delivered some of her best performances. Against Florida State she had the second triple-double in school history with 21 points, 12 rebounds, and 11 assists. She helped Duke defeat Maryland in a

Monique Currie was the MVP of the ACC Tournament in her freshman year and earned a spot on the league's Silver Anniversary women's team selected in 2002.

nationally televised home game by scoring 10 of her team's first 13 points on the way to a career high of 31. Currie then outdid herself in Duke's next contest, when she broke the single-game school scoring mark with 43 points at Miami, on 11-of-18 shooting from the field and 15-of-16 shooting from the foul line. Duke won in double overtime, with Currie getting 15 points in the second overtime while hitting 10 of 10 free throws in the last 93 seconds.

Currie graduated in May 2005 and toyed with heading to the WNBA before deciding to use her medical red-shirt option and return for another college season. After helping the United States win a gold medal at the World University Games she enrolled in a master's degree program, and her teammates were more than happy to have their leader back for another run, because they

Hubie Brown, Chuck Daly, and Vic Bubas made for a formidable coaching staff in 1969.

considered her one of the most menacing players in the country.

"She's such a quality player and she's so tough," said guard Jessica Foley. "She gives the team a mental edge, too. I remember when I first came in I was pretty intimidated by Mo. Now I'm friends with her, but just having her on the team makes us a little more intimidating as a group as well."

"I've always loved Mo's attitude on the court," coach Gail Goestenkors said. "She's going to do whatever it takes to win. She's a warrior. She's one of those players that when you are in a battle, you want her on your team because you know she's going to do what's necessary. She wants the ball in her hands, she's going to take the big shot and she's usually going to make the big shot. There's a mental and physical toughness about her and I think it rubs off on all of her teammates."

Daly, Chuck. He coached the original Dream Team to an Olympic gold medal. He guided the Detroit Pistons to back-to-back world championships. He was inducted into the Naismith Memorial Basketball Hall of Fame and named one of the top 10 NBA coaches of all-time.

But for six years early in his coaching career, Charles Jerome Daly was a key member of Vic Bubas's Duke staff, helping the Blue Devil program compile one of the best major-college records of the decade.

Daly came to Duke from the Pennsylvania high school ranks in the summer of 1963. A few months before his hiring, he had watched the Blue Devils play in the Final Four at Louisville on a scalper's ticket in the farthest row from the court. At the end of his first year in Durham he was in a ringside seat on the bench at the Final Four in Kansas City. "A pretty big jump for me," he recalled. "There's no question that the biggest step I took and the biggest break I got was with Vic Bubas at Duke."

Daly coached the freshman team for his first two years. The frosh went 11 – 4 in 1964 led by Bob Verga, then 13 – 3 in 1965 led by Mike Lewis. When Bucky Waters left Duke to become head coach at West Virginia after the 1965 campaign, Daly moved up to assistant head coach for the next four years — Bubas's final four years — and helped the Devils to a third Final Four in 1966 as well as two NIT berths and three appearances in the ACC final.

When Bubas resigned, the dapper Daly left Duke to become head coach at Boston College for two years and then went to Penn, where he claimed the Ivy League title four times in six years. He made the transition to the pro game as an assistant with the Philadelphia

76ers. He then served as a head coach for Cleveland (41 games), Detroit (nine years), New Jersey (two years), and Orlando (two years), winning 638 games in 14 seasons with two titles (for the Pistons). His winning percentage as a college coach was .709 and as an NBA coach.593. His NBA playoffs record was 75 – 51, with 12 appearances in 14 seasons.

Daly was undefeated as head coach of the 1992 U.S. Olympic team, a collection of NBA legends that went 8 – 0 in Barcelona. Duke's Christian Laettner was the lone collegian on the team, while Mike Krzyzewski was an assistant coach. Daly was elected to the Hall of Fame in 1994 and was named one of the top coaches in NBA history in 1996 during the league's 50th anniversary celebration.

Davidson. Duke and Davidson met for the 100th time during the Blue Devils' 100th season of college basketball in 2005. The two schools first played in 1909, when Duke was still known as Trinity College, and began scheduling each other regularly in 1915. The rivalry was a strong one in the early years, as the Wildcats joined Duke, Wake Forest, N.C. State, and North Carolina in competing for the state of North Carolina's "Big Five" championship. In addition, Davidson became a conference rival of the Blue Devils when the Wildcats joined the Southern Conference in 1937, and the two usually met twice a year until Duke left for the ACC in 1953 – 54.

Duke has dominated the series, winning over 80 percent of the games. Two of the more memorable contests were in the 1963 and 1964 seasons. In 1963 the unranked Wildcats pulled off a shocking 72 – 69 victory over second-ranked Duke. It was the Blue Devils' first loss of that season. Duke also dropped its next game, at Miami, but didn't lose again until reaching the NCAA Final Four. The following season, the two programs met in a February showdown at the Indoor Stadium with Duke ranked fifth in the country and the Wildcats fourth. Duke pulled out this one, 82 – 75, as Jeff Mullins scored 29 points. Davidson star Fred Hetzel, recruited by Duke, had 28 points and 10 rebounds.

Davidson was coached by Duke alumnus Lefty Driesell from 1961 through 1969, during which time it developed into a national power. Davidson won at least 20 games in six of Driesell's last seven years and claimed the Southern Conference regular-season crown in five of

his last six years. Davidson won two of six games against Duke during the Driesell years, the upset in 1963 and an overtime decision in 1969 against Vic Bubas's last team, when the Wildcats were ranked No. 5 in the country.

Duke won 26 of 27 games with Davidson from 1973 through 2006. The only Davidson victory during that stretch was in December 1981, when the Wildcats hit a last-second shot to defeat the Blue Devils in Cameron in the Iron Duke Classic. Duke's average margin of victory in its next 18 consecutive wins over Davidson was about 30 points.

Davidson, Patrick. Joseph Patrick Davidson, a walk-on guard, played in 29 games during his first two Duke seasons, 2004 – 05, and scored four points with five rebounds. All of his points came at the free-throw line, where he was a perfect 4 for 4. One of the leaders of the Blue team in practice, Davidson started one contest in 2005, the Blue Devils' home game with Wake Forest. Davidson played the first two minutes, performed aggressively on defense against the Deacons' point guard Chris Paul, and helped set the tone for one of the team's most significant regular-season victories. At the end of the season, he and fellow reserve Patrick Johnson received the coach's award for commitment and values. Davidson was awarded a scholarship for the 2006 campaign but could not compete because of injury.

A native of Melbourne, Ark., Davidson originally signed with Lehigh out of high school but instead went to Blair Academy in New Jersey for a year of prep school. He was a teammate there of Duke's scholarship signee Luol Deng. Blair had a 25 – 4 record and Davidson was chosen the team's defensive MVP.

In 2006 Davidson was joined at Duke by his brother, Jordan Kenneth Davidson, a 6 – 1 walk-on reserve guard. Jordan also played at Melbourne High for three years before finishing his prep career at Blair.

Davis, Brian. His first impression of Cameron Indoor Stadium was not destined for a Duke basketball recruiting video. As a high school senior making his campus visit, Brian Davis walked into the empty gym in February 1988 and thought to himself, "This isn't Cameron. I've seen high school gyms better than this."

But the next night, with Duke playing N.C. State in

the first game of a weekend doubleheader, one side of the student section started chanting "Brian" and the other side answered "Davis," and the prepster from Capitol Heights, Md., knew where he was. The following day, Davis had even more fun watching Billy King spark a win over Notre Dame with one of the epic defensive performances in school history.

Davis thought about that on the eve of his final game at Cameron in 1992, a win over North Carolina that enabled him and his roommate Christian Laettner to finish with one of the best home records in school history at 56–2. It was one of the many glittery accomplishments of his four-year run, 1989–92, which included four trips to the Final Four, two national titles, and a 21–2 record in the NCAA Tournament.

Brian Keith Davis, a 6–7 forward, appeared in 141 of the Devils' 149 games, with 952 points, 434 rebounds, and 181 assists. He shot 46.5 percent from the field and was a double-figures scorer in his senior year, with an 11.2 average. But Davis's story had very little to do with statistics and more to do with keeping the team's blood flowing as an energizer, defensive stopper, communicator, and leader.

Davis was a perimeter reserve for his first two years, with his most recognized moment coming at the end of the 1990 season. After a timeout huddle, Laettner was preparing to pass the ball in bounds for a final play against Connecticut, a Final Four trip hanging in the balance. Mike Krzyzewski changed his mind on the call after he saw UConn's defense and yelled out, "Special." Davis heard it and knew what to do; as soon as he received Laettner's pass he gave it right back, and Laettner hit the game-winning shot.

Davis started only 11 games in his junior year, but he was frequently a finisher. And no finish was better than his performance in the second half of the NCAA semifinal with UNLV. He played 14 minutes off the bench in the decisive period, hit 5 of 8 shots, and scored 15 points with four rebounds as the Devils stunned the top-ranked Rebels, 79–77. With Duke down by one point at the five-minute mark, Davis slammed home a thunderous dunk to give his team the lead. Then, as the clock raced toward the final minute, he scored on a drive to tie the score at 76 and added a free throw to give Duke another lead.

Brian Davis was a key communicator and defensive stopper for the 1991 and 1992 NCAA title teams.

Davis's best year was his senior season of 1992, when the Blue Devils went 34–2 and he shared captain's duties with Laettner and started all but one game. He made some significant contribution in nearly every game of the campaign, from a 19-point effort in a home rout of Florida State to his tomahawk dunks versus N.C. State for win No. 20. On a trip to UCLA he had 19 points and 11 rebounds, then followed up with a career high of 30 points in a 98–97 comeback victory at Clemson. At the ACC Tournament he was outstanding on the offensive and defensive ends in helping the Blue Devils reach a goal by winning the league championship, the only title that had previously eluded the team during his career. Davis was on the all-tournament first team.

Davis was superb during the NCAA as well, but he suffered a severe ankle sprain that kept him out of the

Johnny Dawkins led Duke in scoring for four straight years and finished with more points than anyone else in school history.

starting lineup for the only time in his senior year, the national championship game against Michigan. Yet he was able to contribute 10 minutes of solid relief as Duke claimed its second national title.

Davis was a player who did not allow basketball to define his entire college experience. He was extremely active on campus and in community outreach efforts, and his summer internships included stints with Sen. Terry Sanford, the Discovery Channel, and a Wall Street firm.

"What I've done is to allow other things besides basketball to be very important in my life," he said. "I think if I would have allowed basketball to be the only thing in my life to determine who I am, then this [final game] would be a sad day. I'd like to play in the NBA someday, too, but I'm not depending on that to make my life satisfying. Once you start to think like that, it's hard to be at peace with yourself, and I'm very much at peace with myself."

Davis played in the NBA during the 1994 season, and he got involved with several entrepreneurial activities, including a partnership with Laettner in a commercial development firm, Blue Devil Ventures.

Davis, William. A reserve for the 1935 team, William Carson Davis, of Collingswood, N.J., lettered and scored 13 points.

Dawkins, Johnny. Adroit, dynamic, and indefatigable, Johnny Dawkins was the original marquee performer who ushered Mike Krzyzewski's Duke program to national distinction. When Dawkins committed to Krzyzewski as a blue-chip prepster, other top recruits were not far behind. When Dawkins took the floor in Durham, his cohesive classmates followed him for four years, through adversity and past doubt, all the way to the national championship game.

Duke lost by three in Dawkins's last contest, against Louisville in the NCAA final in 1986, and Dawkins says he has never got over it. But he sleeps well knowing that he poured everything he had into that Final Four and walked off the court with nothing left in the tank. That made him all the more appreciative, 15 years later, when he was able to experience the national title in 2001 as Duke's associate head coach.

"As a coach, the greatest lesson I've learned is how great it is to see something from beginning to end," he said. "I never completed it in '86, but in 2001 I got to see it in its completion, from start to finish, from the summer workouts and the preseason workouts all the way through the ACC and the tournaments, to finally get to the final game and win it.

"People will see us as a great team that won a championship that year, but no one sees the work and preparation that went into the success of that season. That's something as a life lesson that I'll always take with me from that season, the amount of hard work and preparation that it takes to be successful. People say you're champions, that's great, but they don't see the commitment and the sacrifices that everyone has to make for that to be accomplished."

Johnny Earl Dawkins Jr. made that commitment to excellence as a high school, college, and pro player, and as a coach. A 6 – 2 left-hander from Washington, D.C.,

Iron Men

At the annual Duke basketball awards banquet each season, the team leader in minutes played receives the Iron Duke award. Johnny Dawkins ranks as the undisputed iron man in school history, the only player to lead the team in that category for four consecutive years. Dawkins played 38 minutes in his career opener versus East Carolina and never looked back, averaging over 35 minutes a game for four years, 1983–86.

Thirty-two times in his career Dawkins played at least 40 minutes in a game, more than any other Blue Devil. His sophomore year was his most amazing from the standpoint of stamina. He averaged over 38 minutes a game and had 16 games of 40 or more minutes. Dawkins played 40 minutes for three straight days at the Rainbow Classic. Later, when Duke had back-to-back overtime contests versus Wake Forest and N.C. State, Dawkins went the full 45 against the Deacons and 43 against the Wolfpack.

Statistics for minutes played have been compiled consistently since the mid-1970s. Other notable Duke iron men since then:

— Post man Alan Shaw just about never left the court during his junior year of 1972, with an average of close to 39 minutes a game and at least 11 games of 40 minutes.

— Point guard Bobby Hurley graduated in 1993 with the school record of 4,802 minutes played. He didn't go the distance nearly as often as Dawkins, but he never ran out of gas either. For the biggest games, Hurley rarely took a breather. He played every minute of the Final Four in 1991, for example, and all 45 minutes of the Kentucky overtime game in 1992.

— Shane Battier had 10 games of at least 40 minutes during his senior year of 2001. In four games against Maryland that year he played 42, 38, 40, and 40. In the NCAA tourney he played 26 minutes in the first round, then rested for only one minute total in the next five contests as Duke won the national title.

— Point guard Chris Duhon broke Hurley's career minutes record at 4,813—the most ever by an ACC player—and

was rarely on the bench in his senior year of 2004. He had 11 games of at least 40 minutes, including the ACC championship overtime game against Maryland, when he bruised his ribs while trying to save a ball but still logged 40 of 45 minutes. He was on the floor for 601 of a possible 645 minutes.

— J. J. Redick knew he'd need to play extended minutes in 2005 and prepared for it with extensive preseason conditioning. He'd played 40 minutes only twice before that year but averaged 37.3 minutes with 11 complete games, including all 45 in overtime at Maryland. He missed only 32 minutes of action during the 2005 ACC regular season, and only 36 ACC minutes as a senior in 2006, when he played at least 40 minutes on nine occasions.

Most Games of 40 or More Minutes, Career

1.	Johnny Dawkins, 1983–86	32
2.	J. J. Redick, 2003–06	22
3.	Chris Duhon, 2001–04	20
4.	Jim Spanarkel, 1976–79	19
5.	Bobby Hurley, 1990–93	17
	Shane Battier, 1998–2001	17
7.	Dick DeVenzio, 1969–71	16
8.	Vince Taylor, 1979–82	15
9.	Tommy Amaker, 1984–87	14
	Howard Hurt, 1959–61	14

Fewest Minutes Missed, Season
(Minimum of 800 Minutes Played)

1.	Vince Taylor, 1982	73	(1,037 / 1,110)
2.	Johnny Dawkins, 1984	79	(1,306 / 1,385)
3.	Jim Spanarkel, 1977	81	(1,019 / 1,100)
4.	J. J. Redick, 2005	94	(1,231 / 1,325)
5.	Chip Engelland, 1982	102	(1,008 / 1,110)
6.	J. J. Redick, 2006	109	(1,336 / 1,445)
7.	Johnny Dawkins, 1983	117	(1,003 / 1,120)
8.	Jim Spanarkel, 1979	121	(1,084 / 1,205)
9.	Johnny Dawkins, 1985	138	(1,117 / 1,255)
10.	Chris Duhon, 2003	142	(1,188 / 1,330)

he was the first big-name recruit to align with Krzyzewski as a prep senior in 1982. Mark Alarie, Jay Bilas, and David Henderson joined in, and the foursome made up the heart of Krzyzewski's first championship team. After a year of indoctrination, the group accompanied

the coach on his first three NCAA rides, culminating in his first ACC title and first Final Four in 1986.

Dawkins started all 133 games over four years, scored in double figures in all but four of them, and led the team in points each season, the only player to do so in school history. He finished with 2,556 points, the most ever at Duke until J. J. Redick surpassed that total in 2006. Dawkins is the only Duke player to have taken over 2,000 shots and made over 1,000. He shot 50.8 percent from the floor and 79.0 from the foul line. He never led the ACC in scoring but averaged 19.2 points for his career and placed second in conference points three times, once to Michael Jordan and twice to Len Bias. Dawkins won or shared the Duke MVP award in all four of his years.

As a freshman, Dawkins had to run the team as its point guard in addition to shouldering a scoring load. When Tommy Amaker arrived as the Blue Devils' distributor cap the next year, Dawkins had that responsibility lifted, and the two combined to form one of the most complementary backcourt combos ever in the ACC. Even while he was expected to score, Dawkins continued to involve everyone else in the offense. His assist totals as a sophomore and junior exceeded his freshman output, and he finished with 555 for his career, the first Blue Devil to top the 500 mark. He also had 536 career rebounds.

Dawkins put points on the board in every conceivable manner. He could work either end of the fast break, either end of the alley-oop, drive, pull up, and drain the long ones. His creativity and instincts were accentuated in Krzyzewski's motion offense, as was his coach's confidence in him. Bilas refers to him as the most important player in program history, and Alarie forever marvels at his demeanor. "Johnny was far and away the best player I ever played with, college or NBA, at bringing a confident, no one-can-stop-us attitude to every game. And no one could stop him," Alarie noted.

Dawkins's career high of 34 points came in one of his definitive performances, a complete 40-minute effort to lead the Blue Devils to victory at UNC in 1985. It was the program's last visit to Carmichael Auditorium, a historical house of horrors where Duke had lost 18 straight games. Dawkins went on to earn first-team All-ACC honors and consensus All-America honors, setting up his best season in 1986, when he averaged 20.2 points and co-captained the Devils to a mark of 37–3.

Although they played at a high level all season, February and March were special for Dawkins and his teammates. The university retired his No. 24 jersey before a

game with Oklahoma, making him just the third Blue Devil to receive that honor. In the following week the senior class, which also included reserve Weldon Williams, claimed an emotional win over UNC to close its home career in first place in the ACC. The next week, Dawkins was MVP as the Devils edged their second-biggest rival, Georgia Tech, for the ACC tourney championship.

Once the NCAA began, the nation had a chance to watch Dawkins unleash the full torrent of his ability. In six playoff games he scored 153 points for a 25.5 average, and he single-handedly made sure that the Devils avoided one of the biggest upsets in tourney history by carrying them past upstart Mississippi Valley State in the opening round.

"He just wouldn't let Duke lose, and they were soundly beaten for 30 or 32 minutes," recalled Bucky Waters, the TV analyst for the contest. "He just absolutely took the game over. That was about as good of a one-man performance at the NCAA level that I've seen."

Dawkins had 28 points in the regional final over Navy, including a memorable reverse dunk, and he totaled 24 in each of the Final Four games. A 40-game season might have left some players fatigued at the end, but Dawkins shot 11 of 17 and 10 of 19 in his two Final Four games. Honors included the East Region MVP, the Naismith Award as national player of the year, a spot on the All-Final Four team, and consensus All-America again. He was the first player in Duke history to be named consensus first-team All-America twice.

Dawkins's pro career spanned nine seasons. Unlike in his college career, he had just one season in which he started every game, and he missed the majority of two campaigns because of injury. But he was regarded as a regular throughout, with 303 starts in 541 career contests for the Spurs, 76ers, and Pistons. Drafted with the 10th pick by San Antonio, Dawkins averaged 11.1 points and 27.5 minutes for his career. His best year was 1990, when he started all but one contest, averaged 14.3 points, and dished over 600 assists to help Philadelphia reach the conference semifinals.

After retiring from the NBA, Dawkins spent a year as an administration intern at his alma mater, worked on the radio broadcast team, and was inducted into the Duke Sports Hall of Fame (1996). He joined Krzyzewski's coaching staff for the 1998 season and was elevated to associate head coach in 2000. Duke was ranked No. 1 nationally at some point in each of his first seven years and won seven ACC championships in his first nine.

One of Dawkins's areas of expertise is player development. He learned of the necessity of year-round training while in the NBA but had already gained an appreciation for it while in college, playing with USA Basketball one summer and serving as an alternate for the Olympic team in 1984. He teams with the school's strength-and-conditioning staff to direct individual improvement programs for each player.

Dawson, Jeff. As a high school All-America, Jeff Crawford Dawson almost followed his brother Jim to Illinois, where he was the team captain and the player of the year in the Big Ten. Jeff finally decided in June before his freshman year to come to Duke instead, enjoyed a great season on the frosh team, and played in every varsity game as a sophomore in 1971. But after that one varsity campaign he decided to head back home and transferred to Illinois. A 6 – 1 guard from Downers Grove, Ill., Dawson scored 288 points in his 30-game Duke career, with highs of 22 points against North Carolina, 21 against Virginia Tech, and 20 against N.C. State.

Day, Alison. Recruited by coach Debbie Leonard, Alison Day played her entire career under coach Gail Goestenkors and was in the core group of players that the women's program relied on to reach national respectability. A 6 – 3 center from Hudson, Ohio, Day played in 115 games and started 83 from 1993 to 1996. She scored 1,235 points (10.7 a game) and added 617 rebounds (5.4 a game) while hitting almost 54 percent of her field goals. She also had touch away from the paint, stepping out to the three-point line to hit 60 threes in her last two years.

Day was Duke's leader in field-goal percentage and free-throw percentage three times each. Her best season was 1995, when she topped Duke in scoring average (16.1), was second on the boards (6.6), and earned first-team All-ACC honors for a team that won 22 games and made the NCAA for the first time since 1987. Day had the game-winning shot when Duke knocked off UNC to end the Tar Heels' 32-game winning streak, and she tied the school scoring record with 37 points in a four-overtime NCAA tourney game at Alabama.

Day made the All-ACC second team as a senior in 1996, when she averaged 11.8 points and 6.7 boards while hitting 44 three-pointers. That team posted a record of 26 – 7 and went 12 – 4 in the ACC. Day also made the ACC Honor Roll in all four years.

Dean, Chubby. Major league baseball pitcher Alfred Lovill "Chubby" Dean was a 5 – 11 reserve guard on the Duke basketball roster in 1936 but did not letter. A native of Mt. Airy, N.C., he played seven seasons in the majors between 1937 and 1943 and pitched in 162 games, with a record of 30 – 46.

Decker, Marvin. An asset in Duke's double-pivot offense of the mid-1950s, Marvin Clement Decker played forward and center and was one of the Blue Devils' most effective rebounders. A 6 – 5 native of Bloomfield, N.J., he played freshman ball in 1951, began the 1952 season on the junior varsity, and was promoted to the varsity at midyear because of his excellent performances. He started in 1953 and was the team's No. 2 rebounder with an average of 8.3. In a rout of North Carolina to close the regular season, Decker came up with 19 rebounds. He also showed some scoring punch with a 21-point game against West Virginia and seven others in double figures. As a senior in 1954 he had 15 and 13 points in the first two games but saw mostly relief duty. His career totals: 60 games, 312 points, 350 rebounds.

Defensive Player of the Year. Originally established by a Rotary Club in Houston and named the Henry Iba Corinthian Award in honor of a legendary coach, an award for national defensive player of the year has been given since 1987. Duke senior point guard Tommy Amaker was the first recipient. The National Association of Basketball Coaches took over administration of the award, which had been presented nine times to Duke players through the 2006 season: Amaker 1987, Billy King 1988, Grant Hill 1993, Steve Wojciechowski 1998, Shane Battier 1999, 2000, and 2001, Shelden Williams 2005 and 2006. Battier, Stacey Augmon of UNLV, and Tim Duncan of Wake Forest are the only three-time recipients.

Deimling, Kes. After earning all-state basketball honors and winning a pair of national singles tennis championships in high school, Keston John Deimling lettered for two years for the Duke varsity in 1951–52, scoring 295 points in 60 games. Deimling was the top scorer on the 1950 freshman team and one of the top varsity reserves in 1951, when he averaged 6.9 points a game. His career high of 16 points was against North Carolina, and he scored in double figures seven other times in 1951. His playing time diminished after that season. A 6–4 forward from Oak Park, Ill., Deimling extended his prep tennis success to college as the No. 1 player for the Duke team that won the Southern Conference championship in 1952.

Delaware. Duke and the University of Delaware have met just once on the basketball court, but the connection between the two programs extends beyond that game. The Blue Hens hired three consecutive head coaches who were former Duke assistant coaches: Bill Foster's assistant Steve Steinwedel (1986–95), Mike Krzyzewski's assistant Mike Brey (1996–2000), and former Duke player and coach David Henderson (2001–06). Steinwedel worked at South Carolina in between his Duke and Delaware positions. Brey and Henderson went directly from the Blue Devils to the Blue Hens.

The only game between the two schools was played on December 19, 1995, when Brey brought his first Delaware team to Cameron Indoor Stadium and played Duke close before falling 79–73.

Dement, Mike. A member of Mike Krzyzewski's coaching staff for the 1983 season, Mike Dement spent one year with the Blue Devils. Dement, a native of Louisburg, N.C., and an East Carolina graduate, was listed as a volunteer assistant, with on-campus recruiting as well as floor coaching responsibilities. Eventually he became a college head coach, posting a record of 260–243 in his first 18 years. He coached at Cornell for five seasons beginning with the 1987 campaign, moved to UNC Greensboro for four years, and then took over the program at SMU. He guided the Mustangs to a record of 138–120 in nine years, until his dismissal late in the 2004 season. In April 2005 he returned for a second stint as head coach at UNCG, where he had previously posted a record of 55–56 while leading the program into the Division I era. He had one NCAA bid at Cornell and one NIT bid at SMU.

D'Emilio, Rudy. A 5–11 guard from Philadelphia, Rudolph John D'Emilio enjoyed a standout varsity career, 1952–54. D'Emilio, a three-year starter and two-time team captain, played in 80 games and scored 1,028 points with 330 rebounds. The Blue Devils had a 64–20 record during his career.

D'Emilio teamed with Dick Groat in the backcourt in 1952 and demonstrated his scoring and playmaking ability with a scoring average of 11.2 as well as 100 assists. He delivered 25 points in a victory at UNC. With Groat gone, his scoring increased in the following two years. His career high of 30 points was in 1953 against George Washington, while he totaled nine games of 20 or more points in his last two years.

In an overtime conquest of Wake Forest in 1953, D'Emilio scored the game-winning layup with seven seconds remaining despite playing on a broken toe that kept him out of the next three games. In December 1953 he helped Duke win its only Dixie Classic by leading the team in scoring in three straight games, scoring 19 versus Oregon State, 23 versus Wake Forest, and 24 versus Navy in the final.

D'Emilio was the most valuable player of Duke's last team to play in the Southern Conference. In the first year of ACC play, 1954, D'Emilio made the initial All-ACC first team. He also lettered in soccer during the fall of 1953 for the team that finished as the runner-up in the first official season of ACC play in the sport.

Deng, Luol. Six-time ACC rookie of the week. Unanimous ACC All-Freshman selection. Third-team All-ACC player. Most Outstanding Player at the NCAA Atlanta Regional. Then gone to the NBA. That was the storyline for Luol Deng's one and only season with the Duke basketball team.

A 6–8 forward, Deng made quite an impact on Duke, ACC, and college basketball as a freshman in 2004. He played in all 37 games and started 32 for a team that reached the Final Four, finishing second on the squad in scoring with 558 points for a 15.1 average. He was also the second-leading rebounder, with 255 boards for a 6.9 average. Deng led all freshmen in the ACC in scoring, rebounding, and field-goal percentage. His all-around game made him an asset at nearly every position, and he was Duke's leading scorer during its NCAA Tournament run.

Luol Deng was the ACC rookie of the week six times in his only college season.

high school basketball at Blair (N.J.) Academy and patterned his game after that of former Duke star Grant Hill. After his one Duke season, Deng declared for the NBA draft and was selected by Phoenix with the seventh pick of the first round. Phoenix then traded his rights to the Chicago Bulls. He made the NBA all-rookie first team in 2005.

Dennard, Kenny. There is no shortage of stories about Kenneth Stephen Dennard and his Duke basketball career. One of the most aggressive forwards in school history, he was also one of the most fun-loving and gregarious. He would stop at nothing to pursue a loose ball or rebound, and the same could be said of his personality off the court.

A 6 – 8 native of King, N.C., Dennard was a four-year starter on teams that went to three NCAA Tournaments and one NIT, 1978 – 81. He played in 117 games with 1,057 points, 671 rebounds, and 232 assists. He shot 51.3 percent from the floor and had career highs of 28 points (against Long Beach State) and 16 rebounds (twice). Dennard was recruited by Bill Foster and played for him for three years, then spent his senior season under Mike Krzyzewski, when he and classmate Gene Banks were the co-captains and co-MVPs.

The stories about Dennard began before he even arrived at Duke, when a North Carolina newspaper columnist bet a colleague $100 that Dennard would not score 100 points in his career. That bet was lost early in his freshman season, when Dennard and Banks stepped immediately into the starting lineup, teamed with Mike Gminski to form the "Duke Power Company," and helped the Blue Devils reach the Final Four. Dennard had a 22-point game against Clemson in the ACC Tournament, pumping in shot after shot from the corner, and made the all-tourney second team as his Blue Devils won that event for the first time since 1966.

Near the end of the 1978 season, with Duke about to finish off Villanova for the berth in the Final Four, Dennard provided a punctuation mark with a flamboyant dunk. Dennard will tell you that it was the first reverse dunk ever by a college player on national television. Another first was recorded the following weekend in St. Louis, when Dennard decided to visit fans in the Arkansas section during the Final Four consolation game

Deng played at a high level from the beginning, when he opened his career with back-to-back games of 21 and 20 points. His worst outing was at home against Georgia Tech in March, when he hit just 1 of 14 shots for three points and saw Duke lose a 41-game home winning streak. He bounced back with his best game a few days later, hitting 12 of 16 shots for 25 points in the home finale against UNC. At the Atlanta Regional he had games of 18 and 19 points to lead Duke over Illinois and Xavier. Two plays late in the Xavier game made the difference, as the Blue Devils secured a Final Four berth: Deng saved a rebound and hurled it outside to J. J. Redick for a three-pointer, and on the next possession he rose above the crowd to tip in an offensive rebound that gave Duke a five-point lead.

A native of Sudan who fled to Egypt during a civil war and then moved to London as a youngster, Deng played

Kenny Dennard joined Mike Gminski and Gene Banks on a frontline known as the Duke Power Company.

take an improbable ACC Tournament championship. Duke defeated Maryland 73 – 72 at the buzzer, and Terp fans will forever insist that Dennard undercut their Buck Williams on the decisive play, though nothing was called. Soon after, Dennard and the Devils enjoyed one of the biggest wins in school history when they beat Kentucky at Rupp Arena in their third straight NCAA visit. It was Foster's last victory.

Dennard's free-spirited style was not exactly a perfect match with his new coach Krzyzewski, the Army product who took over for Dennard's senior year. But his all-out hustle on the floor overcame any differences, and the result was his best statistical season, a 10.6 scoring average and a rebounding mark of 6.9 to lead the team. He played more minutes than anyone but guard Vince Taylor, and he was particularly strong in the NIT after Banks went down with an injury. But the enduring story from that season will always be his pass to Banks for the buzzer-beating shot on Senior Day to tie UNC and force overtime. Until it was eclipsed by the pass from Hill to Laettner in 1992 against Kentucky, that ranked as perhaps the most memorable pass in school history.

Dennard played in three NBA seasons after Duke, while also winning a battle against testicular cancer, before becoming a successful businessman in Houston.

at the Checkerdome, barely an hour before he was supposed to take the court and play for the national title. When he returned to the Duke locker room, in time for the pre-game warmup, he was wearing a Razorback hog head.

The next year, NCAA Tournament time was not so giddy. Expected to contend for the championship, the Blue Devils were victimized by a rash of misfortune in the opening week of March Madness. Dennard made his contribution by participating in a late-night pickup game on campus and injuring an ankle, which kept him out of the NCAA game. With guard Bob Bender on the shelf after an appendectomy and Gminski dealing with food poisoning, the Devils were upset by St. John's.

Dennard suffered a more legitimate, serious injury in 1980, a deep thigh bruise that cost him nine games. The team also slumped down the stretch of that season. He returned to the lineup with a gutty performance on national TV at Marquette, and then helped the squad

Denton, Randy. At 6 – 10 and 240 pounds, Randy Denton was the most physically imposing player to wear a Duke uniform when he patrolled the court from 1969 through 1971. He was also one of the best. The leading scorer and leading rebounder for three consecutive years, Denton played in all 84 games and totaled 1,658 points with 1,067 rebounds. He became the second Duke player to reach 1,000 career rebounds, breaking Mike Lewis's all-time school record of 1,051. He never won the ACC rebounding title, finishing second to South Carolina's Tom Owens every year, but no one else in Duke history ever averaged more than his 12.7 boards a game. He also finished among the top 10 scorers in the ACC every year and made the All-ACC team three times, on the second team as a sophomore and junior, the first team as a senior.

A native of Raleigh, where he was coached in high school by former Duke player Howard Hurt, Randall Drew Denton broke the 30-point barrier 11 times and

Randy Denton was the second player in school history to post at least 1,000 points and 1,000 rebounds.

had at least 20 rebounds in eight games. His career scoring high of 37 points was against Clemson in 1970, his best rebounding total of 25 against Northwestern in 1971. That was the second-best board game in Duke history. He also had 23 points in that game, one of several "20–20" days in his career. Another of those was his final college contest, with 23 points and 20 rebounds against St. Bonaventure in the NIT in 1971.

Denton more than held his own against the top centers of his era, excelling in head-to-head battles with players such as Rudy Tomjanovich of Michigan, Dan Issel of Kentucky, and Jim McDaniels of Western Kentucky. As a sophomore he was named MVP of the Sugar Bowl Tournament in leading Duke to the title. He had 35 points in an NIT game with Utah at Madison Square Garden. During his senior year he blitzed Wake Forest with 28 points and 17 rebounds, hitting a lay-in with 17

seconds left for the winning points. During his senior year alone he had 22 double-doubles in points and rebounds, out of 30 games.

A two-time team MVP and All-America in 1971, Denton was a fifth-round NBA draft pick but instead played five seasons in the ABA before closing out his pro career with one year in the NBA. He was enshrined in the Duke Sports Hall of Fame in 1991 and was a charter inductee in the Duke Basketball Hall of Honor in 2001.

DeVenzio, Dick. Known as an advocate for student athletes' rights, Dick DeVenzio crusaded against the NCAA and its stance on amateurism long before it became popular to do so. In 1992 he went so far as to set up a trust fund for Duke recruit Joey Beard, payable upon graduation, to raise awareness for the issue of compensating athletes within a system that was exploding financially at their expense. He wrote countless columns and several books, including *Ripoff U.*, and appeared on national television urging reforms that would benefit athletes beyond their scholarships.

Tragically, Richard Daryl DeVenzio's voice was silenced in 2001 when he died of colon cancer at the age of 52, less than two months after the diagnosis. But while his activism drew much attention, DeVenzio, a former Duke guard, also left behind a legacy of passion for his sport. After playing overseas in the years following his college days, DeVenzio founded a series of basketball camps across the country that reached generations of young players. He also directed the Prep Stars camps.

"I went to his first camp in 1972. He was my childhood hoops hero," said former Duke player Richard Ford. "He got the debate going on players' rights, but that was just a small part of what he did in basketball. His true passion was teaching kids the sport he loved."

DeVenzio's childhood hoops hero was former Duke captain Denny Ferguson, who played high school basketball under DeVenzio's father Chuck, a prep coach in Springdale, Pa. After quarterbacking his Ambridge High team to an undefeated season, DeVenzio then followed Ferguson's college path to Durham and became one of the top playmakers in school history. A deft 5–10 ball handler, he was the regular point guard for three seasons, 1969–71, scoring 693 points and dishing 388 assists in 81 games.

DeVenzio, who was a Parade All-America under his dad's tutelage, dazzled Duke fans with his sparkling performances for the freshman team in 1968. His two steals and a 55-foot shot at the buzzer enabled the Blue Imps to stun UNC, 66–64. He moved right into the starting lineup the next year and was instantly recognized as one of the best passers in the ACC. He posted the first of three straight 100-assist campaigns and twice set a school record for most assists in a game, with the top mark of 12 against N.C. State. DeVenzio also showed off his jump shot to the tune of 12.2 points a game, the best figure of his career. He poured in 28 points to propel Duke into overtime against nationally ranked Davidson; he popped 7 of 7 field goals in a contest against Clemson; and in his first two ACC Tournament games he scored 24 and 19 points to send the Devils to the final. That landed him on the all-tourney first team.

DeVenzio's scoring averages gradually declined over his last two years, but he continued to pace the team in assists. When he graduated he ranked as the school's career assists leader. UPI named him to its Small All-America team, and he was a member of the Academic All-America squad as well.

Dixie Classic. Hall of Fame sports columnist Smith Barrier of Greensboro once described the Dixie Classic as the state of North Carolina versus the world. "It was something the basketball fans of North Carolina happily and eagerly squeezed in between Christmas and New Year's, then talked about in the intervening 51 weeks," Barrier wrote in his book *On Tobacco Road* (1983). The event was a three-day, eight-team tournament that took place in 12 consecutive Decembers, 1949 through 1960, at Reynolds Coliseum in Raleigh. The concept was that the Big Four schools of North Carolina—Duke, N.C. State, Wake Forest, and UNC — would take on four outstanding teams from around the country. Each of the three days featured an afternoon doubleheader and an evening doubleheader, usually before huge crowds, with thousands more fans listening in on radio around the state. Former N.C. State coach Everett Case was the driving force behind the event, which some say was at least as popular as the annual conference tournaments.

Top-notch outside competition was usually on hand, but no outside team ever won the event. N.C. State dominated with seven Dixie titles, followed by UNC with three, Duke and Wake one apiece. Of the 24 available spots in the final over the duration of the event, only seven were claimed by teams outside the Big Four. Five times the championship game featured two local teams. During three straight years, 1955 – 57, the first-place and third-place games were contested entirely by members of the Big Four.

Duke won its lone Dixie title in December 1953, when the Blue Devils beat Oregon State, Wake Forest, and Navy. Duke's only other appearance in the final was in the last Dixie, when it was beaten by UNC. The Devils won the third-place game three times. Duke was also part of one of the event's greatest games when it overcame a 32-point deficit to edge Tulane in 1950.

The best Dixie Classic was in December 1958, when four of the top 10 teams in the national poll were on hand, including No. 1 Cincinnati with Oscar Robertson. N.C. State won that year, while Cincinnati fell to UNC in a marvelous fifth-place game. But three years later, the plug was pulled on the event in the wake of college basketball's point-shaving scandals. After four N.C. State players and one from UNC had been charged with fixing games, administrators within the greater University of North Carolina system eliminated the Dixie Classic as part of their efforts to deemphasize basketball.

Doak, Bob. Trinity's coach for the 1916 season was Robert Doak, who guided the program to a 9 – 11 record. Doak was hired from Elon College, which he coached to the state championship in 1915. During his one year at Trinity, Doak also coached the 1916 track team. He was succeeded in the basketball job by his brother, Chick Doak.

Doak, Chick. Known more for his long affiliation with N.C. State, Charles Glenn "Chick" Doak coached Trinity to its first championship. He guided the basketball team in 1917 and 1918 to records of 20 – 4 and 10 – 5. The 1917 squad, which claimed the state title, is believed to have been the first at a North Carolina college to win 20 games. Doak played collegiate basketball at Guilford College. He came to Trinity in the fall of 1916 from UNC, where he had coached basketball the previous two seasons. He later returned to Trinity to coach the 1920 baseball team before embarking on a 33-year tenure as a professor and coach at N.C. State. The Wolfpack's baseball stadium, Doak Field, was named for him. His wife Frances led several women's organizations and was the first female radio announcer in North Carolina.

Dockery, Sean. A personable point guard recruited from inner-city Chicago, Sean Areon Dockery used his quickness, toughness, and heart to develop into a starter by his junior season at Duke. But long before that, the rest of the Blue Devils frequently referred to Dockery as their best teammate.

"Sean brings the intangibles to this team," said his classmate Lee Melchionni. "He's like the glue that makes everything stick. He may not score the most or have the most rebounds, but he goes out there and gives his heart and soul to the game and to his teammates. To be around him on and off the court, he's a great guy who cares for other people around him."

As a symbolic indication of the Blue Devils' affection for Dockery, senior captain Daniel Ewing wore Dock's blue knee sleeve into battle when his teammate had to miss six games with an injury in 2005, just to keep some of his presence on the floor.

A 6–2 high school All-America who once scored 53 points in a prep game, Dockery played in all 70 Duke contests in his first two years, 2003–04, mostly as a backcourt backup, though he did start twice. As a sophomore he was recognized with the Ted Mann Jr. award as the reserve who contributed most to team morale. After veteran Chris Duhon graduated in 2004, Dockery realized that there was an opportunity to make a bigger impact and went through a grueling off-season program. A focal point was his shooting, as he had connected on just 7 of 36 three-pointers over his first two years. After putting up 1,000 shots a day during the off-season, Dockery hit a team-best 43 percent (24 of 56) from beyond the arc in 2005, shot 47.7 percent overall, and started 22 times in his 27 appearances.

Dockery was known for his defensive ball pressure, getting seven steals in a 2004 game against St. John's. His season high of 15 points was against Davidson in 2005, and his top assists effort of six was on a return to Chicago for a contest against Valparaiso. When Dockery had to miss six games after suffering a knee injury at

Georgia Tech, it was a blow to a team lacking in depth. He returned for the NCAA Tournament and had a strong outing with eight points and three assists in 24 minutes against Delaware State in his first game back.

The son of a high school basketball coach, Dockery played in 133 games and started in 56, with 646 points and 234 assists. He was one of the co-captains for the 2006 campaign. One of the highlight moments of his basketball life occurred in the ACC opener in his senior year, when he connected on a 40-foot shot as time expired to lift the Blue Devils over Virginia Tech, 77–75. After being outscored 12–0 over the last four minutes, Duke trailed 75–74 with 1.6 seconds remaining when Dockery caught a long pass from Josh McRoberts at midcourt, took one dribble, and nailed the game-winning jumper. He finished the game with a career-high 19 points.

Doherty, Marty. After transferring from Colgate, Martin William Doherty split time with Junior Morgan at the center position for the 1954 and 1955 seasons. Doherty, a 6–9 product of Pelham, N.Y., appeared in 52 games with 289 points and 245 rebounds. He scored in double figures a handful of times each season, with a career high of 18 points against South Carolina in 1954.

Domzalski, Taymon. Considered one of the best high school basketball players ever produced in the state of New Mexico, Jerome Taymon Domzalski, a 6–10 center, fulfilled a reserve role for the majority of his four years at Duke, 1996–99. Domzalski was named the top male student athlete in the country after his senior year at New Mexico Military. (He had played at Lovington High in his home town for the previous three years.) Upon arrival at Duke he started 18 of 31 games as a freshman, averaging 6.5 points and 5.0 rebounds while making the ACC All-Freshman team. A knee injury sidelined him for much of his sophomore year, while a back injury cost him a few games in his junior year, when he started eight of 26 contests. He played some important minutes in 1998 after starter Elton Brand was felled by a broken foot. Domzalski appeared in 30 of 39 games for the 1999 Final Four team, averaging 9.9 minutes with one start, on his Senior Day. His career concluded with 100 games played, 424 points, 336 rebounds, and 64 blocked shots.

"You always want to play more," he said before his last home game, "but you always have to look at the team concept. When you lose yourself in that concept, it's a lot easier to embrace a role. It's tough for fans to understand that, and it was tough for me to understand that when I first got here. But if we can put another banner up, I'll do anything."

An excellent student, Domzalski was named the Paine Webber national scholar athlete of the year in 1998 as part of ABC television's coverage of college basketball. He also won the team's Dr. Deryl Hart award for academics in 1997. As a minor league player in the International Basketball League after graduation, Domzalski was named an IBL community man of the year in 2000. He later enrolled in medical school at Duke.

Doughty, Pat. Reserve guard Patrick Jay Doughty saw action in 23 games during his three varsity years, 1970–72, with 26 points and 11 assists. A 5–10 resident of Tempe, Ariz., by way of Herrin (Ill.) High School, he had a pair of six-point games as a junior and played sparingly in 13 games as a senior, with the highlight coming in Duke's upset win over Virginia as he showed off his ball-handling skills to beat the Cavalier press. He won the Ted Mann Jr. award as the reserve contributing most to team morale. He also served as one of the team captains in 1972.

Drago, Tony. Captured at the Battle of the Bulge in the Second World War and held as a prisoner of war for six months, Anthony Charles Drago enrolled at Hartwick College in New York upon his discharge from the Army in 1945. He played basketball there under coach Harold Bradley, who was also the school's athletics director. After Drago's graduation, Bradley hired him as Hartwick's physical education director and freshman basketball coach. Bradley moved to Duke in the fall of 1950 and eventually got Drago to join him for a four-year run on his coaching staff from 1954 to 1957. Drago coached the freshman team for two years (posting 12–5 and 14–3 records), assisted with the varsity, and taught physical education.

Driesell, Lefty. Far better known as a coach than as a player, Charles Grice "Lefty" Driesell was a member of the Duke program from 1951 to 1954 and lettered in his last two seasons. A 6–3 frontcourt player from Norfolk, Va., he was one of the top members of the freshman team in 1951, was unable to play in 1952 because of a mastoid problem, and then played in 45 games in his last two years, with 181 points and 107 rebounds. He scored 13 points in his varsity début against Vanderbilt in 1953 and had his career high of 19 points against Vandy in 1954. He had two other double-figure games in his career against home-state teams, Virginia and Virginia Tech.

Born on Christmas Day in 1931 and inducted into the Duke Sports Hall of Fame in 1993, Driesell gained his greatest athletic notoriety as a college basketball coach. In 41 seasons at four schools, he had a record of 786 wins and 394 losses. His victory total was the fifth-highest in the history of Division I college basketball when he retired in 2003.

Driesell coached Davidson to national prominence from 1961 to 1969, leading the Wildcats to a spot in the final top 10 polls of 1964, 1965, 1968, and 1969. His alma mater was in the market for a head coach when Vic Bubas resigned in the spring of 1969. Shortly after Duke opted for Bucky Waters, Driesell moved to the ACC by accepting the head coaching post at Maryland. Professing his intention of developing the Terps into the UCLA of the East, in 17 years he guided Maryland to ten 20-win seasons, eight NCAA berths, and an NIT title. His best Terp teams were in the early 1970s. He reached the ACC title game three straight years, 1972–74, and finished among the top 15 in the final national poll for five straight years, 1972–76, but didn't make the NCAA tourney in any of those seasons because only the league champion was invited. Driesell was on the losing sideline in perhaps the best ACC game of all-time, a 103–100 overtime loss to N.C. State in the ACC final in 1974.

Driesell returned to the ACC championship game again in back-to-back years, 1980 and 1981, but each time lost by one point, to Duke and North Carolina. He won his lone ACC Tournament crown in 1984, when he beat the Blue Devils in the final at Greensboro and indicated that he'd like to attach the trophy to the hood of his car for a drive across the state of North Carolina. In each of his previous five ACC championship games, his team had lost to either UNC, N.C. State, or Duke.

Driesell was forced to leave Maryland after the 1986

season and the shocking drug-related death of the ACC player of the year, Len Bias, after the NBA draft. He returned to the sideline at James Madison from 1989 to 1997, then headed to Georgia State, where he picked up his 700th career win. He retired just after New Year's Day 2003, 10 games into the season. He had turned around the Panthers, one of the losingest programs in the nation, by directing them to 29 wins and a trip to the NCAA tourney in 2001, where they were ousted in the second round by his former school, Maryland.

Driesell is the only coach to lead four Division I schools to at least 100 wins. He also guided each of his four schools to postseason play, with a total of 13 trips to the NCAA Tournament and eight to the NIT. Driesell's coaching record: Davidson 176 – 65, Maryland 348 – 159, James Madison 159 – 111, Georgia State 103 – 59. His record against Duke: 25 – 22.

Duff, Bob. Forward Bob Duff, of Englewood, N.J., lettered in 1948 when he appeared in nine games and scored 36 points. He played in 11 games with 28 points in 1949 but did not letter.

Duhon, Chris. He was chosen national player of the year in high school, ACC rookie of the year as a college freshman, ACC preseason player of the year entering his junior campaign, and All-America by several outlets after a senior year in which he led Duke to the Final Four. Chris Duhon graduated as the Blue Devils' all-time leader in steals and minutes played while ranking second in assists, but there was only one statistic that ever mattered to him. "I've just gotta go get wins," he once said. Much like the best baseball pitchers, Duhon compiled an outstanding won-lost record during his four years, with 123 victories in 144 games. "Maybe I'll get a Cy Young or something," he quipped. The only Duke player to win more games was Shane Battier, with 131.

From 2001 to 2004 Christopher Nicholas Duhon, a 6 – 1 point guard from Slidell, La., scored 1,268 points and had 819 assists, 489 rebounds, 300 steals, and 162 three-pointers in 4,813 minutes. He started 113 times and averaged 5.7 assists versus just 2.5 turnovers, one of the best ratios in ACC history. But more than any of those numbers, Duhon was known mostly for his floor

Captain Chris Duhon guided Duke to the 2004 Final Four despite a painful rib injury.

leadership, as a two-time captain who influenced teams that put together three 30-win seasons while achieving three ACC titles, two trips to the Final Four, and a national championship.

Duhon played on four distinctly different teams and found a way to matter significantly on each. As a freshman he fit in on a veteran team, brought energy off the bench most of the year, and then, inserted into the starting lineup at the end, helped the Devils go 9 – 0 in the postseason (ACC and NCAA). After that season his leadership capabilities germinated when he was selected captain of a U.S. National Team that won the World Championship for Young Men. USA Basketball recognized those efforts by naming him the organization's male athlete of the year for 2001.

As a sophomore Duhon teamed in the backcourt with

national player of the year Jason Williams, sometimes at point, sometimes on the wing, complementing a core group of juniors who headed to the NBA after the season. As a junior, Duhon faced his biggest leadership challenge as the primary court general on a team loaded with freshman talents. Then, in his last year, he functioned more like the traditional senior captain and point guard, with selfless immersion in the team concept.

"You see a guy like Chris Duhon, with the class that he has," Maryland coach Gary Williams said when asked about players who eschewed college basketball for the pros. "You hope he can have an influence on as many players as LeBron James."

The winner of a national three-point shooting contest in high school, Duhon averaged just 8.8 points a game over his four years and connected on just 41.8 percent of his field goals. But he delivered a host of shots in the clutch, beginning in his freshman year. With time running out at Wake Forest, Duhon took a pass from Williams and hit an off-balance floater at the buzzer to give Duke an 82–80 victory. As a senior, his length-of-the-court drive and reverse layup with 6.5 seconds left beat UNC in overtime in Chapel Hill, while his three-pointer with 36 seconds left was the clinching dagger in a home win over Florida State. He made the All-ACC first team that year.

Duhon was usually so preoccupied with making sure his teammates got their shots that the coaches were always encouraging him to hunt for his own shot more. He picked his spots, and consequently many of his baskets were momentum changers. A prime example was the home game against Wake Forest in 2003, when he erupted for a string of three straight three-pointers late in the first half to pace a victory in a battle of two unbeaten teams. Duhon had his career high of 23 points at Wake later in the year, and posted his career high of 14 assists against the Deacons in 2004.

Considered a superb defender, Duhon made the ACC all-defensive team in 2002 and 2004. He clamped down on a succession of top scoring threats to help Duke win the ACC tourney in 2003 and did the same in the NCAA the following year to carry Duke to the Final Four. He led Duke in steals in his last three years and broke Battier's career school steals record in February of his senior season. The record-breaking theft came when the Devils were locked in a battle with Virginia. Duhon took the ball away from center Elton Brown at the foul line and sprinted for a layup at the other end as part of the most important run of the game.

Duhon was no stranger to adversity but usually handled it well. He came down with severe laryngitis before the Wake game in 2003 but led a major win through his actions instead of words. A few weeks later, Mike Krzyzewski thought that Duhon was putting too much pressure on himself and benched him for the start of the biggest game of the regular season, against UNC — one of only two starts that he missed in his last three years. When he came off the pine he responded with one of his finest floor games, 12 points and 10 assists with two critical shots in the final minutes.

The classic example of Duhon's commitment, though, showed up in the NCAA Tournament in 2004. Barely able to practice because of painful bruised ribs, he threw himself and his body into wins over Illinois and Xavier at the Atlanta Regional as Duke earned a trip to the Final Four. It was a true warrior performance, as Duhon continued to scramble for loose balls, play suffocating defense, and drive fearlessly into the paint to make plays, flinching on contact but never yielding. He didn't score much, but his exercise in toughness provided a clear example. He came up with a career high of 10 rebounds (all defensive) against Illinois and played 40 minutes in the Xavier contest, which went to the wire.

"I have to show strength to these guys," said Duhon, who earlier in his career met with Krzyzewski and asked to be held accountable for his team's performance. "If I take my foot off the gas, it gives them the opportunity to take their foot off the gas. Right now I'm putting the pedal to the metal."

Freshman Luol Deng was named the regional MVP, but it wasn't a unanimous selection. "No way we would be going to San Antonio without Duhon. No way," said Krzyzewski, who may have invested more time and energy in cultivating leadership skills with Duhon than with any other player he coached. "Duhon was the best player and the most important player in Atlanta."

Duhon showed that same toughness as an NBA rookie in 2005. Though not drafted until the second round, he became a starter early in the year for the Chicago Bulls, helped lead them to the playoffs, and then played through the pain of a back injury during the postseason. He was rewarded with a new contract after his initial season and named one of the Bulls' captains. He was also quick to set up a relief fund in 2005 after Hurricane Katrina devastated his native Louisiana, generating over $1 million in support.

Duke Basketball Hall of Honor. The university established its Basketball Hall of Honor in 2001 to recognize the top players who have not had their jerseys retired. To earn enshrinement, a player must be selected either national player of the year, national defensive player of the year, or All-America, be named to the All-ACC team multiple times, or win an Olympic gold medal. The Hall of Honor is located on the concourse at Cameron Indoor Stadium.

Charter induction ceremonies were held on December 2, 2001. The 18 initial honorees were Mark Alarie, Tommy Amaker, Tate Armstrong, Gene Banks, Elton Brand, Chris Carrawell, Randy Denton, Billy King, Ed Koffenberger, Trajan Langdon, Mike Lewis, Jack Marin, Jim Spanarkel, Steve Vacendak, Bob Verga, Bill Werber, Steve Wojciechowski, and Corren Youmans.

The Hall of Honor is also open to outstanding women players who meet the same criteria. Five women were inducted on January 20, 2002: Sue Harnett, Katie Meier, Chris Moreland, Georgia Schweitzer, and Michele VanGorp.

Duke Basketball Report. Described by one of its founders as a neighborhood pub in cyberspace, the Duke Basketball Report (DBR) has emerged as the most popular of the many Internet sites devoted to coverage of the Blue Devil program. With ever-changing content, news updates, and links to stories published elsewhere, DBR provides a place for fans from all across the world wide web to gather electronically in the name of Duke and ACC basketball.

DBR's origin dates to 1991, when Mike Hemmerich and Julian King began posting Duke basketball musings on a Prodigy bulletin board. By 1994 they were periodically sending out a printed newsletter, and in 1996 they went on line. The popularity of their site began to grow, largely by word of mouth. "I was excited when we got 6,000 hits a month," recalled Hemmerich in 2005. "Now we might get two million hits in one day."

Hemmerich is a 1980 Duke grad who later earned law and business degrees from the school, while King is the grandson of former Duke president Dr. Deryl Hart. In 1998 they were joined by another Duke alum, James Armstrong '82, who brought considerable technological expertise to the operation.

A free site with no advertisements, DBR has been a convenient place for fans to check out current events as well as share opinions. It has also conducted numerous charity auctions of tickets and memorabilia to benefit the Duke Children's Hospital. One of the most noteworthy was an auction for a rim from the Final Four in Minneapolis in 1992 that generated a $22,000 donation. The site's address is dukebasketballreport.com.

Duke Sports Hall of Fame. Created in 1975, the Duke Sports Hall of Fame included 114 members through its 2004 induction class. The charter members included legendary basketball coach Eddie Cameron, Duke's first basketball All-America, Bill Werber, and the first Duke player to have his number retired, high-scoring guard Dick Groat. Football coach Wallace Wade, football star George McAfee, and the incomparable Ace Parker, who played a season of basketball amid his football and baseball campaigns, completed the introductory class.

The Hall of Fame was relocated from Cameron Indoor Stadium to the second floor lobby of the Schwartz-Butters Center in 2000. The following 27 inductees either played or coached basketball at Duke: Mark Alarie, Tommy Amaker, Gene Banks, Vic Bubas, Eddie Cameron, Gordon Carver, Harry Councilor, Johnny Dawkins, Randy Denton, Lefty Driesell, Boley Farley, Danny Ferry, Bob Gantt, Gerry Gerard, Mike Gminski, Dick Groat, Art Heyman, Bernie Janicki, Ed Koffenberger, Mike Lewis, Jack Marin, Jeff Mullins, Ace Parker, Jim Spanarkel, Steve Vacendak, Bob Verga, Bill Werber.

Chris Moreland became the first women's basketball player in the Duke Sports Hall of Fame when she was enshrined in 2001.

Duncan, Tim. One of the ACC's and NBA's all-time great centers, Tim Duncan dominated Duke during his four-year career at Wake Forest, 1994 – 97. He averaged a double-double in nine contests with the Devils, 17.2 points and 10.1 rebounds, and had games of 24, 20, 26, and 26

Corey Maggette slapped the backboard after a rim-rattling dunk versus Florida in December 1998.

A Shot He'll Never Forget

Grant Hill, December 1991 versus St. John's

Hill attempted 1,400 shots in his Duke career, and the one most people recall first is the one-handed dunk that he threw down on Kansas in the opening minutes of the national championship game in 1991. But the one that Hill mentions first came in the opening moments of the ACC-Big East Challenge early in the 1992 season.

With top-ranked Duke expecting a real skirmish from seventh-ranked St. John's, the Blue Devils exploded out of the gates to a 14–2 start at the Greensboro Coliseum. One of the baskets in that spurt was a Hill dunk off an alley-oop pass.

"I was hyped up and screaming and yelling, and Coach K was getting us pumped up," Hill said. "It was our first big challenge, on ESPN with Dick Vitale. To me, there was an intensity and passion on that particular play, with my teammates coming over getting pumped up, and we went on to blow them away. There were a lot of plays I had that I remember and enjoyed, but to me that was one of my favorites. It set the tone for that game and set the tone for the season."

Duke had another huge run, 20–3, in the second half that featured another alley-oop from Hurley to Hill. The Devils eventually went up by 31 points before St. John's rallied for a more respectable final score of 91–81. Hill finished with 15 points on 7-of-8 shooting.

points in his last four meetings. Wake Forest defeated Duke eight straight times during the Duncan era, before the Devils knocked off the second-ranked Deacons in Winston-Salem in the last matchup.

Dunk. College basketball rule makers attempted to diminish the impact of the dominant big man when they made the dunk illegal at the start of the 1967 season. That just happened to coincide with the year that Lew Alcindor, 7–2, was first eligible to compete for the UCLA varsity. The ban on dunking continued in effect through 1976, just a couple of years after the graduation of Bill Walton, 6–11, the Bruins' other grand center. Duke coach Bill Foster was president of the National Association of Basketball Coaches in 1976 and supported the return of the dunk. The play became legal again for the 1977 season — just in time for the arrival of Foster's first true pivotman, Mike Gminski, 6–11.

G-Man flushed many a shot during his day en route to breaking Duke's career scoring record. No one dunked more frequently for the Blue Devils than the 6–5 flying forward Robert Brickey, who posted a school high of 56 slams in 1989 and 147 for his career, nearly a third of his field goals. But the unquestioned king of the jam in Duke annals remains Grant Hill, the 6–8 forward who could dunk with power, creativity, and always style.

A baker's dozen of the most memorable dunks in school history, in chronological order:

1. Kenny Dennard's backwards, two-handed dunk against Villanova in the East Regional at Providence in 1978. It helped send the Blue Devils to their first Final Four in over a decade.

2. Gene Banks's windmill over Ralph Sampson at University Hall in 1980. Dennard once called it the most powerful dunk he'd ever seen from a college player other than Shaquille O'Neal.

3. Johnny Dawkins's reverse dunk on Navy late in the first half of the NCAA East Regional final at the Meadowlands in 1986. It came on a fast-break pass from Tommy Amaker. Navy point guard Doug Wojcik was the helpless defender.

4. Guard Phil Henderson's one-handed dunk in center Alonzo Mourning's face to help Duke beat Georgetown in the NCAA East Regional championship game at the Meadowlands in 1989.

5. Grant Hill's one-handed slam on a long lob by Bobby Hurley in the first half of the NCAA title game versus Kansas in 1991 at the Hoosier Dome in Indianapolis. This was voted the best dunk in Duke history by a 1994 fans' poll in *Blue Devil Weekly*. It was immortalized in a two-page spread in *Sports Illustrated*, though Hill always insisted that it wasn't his favorite dunk. (His favorites were an alley-oop versus St. John's and a reverse slam at Canisius the following year.)

6. Grant Hill's one-handed catch-and-slam on Georgia Tech in Atlanta during the regular season in 1992. Brian Davis threw the pass. It was a nice dunk for a point guard — the position that Hill played for 40 minutes in this game while Hurley was out with an injury.

7. Grant Hill's two-handed reverse dunk on Michigan late in the NCAA championship game at Minneapolis in 1992. Hurley threw the pass while Christian Laettner and Tony Lang sealed a clear path to the rim for Hill.

8. Tony Lang's one-handed jam over Iowa's shot-blocker Acie Earl in the closing minutes of a game in Cameron Indoor Stadium in 1993.

9. Freshman Jeff Capel's thunder dunk on a breakaway pass from Chris Collins with 38 seconds left to punctuate an NCAA regional final win over Purdue in 1994.

10. Ricky Price's 360-degree dunk on a fast break in a game with Mercer in December 1997. Price had missed the first semester of his senior year for academic reasons and made this play on his first day back in uniform.

11. Freshman Corey Maggette's dunk against Florida in December 1998, one of the best ever in Cameron. Maggette was streaking down court, went high over the rim for the stuff, then grabbed the rim and slapped the backboard on the way down. Yes, he was called for a technical foul, but nobody cared. Duke won by 30.

12. Dahntay Jones's throw-down on the 6 – 10 center Nick Vander Laan with three minutes left in a win at

Virginia in 2003. Jones drove, rose above the rim, pummeled the basket and the defender, and then did a set of pushups after he crashed to the floor. It was a stunning play that shocked even Jones's father, who had attended almost every one of his son's high school and college games and was accustomed to his high-flying acrobatics.

13. DeMarcus Nelson's eye-popping slam against Seton Hall early in a rout at Cameron in 2006. Sean Dockery threw a high pass and Nelson soared for the catch and fast-break slam in Grant-like fashion. Teammate J. J. Redick called it one of the nastiest dunks he'd ever witnessed.

Dunleavy, Mike. The son of a long-time NBA player and coach, Michael Joseph Dunleavy Jr. brought an exceptional basketball IQ to Duke from his All-America high school days in Lake Oswego, Ore. A smooth forward, he simply understood the game inside and out, and used his all-around skills to help the Blue Devils win three ACC championships and one NCAA title in his three seasons, 2000 – 2002. Yet it took the encouraging words of another coach's son to help Dunleavy refocus for his most luminous moment as a collegian.

Dunleavy was one of Duke's top scoring threats in 2001, but at the Final Four he struggled against Maryland, hitting just 2 of 8 shots for four points. The next day, as Duke prepared for the NCAA final, Dunleavy watched video and met with assistant coach Chris Collins, also the son of an NBA coach. Collins's message was simple: "I just talked to him about going out and being aggressive. If you miss a shot, so what? You don't ever want to be in a situation where you look back later in life and say, 'I had a chance to play in the national championship game and I wish I would have been more aggressive.'"

Dunleavy took those words to heart and had a team high of 21 points in the final against Arizona. Most notable was a set of three consecutive three-point shots in a 45-second span in the second half. Over one seven-minute stretch he scored 18 of Duke's 21 points to help the Devils open up a 10-point lead. A spot on the All – Final Four team was his, along with a championship ring. Just a month before, he had performed a similar feat, exploding for a team high of 24 points in the ACC champion-

Mike Dunleavy hit three three-pointers within a 45-second span to provide a boost in the 2001 NCAA final.

mononucleosis but rebounded to make the ACC all-tournament squad and was named the reserve contributing most to Duke's team morale. The next two years he was one of the best players in the ACC, with averages of 12.6 and 17.3 points. He made the ACC all-tourney team both years and was one of three Duke players chosen first-team All-ACC in 2002, as the Devils won their fourth straight championship.

Having adding some muscle during the off-season to help his work around the basket, Dunleavy averaged 7.2 rebounds and led the squad in blocked shots in 2002, and came up one steal shy of topping the team in that category — all without compromising his ability to shoot and pass the ball. He placed in the top 10 of seven statistical categories in the ACC and enjoyed his best year. He started the campaign by earning MVP honors at the Maui Classic and went on to lead the Devils in scoring nine times. One of his most dominating performances was in Raleigh, when he scored 15 consecutive points in the last four minutes of the first half versus N.C. State. He had 22 overall for the half and 27 for the game as Duke routed the Wolfpack.

In both regular-season games with Wake Forest, Dunleavy had pulsating three-pointers at the halftime buzzer. For the game in Winston-Salem, the shot came from midcourt and was part of his career-best scoring night of 30 points, on 11-of-19 shooting. Dunleavy averaged 19.1 points in conference games, on a team that led the league in scoring and scoring margin. Dunleavy ranked eighth in the conference in rebounding, though his career rebounding high was recorded the previous year with 17 at Clemson.

A second-team All-America as well as an Academic All-America selection, Dunleavy captained the 2002 team along with Jason Williams and Carlos Boozer, and shared the MVP award with Williams. He was named a co-captain for 2003 and would have been the favorite for national player of the year. But before that season began Dunleavy was informed by his well-connected father that his NBA stock might never be higher, so he left early for the pro ranks. Dad's information proved accurate, as Dunleavy was the No. 3 pick in the draft, just behind Yao Ming and Williams. He developed into a starter for the Golden State Warriors by his second year and improved his scoring average in each of his first three

ship game versus UNC to make that all-tourney squad and earn a title. Those were the only two games all year in which Dunleavy led the Devils in scoring.

Dunleavy appeared in 104 games and started 76, including every contest in his sophomore and junior years. He scored 1,371 points for a 13.2 average, had 601 rebounds for a 5.8 average, and dished 225 assists. He made 179 three-point shots. Versatile as well as cunning, Dunleavy saw his game grow with his body while at Duke. He came in as a 6 – 7, 200-pound perimeter player and was listed at 6 – 9 and 220 pounds in his junior year, meaning that he was always adjusting his style to his physical tools. Duke finished No. 1 in the national poll in all three of his seasons.

Coming off the bench as a sixth man in his freshman year, Dunleavy went through a late-season bout of seasons. The Warriors signed him to a long-term $44 million contract at the start of his fourth campaign.

Dwyer, Bobby. Former Wake Forest basketball captain Bobby Dwyer was Mike Krzyzewski's top assistant coach for eight years, five at Army and his first three at Duke, 1981–83. The son of a successful high school coach in Washington, D.C., Dwyer had extensive on-the-court and recruiting duties for Krzyzewski, while also handling many administrative office matters. With his background and contacts in D.C., Dwyer was an important recruiter in that area, especially in the Devils' pursuit of Johnny Dawkins. Dwyer attended almost every game that Dawkins played in his senior year at Mackin Catholic in Washington.

A 1974 Wake grad and three-year letterman for the Deacons, Dwyer left Duke after the 1983 season to accept the head coaching job at Sewanee. In October 1985 he went to William & Mary, where he became head of the school's athletics fund-raising organization.

Dyke, Mac. Coach Mike Krzyzewski's first team in 1981 featured a handful of walk-on contributors, including forward Cornelius McKown Dyke, a 6–7 sophomore from Redlands, Calif. He saw action in three varsity games, making his only field goal attempt for two points.

Easton, Scott. A three-year starter during Mike Krzyzewski's tenure at Army, Scott Easton joined his college coach for one year as a Duke assistant in 1988. Easton had been an officer in the Army for eight years, while also coaching a service team and volunteering at the high school level. He resigned with the rank of captain before joining the Blue Devils, who won the ACC and went to the Final Four during his only season on the staff.

Edwards, Fred. Once described as the ringmaster of Duke's 1938 basketball circus, Fred "Mouse" Edwards co-captained the Blue Devils' first Southern Conference championship team. A 6–2 forward from Bloomsburg, Pa., Edwards helped drive the 1938 team to the tourna-ment championship and scored 12 points in the final 40–30 victory over Clemson. He made the all-tournament second team.

A three-year letterman at center for coach Wallace Wade's football team, Edwards typically joined the basketball team late. He saw more action than expected as a sophomore after Billy Huiskamp had an appendectomy. He was a key alternate as a junior and a starter as a senior. He totaled 276 points in his three seasons.

Edwards, Zeno. A 6–1 guard from Washington, N.C., Zeno Lester Edwards III played in nine games as a sophomore in 1972, with four points, three rebounds, and three assists.

Egan, Floyd. When Duke resumed intercollegiate football in 1920 after a 25-year ban on campus, Floyd J. Egan was chosen to coach the program. At 26, he was hired to run the athletics department, coach several sports, and teach physical exercise. Egan came from New York University, where he had been a four-year player in football, basketball, and baseball. As an Army lieutenant he had also coached NYU to the championship of a national basketball tournament in 1919. At Trinity he coached the baseball program in 1920 and then turned his attention to football, guiding the school to a record of 4–0–1 in its first season back. After his only grid campaign, he led the 1921 Trinity basketball team to a 9–6 mark in his lone season as its coach.

Emma, Tom. Logging almost 3,000 minutes in the Duke backcourt, Thomas Michael Emma, a 6–2 guard from Manhasset, N.Y., was a fixture in the playing rotation during the early years of coach Mike Krzyzewski. From 1980 to 1983 he appeared in 110 games with 784 points for a 7.1 average. He also contributed 245 assists and 196 rebounds.

Recruited by Bill Foster, Emma saw brief reserve minutes for Foster's last team as it claimed the ACC championship. He was at his best at the end of the year, with 18 points in the last two regular-season games. Emma then started all 30 games in 1981, Krzyzewski's first year, and averaged 9.6 points. He showed solid floor leadership with 71 assists against only 50 turnovers and led the ACC in free-throw shooting at 86.1 percent.

Emma started all but five games as a junior, averaged almost 35 minutes a night, and again took care of the ball with minimal turnovers, timely scoring, and excellent work at the foul line (82.7 percent). In 1983 Emma remained a regular as a senior, despite an influx of new talent. He started alongside Johnny Dawkins in the backcourt for 20 of 28 games, played more minutes than everyone but Dawkins and Mark Alarie, and scored in double figures 13 times, raising his career total to 41. He ended his career having hit 214 of 254 free throws for 84.3 percent, at that time the top figure in school history. Two of the most memorable foul shots were in his sophomore year, with three seconds left in the Maryland game to help Duke pull off a 55–54 upset. His scoring high of 19 points was against Stetson in his first career start, and he matched that figure as a senior versus N.C. State. Emma was drafted in the 10th round by the Chicago Bulls but did not play in the NBA.

Engelhardt, Dave. See Trainers.

Engelland, Chip. A 6–4 bomber from Pacific Palisades, Calif., known primarily for his shooting ability, Arthur Edward "Chip" Engelland played in 113 games over four seasons and connected on almost 52 percent of his field goals. And most of his 793 career field-goal attempts were not layups but perimeter jumpers. The three-point shot was in the experimental stage in his senior year, and he made 55 percent from behind the 17-foot-9 arc. He also hit 85 percent from the foul line.

Engelland emerged as Duke's first guard sub in his freshman year of 1980. He started strong, making big plays off the bench at the Big Four Tournament and hitting a shot with two seconds left to send a contest with Boston College into overtime. He played in every game in 1981, again as the first backcourt sub. Engelland moved into the starting lineup in 1982 and averaged 15.2 points a game, sixth-best figure in the ACC, and posted 27 points in a win over Holy Cross at the Meadowlands. He also led the ACC in free-throw shooting with an 87.5 percentage and topped Duke in minutes with 1,008.

Engelland's senior year saw him back in a reserve role behind freshman Johnny Dawkins and classmate Tom Emma to start the season. He did not play at all during four games at midseason. By year's end he had returned to the starting lineup and finished with a scoring average of 12.2. He produced his career best of 30 points in his last home game, a blowout loss to UNC during which he hit 11 of 18 shots, including six three-pointers. He was presented with the Dr. Deryl Hart award as the team's top scholar athlete in his final two years. Engelland finished with 1,025 career points, 168 assists, and 148 rebounds.

Engelland's shooting prowess led him to a professional career in numerous leagues from the Philippines to the Continental Basketball Association and the World Basketball League. When he retired he began teaching the game and working with players at all levels. One of his early clients was Chicago Bulls guard Steve Kerr, who hit the clinching shot in the NBA Finals in 1997. Another was former Duke star Grant Hill. Engelland used his contacts and teaching ability to eventually land a position as an NBA assistant coach.

Erickson, Nicole. Nicole Erickson packed a lot into only two seasons as a Duke women's basketball player. A 5–6 high school All-America from Fullerton, Calif., she spent her first two collegiate seasons at Purdue, then transferred to Duke and became an impact player. She made the All-ACC second team in both 1998 and 1999 while helping the Devils win a pair of regular-season conference crowns and reach the Final Four for the first time in program history.

Erickson was an excellent perimeter shooter who led the 1998 team in scoring at 12.8 points a game. She set a school record with six three-pointers in her second game, against Notre Dame, and finished the year with another school mark, 60 threes in one season. In 1999 she was Duke's No. 2 scorer behind fellow Purdue transfer Michele VanGorp, broke her own three-point record with seven in the Clemson game, and set a new season record for threes with 62.

Known for her mental toughness after a lifetime of playing at an élite level, Erickson was frequently at her best in the biggest games. She made the NCAA all-regional teams in 1998 and 1999 and the All–Final Four team in 1999 after helping Duke to its first championship game appearance. In 1998 her five threes against Louisville propelled the Devils to their first Sweet 16. Once at the Oakland regional, back in her home state,

Erickson had the hot hand again with 20 points against Florida to put Duke in the regional final. In the 1999 regional final her 17 points aided the mammoth upset of Tennessee, while her 22 versus Georgia in the national semifinals (in San Jose, home state again) sparked the Devils to the final.

In addition to her leadership, toughness, and perimeter touch, Erickson excelled at the foul line. Her career percentage of 88.0 (161 of 183) is the best in ACC history, and her 32 consecutive makes at the end of the 1999 campaign is the longest streak in Duke history.

Essex, Rey. One of four walk-on members of the 1987 team, Grant Reynolds Essex saw action in six games and scored three points while claiming seven rebounds. He was a 6 – 6 sophomore from Atlanta.

Evans, Brad. One of the most decorated local athletes to attend Duke, Bradford Lee Evans earned 16 letters at Durham High School and was All-America in basketball as well as football. He quarterbacked the Bulldogs to a state football championship in 1965 and a second-place finish in 1966, while helping the basketball squad to second- and third-place state finishes.

Evans's multi-sport efforts continued at Duke, where he lettered twice in basketball and twice in football. A 6 – 3 guard on the hardwood, he topped the 1968 freshman team in scoring and then became a part-time starter for Vic Bubas's last team. His drives from the wing helped produce 11 points in a win over Wake Forest, and he followed that with his season high of 14 versus Maryland.

As a junior Evans started in the backcourt with Dick DeVenzio and had several highlight performances. Offensively, he hit 10 straight field goals against Penn State for his career high of 26 points. Defensively, he shut down N.C. State's Vann Williford and UNC's Charlie Scott in successive contests.

The son of a Durham police lieutenant, Evans played in 50 games during the 1969 and 1970 seasons, scoring 354 points with 120 rebounds and 105 assists. In football he lettered at end for the 1970 and 1971 teams.

Ewing, Daniel. Three ACC championships, a Final Four trip, and 115 victories defined the career of George

A Texas native, Daniel Ewing closed his junior and senior seasons in NCAA games in his home state.

Daniel Ewing Jr. During his four years, 2002 – 05, Ewing took part in more wins than any other player in the nation. And he played no small role in that success as a two-year starter, two-time captain, and co-MVP.

Ewing, a 6 – 3 guard from Missouri City, Texas, never missed a game in four years and started in 79 of his 138 appearances. Moved to a starting role for the ACC Tournament in 2003, he was a fixture in the lineup for the rest of his career (minus some spot reserve duty) and scored 1,595 points for an 11.6 average. He added 382 rebounds, 293 assists, 217 three-pointers, and 191 steals.

Ewing made his début in Cameron Indoor Stadium as a prep player, when the McDonald's All-America game was held there. His best contest as a rookie was in the NCAA Tournament against Notre Dame, when he erupted for 18 points, almost three times his season average, on 4-of-7 three-point shooting and a 6-of-6 performance at the foul line. He was selected as the reserve contributing most to team morale that year.

Ewing's first major breakthrough was at the ACC tourney in 2003, when he opened the event by pouring in his career high of 32 points against Virginia. He was averaging only 12 points a game and had missed nine of his last 10 three-pointers entering the tourney before connecting on 11 of 16 shots versus the Cavaliers. "I sometimes have a habit of being laid back," he said. "I got some easy baskets and had the chance to penetrate in the Virginia game, but it's really just a mindset — to remain assertive and try to make things happen on defense."

Ewing went on to average 20.7 at the tournament and was named MVP as Duke won its fifth straight title. It marked the first of three straight years for Ewing to land on the ACC All-Tournament first team. In 2004 his 26 points in the opener, versus Virginia again, set the tone for another run to the final, and in 2005 he averaged 15 points across the three days in helping to propel the Devils to another crown.

Ewing played both guard positions during his career and was known as a strong on-the-ball defender. He shouldered more of the point guard responsibilities as a senior after Chris Duhon graduated and recruit Shaun Livingston opted for the NBA. He led the team in assists with 132 and had his best scoring season with a 15.3 average. Ewing, J. J. Redick, and Shelden Williams were regularly referred to as the Big Three of the 2005 team, as they contributed 53 of the club's 78 points a game.

The ACC leader in three-point shooting as a junior (41.1 percent), Ewing had one of his best shooting exhibitions early in his senior year when he hit 10 of 14 shots, including five threes, for 29 points in a home win over Michigan State. Mysteriously his shot left him for a few games, and he was on an 0-for-13 skid when Temple came to visit. But he broke out of it with a strong second half that included a trio of three-pointers plus a fast-break dunk to key the win. Ewing posted his only career double-double in his last home game, when he had 14 points and 10 assists versus Miami. He was named to the All-ACC third team.

Ewing turned in one of his better performances to get his last win, versus Mississippi State in the NCAA Tournament. He had 22 points, more than a third of the team total in a 63 – 55 decision, and made two pivotal plays with the game on the line: a follow shot on a fast-break layup that the Bulldogs had blocked, and a driving bank shot at the one-minute mark. The win sent Duke to the Sweet 16 in Austin, at the same arena where his powerhouse prep team had won two state titles. Ewing had also ended his junior year in the Lone Star State, at the Final Four in San Antonio.

The mild-mannered Ewing was whistled for a surprising four technical fouls during his senior year and had some difficult challenges as the leader of a team that faced constant adversity due to injuries. "Being a senior and point guard, when something doesn't go right it falls back on me," he said. "I have the ball a lot and am able to direct guys. I had to take the positive and negative criticism and try to get better. I just want to be remembered as a winner, a guy who was able to do whatever he had to do for his team to win, played hard and made big plays."

Six weeks after his graduation, the Los Angeles Clippers made Ewing the second pick in the second round of the NBA draft.

Falk, David. Once known as the most powerful sports agent in professional basketball, David Falk has represented the financial interests of several Blue Devils. He was the NBA agent for all-time scoring leader Johnny Dawkins, negotiated Danny Ferry's 10-year contract with the Cleveland Cavaliers, and counted NCAA all-time assists leader Bobby Hurley among his clients. As the agent for Elton Brand, Falk worked out an $84 million free-agent offer for his young power forward with the Miami Heat, though Brand had to stay with the Los Angeles Clippers after they matched it.

Falk has also represented coach Mike Krzyzewski in several business affairs, involving books, speaking engagements, and numerous endorsements for corporations such as American Express, General Motors, and Sony. Falk was also intimately involved in Krzyzewski's talks with the Los Angeles Lakers in the summer of 2004.

Falk broke into the business by working for Donald Dell at ProServ, one of the original sports marketing firms, headquartered in the Washington, D.C., area. He represented Michael Jordan and Patrick Ewing and at one point had signed the No. 1 picks of six NBA drafts. Falk left ProServ in 1992 to form Falk Associates Management Enterprises (FAME), then sold the business in 1998 to SFX Entertainment and became chairman of its SFX Sports Group. He eventually stepped back from that role to concentrate on working with a select group of clients, including Jordan and Krzyzewski. "What motivated me back then was the money," Falk told the *Washington Business Journal*. "Now the money is irrelevant. What keeps me going now are the relationships with those people."

Farley, Roland. A multi-sport standout, Roland "Boley" Farley teamed with classmates Bill Werber and Chalky Councilor to lead Duke into a new era late in the 1920s when the school joined the Southern Conference. The trio started for three straight seasons, 1928 – 30, the last two in their new league. Duke stunned the conference by reaching the tournament finals in each of those years.

Farley, from Danville, Va., scored 65 points in 1929 and 96 for the 1930 team, which he co-captained with Councilor. He also played football and starred in baseball. He was inducted into the Duke Sports Hall of Fame in 1980.

Feinstein, John. Best-selling author John Feinstein, a 1977 Duke grad, enlightened a generation of Duke students with his expert coverage of Blue Devil basketball for the *Chronicle*, the school newspaper. He went on to a noteworthy writing and reporting career with the *Washington Post*, excelled at commentary for ESPN television and National Public Radio, and emerged as a giant in the sports publishing industry with popular, insightful works on a variety of subjects from golf and tennis to baseball and college football. His book on Indiana basketball, *A Season on the Brink*, became the best-selling sports book of all time. Three other basketball books by Feinstein prominently featured Duke players, coaches, and teams: *A Season Inside* (1988), *A March to Madness* (1998), and *Forever's Team* (1989), which detailed the development of the Blue Devils' 1978 NCAA runner-up team and followed the personal stories of every player and coach through the subsequent 10 years. His mys-

tery novel *Last Shot: A Final Four Mystery* (2005) also had a Blue Devil twist, as the main characters are teen reporters at a Final Four involving Duke. Feinstein's *Let Me Tell You a Story* (2004), with Red Auerbach, was his 14th nonfiction book. In 2006 he published *Last Dance: Behind the Scenes at the Final Four*, with a foreword by Mike Krzyzewski.

Ferguson, Denny. A starter for most of his three-year tenure, 1963 – 65, Dennis Henry Ferguson operated in a backcourt that helped the school post a record of 73 – 13 with two Final Fours and two ACC crowns. A 6 – 0 native of Springdale, Pa., he played in 81 games with 409 points and 136 rebounds. He served as captain and was selected most valuable player of the 1965 squad. Duke had a mark of 38 – 4 in ACC games during Ferguson's run. He was at his best in the Final Four in 1964, when his 14 points, five assists, and quarterbacking skills set the tone for a victory over Michigan that propelled the Blue Devils into their first NCAA final.

One of Ferguson's most memorable plays was in a game against Tennessee at Greensboro in 1964. Duke was down by five entering the last minute but tied the score, forcing overtime when Ferguson dove and stole the ball from UT's guard Danny Schultz, then passed ahead to Buzzy Harrison for a layup with nine seconds remaining. The Blue Devils went on to win in double overtime. "We had to have a play like that to survive," Vic Bubas said. "I can't remember a greater steal."

Ferguson, James. A reserve for the 1934 team, James Ferguson lettered and scored nine points.

Ferry, Danny. He had to deal with excess criticism early in his NBA career, but in retrospect, Danny Ferry played hardball and won. Recipient of the Naismith trophy as national player of the year in his senior season at Duke, Ferry was the No. 2 selection in the pro draft in 1989. He made it clear that he had no interest in playing for the Los Angeles Clippers, so when they drafted him anyway and wouldn't trade his rights, Ferry headed to Italy to play his first professional campaign overseas. To salvage some value for their draft pick, the Clippers later worked out a trade with Cleveland, and agent David Falk worked out a 10-year contract valued at

Danny Ferry twice won the McKevlin Award as the ACC male athlete of the year.

A Game He'll Never Forget

Danny Ferry, December 1988 versus Miami

One of Ferry's favorite road trips was a visit to Miami early in his senior year, when he set the ACC scoring record with 58 points in a 117–102 victory. Ferry was 23 of 26 from the field and 10 of 12 from the foul line and had just two three-pointers in an amazing show.

"Max Crowder [a former team trainer] let me have pancakes that night," Ferry recalled. "I had been begging for pancakes before the game for a long time and he finally gave in, that was the first time, and I ended up having 58 points.

"I don't remember one shot I made, I don't remember anything that happened. It was the ultimate zone that I've ever been in. Everything was a blur, but it was a great blur. Everything around me moved so slow and the ball was going in. The whole thing was really a surreal experience, and something I take a lot of pride in. To be able to do that was a pretty neat thing and I'm blown away by it still."

$34 million. After his year abroad Ferry spent an entire decade with the Cavaliers, appeared in more games than any other player in franchise history, and hit the second-most three-pointers in club history. When his deal ran its course, he moved on to San Antonio for three years and was part of the Spurs' title team in 2003.

Rather than languish with an underperforming club, Ferry stuck to his guns, signed the first long-term blockbuster contract of any Duke product, played almost 1,000 games over 13 years, made nine playoff appearances, and became the second Blue Devil alumnus to earn an NBA championship ring (joining Jeff Mullins).

Shrewd behavior should have been expected from Daniel John Willard Ferry. The son of former NBA player and general manager Bob Ferry and a native of Bowie, Md., Danny came to Duke well schooled in the fundamentals, with the court savvy to match. In addition to his genealogy, it didn't hurt that he was coached in high school by the legendary Morgan Wootten of DeMatha. After Johnny Dawkins, he was the next-most influential

and significant prospect recruited by Mike Krzyzewski — a national high school player of the year who declined Dean Smith's overtures and instead cast his lot with the up-and-coming Duke program. His arrival ensured that the Blue Devils would stay around awhile even after the class of 1986 moved on, the critical step toward a continuity of excellence.

One of the most versatile 6–10 players in ACC history, Ferry could dribble, handle and pass the ball, shoot inside and out, rebound at both ends of the floor, and play defense. He knew every move and every trick in the book, never backed down, always maintained a confident demeanor, and demonstrated poise beyond his years from his freshman season on. "Most people need a lifetime to learn what Ferry has known instinctively since he was in swaddling clothes," Curry Kirkpatrick wrote in *Sports Illustrated*.

Even though he stepped into a veteran team, Ferry was called on to start at the beginning of his rookie season while senior post Jay Bilas was recovering from off-season surgery. He got the starting call 21 times, played all 40 games, led the team in rebounding 13 times, and helped the Devils to a record of 37 – 3. In the Final Four he made the winning field goal against Kansas in the semifinals with 22 seconds left and made a critical defensive stop with 11 seconds to go by drawing a charging call.

Ferry started every other game but one the rest of his career, missing just the N.C. State game in his senior season because of injury. He was the best player on the court for most of those outings, sharing the team MVP award with Tommy Amaker in his sophomore year and winning it outright for the next two. He was also named ACC player of the year in his last two seasons and both times won the McKevlin Award as the ACC athlete of the year. Consensus second-team All-America in 1988 and consensus first-team in 1989, Ferry claimed three national player of the year awards as a senior and led Duke to its third Final Four in his four seasons.

Ferry totaled 143 games from 1986 to 1989, with 124 starts. He scored 2,155 points for a 15.1 average, had 1,003 rebounds for a 7.0 average, and dished 506 assists. That made him the first player in ACC history to top 2,000 points, 1,000 rebounds, and 500 assists, so he was a clear-cut selection for the league's 50th anniversary team in 2003. He led Duke in scoring and rebounding in each of his last three years and also led in assists as a sophomore. Most observers considered him the best passing big man in the country during his tenure. "He's the best passer in college basketball since Larry Bird or Bill Bradley," said coach Dave Bliss, then of SMU.

"I like the way Danny Ferry just roams around out there," added Bill Foster, who faced his former school as coach of Northwestern. "He's such a great player you have to play him like you would a guard, a forward, and a center."

Ferry's single best individual performance was at Miami in his senior year, when he scored 58 points, topping Dick Groat's old school record by 10 points and David Thompson's ACC record by one. Ferry was an excellent three-point marksman, but he posted his 58 with the benefit of just two threes. Ferry achieved his rebounding high in his sophomore year at Maryland, when he grabbed 19 to go along with 20 points, seven assists, and three blocks in one of his better all-around shows.

Both those games just skim the surface on his career highlight reel. He had game-winning baskets in overtime versus Clemson and Wake Forest in 1987; won the MVP award at the 1988 ACC tourney in leading Duke to the title; topped the conference in scoring his junior and senior years; poured in 26 points with 10 rebounds against Kansas on the day his jersey No. 35 was retired; and played his heart out in his last game with 34 points and 10 rebounds in a loss to Seton Hall in the Final Four. He just about always excelled against his home-state team, the Maryland Terps, once scoring 33 points at College Park by hitting 10 of 19 from the field and 11 of 12 from the line. There was one stretch of four games in January 1988 when he scored 103 points while hitting 41 of 56 field goals and 13 of 15 free throws.

"I probably haven't seen a player like Danny Ferry since I coached Patrick Ewing in high school," said Boston University coach Mike Jarvis, who fell to the Devils in the NCAA tourney. "Ten years from now I'm going to tell my grandchildren I coached against Danny Ferry. That's how good I think he is."

Perhaps the best part of his story is that Ferry genuinely put the team ahead of his personal game, had fun being part of the group, and reacted with modesty to all the honors and accolades that came his way.

In the NBA Ferry played 917 regular-season games, logged over 18,000 minutes, and averaged 7.0 points. Not superstar scoring numbers, so there were persistent critics. The 1995, 1996, and 1997 seasons were his best statistically, when he played all 82 games each year and started most of the latter two. He averaged 13.3 points in 1996 and 10.6 in 1997. The long-range shooting he displayed at Duke — in the first three years that the three-point shot was installed in college — helped him to deliver 677 triples as a pro.

Ferry performed in 67 playoff games, starting in 11 of 13 contests for the Spurs in 2001 and coming off the bench for San Antonio's title-winning team in 2003. After that he retired and headed to the Spurs front office, before returning to Cleveland as general manager in 2005. He was inducted into the Duke Sports Hall of Fame in 2004.

FIST. One of coach Mike Krzyzewski's most powerful team-building tools has been the concept of the FIST: Five Individuals Standing Together. It reflects the importance of having all five players on the basketball court work in concert to achieve a common goal. No matter how strong five fingers are on an open hand, Krzyzewski has told his players, they will always be more powerful when they come together to form a fist. The notion is so significant that Krzyzewski has kept a sculptured fist in his office and had a fist engraved into his team's 2001 NCAA championship rings. One of the telling images from the 1992 season that culminated in a national title could be observed in the back of Duke's locker room after the win over Michigan: a grease board with FIST written neatly in blue marker, accompanied by the championship trophy draped with a net.

Krzyzewski identifies five key qualities that can make for a successful team: communication, trust, collective responsibility, caring, and pride. "I like to think of each as a separate finger on the fist," he wrote in *Leading with the Heart*. "Any one individually is important. But all of them together are unbeatable."

Fitts, Burton. A 6–3 forward from Winston-Salem, Sanford Burton Fitts played in three games as a senior in 1965, scoring two points.

Fleischer, Bob. Three-year starter Bob Fleischer was the leading scorer for coach Neill McGeachy's only team and coach Bill Foster's first, earning the most valuable player award in both years. A 6–8 frontcourt stalwart from Youngstown, Ohio, he was the most consistent player during a transition period in program history, appearing in all 72 games from 1973 through 1975. He scored 1,139 points and had 817 rebounds to average a double-double (14.6 points, 10.5 rebounds) while hitting 55.9 percent of his shots.

Robert Phillip Fleischer earned All-ACC second-team honors as a senior, when he was the league's No. 4 rebounder and No. 6 scorer while topping the conference in field-goal percentage. He was the No. 2 board man the year before, behind only Len Elmore of Maryland. Fleischer's career high of 33 points was against LSU in 1975. He posted a pair of 31-point conference games versus Virginia and Wake Forest in 1974. His career rebounding high of 19 was against Wake Forest in 1975.

Fleischer put 40 double-doubles in the book, 19 in his junior year and 13 in his 15 games against ACC foes. In the two ACC games in which he missed out on double-doubles, he had 20 points in one and 10 rebounds in the other.

Fleischer, a co-captain as a senior, graduated with the fifth-best rebounding average in Duke history and a field-goal percentage second only to that of Jay Buckley (1962–64) for players with at least 300 made baskets. He was also a two-time Academic All-America selection, and remains the only Duke basketball player to be chosen for an NCAA postgraduate scholarship. Fleischer was a fourth-round NBA draft pick but did not play in the league. He played professionally in Israel and then became a urologist.

Fleming, Bill. Duke played in three straight Southern Conference Tournament championship games from 1950 through 1952, and William McCurdy Fleming was instrumental in those postseason runs. A 6–3 forward from Philadelphia, he lettered in all three seasons and averaged 6.0 points a game, scoring 449 points in 75 games. He was a starter for the 1951 and 1952 teams and averaged 9.7 rebounds in his last season, the first in which Duke officially recorded rebounding statistics.

Flentye, Bill. William Flentye, a 6–2 forward from Aurora, Ill., earned a letter but did not score for the team that was the runner-up in the Southern Conference in 1940. He scored six points in 1939.

Florida State. Florida State University became a member of the ACC on July 1, 1991. The Seminoles upset North Carolina in Chapel Hill in their first conference basketball game, came to Duke for their second ACC road trip, on January 6, 1992, and were blitzed by 16 points. That proved to be a sign of things to come, as the Blue Devils defeated FSU in 24 of their first 29 meetings as league rivals, including all 15 at Cameron Indoor Stadium from 1992 through 2006. Most of those games in Durham were not even close, with all but four decided by double-digit margins.

FSU's five wins in the series were at Leon County Civic Center, all by five points or fewer, four times versus a Duke team ranked in the top 10. Duke's 2002 squad was undefeated and ranked No. 1 in the country when it lost at FSU.

But the Blue Devils have also turned in some excellent efforts in Tallahassee. One of their better long-range shooting exhibitions in school history was in the game there in 1996, when guard Chris Collins hit seven shots from well behind the three-point arc en route to 27 points. That set a school record for threes, with Collins's final bomb of the night serving as a lethal dagger in disposing of the Seminoles. Nine years later, J. J. Redick topped that performance by hitting 8 of 11 three-pointers on his way to 31 points, with Collins watching from the bench as an assistant coach.

Ford, Phil. North Carolina's all-time scoring leader and one of the top point guards in college basketball history, Phil Ford enjoyed many special moments in his 11 games versus Duke over four years, 1975–78. None was better than his final home game in Chapel Hill, when he hit 13 of 19 field goals for 34 points and secured the ACC regular-season championship by hitting a pair of free throws with six seconds remaining. Ford averaged 22.8 points against the Devils and led his team to victory in nine of the 11 encounters.

Ford, Richard. He came to Duke from Durham High School with hopes of playing for the soccer team. A preseason injury scuttled that plan, so Richard Lee Ford decided to try out for the junior varsity basketball team. He made it, and then went on to serve as a practice player and backup point guard for the varsity. Before he graduated in 1984, Ford had earned a scholarship.

A left-hander, Ford played in 11 JV games during his freshman year of 1981, posting a 19.5 scoring average, and moved up to practice with the varsity after Allen Williams suffered an ankle injury. He averaged 19 points in six JV games in 1982 and had the chance to play in four varsity games. He then went on Duke's summer tour of France and spent the entire 1983 season with the varsity, appearing in five games while also working hard in practice to simulate opponents' tendencies. Coach Mike Krzyzewski placed Ford on scholarship for his senior year, when he played in 12 games with two points and four assists. His career totals included 21 games, four assists, four rebounds, and four points, all from the foul line.

Ford was a team co-captain as a senior, when he also won the Ted Mann Jr. award as the reserve contributing most to team morale.

Foreign tours. During Mike Krzyzewski's first 25 years, the Duke program made three basketball-related trips overseas. The first took place in the summer of 1983, when the Blue Devils visited France over the final two weeks of August. Eight players made the tour, which included seven games and stops in eight cities. Duke posted a record of 4–3, with five games against French teams, one against a German team, and one against an Italian team. Johnny Dawkins and Mark Alarie, rising sophomores, were the top two scorers in every game, with Dawkins averaging 25 points and Alarie 23.

In June 1988 the Blue Devils returned to Europe for a 21-day exhibition tour. They visited Greece and Spain, playing in three tournaments and two scrimmages for a total of 10 games. Their record was 3–7. A few of the opponents were national teams in peak form preparing for Olympic qualifying tournaments. Rising senior Danny Ferry averaged 30 points a game on the tour and was selected most valuable player in two tournaments.

In October 2002 Krzyzewski took his team to London for a long weekend during Duke's fall break. The Blue Devils scrimmaged against a team from Belgium and played four games against British pro teams, winning three. Dahntay Jones led Duke in scoring with 64 points in the four games. This trip differed from the first two in that the entire team was able to participate, a key factor for a freshman-dominated club. On the previous summer tours, incoming freshmen were not permitted to participate because they were not yet enrolled in school. In this unique instance, Duke was able to practice 10 days in advance of the trip and play four games while other schools were just beginning preseason drills.

Duke had a tour of Australia scheduled for the summer of 1994, with the Blue Devils expected to play a half-dozen games. But Krzyzewski canceled the tour in May, citing insufficient academic progress by some of his players during the spring semester.

Seven years later, the Duke women's team spent 12 days touring Australia, with visits to sites such as the Sydney Opera House, the Great Barrier Reef, and the

Bill Foster coached Duke to three NCAA bids and two ACC championships.

2000 Olympics facilities arranged around a schedule of four exhibition games with the Australia Institute of Sport, the Brisbane Capitals, and the Sydney Panthers.

Foster, Bill. Regarded as a tireless builder of college basketball programs, William E. Foster was the coach who arrived at Duke during its lowest moment of the turbulent 1970s and guided the Blue Devils back to national prominence in less than four years. His first three seasons were long, often frustrating and agonizing, as Duke won only half of its games, struggled on the road, and remained rooted in the ACC cellar even while he was serving as president of the National Association of Basketball Coaches. Foster's fourth season saw the Devils climb from the outhouse to the penthouse, with an ACC title, a trip to the Final Four, and the first of three straight NCAA Tournament bids before he was off to attempt a reclamation project elsewhere.

Foster, a Pennsylvania native and product of Eliza-

bethtown College, directed the Duke program for six seasons, 1975 – 80. His record was 113 – 64 overall, 31 – 43 in the ACC. During the first half of his tenure Duke went 40 – 40 overall, 7 – 29 in the league. Over the second half of his stay the Devils were 27 – 7, 22 – 8, and 24 – 9 for a total of 73 – 24 and 24 – 14 in the league, with three top 20 national finishes and two ACC championships to accompany the three NCAA bids.

Along with an indefatigable work ethic and a vast basketball background, Foster brought a promotional flair to the school at a time when it was struggling to compete and recruit in an ACC dominated by its local rivals N.C. State and UNC, as well as Maryland. The Blue Devils were only five years removed from the Vic Bubas era when Foster was hired, but he was the team's third coach in three seasons. So along with restocking the talent level, he also dived head first into building excitement among the fan base, with numerous speaking engagements and catchy slogans such as "The Runnin' Dukes" and "Off and Running."

The team wasn't off and running, though, as it lost all but one of its ACC road games in his first three years. The lone conference road win was in 1977 at Virginia, to give the Devils an 11 – 3 mark. But star senior Tate Armstrong suffered an injury in the game and was lost for the rest of the year, and the record ended up at 14 – 13.

Foster's recruiting efforts yielded Jim Spanarkel as ACC rookie of the year in 1976, Mike Gminski in 1977, and breakthrough prospect Gene Banks in 1978. Those were the key pieces that produced a mid-January victory over North Carolina in 1978, and suddenly the Blue Devils were 12 – 3, back in the polls, and being taken seriously again. Foster's 1978 team displayed uncommon youthful innocence and chemistry in placing second in the ACC standings, winning the tournament, and advancing all the way to the national championship game, which it lost to Kentucky.

With all the main components returning in 1979, Duke began the year ranked No. 1 and Foster had the appropriate slogan, "Let's Do It Again." The Devils tied for first in the ACC regular season and remained in the top 10 virtually all year, before the wheels fell off at the end. An odd assortment of injuries and illnesses contributed to the Devils' loss to UNC in the ACC championship and to its infamous Black Sunday NCAA defeat to St. John's a week later in Spanarkel's last game.

Under pressure to recapture their earlier success, the Devils jumped out to a 12 – 0 start in 1980 and returned to No. 1 in the nation. But a loss at Clemson ended the winning streak and ignited two months of struggles — with injuries, bad chemistry, and rumors that Foster was contemplating a departure. Duke went 7 – 7 in the ACC and looked to be headed for an early spring break when it lost by 25 points at UNC in the regular-season finale.

Almost miraculously, Foster's team came back together for one last hurrah. It stormed to the title from the No. 6 seed at the ACC Tournament, defeating the top three seeds on successive days. The day after the ACC crown was secured, Foster announced that he would be heading to South Carolina as head coach. His Duke team didn't allow a hasty exit, however, as it won two NCAA games, including an impressive victory over Kentucky in Rupp Arena in the Sweet 16. The Devils then played Purdue in the regional championship game and fell to Joe Barry Carroll and Co. 68 – 60, and the Foster era was over.

The motives behind Foster's departure were the subject of hot debate. With so many core players in place for three years, recruiting hadn't gone as well as necessary. There was the relentless presence of Dean Smith eight miles down the road, at times overshadowing everything else basketball-related in the area. Foster in later years discounted reported disagreements with his own administration.

Foster spent six years trying to rebuild South Carolina, with one 22-win season as the apex. During his third year, the stress of coaching led to a heart attack that cost him nine games. In 1987 he was forced out and headed to Northwestern, where he also served as interim athletics director. After the Wildcats, he worked as an assistant commissioner for the old Southwest Conference. His complete record as a college head coach: Bloomsburg State (1961 – 63) 45 – 11, Rutgers (1964 – 71) 120 – 75, Utah (1972 – 74) 43 – 39, Duke (1975 – 80) 113 – 64, South Carolina (1981 – 86) 92 – 79, and Northwestern (1987 – 93) 54 – 141. The total: 467 – 409 in 33 seasons. He was the first coach in Division I history to lead four schools to 20-win seasons.

Fox, Paul. A hard-working guard with solid skills, Paul William Fox worked the backcourt for three head coaches in four years — Waters, McGeachy, and Foster — during the transitional 1970s. A 6 – 2 native of Ardmore, Pa., he participated in 68 games, mostly as a reserve, with 150 points and 71 rebounds.

Fox led the 1973 junior varsity in scoring, pouring in 36 points against the Virginia JVs. He also made five brief varsity showings. As a sophomore in 1974 he played in 20 games, starting some at midseason. He registered his career high of 10 points against Yale and had nine against UNC in the Big Four tourney. The end of the UNC game at Cameron was not his favorite, however. With the score tied and just four seconds left, Fox's inbounds pass intended for Bob Fleischer was picked off by Bobby Jones, who hit the winning layup at the buzzer. "Bobby Jones anticipated it greatly," coach Neill McGeachy said. "I don't think it's to Paul's discredit but to Bobby's credit."

Fox was a light-scoring backcourt sub in 1975 who got the chance to start at the end of the year when Tate Armstrong was injured. His eight-point effort in the second half versus Clemson in the ACC Tournament helped keep the Devils close before the Tigers escaped with a two-point win. Fox was knocked out, literally, in the closing seconds as he was trying to foul Clemson center Tree Rollins. Fox played in 25 of 27 games as a senior in 1976. Armstrong and Jim Spanarkel handled the bulk of the backcourt duties, but Fox provided support with 53 percent shooting and got the chance to start again when Spanarkel was injured late in the year. He scored 21 points in the last three games of his career.

Francis, Bob. Before a home game against Penn State on January 3, 1967, Duke coach Vic Bubas temporarily suspended nine players for violating team rules. That left him with just seven players in uniform to face the Nittany Lions. One of the seven was Robert Dean Francis, a 6 – 6 sophomore from West Jefferson, N.C., who was not on the travel roster. Bubas used just six players in the victory, with Francis making his only career appearance in a varsity uniform. The lone sub used in the game, Francis hit 1 of 2 field goals and 3 of 3 free throws for five points. All-America Bob Verga, the only regular starter not suspended, led the way with 38 points.

Franke, Ned. After two years as one of Duke's top junior varsity players, Robert Edward Franke, 6 – 5, from Pinehurst, N.C., made the varsity roster as a junior in 1982. He saw action in three games, with two points and one rebound.

Frazier, Walt. Hall of Famer Walt Frazier faced Duke near the end of his college career at Southern Illinois University. The two schools squared off in the first round of the NIT at Madison Square Garden in 1967, with the Salukis taking a 72 – 63 decision. It was a weary Duke's fourth game in five days, coming on the heels of the ACC Tournament. Frazier had 17 points and nine rebounds. He led his team to the NIT crown before embarking on an NBA career that landed him on the league's 50th anniversary team.

Freshman basketball. Before the 1972 – 73 season, when freshmen became eligible to compete in varsity basketball, most universities fielded all-freshman teams to develop their future players. Freshman teams consisted of recruited scholarship players as well as walkons, were coached by one of the varsity assistant coaches, and played a schedule of 15 to 20 games against other freshman teams, junior colleges, and some prep schools. Often a team's home contests were played as the first game of a doubleheader with the varsity, offering fans an opportunity to observe the stars of the future. After the arrival of freshman eligibility, several schools continued to operate developmental teams more aptly called junior varsity squads, giving young reserves and nonscholarship players a chance to gain game experience.

Freshman basketball at Duke can be traced back to Trinity College roots. The first freshman team in school history was organized in 1923, was coached by the football player W. L. "Ikey" Taylor, and posted a 4 – 4 record. Taylor, an all-state guard on the 1923 gridiron, guided the freshmen in 1924 to a record of 10 – 6 and coached the first freshman team under a Duke banner in 1925 to a 9 – 1 mark and the state title.

Freshman teams were referred to as the Red Devils during the early years, later becoming known as the Blue Imps. Duke had freshman basketball through the 1971 – 72 season and continued to conduct a junior varsity program through 1981 – 82. Here is a look at several noteworthy squads:

— 1930: One of Duke's first great freshman teams, it went 11 – 0 and had no close games. The starting lineup featured Theodore Capelli and Wendell Horne at forwards, Burt Hill at center, and Don Robertshaw and Nelson Colley in the backcourt. Colley was the captain. Robertshaw and Capelli moved directly into the varsity lineup the following year, but Horne proved to have the best overall career. He was the only player who logged three varsity seasons, and after backup work for two campaigns he blossomed into the No. 2 scorer in his senior year of 1933, when he was also president of the student government.

— 1941: After leading Durham High School to multiple state championships and a 69-game winning streak, local products Bob Gantt, Cedric Loftis, and Garland Loftis made their collegiate débuts for the Duke freshman team. Their squad posted an 11 – 2 record and they were the top three scorers, with averages of 14.1, 13.3, and 11.4 points. One of their losses was against the N.C. State freshmen, when their old Durham High teammate Bones McKinney pumped in 22 points.

— 1949: Fans came early to the Indoor Stadium to watch this team in action before varsity games. It averaged over 70 points a game during a year when the varsity scored 70 points only twice all season. Coached by Paul Williamson, these Blue Imps won 15 of 17 games, beat North Carolina's Tar Babies four times, and claimed the Big Four championship. Dick Groat was one of the top performers, but not the only one. Three players from this team were in the opening-day lineup in 1950 as sophomores: Groat, Dick Crowder, and Dayton Allen.

— 1955: Future varsity starters Paul Schmidt, Jim Newcome, Bucky Allen, and Bobby Joe Harris all averaged between 13 and 15 points a game for a squad that won 14 of 17 games.

— 1958: Several core players of the 1960 ACC championship squad got their starts on this freshman team that posted a 13 – 4 record, most notably Doug Kistler, Howard Hurt, John Frye, and Fred Kast.

— 1960: Coached by Bucky Waters during the first year of the Vic Bubas era, this team posted a 10 – 5 record and provided the first collegiate stage for high-profile recruit Art Heyman. He averaged 30 points a game, enjoyed one 47-point outing, and keyed three victories over the rival UNC freshmen.

— 1961: These Blue Imps posted a 16 – 2 record and enjoyed a 15-game winning streak, including victories in all their conference games. Jeff Mullins led the way with 24.7 points and 10.5 rebounds a game, while Jay Buckley averaged 15.3 points and 13.5 rebounds. Seven players from this team moved up to the varsity in the following year.

— 1963: Steve Vacendak averaged 18.7 points and Jack Marin 17.1 for a freshman club that won 14 of 16 games.

— 1964: Coached by Chuck Daly, this team went 11 – 4 and was known for unleashing star guard Bob Verga. He averaged 32.2 points a game and set the Indoor Stadium scoring record with 51 points against the Virginia Tech frosh. He also had a 45-point game against N.C. State and finished with nine games of 30 or more points. Bob Riedy supported him with a double-double season (16.9 points, 13.8 boards).

— 1965: Mike Lewis had one of the best freshman rebounding marks in school history, 17.0 a game, for a 13 – 3 team that enjoyed a 10-game winning streak. Lewis had a 26-rebound night against Davidson.

— 1968: These Blue Imps had six 100-point games and averaged 90 points a night in posting a 12 – 4 record. Future varsity players Brad Evans, Randy Denton, and Rick Katherman all averaged better than 19 points a game while guard Dick DeVenzio ran the show and pumped in 16.7 points.

— 1970: The first undefeated freshman season in 40 years, as a core of blue-chip Bucky Waters recruits went 16 – 0 while averaging 94.5 points a game. The top performers were Jeff Dawson (20.3 points a game), Richie O'Connor (20.7), Gary Melchionni (17.1), and Alan Shaw (14.6). Shaw had a 26-rebound game, matching Mike Lewis's unofficial freshman game record.

— 1972: This was the last year of all-freshman teams before the NCAA permitted members of any academic class to play for the varsity. Duke had a record of 11 – 5. One of the great all-time freshman performances was turned in by Dave Elmer, a 6 – 10 center who scored 40 points to help Duke spoil N.C. State's undefeated season. Elmer's counterpart, Tom Burleson, was held in check for 10 points. Elmer never made it to the Duke varsity, however, as he opted to transfer to Miami of Ohio.

Frye, John. An expert ball handler and playmaker, John Lee Frye was a constant in the Duke backcourt for three straight seasons, 1959 – 61. He played in all 81 games during this period, with 766 points and 211 rebounds. It was no coincidence that the Devils finished with an upper-division ACC record in each of these years, a conference title in 1960, and a 22-win season in 1961.

Frye, a colorful 6 – 0 performer from Huntington, W.Va., had several big games as a sophomore, including an 18-point day in the ACC semifinals versus North Carolina. He tormented Navy in his junior year, with a career high of 23 points in the Birmingham Classic and another 19 in a regular-season meeting. But his most significant shots were from the foul line, as his clutch free-throw shooting helped the Devils cement wins over UNC and Wake Forest to win the ACC Tournament.

Frye was married with a one-year-old son in his senior year, when he had his best career scoring average of 10.0 points even while sophomore Art Heyman was lighting up scoreboards at a 25.2 clip. Frye poured in 25 points in a win over Wake Forest, had the clinching free throws in a victory over Navy, and rang up 50 points in three ACC Tournament games. The team had a 22 – 6 record and reached the ACC final for the second straight season, this time falling to UNC. Frye joined Heyman on the all-tournament team.

Gantt, Bob. One of Duke's best home-grown athletes of all time, Robert Melvin Gantt Jr. was a standout in the 1940s for the basketball, football, and track teams. As an end in football, he became the first Blue Devil to earn first-team All-America honors twice. He also performed in the transplanted Rose Bowl game that was played at Duke on January 1, 1942. Gantt led the 1943 football team in scoring, with one touchdown and 41 extra-point kicks. A 6 – 3 center in basketball, he was a key player on the 1942 and 1943 teams before leaving for military service.

Gantt was the son of an outstanding baseball pitcher who tossed three no-hitters for Trinity College in 1908. He came to Duke from Durham High, where he was part of a powerhouse basketball program along with

Three-sport standout Bob Gantt was the first Blue Devil to play in the NBA.

Gantt is considered Duke's first NBA player, as he performed for the Washington Capitols in the 1947 season. The league was known as the Basketball Association of America at the time but evolved into the NBA three years later. Gantt's coach was Red Auerbach, who had coached Gantt's Norfolk NTS team. Gantt appeared in 23 games and scored 71 points during the inaugural BAA season.

Gantt was inducted into the Duke Sports Hall of Fame in 1981.

Garber Award. Since 1990 the Atlantic Coast Conference has presented the Mary Garber Award to its female athlete of the year. The award is named for a pioneer sportswriter from the *Winston-Salem* (N.C.) *Journal*. Duke basketball star Alana Beard won the award in 2003 and 2004. The only other Duke woman to claim the honor was NCAA tennis champion Vanessa Webb in 1998.

Garber, Don. Three-year reserve Don Garber, from Washington, D.C., scored 46 points for the Blue Devil varsity, 1930–32. He lettered only as a sophomore, in 1930.

Gaudet, Pete. It was no coincidence that Duke started to win basketball games once Pete Gaudet joined the coaching staff. After successive 17-loss seasons, Mike Krzyzewski brought his former Army aide to Durham, where he played a major role in the Blue Devils' success for over a decade. Gaudet, the team's associate head coach, was viewed as Krzyzewski's right-hand man during his 12 seasons, 1984–95. He was an expert in breaking down film, preparing scouting reports and game plans, and overseeing player development, particularly with post players. He maintained an extensive catalogue of film and video clips on all the players for teaching or motivational needs. He was also known for a dry sense of humor that could lighten the mood in the locker room or on the court. The Blue Devils averaged over 28 wins during his first 11 seasons, with NCAA appearances each year, seven trips to the Final Four, and two national titles.

Gaudet, who was Army's head coach for two seasons after Krzyzewski left for Duke, was asked to replace his boss again in 1995 when Krzyzewski had to leave the team in early January for medical reasons. Gaudet was

his fellow Blue Devils Garland and Cedric Loftis. After starring for the Duke freshman team in 1941, he played regularly as a sophomore and started as a junior, when he averaged over 10 points a game. He played in five games in 1944 before entering the service. Gantt totaled 380 career points. One of his big moments was a tip-in in the closing seconds of a game against UNC in 1942 to force overtime.

In 1945 Gantt had the opportunity to play against the Blue Devils when his Norfolk Naval Training Station team visited Durham. He scored 12 points in a lopsided Norfolk victory.

the interim coach for the remainder of a tough season, as the Blue Devils went 4 – 15 without Krzyzewski and finished with a record of 13 – 18. Ten of Gaudet's 15 defeats were by seven points or fewer, with most decided on the final possession.

Gaudet resigned in May 1995 in a move that he attributed to financial circumstances, not the hard-luck campaign. As the assistant who did no off-campus recruiting, Gaudet had been designated the school's "restricted earnings" coach after a cost-cutting NCAA convention imposed limits on college staffs. This meant that he was permitted to earn only $12,000 a year for his coaching duties and $4,000 for operating Krzyzewski's summer camp. A noted instructor who taught a popular coaching class on campus, Gaudet conducted a four-day clinic in Italy a few days after his resignation and was paid more than he could have earned in one month as a restricted earnings coach.

In fact, Gaudet was the face of the movement to end the restricted earnings designation. In 1993 he filed a lawsuit challenging the NCAA's right to make its cost-cutting rulings retroactive. He asserted that contracts in place before the regulations were enacted, which would pay him at least $25,000 annually to coach and $50,000 to run the summer camp, could not be invalidated. Ironically, a week after Gaudet announced his resignation, a U.S. District Court judge in Kansas City ruled that the NCAA's earnings restrictions violated federal antitrust laws.

By that time there was no turning back for Gaudet. He spent a year teaching courses at Duke and appearing at clinics before being hired as an assistant coach at Vanderbilt. In 1999 he moved from the men's staff to the women's staff, then followed head coach Jim Foster to the Ohio State women's program in 2002.

Gebbie, Tom. Reserve center Thomas Gebbie, a 6 – 7 engineering student from Chicago, played in three games in 1962, scoring three points.

Georgia Tech. It was Super Bowl Sunday in 1990, and the Cameron Crazies had a super-sized treat for Georgia Tech's Dennis Scott. Cognizant that Scott had shed over 20 pounds since the previous season, the students decided to shower him with temptation by littering the

A Shot He'll Never Forget

Mike Dunleavy, 2000 versus Georgia Tech

Dunleavy once had a remarkable half-court shot to beat the halftime buzzer at Wake Forest, and in 2001 he nailed a trio of three-pointers within 45 seconds of the second half to help Duke beat Arizona in the NCAA title game.

But one of the shots he'll never forget came in his freshman year at Georgia Tech. Just before the half he got the ball on the right wing, eluded defender Shaun Fein with a quick fake, dribbled toward the basket, did a 360-degree spin around Clarence Moore, and swooped under center Alvin Jones for a reverse layup on the left side of the hoop to give the Devils a 45 – 31 lead at the break. Coach Mike Krzyzewski was so amazed that he high-fived Dunleavy as he trotted off the court.

"I've never seen anything like that, right before the half. That was some shot," Tech coach Bobby Cremins said.

"I don't really even know what I did, but I spun around and did a reverse layup under and over a few guys, and I think it's the only time I've ever been on SportsCenter," said Dunleavy, who finished with 10 points off the bench in a 19-point victory. "It was just a funny moment, but it was a pretty good move, too."

court with Twinkies, doughnuts, and other junk food during his pre-game introduction. Scott's response? He hit 11 of his first 13 shots and went on to score 36 points. Duke, however, overcame a 12-point deficit to win the game 88 – 86, thanks mostly to superlative bench play. With senior Robert Brickey out with an injury, sophomore Brian Davis and freshman Thomas Hill received extended minutes. Davis led with 16 points and was strong down the stretch, while Hill played ball-denial defense against Scott with the game on the line.

The 1990 season ranks as one of the better ones in the annals of the Duke-Tech series. Just two weeks before Super Sunday, Duke picked up a tense 96 – 91 decision in Atlanta to hand the Yellow Jackets their first loss after a 10 – 0 start. Both clubs were ranked in the national top 10. The game was billed as a battle of freshman point guards, and Bobby Hurley scored 15 points with 11 assists while Tech's Kenny Anderson countered with 24 points and 11 assists. Scott also contributed big with 30 points, but Duke rallied with a 17 – 4 run fueled by Phil Henderson and Christian Laettner. It was the Devils' first victory in Atlanta since 1984. Tech avenged both losses by knocking Duke out of the ACC Tournament in the semifinals, and both clubs advanced to the Final Four in Denver but didn't square off there.

Duke was the opposition when Tech opened its Alexander Memorial Coliseum in 1956, and the two played sporadically before the Yellow Jackets joined the ACC race in 1980. But the rivalry warmed up considerably with coach Bobby Cremins's arrival in 1982, a year after Mike Krzyzewski was hired at Duke. The two developed a close friendship, and their games were just about always intense and down to the wire. The Yellow Jackets probably ranked as Duke's second-biggest rival during the mid-1980s, when both schools were trying to build quality programs at the same time, with an anchor class recruited in the same year. Duke's class was led by Johnny Dawkins and Tech's by Mark Price, and their teams were an even 5 – 5 against each other over four years entering their last meeting, in the league championship game in 1986.

The Jackets were one of just two teams in 1986 to defeat Duke in the regular season, when Price, Bruce Dalrymple, and Craig Neal outplayed Duke's backcourt in Atlanta for an 87 – 80 decision. Tech was the hot team at that time, winning its 15th straight game and moving to the top of the ACC standings. But that was the last contest that Duke dropped until the Final Four. A 68 – 67 victory over the Yellow Jackets in the ACC final gave Krzyzewski his first conference championship.

Duke posted a 28 – 16 record versus Tech during the Cremins years (1982 – 2000). Wins in Atlanta were particularly hard to come by. Duke won there in 1984 by one point on a free throw by David Henderson, but lost there over the next five years before ending the drought in 1990. Duke-Tech in Atlanta usually went down to the last possession or two, as in 1993 when the Devils entered the game 10 – 0 and ranked No. 1 before absorbing an 80 – 79 loss.

Duke won 15 straight games against Georgia Tech from 1997 to 2004. Tech ended the futility by whipping

Duke in Cameron in 2004 to snap the Devils' 41-game home-court winning streak, the longest in the nation at the time. Duke found redemption with a victory in the ACC semifinals, winning handily with a clinical second half in which it committed no turnovers and scored on 20 of its last 22 possessions. As in 1990, both schools went on to reach the Final Four, this time in San Antonio, but did not face each other. One year later they met in the ACC final, with Duke claiming a 69 – 64 decision. The Devils never trailed, but they needed every one of J. J. Redick's 26 points and a tip-in by Shelden Williams of a missed free throw to secure their 19th triumph in 20 games over the Yellow Jackets.

Gerard, Gerry. When Eddie Cameron left his basketball coaching post to take over the football program during the Second World War, Duke didn't have to look far for his replacement. Assistant coach Kenneth Carlyle "Gerry" Gerard was elevated to the head coaching role and remained there for eight years, 1943 – 50, compiling a record of 131 – 78.

A native of Indiana, Gerard played football at Illinois and was the backup to the famed All-American Red Grange. When Gerard came to Duke in 1931, it was to run the intramural sports program. Four years later he started the soccer program, and he coached the squad for its first 11 years. He officiated football and basketball games and was also known for his work as a local radio announcer in those sports. He became Cameron's assistant basketball coach in 1941 and served for two years before his promotion. Even after moving up he continued to officiate football contests, occasionally missing an early-season basketball event to fulfill a football obligation.

Gerard coached the Blue Devils to the Southern Conference championship game in six of his eight years and won two titles, in 1944 and 1946. He was named league coach of the year in 1948 and 1950.

One of Gerard's best teams was his first, in 1943, with a mark of 20 – 6 overall and 12 – 1 in the conference. It was stocked with Durham natives and won 16 of its last 17 games before falling to George Washington in the Southern final. Duke won the league tourney the next year in improbable fashion, as it entered the event with a 10 – 13 record. The Devils blew out William & Mary before defeating State and Carolina for the crown and an even 13 – 13 record.

The 1946 team was another of Gerard's best, as it went 12 – 2 in the conference season and rode the scoring of Ed Koffenberger to the tourney crown. The Devils finished the year with a record of 21 – 6. Koffenberger set Duke's career scoring record in the following year as Duke went 19 – 8, but the Devils bowed out of the Southern Conference tourney in the first round, even though it was held on their home floor for the first time.

Gerard's health began to deteriorate at the end of the 1949 season. He was able to return in 1950, but in November 1950 he took a leave of absence because of illness. His two-year battle with cancer came to an end in January 1951 at the age of 47. In December 1951 Duke and UNC met in a benefit game for Gerard's family, and in 1987 Gerard was inducted posthumously into the Duke Sports Hall of Fame.

Gilbert, Richard. A 6 – 1 reserve for the 1943 team and a starting forward in 1944, Richard M. Gilbert played in 40 varsity games, lettered in both years, and scored 80 points. He was from White Plains, N.Y.

Glasow, Carl. He received a mechanical engineering degree from Cornell as a Navy V-12 student and a master's in physical metallurgy from Rochester. Then Carl Edward Glasow came to Divinity School at Duke and played basketball for one season, 1952. A 6 – 4 center from Rochester, N.Y., he scored 75 points with 88 rebounds in 20 appearances. He had previously lettered for two seasons at Cornell.

Gminski, Mike. The finest center in Duke history was also one of the program's youngest players. Michael Thomas Gminski was only 17 years old when he enrolled at the school and turned 20 just before the start of his senior year. But he had a game, and consequently a career, that transcended his youth. During his four seasons, 1977 – 80, Gminski became Duke's all-time leader in points, rebounds, and blocked shots. He was just the fourth Blue Devil to earn first-team All-ACC honors three times and the second to make All-America three times. He was also a three-time Academic All-America.

A 6 – 11 product of Monroe, Conn., Gminski was in

Center Mike Gminski graduated as his school's all-time scoring and rebounding leader.

an accelerated academic program in high school. Duke player Terry Chili heard during a summer camp that Gminski planned to finish high school a year early and tipped off his coaches, who started the recruiting process before most schools knew that the big guy was available. Gminski had notified some schools of his intentions, but Duke hadn't been one of them.

Gminski stepped immediately into coach Bill Foster's lineup, played nearly 35 minutes a game as a freshman, averaged a double-double with 15.3 points and 10.7 rebounds, and was named ACC co – rookie of the year. Duke logged just a 14 – 13 record and placed last in the ACC, but it pivoted back to national prominence in 1978 with Gminski as one of the central figures. Dominant on the offensive end and an anchor of the club's 2 – 3 zone defense, Gminski helped Duke to marks of 27 – 7, 22 – 8, and 24 – 9 in the next three years. The Devils won the ACC Tournament in his sophomore and senior seasons, played in the NCAA tourney three times, and battled Kentucky for the national championship in 1978.

Gminski is the only four-year player in Duke history to average double figures in points (19.0) and re-

The Shot He'll Never Forget

Mike Gminski, 1980 versus Maryland

The shot most people will never forget from the 1980 ACC Tournament was Albert King's soft miss in the closing seconds that Duke rebounded as time ran out. It stands as one of the most controversial plays in tournament history. Did Kenny Dennard really undercut Maryland's Buck Williams, who was poised for the offensive rebound? No official's whistle blew, leaving Duke to celebrate a championship.

But that is not the shot that Duke All-America Gminski thinks of first. A few seconds earlier, Duke trailed 72–71 when Vince Taylor started to drive, pulled up for a shot, and missed. Dennard tapped the rebound from one side of the basket to the other, where Gminski was open for an easy lay-in with nine seconds left. They were the winning points in a 73–72 victory.

Gminski recalls the play fondly because of the way it helped erase the sting of some early frustration that year.

"It was my senior year, we had a lot of high expectations, and for a lot of reasons ended up in the middle of the pack with the sixth seed for the tournament," he said. "To beat the three, two, and one seeds on consecutive days, that was a special tournament for me."

The win got the Blue Devils into the NCAA Tournament, which they would have missed without the automatic bid.

---

bounds (10.2) for a career. He and Christian Laettner are the only two to make the ACC All-Tournament team four times; Gminski was on the first team for three of those years. He also shared the team MVP award three times. He played in 122 games with 2,323 points, 1,242 rebounds, and 345 blocked shots. (Laettner, Johnny Dawkins, and J. J. Redick later passed him on the scoring chart, while Shelden Williams broke his rebounding and blocks records in 2006.) Gminski hit 53.1 percent of his floor shots and was excellent at the foul line, 79.2 percent. He also had the distinction of never fouling out of a college game.

Though there were no ESPN pundits to slap nicknames on every player and video clip during Gminski's time, NBC analyst Al McGuire often referred to G-Man as the big "aircraft carrier" that successful teams needed. Fos-

ter surrounded Gminski with all the key elements—a crafty floor leader in Jim Spanarkel, a dynamic forward in Gene Banks, solid point guards in Bob Bender and John Harrell, and a hustling workman in Kenny Dennard. When most of the parts were in working order, the Devils were difficult to beat. Their chemistry in 1978 was especially effectual in showing that Duke could compete again on the national stage. After their runner-up finish, the Devils were ranked No. 1 at various points over Gminski's last two years. Before 1978 Duke hadn't sniffed a national ranking in over six seasons.

Gminski had his career scoring high of 33 points against Virginia Tech during the 1978 season, and totaled 20 or more points in six of his team's eight postseason games, including a 29-point outing against Notre Dame in the Final Four to power Duke to the final. One of his best games in 1979 was a Super Sunday showdown at N.C. State, in which he paced a victory with 31 points. When Duke welcomed McGuire and NBC to Cameron for a rare national TV date against the announcer's former school, the aircraft carrier had 22 points and nine rebounds to torpedo Marquette. Gminski was named ACC player of the year in 1979, but the campaign ended in disappointment with an upset to St. John's in the NCAA. Gminski scored 16 points but was not close to full strength because of illness.

As a senior Gminski paced Duke to five championships: the first Hall of Fame Tip-Off Classic versus Kentucky, the Big Four Tournament, the Industrial National Bank Classic, the Iron Duke Classic, and the ACC Tournament. The ACC regular season was a disappointment at 7–7, but the last home game was a career highlight. Just before tipoff, Duke announced that G-Man would be the first athlete to have his jersey retired since Dick Groat almost three decades earlier. The man of the hour scored 29 points and had a career high of 19 rebounds to lead an overtime win versus Clemson. Ten days later he scored the game-winning basket off a rebound as Duke topped Maryland for the ACC crown. It was the last of his 191 career points in the ACC tourney, tying Art Heyman for the most in school history (another mark later topped by Redick).

Gminski averaged 2.8 blocked shots a game over four years, one of the 10 best marks in ACC history. Much like Mike Krzyzewski's best shot blocker, Shelden Williams, Gminski kept many of his rejections in play for his teammates to retrieve. Once each year he blocked nine shots in a single game, the school record until Cherokee Parks had 10 in the 1994 ACC Tournament. His most celebrated block party was in the NCAA regionals in 1978, when he rejected three straight Penn shots to turn around a game that the Devils won 84 – 80. G-Man had seven blocks that day.

The No. 7 pick of the pro draft, Gminski enjoyed the longest NBA career of any Duke alumnus, with 14 seasons and 938 games. He scored over 10,000 points and had nearly 6,500 rebounds. His best year was 1989, when he started all 82 games and averaged 17.2 points, teaming with Charles Barkley to help the Philadelphia 76ers reach the playoffs. He started all but one contest the next year as the Sixers won their division. Overall he made five playoff trips with the Nets, two with Philly, and one with the Charlotte Hornets.

After retirement Gminski joined the Hornets' broadcast team for eight seasons and then became the television analyst for the ACC's Sunday night game of the week on Fox Sports Net. In 2004 he also joined the fold of CBS analysts for the NCAA Tournament. The ACC named Gminski to its 50th anniversary team, and he was enshrined in both the Duke Sports Hall of Fame (1996) and the North Carolina Sports Hall of Fame. Gminski has served as chairman of the board of advisors for Duke Children's Hospital.

Godfrey, George. A 6 – 0 guard from Jacksonville, Fla., George Godfrey was a reserve in 1948 and 1949. He played in 26 games and scored 36 points. He earned a letter in 1948.

GoDuke.com. The official website of Duke athletics, GoDuke.com was launched in 1997 as a source for news and other information on all varsity sports at the university. But its heaviest traffic is generated by the basketball program. The site publishes all basketball-related news releases from the sports information department, transcripts of major press conferences, pre-game facts and notes on every contest, and post-game coverage that includes box scores, locker-room quotes, and photos. It also links to radio game broadcasts and daily audio updates from Mike Krzyzewski.

From 2001 to 2005 Gail Goestenkors coached the Duke women to five straight 30-win seasons and 157 victories, the second-highest total in the nation.

Duke's first Internet home page for athletics made its début in 1996 as part of the university's duke.edu site. Since the move to GoDuke.com in 1997, the features on the site have continually expanded. The site has been relaunched several times with new and updated designs, most recently on July 1, 2005, with increased emphasis on premium audio and video services.

Goestenkors, Gail. She was only 29 years old and had never been a head coach when the job opened. But if the risk in hiring her was great, so too was the reward for both parties in the union of Gail Ann Goestenkors with Duke University. The school's prescience resulted in the development of one of the premier women's basketball programs in the country, while the coach evolved into one of the most widely respected and admired figures in her sport.

Interest in Duke basketball was at an all-time high in the spring of 1992, as the men's program basked in the afterglow of back-to-back NCAA championships. Astute observers recognized similar potential in the women's program if the appropriate commitment were made. Assured that the resources needed to excel would be available, Goestenkors, a native of Waterford, Mich., shared her championship vision with the search committee charged to replace Debbie Leonard, including details on every recruit she would pursue for the next three years. Her plan, foresight, and energy led to an offer. After one year as a graduate assistant at Iowa State and six as an ace recruiter for Purdue, Goestenkors was a head coach for the first time. "My goal is to prove you right," she told director of athletics Tom Butters.

Using as a model Tara VanDerveer of Stanford, the 1990 and 1992 NCAA champ, Goestenkors aimed to take Duke to the Final Four in five years. It didn't happen quite that quickly, as her first team posted a losing record and her second was just five games over the break-even mark. "It's good that I was naïve. I didn't know any better. In my case, ignorance was bliss," she later recalled. But in the third season, 1995, the Blue Devils emerged as contenders in the ACC while returning to the NCAA Tournament for the first time since 1987. They haven't missed that event since, and in 1999, after upsetting almighty Tennessee, the Duke women were playing at the Final Four for the national title. The program had gone from the bottom of the conference to the national penthouse in just seven years.

With superb recruiting as the backbone, Goestenkors took Duke to three more Final Fours (2002, 2003, 2006), began an unprecedented run of dominance in the ACC with five straight tournament crowns from 2000 through 2004, and had six straight 30-win seasons from 2001 through 2006. Before her arrival, the program had won only two ACC tourney games and one NCAA game, and had posted just one 20-win campaign while operating on a proverbial shoestring.

Through the 2006 season, her 14th at the helm, Goestenkors owned an overall record of 364–97 and had reached 300 wins faster than any other coach in ACC history. Her conference record was 165–55, with seven regular-season titles, and her ACC tourney record was 25–9, with five championships. In 12 consecutive NCAA visits, her 34–12 record represented a winning percentage of 73.9, the third-highest among active coaches, behind only UConn's Geno Auriemma and Tennessee's Pat Summitt. The Blue Devils had been ranked in the final top 10 nine straight times and had enjoyed five No. 1 seeds in the NCAA tourney between 2001 and 2006. Goestenkors had been named ACC coach of the year six times and national coach of the year four times.

While flourishing on the recruiting trail, Goestenkors also proved that she was one of the better X-and-O coaches in the nation, annually molding strategy to fit the talent on hand while insisting on defense first. Motivating players and fostering team chemistry became strengths as well. Two of her better teams, the one that went to the Final Four in 2002 after going 19–0 in the ACC and the team that won 31 games in 2005, had rosters of only eight players.

"She's a little lady, but gets the most out of you," said her best player, Alana Beard. "She's going to push you. She's not going to let you settle for anything less."

"For a woman role model, I could not have picked anybody better," said another former star and assistant coach, Georgia Schweitzer. "As far as I'm concerned, she is the best college coach in America. She always has us ready for the game, and if the strategies aren't working, she changes. I've played on other teams where the coaches have a mentality where they're never going to change. But she adjusts to the players and listens to the players if they tell her something's not working."

Goestenkors built her juggernaut in the shadow of the premier men's program in the nation, a situation that she embraced from her first moment on campus. "Mike's been a tremendous supporter for us," Coach G said of Coach K. "We've never felt like we're in a shadow. I've always felt like the men's basketball program sheds light on every other aspect of the university, not that they cast shadows. I think we've used that to our benefit, and a lot of departments within the university have seen more success and more interest because of the national exposure our men get."

A point guard from Saginaw Valley State from the

class of 1985, Goestenkors once dreamed of coaching the Michigan Wolverines in her native state. When that job opened in 1996 she instead recommended a friend. She also resisted overtures from the WNBA after her breakout experience in the Final Four in 1999.

"When I first got this job, I didn't know that it would necessarily be the job I would want to end with," she said on the eve of her 10th Duke season. "It was my first head coaching job and usually you bounce around a little bit. I looked at a couple of those other jobs within the first five years or so, but now I've come to realize that this is my dream job. You don't know that when you are young and growing up, but now that I've had a chance to compare it . . . I just can't honestly think of a better job in the country than this job. I guess I didn't think I'd be here 10 years, and now I can't imagine being anywhere else."

But she can imagine coaching other teams — such as with USA Basketball. She was an assistant coach for the 2002 national team that won the World Championship and for the 2004 USA team that won the Olympic gold medal. During the summer of 2005 she was head coach for a national contingent that won the Under-19 World Championship in dominating fashion; it was named USA Basketball's team of the year, and she was named the organization's coach of the year.

Goetsch, Scott. Playing time proved limited for Scott Douglas Goetsch during his four years at Duke, the final three of which coincided with the career of the Blue Devils' greatest center, Mike Gminski. But Goetsch handled his role as a 6 – 9 reserve post player by always delivering quality minutes and always pushing Gminski to be at his best during practice.

Goetsch, from Chatsworth, Calif., appeared in 94 career games and scored 185 points with 167 rebounds. He shot 58 percent from the field. During his freshman year of 1976 he played in the junior varsity games, once grabbing 20 rebounds versus UNC, while making six appearances for the varsity. For the next three years he saw backup duty in just about every varsity game.

As a sophomore Goetsch had the best contest of his career, with 12 points and eight rebounds against Davidson, and he earned a start late in the year against Virginia. He won the Ted Mann Jr. award as the reserve contributing most to team morale. Goetsch averaged 2.9

points and 2.2 rebounds while shooting 62 percent as Gminski's backup for the team that reached the Final Four in 1978, and he had several highlight moments. He came off the bench to score 11 points at SMU, had an important basket in a road win at Maryland, and hit a jumper over his high school rival Bill Laimbeer in the Devils' NCAA semifinal win against Notre Dame. As a senior in 1979 he saw reserve action in all but one game. He later graduated from Duke Law School in 1982 and joined a firm in Baltimore.

Goetz, Lou. As the right-hand man to head coach Bill Foster, assistant coach Lou Goetz was an integral factor in Duke' reemergence as a national power in the late 1970s. A native of Passaic, N.J., he began his association with Foster in the 1960s when Foster recruited him to play for Rutgers. After playing on two NIT teams, Goetz graduated in 1969 and joined Foster's coaching staff, before following his boss to Utah and eventually to Duke, where he worked for four years, 1975 – 78. Goetz had a hand in every aspect of rebuilding the Duke program, on the court and off. The day after the Blue Devils lost to Kentucky in the national championship game in 1978, Goetz accepted his first head coaching position at Richmond, where he worked for three years before resigning to enter private business.

Goetz enjoyed another connection to Duke basketball. While in Durham he met Tracy Groat, the daughter of two-sport All-America Dick Groat. The two were married in December 1977.

Goins, Connie. A smooth 5 – 10 guard from Frankfort, Ky., Connie Goins was a regular in the lineup for women's coach Debbie Leonard in the mid-1980s. She played in 101 games from 1983 to 1986 and started 96 times, with a career scoring average of 11.3 on 1,140 points. An all-around player, Goins also had 461 rebounds and 297 assists. She led the Devils in assists as a senior, had a 30-point game as a junior, and graduated with more free throws made than anyone in school history to that point, except her teammate Chris Moreland.

Goins, a four-time ACC Honor Roll member, was the second player in Duke history to earn All-ACC honors. She made the second team in 1986, when she averaged 13.5 points, 5.2 rebounds, and 4.5 assists for the first Duke team ever to win at least 20 games and play in the postseason (in the WNIT). Moreland previously made the All-ACC second team in 1985 and was a first-team pick in 1986.

Golden, Dave. After pacing the 1966 freshman team in scoring, backcourt whiz David Duane Golden stepped up to the varsity and poured in 25 points against Michigan in his second game. That was easily the high-water mark of his sophomore season, but Golden went on to earn a starting berth during coach Vic Bubas's last two seasons. In three years, 1967–69, Golden scored 752 points and had 153 rebounds in 80 games. A 6–0 native of Pekin, Ill., known for his long-range shooting touch, Golden had his best marks in 1968 when he averaged 13.1 points even though he was coming off summer knee surgery. His career high of 26 points came twice in that year, two games apart, against Clemson and N.C. State. He hit 12 of 16 shots versus the Tigers. Golden had another handful of 20-point outings and finished off his home career with 10 points in a memorable upset of UNC in 1969. That was also Bubas's last home game.

Gomez, Rick. A 6–3 guard from Rosselle, N.J., Ricardo Anthony Gomez was a member of coach Bill Foster's first Duke recruiting class, but he didn't last long. Gomez played in five junior varsity games and nine varsity games as a freshman in 1975, then appeared in just five games in 1976 before leaving school at the end of his sophomore year. He totaled 14 points for his varsity career.

Goodman, Jon. A walk-on member of the 1987 team, Jon Christopher Goodman played in 10 games and had six points with three assists. He was a 5–9 freshman guard from Pocatello, Idaho, and his sister Dawn was a member of the varsity cheerleading squad.

Gordon, Dick. Although he didn't earn many accolades, Richard Gordon was a scrappy 6–0 guard whom coach Gerry Gerard could depend on in the late 1940s. Gordon, from Jacksonville, Fla., lettered during four postwar years, 1946–49, and became the first Blue Devil to appear in at least 100 varsity games. He totaled 432 points in 101 career contests.

Gordon started every varsity game as a freshman in 1946, when Duke won the Southern Conference Tour-

nament. He was a part-time starter in 1947, then came off the bench for much of the rebuilding year of 1948, when he missed the only four games of his career. Gordon was back in the lineup as a senior in 1949, when he was team co-captain. Duke's record during his career was 70–35.

Graduation rates. The rafters of Cameron Indoor Stadium have got crowded over the years, with banners representing the Blue Devils' major accomplishments, such as Final Fours and championships. One of the program's policies is that no banner goes up, no matter how exemplary the team, until all of its senior players have graduated. The school hasn't had to withhold many banners, because the graduation rate has been stellar.

Beginning with the 1976 freshman class that included Jim Spanarkel, the first 2,000-point scorer in school history and the captain of the team that reached the Final Four in 1978, Duke has graduated over 90 percent of its recruited scholarship basketball players who stayed for four years. From the 1976 freshmen through the 2002 freshmen, 68 of 75 recruited players graduated. Of the seven who did not, five left school early to turn professional. These figures do not include 10 recruited players who transferred from Duke during that period, at least eight of whom graduated from their second school. Since 1976 only two players who didn't transfer or turn pro have failed to graduate.

That compares favorably with the university's overall graduation rate of 93 percent for the student body at large and is well above the national graduation rate for basketball players, which has been listed at between 40 and 45 percent annually since the NCAA began tracking data in 1984.

Graham, Otto. One of the great quarterbacks in pro football history, Otto Graham twice played basketball against Duke. A football star at Northwestern, Graham went to Carolina Pre-Flight in 1944 during the Second World War and helped direct the Cloudbusters to a pair of victories over the Blue Devils. On December 29, 1944, Graham hit 11 field goals and scored 27 points before a crowd of 2,000 at UNC's Woollen Gym to aid a 58–43 win by Pre-Flight over the Blue Devils. A couple of weeks later, on January 10, 1945, Graham had 18 points as Pre-Flight overcame an early 17–6 deficit to defeat Duke

49 – 45 in Durham. Graham launched his Hall of Fame football career with the Cleveland Browns in 1946.

Gray, Irving. A 5 – 11 guard from Freeport, N.Y., Irving Gray lettered as a sophomore for the team that won the Southern Conference championship in 1946, scoring 30 points in 19 appearances. He returned to play in six games in 1947, went scoreless, and did not letter.

Gray, Steve. Once described by coach Bill Foster as a workaholic, Stephen Biagio Gray may have spent more time in the gym training than any of his contemporaries in the late 1970s. Gray, a 6 – 2 guard from Woodland, Calif., played in 88 games from 1976 to 1979, mostly as a reserve. He posted career totals of 223 points and 119 assists.

After limited playing time in 10 games as a freshman, Gray had a chance to make a bigger mark during the second half of his sophomore season when star guard Tate Armstrong was lost to a wrist injury. Gray moved into the lineup and averaged 38.7 minutes over a seven-game stretch. But with Duke struggling to win ACC games, Gray committed a couple of memorable mistakes in narrow home defeats. He lost the ball off his foot at the end of the N.C. State game and threw a pass away off the rim at the end of the Maryland game, and Duke dropped both by a single point. Foster turned to reserve Bruce Bell to run the offense for the rest of that year.

After a solid preseason, Gray started the first 10 games of 1978 and helped the Devils to a record of 8 – 2. Then Foster plugged John Harrell into the lineup and moved Gray to the bench for the rest of the year. He had 82 points and 30 assists as Duke won the ACC and reached the Final Four. Perhaps Gray's most frustrating season was as a senior in 1979, when he saw very little playing time in 26 appearances.

Gray's top scoring game was for 14 points versus Wake Forest at the Big Four Tournament in his junior season. Aside from being a hard worker and good defensive player, Gray was also an excellent free-throw shooter, hitting 85 percent for his career. In 1978 he was the team's top scholar athlete as the winner of the Dr. Deryl Hart award.

After graduating in 1979, Gray spent a couple of years traveling and playing semiprofessional basketball until he was injured in a car accident. He entered the computer industry after that and later reunited with his former teammate Kenny Dennard, joining him in business in Houston.

Great Alaska Shootout. Duke's first trip to the Great Alaska Shootout, in November 1995, provided an important stepping stone for a team that was reeling from a losing record in the previous season. With coach Mike Krzyzewski back on the bench, the Blue Devils defeated Old Dominion, Indiana, and Iowa to win the title. In the ODU game Duke's co-captain Jeff Capel faced a team coached by his father. The Indiana game matched Krzyzewski against his college coach Bob Knight. The Iowa game featured a 30-point explosion by Duke's other co-captain Chris Collins, though he was not named most valuable player. The one down note for Duke was that sophomore guard Trajan Langdon, an Anchorage native and the best basketball player ever produced by the state, was unable to play in his home town because of injury.

Duke returned to the Shootout in November 1998 with one of its best teams, led by fifth-year senior Langdon. Ranked No. 1 in the country, the Devils got past Notre Dame and Fresno State before falling to Cincinnati 77 – 75 on a last-second dunk. Duke overcame a 19-point deficit in that contest and didn't lose again until the national championship. Langdon enjoyed games of 20, 26, and 13 points in the tournament he always dreamed of playing in, and the attention that he received from the locals was nothing short of hero worship. When the favorite son was introduced before the games, nearly every person in Sullivan Arena was standing, creating a roar that would have made Cameron Indoor Stadium proud.

Duke's third Thanksgiving in Alaska was in November 2003, when the Blue Devils again reached the championship game before falling to Purdue.

Green, Ted. A 6 – 3 post man from Harrisburg, Pa., Ted Green came to Duke from Princeton in 1945, earned a letter, and scored 51 points.

Duke versus Maryland in the 2004 ACC final at the Greensboro Coliseum.

Greensboro Coliseum. The history of ACC basketball could not be written without devoting a significant chapter to the Greensboro Coliseum. From 1967 through 2006 the ACC Tournament was held in Greensboro 21 times. On ten of those occasions, the championship team went on to reach the Final Four of the NCAA Tournament. Three times that team was Duke, in 1978, 1986, and 1988. Overall Duke won six of the first 21 ACCs held in Greensboro.

Built on the site of an old fairgrounds, the coliseum opened in October 1959 with a capacity of about 9,000 seats. Villanova played N.C. State in the first college basketball game there. The facility ended a 13-year monopoly by Reynolds Coliseum on the ACC Tournament when it hosted the 1967 event, before the league took its postseason extravaganza to the bigger Charlotte Coliseum for the next three years. A massive renovation that increased capacity to almost 16,000 brought the ACC back to Greensboro in 1971, and the tourney stayed through the rest of the decade, save a side trip to Landover, Md., in 1976.

It was during the 1970s that Greensboro and its coliseum cemented themselves as the epicenter of ACC bas-

ketball. The 1971 championship game had one of the most astonishing finishes ever, with South Carolina's 6–3 guard Kevin Joyce winning a jump ball against North Carolina's 6–10 center Lee Dedmon with six seconds left, tapping the ball to his teammate Tom Owens for the decisive score.

In 1973 N.C. State's David Thompson hit a pair of free throws in the waning seconds of the ACC final against Maryland to give his team a two-point win and a perfect season of 27–0. A year later, the two combatants engaged in the game that is generally regarded as the finest in ACC history, a 103–100 overtime win for the Wolfpack. Two weeks afterward, State nudged UCLA in double overtime on the same floor to end the Bruins' long NCAA title run. The Pack then defeated Marquette for the national title, ending perhaps the most significant month in the state's basketball history, all at the Greensboro Coliseum.

In 1975 the entire ACC Tournament was decided by a total of 20 points. In 1978 a cinderella Duke team ended a long dry spell by returning to the top, and in 1980 the Blue Devils capped off a title run from the sixth seed by edging Maryland at the buzzer. Concurrent with all these ACC spectacles was the creation of the Big Four Tournament, also in Greensboro. It featured Duke, N.C. State, Wake Forest, and UNC, ran for 11 seasons (1971 – 81), and frequently featured games just as pulsating as the March contests, with publicity to match.

Duke made its début in Greensboro Coliseum on January 3, 1961, with a victory over Navy in which Art Heyman set an early stadium scoring record with 28 points. When Navy got close late in the game, Heyman scored seven points in 93 seconds to wrap it up. Interestingly, each school's football team had played in a major bowl game the day before, Duke at the Cotton, Navy at the Orange. The Midshipmen had one player who competed in both sports, flying from Miami to Greensboro for the hoops game.

Duke continued to play at least one game a year in Greensboro for over a decade. In December 1961 Duke played Wake Forest in the coliseum to fill a scheduling gap left by the demise of the Dixie Classic. The contest was in addition to their home-and-home ACC games and didn't count in the league standings. That holiday arrangement continued through 1970. Also in the 1960s, Duke played Virginia Tech in several season openers at the coliseum. In 1971 the Blue Devils played almost as many games in Greensboro as they did at home, with seven appearances. The Blue Devils also made at least one annual trip to Greensboro through most of the 1980s, as Wake Forest played its home games at the coliseum from 1982 to 1989.

Along with the Final Four in 1974, Greensboro hosted numerous NCAA Tournament games. Duke opened tournament play there five times — 1986, 1989, 1992, 2001, and 2006 — and won all 10 games. Four of those teams wound up in the Final Four and two won the national title. From 1986 through 2006, Duke played 43 games at the Greensboro Coliseum and won 36 of them. Overall, Duke played more than 100 games in the coliseum from 1961 through 2006.

The coliseum, renovated again in 1994 to remain competitive with 20,000-seat structures in Charlotte, Raleigh, and Chapel Hill, also proved fertile territory for the Duke women's basketball team. It was the site of the Blue Devils' upset of defending national champion Tennessee in 1999 for the school's first trip to the Women's Final Four. By the end of the 2006 season, the

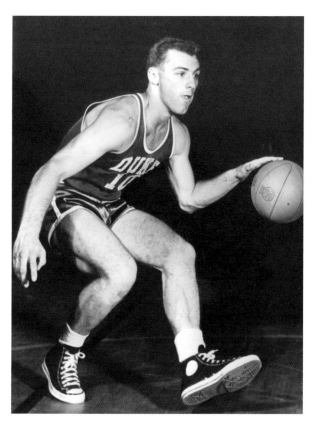

Future Major League Baseball star Dick Groat was the first Blue Devil to have his jersey retired, in 1952.

Duke women had played in six ACC Tournament finals in Greensboro, with five titles and an overall record of 20 – 2 in the building.

Groat, Dick. His most memorable moment in sports? That's an easy question for Dick Groat. It came at the World Series in 1960, when his Pittsburgh Pirates beat the New York Yankees 10 – 9 in the seventh game on one of the most famous plays in baseball history, Bill Mazeroski's home run in the bottom of the ninth inning.

"Watching from the dugout, seeing Maz's ball go over the fence, was the greatest thrill I've ever experienced," Groat told a baseball publication 20 years afterward. "It was especially thrilling for me, growing up in the Pittsburgh area, playing for the Pirates and then seeing us with our first pennant in 33 years."

Groat, a shortstop named five times to the All-Star team, led the National League in batting that year with a .325 average, was chosen the league's MVP, and had delivered a key blow of his own against the Yankees, igniting a late-game rally with a run-scoring single in the seventh inning. It was one of many clutch performances that he turned in during his 14 years in the major leagues.

Such feats surely add luster to Groat's status as a distinguished alumnus, but in Duke circles, Groat's name will always be associated more with basketball than baseball. He played both sports as a collegian and was All-America in both, but it was in basketball that he emerged as one of the most revered figures in the university's athletic heritage. He wasn't the school's first All-America selection, but by the time he made his last bucket in 1952 he was inarguably the best basketball player the institution had produced in nearly half a century of competition.

Richard Morrow Groat, a 6–0 guard from Swissvale, Pa., played three varsity seasons, 1950–52, and set every record in the book. Many remained on the books for decades afterward. His sophomore year was incomplete, as he had to leave school on an academic infraction after averaging 14.5 points in the first 19 games. But the fireworks really began in his junior year. In the opening contest he scored 31 points to set a new single-game Duke record — and proceeded to top it three more times that year. He totaled 831 points to establish a new national scoring record for one season, and in the process became the first Duke player to pass 1,000 points for a career.

The next year, as a senior, Groat finished second in the nation in scoring and led in assists. He extended his individual game record to 46 points, then to 48 in his home finale with UNC. He closed his 82-game varsity tenure with 1,886 points, the most in school history, and his career average of 23.0 was the best as well.

Just how durable were those standards?

— His career points total lasted over a decade, until Art Heyman slipped past in 1963. Heyman's career average of 25.1 also topped Groat's 23.0 average, but only two other players in Duke annals have even reached 20.0 for a career.

— Groat's single-game record of 48 points stood for 37 seasons, until Danny Ferry had a 58-point night in 1988–89.

— His 831 points in one season lasted even longer, until Jason Williams totaled 841 in 2001. And only two Duke players have had a better single-season scoring av-

erage than Groat's 26.0 in 1952: Bob Verga's 26.1 in 1967 and J. J. Redick's 26.8 in 2006.

— Groat's mark of 229 assists in a year lasted until Tommy Amaker had 241 in 1986, though that's somewhat deceiving because assists statistics were not compiled consistently in the 1950s and 1960s.

Groat played his sophomore year under coach Gerry Gerard, learned the finer points of the game during three months of instruction from Red Auerbach, and played his last two years under Hal Bradley. Duke had records of 20–13 and 24–6 during Groat's last two years and was unable to win the Southern Conference, but Groat was chosen MVP of the tournament both times anyway as its leading scorer and playmaker.

While his hallmark game was the finale with UNC in which he hit 19 of 37 field goals and 10 of 11 free throws, Groat was rarely better than in the second half of a contest with Tulane in the Dixie Classic in his junior year. The Blue Devils trailed by 32 points in the first half, but Groat led an inspired second-half charge as Duke regrouped and won 74–72. He finished with 32 points, including 24 in the second half that topped Tulane's entire team total of 16.

Along with winning All-America and national player of the year honors, Groat won the McKevlin Award twice as the top athlete in the Southern Conference and the Teague Award as the most outstanding amateur male athlete in the Carolinas. His baseball accomplishments undoubtedly aided the cause, as he batted .386 and .370 in 1951 and 1952 while pacing the Blue Devils to a pair of league championships and a trip to the College World Series. An All-America in two sports, Groat became the first Duke athlete to have his jersey retired when the school retired his basketball No. 10 at a baseball game with UNC.

Groat signed a $25,000 contract with the Pittsburgh Pirates in 1952 and went directly to the majors without spending a day in minor league baseball. Joining the team in midseason, he quickly became the starting shortstop. He was also drafted by the Fort Wayne Pistons of the NBA with the third pick of the first round and signed a $10,000 deal with them. He played professional basketball during the 1953 season, with the Pistons flying him back and forth to Duke so that he could complete his academic requirements. He never practiced with Fort Wayne but still averaged almost 12 points a game.

The Pirates eventually called a halt to that exercise. Groat spent two years in the Army, where he played basketball for service teams and once faced his alma mater in an exhibition. Upon his discharge Groat concentrated on baseball for the remainder of his pro career, playing in 1,929 games with 2,138 hits and a .286 average. He was traded from Pittsburgh to St. Louis in 1963 and helped the Cardinals beat the Yankees in the World Series in 1964.

A charter inductee in the Duke Sports Hall of Fame (1975), Groat was a manufacturer's rep in the steel business for several years. He remained involved in athletics as the co-owner of a golf course in Pennsylvania and as a radio broadcaster for University of Pittsburgh basketball games since 1979. Over 50 years after his college hoop days ended, he told a reporter for the *Pittsburgh Tribune-Review* that he often wondered during his all-star baseball career if he'd chosen the right sport.

"To me basketball is the epitome of a team game," he said. "Baseball should be played that way, but the modern-day baseball player doesn't play it that way, advancing runners, taking strikes, all the things that the two world champions I played on did.

"I still get a thrill going to see a basketball game."

Hall, Cameron. Sidelined by a back injury in 1976 during his true freshman season, Cameron Murray Hall came off the bench to fortify Duke's inside game during the 1977 campaign. A 6–9 forward from Canada, Hall played in all 27 games and averaged 4.3 points and 2.1 rebounds. He then played sparingly in seven games at the beginning of the 1978 season. Foreseeing limited playing time, he decided to leave the program but remained in school and graduated on time in 1979. His career totals included 34 games, 140 points, and 67 rebounds.

Before coming to Duke, Hall was the only high school player named to the Canadian National Team and performed in the Pan American Games in 1975. In the following year he played for Canada in the Montreal Olympics and was the top frontcourt reserve as his country took fourth place. Hall put that experience to good use during the 1977 Duke season.

Hall, Jeremy. A walk-on from Sarasota, Fla., Jeremy Robert Hall played in 10 games as a freshman for the 1996 team, scoring four points with one rebound. He was invited to help out at practice early in the year and was added to the roster after standout guard Trajan Langdon was ruled out for the season because of a knee injury. One of Hall's field goals came on a layup in the closing moments of the regular-season home finale, throwing a scare into UNC as the Tar Heels watched a 15-point lead slip to five before holding on to win.

Hall, Tyish. Joining Kira Orr and Windsor Coggeshall in Gail Goestenkors's first Duke recruiting class, Tyish Hall was one of the key post players when the Blue Devil women were developing into a conference contender. A 6–3 forward from Centreville, Va., she earned All-ACC second team honors as a junior and senior and helped anchor three teams that advanced to the second round of the NCAA Tournament.

Hall played in 109 contests from 1994 to 1997 and started almost every one in which she was healthy over her last three years. She finished with 1,286 points for an 11.8 average, plus 632 rebounds for a 5.8 average. She hit 63.0 percent of her field goals, still the top all-time figure in Duke women's history. In 1996 her field-goal percentage of 65.5 set a new ACC record and was the second-best in the nation for that season.

In Duke's first NCAA Tournament game of the Goestenkors era, Hall demonstrated that shooting touch with a 9-of-9 performance from the field for 22 points in a win over Oklahoma State. She followed that with a double-double of 12 points and 13 rebounds in a four-overtime marathon at Alabama.

Hall was the leading scorer (15.1), rebounder (7.0), shooter (65.5), and shot blocker for the 1996 team, which posted a record of 26–7 and went 12–4 in the ACC.

Hamilton, Roger. A 6–3 reserve from Westerly, R.I., Roger Hamilton played in the Davidson and Clemson games in 1962, scoring two points. He made a more lasting contribution to Duke later in life when he championed the fund-raising efforts that led to the construction of the school's indoor tennis facility.

Harding, Lindsey. She didn't get taller, but Lindsey Marcie Harding went through a definite growth spurt in 2005. Forced to sit out the season for violating team rules, she matured while studying every game situation more closely from the bench. When she returned to action in 2006, she was one of the most polished performers for the Blue Devils' Final Four team.

A 5 – 8 point guard from Houston, Harding was a spot starter for the 2003 Final Four team and a lineup fixture for the 2004 ACC championship team. She made the All-ACC third team and the all-defensive team that year, but she was even better in 2006 after her year off. Harding was Duke's catalyst at both ends of the floor, spearheading the defense with her ball pressure and igniting the offense with her speed and decision making. She posted a career high of 19 points a couple of times, but her signature game was Duke's home victory over top-ranked Tennessee, when she had 15 points and eight steals and pestered the Lady Vols for the entire evening.

"Lindsey was amazing," coach Gail Goestenkors said. "If there's a better defensive player in the nation, I'd like to see her. She did a little bit of everything on the defensive end and really disrupted so many things that they wanted to do. Then on offense she took it to the basket when she needed to, she hit the little pull-up jumpers, and she got the ball to the open player and ran the offense for us. She had an exceptional game."

Harding was named to the All-ACC second team and was chosen the league's defensive player of the year by the 12 head coaches. With one year remaining in her collegiate career, she had totals of 835 points and 448 assists in 106 games, and was well within reach of challenging the school career assists mark of 533.

Hardy, Rob. Enamored with Duke from his days at Vic Bubas's summer camp, Robert Moss Hardy Jr. was able to live out a dream by playing basketball for the Blue Devils in the late 1970s. A 6 – 3 walk-on who grew up in Kentucky and attended high school in Columbus, Ohio, Hardy played for the junior varsity in 1976 and led the JV team in scoring with a 17.2 average in 1977, his sophomore year. He also saw action in six varsity contests that year.

Hardy's enthusiasm on the bench and hard work in practice earned him a spot on the varsity roster in 1978

and 1979, as well as a scholarship. He played in 13 games for the 1978 Final Four team and appeared in nine games in his senior year. His career totals included 28 games, 22 points, and 12 rebounds. Though he never saw major minutes, he was considered an invaluable ingredient in the chemistry of the 1978 team. Hardy went to law school at Louisville and later returned to Frankfort, Ky., to help run his family's insurance business.

Harner, Harry. During his lone season at Duke in the midst of the Second World War, Harner, of Staunton, Va., started at a guard position, played 25 games, and scored 160 points to help the Blue Devils win the Southern Conference title in 1944. A former Washington & Lee student, he made the all-tournament second team.

Harnett, Sue. A charter inductee in the Duke Basketball Hall of Honor at Cameron Indoor Stadium, Sue Harnett, a 6 – 4 center from Staten Island, N.Y., ranks as one of the best players in the history of the women's program. She patrolled the paint from 1987 to 1991, playing in 117 games while averaging 15.3 points and 7.7 rebounds. As a freshman she played for the Blue Devils' first NCAA Tournament team, and as a senior she became just the second Duke player to be selected All-America when Fast Break named her to its third team.

Harnett totaled 1,785 points to finish No. 2 on the school career scoring chart, behind Chris Moreland. Alana Beard and Monique Currie are the only players since then to pass Harnett. She also finished second to Moreland in career rebounds with 899, and only one other player has since moved past her, Iciss Tillis.

Harnett averaged 19.5 points and 8.2 rebounds in 1989 and made the All-ACC second team. She seemed destined for a banner senior year in 1990 until sustaining knee damage in the fifth game. The injury occurred in the final of the Duke Dial Classic, for which Harnett was named MVP with 26 points before getting hurt. But she was lost for the remainder of the season. After grueling rehabilitation, she returned for another senior year in 1991 and averaged 32 minutes while starting every game. She had 17.5 points and 8.8 rebounds a game and again made the All-ACC second team.

Harnett was named to 10 all-tournament teams and earned the tourney MVP award five times in her career.

Sue Harnett set the Duke women's record for most points in a game with 37 at VCU, on the same day that Danny Ferry set the men's record with 58 at Miami.

Her best game overall was at Virginia Commonwealth in December 1988, when she scored 37 points and grabbed 18 rebounds. The point total set a Duke school record that stood until Alana Beard had 41 in 2003. Harnett's record-setting performance happened on the same day that Duke senior men's star Danny Ferry set the school and ACC scoring record with 58 points at Miami.

Harnett was the second high school All-America women's player to sign with Duke, following Moreland. She twice made the Parade team and was New York's state player of the year as a prep senior.

Harrell, John. The starting point guard for Duke when it reached the Final Four in 1978, John David Harrell III played a major role for one of the school's most fondly remembered units. He performed in 63 games over two seasons while scoring 231 points and dishing 98 assists.

Harrell starred locally at Durham High School and then enrolled at N.C. Central, where as a freshman he averaged 19 points a game while earning conference rookie of the year honors. With turmoil surrounding the Central program, a family friend suggested that Harrell transfer to Duke. He was accepted, sat out the 1977 campaign because of transfer regulations, and then emerged as the 1978 starter 11 games into the year when he helped the Devils win a road test at Maryland. An excellent ball handler blessed with quickness, he could run the break as well as the half-court offense. He averaged just 1.2 turnovers while scoring 5.1 points that year. His scoring high was a 13-point effort versus Maryland in the ACC Tournament, but his highlight moment was at the Final Four, where he nailed two free throws with nine seconds left to clinch a victory over Notre Dame and send Duke to the final.

Harrell's 1979 season proved not as glorious. He and Bob Bender had shared playing time down the stretch run in 1978, with Bender coming off the bench. Coach Bill Foster decided to make Bender the starter in 1979 and bring Harrell off the bench. Harrell averaged two points a game and was playing so little toward the end of the season that he opted to graduate that spring rather than come back for his fourth year of eligibility in 1980.

Harris, Bob. "They throw it the length of the floor. Laettner catches, comes down, dribbles, shoots, scooores! Christian Laettner has hit the bucket at the buzzer. The Blue Devils win it, 104 to 103. Look out Minneapolis, here come the Blue Devils!"

Not only does Christian Laettner's bucket at the buzzer in the NCAA Tournament of 1992 rank as one of the most memorable plays in school history, but its description on radio by veteran announcer Bob Harris stands as the most famous broadcasting call the program has ever known. Replays of the magic moment began on the team's charter flight home from Philadelphia following the overtime victory over Kentucky, and continued well into the future. The game was televised by CBS Sports, but it is Harris's definitive radio call that usually accompanies the videotape in promos, advertisements, special features, and other broadcast reflections on the classic finish. A clip of the shot at the Basketball Hall

Bob Harris celebrated his 30th season as the "Voice of the Blue Devils" in 2006.

of Fame included Harris's description, and it was once rated the second-most recognizable basketball call ever, behind Johnny Most's "Havlicek stole the ball! Havlicek stole the ball!" during a Boston Celtics game.

Harris has been the play-by-play announcer for Duke basketball games since 1976. A native of Albemarle, N.C., he moved to Durham in 1975 as a salesman for local station WDNC. He also hosted a sports talk show and worked as the color man for several Duke football games. He got the chance to do his first play-by-play for the Blue Devils at the Big Four Tournament in January 1976, when veteran announcer Add Penfield was ill. When Penfield was unable to make a trip to Maryland a few weeks later, Harris got the nod again. Thus began his long, distinguished career as the "Voice of the Blue Devils."

The 2006 season was Harris's 30th as the play-by-play man for basketball and included his 1,000th Duke hoops broadcast. He missed only 12 games during his first 30 years — two because of illness, one because of his father's death, and the others because of conflicts with football broadcasts.

Working from the "crow's nest" overlooking the floor in Cameron Indoor Stadium, and courtside at arenas all over the country, Harris has witnessed many of the signature moments in Duke history and brought them to life for his listeners. Final Fours, ACC championships, classic confrontations with archrivals, buzzer beaters and blowouts, nearly 100 NCAA Tournament games — Harris has been on hand for them all, providing Duke fans with their team's story every night, from his exclusive pre-game interview with the head coach through his post-game visit to the locker room, win or lose. Viewing the action through Duke blue lenses, his popularity among fans is such that many turn down the audio on television broadcasts to listen to his account. When Duke fans hear "How sweet it is!" they don't think of Jackie Gleason but of Harris punctuating his call on the Duke Radio Network of a momentum three-pointer or dunk.

A two-time broadcaster of the year in North Carolina, Harris was influenced early by such pioneers as Penfield, Ray Reeve, and Charlie Harville, as well as by Brooklyn Dodgers broadcasts that he could pick up on summer nights during his youth in Albemarle. He followed the exploits of Hal Bradley's Duke teams in the mid-1950s, UNC's NCAA title team in 1957, and Everett Case's program at N.C. State, the school he attended in the early 1960s. He became a full-fledged Duke enthusiast when he began working for the radio team in 1975–76, and there hasn't been anyone more loyal to the program in the 30 years he's been behind the microphone.

"The thing I'm most proud of career-wise," he wrote in 1998, "is the fact that I have been able to work for a university like Duke — one that has so much tradition and so much prestige. Hopefully, I've been able to add to that. To have the opportunity to work with, and develop relationships with, so many great coaches and so many student athletes is really an honor."

Harris's color announcers on basketball broadcasts have included Glen Smiley (1976–77), Johnny Moore (1978), Danny Highsmith (1978–87), Mike Waters (1988–92), Tony Haynes (1993–98), and John Roth (1999–). Other analysts he's worked with include former players Bob Bender (1983), Jay Bilas (1988, 1993–96), Johnny Dawkins (1997), and Steve Wojciechowski (1999), and former actor Matthew Laurance (sideline analyst, 2000–).

Along with his game broadcasts, Harris has hosted the weekly coaches' television shows and conducted five-minute daily interview programs with the coaches for local and Internet broadcast. And he has been extremely involved in community service, with countless celebrity appearances as well as behind-the-scenes work for a host of charitable causes, along with his wife Phyllis.

In 2006 Harris was honored with induction into the North Carolina Sports Hall of Fame.

Harris, Bobby Joe. After leading the 1955 freshman team in points and assists, Bobby Joe Harris, a 5–11 guard, moved on to the varsity and took up residency in the starting lineup for three straight seasons, 1956–58. He played in 75 games, with 744 points and 253 rebounds. Duke had an ACC record of 29–13 during his years as the backcourt leader, with two third-place finishes and a regular-season title in 1958.

A prep All-America from King, N.C. (and no relation to broadcaster Bob Harris), Harris turned in dozens of fine performances, scoring 22 points against N.C. State in 1956, 26 against South Carolina in 1957, and 20 against Wake Forest in 1958, when he put on a free-throw shooting clinic by hitting 14 of 16. His career-best effort of 28 points was against Clemson in his junior year.

When Duke rallied to defeat Kentucky at the Indoor Stadium in 1957, Harris played a huge role in the Blue Devils' 10–0 run to finish the game. As a key in the full-court press defense, Harris made a steal that led to his backcourt mate Bucky Allen's winning layup with 15 seconds left in the 85–84 decision.

Harris was Duke's most valuable player in 1957 and a co-captain in 1958.

Harrison, Buzzy. Starting at guard for three of coach Vic Bubas's best teams was Frank Late "Buzzy" Harrison, a 6–3 student athlete from South Charleston, W.Va. Harrison's No. 34 could be seen on the floor for 83 of 86 games over three years, 1962–64, helping his school to two ACC championships, two Final Four berths, and a record of 73–13. Harrison scored 675 points with 267 rebounds. He made the ACC all-tournament second team in 1963 and the All-ACC second team in 1964.

Harrison was one of five starters to reach double figures in the NCAA semifinal with Michigan in 1964,

scoring 14 points to help send the Devils to their first national championship game. In the ACC final in 1963 his defense was recognized as a critical element to the team's victory over Wake Forest. He scored 18 in the semis that year against N.C. State.

As a sophomore in 1962, Harrison had 15 points in his third varsity game, versus Louisville, and 15 more in the next, against Clemson in his ACC début. Because of a preseason ankle injury he missed the first three games of 1963 and had to work his way back into the lineup. In a rout of Wake Forest that year he went for 18 points on 8-of-10 shooting and also plugged N.C. State for 18 in the ACC tourney. The one time he led Duke in scoring during his three years was his last regular-season game, a trip to UNC in 1964, when he delivered 28 points in a lopsided victory. He also made a clutch layup in the Tennessee game that year, tying the score with nine seconds left in regulation. It was his only field goal of the day. His team went on to win in double overtime.

Off the floor, Harrison was president of the local chapter of the Fellowship of Christian Athletes and spent a summer working in Nicaragua on a trip sponsored by a campus religious group. He was also named Academic All-America in 1963.

Harscher, Frank. A 6–3 guard from Lexington, Ky., Frank Harscher played in 15 games for the 1964 team, scoring 23 points. The team won the ACC title and played in the NCAA final. It was captained by Jeff Mullins, who was a teammate of Harscher in high school. Harscher transferred after his first two years at Duke.

Hart, Deryl. Beginning in 1976, the outstanding student athlete on the Duke team was presented with the Dr. Deryl Hart Award. Julian Deryl Hart, a native of Georgia, came to Duke in 1930 upon the opening of the medical center and founded the department of surgery. He was a surgeon and faculty member for 30 years, then in 1960 was named president pro tem of the university when Hollis Edens resigned from the post. The pro tempore label was subsequently removed, and Hart served as president until his retirement in 1963. Terry Chili was the first recipient of this academic honor. Quin Snyder (1987–89) and Shane Battier (1999–2001) won it three times apiece.

Hartley, Howard. Howard Hartley, a forward from Ravenswood, W.Va., lettered for the team that won the Southern Conference title in 1944 and scored 25 points in eight games. He came off the bench to score eight key points in the championship game victory over UNC. He also lettered as a back on the 1943, 1946, and 1947 Duke football teams and played in the NFL from 1948 through 1952.

Hartness, W. R. William Robert Hartness of Mooresville, N.C., was one of the top scorers for Duke's freshman team that won the state championship in 1925, then lettered as a sophomore in 1926.

Hathaway, L. B. Considered the best defensive guard in the state during his era, Loyd Bryan Hathaway was a rare four-year starter for Trinity from 1918 through 1921. A product of Hobbsville, N.C., he was president of the sophomore class in 1919 and captain of the basketball team in 1920 and 1921. His 1920 team won the second state championship in Trinity history and was the first team in school history to play archrival North Carolina in basketball. Hathaway also played varsity tennis and baseball.

Hawaii trips. Duke visited Hawaii for basketball tournaments seven times in coach Mike Krzyzewski's first 22 years. Duke won four of the tournaments and posted a 17–3 record overall.

The Blue Devils' 1984, 1990, and 1995 teams competed in the Rainbow Classic in Honolulu, winning the 1990 event by defeating host Hawaii in the final. The 1993, 1998, and 2002 teams all won the Maui Invitational in Lahaina, with the 1998 club knocking off top-ranked Arizona in the final. The 1987 team opened the season at BYU-Hawaii's Thanksgiving tourney, falling to Illinois in the championship game.

Hayes, Charlie. A 5–10 forward, Charles Marvin Hayes, of Williamsport, Pa., lettered as a senior for the 1933 team that played for the Southern Conference championship. He scored 64 points, the sixth-best figure on the club.

Heaps, Jay. One of Duke's all-time greatest soccer players, Jay Heaps also played for the basketball team and lettered for four years, 1996–99. He saw action in 30 basketball games, with eight points and 15 assists. A 5–9 guard from Longmeadow, Mass., he was a crowd favorite at Cameron Indoor Stadium, earning the fans' enduring admiration with his play at the end of the Senior Day contest against UNC in 1996. With the Tar Heels up by 15 points in the closing moments, Mike Krzyzewski emptied his bench. In about 90 seconds of hectic action, Heaps had three assists and one steal. Baskets by his fellow subs Todd Singleton, Jeremy Hall, and Baker Perry made it a five-point game with 22 seconds left, and Krzyzewski sent his starters back to the court. UNC held on for an 84–78 victory. Heaps's first career basket, a three-pointer, came against Maryland a week later in the ACC Tournament, when he also had three assists and a steal.

John Franklin Heaps III joined the team as a freshman in January 1996 after the roster had been reduced to seven recruited players because of injuries. To help quench his love for the game, Heaps had been helping out the Duke women's program as a scrimmage player in practice. He spent the rest of his career with the men's team when he wasn't playing soccer. During his first three years at Duke, Heaps would pack his spring days with off-season soccer workouts in the morning, then basketball practice in the afternoon.

Heaps was a star on the soccer field, earning All-ACC honors for four years and All-America twice. As a senior in 1998 he picked up national player of the year honors presented by the Missouri Athletic Club and was chosen national scholar athlete of the year by the coaches' association. He finished his career ranked third in Duke history in goals (45) and fourth in assists (37). He either scored or assisted on game-winning goals 23 times as a Blue Devil.

Heaps played in only four basketball games early in his senior year, graduating a semester early so that he could concentrate on launching his pro soccer career that spring. Still, coach Mike Krzyzewski awarded him a basketball letter for the 1999 season. Heaps was the second pick of the Major League Soccer draft and was chosen MLS rookie of the year in 1999.

Former sixth man David Henderson (right) returned to Duke to launch his coaching career.

Hedrick, Bull. A backcourt mainstay for four years, 1909 – 12, Henry Grady "Bull" Hedrick, of Lexington, N.C., captained the 1911 team as a senior and played as a law student in 1912. As a junior in 1910 he was also president of the Trinity YMCA. Hedrick later became a law professor at Trinity.

Henderson, David. He started almost every game in his freshman and senior seasons, but David McKinley Henderson may be best remembered for the role he fulfilled in between. During his sophomore and junior years, Henderson, a 6 – 5 native of Drury, N.C., thrived and built a reputation as the Blue Devils' sixth man, or "sixth starter" as coach Mike Krzyzewski called him. There was no doubt that he was one of the best players on the team during his era, 1983 – 86. He was also one of the most valuable, able to contribute offensively and defensively off the bench. And whenever a game was on

the line at the end, Henderson was always one of the players Krzyzewski wanted on the floor.

Initially Henderson was not enthralled with the sixth-man role, but his coach encouraged him to embrace it. "Coach told me I would be on the floor when the game was decided. Once I knew I was going to play in the crucial moments, I was all for it," Henderson told historian Jim Sumner. "Coach thought that I was tough enough to deliver lots of things off the bench, play [defense], bring energy and toughness to the team. I could do a lot of things, fill a lot of roles."

Henderson played in 128 games and started 65. He had 24 starts as a freshman and 39 as a senior. There was just one start in each of his sophomore and junior years. But regardless of his place in the lineup, he was on the floor for an average of 26 minutes a game. He totaled 1,570 points for a 12.3 average and had 513 rebounds for a 4.0 average. He had a scoring average in double figures for his last three years, with a best of 14.2 as a senior.

Henderson was in on the ground floor of Duke's revitalization under Krzyzewski, as part of his first significant recruiting class. But he never made the All-ACC team and didn't receive much acclaim with Johnny Dawkins and Mark Alarie on his squad. Another classmate, Jay Bilas, later an ESPN analyst, called him one of the most underappreciated players in school history. "Henderson was the toughest person I have ever been around," he noted, "and was as responsible for providing our teams with a will to win and compete as any player during that era. David Henderson backed down to no one and would not let his teammates back down. Had he played at another ACC school, Henderson would have been All-ACC."

Henderson's strength, athleticism, and jumping ability made for an impressive physical package. One year during preseason practice he pulled the rim out of a glass backboard with one of his dunks, and he had a slam in the game against Washington in 1985 that was one of the most ferocious ever witnessed in Cameron. He had a game-winning shot to beat William & Mary in 1984 when the Devils were just learning to win on the road and also hit a free throw with no time on the clock at Georgia Tech that year to get a 69 – 68 victory. He was Duke's leading scorer with 22 points against Pepperdine in 1985, Krzyzewski's first NCAA victory.

Most of Henderson's highlights, though, were team efforts during the 1986 season, in which Duke went 37 – 3, won the ACC, and played for the national title. At the beginning of the season he delivered his career high of 30 points against Kansas and pocketed the MVP trophy at the Preseason NIT. He had his second-best game of 28 points against Oklahoma, making sure that the Blue Devils beat the Sooners on the day his buddy Dawkins's jersey was retired. In his last home game against UNC he led the team with 27 points and a couple of satisfying backdoor plays, as the Devils completed an ACC regular-season crown. Then he joined Alarie and Dawkins on the all-tourney team when Duke claimed the ACC Tournament for the first time under Krzyzewski.

Henderson performed briefly in the NBA in 1988 but enjoyed most of his professional success overseas in France, Israel, and Turkey. He then turned to coaching and was hired by Krzyzewski before the 1998 season. He remained on the staff for three years, before he was hired as head coach at Delaware on his 36th birthday, July 21, 2000. His first team posted a 20 – 10 record. Through five seasons he had a mark of 76 – 72, but was dismissed after a 9 – 21 record in his sixth year.

Henderson, Phil. After missing most of his freshman season because of academic difficulties, Phillip Terry Henderson, a 6 – 4 guard from University Park, Ill., developed into an offensive force on the Duke perimeter. In four seasons, from 1987 through 1990, he totaled 1,397 points in 115 games for an average of 12.1. He also had 330 rebounds and 217 assists and made 128 three-point shots.

Henderson picked up his first career start in 1988 versus Notre Dame on national television. He enjoyed some scoring outbursts in ACC contests, including a 19-point game against Wake Forest and two key three-pointers against N.C. State in the ACC Tournament on Duke's run to the title. In his junior year he started all 36 games and averaged 12.7 points, peaking during postseason play. He scored 16 in a loss to UNC in the ACC final, then averaged 17.4 in the NCAA Tournament as Duke streaked to the Final Four. After making the ACC All-Tournament team, he was an easy selection to the All-East Regional team when he scored 21 points against Minnesota and 23 in the regional final against Georgetown. He made

one of the most memorable plays in Duke history versus the Hoyas, when he drove into the lane and dunked over center Alonzo Mourning.

Henderson flirted with transferring back to his home state of Illinois but ultimately turned his senior year into his best year on the court. He led Duke in scoring with an 18.5 average and teamed with his fellow seniors Robert Brickey and Alaa Abdelnaby to drive the Blue Devils to an improbable Final Four. Sharing the team's most valuable player award with Christian Laettner, Henderson was a second team All-ACC pick and made the all-tournament teams at the Rainbow Classic, ACC Tournament, East Regionals, and Final Four. He missed scoring in double figures just three times and dropped his career high of 29 points on the Citadel. He also had three 28-point games, all in big-time games: versus Arizona at home, UCLA in the regionals, and Arkansas in the Final Four.

Rarely the outspoken type, Henderson issued some strong words in the locker room as a senior after a semifinal loss in the ACC Tournament when he suggested that the young players on the roster needed to grow up. He backed up his statements by averaging 22.3 points in the NCAA and ACC tourneys. After delivering one of the most memorable dunks in school history in the 1989 NCAA, he had one of the key three-pointers in the 1990 Final Four, stopping to measure a wide-open look for what seemed like several seconds before pulling the trigger. Duke went on to win handily.

Henderson was a second-round draft pick by the Dallas Mavericks but never played in the NBA.

Hendrickson, Evan. Duke won its first conference championship in 1938 with a victory over Clemson in the Southern Conference final. A reserve letterman for that team was Evan Hendrickson, who scored 28 points. Hendrickson was the younger brother of former Duke football and basketball competitor Horace Hendrickson.

Hendrickson, Horace. After starring at quarterback for the 1933 football team that barely missed a Rose Bowl bid, Horace James Hendrickson reported to the basketball team (along with his backfield coach Eddie Cameron) and lettered as a senior reserve in 1934. He scored eight points. A native of Beaver Falls, Pa., he played four years of football and four years of baseball. Hendrickson later went into coaching, with positions that included a two-year run as head football coach at N.C. State, 1952–53. During the 1949–50 and 1950–51 academic years, he was a Duke football and basketball assistant coach.

Herbert, Dick. One of the twentieth century's top sports journalists in North Carolina got his start as a member of the Duke basketball program. Richard C. Herbert, of Harrisburg, Pa., was an assistant manager of the basketball squad for three years and the head manager in his senior year of 1935. He also worked as the sports editor of the school newspaper (the *Chronicle*) and the yearbook (the *Chanticleer*).

Herbert achieved his greatest fame and success, though, after graduation, when he developed into one of the most influential media members in the state. A stickler for truth and accuracy, Herbert enlightened readers of the *News & Observer* of Raleigh during his 29 years as sports editor, penning nearly 10,000 columns before retiring in 1971. Later he was known for edifying listeners on a variety of historical sports topics as a frequent guest on a popular radio call-in show in Raleigh. He witnessed much of that history first-hand, having covered the Atlantic Coast Conference from its inception. And he always took a keen interest in what Duke was doing, on the hardwood and elsewhere in athletics.

Herbert was the first journalist to serve as president of both the football and basketball national writers' associations and the first to be honored by the Naismith Memorial Basketball Hall of Fame with the Curt Gowdy Media Award (1990). He was enshrined in the North Carolina Sports Hall of Fame (1977), the Duke Sports Hall of Fame (1984), and the U.S. Basketball Writers Association Hall of Fame (1988).

In March 1996 Herbert was at the ACC Tournament to receive the Marvin "Skeeter" Francis Award for distinguished service, awarded annually by the Atlantic Coast Sports Writers Association, a group that Herbert had served as executive secretary for 23 years. But he suffered a stroke at the tourney and died shortly after at the age of 82.

Herbster, Ron. A 6–2 left-handed guard from Chester, Pa., and a three-year letterman, Ronald William Herbster played in 85 of Duke's 86 games from 1963 through 1965, with 281 points and 105 rebounds. Though hampered by knee problems, he started a few games and was always in the hunt for starter's minutes on three very talented teams. As a senior he was selected the first winner of the Ted Mann Jr. Award for the reserve contributing most to team morale. Mann, who died in the summer of 1964, was one of Herbster's teammates and classmates.

Herrick, Albert. Three-year letterman Albert "Bud" Herrick, a 6–3 center from Lebanon, Ohio, scored 217 points during his varsity career, 1935–37. He was a second-teamer as a sophomore and a starter as a junior and senior.

Heyman, Art. Of all the outstanding basketball players to grace the ACC stage in its first half-century, only two were unanimously chosen to the All-ACC team three times. Not Michael Jordan. Not Ralph Sampson. Not Tim Duncan or Christian Laettner. The only two were N.C. State superstar David Thompson and Duke great Arthur Bruce Heyman. Thompson worked his magic in the mid-1970s as the league's only three-time scoring king and the catalyst for a Wolfpack national championship. Heyman made no less an impact in the early 1960s as the pioneer player around whom coach Vic Bubas constructed Duke's first national powerhouse teams.

Heyman was the best point producer in school history, bar none. Over 40 years after graduation, his 25.1 scoring average still stood as the best career mark ever at Duke and the fifth-best in ACC annals. He didn't have the most picturesque shot, but he put points on the board in every conceivable fashion, from jumpers and putbacks to bullish drives and foul shots. In fact, he went to the free-throw stripe more times (853) than any player in school history except Laettner, who had only 32 more attempts while playing 69 more games.

Heyman was also an exceptional, relentless rebounder. Despite standing only 6–5, he averaged at least 10 rebounds a game every year and 10.9 for his career. That mark places him higher than every other player in school history except centers Randy Denton, Mike Lewis, and Bernie Janicki. And Bubas often remarked

Art Heyman was named MVP of the 1963 Final Four even though Duke didn't play for the championship.

A Shot He'll Never Forget

Art Heyman, 1961 versus Navy

Vic Bubas once said that if he had to put the ball in one player's hands to win a game, it would be Heyman, his national player of the year and star of the team that went to the Final Four in 1963.

Well, Bubas did exactly that in the 1961 Navy game, when Heyman was a sophomore.

"Navy had good basketball back then, and we were down by one point," Heyman said. "We got in the huddle and everybody was screaming what to do, and I couldn't believe it because at timeouts then you never opened your mouth. Then Vic said, 'Okay, everybody shut up. Give the damn ball to Heyman and let him do what he wants to do,' and I scored and we won the game."

Trailing 71–70 in the final minute, Heyman dribbled the ball the length of the court, weaved around four defenders, and banked in a layup with 32 seconds left to put Duke ahead 72–71. Teammate Johnny Frye then connected on some free throws and the Devils had a 75–73 victory. Heyman finished with 26 points.

on what a gifted passer Heyman was. Complete assists records weren't compiled during his era, so there's no telling how many assists he racked up by feeding teammates such as Jeff Mullins. But he did produce the first triple-double at Duke when he had 21 points, 18 rebounds, and 10 assists versus Virginia in the ACC Tournament in 1963.

Heyman's value extended beyond his considerable statistical production. His toughness, presence, competitiveness, and combativeness made him the central figure in Bubas's Duke development project. There is no exaggeration in the old story about Bubas's heading immediately to Rockville Centre, N.Y., to make a pitch for Heyman as soon as he was formally hired in the spring of 1959. Heyman had committed to UNC but instead became the blue-chipper who got the Blue Devils going and attracted other top talents (not to mention stoking the fire with UNC). It's worth noting that while the Devils had enjoyed many weeks in the national polls during the 1950s, the club's profile rose dramatically as soon

as Heyman stepped on the floor in 1961. His arrival set in motion a six-year period in which Duke was ranked in the Associated Press national top 10 poll every week except for one early in his junior year.

Duke didn't retire jerseys during the 1960s, but when that practice became more prominent a couple of decades later, it bothered Heyman's sidekick Mullins not to see his teammate's No. 25 in the rafters. "I thought it was a major oversight," Mullins said, "simply because at one moment in time, for one split moment, Art Heyman was the greatest player in college basketball. For many years, he was the only [Blue Devil] who could lay credit to that." The oversight was corrected when No. 25 was retired in 1990, 12 years after Heyman was inducted in the Duke Sports Hall of Fame and 13 years before he was named to the ACC's 50th anniversary team.

Heyman played in 79 games during his varsity career, 1961–63, and graduated as the all-time scoring leader with 1,984 points. His yearly scoring marks were 25.2, 25.3, and 24.9, the last leading the conference. He shot

45.1 percent from the field and easily would have been the first 2,000-point scorer had he been able to hit better than 65.4 percent from the foul line. He totaled 865 rebounds, with yearly board marks of 10.9, 11.2, and 10.8. Heyman led Duke in scoring and rebounding each year. He was an All-America every season and national player of the year as a senior, when he swept all the ACC awards — player of the year, tournament MVP, athlete of the year.

Heyman's legendary moments were many, but some of the most significant occurred in the rivalry with UNC. The Tar Heels were the first team to beat him as a sophomore, when they ended Duke's 9–0 start with a victory in the Dixie Classic. Heyman got off to a hot start in that game, but in the second half Doug Moe and his mates shackled him. Duke and Heyman extracted revenge when the Heels visited Durham, as Heyman poured in 36 points in a performance that he always ranked as one of his most memorable. No choir boy on or off the floor, he gave UNC's guard Larry Brown a hard foul in the closing seconds. Brown came up swinging, and soon the court was swarming with fisticuffs, in one of the biggest brawls in league history. Heyman, Brown, and UNC's Donnie Walsh were eventually suspended for the rest of the ACC regular season. There were protests that Heyman had simply been defending himself, but the conference had a point to make. From Duke's and Heyman's perspectives, the disruption cost them an NCAA run; they were unable to rekindle their chemistry for the postseason and lost in the ACC title game to Wake Forest.

The Deacons and Devils waged many wars during the Heyman era. In 1961 they met in back-to-back games just before Heyman's suspension began. He and Billy Packer matched 31-point outings as Duke won the first game. Five days later Heyman had 31 again and Packer 25, but Wake won on the strength of Len Chappell's 38. Duke won two of three the following year with Heyman scoring 33, 26, and 18. "Heyman's just too much," Packer said. "Art is in a class all by himself. I don't know what you can do against a guy like that. He's just simply great."

Heyman irritated ACC foes with a litany of 30-point outbursts but saved his best for last when he posted career highs of 40 points and 24 rebounds in his final home game against North Carolina. The Blue Devils won easily to complete a perfect 14–0 league season and give Heyman a 5–2 record against his biggest rival. It always remained one of Heyman's favorite days, as much for the outcome as for a special halftime ceremony when he was honored by his fellow students.

"You could really sense the love that night," he recalled many years afterward. "I had a lot of honors, but the greatest honor I ever received, people don't realize this, was when the student body gave me the plaque for how I brought everybody together with basketball. That was the greatest honor I ever received, from the students."

Heyman led his team to the ACC title the following week and then helped them reach their first Final Four. Duke dropped the national semi to Loyola of Chicago before beating Oregon State in the consolation game. Heyman scored 51 points in the two games and was so impressive that he was named Final Four MVP even though his team didn't reach the final, much less win it.

Heyman became the first Duke player to be selected No. 1 in the NBA draft, made the all-rookie team with the New York Knicks, and played six pro seasons, for seven teams. In 1968 he moved from the NBA to the ABA, where he enjoyed his best pro year, averaging 20.1 points for the Pittsburgh Pipers. He teamed with Connie Hawkins to lead the Pipers to the title; they outdueled New Orleans and his old nemesis Moe in the finals.

Hibbitts, Harold. A junior college transfer from Pikeville, Ky., forward Harold Hibbitts lettered for the 1949 team. He scored 47 points in 18 games.

High School All-Americas. Through the 2005 recruiting season, Duke had 42 players who'd been named to the McDonald's High School All-America team and 64 to the older Parade Magazine All-America team. McDonald's traditionally names a 24-player team composed of seniors, while Parade usually recognizes 40 players, listed on four 10-player units, without regard to class. The list below does not include players who signed with Duke but never matriculated, or players who transferred to Duke.

McDonald's All-Americas

1977	Gene Banks
1978	Vince Taylor
1982	Johnny Dawkins
1983	Tommy Amaker, Martin Nessley
1985	Danny Ferry, Quin Snyder
1986	Alaa Abdelnaby, Phil Henderson
1987	Greg Koubek
1988	Christian Laettner, Crawford Palmer
1989	Bobby Hurley, Bill McCaffrey
1990	Grant Hill
1991	Cherokee Parks
1992	Chris Collins
1993	Joey Beard
1994	Trajan Langdon, Ricky Price, Steve Wojciechowski
1995	Taymon Domzalski
1996	Nate James
1997	Shane Battier, Elton Brand, Chris Burgess
1998	Corey Maggette
1999	Carlos Boozer, Mike Dunleavy, Casey Sanders, Jason Williams
2000	Chris Duhon
2001	Daniel Ewing
2002	Sean Dockery, J. J. Redick, Shavlik Randolph, Michael Thompson
2003	Luol Deng
2004	DeMarcus Nelson
2005	Eric Boateng, Josh McRoberts, Greg Paulus
2006	Gerald Henderson, Jon Scheyer, Lance Thomas

McDonald's All-America Women

2002	Mistie Bass Williams, Brooke Smith
2003	Alison Bales, Brittany Hunter
2004	Chante Black, Wanisha Smith
2005	Carrem Gay, Abby Waner
2006	Joy Cheek, Bridgette Mitchell

Parade All-Americas

1959	Art Heyman (1)
1960	Jeff Mullins (1)
1961	Brent Kitching (2), Hack Tison (2)
1964	Mike Lewis (1)
1965	Dave Golden (3), Steve Vandenberg (4)
1967	Dick DeVenzio (1)
1968	Don Blackman (5)
1972	Dave O'Connell (3)
1975	Bob Bender (2)
1976	Gene Banks (1)
1977	Gene Banks (1)
1978	Vince Taylor (2)
1982	Johnny Dawkins (3), Mark Alarie (4)
1983	Tommy Amaker (3), Martin Nessley (3)
1984	Danny Ferry (2), Kevin Strickland (3)
1985	Danny Ferry (1)
1986	Alaa Abdelnaby (4), Phil Henderson (4)
1987	Greg Koubek (2), Christian Laettner (3)
1988	Christian Laettner (2), Crawford Palmer (3), Bobby Hurley (4)
1989	Bobby Hurley (1), Bill McCaffrey (4)
1990	Cherokee Parks (1), Grant Hill (3), Tony Lang (3)
1991	Cherokee Parks (1), Erik Meek (2)
1992	Joey Beard (3)
1993	Joey Beard (2), Jeff Capel (4)
1994	Trajan Langdon (2), Ricky Price (4)
1995	Taymon Domzalski (2), Chris Carrawell (4)
1996	Mike Chappell (4)
1997	Shane Battier (1), Elton Brand (1), Chris Burgess (1), William Avery (3)
1998	Corey Maggette (2)
1999	Jason Williams (1), Carlos Boozer (1), Casey Sanders (2), Mike Dunleavy (3)
2000	Chris Duhon (1)
2001	Shavlik Randolph (2), Shelden Williams (4)
2002	Shavlik Randolph (1), J. J. Redick (2), Michael Thompson (4)
2003	Luol Deng (1)
2004	DeMarcus Nelson (2)
2005	Josh McRoberts (1), Greg Paulus (2), Jamal Boykin (3), Eric Boateng (4)
2006	Jon Scheyer (1), Gerald Henderson (2), Lance Thomas (2), Brian Zoubek (4)

Parade All-America Women

1983	Chris Moreland (3)
1984	Chris Moreland (2)
1985	Sue Harnett
1986	Sue Harnett

1993   Kira Orr (4)

1994   Payton Black (2), Jennifer McGinnis (4)

1995   Hilary Howard

1998   Krista Gingrich (2)

1999   Michele Matyasovsky (2), Sheana Mosch (2), Olga Gvozdenovic (3), Iciss Tillis (3)

2000   Iciss Tillis (1), Alana Beard (2), Rometra Craig (2), Vicki Krapohl (4)

2001   Monique Currie (2), Wynter Whitley (2), Mistie Bass Williams (2)

2002   Brooke Smith (1), Mistie Bass Williams (2), Lindsey Harding (2)

2003   Alison Bales (1), Brittany Hunter (1)

2004   Wanisha Smith (1), Chante Black (3), Laura Kurz (4)

2005   Abby Waner (1), Carrem Gay (3), Brittany Mitch (3), Keturah Jackson (4)

2006   Joy Cheek (2), Bridgette Mitchell (2)

Hill, Grant. No player in Duke history quite compares with Grant Hill. There have been better shooters, better scorers, better rebounders, better passers, better defenders, and better leaders. But if any others combined all those essentials into a more complete all-around package than Hill did, the list is a short one. During his senior year, when it came time for Duke officials to decide if Hill's jersey should be retired, a previous guideline that national player of the year recognition should be a prerequisite was easily ignored in favor of a more fundamental question: Could anyone else wear No. 33 and do it justice? The answer was an unequivocal no. Hill channeled his extraordinary skills into the team concept for four years and played an instrumental role in helping the Blue Devils reach three NCAA finals, two of which they won. Duke averaged 29.5 wins a year during his career and won the ACC regular season three times.

Grant Henry Hill played in 129 games from 1991 through 1994. Only once, in his senior year, did he make it through an entire season unscathed by injury, but still he started 125 times and averaged 30 minutes a game. Hill scored 1,924 points for a 14.9 average, had 769 rebounds for a 6.0 average, dealt 461 assists, and twice led the team in steals. As a senior he topped the Duke stats sheet in points, assists, and steals while ranking second in rebounds and blocked shots. He hit 53.2 percent of

A national defensive player of the year in 1993, Grant Hill set the NCAA Tournament record for career steals.

his career field-goal attempts and even showed off long-range shooting skills in his last year, when he made 39 of his 44 career three-pointers.

A creative flair accompanied Hill's high marks for technical merit. No one dunked the ball with more artistry, ran the fast break with more grace, defended with more athleticism, or reacted to the spectacular with more humility. Big plays? The list was lengthy. His one-handed alley-oop was the signature moment of Duke's first NCAA title victory over Kansas. His perfect pass to Christian Laettner set up the most memorable shot in NCAA Tournament history versus Kentucky. His defense took national player of the year Glenn Robinson completely out of the regional final in 1994.

Yet a few years after graduation, when asked about his favorite shot and best game, Hill settled on a dunk against St. John's early in his sophomore year, because he thought it helped set a tone for the season, and a game at Virginia in which he hit just a couple of field goals while trying to get everyone else on the team involved in the action.

Hill's career scoring high came in his senior year against Clemson, when he had 33 points in a performance that Krzyzewski called one of the best ever at Duke. After Hill sustained a bump on the cheek while diving for a loose ball, the coach took him out for a few minutes. He returned to the court with Duke trailing the Tigers and proceeded to score on a reverse under the basket, a three-pointer from the wing, an eight-footer from the baseline, a dunk, and several free throws. The dunk was the most impressive, as he pursued an errant pass, knifed through the heart of the defense, and finished with a two-handed slam. When the spurt ended, Hill had scored 15 of his team's 17 points, the Devils were back on top, and everyone knew what it was like to see Hill take the ball in his gifted hands and dominate. Along with the points, he also had nine rebounds and six assists.

Hill was national defensive player of the year as a junior and played even better as a senior, though he didn't repeat. He was first-team All-ACC in his last two years, first-team All-America and ACC player of the year as a senior, and All–Final Four twice. He set an NCAA tourney record for career steals (39) and was chosen to the ACC's 50th anniversary team.

A 6–8 product of Reston, Va., and son of former NFL great Calvin Hill, Grant later became Duke's most accomplished NBA player and the most successful in translating his personal appeal into lucrative endorsement deals. He was the No. 3 draft pick after graduation, was co-winner of the NBA rookie of the year award in 1995, and was chosen to the All-Star Game six times in his first decade as a pro. In fact, he made NBA history in 1995 when he became the first rookie ever to finish as the leading vote getter for the All-Star Game.

After his second pro season Hill was named to the 1996 Olympic team and helped the USA win a gold medal in Atlanta, though he was injured for the final game. He was chosen for the 2000 Olympic team as well but had to relinquish his spot because of ankle surgery. After his troublesome ankle ailments forced him to miss most of three seasons, Hill returned to form in 2005 by averaging 19.7 points for the Orlando Magic, while winning the league's sportsmanship award. In the summer

of 2005 he was honored with a locker dedication at the Naismith Memorial Basketball Hall of Fame recognizing his many achievements.

Chairman of the Duke Basketball Legacy Fund, Hill and his wife, the pop singer Tamia, endowed a basketball scholarship at his alma mater. An avid art collector, Hill selected 46 of his favorite pieces for a two-year national tour and book. The exhibit, entitled "Something All Our Own: The Grant Hill Collection of African American Art," made stops at several art museums across the country, concluding in 2006 at Duke's new Nasher Museum of Art.

Hill, Thomas. Three players whose jerseys were retired accompanied Thomas Hill throughout most of his Duke basketball journey. But if he ever worried about being overshadowed by Christian Laettner, Bobby Hurley, or Grant Hill, he never showed it. A 6–5 guard from Lancaster, Texas, he made an impact in each of his four years, 1990–93, and started most of his last three seasons while helping the Blue Devils win 82 percent of their games and two national titles.

"That's something I really can't worry about," he said in an interview near the end of his senior year, when asked about his place among superstar teammates. "To me the most important things are playing well and winning. Those things have happened here for me, and overall I'm pretty happy about things.

"It was funny last year at the NCAA Tournament, when I was sitting at the interview table with Christian and Bobby, and nobody directed any questions to me. Finally, Christian said something about it and told the reporters to ask me a question. I felt kind of left out, but we were able to joke about it."

"In another program he might have gotten more attention," Mike Krzyzewski said, "but he has been a great asset to our championship teams and has always taken a positive approach to the game."

The son of a hurdler who won a bronze medal at the 1972 Olympics, Thomas Lionel Hill II played in 141 of 145 games during his career and started 88, including all but two in the 1992 and 1993 seasons. He scored 1,594 points for an 11.3 average and added 488 rebounds with 177 assists and 194 steals. He made 51.9 percent of his field goals and 72 percent of his free throws. The Blue

Thomas Hill made the All-ACC third team for three straight seasons.

Devils won 82 percent of their games during his career, including marks of 18 – 2 in the NCAA tourney and 57 – 3 at Cameron Indoor Stadium.

Hill came off the bench as a freshman with several solid outings before making a name for himself as a sophomore when he scored 16 points in a win at Oklahoma before a strong family contingent and a national television audience. (His father was a University of Oklahoma administrator at the time.) He was selected the CBS player of the game, then was the NBC player of the game for his role in a win at Notre Dame. Against Georgia Tech he scored 20 points and had the game-winning basket as time expired. Hill was in and out of the starting lineup for the first half of the season, but in mid-February he joined the first five for good. It was a role he maintained for the rest of his career, as he developed into a consistent double-figures scorer.

Hill was one of the unsung heroes of the Blue Devils' win over Kentucky in 1992 with 19 points, making

a leaning jumper with 1:03 left that ultimately sent the contest into overtime. He scored 27 points in two Final Four contests that year as Duke won a second straight title. He finished as the team's second-leading scorer for the tournament.

Krzyzewski said his most exciting moment during the NCAA final in 1992 was when Hill missed a shot but somehow wound up with the loose ball and put it in for a score. "It's that kind of competitiveness which sets him apart," he noted. "I'm sure other teams have competitive kids, but Thomas goes further than anyone I know."

Hill's top scoring average of 15.7 points came in his senior year, when he co-captained the team with Hurley. He also matched his career scoring high that year with 26 points against Georgia Tech. Hill improved his perimeter shooting throughout his tenure and finished with 95 three-pointers. But he was best known for turning defense into offense as one of the Devils' top finishers on fast breaks.

Hill was voted to the All-ACC third team for three straight years and won the Dr. Deryl Hart award as the team's top scholar athlete in 1993. He was a second-round NBA draft pick but was never able to land on a regular-season roster.

Hobgood, Langhorne. Langhorne Hobgood, a 6 – 6 center from Durham, scored 19 points for Duke's team that won the Southern Conference championship in 1938, the only season he earned a letter. Hobgood played but did not letter for the 1940 team that opened the Indoor Stadium.

Hodge, Willie. In the first group of recruits at the onset of freshman eligibility, Willie Hodge, a 6 – 9 forward from San Antonio, played in 102 games from 1973 through 1976 and totaled 1,117 points with 605 rebounds. Considered inconsistent early in his career, Hodge showed improvement in every season and capped off his Duke days with averages of 16.9 points and 7.8 rebounds as a senior co-captain.

Willie Alexander Hodge III was a frontcourt fixture in the starting lineup for his last two years and responded by scoring in double figures almost every time out. From the middle of his junior year through the end of his career, Hodge scored at least 10 points in 41 of 44 games.

Statistically, Hodge's best game was versus East Carolina in 1976, when he had 35 points and 16 rebounds. The two games before that, he had 29 in a narrow loss to Tennessee and 26 in a two-point win over Virginia. Later that season he had a six-game run in which he averaged 21.5 points and 10.5 rebounds. Duke won three of the contests and dropped two only narrowly.

Hodge's aggressiveness was applauded, but he did close his career with a dubious school record, for fouling out of more games than anyone else. He was disqualified 14 times as a senior and 25 times for his career.

Hodge was a fifth-round NBA draft pick but did not play in the league.

Hoffman, John. A starting guard and senior co-captain of Duke's first Southern Conference championship team, John Hoffman was one of the Blue Devils' "never a dull moment boys" of 1938. So dubbed because of their colorful antics and rollercoaster results, the Devils owned a 10 – 9 record in late February before finishing with a five-game winning streak, including three wins at the conference tourney. Hoffman scored 169 points during his three years as a letterman, 1936 – 38. A 6 – 1 native of Fort Wayne, Ind., he was a reserve in his first two years before solidifying a starting job as a senior.

Holley, Chuck. The opening jump ball for the first game played at the Indoor Stadium was controlled by Charles Holley, a 6 – 3 junior from Ford City, Pa., who was a three-year starter in the pivot. Holley scored 435 points during his career, 1939 – 41, and led the Devils with 203 points as a senior. Holley was at his best late in his career, when he helped Duke beat powerhouse North Carolina twice in one week. After the Devils handed UNC its first conference loss in the regular-season finale, the two teams met in the first round of the tournament. Holley scored 10 points and helped hold in check UNC's George Glamack, who led the nation in scoring. The previous year Glamack had scored 18 points to key a Tar Heel rout of Duke in the Southern Conference final. After the big win over UNC, Holley had a game-high 16 points in a victory over South Carolina in the championship game and was named first-team all-tournament.

Hollingsworth, Wright. A forward from Rome. Ga., Wright Hollingsworth lettered for the team that won the Southern Conference title in 1944 and scored 12 points in 11 games. He attended Tennessee before military training brought him to Duke.

Home courts. Duke had four home courts during its first century of intercollegiate men's basketball, two on East Campus and two on West. All remain standing in their original locations. Cameron Indoor Stadium, considered one of the most hallowed on-campus arenas in America, has been the home of the Blue Devils longer than any other facility. It celebrated its 65th anniversary on January 5, 2005, with a game against Princeton in which Duke's team wore "throwback" uniforms.

Notes on Duke's four home floors:

Angier B. Duke Gym: Erected in 1898 when Trinity College had a total enrollment of 149 students. Located on what is now known as East Campus, which was the only campus at the time. Nicknamed "the Ark" because of the long, plank-like walkway leading up to the front door. First varsity basketball game on March 2, 1906, when Trinity lost to Wake Forest 24 – 10. Last game on March 12, 1923, when Trinity beat Guilford 45 – 32. Named for the grandson of Washington Duke, whose funding relocated Trinity College in Durham. Angier's father, Benjamin Duke, donated the money for the school's first gym and had it named for his son, who was just 14 at the time. Angier later attended Trinity and graduated in 1905, just before basketball was introduced. Playing surface at the Ark measured just 32 feet by 50 feet, tiny by modern standards, but only a few feet smaller than the YMCA court where James Naismith invented the sport.

Alumni Memorial Gym: Opened in 1923 when Trinity College had a total enrollment of 922 students. Located on East Campus, which was the only campus at the time. Cost of construction listed at $111,979 on the initial contract and later rounded off to $150,000. A gift of $25,000 was provided by Angier B. Duke, namesake of the first gym on campus, and his sister Mary. Seating for 1,440 fans downstairs and 600 on the upstairs balcony, for a total of just over 2,000. First game on January 7, 1924, a win over Mercer. Last game on February 22, 1930, when

ACC Home Courts

School	Arena	First Game	Capacity
Boston College	Conte Forum	November 26, 1988	8,606
Clemson	Littlejohn Coliseum	November 30, 1968	11,020
Florida State	Leon County Civic Center	November 29, 1981	12,500
Georgia Tech	Alexander Memorial Coliseum	November 30, 1956	9,191
Maryland	Comcast Center	November 24, 2002	17,100
Miami	Convocation Center	February 4, 2003	7,000
North Carolina	Dean Smith Center	January 18, 1986	21,572
N.C. State	RBC Center	November 19, 1999	19,722
Virginia	John Paul Jones Arena	2006–07 (scheduled)	15,000
Virginia Tech	Cassell Coliseum	January 3, 1962	10,052
Wake Forest	Lawrence Joel Coliseum	November 11, 1989	14,407

senior captain Boley Farley directed a rout of Davidson. Named to honor Trinity alumni who lost their lives in the First World War. Popularly referred to as East Campus Gym, then made a part of the Brodie Center, but the official name remains Alumni Memorial Gym.

Card Gym: Opened in 1930 when Duke had an enrollment of 1,858 undergraduate students. Located on the newly minted West Campus. Cost of construction listed at $345,557. Capacity about 3,500, although a crowd of 5,000 reportedly jammed in for a game against UNC in 1933. First game on December 19, 1930, a 22–21 loss to Villanova in the final minute. Duke's George Rogers scored the first varsity basket in the facility. Last game on December 16, 1939, a 59–28 rout of Hampden-Sydney. Named for Wilbur Wade "Cap" Card, who founded the basketball program in 1905–06. When it opened, the building was simply called the Duke Gym. It was not dedicated in Card's honor until February 15, 1958, 10 years after his death.

Cameron Indoor Stadium: Opened in 1940 when Duke had an enrollment of 2,796 undergraduate students. Adjacent to Card Gym on West Campus. The facility was built in only nine months at a cost of $400,000. Seating capacity initially listed at 9,500, with 6,000 theater seats upstairs and room for 3,500 in the lower bleachers. Capacity was soon changed to 8,800 and then to 8,564 in the late 1970s and 9,314 beginning with the 1989 season, after bleacher renovations. Crowd of 8,000 attended the

first game, on January 6, 1940, when Duke beat Princeton 36–27. Glenn Price of the Blue Devils scored the first five points in the new arena, which at the time was the largest gym south of Philadelphia. First sellout of 8,800 was on February 16, 1946, for game against UNC. Named for former coach and athletics director Edmund M. Cameron on January 22, 1972. When it opened, the building was usually called the new Duke Gymnasium, given its proximity to the old gym. It gradually became known as Duke Indoor Stadium, distinguishing it from Duke Stadium, the football facility before its dedication as Wallace Wade Stadium in 1967. The original floor was replaced and the baskets suspended from the ceiling as part of a $650,000 renovation in 1977. Another major facelift was a $2 million renovation in the summer of 1988. The floor was replaced again in the summer of 1997. The floor was named Coach K Court on November 17, 2000, after Mike Krzyzewski's 500th Duke victory, over Villanova. The refurbished and expanded concourse was named for former coach Vic Bubas on February 4, 2001. Duke owned a record of 689–142 in its first 67 seasons at the Indoor Stadium. The school's longest home-court winning streak stood at 46 games, from 1997 to 2000. Dick Groat's 48 points versus UNC in 1952 is recognized as the stadium scoring record, but the most points ever recorded in the building were from Bob Verga, who scored 51 against Virginia Tech in a 1964 freshman game.

See also Cameron Indoor Stadium.

Horne, Wendell. One of the standouts for an undefeated freshman team of 1930, Oliver Wendell Horne, of Vienna, Ga., lettered for three solid seasons on the varsity, 1931–33. A 6–0 forward, he finished with 197 points, getting 143 of them in 1933 when he started for a 17–5 team. One of his best efforts that year was a 13-point showing to key a win over Washington & Lee in the conference semifinals. He also served as president of the student government.

Horvath, Nick. Early in his freshman season, Nick Horvath, a 6–10 forward, banked in a three-point shot with 14 seconds remaining to give Duke an 84–83 overtime victory over DePaul. It was an early marker on a journey that culminated in 2004 when Horvath graduated as the first player in school history to earn five letters in basketball.

A native of Shoreview, Minn., Nicholas Alexander Horvath played in 32 of the team's 34 games during his freshman year of 2000, showing off his touch with 36.0 percent shooting from three-point range and a 3.3 scoring average. A foot injury shortened his sophomore year to six games, and he was granted a medical hardship from the NCAA to gain another year of eligibility. Even though he didn't play during most of 2001, his support behind the scenes led Mike Krzyzewski to award him a letter after Duke claimed the NCAA title in Minneapolis, near his home.

Horvath returned to see limited duty as a reserve in 2002 and earned more extensive playing time in 2003, when he started eight games. He averaged six minutes a game for the team that reached the Final Four in 2004, playing a season high of 17 minutes against Maryland in the ACC final. His career totals included 133 games with 11 starts, 347 points, 276 rebounds, and 30 three-pointers made. His high games were for 16 points against UCLA and 12 rebounds against Florida State, both during the 2003 campaign.

Horvath's leadership prompted the coaches to make him a team captain during February 2003, and he maintained that role through his fifth season. An excellent student, he received the Dr. Deryl Hart award as the team's top scholar athlete in his final two years, before graduating with double degrees in physics and English. He also received a coach's award for team commitment in his senior year.

Anatomy of a Game-Winning Shot

Nick Horvath, December 1999 versus DePaul

Horvath was a freshman getting his first college start in this December contest, but he only played four minutes because of foul trouble. Still, he made the most of his time, with eight points on perfect 3-of-3 shooting, including the decisive three-pointer in overtime for an 84–83 victory. Taking a pass from Mike Dunleavy, Horvath banked in the winning shot with 14.6 seconds left. Then Chris Carrawell played tight defense on DePaul star Quentin Richardson and the Blue Devils celebrated their 39th consecutive home-court victory, setting a new ACC record (which eventually reached 46 games).

Horvath remembers the shot vividly for several reasons.

"I was so sick that day that I could barely stand. Every time I'd take a breath in, my throat would catch and I'd have a coughing fit," he said. "Right before I went in at the end of overtime, Coach K said, 'If you get the ball, shoot it.' So I let it go.

"There was this guy, Steven Hunter, a seven-footer for their team, jumping at me. I was looking at him and I let it go real quick, and he actually hit my hand as I let the ball go. I let it go really hard because I wanted to get it over him, and fortunately I was facing the hoop straight on, so even though it was long it went off the backboard and went in.

"Of all the nights that I wanted to go out and celebrate, I was so sick that I went home and decided to take a little nap before I went out, and the next time I woke up it was 10 the next morning."

Howard, Emma Jean. When Duke was in the process of elevating its women's sports programs in the early 1970s, the school hired Emma Jean Howard as the head coach of two teams — women's basketball and volleyball. A native of Rock Hill, S.C., and a 1968 graduate of Winthrop, Howard had been coaching her alma mater's volleyball team when she joined the Duke staff in 1974. She guided the Blue Devil basketball team for three years and the volleyball team for six, through 1979, while also teaching physical education.

Howard's first basketball team in 1974–75 competed in the state's Division II of the old AIAW, against schools such as Elon and Campbell. It posted a 6–7 record and placed second in the state, but basketball was operated more like a club sport. Women's athletics merged with the men at Duke in 1975, so the 1975–76 season is regarded as the first official season of varsity women's basketball. Howard's team went 0–14 that year and 2–12 in 1976–77. Duke made a bigger commitment to the sport in 1977 by moving up to Division I and hiring Debbie Leonard to guide the team, while Howard remained with volleyball. Her 1976 volleyball squad went 36–6 and advanced to the AIAW nationals, while the 1977 and 1978 teams reached the 20-win mark.

Howard, Hilary. At the Women's Final Four in 1999, a reporter asked Duke's All-America Michele VanGorp if she thought that Hilary Howard, the team's 5–6 point guard, looked more like a sorority girl than a basketball player. "She is a sorority girl, you're right," quipped VanGorp. "She belongs to a sorority we like to refer to as Visa Visa Mastercard."

But VanGorp took exception to the insinuation that Howard wasn't athletic enough. "She's very athletic. I mean, she doesn't look like she is, but she's fairly quick on her feet. She can pretty much guard anyone out there. And a lot of times we give her the toughest defensive assignment. She puts up with all the pain in her [injured] feet and goes out there and plays hard every day. It's like they say, you can't judge a book by its cover, because it's really what's inside that counts."

What counted most for Howard was her floor leadership, playmaking, and defensive tenacity. She started 110 times in 121 appearances over her four years, 1996–99, and shared a central role in Duke's rise to national prominence. She was a member of the first Duke recruiting class to play in four NCAA Tournaments and was the starting point guard for the first two teams to get past the second round of the tourney, culminating with the Final Four berth her senior year.

A product of Scarsdale, N.Y., Howard led Duke in assists her last three years, became the first Blue Devil to top the 500 mark in career assists, and finished up as the school's all-time leader with 533. Alana Beard at 509 was the only other Blue Devil to reach 500. Four times Howard dealt 11 assists in a game, one short of the school mark. Howard also scored 986 points, had 381 rebounds, and hit 132 three-pointers.

Howard was a first-team All-ACC pick in 1998, when her heady play helped Duke to its first regular-season conference title, a 24–8 mark, and a trip to the regionals of the NCAA. She made the second team a year later when a team loaded with seniors compiled a mark of 15–1 in the ACC and 29–7 overall. She and VanGorp were the only players to start every game for that Final Four team.

Hubbell, David. David Hubbell scored 12 points as a reserve center for the 1941 and 1942 Southern Conference champs, earning a letter for the 1942 campaign. He got in one game and scored one point in 1943 before graduating in January that season. A 6–3 native of Durham, he had never played organized basketball before joining the 1940 Duke freshman team.

Hughes, Tommy. Duke's starting lineup for the first half of the 1950 season featured three multi-sport standouts: Dick Groat, a sophomore baseball whiz, along with two senior football ends, Corren Youmans and Thomas Hughes. Youmans was the only one still in the basketball lineup at the end of the year, as his backcourt mates Groat and Hughes left school because of academic infractions. It was a premature conclusion to an otherwise solid career for Hughes, a 6–0 product of Sumter, S.C.

Before his departure, Hughes started the better part of three seasons, 1948–50, and scored 533 points in 72 games. His best average, in 1948, was 8.4 points. The Blue Devils reached the Southern Conference final in that year, and he made the all-tournament second team. The next year Duke didn't qualify for the tourney (held on its home court), but Hughes was a second-team all-conference pick for his play during the regular season. In 1950 he and Youmans were co-captains.

In football Hughes lettered for three years, 1947–49, and caught 46 passes for 636 yards with two scores. He was the team's leading receiver in 1948 and 1949.

Huiskamp, Billy. A 5–6 outfielder for the baseball team, William Huiskamp was a sub for the 1934 basketball Blue Devils before earning letters in 1935 and 1936. A native of Keokuk, Iowa, he scored 94 points in 1935 and 109 in 1936. Huiskamp saw first-team action both years but missed part of the 1936 season because of an appen-

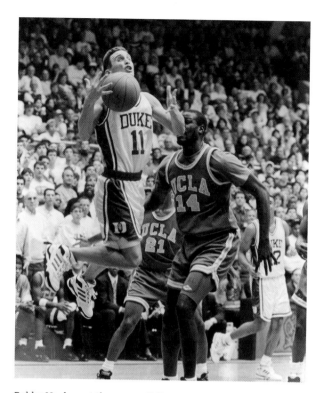

Bobby Hurley set the NCAA all-time assists record at 1,076.

dectomy. He received some all-conference votes even though Duke lost in the first round of the tournament. Huiskamp had a .400 batting average and perfect fielding mark as the regular rightfielder for the 1935 baseball team and lettered in the sport for three years, 1934–36.

Hurd, Stacy. A 6–1 product of Troy, N.Y., Stacy Hurd was a reliable double-figures scorer for the Duke women during the early 1980s. She played in 104 games with 60 starts over four years, 1981–84, finishing with 1,241 points for a career average of 11.9 a game. She also had 595 rebounds for a 5.7 average.

Hurd had a career best of 31 points versus Wake Forest in her freshman year. That stood alone as the freshman scoring record until 1985, when Chris Moreland matched it. Alana Beard's 33 points versus Maryland in 2001 was the only freshman figure to top Hurd's.

Hurd led Duke in points scored during each of her first three seasons and became the first Blue Devil woman to top 1,000 career points in 1983, her junior season. She made the ACC Honor Roll and was an honorable mention Academic All-America in her last two years.

Hurley, Bobby. Long before there were UNLV nightmares to terrorize him or Michigan players to denigrate him, there was someone a lot closer to home challenging Bobby Hurley's moxie on the basketball court. His dad.

Bob Hurley Sr., the Jersey City probation officer and ultra-successful high school coach, once upon a time played a little hoops himself. And when he went one-on-one against his first born, father-son comradeship often took a backseat to the cutthroat competition that always ensued.

"I used to do all the little things to disrupt him," said Hurley Sr., who played collegiately at St. Peters before launching his legendary coaching career at St. Anthony High. "I would talk to him during the games. I would shoot a shot and say it was good — all the stuff to distract him. For the longest time, I would be able to get into his head."

By the time Hurley's Duke career wound down in 1993, no one could distract, disrupt, or get into his head any more. As one of the great point guards in college basketball history, he was the floor conductor during an unparalleled period of accomplishment. The Blue Devils played in three national championship games and won two, while he set the NCAA record for career assists and the unofficial Duke record for the most key three-point shots. He played every minute of the Final Four in 1991, was MVP of the Final Four in 1992, and presided over an era in which the Blue Devils won 82 percent of their games, including an 18–2 mark in the NCAA tourney.

Winning was always the most important thing to Hurley, an attitude that he developed through interaction with his father and through countless pickup games on the playgrounds of his native New Jersey and New York. He was very much a playground product, toughened not at a manicured goal hanging from a suburban garage but on the cement surfaces of some rough, inner-city, neighborhood courts. Usually he was one of the smallest or youngest on the court, and frequently one of the only white kids. "I think you learn toughness because you need to win when you are on the playground," Hurley said. "If it's a good playground, when you lose you are going to be sitting there at least an hour to get back on."

Robert Matthew Hurley never had to worry about being on the court at Duke. He was a starter from his first practice as a freshman and appeared in 140 games, missing just five with a broken foot. He scored 1,731 points for an average of 12.4 and dished 1,076 assists, the NCAA career record. He averaged 7.7 assists a game and led the ACC in that category in 1992 and 1993, the first Duke player ever to do so. He also set the school's single-game (16) and single-season (289) assist marks, and his 264 three-pointers stood as the Duke career mark when he graduated. He wasn't the best shooter by percentage (41.0 for his career) but he was one of the most fearless, never hesitating to pull the trigger when a big basket was required.

Hurley connected on the biggest three-point shot in school history with 2:14 left to play in the NCAA semifinals against UNLV in 1991. The basket proved the key play in Duke's victory, an upset of the defending NCAA champs and top-ranked team in the country. The previous year, as a freshman, Hurley had been bothered by nightmares after the Runnin' Rebels routed Duke by 30 points in the national championship game.

Over four years Hurley always put himself in position to deliver the big play, big pass, or big shot when it was needed most. The three against UNLV was only one of his many momentum-changing baskets. When Duke was involved in a close game between 1990 and 1993, chances are that Hurley stepped up with a major shot during crunch time or fed one of his teammates in position to score. When Duke pulled off its miraculous win over Kentucky in the regionals in 1992, it was Hurley who had the presence of mind to call a timeout with 2.1 seconds left. When no one else could hit in the semifinals versus Indiana, Hurley had six three-pointers and 26 points to make sure that his team reached the final game. When the team went to the halftime locker room trailing mouthy Michigan, it was Hurley who erupted first, verbally challenging others to elevate their play. A repeat NCAA crown resulted.

One of the best stretches of Hurley's career was his last month or so, after his teammate Grant Hill was sidelined by an injury. Hurley began dispatching assists in double-digit doses to help the Blue Devils compensate for Hill's absence. A typical performance was put in against UCLA the day the university retired his No. 11 jersey. He scored 19 points and dished 15 assists to account for 50 of the team's 78 points. In the very next game, his home finale against Maryland, he again scored 19 while dealing 12 assists, including the NCAA record breaker on a lob to Erik Meek with 11:02 to go in the first half.

Hurley scored his career high of 32 points in his last game, a second-round loss to California in the NCAA. He played every minute of that contest and added nine assists with just one turnover. His team trailed by 18 points in the second half, before he finally tied the score on a three-pointer with under four minutes to go.

A slight six-footer, Hurley looked like any other average college student — until he stepped on the basketball court. There he reigned supreme as one of the best play-makers the ACC has ever known, an easy selection to the league's 50th anniversary team. He also won the team's top academic honor, the Dr. Deryl Hart award, in his junior year.

Hurley was the seventh pick of the NBA draft in 1993 and signed with the Sacramento Kings. But tragedy interrupted his rookie season when he was thrown from his truck in a traffic accident on his way home from a game. He suffered multiple injuries, some life-threatening. He eventually returned to play in parts of four more NBA seasons before retiring in 1998.

Hurt, Howard. Highly recruited in football and basketball out of Beckley, W.Va., Howard Preston Hurt was so widely respected on campus that he was selected as Duke's solo team captain in two consecutive years. A versatile 6 – 3 leader, he played in 80 of the program's 81 games from 1959 through 1961, in the frontcourt and the backcourt, delivering solid to spectacular performances regardless of position. His scoring averages were 15.7, 13.4, and 12.3, and he was usually one of the better rebounders on the court because of his hustle and desire. His career totals included 1,095 points and 575 rebounds.

"Inch for inch and pound for pound, we don't think there are too many better than Howard. He always gives way over 100 percent," coach Vic Bubas once noted. Hurt was voted Duke's most valuable player by his teammates as a sophomore, when he made the All-ACC second unit. He was the leading scorer for the team that won the ACC championship in 1960 and repeated second-team all-league honors in both 1960 and 1961.

Hurt had a pair of 28-point games as a sophomore,

versus North Carolina and Wake Forest, and totaled 52 points in the Blue Devils' ACC Tournament sweep in his junior year, when he was named to the all-tournament team. He was consistently excellent in 1961, beginning with an 18-point game in overtime versus LSU to open the year and continuing through a 20-point game to close the regular season against UNC. After his senior year he was the 95th pick in the NBA draft but did not play in the league. Later, as a high school coach at Enloe in Raleigh, Hurt helped develop one of Duke's best centers, Randy Denton.

Hyde, Henry. Henry J. Hyde of Chicago played in the backcourt and frontcourt for the 1944 Southern Conference championship team while he was attending the Navy V-12 program at Duke. He scored 53 points in 22 games. Hyde served in the South Pacific during the Second World War and then in the U.S. Naval Reserve from 1946 through 1968, retiring at the rank of commander. A graduate of Georgetown University, which he attended before and after his brief stay at Duke, Hyde has been a member of the U.S. Congress since 1975, representing the sixth district of Illinois in the House of Representatives.

Indiana. Before 2006 two of college basketball's most storied programs, Duke and Indiana University, met five times, all on neutral courts in tournament play. The first-ever meeting, in the Sweet 16 of the NCAA Tournament in 1987, pitted Duke coach Mike Krzyzewski against his mentor Bob Knight for the first time. The Hoosiers won by six points and went on to claim the NCAA title.

Krzyzewski's team bested Knight's when they next met, in the NCAA semifinals in 1992. Marty Clark's five free throws in the final 87 seconds made the difference in an 81 – 78 victory. Duke then went on to beat Michigan for the title.

Duke topped Indiana again in November 1995 in the semifinals of the Great Alaska Shootout and won the championship the following night. A year later, in another early-season showcase, Indiana whipped Duke in the championship game of the Preseason NIT. Knight watched his 6 – 8 junior Andrae Patterson light up an

A Moment He'll Never Forget

Jason Williams, 2002 versus Indiana

Playing in the Sweet 16 in Lexington, Ky., Duke trailed Indiana by four points with 11 seconds to go. Freshman Daniel Ewing fired off a shot and Williams tracked down the long rebound, stepped back behind the three-point line, and connected on a stunning jumper with 4.2 seconds to play. Plus the Hoosiers fouled him, giving Duke a chance to tie the game. Unfortunately Williams missed the free throw, Carlos Boozer missed a hurried follow-up, and the Devils saw their season end with a 74–73 defeat.

But that's one of those moments—along with his clutch jumpers during the Miracle Minute at Maryland in 2001 and his 38-point outburst to lead an overtime win over Kentucky—that Williams will never forget.

"Every kid dreams of being in that situation and being the go-to guy," he said. "I missed the free throw and Carlos got a putback and missed that and we lost the game, but I love being in situations like that. I love hitting shots like that."

assortment of Blue Devil defenders for 39 points to carry the Hoosiers.

Duke and Indiana met again in the NCAA Sweet 16 in 2002 at a location friendly to neither side — Rupp Arena in Lexington, Ky. Duke's hopes of a repeat NCAA title were dashed when Indiana made a late 10 – 0 run to pull out a 74 – 73 victory in a game that the Blue Devils appeared to have in the bag with a 14-point lead. The Hoosiers, under coach Mike Davis, eventually fell to Maryland in the NCAA final.

In 2006 the first Duke-Indiana game at a home site took place when the Blue Devils visited Bloomington during the ACC – Big Ten Challenge. A packed house of 17,343 at Assembly Hall was quieted early when Duke rocketed to a 16 – 2 start. Senior J. J. Redick led a poised Duke effort with 29 points as his team withstood a late Hoosier spurt. The Blue Devils prevailed 75 – 67, making them 7 of 7 in the ACC – Big Ten event.

Iowa. Duke owns a 7 – 1 record against the Iowa Hawkeyes. Six of the eight games have been played at neutral sites, plus one each at the schools' home arenas.

The most significant wins for Duke were in the NCAA Tournaments in 1991 and 1992, each time in the second round during national championship marches, and in the Great Alaska Shootout championship game during November 1995. Chris Collins exploded for 30 points in that one.

The home-and-home series spanned the 1993 and 1994 seasons, with Duke winning both games. Iowa's lone victory was in the opening game of the Rainbow Classic in December 1994. The top-ranked Devils pounded the seventh-ranked Hawkeyes 80–62 at the United Center in Chicago during the ACC–Big Ten Challenge early in the 2002 campaign. Jason Williams, Carlos Boozer, and Mike Dunleavy combined for 65 points.

Issel, Dan. When he graduated from Kentucky he was the school's all-time scoring leader, and when he retired from the NBA he was pro basketball's fourth-best point producer ever. Hall of Famer Dan Issel was averaging 35 points a game when he led his top-ranked Wildcats against Duke in the Kentucky Invitational during December 1969. Issel had 20 points and seven rebounds but was outplayed by Duke center Randy Denton, who had 28 points with 21 boards. Issel's team won the game, though, to hand Duke coach Bucky Waters his first defeat after a 6–0 start.

Jackman, Bill. After leading his high school to the Nebraska state title as a senior, William David Jackman headed to Duke as a member of coach Mike Krzyzewski's first blockbuster recruiting class. A 6–8 forward, he was the first player of the six-man class to commit to the Blue Devils. But Jackman lasted just one year in Durham. He played in 27 of Duke's 28 games in 1982–83, scoring 87 points and grabbing 44 rebounds, with highs of 12 points against Davidson and 11 against Maryland. After the season he transferred to Nebraska and completed his career in his home state.

Jackson, Doug. A slick-shooting point maker for the 1967 freshman team, Douglas Ray Jackson saw a promising career derailed by a knee injury. He played in three games in 1968, missed all of 1969 after surgery, and played in just one contest in 1970. A 6–5 forward from Overland Park, Kan., he scored six career points.

James, Carl. Although he was best known for his affiliation with Duke and intercollegiate football, Carl C. James was intricately involved with the Blue Devil basketball program as the school's athletics director in the 1970s. Named the replacement for retiring legend Eddie Cameron in 1972, James had to navigate turbulent seas during the following two years in trying to set the basketball program on course for the future.

With head coach Bucky Waters's resignation in September 1973, just a month before the start of preseason training, James wanted to land a so-called supercoach to guide the Blue Devils' fortunes. James took aim at the recently retired Kentucky icon Adolph Rupp and persuaded him to steer the ship for a season while he searched for a permanent coach. But Rupp had to back out at the last minute, and James named assistant Neill McGeachy to the post three days after practice started.

Faced with a late start and only a one-season commitment from the administration, the young coach was placed in an impossible position. The Blue Devils posted a 10–16 record in 1974 and McGeachy's contract was not extended. That's when James brought in Bill Foster from Utah to rebuild. Foster had the school back in the Final Four in 1978, a year after Tom Butters had replaced James in the AD's chair.

A Raleigh native, James played football for Duke from 1949 to 1951 and threw the discus for the track and field team. He returned in 1954 to serve as an assistant to the athletics director. His actual role was to recruit football players for coach Bill Murray, and he helped stockpile the talent for several outstanding bowl and championship clubs. He left in 1966 for private business and came back as associate AD in 1969.

James's administrative career also included stints as athletics director at Maryland, executive director of the Sugar Bowl, and commissioner of the Big Eight Conference. He retired in 1996 after helping the Big Eight add four Texas schools to become the Big 12 Conference. James was enshrined in the Duke Sports Hall of Fame (1990) and the North Carolina Sports Hall of Fame (2000). He died in 2004 at the age of 75.

James, Nate. An unusual set of circumstances descended on Duke after a run to the Final Four in 1999. Three players opted to leave early for the NBA and a fourth decided to transfer. With coach Mike Krzyzewski at home recovering from hip replacement surgery in the spring, he received a visit from his only three returning scholarship players — Chris Carrawell, Shane Battier, and Nate James. They wanted to assure their coach that they would be back and were prepared to lead an otherwise youthful team into new territory. Carrawell evolved into the ACC player of the year in the following season, while James and Battier were the rocks of leadership upon which the team that won the national championship in 2001 was built.

James, a 6–6 product of Washington, D.C., had ironically been the subject of numerous transfer rumors earlier in his career. He suffered ruptured tendons in his right thumb that sidelined him for the first 14 games of his freshman year, and endured a high ankle sprain that cost him all but six early games the next year. While some suggested that the hard-luck story of his first two seasons would lead him to seek a new start elsewhere, James instead applied for a medical hardship to earn an extra season of eligibility and went about establishing himself as one of the most dedicated of Blue Devils. Chosen as the reserve who contributed most to team morale in 1999, when Duke was the national runner-up, he put in countless hours of off-season preparation for 2000 and started all but one game while averaging 11.0 points. Then he teamed with Battier as co-captain in 2001, started most of the year, and averaged 12.3 points as the Devils won the NCAA championship.

Nathaniel Drake James played in 135 games from 1997 to 2001, with 63 starts. He scored 1,116 points, had 500 rebounds, and shot 47.3 percent from the floor. While known mostly for defense and rebounding, he could also hit the occasional three-pointer, with 111 made during his career. Duke won or shared the ACC regular-season championship in all five years that James was on the team, a feat achieved by no other player in league history. Duke had a 71–9 mark in conference games during his career, though in one of those years he did not play in any league games.

James brought a warrior mentality to the court that set an example for his teammates and contributed to

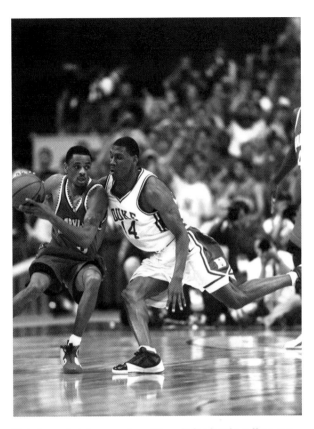

Nate James's defense on Juan Dixon helped Duke rally to top Maryland in the 2001 Final Four.

many victories. Sometimes that meant scoring, as in the 26 points he had versus Texas to help Duke win the Preseason NIT semifinals in 2001, or the career high of 27 points that he scored at Clemson later that year, on 10-of-14 shooting. But usually James's warrior spirit showed in the way he went after loose balls and rebounds, the way he defended, the way he attacked weight training workouts despite a variety of ailments — all activities that led one publication to name James the ACC's most underrated player. ACC coaches, meanwhile, named him to the league's all-defensive team in 2001, while the media voted him third-team All-ACC.

"Being injured taught me how a sport can be taken away from you and it made me appreciate it more. It made me a hungrier player," he said.

Three of James's most noteworthy moments were against Maryland in 2001. In the final seconds at College Park, not far from his home, he hit a pair of clutch free throws in the face of an antagonistic crowd to send the game into overtime. In the ACC semifinals, his penchant for finding offensive rebounds led to the winning tip-in just moments before the buzzer. And in the second half of the NCAA semis in 2001, James stepped up and volunteered to stop Terp star Juan Dixon, who had torched the Devils for 16 points in the first half. Dixon scored just three more points and Duke rallied to win.

One of James's most significant contributions to the NCAA crown, though, was the way he handled his move out of the starting lineup late in the year. Then a fifth-year senior, he had started 29 straight games heading into the regular-season finale at UNC. But Krzyzewski wanted to rework the lineup after an injury to Carlos Boozer, so he decided that he needed to have James come off the bench. James accepted the move and still played 24 minutes a game in the Devils' nine postseason contests, which netted ACC and NCAA trophies. Krzyzewski wrote in his book *Five-Point Play* (2001) that James may have been the biggest winner of all: "When he walked off the court in Minneapolis, he was not only a champion in basketball — Nate James was a champion in life."

Jamieson, Bob. A prep All-America in football and an all-state selection in basketball, Robert James Jamieson was a reserve for the 1961 through 1963 Blue Devils. He played in 30 games, with 50 points and 53 rebounds. A 6 – 5 frontcourt player from Greensboro, N.C., Jamieson had one of his best efforts in helping Duke beat Wake Forest in Greensboro in 1962.

Janicki, Bernie. In the regular-season finale against North Carolina in 1952, Bernard Aloysius Janicki posted a school record that might never be broken. He grabbed 31 rebounds in the contest as Duke blasted the Tar Heels by 30 points. A 6 – 3 forward from Ambridge, Pa., he came to be known for his board work in his three varsity seasons, 1952 – 54, grabbing 923 rebounds in 83 games for an average of 11.1. He also scored 1,247 points, an average of 15.0.

Janicki's sophomore year ranks as the best rebounding season in school history. Along with his single-game record, he totaled 476 rebounds for a 15.9 average. Neither figure has since been eclipsed. Mike Lewis in 1968 is the only other Duke player to claim at least 400 rebounds in one year.

Janicki averaged double figures in points and re-

bounds in each of his first two seasons and led the Devils in scoring in each of his last two. He played 63 games in which he scored in double figures, scoring 30 points against South Carolina in 1953, 28 against Penn, 26 against Southern Cal, and 25 against N.C. State. In eight career contests against the Wolfpack he averaged 18 points, scoring at least 20 in half his meetings with the Blue Devils' most prominent opponent of that era. In a memorable battle with the Pack in 1952, Janicki's one-handed shot from near midcourt with seven seconds left forced overtime. The Devils eventually lost in double-overtime despite Janicki's 20 points.

Although he never made an all-conference team, Janicki was one of the team captains in his last two seasons and the team most valuable player as a senior. He was enshrined in the Duke Sports Hall of Fame in 1992.

Jankoski, John. John E. Jankoski started at forward for the 1928 and 1929 teams, his only seasons on the varsity. He scored 41 points for the 1929 team, which had a 12 – 8 record in Eddie Cameron's first season. A native of Milwaukee, he also played three years as a halfback and fullback for Duke football after captaining the freshman football team in 1926.

Jersey retirements. During the first century of Duke basketball, the jersey numbers of 11 all-star men and one woman were retired by the university. Dick Groat's No. 10 was the first, with the ceremony taking place at a baseball game during his senior year of 1952. Duke didn't retire another number for almost 30 years, until Mike Gminski's senior game in 1980. Nine of the 11 retirement ceremonies took place between 1986 and 2003, though two of those were for players who performed in the 1960s. Here is a list of all retirement ceremonies, in the order that the players completed their college eligibility:

10	Dick Groat	May 1, 1952
25	Art Heyman	March 4, 1990
44	Jeff Mullins	December 6, 1994
43	Mike Gminski	February 20, 1980
24	Johnny Dawkins	February 22, 1986
35	Danny Ferry	February 18, 1989
32	Christian Laettner	February 26, 1992

11	Bobby Hurley	February 28, 1993
33	Grant Hill	February 27, 1994
31	Shane Battier	February 21, 2001
22	Jason Williams	February 5, 2003
20	Alana Beard	January 24, 2004 (first woman's jersey retired)

Johnson, C. B. After a solid season on the 1959 Duke freshman team, Charles Berdine Johnson was elevated to the varsity in 1960. A 6 – 3 sophomore forward from New Orleans, he made his only career appearance during coach Vic Bubas's first year, going scoreless against Virginia.

Johnson, Dick. Performing for coach Harold Bradley's first two Duke teams in basketball and coach Jack Coombs's last two in Duke baseball, Richard Allan "Footsie" Johnson played an important role in numerous Blue Devil victories. A 5 – 11 native of Dayton, he lettered for the 1951 and 1952 basketball teams, each of which won at least 20 games and played for the conference championship. The 1952 team was the first in school history to appear in a final national poll. Johnson totaled 196 points in 58 games, with a high of 12 versus Temple. In baseball Johnson had 100 base hits over the 1951 and 1952 campaigns for a .361 career batting average. He helped the 1952 team post a 31 – 7 record and advance to the College World Series. After the season he signed with the Chicago Cubs and eventually played eight games in the major leagues in 1958.

Johnson, Patrick. He never played high school basketball, but Patrick Brooks Johnson developed into a solid backup reserve for the Blue Devils. A 6 – 9 native of Atlanta, he concentrated on baseball as a prepster, pitching and playing first base for four years. At Duke he made a brief attempt to continue his baseball career but gave up the sport and played intramural basketball as a freshman. He then walked on to the basketball team as a sophomore in October 2002.

Johnson's size proved a valuable asset in practice, and he appeared in five games during 2003 and 13 in 2004. Johnson's steady development led to a scholarship for his senior year of 2005, when he played in 22 games and was chosen to start against Wake Forest. He spent much of the season playing in a shoulder harness after suffering an injury in the N.C. State game. Johnson and walk-on Patrick Davidson received the coach's award for their commitment and values.

Johnson had 26 points and 35 rebounds in 53 appearances, with highs of six points versus Seton Hall in 2006 and six rebounds plus three assists in 10 minutes versus Virginia Tech in 2005. With one year of eligibility remaining after graduation, he played as a graduate student in 2006.

Johnson, Rick. During Mike Krzyzewski's first two seasons in Durham, Rick Johnson was one of his assistant coaches, with the primary responsibility of operating the junior varsity team. Johnson guided that program for the 1981 and 1982 campaigns, the final two years that Duke had JV ball. Johnson had played for Krzyzewski at the United States Military Academy Prep School in Fort Belvoir, Va., and had graduated in 1980 from Mississippi, where he was a student assistant coach for Bob Weltlich.

Jones, Bobby. Considered one of the top defensive players in NBA history, Hall of Famer Bobby Jones demonstrated those instincts as a collegian when he picked off a pass and scored the winning layup at the buzzer to stun Duke in 1974. Jones faced the Blue Devils nine times in his three years at North Carolina, 1972 – 74, and picked up eight wins. UNC was ranked in the top 10 for all but one of those games. Jones averaged 13.7 points against Duke, with a high of 24 when the Tar Heels rallied to beat the Devils in overtime in his final home game.

Jones, Dahntay. A menace on defense and explosive off the drive, Dahntay Laval Jones was a pivotal figure for a pair of ACC championship teams in 2002 and 2003. A 6 – 6 forward from Trenton, N.J., and a transfer from Rutgers, he played in 68 games during his two-year Duke career and totaled 975 points for a 14.3 average. He also had 326 rebounds.

In two years at Rutgers, 1999 and 2000, Jones started 59 of 63 games and scored 836 points. He made the Big East all-rookie team as a frosh and led the Scarlet Knights in scoring as a sophomore. After transferring to

After transferring from Rutgers, Dahntay Jones scored 975 points in two Duke campaigns.

Duke he had to sit out the 2001 national championship season, but still he made a contribution by excelling in practice sessions. He was awarded a letter despite not playing a game, and he received the Ted Mann Jr. plaque as the reserve contributing most to team morale.

Jones moved seamlessly into the Duke lineup in 2002 and was considered the team's defensive stopper, frequently assigned to deny the ball to opposing top guns. He made the ACC's all-defensive team as selected by the coaches, averaged 11.2 points a game, and delighted Blue Devil fans with his above-the-rim game. He was Duke's most flamboyant dunker for two years in a row, but he also drilled 59 three-point shots to demonstrate the versatility in his game.

Jones led Duke in scoring and ranked fifth in the ACC in 2003 with a 17.7 average. He was a first-team All-ACC selection and a repeat pick for the all-defensive team as well as team MVP. One of his best games was at home against UNC, when he had 23 points and 13 rebounds.

With the score tied at 61, Jones hit two foul shots, a three-pointer, and a dunk to put the Blue Devils ahead for good at 68–63. Chosen as the team's most valuable player, he was instrumental in Duke's fifth straight ACC Tournament title and virtually unstoppable in the Devils' three NCAA Tournament games. He recorded his career scoring high of 28 points in a second-round contest with Central Michigan, and his 24.7 average led all scorers in the 2003 tourney.

Jones was the 20th pick in the first round of the NBA draft in 2003, going to the Memphis Grizzlies in a trade by the Boston Celtics.

Jones, Ray. Well-traveled and energetic, Raymond Robert Jones enjoyed a two-year stop in Durham as an assistant coach for Bill Foster for the 1977 and 1978 seasons. A LaSalle graduate, he was a tireless recruiter for the Blue Devils, always on the road in search of talent. He also worked with the junior varsity program. Jones left Duke after the Devils reached the Final Four in 1978, when he was not promoted within the staff after another assistant's departure. But he reunited later with Foster as an assistant at South Carolina and made several other stops on his basketball journey before becoming an NBA scout.

Jordan, Michael. The greatest player in modern basketball history was a dominant performer in seven games against Duke during his college days at North Carolina, 1982–84. Michael Jordan averaged 23.0 points in the series and twice hit for 32 points. His team was ranked No. 1 in the nation for four of the meetings, and he was a perfect 6–0 against the Devils heading into the ACC Tournament semifinals in 1984. UNC had gone undefeated in the league that year while Duke, dominated by sophomores, had checked in at 7–7. But the Blue Devils pulled off the upset despite Jordan's 22 points, handing him a most frustrating defeat in his final ACC contest. Jordan was on the 1992 Olympic team for which Mike Krzyzewski was an assistant coach.

Joyce, Marty. Martin J. Joyce did not play high school ball because of injuries. After graduation he entered the military and developed his game playing on service teams. When he enrolled at Duke in 1956–57 he was a 24-year-old member of the freshman team. A 5–11 guard from Philadelphia, he saw reserve action for the 1958 and 1959 varsity teams, with 18 games, 18 points, and 14 rebounds. His steady court manner led to his selection as a team co-captain for the 1959 club.

Junior varsity basketball. See Freshman basketball.

K Academy. Coach Mike Krzyzewski established the K Academy in 2003 as a unique basketball fantasy camp for adults 35 years and older. The annual event attracts participants from around the country. Former Blue Devil greats join the coaching staff as the camp "counselors" for four days of competition and social events that give campers total immersion in the Duke basketball culture. With tuition costing $10,000 by the summer of 2005, the K Academy was designed as a fundraiser for the Duke Basketball Legacy Fund as well as for outreach efforts such as the Emily Krzyzewski Family Life Center in Durham.

K Lab. On June 26, 1998, Duke christened the Michael W. Krzyzewski Human Performance Lab. The facility, within the Duke Sports Medicine complex, was created primarily to conduct research on athletic performance with the goal of preventing injury. Sophisticated equipment and specialists in orthopedics, kinesiology, biomechanics and physical therapy helped the K Lab to produce over 25 publications in scientific journals and over 120 conference abstracts and presentations in its first seven years.

Kalbfus, Jack. After leading the junior varsity in scoring in 1954, John Paul Kalbfus earned plenty of playing time for the varsity in 1955. A 6-3 forward from Greensburg, Pa., he scored in double figures in six of his first seven games, topped by a 21-point night against Minnesota in the Dixie Classic. As a junior in 1956 he moved to guard to offset the departure of Don Tobin and played in the first 14 games, with a high of 19 points against Wake Forest and an average of 8.3. But he was academically ineligible for the second half of the season and concluded his career with totals of 38 games, 291 points, and 113 rebounds.

Kansas. Duke and Kansas, two of the oldest and winningest programs in college basketball, haven't played each other very often, but most of the games have had championships at stake. The schools had a home-and-home series spanning the 1988 and 1989 seasons, with Duke winning both contests. Each of the other six has been in tournament play on neutral courts, with Duke winning four times.

The first Duke-Kansas contest took place early in the 1986 season, when the teams met in New York for the championship of the Preseason NIT. Duke pulled out a narrow win, a key early accomplishment and confidence booster for a team that went on to the Final Four. David Henderson's career high of 30 points led the attack and earned him tournament MVP honors. Duke and Kansas met again at the end of the season in the Final Four, with the Devils taking another narrow win to reach their first national title contest under Mike Krzyzewski.

During the 1988 season Duke made its only visit to the historic Allen Fieldhouse in Lawrence and claimed an overtime victory behind 21 points from Quin Snyder, who had been recruited by Kansas coach Larry Brown. The teams met again in the Final Four a few weeks later in Kansas City, with the Jayhawks taking a semifinal victory on the way to the national title. Danny Manning led Kansas with 25 points and 10 rebounds, after scoring 31 points in the regular-season meeting.

Duke routed Kansas the following year on a snowy day in Durham. Danny Ferry celebrated the retirement of his jersey No. 35 with 26 points and 10 rebounds. That was Roy Williams's first season on the Jayhawks bench. When DU and KU next met, Williams had just defeated his mentor Dean Smith in the NCAA semifinals in 1991 to set up a championship contest with the Blue Devils. Duke won 72-65 in Indianapolis to claim its first national title. Christian Laettner and Billy McCaffrey were the scoring leaders, while Bobby Hurley played a near flawless floor game.

Duke and Kansas also squared off in the NCAA tourneys of 2000 and 2003. The Devils won in the second round in 2000 by 69-64, as Shane Battier had one of his best days with 21 points and eight blocked shots, while freshman Carlos Boozer was strong in the post. In 2003, during Williams's last NCAA tourney with Kansas, his team defeated Duke 69-65 in the Sweet 16. Although Duke endured a cold shooting night, the game was one of the better-played ones of the tournament that year. Senior Dahntay Jones closed his career with a 23-point effort and Chris Duhon played an excellent floor game in putting his team on top throughout the contest while holding his future Chicago Bulls teammate Kirk Hinrich to 1-of-9 shooting. But Nick Collison's 33 points and 19 rebounds were too much for Duke to overcome.

"This was one of the most competitive games I've ever played in," Jones said. "It was two special teams, two teams competing for 40 minutes. That was a battle out there. It turned in their favor, but they've got one of the great players in college basketball and he played like a man tonight."

Kast, Fred. In Harold Bradley's final season of 1959, Frederick Wesley Kast demonstrated a fine shooting touch as a sophomore forward. A 6–7 native of Rahway, N.J., he continued to develop under new coach Vic Bubas and posted his best game of 14 points versus North Carolina in 1960. He did not play in 1961 but returned to finish his career by coming off the bench in 1962. He totaled 57 varsity appearances, with 243 points and 167 rebounds.

Katherman, Rick. One of the uncanny long-distance shooters in school history, Richard Ross Katherman averaged 12.3 points a game during his varsity career, 1969–71. He was the No. 2 scorer for Vic Bubas's last team and Bucky Waters's first team and missed only two contests during his tenure, appearing in 82 games with 1,005 points and 362 rebounds.

Sometimes referred to as "the rifleman" for his marksmanship on the perimeter, Katherman led Duke in scoring seven times as a sophomore and had seven 20-point games. The best: 25 points and 13 rebounds versus Maryland (on 12-of-19 shooting) and 25 points with 12 rebounds versus East Tennessee. He also delivered a 10-of-14 shooting exhibition against Wake Forest. A 6–7 forward from Manchester, Mass., he hit the 25-point mark again as a junior against Clemson. As a senior he began the year on the bench but earned his starting spot back with strong games against Northwestern and Santa Clara. He continued to show his offensive punch with a pair of 21-point days versus N.C. State, one of those despite a high fever.

Duke played five games in Madison Square Garden in 1971, one in the regular season and four in the NIT. Katherman scored 68 points in those contests and went over the 1,000-point mark in his final NIT game. He was an eighth-round NBA draftee but did not play in the league.

Kauffman, Carey. The daughter of a former NBA player and the sister of two fellow ACC players, Carey Kauffman was one of the standout performers during Gail Goestenkors's early years. She was a reserve for coach Debbie Leonard's final team in 1992 and started the next three years under Goestenkors, leading the team in scoring, rebounding, or both for each of those campaigns.

Kauffman, a 6–3 forward from Lilburn, Ga., played in 111 games from 1992 to 1995 and scored 1,228 points with 726 rebounds while starting 80 times. She earned second-team All-ACC honors in her junior and senior seasons and was one of the pivotal figures for Goestenkors's first NCAA team in 1995. Kauffman averaged 14.1 points and 8.4 rebounds that year, and set the Cameron Indoor Stadium scoring record for women with 35 points against UNC Asheville. She also had her career high of 19 rebounds in that game. Kauffman graduated as the No. 5 rebounder in Duke history.

Kauffman's father Bob played for seven years in the NBA, 1969–75, while her sisters Lara and Joanna played at Georgia Tech in the 1990s.

Kelley, Doug. A three-year letterman, 1926–28, Douglas L. Kelley, from Wilmington, N.C., was the captain of the 1928 Blue Devils. It was his second Duke captaincy, as he had previously led the 1925 freshman team to a 9–1 record and a state title. Kelley also played three seasons of varsity football as an end and placekicker.

Kennedy, Joe. Possibly Duke's first scholarship basketball player from famed DeMatha High School, Joseph Aloysius Kennedy developed into a key contributor during his junior and senior seasons. A 6–6 forward from Bowie, Md., he appeared in 62 games over three years, 1966–68, with 454 points and 265 rebounds. After providing frontcourt depth for two seasons, he blossomed as a regular in 1968 with averages of 12.0 points and 6.1 rebounds. His two best scoring games came that year, with 24 and 22 points against Virginia. He played professionally after Duke, with two seasons in the NBA and one in the ABA.

Kentucky. Faced with their second defeat near the end of a long regular season, the top-ranked Blue Devils of 1992 tried their home run play in the closing seconds at Wake Forest. But the pitcher, Grant Hill, threw a curve ball and the Devils were unable to get off a shot. About a month later, when faced with more dire circumstances, Duke had a second chance to call home run again. The Devils trailed Kentucky by a point with 2.1 seconds remaining in overtime at the NCAA East Region championship game. If they couldn't score, their glorious season would be over. This time, though, the pitcher threw a perfect strike, Christian Laettner made the catch, the move, and The Shot, and the Devils were 104–103 victors in a game that many have called the greatest in NCAA tourney history. Nine days later Duke won its second straight national title.

While the outcome may always torment Kentucky supporters, the contest was so entertaining and dramatic that the NCAA tried to recapture the magic several times in subsequent years by assigning the Blue Devils and Wildcats to the same regional bracket of March Madness. Those designs materialized in 1998, and Kentucky fans enjoyed at least a touch of redemption when their Wildcats erased a late 17-point Duke lead to win 86–84 for a spot in the Final Four.

Led by that pair of NCAA thrillers, the Duke-Kentucky rivalry can stand head and shoulders above most others in college basketball. In 19 all-time installments, it has dished up more than its share of classic confrontations and fascinating subplots. The two teams have met five times in NCAA play, twice each in the Jimmy V Classic, the Hall of Fame Tip-Off Classic, and the Kentucky Invitational, and five times in the regular season. Fourteen of the 19 meetings have been decided by seven points or fewer, five in overtime. Kentucky has been rated either first or second in the nation for six of the meetings, while Duke has been No. 1 or No. 2 five times. The Wildcats won 10 of the first 12 games, Duke six of the last seven. All but two of the games since the 1950s have been staged at neutral sites.

Kentucky's coach Adolph Rupp brought his Wildcats to Duke twice in the 1950s, and one of the meetings resulted in a stunning come-from-behind Blue Devil win. Duke finished the game with a 10–0 run, and its only lead was the final one, 85–84. Rupp was less than impressed, as the stadium was not full for the encounter. Duke also

played in Lexington a couple of times in the 1950s and was defeated by the top-ranked Wildcats at the Kentucky Invitational in December 1969, even though center Randy Denton outplayed bluegrass hero Dan Issel.

The Blue Devils returned to pick up a most significant win at Rupp Arena in 1980, upsetting fourth-ranked Kentucky 55–54 to advance in the NCAA. One of the Duke stars that day was guard Vince Taylor, who grew up in Lexington. The game proved to be the final Blue Devil win for All-America Mike Gminski and coach Bill Foster.

Before meeting in the 1980, 1992, and 1998 regionals, the Devils and the Cats played two times in the Final Four. Kentucky won both times, but not without a fight. In the semifinals in 1966, UK was ranked No. 1 and Duke No. 2. Coach Vic Bubas had one of his better teams, but his scoring star Bob Verga was hospitalized with strep throat during the week of the game and was not at full strength. Kentucky claimed the biggest "what if?" contest in Duke history and advanced to the final before losing to Texas Western. In 1978 a youthful Duke team brought cinderella enthusiasm into the NCAA final with No. 1 Kentucky and kept most of the Wildcats' weapons in check. But Jack Givens pierced the 2–3 zone and poured in 41 points to cut down the Devils 94–88.

"I never assumed we would get back to the finals," Foster told historian Jim Sumner 25 years later. "Too many things have to go right. I was devastated by the loss and still feel a strong sense of disappointment. I still haven't completely gotten over it." Kentucky fans of 1992 could relate.

With the schools ranked second and third in the nation in November 1979, Duke edged Kentucky in the first Hall of Fame Tip-Off Classic in Springfield, Mass. They were brought together again for the event's 10th anniversary, and No. 1 Duke won that game in a 25-point rout, the most lopsided outcome in series history.

When the teams squared off at the Jimmy V Classic in the 1999 and 2002 seasons, both were again highly ranked and the match-ups were highly anticipated. With his team down by 12 in the second half of the 2002 game, Duke guard Jason Williams moved from the wing to the point and took over. On an assortment of clutch three-pointers, drives, and free throws, he scored 23 of the Blue Devils' final 31 points in regulation and finished with a career high of 38 as Duke won 95–92 in a battle royale typical of the entire series.

"I just rode him as much as a jockey could ride a horse. You just kept calling his number and he kept responding," Krzyzewski said of Williams. His teammate Mike Dunleavy, who stood out in the overtime, added: "He's been doing that for two years. You don't want to always expect it out of him but it's something he does. He is the best player in the country and he proved it again tonight."

While match-ups between Duke and Kentucky have usually been characterized by an intensity befitting two of the country's all-time great programs, it was the match-up in 1992 that made Duke the target of perpetual scorn for many Wildcat fans. Although Krzyzewski delivered one of the great lessons in sportsmanship by heading for the retiring UK radio announcer Cawood Ledford moments after the game to express his admiration for Kentucky's efforts, another image remained etched in the hearts of the Wildcat faithful: Laettner stepping on a fallen UK player in the lane. That he later hit the winning shot cemented his position as public enemy No. 1 to UK followers.

Kiker, Paul. One of the early standouts for Trinity was Paul J. Kiker of Polkton, N.C. He entered school in the fall of 1906 and graduated in 1911, starring at forward and center for Trinity during most of that time. The first portion of his career overlapped with that of his brother, William Black Kiker, who graduated in 1909. The brothers were in the starting lineup together in 1908. Paul was out of school during William's senior year, then returned to captain the 1910 team and start for the 1911 team. Paul also served as manager of the *Trinity Chronicle* his senior year.

King, Billy. The quintessential example of a player who made a major impact without scoring major points, Billy Matthew King, a 6–6 forward from Sterling Va., affixed an indelible stamp on Duke basketball during the mid-1980s. One of the best defensive players in school history and one of the ultimate leaders of the Krzyzewski era, King averaged just 4.5 career points a game but commanded playing time with everything else he brought to the court.

Billy King delivered a defensive masterpiece versus Notre Dame in 1988.

From 1985 through 1988 King played in 135 games with 64 starts, 602 points, 390 rebounds, and 140 steals. The numbers don't mean as much as his having played in every game in which he was healthy for all four years and having averaged almost 30 minutes of court time in his last two years. The only four games he missed were late in the 1987 season, when he suffered a broken wrist at Notre Dame. Like Tate Armstrong at Virginia a decade earlier, King ignored the pain and played the rest of the game, logging 39 minutes in the overtime loss. He had surgery the next day and, unlike Armstrong, was able to return for the final month of the season. During that month he had one of his best clutch efforts when Duke beat Xavier in the NCAA tourney. King had a steal and a dunk to tie the score with three-plus minutes to play, and he hit a free throw with six seconds left to help ensure the outcome. That was unusual because free-throw shooting was not a strength; in 280 career attempts he converted just 48 percent.

King was used mostly as a defensive specialist in his freshman year, and that label stuck through graduation. He almost always drew the opposing team's top offensive perimeter threat in his last two years, and he usually kept it in check. A few of his defensive performances took on legendary proportions in Duke annals. In 1988 he hounded Notre Dame's ace David Rivers into a 3-of-17 shooting day in a nationally televised victory at Cameron Indoor Stadium. Later, in the NCAA regional final against Temple, his defensive work led to a nightmare day for the Owls' star freshman Mark Macon, who shot 6 of 29 as Duke posted an upset and made it to the Final Four. King won the Henry Iba Corinthian award as the nation's best defensive player. He made a habit of trying to be the best defender every day, not just for marquee games.

Though he was an excellent one-on-one defender, King was most valuable because he completely understood Krzyzewski's team defense concepts. His exceptional ability as a communicator not only helped his teammates make the necessary defensive adjustments but also made him one of the most influential leaders in the program. "He and Shane Battier are the two guys who could communicate the best in a group setting on the court that I've ever coached," Krzyzewski said.

King was one of the Blue Devils' most active players off the court, with speaking engagements and outreach appearances. He hosted a show on the student cable TV station and after graduation worked briefly in commercial television as a basketball analyst. Then he got into coaching, first joining Duke alumnus Bob Bender's staff at Illinois State. In 1993 he made the move to the NBA, landing a spot on the Indiana Pacers' staff through his connection with head coach Larry Brown, who had tried

recruiting him to Kansas during his high school years. When Brown moved to the Philadelphia 76ers after the 1997 season, he persuaded the team's owner, Pat Croce, to give King a shot in the front office. By 1998 King was the team's general manager. During the spring of 2003, *Sports Illustrated* listed him No. 35 in a ranking of the most influential minorities in sports. A few weeks later, King's dominion grew significantly when he was named president of the Sixers.

King was a charter inductee in the Duke Basketball Hall of Honor in 2001.

Kistler, Doug. He never made the All-ACC team, but few could ignore Douglas Carr Kistler's influence on the Blue Devils' first major ACC accomplishment. In coach Vic Bubas's first campaign of 1960, Kistler became the first Duke player to be selected most valuable player of the ACC Tournament while leading the Blue Devils to the championship. As a lanky 6–9 junior forward, Kistler dropped 26 points on South Carolina in the opening game of the event, then helped the Devils avenge earlier losses to North Carolina and Wake Forest to claim the title. He scored 22 in the championship game. The crown carried with it an automatic bid to the NCAA tourney, and Kistler jump-started Duke's run to the national quarterfinals with another 26-point outburst in a first-round contest versus Princeton in New York. It was one of his best performances, featuring 9-of-10 shooting from the field and 20 points in the first half. He also had a team high of 20 points in an Elite Eight loss to NYU. Earlier in the year he had games of 23 and 22 points against Virginia and added 18 rebounds in one of those, the team's best board game of the year.

A native of Wayne, Pa., Kistler started all three of his varsity years, 1959–61, and scored 932 points with 756 rebounds in 81 games. He averaged 10.0 points and 9.0 rebounds as a sophomore and better than that in each of his succeeding years, putting to good use his blend of height, speed, and shooting acumen. Consistency was his calling card on the boards. He was one of the ACC's top 10 rebounders in all three years and ranked seventh in the league in field-goal percentage as a senior. The highest-scoring game of his career, 31 points against South Carolina in 1961, featured 15 field goals.

Kistler was a third-round NBA draft pick and played five games for New York in the 1962 season. He went on to become a successful high school basketball coach in North Carolina, directing Durham Jordan to a state championship, but tragically lost his life in a head-on collision with a drunk driver in 1980.

Kitching, Brent. Though he spent two years in the shadows of the future Duke Hall of Famers Art Heyman and Jeff Mullins, Brent Gordon Kitching, a 6 – 7 forward from Sharon Hills, Pa., appeared in 62 games during his three varsity campaigns, 1963 – 65, with 235 points and 103 rebounds. Duke won two ACC crowns and went to a pair of Final Fours. He saw action in the NCAA final with UCLA in 1964 and scored two points.

Knight, Bob. One of college basketball's winningest coaches in Division I, Robert M. Knight finished the 2006 season with 869 career victories, behind only Dean Smith (879) and Adolph Rupp (876) in the NCAA record book. Knight was the college coach, mentor, then Hall of Fame presenter for Duke's Mike Krzyzewski.

When Knight was the head coach at Army, Krzyzewski was his point guard from 1967 to 1969 and his captain as a senior. With his tough, demanding style, Knight helped develop Krzyzewski into a fierce defensive specialist and leader. He was also there with memorable compassion when Krzyzewski's father died suddenly during his senior year.

A few years later, in 1975 after leaving the service, Krzyzewski worked as a graduate assistant for Knight at Indiana, when the Hoosiers posted an undefeated regular season and finished 31 – 1. Krzyzewski then secured his first head coaching job, at Army (1976 – 80), before proceeding to Duke upon recommendations by Knight.

Krzyzewski was Knight's assistant coach at the Pan American Games in 1979, an event not without controversy. Knight was ejected during the opening game and had a much-chronicled confrontation with a policeman at a practice session on the team's path to the gold medal. Krzyzewski also worked as an Olympic Trials assistant for Knight in 1984 during the development of the USA team that went on to win gold in Los Angeles.

Krzyzewski has always acknowledged Knight's influence on his basketball career and life. The two have exhibited many of the same philosophies, preparation techniques, and game strategies, but it would be a mistake to consider Krzyzewski a coaching clone of Knight. "We're different personalities," Krzyzewski said in the early 1990s. "He likes to hunt and I like to go to the beach. He likes to fish and I like to eat fish. My only pet peeve is when somebody asks if I called him to find out what I should do." One thing the two have shared is long-term success. They were the two youngest coaches in Division I to reach 700 wins, and each has won three national titles, behind only John Wooden (10) and Rupp (4). The year before Knight won his third, he was in Dallas for Krzyzewski's first Final Four, spoke to the team, and supported the Blue Devils all weekend.

Krzyzewski and Knight coached against each other four times while Knight was at Indiana, all in tournaments, because neither would consider scheduling a regular-season meeting. Indiana beat Duke in the Sweet 16 in 1987 on the way to Knight's third national crown, while the Blue Devils topped the Hoosiers in the Final Four in 1992 on their way to Krzyzewski's second title. Their relationship became rocky at that time after Knight barely spoke to Krzyzewski during the post-game handshake and ignored him in the corridor outside the press room. They didn't speak for almost a year and reportedly had very little contact for the next few years. They met on the court again in November 1995 at the Great Alaska Shootout (Duke won) and in November 1996 at the Preseason NIT (Indiana won).

The two coaches haven't faced each other since Knight went to Texas Tech in 2002, but they shared a stage in 2001, when Krzyzewski asked Knight to be his presenter upon his induction at the Naismith Memorial Basketball Hall of Fame. Knight had been inducted in 1991.

Krzyzewski is not the only Duke figure to have been influenced by Knight. Bob Bender, former point guard and assistant coach, spent his freshman year on Knight's 1976 NCAA title team before transferring to Duke. "Coach Knight always stressed the importance of preparing yourself consistently," Bender said. "Not for an opponent, but to play to your potential. I took that from my experience at Indiana, and I've always still believed in it."

Kodak All-America. The oldest and most prestigious All-America honor in women's college basketball is the annual 10-player Kodak All-America team. Five Duke players have been named to the Kodak team: Michele VanGorp (1999), Georgia Schweitzer (2001), Alana Beard (2002, 2003, 2004), Iciss Tillis (2003), and Monique Currie (2005, 2006).

Koffenberger, Ed. The Second World War years were unlike any other period in school history for intercollegiate athletics, and the same could be said for the career of Edward Leroy Koffenberger. He not only attended both Duke and North Carolina, but he also played sports for both archrivals during the same year. He performed in three varsity sports as a Blue Devil and became an All-America in two, one of which he learned at UNC and perfected at Duke.

A 6–2 native of Wilmington, Del., Koffenberger joined the Navy V-12 program after his high school graduation and was dispatched to UNC for officer training. He played football for the Tar Heels during the fall of 1944 but was transferred to Duke when he asked about studying engineering. He finished the 1944 football season with Duke, then moved on to basketball and earned second-team All-Southern honors. In the following year he again played end for the football team before turning in a superb basketball campaign in which he scored 317 points, the most in school history to that point. He gave up football but continued to star on the hardwood, breaking his own scoring record with 416 points in 1947, his final season.

Koffenberger played in all 76 games and totaled 923 points for his three-year career, establishing the school's all-time scoring mark at the time. He was a team captain in 1946 and 1947 and was named to the Helms Foundation All-America team in both years.

Koffenberger became the first player in school history to score 30 points in a game, against Washington & Lee in his senior year. He enjoyed numerous other outstanding games, including one at Madison Square Garden in 1947 that Duke lost in double overtime to NYU. Koffenberger scored 17 points and had a driving layup plus a free throw with 10 seconds left to force the first OT. He also sent a game at UNC in 1946 into overtime, as Duke pulled off an upset to hand the Tar Heels their only league defeat. Later that season he was a major factor when Duke won the conference tournament. Koffenberger was the starting center for the first two sellouts at the Indoor Stadium, the UNC games of 1946 and 1947.

All the while, Koffenberger was emerging as a standout player in lacrosse, a sport that he never played in high school but picked up when he was at UNC. There was no varsity team at Duke in 1945 because of the war, so Koffenberger played for a club team. Varsity lacrosse returned in 1946 and Koffenberger played for his last two years, earning honorable mention All-America as a senior. The 1946 team pulled off one of the major upsets of the day when it whipped Maryland, a perennial power, 12–4 in its season opener.

Koffenberger won the Teague Award as the top amateur athlete in the Carolinas in 1947 and had an opportunity to play professional basketball. Instead he decided to put his engineering degree to use and went to work for DuPont, remaining with the company for 42 years before retiring. He was enshrined in the Duke Sports Hall of Fame in 1980 and was a charter inductee in the Duke Basketball Hall of Honor in 2001.

Kolodziej, Tim. Breaking into the regular lineup as a junior, Timothy Michael Kolodziej was a valuable frontcourt performer who contributed clutch shooting from the corners and savvy passing on the fast break. A 6–5 forward from Amsterdam, N.Y., Kolodziej played in only six games as a sophomore in 1966 before becoming a regular in 1967 and 1968. He totaled 60 appearances with 417 points and 230 rebounds. Duke played in one Final Four and two NITs during his career. Kolodziej led Duke in scoring in his final game, with 16 points against St. Peter's in the NIT in 1968. His career high of 19 points came twice in 1967, versus Virginia and N.C. State. As a senior he won the Ted Mann Jr. award as the reserve contributing most to team morale.

Koubek, Greg. The co-captain of Duke's 1991 NCAA championship team, Gregory Peter Koubek played in all but one game over his four seasons, 1988–91. But that one miss, on a visit to Oklahoma in his senior year, had him briefly contemplating an early end to his career during the Blue Devils' Christmas break. Koubek wasn't happy with how his final year had been progressing, but he stuck it out and made some significant contributions down the stretch. Most notable was a performance at Georgia Tech in which he dived for an offensive rebound in the waning seconds and flipped it to Bobby Hurley, who spotted Thomas Hill for the winning basket as the clock expired. It was an example of the hustle and desire that Koubek brought to the floor for four years.

A 6–6 native of Clifton Park, N.Y., Koubek played in 147 games and Duke won 116 of them. Only Christian Laettner played in more games and only five other players were involved in more wins. Usually a reserve, Koubek started 26 games, including the six NCAA tourney contests in his final year. Koubek became the first player in NCAA history to see action in four consecutive Final Fours. For his career he scored 717 points, with 364 rebounds and 104 assists. He was a 42.6 percent shooter and hit 80 three-pointers.

Koubek earned one start in his sophomore year and marked the occasion with 19 points against Harvard. He got a chance to start several games during his junior year when Robert Brickey was injured, and in the first game of that stretch he had one of his best efforts, with 16 points and nine rebounds at Georgia Tech. He also sent the Michigan game that year into overtime with a basket at the buzzer.

Along with his heroics against Tech in 1991, Koubek delivered a game-sealing jumper against UNC at Cameron and had a career high of 21 against the Tar Heels in Chapel Hill, where his free throw with 17 seconds left sealed a victory. Koubek notched 18 points versus UConn in the Sweet 16 of the NCAA tourney. In the championship game against Kansas he scored just five points — but they were the first five points, to get the Devils off to a winning start.

Kramer, Pete. A 6–4 forward from Camp Hill, Pa., and a frequent starter throughout his three varsity seasons, 1973–75, Peter Joseph Kramer scored 786 points with 253 rebounds and 117 assists in 76 games. After a solid sophomore season he was named the reserve contributing most to team morale. Down the stretch of his junior season he averaged almost 13 points in the last 13 games as one of the team's most consistent offensive performers. He had a season high of 20 against Georgia Tech and 15 against UNC before the Tar Heels rallied for an overtime win. Kramer's best season was in 1975 under new coach Bill Foster, when he was the team's second-leading scorer at 15.1 a game. He was in double figures in all but five games that year, with highs of 27 versus N.C. State, 26 versus South Florida, and 24 versus LSU. He was the No. 10 scorer and No. 6 free-throw shooter in the league.

Krause, Barb. The first rebounding standout in Duke women's basketball history, Krause, a 5–10 forward from Freeport, Maine, played for three years for the Blue Devils, 1979–81, and led the club on the boards every season. Krause had 732 rebounds in 74 games for an average of 9.9, the second-best figure in the Duke record book and the sixth-best all-time average in ACC history.

Krause attended Bowdoin College in her home state as a freshman, then became the first transfer in program history. She made an immediate impact on the Blue Devils, leading the ACC in rebounding with a 10.7 average in her first season. She also posted the top two board games in school history that year, with 24 against Catawba and 23 against Georgia Tech. No one else at Duke before or since has had more than 20 in a game, and her top two figures remain among the top four in ACC women's basketball history. (Krause's 24 against Catawba are the second-best ever by an ACC player, her 23 against Tech the best ever in an ACC game.)

Krause also led Duke in scoring in her first two years and finished just a point behind team leader Stacy Hurd in her senior year. She came up just short of the 1,000-point club with 998, for a career average of 13.5 a game. She hit almost 54 percent of her field goals and led the ACC in free-throw shooting as a senior at 80.4 percent.

Krause played before the NCAA era, when women's basketball was governed by the AIAW. She made its all-state team for North Carolina in her senior year.

Krzyzewski, Mike. The silver anniversary coaching season of 2005 was widely proclaimed the best of Mike Krzyzewski's career. Faced with unforeseen off-season personnel losses and a series of in-season physical casualties, Krzyzewski was constantly forced to reinvent a team lacking in depth, yet still it produced exceptional results: 27 victories, a sixth ACC championship in seven years, and a No. 1 seeding in the NCAA Tournament for the seventh time in eight years. Krzyzewski described the campaign as unique, pointing to the heart and character that the Blue Devils displayed daily as well as to the toughness forged within his unit as a result of adapting to excessive injuries.

But in reality, there were far too many superlative coaching efforts in Krzyzewski's first quarter-century as the leader of Duke basketball to rank any one of them as his best. Equally compelling cases could be made for the jobs he did in 1987, 2000, and 2003, when he molded Sweet 16 teams from young squads that had to replace several veterans from the previous year. Or 1990, when he guided a disjointed, 15th-ranked contingent to the national championship game. Or 1991, when his team conquered undefeated UNLV at the Final Four and beat Kansas for its first NCAA crown. Or 1992, when the Blue Devils wore a No. 1 target on their backs from beginning to end in claiming a second straight NCAA title. And then there was 2001, when he totally overhauled his team in the final week of the regular season, just in time for its march to a third national championship.

With 10 Final Fours, three NCAA titles, 10 ACC Tournament championships, and over 700 victories to his credit, Michael William Krzyzewski stands not only as Duke's most accomplished coach but as one of the handful of élite coaches in college basketball history. John Wooden and Adolph Rupp are the only two to win more national championships. Wooden and Dean Smith are the only two to reach more Final Fours. Bob Knight was the only one to win 700 games at a younger age. No one has won more NCAA Tournament games than Krzyzewski, and no one has come close to his conference superiority in winning five straight ACC tourneys or reaching the league final for nine consecutive years.

Duke fielded successful basketball teams before Krzyzewski's arrival and owns a distinguished tradition replete with outstanding players, coaches, and seasons, but it was thoroughly appropriate that Krzyzewski should have been the first person affiliated with the university to be inducted into the Naismith Memorial Basketball Hall of Fame, a ceremony held in 2001 just before the start of his 22nd season.

Born in Chicago on February 13, 1947, Krzyzewski acquired from his parents the work ethic and many of the values that have shaped his life. His father was

In 2005 Mike Krzyzewski became the all-time leader in NCAA Tournament coaching victories.

an elevator operator of Polish background who had to change his name to Kross so that he could get a job, and his mother scrubbed floors at the Chicago Athletic Club. After graduating from Weber High School, Krzyzewski enrolled at the U.S. Military Academy in West Point to play basketball for Knight. He was Knight's point guard for three years and team captain as a senior in 1969, when he helped the Cadets reach the NIT. It was under Knight's tutelage that the principles of man-to-man defense became ingrained in Krzyzewski.

After his service commitment ended, Krzyzewski was hired by Knight as a graduate assistant coach at Indiana for one season, 1975, then as the head coach at Army on Knight's recommendation. Krzyzewski served his alma mater for five years, 1976–80, compiling a record of 73–59 with one trip to the NIT. Based on another recommendation from Knight, plus the prodding of associate athletics director Steve Vacendak and his own gut instincts, former Duke athletics director Tom But-ters appointed Krzyzewski to guide the Blue Devils after Bill Foster departed for South Carolina in the spring of 1980. It was considered a daring and startling move for a program that had been to three straight NCAAs and won two of the previous three ACC titles.

Krzyzewski coached Foster's players to the NIT in 1981, but overall his early Duke years were a struggle, as he labored to implant his defensive principles and re-cruit the talent needed to compete in the ACC without the benefit of credibility or a proven record. He missed out on several quality recruits in his second year and needed a triple overtime win over Clemson in the last home game just to reach 10 victories. His third team was buoyed by an influx of talent, but it hit a nadir with a home loss to Wagner and a humiliating 109–66 defeat to Virginia in the ACC Tournament. This at a time when Duke's local rivals were winning back-to-back NCAA titles — UNC in 1982, N.C. State in 1983.

The amelioration of Duke basketball under Krzyz-ewski began in 1984. Entering the season, Krzyzewski's four previous teams had gone 9–17 (at Army), 17–13, 10–17, and 11–17, and there were grumblings within the fan base that Butters's decision was not at all pre-scient. It was especially annoying to many that the coach refused to back off from his man-to-man defense in favor of an occasional zone to hide some of the inad-equacies on the roster. But Krzyzewski stayed true to his plan, and in 1984 everything changed. He brought in his first true point guard — and one of his best — in Tommy Amaker and put the ball in his capable hands from day one. He added Pete Gaudet to his staff and benefited im-mediately from the presence of an older, more experi-enced coach. He stood up to the public perception that the ACC belonged to UNC and coach Dean Smith, and decried a "double standard" in the league. Butters saw enough progress by midseason to award Krzyzewski a significant contract renewal. Nearly every one of Duke's ACC contests was excruciating that year, with over half decided by one possession and 12 of the 14 by six points or fewer. Krzyzewski proved his mettle by directing his sophomore-laden squad to a break-even mark in the regular season and capped it with one of his most pivotal victories when the Devils upset No. 1 UNC in the tourna-ment semifinals. Overall Duke won 24 games, played in

its first ACC final, and advanced to its first NCAA under Krzyzewski. There was no looking back.

Duke's 1984 sophomores were the seniors in 1986 for Krzyzewski's national breakthrough season: a 37–3 record, ACC championship, No. 1 ranking, Final Four. Louisville stopped Duke in the NCAA final, but the Blue Devils captured the fancy of basketball fans across the country with their articulate players, obvious team chemistry, and rising young coach. It was during the ensuing decade that Krzyzewski cemented his stature as one of the greats in the game. In the nine years from 1986 through 1994 the Blue Devils went to seven Final Fours, a Wooden-like run during an era of parity. Duke played in the national championship game in five of those nine years, winning two and coming agonizingly close in two others. Midway through the run Krzyzewski picked up a tag from some in the media as a coach who couldn't win the big one, but he kept delivering big-game results, such as upsets of Temple, Georgetown, and Connecti-cut in consecutive NCAA regional finals, a domination of higher-ranked Arkansas in the semifinals in 1990, a 79–77 conquest of seemingly invincible UNLV in the semis in 1991, and a miraculous overtime finish against Kentucky in 1992 to get his team to the Final Four for the chance to repeat the title.

With television coverage of college basketball growing to a saturation point during the decade, a visible Duke became one of the programs that young players grew up dreaming about — a considerable recruiting factor a decade later. But the national titles and successive Final Fours also took a physical toll on Krzyzewski, who coached in the 1992 Olympics and emerged as a leading figure on nearly every issue for the National Association of Basketball Coaches. He underwent back surgery in the fall of 1994, tried to return to the court too soon, and eventually had to miss most of the 1995 season because of his back and the exhaustion from spreading himself too thin for a period of several years. Duke struggled to a record of 13–18 in 1995, including 4–15 in games without Krzyzewski and 2–14 in the ACC, good for last place.

Armed with a renewed perspective, the coach recon-structed his program over the next few seasons. By 1998 Duke was back at No. 1 with a record of 32–4 overall and 15–1 in the ACC. In 1999 it won 37 games, returned to the Final Four, and won the first of five straight ACC titles. From 1999 through 2002 it also finished No. 1 in the final national poll four times and won a third NCAA crown. In 2004 the Devils played in the Final Four for a 10th time under Krzyzewski. The coach finished his 26th year in 2006 with a record of 680–191 for Duke and 753–250 overall.

Among the many pillars undergirding Krzyzewski's legendary career are his abilities to recruit and motivate, and both of these stem from the emphasis that he places on developing personal relationships with his players. Those relationships are formed during the recruiting process. "He was just naturally likable," noted Danny Ferry, two-time ACC athlete of the year. "I think a big reason why was a warmth and a sense of humor, which was kind of surprising. And you just trust him. You know what he is saying is how he feels, and his word is his bond. Those are great things to be able to look at when you are looking at schools and you are meeting coaches.

"He has a great ability to make you feel good about yourself, to make you feel confident about yourself," Ferry added. "Being around a person like that in the recruitment process, you want to see him. When you're playing, you want to be around him. How he treats you, the way he crafts what he says to you, is really uplifting and you want to be around that."

Because of the open communication, honesty, and trust that those relationships are based on, Krzyzewski's gifts as a motivator can take root in fertile territory. Players understand that his methods, strategies, teaching points, and exhortations are aimed at growth and dedicated to the team-building concept of creating an entity bigger than any of the individuals involved.

"So many people think coaching is about X's and O's and substitutions, but coaching is about building trust with a group, building relationships," said former player and assistant coach Chris Collins. "So when you get to an NCAA Tournament and it's a tie game with 10 minutes to go, or you're losing to a 16 seed in the first half, and people are a little rattled, you have that trust, you have that base where we're going to get this done.

"Coach K does an amazing job of spending time with our guys on an individual basis, getting to know our guys. He coaches every player differently. Some guys you

have to yell at to get them jump-started. Some guys you have to hug them more and be more positive. He tries to really do his best to get the most out of our guys for the best of the unit."

"Everybody gets motivated in different ways and his understanding of that was very impressive," said former guard Trajan Langdon. "He would push different buttons with me than he would with Wojo [teammate Steve Wojciechowski]. He would get on me in different ways because he knew that would motivate me differently. Day in and day out, game in and game out, no matter who we were playing, we were ready to go. I think that's the most inspiring thing about Coach K to me—his ability to motivate, not only himself but the team."

One of Krzyzewski's pet phrases within the team is "next play," the notion of continuing to move forward during a game and a season rather than dwell on a particular success or failure. His career is rife with instances of teams progressing to the next play with spectacular results, from the way it dealt with injuries to Billy King (1987) and Robert Brickey (1990) in his first decade, to losses of Bobby Hurley and then Grant Hill on the way to the NCAA title in 1992, to playing most of the 1998 season without Elton Brand and the 1999 ACC tourney without Langdon. Krzyzewski may have been incensed with senior Chris Carrawell for eschewing explicit instructions in the closing seconds of a one-point loss to St. John's in 2000, but he moved on quickly; a few days later he was at his passionate best in talking with his players about how important it was for them to win the final home game for Carrawell.

But "next play" was never illustrated more graphically than at the end of 2001, when a broken foot suffered by Carlos Boozer during the last week of the regular season led to an extreme makeover that catapulted a believing bunch of Blue Devils to a national title. Perhaps that approach works so well for Krzyzewski because he remains grounded in reality instead of expectation and perception. He has never forgotten what it was like to post an 11–17 season and end it with a 43-point loss in the ACC Tournament.

Despite his sterling record, Krzyzewski has endured his share of detractors. Some say that he works game referees to excess, while others criticize his use of profane language. He was roundly condemned for a locker-room incident with student reporters that was laced with invectives. There were cynics in 2005 who suggested that he was so manipulative as to feign a dizzy spell during a game in an attempt to influence officials' calls. There is no doubt that Krzyzewski can be demanding to play for, but he doesn't drive anyone harder than he drives himself, which is why he is second to no one in game preparation and motivation. Physically, he has had to deal with back surgery and two hip replacements. Emotionally and pragmatically, he has had to adjust to changing times in which some of his best talents have departed the fold prematurely for pro careers. In a "Sports Century" program on ESPN Classic, Krzyzewski's daughter Lindy suggested that her father felt betrayed when his players left college early, but that hasn't prevented him from totally investing in his players' careers or helping them in any way after they've moved on.

From humble origins, Krzyzewski has grown into more than a basketball coach. In addition to teaching and leading his players, he has become one of the university's most valuable assets and its most recognizable figure — as a philanthropist for university scholarships, fund raiser to endow his own program, long-standing supporter of the Duke Children's Hospital, prominent ambassador for the school's academic and athletic missions, and even faculty member for the Fuqua School of Business. Duke president Nan Keohane presented him with the school's highest honor in 1997, the University Medal, and her successor Richard Brodhead was not attempting to be humorous with his reaction to the Los Angeles Lakers' courtship of Krzyzewski during his first week on the job in 2004: "To become known as the person who lost Coach K on your first day would be a dubious fame."

Krzyzewski has been ACC coach of the year five times and national coach of the year eight times, and has posted more 30-win seasons (nine) than any other coach in history. His team has been ranked No. 1 in 13 seasons, had 35 NBA draft picks, and graduated over 90 percent of its players while filling the rafters of Cameron Indoor Stadium with championship banners. Krzyzewski's world is one of never-ending high expectations and close scrutiny, not to mention envy — to the point that he was criticized in some circles for appearing in a ubiquitous American Express television commercial in 2005 that touted teaching and leadership.

"It's great to be away from Duke now and appreciate what he has done and what he continues to do," said Shane Battier, one of his consummate pupils and national player of the year in 2001. "When you are there you sort of take him for granted. You expect him to win 30 games every year, you expect him to graduate all his players and you expect him to do the right thing. When you get to the world outside of Duke, you realize that very few individuals can do it, and nobody does it better than Coach. I respect him even more since I left the program."

During the fall of 2005, Krzyzewski was appointed to a three-year term as the first head coach of a new USA Basketball national team program aimed at returning the United States to global basketball supremacy. His primary charge was to coach his country at the FIBA World Championship in 2006 and the 2008 Olympics.

See also Butters, Tom; Coaches' contracts; Coach K Court; Foreign tours; K Academy; K Lab; Knight, Bob; Krzyzewskiville; Naismith Memorial Basketball Hall of Fame; Quotations; Shoe deals; USA Basketball; Steve Vacendak; and entries on several of Krzyzewski's players, assistant coaches, and opponents.

Krzyzewskiville. Admission of undergraduate students to Duke basketball games has traditionally been first-come, first-served. No lottery system, no tickets, just a line forming at the door to the arena and the required presentation of a valid ID card. Once inside, students are free to fill any of the vacant bleacher seats that ring the court.

Krzyzewskiville, also known as K-ville, is the area outside Cameron Indoor Stadium where students wait their turn to enter. A few students had occasionally slept outside the gym to claim spots at the front of the line before Mike Krzyzewski arrived at Duke in 1980–81. But during the 1986 season the practice got a noticeable boost when a handful of undergrads erected tents a couple of nights before the finale with UNC, allegedly after playing several rounds of a college drinking game. Others joined in, and a tradition was born.

Initially most people referred to the area as Tent City, but at some point the students put up a hand-made sign calling it Krzyzewskiville and listing the tent population, which they kept crossing out in favor of a bigger one as more students set up camp.

With power and Internet access available, Duke students can keep up with their studies while camping in Krzyzewskiville outside Cameron Indoor Stadium.

Over the years, the impromptu village has become increasingly structured, with rules governing how many students can be in one tent and how long they must be there to reserve a spot, and with line monitors appointed to oversee the entire operation. This "tenting" operation is generally used to determine a place in line for two home games a year: North Carolina and one other. It has become common for hard-core student enthusiasts to put up their tents over the Christmas break, even before the spring semester begins.

Some of the creativity for which the fans are known inside the arena has been on display in Krzyzewskiville.

The tents are numbered, and many students will add a name to honor a Duke player. During Dahntay Jones's senior year, tent No. 30 (his jersey number) was labeled "Dahntay's Inferno." One year, a tent near the front of the line was called the Waldorf Hysteria. University concessions personnel occasionally provide food to the masses, and Krzyzewski has been known to have pizzas delivered. When Duke landscaped the whole plaza area outside the gym, Internet ports were added to the light poles so that students could use their laptop computers more effectively while tenting. The upgrade was financed by a contribution from a former sports editor at the *Chronicle*, Jeff Gendell.

The most noteworthy event connected with Krzyzewskiville takes place the night before the annual UNC home game, when the head coach gathers all the campers to thank them for their commitment and talk with them about his team and the game, usually sharing some piece of strategy or insight. In 2001, for example, he told them how important they were as the team's sixth man, explained some of his team-building strategies, and even wore the same "Sixth Man" T-shirt as many of the students. And he told them he would have it on under his suit during the game the next night.

Kuhlmeier, Ray. Guard Raymond John Kuhlmeier Jr., of Aurora, Ind., was a three-year backup, 1968–70. He played in 29 games, with 91 points and 30 rebounds. A 6–2 engineering student who won conference championships in four sports during high school, he fittingly had his career high of 10 points in his final home game, helping the Blue Devils to upset 19th-ranked North Carolina 91–83 in 1970.

Kulpan, Jim. Contributing at forward and center, James N. Kulpan, a 6–6 player from Norfolk, Va., lettered for the 1950 and 1951 teams, with each reaching the championship game of the Southern Conference Tournament. Kulpan scored 227 points in 58 games.

Kunkle, Charlie. Forward Charles Kunkle, a 6–2 native of Johnstown, Pa., lettered for three seasons, 1934–36. After a broken hand ended his sophomore season, he was in the starting lineup for his last two. Kunkle was the leading scorer for the 1935 team and the captain of the 1936 team. Duke posted a 56–20 record during his

career. Kunkle's basket in the last seven seconds was the difference in a 35–34 win over Davidson in 1935.

Lacy, Rudy. Though not a consistent starter, Clayton Rudolph Lacy played a prominent role for the three seasons in which he lettered, 1952–54. He appeared in 70 games, with 448 points and 264 rebounds, while serving as a co-captain in his junior year of 1953. A 6–4 frontliner from Union City, N.J., Lacy had his career high of 20 points against Wake Forest in 1953, appropriate perhaps because five of his 17 double-figure scoring games came against the Deacons. Another of those was a 14-point effort in the 1954 campaign to help the Devils knock off the Deacs in the Dixie Classic semifinals on the way to their only title in that event. Lacy's best individual stretch was at the start of the 1953 campaign, when he had 77 points in the first five contests.

Laettner, Christian. In 2002 the *Sporting News* enlisted senior writer Mike DeCourcy to select and rank the top 100 players in the history of college basketball for its book *Legends of College Basketball*. The list began with Lew Alcindor, Bill Walton, Oscar Robertson, Bill Russell, Pete Maravich, David Thompson, Elvin Hayes, and Larry Bird, Hall of Famers all. Then, at No. 9, came Christian Laettner, the first representative from the 1980s and beyond. Only a handful of choices in the book were accompanied by the rationale behind the ranking, and one was Laettner. Why was he so high on the chart? "Although Christian Laettner did not achieve the same pro stardom as many at the top of the list," *TSN* explained, "he was the greatest player in the history of the NCAA Tournament and the college game's best pressure player."

If the greatest players in Duke and ACC history were similarly rated, Laettner undoubtedly would find himself at or very near the top of the poll, much as the Blue Devils were throughout his four-year reign, 1989–92. And the primary reasons would mirror DeCourcy's logic. Laettner was the supreme clutch performer, and he won games when they mattered most. He started for four Final Four teams—the only person ever to do that—and played 23 NCAA Tournament games, one shy of the maximum possible. Duke lost in the semifinals in his fresh-

One of Duke's most competitive players ever, Christian Laettner scored more NCAA Tournament points (407) than any other player in college basketball history.

And some of Laettner's NCAA points remain among the most memorable in event history: The shot to beat Kentucky in 1992, of course, capping a perfect shooting night; his free throws with 12.7 seconds left to give Duke its remarkable win over unbeaten UNLV in the semis in 1991; and the last-second game-winner when the Devils edged UConn in the regional final in 1990. In fact, Laettner's performance in NCAA regional championship games could not have been better. He missed only three field goals and three free throws in four appearances, two of which he won in overtime.

Overall Christian Donald Laettner played in 148 games, a Duke record, and started 128. The team was 122–26 with him on the court (21–2 in the NCAA tourney). So it's easy to see why practically every coach and player who was with him in Durham would list winning games as his best attribute. (In the only game that Laettner missed, the opener of his senior year, the Devils won handily over East Carolina.) Laettner totaled 2,460 points for a 16.6 average and added 1,149 rebounds for a 7.8 average. Both the scoring and rebounding totals ranked second in Duke history at the time. Laettner hit 57.4 percent of his career field goals, a figure that stood fourth in school history. It bears pointing out that he attempted 1,452 shots in his career, while almost everyone else on the top 10 list of percentages took fewer than 1,000.

A 6–11 native of Angola, N.Y., Laettner took many of his shots in that high-percentage territory around the basket, but he also made and attempted more free throws than anyone in Duke history, and he hit 48.5 percent from three-point range. That ranked as the top percentage in the Duke record book for anyone with at least 75 made threes (he made 79 of 163, significantly fewer than the No. 2 long-range shooter, Trajan Langdon, who hit 42.6 percent of 802 attempts). By any measure, Laettner

man year, then played for the title in each of the next three seasons and won two. Laettner scored 407 points during his NCAA tenure, an all-time record. It is a standard that will be difficult to surpass given the transient nature of modern college careers. Since Laettner graduated, only one player has even topped 300 NCAA points: Corliss Williamson of Arkansas (303, 1993–95).

Christian Laettner's Record in NCAA Regional Championship Games

Year	Region Final	Field Goals	Free Throws	Points	Result
1989	Georgetown	9–10	6–7	24	85–77
1990	Connecticut (OT)	7–8	9–11	23	79–78
1991	St. John's	5–6	9–9	19	78–61
1992	Kentucky (OT)	10–10	10–10	31	104–103
Totals		31–34	34–37	97	4–0

The Shots He'll Never Forget

Christian Laettner, 1992 versus Kentucky

Undoubtedly the most famous shot in Duke basketball history was turned in by Laettner to give the Blue Devils a 104–103 overtime victory over Kentucky in the 1992 NCAA regional final at Philadelphia. With 2.1 seconds left, Grant Hill threw the long baseball pass to Laettner, who made the catch, the move, and the 17-foot turnaround jumper to enter the history books.

That was one of many critical shots by Laettner, Duke's ultimate clutch player. He sent Duke to the Final Four in 1990 with a buzzer-beater against UConn, and he helped the Devils win the UNLV semifinal in 1991 by hitting a pair of free throws with 12.7 seconds on the clock, after the Rebels tried to ice him with a timeout. Those were just a few of his memorable moments.

"The best thing I can say about going to Duke and playing there is that you know you are going to be involved in a lot of games like that," Laettner said. "I didn't want to end my career and say I just remembered one game. You do that if you go to a lesser school. I came to Duke because I wanted to have millions of memories like that, and I did, from my freshman year all the way to my senior year."

was an exceptional shooter. As a sophomore he led the ACC in free-throw shooting, as a junior he topped the conference in field-goal percentage, and as a senior he ranked first in three-point shooting with 55.7 percent, a league record.

Laettner's most significant honors included national player of the year in 1992, All-America three times, ACC All-Tournament team four times (there's that clutch characteristic again), ACC athlete of the year twice, Final Four MVP in 1991, NCAA East Regional MVP in 1990 and 1992, ACC player of the year in 1992, and co-MVP of the team three times. He was an obvious choice for the ACC's 50th anniversary basketball team and was one of six Blue Devils on the conference's list of its best 50 athletes from all sports.

Laettner recorded his career high of 37 points against UNC Charlotte in 1991. His top rebounding mark of 19 was against Virginia in 1990. He had five 30-point

games in his senior year, including 32 versus Virginia the night his jersey No. 32 was retired, and a mammoth performance with 33 points and 16 rebounds against Maryland in the ACC tourney. His 31 against Kentucky marked his NCAA high. He had 28 in the win over UNLV and scored 15, 18, and 19 in his three NCAA finals. In 1991 and 1992 he outdueled Shaquille O'Neal to lead the Blue Devils to impressive wins over LSU.

Laettner played with an intense competitive fire and an arrogant confidence that bothered opponents, fans, and sometimes teammates. He did not hesitate to say whatever was necessary behind closed doors to draw the best out of his team. He also appreciated the rare occasions when others did that to him, such as at halftime of the NCAA final in 1992. Duke found itself trailing Michigan at the break and Laettner had seven turnovers with only two baskets while dealing with the Wolverines' double- and triple-teaming defense. After pointed comments from his coach and a couple of teammates, he scored twice in the first 45 seconds of the second half, and Duke went ahead to stay.

Few players in Duke history have been the subject of as much scrutiny as Laettner, by fans and media alike. His matinee-idol handsomeness made him a favorite of many, but he was also a virtual lightning rod for controversy and attention during his last two years, and the verbal abuse that he received in some road arenas, notably at LSU, was unmerciful. When Laettner stepped on a fallen Kentucky player in the 1992 regionals, and received a technical foul but no ejection, the issue raged on into Final Four week. After the championship was won that year, a North Carolina newspaper created national headlines with a story that said Laettner might have violated NCAA rules for agreeing to keep a diary for *GQ* magazine. In reality, the project had received prior approval, but where coverage of Laettner was concerned, the facts were sometimes not permitted to get in the way of a sensational story.

After his senior season Laettner, the unanimous national player of the year, was the only collegian added to a team of NBA legends headed for the 1992 Summer Olympics. Laettner came off the bench for spot minutes in all eight games in Barcelona and scored 38 points with 20 rebounds to earn a gold medal. He was the third pick in the NBA draft, behind O'Neal and Alonzo Mourning, and made the league's all-rookie team in 1993. That was one of his best seasons, with 18.2 points and 8.7 rebounds in 81 starts.

Laettner averaged 16.6 points over his first six seasons in the pros (for Minnesota and Atlanta) and made the All-Star Game in 1997, when he started every contest and had 18.1 points plus 8.8 rebounds for the Hawks. He missed most of the 1999 season with an achilles injury suffered during an off-season pickup game at Duke during the NBA lockout. But he rebounded to start every game in 2000 for the Detroit Pistons and averaged 12.2 points. That was his last year as a consistent double-figures scorer, though he continued to start or play quality reserve minutes in subsequent years for the Washington Wizards.

The 2005 season was Laettner's 13th year, with his sixth team (Miami). He had career totals of over 11,000 points in 868 regular-season contests and had appeared in 45 playoff games. His scoring high in the NBA was the same as in college, 37 points, against Chicago in 1997.

Laettner donated $1 million to his high school in New York in 2000 and always remained close to the Duke program, returning for alumni games, reunions, off-season training, and the K Academy. He also maintained business interests in Durham as a partner with his former roommate Brian Davis in Blue Devil Ventures, a commercial property development firm. In 2005 he and Davis donated $2 million to the Duke Basketball Legacy Fund to endow a scholarship and help build a training and academic center adjacent to Cameron.

Lakata, Bob. After leading the junior varsity in rebounding in 1954, John Robert Lakata embarked on a varsity career that saw him play in 68 games over three seasons. A 6–7 product of Johnson City, N.Y., he scored 431 points with 394 rebounds as a front-court regular in the 1955, 1956, and 1958 campaigns. He was not in school in 1957. Statistically Lakata's best year was 1956, when he averaged 7.8 points and 7.2 rebounds. He had a 20-point game against South Carolina early that season, which proved to be his career high. His high in rebounding was 23 against Temple in 1955.

Lamley, Herky. After leading the freshman team in scoring in 1952, Howard Foote Lamley had a two-year

varsity experience in which he played in 47 games with 246 points and 212 rebounds. A 6–5 forward and rugged rebounder from Haverton, Pa., he lettered as a reserve in 1953, did not play in 1954, and then returned to see action in all 28 contests of 1955.

Lang, Antonio. "Had Tony Lang not cut his fingernails that day, we might have won a third national championship," former All-America Grant Hill recalled a decade after the conclusion of his Blue Devil career. Hill was talking about the NCAA title game matching Duke and Arkansas in 1994. The Razorbacks secured a 76–72 win when Scotty Thurman's jumper in the closing minute beat the shot clock and just missed grazing the fingertips at the end of Lang's extended right arm.

That was the final game of a highlight-reel career for classmates Lang, Hill, and Marty Clark. Antonio Maurice Lang had been the final signee of the original five-

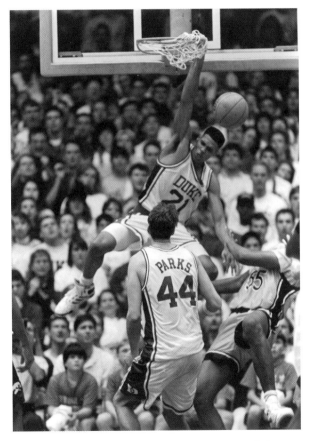

Tony Lang helped Duke to win two NCAA crowns and almost 84 percent of its games over four years.

player class in the spring of 1990. By graduation day, he and his mates stood as the winningest class in school history, with a record of 118 wins and 23 losses for a success rate of 83.7 percent. They had played in three national championship games with two titles, winning three ACC regular-season crowns and one ACC Tournament.

Lang was no small contributor to those efforts. A 6 – 8 forward from Mobile, Ala., he competed in 135 games with 1,012 points and 586 rebounds. He was an occasional starter during his first two seasons, 1991 and 1992, and a regular starter for his last two, with a career total of 87 starts. His final season was his best, when he averaged 12.5 points and 5.4 rebounds as a co-captain while making the All-ACC third team and the All – Final Four team. He also received the team's Dr. Deryl Hart award as the top scholar athlete that year.

Lang was blessed with talent but found a place on the floor mostly because he always put his heart on the line. That became obvious in his freshman year when he suffered a head injury against North Carolina that required 10 stitches but still returned to the floor to play the second half. As a sophomore Lang had settled into the role of key bench contributor for the 1992 powerhouse team, but he was always ready. When Bobby Hurley suffered an injury in midyear, Lang was in the starting lineup for Duke's next game against LSU and Shaquille O'Neal. He had 12 points, five rebounds, and three assists in an impressive road win and never came out of the lineup for the rest of the year. Or the rest of his career, for that matter. He started the final 18 games of the 1992 season, all but four in 1993, and every game in 1994. Only a hairline fracture of his sinus cavity knocked him out of the lineup in 1993.

Lang's highlights were many. There was a go-ahead slam dunk in the closing seconds against Maryland in 1992 and a player-of-the-game performance with 16 points against Seton Hall in the NCAAs, the game preceding the epic contest against Kentucky. There was his overtime spark against Oklahoma in 1993, when he helped save a game in which Duke had blown a 20-point lead, as well as a ferocious dunk in a win over Iowa. Against North Carolina that year he hauled in a pass from Hurley and delivered a fast-break dunk that ignited a decisive run in which his team scored on its last 11 possessions. In 1994, when he and Hill were the glue

for an evolving squad, there was his career-best of 26 points against Florida State, followed by his team-leading efforts against Temple on the day classmate Hill had his jersey retired, his 19 points in the NCAA regional final against Purdue, and his solid play in the Final Four that had Duke within a fingernail of hoisting a third trophy.

Lang was a second-round draft pick of the Phoenix Suns and played parts of six seasons in the NBA, 1995 – 2000. His most productive years were 1996 and 1997, when he appeared in 105 games for Cleveland.

Langdon, Trajan. Before J. J. Redick came along to create debate, Trajan Shaka Langdon was regarded as perhaps the best pure perimeter shooter in modern Duke history. He had taken and made more three-pointers than any other Blue Devil and also ranked first in career free-throw percentage. Late in his senior year of 1999, after one of his deadly shooting exhibitions had conquered another opponent, Mike Krzyzewski said, "He is the best shooter I have ever had. He doesn't take many shots to score his points. He is an incredibly efficient shooter and releases quickly. Some of his shots are made before he gets the ball because he has beaten his man. He works hard when he doesn't have the ball so he gets good looks."

Langdon, 6 – 3, was a rarity on several fronts in addition to his shooting capabilities. He was Duke's first recruit from Alaska, an Anchorage native who was revered across his home state. His undergraduate career spanned five seasons, as he missed one year because of injury. He was the first Krzyzewski player, and only the fifth in Duke history, to earn All-ACC first-team honors three times. In many ways he was the quintessential Blue Devil basketball hero: an all-star player, the prototypical team leader from his freshman year on, and an exceptional student who twice won the team's Dr. Deryl Hart award as its best scholar.

Though he was a top recruit after leading his prep team to three state titles, Langdon came to Duke as a non-scholarship walk-on player. The San Diego Padres signed him to a professional baseball contract that covered his college education for four years in exchange for his agreeing to play a certain number of days each summer in the team's minor-league system. His baseball career didn't take off, but his basketball career saw

At the free-throw line and the three-point arc, Trajan Langdon was one of the most accurate shooters in ACC history.

him play in 136 games from 1995 through 1999, with 129 starts. He scored 1,974 points for a 14.5 average, and added 389 rebounds with 255 assists. From three-point range he hit 342 of 802 attempts for 42.6 percent, and he made 86.2 percent of his 448 free throws. He averaged just under 29 minutes a game and scored in double figures in each of his four active seasons. In 1997 he led the ACC in free-throw percentage with 89.7, and in 1999 he topped the league in three-point shooting at 44.1 percent.

Langdon found a home in the starting lineup in his freshman year, but Duke suffered through a 13 – 18 season with Krzyzewski absent for health reasons. After the season, Langdon played for USA Basketball at the Junior World Championships and saw action in every game despite a sprained ankle. Then he reported for pro baseball duty to the Idaho Falls Braves and hit his first home run, but he developed an injury in his left leg while overcompensating for his ankle problem. He was unable to play in a single basketball game in 1996, including the Great Alaska Shootout, which Duke entered for the first time

ever because of Langdon's connection. He watched from the bench as the Blue Devils won it. Duke medics labeled Langdon's injury a stress reaction and it led to two surgeries in Los Angeles to repair cartilage damage, plus over a month on crutches.

Langdon returned in 1997 with uncommon hunger after his two seasons of adversity. He led Duke in scoring, tied the old school record for three-pointers with seven against UNC, and poured in his career high of 34 points against Clemson, the highest-scoring game by an ACC player in a conference game that year. In 1998, as one of the team captains, he finished second in scoring to senior Roshown McLeod and matched his career high with 34 points in a rout of UCLA, hitting 11 of 16 from the field. The team enjoyed a 32 – 4 season, its first 30-win campaign since 1992. Afterward, with NBA players unavailable because of a labor dispute, Langdon was named to the USA team that took a bronze medal at the FIBA World Championship.

Langdon's best collegiate year was his last one in 1999, when he again placed second on the team in scoring, this time with a 17.3 average that trailed national player of the year Elton Brand at 17.7. The two were chosen co-MVPs. Duke returned to the Great Alaska Shootout to start the year, and Langdon was practically worshipped by the locals, his every move closely scrutinized. Unfortunately, Duke was clipped by Cincinnati at the buzzer in the final game, denying the native son a title in the event he had always watched as a youngster. But he and his team recovered to turn in one of the most impressive campaigns in school history, not losing another game until the NCAA final. Late in the season, Langdon had a new perspective on that early adversity.

"People kept telling me that injuries and different things happen for a reason," he said. "I can look at it now and say, although it was very difficult then, I am very happy that I am able to be a senior captain on this unbelievable team."

Langdon earned second-team All-America honors and charted his third straight All-ACC season as the Devils went 19 – 0 against conference foes. Mike Gminski had been the last Devil to earn All-ACC three times (1978 – 80). Early in the year Langdon dropped seven three-pointers on Michigan to help hand the Wolverines their most lopsided loss in school history. Twice he lit up Chicago's United Center, with 23 versus Michigan State and 25 versus DePaul. His best ACC showing of the year was 26 points at Wake Forest. A foot injury in the ACC Tournament opener took him out of the event, but he returned for the NCAA tourney and was selected MVP of the East Region after Duke topped Temple to earn a trip to the Final Four. Langdon hit three straight long bombs as part of a 17 – 2 run that broke the game open. He scored 25 in his final contest, a loss in the championship game to UConn.

Langdon was a lottery pick in the NBA draft in 1999 and played three injury-plagued seasons for the Cleveland Cavaliers before continuing his pro career successfully overseas. In 2001 he was a charter inductee in the Duke Basketball Hall of Honor.

Latimer, Dick. Reserve guard Richard Lee Latimer lettered for three seasons, 1950 – 52, and scored 125 points in 66 games. One of his top efforts was a 10-point game in a close loss to tenth-ranked N.C. State in 1951. Latimer, 6 – 2, was from Bethesda, Md.

Legacy Fund. Created in January 2000, the Duke Basketball Legacy Fund took aim at fortifying the financial foundation of the Blue Devil program. Guided by associate athletics director Mike Cragg, the fund was intended to build an endowment for scholarships, coaches' salaries, and the operating budget; create a capital fund for basketball facilities; and meet other future needs to ensure the program's strength well beyond the coaching days of Mike Krzyzewski. In its first four years, the fund attracted 28 partners at a minimum of $1 million apiece. It also gave rise to a venture capital co-investment fund that welcomed 16 members at $50,000 apiece in its first two years. Former star player Grant Hill was the first chairman of the Legacy Fund. The fund's first nine endowed scholarships, through 2005 – 06, were named for Grant and Tamia Hill, David T. Borman, Bill Jessup, Kevin and Gayle Compton, Gunnar Peterson, Captain Bill Krzyzewski, Gopal Varadhan, Christian Laettner and Brian Davis, and Michael and Candace Olander.

Legends of College Basketball. Seven former Blue Devils were ranked among the top 100 college players of all time in the book *The Sporting News Selects Legends of College Basketball* (2002).

Christian Laettner made the top 10, checking in at No. 9. The other Duke greats recognized in the book: Bobby Hurley (28), Jason Williams (37), Shane Battier (54), Danny Ferry (71), Johnny Dawkins (78), and Art Heyman (83). All had their college jerseys retired. The book was written by Mike DeCourcy.

Legends Weekend. See Alumni games.

Leonard, Debbie. Writing in the school newspaper midway through the 1978 season, columnist Jim Mazur likened Duke's challenge in women's basketball to "a match race between Seattle Slew and a $3,000 claiming horse." Debbie Leonard was in her first season as the Blue Devils' coach and the task before her was daunting. When her club took the floor against an ACC team, the opposing roster normally included several scholarship players; she had just three and only one was a starter. Not surprisingly, the Devils' record was 1 – 19 that year.

But Leonard remained on board for 14 more years as the coach of Duke women's basketball and led the program to many noteworthy achievements, including its first national ranking, its first 20-win season, its first invitation to the NCAA Tournament, and a 100 percent graduation rate. Her overall record in 15 years, 1978 – 92, was 213 – 189, and 69 – 119 in the ACC. Nine of her teams were .500 or better, and all but three had winning records at home. In short, Leonard did about as much as she could given the level of support that existed for her sport at the time.

A native of Lexington, N.C., and a 1974 graduate of High Point College, Leonard was hired by athletics director Carl James in the spring of 1977 after she'd spent one year as an assistant coach for UNC Greensboro. James, formerly a renowned football recruiter for the Blue Devils, had moved Duke up to the Division I level within the North Carolina AIAW and signed three players to scholarships before landing Leonard, with the promise of more aid to come. But he resigned later that summer, and when Tom Butters took his place, scholarships in the non-revenue sports were put on hold because of budgetary concerns.

Consequently, the Blue Devils found themselves at a personnel disadvantage for Leonard's first few seasons. In 1978 two ACC powers, Maryland and N.C. State, administered 70- and 82-point spankings to Duke in back-

Debbie Leonard coached the Duke women to 213 victories in her 15 seasons.

to-back games. Maryland added insult to injury by practicing on Duke's floor immediately afterward because it didn't get a good enough workout during the game.

Gradually Leonard was able to add scholarship talent and guide Duke to respectability. In the early 1980s she coached the Devils to their first wins over Maryland, N.C. State, North Carolina, and Virginia. After recruiting high school All-America Chris Moreland in 1985, there was a noticeable turn forward as Duke made its first appearance in the Associated Press poll during the 1986 campaign, went to the NCAA Tournament in 1987, and was ranked as high as ninth nationally in 1988. From 1985 to 1988 Duke won 76 games against 38 losses and broke even in the ACC, with a best mark of 21–9 overall in 1986.

After Moreland's departure, Duke was ranked for three weeks in 1989 but dropped out of the polls and struggled in subsequent years with a series of injuries to

key recruits. Leonard left the post after a 14–15 record in 1992 and turned to a career in insurance while also analyzing games on television.

Lewis, Cliff. A star halfback on the 1944 Duke football team as well as a 5–10 guard in basketball, Cliff Lewis, from Cleveland, played a pivotal role in the Blue Devils' defeat of Alabama in the Sugar Bowl on January 1, 1945. His football commitment made for a late arrival to the Duke basketball team, but he was able to handle the transition and earned a letter while scoring 39 points.

Lewis went on to greater athletic fame as an NFL player. He was the Cleveland Browns' first quarterback in 1946, moving to safety when Otto Graham came on board. Lewis later became a sports executive, joining the New York Yankees organization in 1973. He was a Yankees vice-president when he died in 2002 at 79.

Lewis, Henry. Forward Henry Lewis, a 5–8 native of Brooklyn, lettered for the 1932 and 1933 teams and scored 160 points. He scored 15 points in 1933 before withdrawing at the start of the spring semester. His brother Fred Lewis was a guard on the 1932 and 1933 teams but did not play enough to letter.

Lewis, Jim. The first black assistant basketball coach in Duke history, Jim Lewis served on the staffs of three head coaches during his five-year tenure with the Blue Devils. He came to Duke in June 1971 to work for Bucky Waters, for whom he'd played at West Virginia in the 1960s. Lewis was on Waters's last two Duke staffs, assisted Neill McGeachy during his one season as head coach in 1974, and remained for Bill Foster's first two campaigns before departing at the end of the 1976 season for a job at Tulane.

Later in his coaching career Lewis made the shift from men's to women's basketball. He was head coach of the women's team at George Mason for 14 years, becoming the winningest coach in school history. He then coached the WNBA's Washington Mystics during the first two years of their existence. In April 2000 he was hired as the head women's coach at Fordham. All the while, he enjoyed numerous assignments working with women's teams for USA Basketball.

Lewis, Mike. Sometimes referred to as the Missoula Mountain, Michael James Lewis, 6–7, from Missoula, Mont., was one of the most effective centers and outstanding rebounders in school history. In three varsity seasons, 1966–68, he averaged double figures in points and rebounds every year, finishing with totals of 1,417 points and 1,051 boards in 84 games. He was the first player in Duke history to record at least 1,000 rebounds and the first to lead the ACC in rebounding, and his career rebounding average of 12.5 was topped only by Randy Denton at 12.7.

Strong and rugged, Lewis honed his muscles by working for his dad in a sawmill. At Duke he stepped into a prominent role immediately, starting as a sophomore for the 1966 team that many regard as the best in coach Vic Bubas's tenure. He led the ACC in rebounding and was third on his team in scoring, behind all-stars Jack Marin and Bob Verga, as the Devils won the ACC and advanced to the Final Four. In the semifinals of the ACC Tournament, his free throw with four seconds left gave Duke a 21–20 win over UNC in one of the famous slowdown games in early league history. In the semifinals of the NCAA tourney against Kentucky, his 21 points were critical when Verga was under the weather, though the Devils lost by four points.

As a junior, Lewis ranked second in the ACC in rebounding and field-goal percentage while landing a spot on the All-ACC second team. He posted three 30-point games, including 33 versus West Virginia, and had one of the most eye-popping statistical lines of his career with 30 points and 24 rebounds against Wake Forest. Lewis missed the only game of his career in 1967, when he and several teammates broke curfew one night and were suspended by coach Vic Bubas.

With Verga graduated, Lewis was the leading scorer, captain, and most valuable player of the 1968 team. He ranked first in the ACC in rebounding for a second time, third in field-goal percentage, and fourth in scoring with his career high of 21.7 points a game. His rebounding average of 14.4 that year was second in school history only to Bernie Janicki's 15.9 in 1952. Lewis had eight games of 30 or more points, with a career best of 35 versus Wake Forest. Against N.C. State he had 34 points and 22 rebounds, while hitting 12 of 13 free throws. He also had a 22-rebound game versus Temple.

Mike Lewis scored 23 points in a rout of Wake Forest at the 1966 ACC Tournament.

Lewis scored 18 points with 18 rebounds in his final home game against UNC, then fouled out and watched his sub, Fred Lind, heroically help the Blue Devils pull out a triple-overtime thriller. "It was agonizing watching from the bench, but I loved the way it turned out," Lewis told historian Jim Sumner. "The best thing was the incredible reaction of the students. It was important to them and it was important to us."

Lewis was chosen first-team All-ACC and made some All-America teams. He was drafted by the Boston Celtics but opted to play professionally in the ABA, where he worked for six seasons before suffering an injury. He was enshrined in the Duke Sports Hall of Fame in 1985 and was a charter inductee of the Duke Basketball Hall of Honor in 2001.

Liccardo, Jim. Considered a steady and valuable reserve, James Frank Liccardo played in 58 games in three years on the varsity, 1965 – 67. He scored 121 points with 118 rebounds. Duke played in three ACC championship games and a Final Four during Liccardo's career. He achieved his scoring high of 11 points in the season opener against Virginia Tech in 1966. As a senior he was the second winner of the Ted Mann Jr. Award for the reserve contributing most to team morale. Liccardo was a rising sophomore when Mann died in the summer of 1964. He also was a top pitcher for the Duke baseball team.

Lilly, Bill. William B. Lilly, a starting guard from Albemarle, N.C., was selected captain of the 1908 Trinity team as a 24-year-old sophomore. His season, and life, came to a tragic end when he died of pneumonia on February 18, 1908.

Lind, Fred. His legacy was established and permanently etched into Duke basketball lore on the basis of one shining moment in March 1968. Frederick Gustave Lind had played an insignificant number of minutes and had never faced North Carolina, but he became a royal blue hero for the ages when he came off the bench to spark the Blue Devils over the third-ranked Tar Heels in triple overtime, 87 – 86. Then a 6 – 7 junior who had scored only 23 points in his career, Lind took over inside when Mike Lewis fouled out and proceeded to score 16 points, grab nine rebounds, and hit two free throws that forced overtime in perhaps the greatest contest between Duke and UNC ever played. He also hit a jump shot with seven seconds left to force the second overtime and had a critical series of plays in the third, including a hook shot, a blocked shot, and a rebound.

"I was pretty loose and didn't feel too much pressure," he recalled. "It was just one of those things where I felt like I had a lot of confidence."

A native of Highland Park, Ill., Lind showed plenty of potential on the 1966 freshman team with games such as the one against Southwood, when he had 27 points and 19 rebounds. But he played in only six varsity games as a sophomore — one of those a start against Penn State — and was used sparingly as a junior until his breakout versus the Tar Heels.

Lind emerged as a starting forward in 1969 and averaged 10.5 points with 7.9 rebounds. He opened that senior year with his first 20-point effort against Virginia Tech, had his career best of 23 against West Virginia, and delivered 18 points with 10 rebounds on his Senior Day game against UNC, again assisting in an upset of the nation's second-ranked team on coach Vic Bubas's final appearance at the Indoor Stadium. "That game was at least as special or more special to me because it was Coach Bubas's last game," he remembered.

Lind closed the season ranked seventh in the ACC in field-goal percentage at 54.6, and he scored in double figures in almost half of Duke's games in 1969, after entering the year with only 61 career points to his credit.

Lind played in 52 games, with 355 points and 281 rebounds, and was selected as the team's most valuable player as a senior. He went to law school at DePaul and was hired in the public defender's office in Guilford County (Greensboro), N.C., in 1974, launching a long career in which he represented clients who could not afford to hire an attorney.

Linney, Larry. After spending two years on the junior varsity, Larry Rolando Linney was promoted to the varsity roster by coach Bill Foster for the 1980 season and remained there in 1981 under coach Mike Krzyzewski. He appeared in 39 varsity games, with 79 points, 49 rebounds, and 22 steals. A 6 – 4 swingman from Asheville, N.C., Linney provided depth at the forward and guard positions. He earned extensive action as a senior in 1981, playing 248 minutes in 26 games. As a JV player he averaged 18.8 points and 11.0 rebounds as a sophomore in 1979. He later served as a North Carolina state representative.

Litz, Steve. A 6 – 5 forward from Pittsburgh, Stephen Francis Litz played in 17 games as a backup over two seasons, 1970 and 1971, scoring 36 points with 25 rebounds. He connected on 13 of 19 field goals and had his biggest moment late in an overtime win versus Wake Forest in 1970, when he grabbed the rebound that sealed the outcome.

Loftis brothers. Duke's usual starting five in 1943 included four players who had gained fame as local heroes when Durham High School was the top program in the state: the 1941 prep grad Gordon Carver and the 1940

After helping Durham High win 69 straight games, brothers Cedric and Garland Loftis played together at Duke.

recruiting trio of Bob Gantt, Cedric Loftis, and Garland Loftis. Gantt and the Loftis brothers were members of a platoon of sophomores who came off the bench to help Duke win the Southern Conference in 1942. In 1943 all three moved to the starting lineup, with the Loftis brothers holding down the backcourt jobs. They were joined by the local sophomore Carver as well as veteran John Seward to form a nucleus that carried the Devils to a 20 – 6 record, 12 – 1 in the league.

Cedric, 5 – 11, may have been the best offensive guard in the conference in 1943 and led Duke in scoring with 293 points. He made the all-tournament second team as a sophomore in 1942 and moved up to the first team in 1943. Garland, 5 – 10, had an excellent long-range shot and was an accomplished defensive player.

The two had played together since grammar school, but that 1943 season was the last time they played together at Duke. After the war, Cedric played semipro ball. As a member of the Hanes Hosiery team, he nailed

a shot with four seconds left to knock off the Blue Devils 58 – 57 in the 1948 – 49 season opener. Garland, meanwhile, returned to Duke as a 24-year-old senior on the 1947 team and started in the backcourt.

Cedric Loftis had 493 points in his varsity career, which spanned two years and 49 games. Garland Loftis totaled 388 points in three years and 66 games.

Long, Earl. Coming to Trinity from Guilford College during the First World War, Earl Long played one season of varsity basketball, 1918, and led the team in scoring with 144 points. A native of Milton, N.C., he was the Trinity captain in his lone year.

Love, Reggie. For four autumns from 2000 through 2003, Reginald LaMonte Love worked as a scholarship wide receiver for the Duke football team. A 6 – 4 native of Charlotte, he appeared in 40 games and caught 75 passes with six touchdowns. During his freshman and sophomore years, Love moonlighted as a walk-on reserve for the basketball team. He played in 21 games for the 2001 team, which won the NCAA championship, and 16 more for the 2002 team before leaving the roster late in the season to concentrate on football. Then, surprisingly, he resurfaced at Cameron two years later. After being released from the Green Bay Packers training camp in the summer of 2004, he returned to school, added a second major, and played basketball as a fifth-year senior for the 2005 team.

Love's basketball contributions in 2001 were noteworthy because he helped the Blue Devils compensate for the loss of their injured center Carlos Boozer just before the start of postseason play. Love's inspired effort, particularly on defense, provided a lift in the ACC Tournament in 2001, when he appeared in all three games for 38 minutes and scored eight points while grabbing 10 rebounds. His defense helped turn around the ACC tourney opener against N.C. State, and he had a career high of eight rebounds in the ACC final against North Carolina. He also played in three NCAA Tournament games, going 3 for 3 from the floor while blocking two shots. During most of the 2001 season he was going through football workouts and spring practice while also playing basketball.

Love provided leadership, inspiration, and production for the 2005 team. He played in 21 games and had 33 points with 57 rebounds. When the team lost Shavlik Randolph to mononucleosis, Love was primed to move into the lineup and received his first career start in the ACC opener against Clemson. But he broke his right foot in the contest and had to miss the next 12 games. Nevertheless, he was named a co-captain at midseason and came back to help the Blue Devils win the ACC title.

For his career, Love totaled 75 points and 108 rebounds in 58 games, with four starts. After his second senior year he turned his attention back to pro football, signing with the Dallas Cowboys. He was released after trying out at linebacker.

Lyons, Pat. After playing intramural basketball as a freshman, Pat Lyons, a 6–2 center from Norfolk, Va., made the varsity in 1948 and appeared in 21 games with 32 points to earn a letter. He also lettered at end for the 1948 Duke football squad.

Mack, Connie, Jr. A 6–5 center and the son of major league baseball legend Connie Mack, Cornelius McGillicuddy Jr. had a profound impact on the 1934 Duke basketball team. His arrival from the freshman squad allowed team star Jim Thompson to move to his more natural forward position. Mack was a force in his own right, scoring 146 points to help Duke reach the Southern Conference final. He was an honorable mention pick for the all-tournament team. Mack then had an equally profound influence on the 1935 team: when he did not return to school, coach Eddie Cameron was forced to resume his search for a big man.

Madison Square Garden. Duke made dozens of visits to New York City during its first century of basketball, enjoying several noteworthy evenings at the world's most famous arena, Madison Square Garden. The original Garden, built in 1925 for $5 million at Eighth Avenue and 50th Street, had an extensive college basketball menu, beginning in 1934 with a doubleheader that attracted over 16,000 fans. In 1938 the National Invitation Tournament began at the Garden, and soon college basketball became a mainstay at the facility. During the 1945–46 season, for example, the Garden hosted 21 college twinbills, the NIT, and the NCAA finals.

Duke's first appearance at the Garden was on January 1, 1944, when the Blue Devils dropped an overtime game to Long Island University despite 27 points from Gordon Carver. A crowd of 16,108 attended. After the war the Devils returned to play New York University in January 1947 and January 1948 and lost both games, before crowds of 18,034 and 17,931.

Several NCAA Tournament games in the 1940s and 1950s were held at Madison Square Garden, including Duke's first appearance. The Blue Devils lost to Villanova in a first-round NCAA tripleheader in 1955. Duke also played NYU again at the Garden twice in the 1950s, beat Princeton there in the opening round of the NCAAs in 1960, and made its first NIT trip to the Garden in 1967.

The Blue Devils dropped their NIT opener to Southern Illinois, which went on to win the event. The following season, on February 8, 1968, Duke and Southern Illinois met again in the facility's final college basketball doubleheader. Behind 28 points and 18 rebounds from center Mike Lewis, the Blue Devils gained a measure of revenge with a 24-point win over the Salukis, before a crowd of 5,487. NYU then topped Manhattan in the nightcap to close out the old Garden's college card.

A new $43 million Madison Square Garden complex opened at Seventh Avenue and 33rd Street, atop Penn Station, the following week, and Duke was back in March for another NIT visit. The Devils also made NIT trips to the Garden in 1970 and 1971, twice appeared in the ECAC Holiday Festival there (losing all four games), and made five trips to the Garden for the Preseason NIT. Duke won the Preseason NIT with tense victories over St. John's and Kansas to jump-start the 1986 season, with David Henderson earning most valuable player honors. The 2001 Blue Devils, eventual NCAA champs, won the Preseason NIT at the Garden in a defensive duel with Temple. Jason Williams and Carlos Boozer combined for Duke's final 26 points in that game, including a 9–0 run over the final three minutes. Boozer finished with 26 points to earn MVP accolades. The title helped Williams forget about his Duke début at the Garden the previous season, when the Blue Devils dropped a pair of games in the Coaches vs. Cancer Classic. Duke's 2006 season likewise began with a title at the Garden in the newly named NIT Season Tip-Off. J. J. Redick scraped together a hard-fought 31 points in a semifinal win over Drexel, while Shelden Williams scored 30 to key a championship game victory over Memphis, 70 – 67. Williams's total included a tip-in with 32 seconds left to break a 67-all tie, and he was named the event's MVP.

Home-and-home series with St. John's brought Duke to the Garden in 1999, 2001, 2003, and 2005. An exciting overtime Duke win in 1999 marked the first home sellout for St. John's in several years. The 2003 contest had a stunning finish, as an underdog Red Storm scored the final 12 points of the game and hit a free throw with no time left on the clock to win by one point.

Noting the intense enthusiasm demonstrated by their northeastern alumni base in attending those games, the Blue Devils arranged a nonconference battle with Texas during December 2003 that packed the Garden with 19,558 fans, most of them in Duke blue. A similar battle with Oklahoma drew similar support in December 2004. Through the 2006 season, Duke's record at the current Garden location was 19 – 13, including 8 – 2 in the Preseason NIT and 3 – 4 in the postseason NIT.

Maggette, Corey. The only scholarship freshman on the top-ranked 1999 team, Paul Antoine "Corey" Maggette wowed college basketball audiences with a show that usually took place above the rim. A 6 – 6 forward and Parade All-America from Fenwick High School in Bellwood, Ill., he only started three games but was a high-impact contributor. More of an athlete than a refined basketball player, Maggette played in 39 games and had 414 points for a 10.6 average, the fourth-best on the club. He also had 151 rebounds for a 3.9 average.

Maggette made his début with 17 points in the season's first game, Duke's highest opening point total in 10 years. Three games later he had his first 20-point outing, versus Notre Dame. At UNC in the regular-season finale he enjoyed confounding the Tar Heels with a 14-point, 11-rebound effort in which he was a terror on both ends of the floor. His first career start was a week later in the ACC Tournament semifinals against N.C. State, when he delivered his season best of 24 points, stepping in for senior Trajan Langdon, who had suffered a foot injury the previous day.

Maggette had 29 dunks and 29 three-pointers, a measure of his threat as an inside-outside force. The dunks were more memorable. Against Florida he exploded for five, including one in which he slapped the backboard, drew a technical foul, and sent Cameron Indoor Stadium into a frenzy. At Chapel Hill he drove around Jason Capel for a two-handed rim-rattler that gave the Devils a 20-point lead. Another dunk that made a lasting impression was in the NCAA regional final against Temple, when he threw down an offensive rebound with one hand to put an emphatic finishing touch on the first half.

Maggette's association with Duke was not without controversy. Against the recommendation of Mike Krzyzewski, he opted to enter the NBA draft after his freshman year and was chosen with the 13th pick of the first round. After working as a reserve who played less than 20 minutes a game his first two seasons, Maggette

High-flying Corey Maggette left college for the NBA after starting just three games in his freshman year.

continued to develop his skills and had bloomed as a bona fide NBA star by his fourth season, when he was a starter and consistent scoring threat for the Los Angeles Clippers. As a fifth-year pro blessed with a lucrative new contract in 2004, Maggette had one of the better scoring averages in the league at 20.7 points a game.

Maggette was the subject of an NCAA investigation upon his departure from Duke. As a high school player in 1997 he accepted $2,000 from Myron Piggie to play for his summer team, the Children's Mercy Hospital 76ers. The payments were made before Duke began seriously recruiting Maggette, and university officials were unaware of them until legal allegations were made against Piggie during Maggette's rookie season in the NBA. The NCAA closed its case on the matter in 2003 without sanctioning Duke, saying it was convinced that the school could not have known of the issue while Maggette was on the team.

Mainwaring, Rick. A 6–3 guard from Center Valley, Pa., Richard Douglas Mainwaring played two years of junior varsity basketball and spent one season with the varsity. As a freshman in 1975 he was one of the JV team's top shooters and poured in 19 points in his best outing. He moved up to the varsity roster for his junior year of 1977 and appeared in eight games, with three points and three rebounds. Mainwaring won the Dr. Deryl Hart academic award in 1977 as the team's top student athlete.

Mann, Ted. Aside from a five-year tour of duty in the Navy during the Second World War, Glenn Edward "Ted" Mann spent over 46 years employed by the Duke athletics department, providing information to the media and promoting Blue Devil teams, particularly in the sports of football and basketball.

Born in Kentucky and raised in Arkansas, Mann was named sports editor of the *Greensboro (N.C.) Record* in 1926 at the age of 19. In 1927 he enrolled at Duke, where he worked as a student publicist. Upon graduation in 1931 he was named the university's first full-time director of sports information, a position he held until stepping down in 1966 to become a special consultant to athletics director Eddie Cameron. Mann retired from Duke in January 1973, was inducted into the Duke Sports Hall of Fame in 1979, and died on May 6, 1986.

Mann was considered a leader and a legend in his profession. Many of the techniques that he pioneered to serve the media and publicize his teams and players became standards in the industry. From his daily news bulletins and frequent releases to his players' home-town newspapers, to his warm hospitality and his popular "dots-and-dashes" columns in game programs, Mann always strived to put Duke's best face forward.

Mann once described his approach to his job as a "hell-for-leather bombastic style." Former university president Terry Sanford noted that the title of sports information director fell far short of characterizing his role: "For many, he was Duke: congenial, knowledgeable, tireless; quick with a statistic or a tall tale. He was toastmaster for the university. He won respect for far more than sports."

Mann wrote the history of Duke football, *A Story of Glory*, published in 1985. He was a charter inductee in the College Sports Information Directors Hall of Fame and the first sports information director to be inducted into the North Carolina Sports Hall of Fame. Duke's football press box is named in his honor.

Mann, Ted, Jr. The son of Duke's long-time sports information director, Glenn Edward "Ted" Mann Jr. played one year of freshman basketball and two on the varsity before his tragic death at the start of his senior year. A 6–5 forward, he averaged 15 points a game for the 1962 freshman team that went 14–2. As a sophomore he moved up to the varsity, started the 1963 season opener against Davidson, and played a total of 12 games, with two points and 10 rebounds. He saw action in 17 games as a junior in 1964, with 18 points and 19 rebounds. Mann had three points and two rebounds in the NCAA championship game against UCLA in 1964.

The NCAA final proved to be his last game. Mann, who was known as a scrappy, team-oriented player and was social chairman of his fraternity, was involved in a swimming accident at Fire Island, N.Y., on Labor Day 1964 and died five days later, September 12, stunning the Duke community. Since the 1965 season the basketball program has recognized the reserve contributing most to team morale with the Ted Mann Jr. Award, first presented by the Kappa Sigma fraternity.

Maravich, Pete. The all-time scoring leader in NCAA basketball history, Hall of Famer Pete Maravich never played against Duke during his three-year varsity career at Louisiana State. But he made one visit to Duke Indoor Stadium while playing for Southwood (formerly Edwards Military Institute) of Salemburg, N.C., in between his career at Raleigh's Broughton High and his LSU days. On December 10, 1965, in a preliminary game before a showcase varsity battle between Duke and UCLA, the Blue Imps freshman team hosted Southwood and won convincingly despite 27 points from Maravich. Duke routed Maravich's team again later in the year in a game played at Clinton (N.C.) High School.

Marcovecchio, Joe. A 6–2 guard from Atlanta, Joseph Marcovecchio played in two games as a sophomore in 1957 and went scoreless, with one rebound.

Marin, Jack. Duke icon Vic Bubas called John W. "Jack" Marin the best all-around player he coached, but the label could have applied to more than basketball. After earning All-America honors for the Blue Devils, Marin was accepted into medical school at Duke but opted instead for the NBA. He had a most productive tenure as a pro, returned to Duke to attend law school, became a successful attorney and agent, and starred on a celebrity golf tour. Marin did everything well, not just basketball.

The solid fundamentals that Bubas always praised in Marin were honed under the direction of legendary coach Edward McCluskey, who guided Marin's high school development in Farrell, Pa. A 6–6 left-handed forward, Marin spent an obligatory year on the Duke freshman team before playing in all 86 varsity contests the next three seasons, 1964–66. Over that span the Devils posted a 72–14 record, finished first in the ACC race in all three years, won two conference tourneys, and reached the Final Four twice.

Marin came off the bench for a veteran team in 1964, then started the next two campaigns. He totaled 1,275 points for a 14.9 average and added 695 rebounds for an 8.1 average. He made an even 50 percent of his field goals and 75 percent of his foul shots. During his two years as a starter, Marin averaged 19 points and 10 rebounds, made the All-ACC first team both times, and was se-

Lefty Jack Marin averaged 19 points and 10 rebounds over his junior and senior seasons.

lected second-team All-America as a senior. He finished second to Bob Verga in scoring on the 1965 team and edged Verga for the team scoring crown in 1966, when he shared Duke MVP honors with his classmate Steve Vacendak. Marin led the ACC in field-goal percentage with a 54.6 mark in 1965, a remarkable feat considering how much he shot from the perimeter.

Marin was a factor in just about every contest during his last two seasons. He had a handful of 30-point games in 1965, including a 35-point effort against Notre Dame. He notched his career rebounding high of 21 versus Navy. In 1966 he posted his career high of 36 points against Wake Forest, had 35 in the other Wake game that year, and matched Cazzie Russell's 30-point effort when Duke edged Michigan in overtime in Detroit. He had 40 points combined in two NCAA East Regional games to get Duke to the Final Four, hitting critical free

The Streak He'll Never Forget

Jack Marin, February 1965

Before he became one of Duke's most productive NBA players, Marin thrived during a pro-like slate of games in his junior year. After taking two weeks off for semester exams at the end of January 1965, the Blue Devils returned with eight games in the first 20 days of February. Marin hit 4 of 13 shots for 11 points and 12 rebounds in a game against Maryland on February 1, then went off on a streak where he could not be stopped. Over the next seven games he averaged 27.4 points and 12.4 rebounds while hitting nearly 70 percent from the floor.

Marin hit 74 percent of his shots and averaged over 28 points a game for the first five games in the string, all of which were played in 11 days. He cooled off slightly with 15 points at South Carolina before erupting for his season high of 35 against Notre Dame at Chicago Stadium. Duke won all of Marin's magnificent seven, only three of which were at home.

"I was making three of every four shots for awhile there. It was really wild, especially for an outside player," recalled Marin, the No. 2 point man for one of the school's most prolific offensive units. "We averaged 92 points a game that year, and we'd have averaged 105 a game with the three-pointer. We just ran people out of the gym."

Marin's Magnificent Seven

Date	Opponent	FGs	Pts	Rebs	Result
Feb. 3	N.C. State	14–17	32	11	W
Feb. 6	West Virginia	11–16	32	9	W
Feb. 9	N.C. State	12–18	27	10	W
Feb. 11	Virginia	10–14	25	10	W
Feb. 13	Wake Forest	12–15	26	17	W
Feb. 17	South Carolina	7–11	15	16	W
Feb. 20	Notre Dame	14–26	35	14	W
Totals	7 games	80–117	27.4	12.4	7–0

throws in a two-point win over St. Joseph's to open the tourney.

One of Marin's top performances was in his penultimate college game, when he scalded Kentucky for 29 points in the Final Four. The Blue Devils dropped a four-point decision, however, and Bubas's best team was denied a chance to play for the NCAA crown, making it a bittersweet occasion for Marin.

"My matchup was Pat Riley [who scored 19 points and fouled out]. It was certainly memorable, but also a painful moment," Marin recalled. "It was such an important game, with two southern teams that had swapped first and second [in the polls] throughout the season. We played a pretty good game without Verga and I think it was a well-played game. Unfortunately, we came up short."

Marin had every intention of enrolling in Duke medical school after graduation, but he was the fifth pick of the NBA draft and went instead to the Baltimore Bullets. He made the all-rookie team in 1967, the initial achievement of a long pro career that could stand next to any posted by a Duke alumnus. He rarely missed a game during his entire 11 seasons, and played the full 82-game schedule for four straight years. He scored over 12,000 points, second among former Blue Devils only to Jeff Mullins, who played one more year. Marin's 849 career regular-season games topped all Duke grads until Mike Gminski, Danny Ferry, and Christian Laettner came along with lengthier tenures.

Marin was one of the NBA's best free-throw shooters, hitting 84 percent for his career and leading the league at 89 percent in 1972. That season was his best, with a 22.3 scoring average. He made the All-Star Game that year and the next, after a blockbuster trade to Houston for Elvin Hayes. Marin appeared in the playoffs in seven of his 11 years and had 51 postseason games. The highlight was a trip to the NBA Finals in 1971 after a 42–40 regular season, although Baltimore was swept by Lew Alcindor and Milwaukee. Marin averaged 20.6 points in 18 playoff games that year.

Upon retirement, Marin enrolled in law school at Duke, finishing in 1980. Eight years into his practice, he began representing players as well and specialized in helping American cagers secure employment in foreign leagues. He later was named outside counsel for the NBA's retired players association, and he has been active in lobbying the league to increase the pensions of former players. An avid golfer, he was in on the ground floor when the Celebrity Players Golf Tour was formed in 1997, and he has been a successful participant in several events a year, along with winning six club championships in Durham.

Marin was inducted into the Duke Sports Hall of Fame in 1978 and was a charter member of the Duke Basketball Hall of Honor in 2001.

Martin, Hip. Linville Kerr "Hip" Martin enjoyed a distinguished career for Trinity. A guard from Winston-Salem, he captained the 1916 and 1917 squads and was the team leader in scoring in 1917 with 266 points while playing as a first-year law student. Then he joined the Army during the First World War and returned to finish his law studies in 1920, when he again led the team in scoring. The 1917 and 1920 teams were Trinity's first to win state championships, and the 1917 team was the first in school history to win 20 games. Cap Card, Trinity's first coach and a keen observer of the sport for many years, once called Martin the greatest running guard ever produced in the state of North Carolina.

Martin, Bill. A 6–0 guard from Portsmouth, Va., William Martin played in the backcourt for four seasons, 1947–50. Known for his long shot, he came off the bench in 1947, earned some starts in 1948, and was back in relief for most of 1949. He scored 198 points in 76 games.

Maryland. Duke and Maryland made history on March 1, 1995. For the first time ever, an ACC basketball game was played with neither team's head coach in attendance. Mike Krzyzewski had been out with health problems for almost two months, while Maryland's Gary Williams was hospitalized with pneumonia. The game hardly suffered from their absence. Senior Cherokee Parks, playing for the last time at home, hit two free throws with 29 seconds left to tie the sixth-ranked Terps, before eventual ACC player of the year Joe Smith scored on a tip-in with one second left to give Maryland a 94–92 victory. Smith finished with 40 points and 18 rebounds, while Parks had 20 points and seven rebounds in his swan song.

In many ways, it was a typical Duke-Maryland game: tense, down to the wire, unpredictable. With the Devils struggling and the Terps ranked in the top 10, neither of their games that year figured to be a nail-biter. But both came down to a last shot; earlier at College Park, Smith had blocked Erik Meek's final attempt out of bounds at the buzzer to preserve a 74–72 win. The following

Jason Williams led Duke to three wins in four tries against Maryland in 2001, the last at the Final Four.

year, the Terps were victimized at home when Ricky Price canned a rainbow three-pointer from the corner as time expired, silencing a Cole Field House crowd that was poised to celebrate.

The Terps and Devils played 159 times in the first 101 years of Duke basketball history, with Duke leading the series, 101–58. That margin was built during two prolonged periods of dominance. From 1962 until the end of his reign in 1969, Vic Bubas's teams owned a 16–1 mark against Maryland. Mike Krzyzewski's teams later rolled up a 21–2 record versus the Terps from 1985 until the double dose of Smith heroics in 1995.

But even the best Duke teams have been subject to a Maryland uprising, and vice versa. In 1985, 2003, and 2005, the Terps welcomed undefeated Duke teams to College Park and sent them home with their first defeats. Duke's 2000 team was riding a 31-game ACC winning

A Zone He'll Never Forget

Shane Battier, 1999 versus Maryland

One of Duke's most impressive wins in 1999 came when the second-ranked Devils routed seventh-ranked Maryland 95–77 at Cameron. Sophomore Battier led the way with 27 points, then a career high, on 10-of-13 shooting, and a perfect 4 for 4 from three-point range. Battier was unstoppable, and he still remembers one shot in particular.

"I had this running floater in the middle of the lane," he recalled. "After I hit that shot, I realized that I was in the zone. You don't really realize it until you are in the middle of it, and I had never had that feeling before in Cameron. I felt like everything I threw up was going to go in. I'll never forget that sensation. It was the best game I'd had to that point in my career, and that one shot symbolized that night for me. I was unconscious, just throwing up anything and it was going in."

streak before Juan Dixon and the Terps shut it down with an upset in Cameron. Conversely, during Maryland's powerhouse years in the 1970s, Duke knocked off highly-ranked Terp teams in Cameron in 1972, 1973, and 1976 and just missed doing so in 1974.

Duke beat Maryland for ACC titles 20 years apart, in 1980 and 2000. The 1980 run was particularly satisfying for a Duke team that was disappointed in its season; it was seeded sixth entering the tourney, while Maryland was first. Maryland also beat Duke for ACC championships 20 years apart, in 1984 and 2004. The 1984 win was a shining moment for Maryland's coach Lefty Driesell, a Duke alumnus, and came a day after the Devils posted one of their biggest early wins under Mike Krzyzewski by ousting top-ranked UNC. The outcome in 2004 was a real downer for the Devils, as they led by 12 with 4:58 to go. A 15–3 run to close out regulation enabled the Terps to force overtime and deny Duke a sixth straight ACC crown. This time Maryland was the sixth seed and the Devils were first.

A high point in the rivalry came in the 2001 campaign, when the two schools met four times, with each game worthy of being called a classic. Fueled by Jason Williams, Duke made a miracle comeback in the final

minute and won in overtime at College Park. The Terps then came to Durham and spoiled Senior Day for Duke star Shane Battier. In the ACC Tournament semifinals Nate James scored on a tip-in in the dying seconds to advance his team to the championship game. Then at the Final Four, Maryland cruised to a 22-point lead before Battier, Williams, and Carlos Boozer paced Duke to a 95–84 win and a spot in the NCAA final. Duke won three of the four contests and took the national championship. A year later, as many observers began labeling Duke-Maryland the best rivalry in the country, the two schools split in the regular season and the Terps claimed NCAA laurels.

The contest in 1995 notwithstanding, coaching matchups have certainly added to the texture of the series. Duke student fans delighted in poking fun at Driesell during the 1970s and 1980s, while Krzyzewski's head-to-heads with Maryland alumnus Gary Williams have been among the more closely scrutinized battles of every college season. Contentious fan behavior has also colored the rivalry at various points. Duke students were criticized nationwide for their crude treatment of Maryland's Herman Veal in 1984, while Terp fans showered J. J. Redick with vulgarities in 2004 and threw objects at Duke players' parents after knocking off the top-ranked Blue Devils in 2002.

One of the early powers in women's basketball, Maryland defeated the Duke women in their first 11 meetings and in 27 of 33 from 1978 through 1994. Duke turned it around and lost to the Terps just six times from 1995 through 2006. That included a run of 14 straight Duke victories before Maryland defeated the Blue Devils in the semifinals of the 2006 ACC Tournament. One month later the two played for the NCAA championship, which Maryland won 78–75 in overtime. When Duke and Maryland met at the Comcast Center in College Park on February 13, 2005, the announced crowd of 17,243 set a new record for attendance at an ACC venue.

May, Reynolds. A letterman for the 1934 and 1935 teams, reserve Reynolds May, from Dothan, Ala., totaled 27 points in two years. He also played on the baseball team.

Mayer, Ronnie. Between the departure of Dick Groat and the arrival of Art Heyman, Duke's most prolific offensive player was Ronald Bruce Mayer. A 6–4 forward from Avalon, Pa., he could shoot, drive, and score off the boards, to the tune of 1,647 points in 105 games during his four years of varsity action, 1953–56.

After leading Avalon High to an undefeated season as a prep senior, Mayer stepped immediately onto the varsity roster as a true freshman and was a starter by the end of the year. He rarely left the lineup during the next three years, missing only three games in his entire career, with scoring averages of 12.9, 21.7, and 22.1 in his final three campaigns. He finished sixth in the ACC scoring race in 1955 and fourth in 1956. Additionally, he was the league's fourth-best rebounder in 1955 with a 12.4 average, becoming the first Blue Devil in the ACC era to average a double-double. His exploits landed him on the All-ACC team three times — a pair of second-team berths sandwiched around first-team honors in 1955, when he was also Duke's most valuable player and team co-captain.

Mayer opened his junior year with a 31-point explosion against Clemson, and it was a sign of things to come. Coach Harold Bradley could rely on him to contribute at least 20 points to the cause in nearly every game. He scored 31 again in the second meeting with Clemson in 1955 and had 10 games of at least 30 points in his last two years. His 30-point night against Pittsburgh in 1955 included a 14-of-18 effort at the foul line, while his 34 points against Virginia in the second ACC Tournament marked Duke's best scoring effort in the event until Bob Verga had a 35-point game in 1967 (also versus Virginia). The only other Duke player to top Mayer's ACC mark was J. J. Redick, with 35 against N.C. State in the 2005 tourney.

One of Mayer's best games of 1955 was a two-point win at Wake Forest in which he totaled 19 points and made nearly every play down the stretch. With Wake on top and freezing the ball, Mayer made two steals and turned both into baskets, tying the score with 1:15 remaining. Then he scored on a rebound basket with 18 seconds left to give the Blue Devils their first lead of the game and rebounded Wake's last shot to seal it.

Mayer's career high was a 38-point effort against Maryland in his senior season, but one of his favorite

Ronnie Mayer was Duke's most prolific offensive player during the mid-1950s.

games was earlier that year, when he had 32 points on a homecoming trip to play Penn. He finished his career with averages of 15.7 points and 9.1 rebounds a game. He was a fourth-round NBA draft pick but never played in the league.

McAdoo, Robert. Hall of Famer Robert McAdoo faced Duke three times in his lone season at North Carolina, 1972. He scored only three points when the Blue Devils upset his third-ranked team on the day the stadium was named for Eddie Cameron. McAdoo came back to score 23 against Duke in a win at Chapel Hill in the regular-season finale and added 17 when the Heels topped the Devils in the ACC Tournament. After the season he left school as a junior under the hardship rule and launched his pro career.

McBride, Elliott. A 5–11 guard from Winston-Salem, Robert Elliott McBride played in four games as a senior in 1965, scoring seven points.

McCaffrey, Bill. His smooth but deadly jump shot was forged in the driveway of his home in Allentown, Pa., where a young Bill McCaffrey played hoops with his older brother Ed, an All-America football player at Stanford, and his older sister Monica, a basketball player at Georgetown. Once at Duke, McCaffrey could often be found alone in the gym at night, further refining the jumpers that were so hard for opponents to contain.

William Joseph McCaffrey, a 6–3 guard, enjoyed an excellent two years with the Duke program, culminating in 1991 when he made the All–Final Four squad as a sophomore while helping the Blue Devils to their first national title. In the NCAA championship game versus Kansas he came off the bench and hit his first six shots, finished with 16 points, and fueled the decisive run of the second half. For the season he started 21 times, averaged 11.6 points, and played more minutes than anyone except Christian Laettner and Bobby Hurley. One of his better regular-season outings was against Kenny Anderson and Georgia Tech, when McCaffrey responded to Grant Hill's absence in the Duke lineup by drilling 12 of 19 shots for 29 points in a one-sided victory.

McCaffrey also had a solid freshman year, averaging 6.6 points. His Duke totals were 78 games played, 691 points, 105 assists, and 95 rebounds.

After winning the NCAA title, McCaffrey decided to transfer to Vanderbilt to conclude his career. He won even more acclaim with the Commodores, earning SEC player of the year and All-America recognition before graduating in 1994. He averaged over 20 points a game in each of his seasons at Vandy.

McCaffrey played professionally in Europe for five years. After retiring he spent some time tutoring players one on one and volunteered to help Missouri coach

Quin Snyder for a few months. Then in the summer of 2001 he was hired as an assistant coach at St. Bonaventure by his former Vandy coach, Jan van Breda Kolff. He later served as an assistant at Maine. McCaffrey maintained communication with his former Duke teammates and coaches as well, and returned to campus in 2001 for a 10-year anniversary celebration of the 1991 NCAA crown.

McCahan, Bill. A two-sport college standout in the early 1940s, William Glenn McCahan is on the short list of Blue Devil alumni to play both professional basketball and baseball. McCahan, 5–10, lettered for both Duke teams from 1940 through 1942, and after the Second World War he played both sports for pay. A native of Langhorne, Pa., he played 27 games for Syracuse in the National Basketball League in 1947, scoring 94 points, and appeared in parts of four seasons as a pitcher for the Philadelphia Athletics, 1946–49, with a record of 16–14 in 57 games. He posted 17 complete games in 40 career starts in the big leagues.

At Duke McCahan came off the bench for his first two basketball years and then started at guard as a senior. He was named to the United Press all-conference first team in 1942, when he scored 163 of his 219 career points. Duke played in the conference championship game in all three of his years, won the title in the last two, and had an overall record of 55–17.

McCarthy, Tara. Duke's first scholarship women's basketball player was Tara McCarthy, a 5–8 guard from Garden City, N.Y. McCarthy arrived at Duke in the fall of 1977 and played for coach Debbie Leonard's first three teams. She averaged 16.6 points and 2.0 assists in her first year to lead all ACC freshmen in both categories and earn a place on the all-state team.

McCarthy played three varsity seasons, appearing in 67 games. She totaled 879 points (a 13.2 average), plus 246 rebounds and 212 assists. During her career Duke improved from 1–19 to 11–11 to 14–13 while playing with fewer scholarships than most of its competition.

"I feel really fortunate," recalled McCarthy, now a pediatrician and public health planner. "Duke provided me so many opportunities in terms of the education I got and in terms of the challenges that came about with being in the initial class on scholarship. It was hard those first few years trying to build a program, but it was well worth it."

McClure, David. A 6–6 freshman on the 2005 team, David James McClure, of Ridgefield, Conn., played in 25 games. He had 43 points and 34 rebounds while averaging 7.4 minutes. He started the first two games of the season and one in December against Toledo, Mike Krzyzewski's 700th career victory. McClure's best game was the ACC Tournament opener versus Virginia, when he played his season high of 20 minutes and had season bests of nine points and five rebounds.

McClure led his Trinity Catholic prep team to a 101–7 record and three state titles. He missed seven games in the middle of his first year at Duke because of surgery on an ailing knee. After the season he had a more extensive procedure performed that required lengthy rehabilitation, keeping him out of the entire 2006 campaign.

McDonald's All American Game. Cameron Indoor Stadium played host to the 24th McDonald's High School All American Game on March 28, 2001. The West team, featuring Duke recruit Daniel Ewing and his high school teammate T. J. Ford in the starting backcourt, overcame a 15-point halftime deficit to defeat the East 131–125. Eddy Curry led the West with 28 points to earn most valuable player honors, but it was Ewing and Ford who sparked the late-game rally. Ewing scored eight of his 10 points down the stretch and added seven rebounds. Dajuan Wagner topped the East with 25 points, as a national television audience and 72 NBA scouts observed the action. Ewing's McDonald's jersey was later framed and hung in the McDonald's on campus.

See also High School All-Americas.

McGeachy, Neill. No coach in modern Duke history faced more difficult circumstances than Neill R. McGeachy. When Bucky Waters resigned in September 1973, athletics director Carl James had barely a month to find a successor before the start of preseason practice. He reportedly tried to hire the retired Kentucky legend Adolph Rupp, but when that fell through he turned the job over to McGeachy three days after practice began. McGeachy had been Waters's assistant and enjoyed the

Duke recruit Daniel Ewing drove past Dajuan Wagner at the 2001 McDonald's All American Game at Cameron Indoor Stadium.

support of the players, but he did not step into a very promising situation. He was given just a one-year contract, the team was coming off the school's first losing season in over three decades, and the schedule was one of the most demanding in the country, mainly because the ACC was top-heavy with national powers that year. Duke had nine games against teams that finished in the top 10 nationally, including the defending national champ N.C. State, Maryland, UNC, and Notre Dame.

The season started on an ominous note. When Chris Redding dunked in pre-game warm-ups before the opener with East Carolina, a technical foul was called to begin the game. ECU was up 3–0 before Duke even touched the ball. The Devils won the game but in many ways were behind all year. They finished with a 10–16 record, went 2–10 to place at the bottom of the ACC, and endured two of the most emotional losses ever to UNC. In the game at Cameron, the Devils had only to inbound the ball to get to overtime but instead saw the Tar Heels' Bobby Jones steal the pass and score a winning layup at the buzzer. In Chapel Hill, Duke was on the verge of a major upset with an eight-point lead and only 17 seconds remaining, but the Heels rallied miraculously and won in overtime. The only real highlight of the season was a 10-point win over Virginia that was Duke's 1,000th basketball victory.

On the morning of the final UNC game, Duke's athletic council met and decided not to extend McGeachy's contract. The search was on for a new coach and culminated less than a month later with the hiring of Bill Foster. McGeachy was named an assistant at Wake Forest. He later went into private business, was involved heavily in promoting and marketing sporting events, and became athletics director at his alma mater, Lenoir-Rhyne College.

A native of Statesville, N.C., McGeachy was coached in high school by Dave Odom. He spent two years as an assistant to Terry Holland at Davidson, one year as the Duke freshman coach, and one as Waters's top assistant before being named his replacement.

McGillicuddy, Cornelius, Jr. See Mack, Connie, Jr.

McGrane, Art. Guard Arthur J. McGrane, a 6–1 product of New London, Conn., lettered for the 1943 team, scoring 20 points in 19 appearances.

McKaig, Stuart. A 6–1 native of Toledo and three-year letter winner, Albert Stuart McKaig experienced backcourt reserve duty from 1965 through 1967. McKaig, who prepped in Charlotte, played in 49 games with 60 points and 41 rebounds. He earned his most extensive playing time as a senior, when he posted his career high of eight points against Penn State. McKaig started that game, in which coach Vic Bubas used only six players after suspending nine team members for violating training rules.

Attending Duke on a Navy ROTC scholarship, McKaig abandoned his initial plan to compete in golf for the chance to play under Bubas. He was a favorite of ACC television analyst Bones McKinney, who called him "Buzz saw" for the way he was all over the court in the Devils' pressure defense. Near the end of a contest

with Maryland in 1967, McKaig got a steal and scored a basket, then moments later picked off the inbounds pass and got the ball to Bob Verga for a three-point play as the Devils won a close one. "I would like to have a team of Stuart McKaigs," Bubas said. "His hustle, attitude, and spirit serve as an inspiration to the rest of the players."

McKaig won the Ted Mann Jr. award in 1967 as the reserve contributing most to team morale. Duke played in three ACC finals and one Final Four during his tenure.

McKevlin Award. Each year the Atlantic Coast Conference presents the Anthony J. McKevlin award to its male athlete of the year. The award is named for a former sports editor of the *News & Observer* of Raleigh and is selected by the Atlantic Coast Sports Writers Association. Duke basketball players earned the award eight times in the first 50 years of conference history: Art Heyman in 1963, Jeff Mullins in 1964, Danny Ferry in 1988 and 1989, Christian Laettner in 1991 and 1992, Elton Brand in 1999, and Shane Battier in 2001. Four other Duke athletes also earned the McKevlin: Joel Shankle (1954) and Dave Sime (1956) in track and Mike McGee (1960) and Clarkston Hines (1990) in football. Duke athletes won five straight McKevlins from 1988 to 1992, a streak unmatched by any other ACC school.

McLeod, Roshown. The first player to transfer into the Duke program under Mike Krzyzewski, Roshown McLeod was an all-star performer for the Blue Devils during the 1997 and 1998 seasons. A 6–8 forward from Jersey City, N.J., he competed in 69 games and scored 941 points for a 13.6 average. He also had 376 rebounds for a 5.4 average. He was a starter 57 times and led the 1998 team in scoring with a 15.3 average while earning first-team All-ACC and third-team All-America honors.

McLeod began his college career at St. John's in 1994 and came off the bench for most of two seasons before heading to Duke. After sitting out the 1996 campaign as a transfer, he started nearly every game in 1997 as Duke claimed the ACC regular-season championship. Krzyzewski opted to use him off the bench early in his senior year, but in late December McLeod returned to the starting lineup and played too well to be replaced. Game after game McLeod hit the shots and made the plays that carried the Blue Devils to a 15–1 finish in

Roshown McLeod had much to celebrate when Duke rallied to defeat UNC at his final home game in 1998.

the ACC, more than compensating for the absence of the injured freshman standout Elton Brand. Against N.C. State in Raleigh he had his career game of 27 points and 10 rebounds, connecting on 12 of 18 shots and during one stretch hitting 16 straight points. On his Senior Day against UNC he totaled 23 points and had the game-winning layup in the final minute as Duke rallied from 17 points down to present Krzyzewski with his 500th career victory.

Named Duke's most valuable player, McLeod was chosen in the first round of the NBA draft by the Atlanta Hawks, with the 20th pick. His four-year pro career was punctured by injuries and finally halted by a rare nerve injury in his knee. During the 2003 college season he returned to Cameron Indoor Stadium on the visitor's bench as an assistant coach to Fairfield's Tim O'Toole.

McNeely, Doug. Mike Krzyzewski's first scholarship recruit at Duke was Douglas Eric McNeely, a 6–5 swingman from El Paso. After seeing limited action as a freshman in 1981, McNeely developed into a starter as a sophomore and then finished his career as a reserve his final two seasons when Krzyzewski infused the roster with more talent. McNeely played in 85 games, with 231 points and 163 rebounds.

McNeely's best season statistically was 1982, when he started 15 of 25 games and averaged 4.6 points with 3.2 rebounds. He had his career high of 14 points against UNC that year. As a junior he played in 10 games and started one before sitting out most of the year with personal problems. He returned in his senior year and played in every game as part of the regular rotation, averaging 11.4 minutes as Duke advanced to the NCAA Tournament.

McRoberts, Josh. Considered one of the top high school players in the 2005 senior class, Joshua Scott McRoberts was a freshman for the 2006 Duke team. A

6 – 10 power forward from Carmel, Ind., he was a McDonald's and Parade All-America in high school and was rated the best player at his position by some recruiting services. At the McDonald's All-America game he scored 17 points with 12 rebounds and received the John Wooden MVP trophy. He also won the Morgan Wooten award as the national prep player of the year and was named the national senior athlete of the year by the National High School Coaches Association. McRoberts came off the bench in the season opener of his first Duke season, then moved into a starting front-court role. He averaged 8.7 points and 5.3 rebounds, with a high game of 17 points versus UNC.

Meadowlands. Located in East Rutherford, N.J., the Meadowlands sports complex played host to several major achievements in the first 100 years of the Duke basketball program. The complex includes Giants Stadium, a horseracing track, and a basketball arena, which was once known as Brendan Byrne Arena and later became Continental Airlines Arena. It is the home of the NBA's New Jersey Nets.

Duke competed in five NCAA Tournament regionals hosted by the Meadowlands and won all five to earn trips to the Final Four. Duke's first under Mike Krzyzewski was in 1986, after the Devils beat David Robinson and Navy at the Meadowlands. Final Four appearances in 1988, 1989, and 1990 also followed triumphs at the Meadowlands. Duke upset higher-ranked Temple and Georgetown in the 1988 and 1989 regional finals, then rode a last-second shot by Christian Laettner to upset Connecticut for a Final Four berth in 1990. Duke also won an NCAA regional at the Meadowlands in 1999.

Duke's first Meadowlands experience was a victory over Holy Cross in 1982, a contest nationally televised on ESPN. Duke later waged battles with Notre Dame (1985), Alabama (1987), Arizona (1989), Rutgers (1993), and Texas (2006) at the arena and faced Kentucky twice there in the Jimmy V Classic (1999 and 2002 seasons).

Duke's success led fans and foes alike to refer to the facility as a home away from home for the Blue Devils, or Cameron North. Duke's only loss in its first 18 games at the Meadowlands was a 77 – 75 defeat to second-ranked Arizona in February 1989.

Little-known fact: the Meadowlands was built by a Duke man, Francis Werneke, a Jersey City native who received his civil engineering degree from Duke in 1941. He did the project after his retirement as a construction manager from the Port Authority of New York and New Jersey. While with the Port Authority he directed the building of several landmarks, including the twin towers of the World Trade Center and the third tube of the Lincoln Tunnel.

Meagher, Dan. Tough, aggressive, scrappy, no-nonsense. Dan Gerard Meagher brought these qualities and more to Mike Krzyzewski's early teams as a prominent frontcourt figure from 1982 to 1985. A 6 – 7 forward from St. Catharines, Ontario, Meagher competed in 118 games with 756 points and 476 rebounds. He averaged a career-best 8.0 points as a senior, and he contributed as an enforcer and hustler from day one. An early symbol of the pressure man-to-man defense preferred by Krzyzewski, Meagher won or shared the team's True Blue award (for the most charges taken) in all four years.

Meagher was primarily a reserve in his first two years, playing the most minutes of any freshman in 1982 while bringing instant intensity off the bench. He then started every game in 1984 and all but one game in 1985 as the Blue Devils posted 20-win seasons and returned to the NCAA Tournament. His best clutch moment was in 1984, when he hit key free throws in an overtime win at N.C. State. His career scoring high of 20 points was in 1984 against Loyola (Md.), but he was frequently in double figures in his last two years. He once had 14 rebounds against Louisville.

Concurrently with his Duke success, Meagher was one of the top performers for the national team in Canada. In the summer of 1983 he helped his country upset the United States in the semifinals at the World University Games when he had 15 points and 10 rebounds in a nationally televised battle. The USA team featured his Duke teammate Johnny Dawkins. Meagher added another 15 points in a gold medal win over Yugoslavia. The next summer Meagher helped Canada to fourth place at the Summer Olympics in Los Angeles. After college Meagher was drafted in the sixth round by the Chicago Bulls but never played in the NBA.

Opposing coaches occasionally insinuated that Meagher was a dirty player, but his relentless physical play and spirit made him a favorite in Cameron Indoor Stadium and popular among the student body. He never won many accolades, but his having started 79 games during a time when Duke's roster was being restocked with blue-chip recruits offered a clear indication of his contribution to a successful rebuilding project.

Means, Andy. He saw action in just 17 games, but Andrew T. Means, a 6–5 guard from Indianapolis, made some valuable contributions to Duke basketball behind the scenes and as a practice player during a three-year career that concluded in 2004. Means roomed with the basketball recruits Chris Duhon and Andre Sweet in his freshman year, then joined the team as a walk-on for the 2002 and 2003 seasons. He totaled 12 points and 14 rebounds in 47 minutes of action and made his only two career three-point attempts. A quality leader and a hard worker for the Blue Team in practice, Means was awarded a scholarship for his senior year of 2004, but he suffered a shoulder injury that required surgery and was unable to play the entire season.

Meek, Erik. The summer before he was to matriculate to Duke, Erik Meek, a 6–10 center, was jogging in his native southern California when he was hit by a drunk driver. The accident had far-reaching consequences for Meek's basketball career, leaving him in a wheelchair for two months and limiting his conditioning and development during his freshman year. When his first season was over he needed surgery to remove scar tissue in his knee, requiring him to spend much of the summer in a cast. Though he was one of the team's hardest workers, it took awhile for his body to catch up to his level of determination; he barely averaged 10 minutes a game in his first three years. Finally in excellent health going into his senior year, he initially planned to red-shirt so that he could more fully develop for a breakout fifth season. But just before the campaign started, he was feeling so good about his game that he decided to play anyway, and he had his best year as a fixture in the starting lineup. The team, though, had one of its poorest years, with a 13–18 record after playing in the Final Four in two of his previous three years.

Erik Joal Meek, from Escondido, Calif., appeared in 122 games over his four years, 1992–95, with starts in 36. He scored 613 points, had 520 rebounds, and shot 59.8 percent from the field. During his senior year he averaged 10.3 points and 8.3 rebounds, a figure that ranked second on the team only to his fellow California big man and classmate Cherokee Parks. The two shared team MVP honors and were co-captains along with senior guard Kenny Blakeney. Meek was also chosen the outstanding scholar athlete on the 1995 team with the Dr. Deryl Hart award.

Meek's career scoring high was 21 points versus Boston University in his sophomore year. His best rebounding game was 13 against Georgia Tech at the Rainbow Classic in his senior year. In fact, Meek had several excellent games against the Yellow Jackets. In 1994 he came off the bench to contribute 10 points, 10 rebounds, two steals, and a block in a three-point victory at Atlanta. In 1995 he averaged 13.7 points and 10.3 boards in three meetings with Tech.

Meek was a second-round draft pick by Houston but never made an NBA roster. Instead he played several years professionally overseas.

Meier, Katie. When the ACC celebrated its golden anniversary by naming the top 50 all-time best players in each sport, guard Katie Meier was one of five Duke players chosen to the women's basketball team. Meier was the Blue Devils' top career assists maker and No. 3 scorer when she completed her career in 1990, but her value and impact could be judged even more graphically by reviewing the team's record during her tenure.

During Meier's first two years, Duke made its first two postseason appearances ever, in the WNIT and the NCAA Tournament. The Blue Devils then got off to a 12–0 start in her junior year before heading into a January game at Maryland. Meier damaged knee ligaments in that game and was hobbled or out of the lineup for the rest of the season; the team won just five of its last 16 games. Meier then spent her senior year on the sideline rehabilitating from surgery, and the team's record fell to 12–16 without her. When she returned for a fifth year, Duke had a winning record again at 15–13, though it could have been much better had starting center Sue Harnett not also gone down with a knee ailment, in the fifth game.

A 6–0 guard from Wheaton, Ill., Meier played in 109 games from 1986 to 1990, scoring 1,761 points for a ca-

Katie Meier recorded the first triple-double in Duke women's basketball history during Duke's first-ever NCAA Tournament game in 1987.

reer average of 16.2. She also had 409 assists and 670 rebounds. She was selected ACC rookie of the year in 1986, when she averaged 14.6 points, then closed her career by earning All-ACC first-team laurels in 1990. Meier averaged career highs of 18.9 points and 8.9 rebounds in 1990 and led the team in nearly every category while carrying it on her shoulders in game after game. She played over 1,000 minutes and was on the court for 520 of a possible 560 minutes in ACC contests. Many of her points were a result of sheer hard work; she made only eight three-pointers in her career but worked for shots and was often rewarded with trips to the free-throw line. Her 447 made free throws are the fifth-most in ACC history. Meier also notched the first triple-double in Duke

women's history with 16 points, 11 rebounds, and 10 assists in an NCAA game with Manhattan in 1987.

Meier spent her off-the-court hours at Duke preparing to be a high school English teacher. While playing professionally overseas she volunteered to coach a team of 15-year-olds in her spare time, and soon coaching became her passion. She landed an assistant coaching position at UNC Asheville, moved to Tulane for seven years, and was hired to her first collegiate head coaching job at Charlotte. In four years Meier guided the 49ers to a 76–45 record, and she directed the team to its first NCAA appearance in 2003. In 2006 she returned to the ACC as head coach at Miami. To date she is one of just 13 women to play and coach in the NCAA women's tourney. Meier was one of the charter inductees in the Duke Basketball Hall of Honor in 2002.

Melchionni, Gary. He had more than one great game as Duke's playmaker of the early 1970s, but a memento from Gary Melchionni's best contest remained with him long afterward. When he poured in 39 points to key an upset of third-ranked Maryland in 1973, his teammates and friends later presented him with a game ball denoting the accomplishment — a game ball that his son Lee saw on display in the Melchionni household as he was developing his early affection for Duke.

A 6–3 guard from Woodbury, N.J., Gary Dennis Melchionni was a senior in 1973 when he directed one of the Blue Devils' biggest upsets. He hit 17 of 25 shots and late in the game repeatedly drove the ball inside for layups against a spread-out Maryland defense. Duke led one of Lefty Driesell's best teams by 15 points in the closing minutes and won 85–81. The performance clearly helped Melchionni earn a spot on the All-ACC first team despite the Blue Devils' losing record. Junior stars Bobby Jones of UNC and Len Elmore of Maryland, 1972 ACC player of the year Barry Parkhill of Virginia, and Wake's Tony Byers, the No. 2 scorer in the league, all placed behind Melchionni on the second team. But it was not a one-game season for Melchionni, as he scored in double figures in all but three games and averaged 15.8 points against the league.

In his three years on the varsity, 1971–73, Melchionni played in 77 games, with 803 points, 207 rebounds, and 184 assists. He shot over 80 percent from the free-throw stripe every year. His sophomore season was a hard-luck story, as mononucleosis limited his playing time in the first 15 games while other injuries hampered him later. Still, he was noted for a fine game against South Carolina in which one of his plays was described as among the best in Indoor Stadium history: a steal followed by a diving save into the press table and then a successful outlet pass.

An ankle injury kept Melchionni out of four games early in his junior year, but he returned to average 11.7 points and make the All-ACC second team while serving as co-captain. Duke had three upsets of nationally ranked teams, and he performed well in all of them, with 12 points versus UNC, 16 versus Virginia, and 11 versus Maryland. He was also listed as an Academic All-America. Melchionni repeated his co-captain duties as a senior, when he was voted the team's most valuable player.

Melchionni, whose two older brothers had starred for Villanova, was a second-round NBA draft pick by the Phoenix Suns and played two years in the league. He remained closely connected to Duke, as president of the alumni association and a Duke parent: his daughter Monica graduated from Duke and his son Lee played for the Blue Devils, 2003 – 06.

Melchionni, Lee. For as long as he could remember, Lee Matthew Melchionni wanted to play college basketball at Duke. His father Gary was an All-ACC playmaker in the 1970s, his cousin was a Blue Devil lacrosse player, and his older sister attended the school. After an all-state high school career, Melchionni had the chance to realize his dream as a member of the Devils' top-rated recruiting class of 2002. Technically he was considered a walk-on as a freshman, since his six-player class was one over the NCAA limit on scholarship offers for a single year. But he was on scholarship for the rest of his career and emerged as quite an asset, particularly with his accurate left-handed perimeter shooting stroke.

A 6 – 6 forward from Lancaster, Pa., Melchionni came off the bench in 48 games in his first two years, 2003 – 04, and scored only 62 points. But he recognized that an opportunity to contribute more awaited him in 2005, and he took advantage. He played in all 33 games, started 14, and averaged almost 22 minutes of action. His scor-

ing average of 7.7 points ranked fourth on the team, and his 57 three-pointers added a major dimension to the offense. With J. J. Redick and Daniel Ewing usually occupying the top perimeter defenders, Melchionni capitalized by knocking down numerous key shots.

Melchionni carried the team in the first half of a win versus St. John's in Madison Square Garden. With Redick, Ewing, and Shelden Williams combining to shoot 0 for 12 in the half, Melchionni scored 14 of his 16 points in the first 20 minutes. He had a pair of key threes in the ACC opener versus Clemson, had five threes in the season finale at UNC, and matched his career highs of 16 points and nine rebounds versus Virginia in the ACC Tournament. One of his most significant outings was at Georgia Tech, when he broke a 49 – 49 tie with a three-pointer at the 3:15 mark, then popped another with 1:26 to play to seal a 60 – 56 victory.

Though he started several games, Melchionni earned the team's Ted Mann Jr. award as the reserve who contributed most to team morale in 2005. His overall improvement was impressive, as he evolved from a player who averaged barely one field-goal attempt a game over two years to an integral scorer and energizer. Just before the 2006 season began, he was named one of the squad's four senior co-captains. He totaled 117 games with 19 starts, 521 points, and 260 rebounds for his career.

Metzler, Robert. A 5 – 10 guard from Reading, Pa., Robert James Metzler played in 11 games as a reserve for the 1943 team and lettered while playing in five games for the 1944 team. After the war he returned to play in two games for the 1947 team. He scored seven points in 18 career contests.

Mewhort, Buzz. Playing behind Art Heyman and Jeff Mullins limited the court time for Donald Milton "Buzz" Mewhort, a 6 – 4 forward from Toledo, but Duke's coaching staff considered him a dependable player with a good outside shot and a knack for rebounding. He played in 71 games over three years, 1960 – 62, with 346 points and 225 rebounds. Mewhort posted his best numbers as a senior, with 6.8 points and 4.2 boards, when the Devils placed second in the ACC. As the starting center against West Virginia he came up with nine points and 16 rebounds. The next game, against Wake Forest, he pumped in 20 points on 9-of-11 shooting. By the end of the year, some were calling him the best sixth man in the nation. He provided ample evidence by coming off the bench to drill long shots in a pair of wins versus UNC. In the regular-season finale against the Heels, Mewhort hit three straight bombs and scored all 13 of his points in the last nine minutes on 5-of-7 shooting as Duke won by eight.

Duke had a 42 – 11 record during Mewhort's last two seasons. The co-captain with Heyman in 1962, he also was prominent in campus activities and was chosen for a senior leadership fraternity.

Michigan. For years Duke publicists used a quote from the former All-America Jack Marin to describe the atmosphere at Cameron Indoor Stadium. Marin, a star in the 1960s, compared the deafening decibel level to the roar of a jet engine. The game Marin was recalling when he made the comparison was a battle with the University of Michigan, one of the Blue Devils' top non-conference rivals in two distinct eras of program history.

The series began during the reign of coach Vic Bubas. Duke and Michigan played every December from 1963 through 1970, plus once at the Final Four. After a layoff of nearly two decades, the rivalry was renewed under coach Mike Krzyzewski, and the two teams played every December from 1989 through 2002, plus once at the Final Four. The rivalry was not renewed once former Duke player and coach Tommy Amaker became the Michigan coach. Neither he nor Krzyzewski wanted to face each other in a regular-season contest. Overall there were 24 match-ups, with Duke winning 17.

The series opener in December 1963 pitted top-five teams, with Michigan rolling to victory behind the play of Cazzie Russell. But that outcome provided Duke with plenty of incentive when the two teams met in March at the Final Four. Russell was spectacular again with 31 points, but Blue Devil seniors Jeff Mullins and Jay Buckley guided Duke to an 11-point win that enabled the school to play in its first NCAA title contest.

Michigan was No. 1 in the nation when it came to Durham in December 1964 and knocked off No. 5 Duke. That was the game where the crowd was as loud as a jet engine, according to Marin. The specific moment he remembered was late in the game, after Duke had rallied

to tie the score and then stole the ball. The Wolverines were able to escape, though, with a seven-point win.

The following year, Duke was No. 1 and Michigan No. 3 when the schools met at Cobo Hall in Detroit for one of the best contests in the first portion of the series ledger. Russell put the Wolverines on top by 10 with under four minutes to play, but Marin and Bob Verga rallied Duke to force overtime, and the Devils prevailed 100 – 93. Marin finished with 30 points and Verga with 27. "It was the greatest comeback any Duke team of mine has ever staged," Bubas said afterward.

When the series was renewed in December 1989 in Ann Arbor both teams were in the top 10, with Michigan coming off its national championship run the previous spring under coach Steve Fisher. Duke forced overtime, but the Wolverines pulled out a 113 – 108 classic. Two years later, Duke was the defending NCAA champ and Michigan was stocked with a freshman class billed as the Fab Five, featuring Chris Webber, Jalen Rose, and Juwan Howard. The No. 1 Blue Devils pulled off a narrow 88 – 85 win in Ann Arbor, then beat the Fab Five at the close of the season by 20 points to claim their second straight NCAA crown. Duke blew the game open in the second half and scored on its final 12 possessions, sparked by the Final Four MVP, Bobby Hurley.

After that game, Hurley pulled out a T-shirt with the message "You can talk the game, but can you play the game?" on the front, and "Duke, we can play the game" on the back. It was a reference to several inflammatory comments made by the Michigan freshmen before the Final Four. When the two schools had their regular meeting in December 1992, there was more talk from the Wolverines as they came into Cameron ranked No. 1 for the rematch. But No. 4 Duke held serve on its home floor with a 79 – 68 victory in one of the most hyped non-conference regular-season contests of the Krzyzewski era.

With the syndicator Raycom owning the television rights, the Saturday night showdown was picked up in 46 of the top 50 TV markets. There were over 200 requests for media credentials, ticket scalpers could name their price, and students camped out for seats over a week before tipoff. Senior point guard Hurley was at his best in making sure that the home fans went home happy. With the Wolverines on an 8 – 0 run, Hurley came off a screen set by sophomore Cherokee Parks and hit the biggest shot of the contest, a three-pointer at the 7:48 mark, to regain momentum for the Devils. He finished with 20 points and his classmate Thomas Hill was all over the court in scoring 21. "The way they talk, you'd think they were 3 – 0 against us," Hurley said of the Michigan youngsters, who were actually 0 – 3. "They didn't talk much during the game. Maybe they are growing up a little."

Duke picked up its fifth straight win over Michigan in December 1993 as senior Grant Hill turned in one of his typical all-around games with 18 points and expert leadership. He also made one of the better defensive plays of his career in blocking a three-foot shot by Howard when the game got tight in the closing minutes. Before that game in Ann Arbor, appropriately enough, Michigan retired the jersey of former great Russell, who always played so well against the Devils in the 1960s. "I always looked at this game as a measuring stick to see where we were as a team," Russell said.

The Devils ran their streak over the Wolverines to six straight in December 1994, overcoming one of the great runs by an opponent in Cameron history as Michigan logged a 24–0 spurt in the first half. The Wolverines finally beat Duke three straight times in the mid-1990s. Duke countered by decisively winning the next five contests in the series, topping the 100-point mark four times. Amaker was on the opposing sideline for the last two, in December 2001 and December 2002.

Michigan State. Walking through a Michigan airport in the middle of the night, Mike Krzyzewski tapped into his mental reservoir and conjured up the perfect analogy. "This reminds me of what our 1990 – 91 team did at Oklahoma," he said, about an hour after his 2003 – 04 team had dismantled Michigan State 72 – 50 on the Spartans' raucous home court.

Krzyzewski's 1990 – 91 team had gone to Norman, Okla., in December, stared down a record crowd, shut down high-scoring Brent Price, and claimed a 90 – 85 victory in a nationally televised performance that ended a 51-game home winning streak for the Sooners.

"That was a game that showed that team what it could become," Krzyzewski recalled. "This game could do the same for this team."

The 1991 Duke team went on to become national champions. The 2004 team didn't duplicate that feat but did reach the Final Four, and its win at East Lansing in the ACC – Big Ten Challenge was the starting point after a lukewarm opening to the season in bone-chilling Alaska. It was one of seven all-time meetings between the two schools, all in a tournament or special event.

The Spartans and Blue Devils were tied in the polls at No. 6 for the headliner at the Breslin Center in December 2003, and the home folks were clearly primed for a nationally televised showcase performance. Duke was in an atypical role as an underdog in an arena where the Spartans had vanquished 76 of their previous 80 foes. But sparked by new starters Shavlik Randolph and Sean Dockery, the Devils forced 17 first-half turnovers and went on a 20 – 2 run to take control of the game.

Michigan State was sent to Durham for the following season's ACC – Big Ten Challenge, and the Devils were up to the task of defending their home court. But the December 2004 battle was much closer, with Duke winning 81 – 74. It was a one-point game late when Dockery hit an off-balance jumper to give Duke a lift. J. J. Redick and Daniel Ewing hit 29 points apiece to spearhead the attack.

The Spartans had both those December games on their minds when they met Duke in the NCAA Tournament Sweet 16 in 2005. They talked about getting coach Tom Izzo his first win over Duke and accomplished the mission 78 – 68, primarily on the strength of a perimeter defense that disrupted Duke's guards and forced 22 turnovers.

"You've got to give Michigan State credit for speeding us up," said Redick. "They put that full-court pressure on us and when we got inside of half-court we were sped up and didn't take care of the ball. They were really physical and we weren't as strong with the ball. That's got to be on us, to be strong with the ball."

Michigan State beat Duke in December 1958 in the Dixie Classic, but the two teams never met again until the NCAA tourney in 1994. Duke won that game, as well as two physical, six-point duels in the 1999 season. One was in the Great Eight in Chicago, the other in the Final Four — the first and last stops on a 32-game winning streak. Elton Brand's 18 points and 15 rebounds set the tone in the national semis to move the No. 1 Blue Devils past the No. 2 Spartans.

Overall, through 2006 there were seven Duke-

Michigan State games on the books, five on neutral courts, with the Devils owning a 5 – 2 record.

Miller, Alex. A 6 – 1 reserve forward from Millersburg, Ky., Alex Miller scored eight points for the team that won the Southern Conference championship in 1942, then lettered for the 1943 team when he scored 13 points in 12 contests. Miller returned after the Second World War and played in two games for the 1947 team. He had 18 career points.

Miller, Don. A 6 – 4 reserve forward from Miami Beach, Donald Ira Miller saw reserve action during the 1957 and 1958 seasons. He played in 39 games with 117 points and 63 rebounds. After playing sparingly for most of the 1957 campaign, he had the best stretch of his career over the last six games, when he scored 57 points and helped Duke to three ACC wins. He had a career-best 16 points against Virginia during that run.

Minor, John. John Travis Minor, from Batavia, N.Y., saw backup duty for three teams, 1937 – 39, and lettered for the latter two years. He scored 95 points, over half in his senior season.

Mock, Bill. After Bill Werber became Duke's first All-America in 1930, the school waited 10 years to decorate its second All-America. The honoree was William Mock, a 6 – 2 forward for the 1940 and 1941 squads. Mock, from Altoona, Pa., came off the bench most of 1940 and was the leading scorer for the 1940 conference runner-up team, a unanimous selection to the all-tournament squad, and a member of the All-America third team chosen by NEA. He did not repeat those honors in 1941 but was the fifth-leading scorer for the Blue Devils' conference championship team. He totaled 292 points in his two campaigns as a letterman. Mock hit the winning shot in a victory over UNC in 1941 with 2:09 to play, allowing Duke to freeze the ball for most of the remaining time.

Moore, Tony. With his athleticism and leaping ability, Antonio Maurice Moore showed promise as a reserve forward early in his career. But just as he was on the verge of bigger things, he was declared academically ineligible and his Blue Devil days came to an end.

Moore, a 6 – 7 forward from Washington, D.C., played in parts of four seasons, from 1993 through 1996. He totaled 56 games, with 142 points and 106 rebounds, while hitting 61 percent of his field-goal attempts. His freshman year consisted of just 12 appearances because of knee and shoulder injuries. He played a combined 37 games in his sophomore and junior years, mostly in relief roles, though he did start the Boston University game in 1995. He also hit his career scoring high that year, with 13 points against South Carolina State.

As a senior Moore started five of the first seven games and was averaging 5.1 points, 4.0 rebounds, and 24.6 minutes of playing time. He was just beginning to blossom on the court as a quality inside player when he was dismissed from school at the end of the fall semester for academic reasons.

Moreland, Chris. The first women's basketball player enshrined in the Duke Sports Hall of Fame, Chris Moreland was one of the ACC's dominant players during the 1980s. She was the league's rookie of the year as a freshman, its player of the year as a junior, and one of its top scorers and rebounders of all time when she graduated.

Moreland was the first high school All-America to commit to Duke during the Debbie Leonard era. Her arrival instantly upgraded the Blue Devils from a perennially mediocre team to one that had a chance to win almost every game. Duke posted a 19 – 8 record in Moreland's first year, played in the postseason her next two years, and got off to a 12 – 0 start in her senior year before an injury to her fellow standout Katie Meier derailed the season.

"Every up-and-coming team like ourselves needs one quality player to propel us to a higher level," Leonard said. "Chris Moreland has been that player for us. Without her, we probably would not have been able to sign many of our recruits. She has had more impact on our program than any other player."

Moreland averaged 20.1 points and 11.1 rebounds over her 111 games, the only women's player in Duke history to average a double-double for a career. No other player in school history has averaged double-figure rebounds or at least 20 points for a career. Moreland's 2,232 points were the Duke record until Alana Beard set a new mark in 2004. Her point total remains fifth in ACC history and

When Chris Moreland graduated in 1988, she had the best career rebounding average and second-best scoring average in ACC women's basketball history.

her rebound total of 1,229 is fourth, while her rebound average of 11.1 is the best the conference has ever seen. Moreland attempted more free throws than anyone in ACC history (868), and her 576 free throws made are second only to Beard's 582.

Duke never had an All-ACC player before Moreland; she made the All-ACC every year, the first team in 1986 and 1987, the second team in 1985 and 1988. She was also the first Duke player to make an All-America team when the Women's Basketball News Service placed her on its first team in 1988.

Statistically Moreland's best season was 1986, when she averaged 23.0 points and 11.8 rebounds while hitting 58 percent of her shots. A 6–1 native of Alexandria, Va., she contributed 20.9 points and 10.5 boards in 1987, when she became Duke's first ACC player of the year

and guided the team to its first NCAA tourney. Her top scoring performance was 34 points, which she delivered three times; her rebounding high was 20 versus North Carolina on her last trip to Chapel Hill. One of her best wins was a 68–66 decision over N.C. State in the final game that she and fellow senior Paula Andersen played at Cameron Indoor Stadium.

In September 2001 Moreland was inducted into the Duke Sports Hall of Fame as its fifth female honoree. Five months later she was one of five charter women inductees in the Duke Basketball Hall of Honor.

Morgan, Junior. The starting center for most of his three years, 1954–56, Eben Cornelius Morgan Jr., of Asheboro, N.C., appeared in 79 games with 713 points and 643 rebounds. He averaged double-figures scoring and over nine rebounds a game in each of his last two years. Strong and rugged at 6–7, Morgan had a rare 20–20 game in his senior year when he collected 29 points and 21 rebounds against Navy. But that was not his career scoring high. In a game against Virginia in 1955 he erupted for 33 points. Morgan was a seventh-round NBA draft pick but did not play in the league.

Morgan, Merrill. After an unsuccessful bid to make the varsity in 1958, Merrill Smith Morgan landed a reserve role for the following three seasons, 1959–61. A 6–3 guard from Montclair, N.J., he played in 29 games with 70 points and 26 rebounds. Most of his offensive production was in his initial varsity campaign, when he posted a career best of 20 points against Villanova.

Morris, John. A 6–2 guard from Roxboro, N.C., John Morris was unable to make the varsity roster in 1958 but came back for a successful bid in the following year. He played in one game as a junior in 1959, going scoreless against West Virginia.

Morrison, Harold. After getting off to a slow start because of nagging injuries in his freshman year, Harold Lawrence Morrison Jr., a 6–7 forward, went on to play 93 games from 1976 through 1979. He scored 240 points and had 193 rebounds. Morrison was the starting power forward for most of his sophomore year in 1977, when he averaged 5.5 points and 4.3 rebounds. When freshmen Gene Banks and Kenny Dennard arrived in 1978, Morrison moved to the bench but still played an important supporting role as a frontcourt reserve for the team, which was the ACC champion and an NCAA finalist that year. His playing time dwindled in the second half of the season after he suffered an injury. Morrison played in 27 of Duke's 30 games during his senior year of 1979 but did not get extensive minutes. A native of West Orange, N.J., he went into hospital administration and then became an insurance executive.

Mosch, Sheana. No one really knows the answer to this question, but Sheana Mosch would ask it anyway—in ink, in all caps, on the tops of her basketball shoes.

HWJP — How would Jesus play?

"I think you could break it down into two things," she would say. "I think he'd work his butt off and have a good attitude, those two things."

Those are the two things that Mosch concentrated on during her career as a Duke women's basketball player. The philosophy served her well, as she was one of only a few in program history to never miss a game over four years. She appeared in more contests, 140, than any other Blue Devil—and also played in the most wins, 124, before Mistie Williams topped those records in 2006.

A 5–10 guard from Clearfield, Pa., Mosch learned the game from her father George and by devouring every book, magazine article, and videotape that she could find about the former LSU and NBA star Pete Maravich. Mosch could duplicate many of his ball-handling skills in middle and high school, and her Duke teammates would sometimes see her working on them in the gym. But she never threw behind-the-back or between-the-legs passes during games. She was more substance than flash, fulfilling whatever role her coaches needed.

Mosch totaled 1,283 points with 500 rebounds and 271 assists from 2000 to 2003. She played on four ACC championship and two Final Four teams, and made the All-ACC third team as a sophomore and the NCAA Tournament all-region team in 2002.

Regarded as an excellent driver and finisher, Mosch enjoyed the best offensive flurry of her career as a sophomore when scoring leader Alana Beard went down with an injury. With her team in need of points, the modest

Mosch reeled off a four-game string in which she had 25, 29, 30, and 22 points, all versus ACC teams, with three of the games on the road. She hit 42 of 59 shots during the run, and attempted just six three-pointers. Everything else came on drives, fast breaks, putbacks, or medium jumpers after she worked herself free on screens. The highlight performance was against Clemson, when she hit 12 of 12 shots for 30 points while also grabbing 11 rebounds and dishing six assists. Her 29 points in the UNC game included 13 straight in overtime to key a victory.

Then when Beard returned to the lineup, Mosch went back to scoring her usual 8–10 points. That's also what Mosch averaged as a senior when she came off the bench for all but six games while helping the Devils to the Final Four.

Moses, George. He arrived at Duke in the fall of 1974 as a 26-year-old junior college transfer. Older than everyone else on the team, George Isaac Moses, a 6–5 forward from New York, had a short career in which he made his mark mostly as a relentless rebounder. In 35 career games he grabbed 316 rebounds for a 9.0 average and reached double figures 15 times. He also scored 279 points for an 8.0 average.

Moses served in the military after high school, then went to Schreiner Junior College in Kerrville, Texas, where he once had 37 points and 30 rebounds in one game. Neill McGeachy's Duke staff was one of over 200 to recruit him, though by the time he reached campus Bill Foster had taken over on the Blue Devil bench. Moses helped Duke get off to a 6–2 start in 1974–75, averaging 7.0 points and 6.8 rebounds as a solid, steady sixth man. Then he was declared academically ineligible and was lost for the rest of the year. He returned the following season, however, and was a true force on the boards. He played in all 27 games and averaged 9.7 rebounds, ranking fifth in the ACC. His top efforts were back-to-back outings of 17 and 18 rebounds against Maryland and Clemson. He also contributed 8.3 points that year and was second on the team in assists with 80, but fouled out nine times.

Moss, Pete. Paul Elliott "Pete" Moss lettered for the first two Duke teams, 1925–26, and captained the 1926 squad as a senior. He was from Forest City, N.C.

Moyer, Bob. Bob Moyer, a 6 – 0 guard from Harrisburg, Pa., scored two points but did not letter for the 1940 team, then lettered but went scoreless as a reserve on the 1941 team, which won the conference title.

Mullen, Jack. When he first made the varsity in 1960, Charles Franklin "Jack" Mullen was a 24-year-old sophomore who had been in the Navy. Playing on service squads, he made the All-Navy team in 1958. He played three years for coach Vic Bubas, 1960 – 62, lettering for the first and last. A 5 – 11 guard, he started for most of the 1960 season and was the spearhead of a 1–1–3 defense employed down the stretch as Duke won the ACC title and reached the Elite Eight of the NCAA. Known for his quarterbacking skills, Mullen was praised for his role in a victory over South Carolina in 1961 even though he scored just four points. He missed most of 1961 and the first part of 1962 because of academic problems. But when he returned, he was a spark off the bench. In just his third game back he hit his career high of 17 points on 7-of-8 shooting in a home win over UNC and energized the Devils as a reserve in the season finale at Chapel Hill. His career totals: 56 games, 263 points, and 188 rebounds.

Mullins, Jeff. The scene: Greensboro Coliseum, January 1964, Duke versus Tennessee. The eighth-ranked Blue Devils trailed by five with barely a minute to go but tied the score to force overtime. They were down by five again in the extra period but rallied to earn a second OT. Finally, before the largest crowd to watch a basketball game in the arena's first five years, Duke broke the tie and pulled out a 67 – 65 victory — only after a last-ditch Volunteer shot banked in a fraction of a second too late.

There were plenty of heroes to go around in the Duke locker room, but one stood above the others. Jeffrey Vincent Mullins had hit the shot to tie the score with 1:09 left in the first overtime. He'd given the Devils the lead for good with 1:19 left in the second overtime and tacked on a critical free throw with three seconds left. The box score showed him with 33 points, then a career high, on 14-of-27 shooting, plus 12 rebounds.

"If there was ever an All-American effort," coach Vic Bubas said, "Jeff gave it to us tonight."

Jeff Mullins and Art Heyman averaged over 20 points a game in guiding the 1963 team to Duke's first Final Four.

In truth, Mullins gave an all-star effort virtually every night that he donned a Duke uniform. A 6 – 4 New Yorker who prepped in Lexington, Ky., he eluded the intense recruiting efforts of Adolph Rupp, then joined the Duke program and became one of its brightest stars. He and Art Heyman teamed during his first two years on the varsity to form one of the most lethal one-two punches in Duke annals. Mullins was just as successful as the team's senior leader after Heyman's departure. He played in all 86 games during his three seasons, 1962 – 64, and scored in double figures every time, a streak unrivaled in Duke history. Furthermore, he was the team's leading scorer in 41 of his 86 games.

Mullins averaged at least 20 points a game every season and finished with a 21.9 mark on 1,884 points. He was a smooth jump shooter, excelled in transition, could drive and draw the foul, and scored frequently on the offensive boards. He totaled 776 rebounds for his career, a 9.0 average, especially eye-opening given his size. And the grace with which he performed every function on the court was usually likened to either ballet or poetry by the scribes of his era.

A Game He'll Never Forget

Jeff Mullins, 1964 versus Villanova

Mullins owns the distinction of scoring in double figures in all 86 games that he played for the Blue Devils. He notched his career high late in his senior year, with 43 points against Villanova in the first round of the NCAA Tournament at Reynolds Coliseum. The best-remembered shot from that game was Mullins's half-court heave at the halftime buzzer. That gave him 28 points in the opening 20 minutes, on 12-of-15 shooting.

"Villanova was a very good team, with some guys who played in the pros for a long time," Mullins recalled. "They played a helter-skelter zone. I won't say it was like the Temple zone, but it was a different zone. Basically it was a four-man zone and they gave Wally Jones the freedom to do just about anything. He could double-team the ball, he could roam. We prepared for that, and it was hard to prepare for, but fortunately I had an awful lot of open looks against it and the shots were going in. So we were able to beat a very good Villanova team."

Duke won 87–73. Mullins finished the day hitting 19 of 28 from the field and 5 of 6 from the line. He had three straight baskets in a 78-second span of the second half to help the Devils open up a lead.

"There's nothing you can do to slow him up," N.C. State coach Everett Case said. "He'll shoot your eyes out. And when he goes on the fast breaks, he shoots from 30 and 40 feet out and makes them."

"Jeff was the greatest player I ever played with and the nicest person I ever played with," Heyman recalled.

Mullins and Heyman combined for over half of Duke's points in the two years they worked together, leading the Devils to a 47–8 record, the school's first undefeated ACC season (14–0 in 1963), and its first Final Four. Duke then went 26–5 in 1964 and 13–1 in the conference, the lone loss a one-pointer to Wake Forest when Mullins missed a last-second shot. He atoned by scoring 24 against the Deacs in the ACC final and was chosen tourney MVP.

Mullins was All-ACC first team for three years, one of just five Duke players to earn that distinction. He was one of the top three vote getters in all three years, and a unanimous selection in 1964 when he was named ACC player of the year and ACC athlete of the year. He also made the ACC All-Tournament first team three times. Mullins had some of his best performances in the NCAA Tournament, leading his team in scoring in five of his eight tourney games. He had his career high of 43 versus Villanova—the most ever by a Blue Devil in the tournament—and 30 versus UConn in the two games that secured the team's Final Four berth in 1964. He also served as Duke's senior class president.

After leading Duke to its first NCAA final, Mullins became the first Blue Devil to play in the Olympics, winning gold in Tokyo. He then headed to the NBA as the No. 5 draft pick, becoming the first Duke grad to make the All-Star team and the first to win an NBA championship ring.

Mullins played in the NBA for 12 seasons, 1965–76, and scored over 13,000 points, more than any other Duke alumnus. He spent his first two years in St. Louis with little fanfare, then enjoyed a productive decade with the San Francisco (later Golden State) Warriors. He averaged 16.2 points for his career and scored better than 20 points a game for four straight years, 1969–72, making the All-Star Game three times. He posted career highs of 22.8 points and 5.9 rebounds in 1969.

Mullins participated in the playoffs in 10 of his 12 years and played in 83 postseason games with a 13.1 scoring average. He made his first appearance in the NBA Finals in 1967, his first year with the Warriors, and posted an average of 17.7 in the playoffs. He hit for 25.1 points a game in the 1968 playoffs and averaged 8.1 in the 1975 playoffs while helping Golden State win the championship.

Mullins's basketball days were hardly over after his pro retirement. He worked in administration at Duke, analyzed games on television, and operated Jeff Mullins Chevrolet in Apex, N.C. Presented with an opportunity to coach the UNC Charlotte basketball program, he served for 11 seasons, 1986–96. He won 182 games and took the 49ers to three NCAA tourneys and two NITs. His 1991 and 1992 teams faced his alma mater in Cameron.

During the 1994–95 season Mullins took a December break to visit Duke for the retirement of his No. 44 jersey. The school did not retire any numbers during the

Daughter Lindy, wife Mickie, and daughters Jamie and Debbie joined Mike Krzyzewski at his 2001 Hall of Fame enshrinement.

Bubas era but decided to retire Heyman's and Mullins's numbers in the 1990s. Mullins had long since been inducted into the Duke Sports Hall of Fame (1978). He was also enshrined in the North Carolina Sports Hall of Fame and the Golden State Warriors Hall of Fame. The ACC named him to its 50th anniversary team.

"I look back very fondly on my total basketball career, from playing high school basketball in Kentucky to a world championship in the NBA and the Olympic experience," he said 40 years after graduation, "but my memories of playing at Cameron and at Duke stand right up there with every key memory I have in basketball. It was just a wonderful time and a wonderful place to play."

Murray, Terry. A 6–5 forward from Atlanta, William Terrence Murray played in one game for the 1964 team, with no points and two rebounds.

Naismith Memorial Basketball Hall of Fame. Significant contributors to the game of basketball have been inducted in the Naismith Memorial Basketball Hall of Fame since 1959. One of the charter inductees was Dr.

James Naismith, who invented the game in 1891 and made the first financial contribution toward the development of the Hall of Fame. A facility to house the Hall first opened in 1968 at Springfield (Mass.) College. The current facility, occupying 80,000 square feet, opened in 2002 in Springfield.

Coach Mike Krzyzewski became the first representative from Duke to be enshrined, joining the Hall of Fame on October 5, 2001, along with John Chaney and Moses Malone. Krzyzewski was elected in his first year on the ballot. His college coach, Bob Knight, presented him for induction.

"Certainly when a coach gets inducted, it's because he's had great players who formed great teams and had amazing assistant coaches. I hope that all those youngsters who have played for me and the people who have worked with me will share in this honor," Krzyzewski said.

"I really believe that this is not an accomplishment, but an honor. Winning a national championship is an accomplishment because you are competing against other people. Professionally, it's the ultimate honor that you can receive. Given the love I have for coaching, to be put as a coach into the Hall of Fame could not be any better."

Former Duke assistant coaches Chuck Daly and Hubie Brown are also Hall of Fame members. Daly was inducted in 1994, Brown in 2005, primarily for their successes in professional basketball. Their boss at Duke, former head coach Vic Bubas, received the Hall of Fame's most prestigious honor short of enshrinement in 1996 when he was recognized with the John Bunn Award. The honor has been presented annually since 1973 to someone who has contributed greatly to the game on or off the court.

Naktenis, Pete. Best known as a left-handed baseball pitcher who went on to perform in the majors, Peter Ernest Naktenis lettered as a 6–1 center for the 1935 basketball team. A reserve in 1934, Naktenis had never played in a varsity game but was thrust into a prominent role when starting center Connie Mack Jr. did not return to school in 1935. He finished with 103 points, one of the top figures on a balanced statistical sheet that year. A native of Aberdeen, Wash., he pitched in 10 major league baseball games, with a record of 0–1.

National Invitation Tournament. During an era when the National Invitation Tournament (NIT) enjoyed prestige on par with the NCAA tourney, the Atlantic Coast Conference would not permit its teams to participate in it. Duke finally became the first school to appear in the NIT as an ACC member in 1967, when the Blue Devils headed to New York and lost a first-round game to the eventual champion, Southern Illinois. Duke was also invited to the NIT in 1968, 1970, 1971, and 1981. The Blue Devils' best run was in 1971, when they lost to eventual champ North Carolina in the semifinals. In five NIT appearances Duke posted a record of 5–6.

The Preseason NIT, bringing together 16 teams under various corporate title sponsors such as Chase, Dodge, and TiVo, was launched in the fall of 1985. With two rounds on campus sites, followed by the semis and finals in New York during Thanksgiving week, it soon developed into one of the premier early-season events in college basketball. Duke won the championship of the inaugural Preseason NIT, edging St. John's and Kansas in tense battles at Madison Square Garden. The Blue Devils also participated in 1990–91, when they lost to Arkansas in the semifinals (though they would eventually prevail

Gene Banks was available for a pre-game TV interview with alumnus Jeff Mullins after breaking his wrist in a 1981 first round NIT game.

as NCAA champs); in 1996–97, when they lost to Indiana in the title game; in 2000–01, when they nipped Temple in the final; and in the 2005–06 incarnation known as the NIT Season Tip-Off, managed for the first time by the NCAA. The Blue Devils got past athletic Memphis in the final to claim their third title in the event and improve their all-time Preseason NIT record to 18–2.

Preseason NIT most valuable players from Duke: David Henderson 1985–86, Carlos Boozer 2000–01, Shelden Williams 2005–06.

NBA draft. The National Basketball Association has used a draft to bring new players into the league since 1947, with the selection order inversely related to the teams' order of finish during the preceding season. In 1985 a lottery was added to determine the order at the top of the draft for the teams that had not made the playoffs. Beginning in 1989 the draft was limited to two rounds.

Dick Groat was the first Duke player selected in an NBA draft, though he spent most of his professional

Grant Hill got the traditional draft-day handshake from NBA commissioner David Stern in 1994.

career playing another sport, baseball. Art Heyman and Elton Brand were the only No. 1 picks from Duke through the 2005 draft. In 1999 Duke had four players chosen among the top 14, and in 2002 Jason Williams and Mike Dunleavy became just the second pair of teammates to be selected among the first three picks.

Seven Duke draftees went on to be named to the NBA All-Rookie team: Art Heyman (1964), Jack Marin (1967), Christian Laettner (1993), Grant Hill (1995), Elton Brand (2000), Shane Battier (2002), and Luol Deng (2005).

NBA early entrants. Elton Brand in 1999 became the first Duke player to make himself available to the NBA draft before completing his college eligibility. The consensus national player of the year, he had the blessing of his coach. In 2004 Duke lost its top recruit to the draft when point guard Shaun Livingston, who had signed a letter of intent with the Blue Devils, opted to go directly

from high school to the pros. He was the fourth pick in the draft. (See page 274.)

NCAA Tournament. The National Collegiate Athletic Association conducted its first men's basketball championship tournament after the 1939 season. Eight teams competed in a one-week event that ended when Oregon defeated Ohio State in the title game at Evanston, Ill. During its early years the tourney was overshadowed by the National Invitation Tournament (NIT) in New York. Schools could play in both tournaments, and in 1950 CCNY became the only team to win both in the same season.

From humble origins the NCAA Tournament grew into one of the most popular sporting events in the United States, as well as a lucrative commercial enterprise responsible for most of the NCAA's revenue, thanks to a $1 billion TV contract with CBS Sports. The field expanded

These are the Duke players chosen in the first round of the NBA draft, with the number of games they played in their NBA careers through 2006:

Year	Player	Team	Pick	Games
1952	Dick Groat	Fort Wayne	3	26
1963	Art Heyman	New York	1	147
1964	Jeff Mullins	St. Louis	5	804
1966	Jack Marin	Baltimore	5	849
1977	Tate Armstrong	Chicago	13	92
1979	Jim Spanarkel	Philadelphia	16	259
1980	Mike Gminski	New Jersey	7	938
1986	Johnny Dawkins	San Antonio	10	541
1986	Mark Alarie	Denver	18	325
1989	Danny Ferry	L.A. Clippers	2	917
1990	Alaa Abdelnaby	Portland	25	256
1992	Christian Laettner	Minnesota	3	868
1993	Bobby Hurley	Sacramento	7	269
1994	Grant Hill	Detroit	3	549
1995	Cherokee Parks	Dallas	12	472
1998	Roshown McLeod	Atlanta	20	113
1999	Elton Brand	Chicago	1	447
1999	Trajan Langdon	Cleveland	11	119
1999	Corey Maggette	Seattle	13	412
1999	William Avery	Minnesota	14	142
2001	Shane Battier	Memphis	6	315
2002	Jason Williams	Chicago	2	75
2002	Mike Dunleavy	Golden State	3	236
2003	Dahntay Jones	Boston	20	72
2004	Luol Deng	Phoenix	7	61
2006	Shelden Williams	Atlanta	5	—
2006	J. J. Redick	Orlando	11	—

to 16 teams in 1951 and to 22 in 1953, fluctuated between 22 and 25 through 1974, and then grew to 32 teams in 1975, the same year that several teams from the same conference were allowed to be invited. The size of the field increased to 40 teams in 1979, to 48 in 1980, and to 64 in 1985. A play-in game with a 65th team was added in 2001.

Duke's first NCAA appearance was in 1955, as a replacement for the ineligible ACC champion N.C. State. The Blue Devils received their first automatic bid as ACC champions in 1960, reached the Final Four for the first time in 1963, played for the national championship for the first time in 1964, and won their first NCAA crown in

1991. In 1992 Duke became the first school since UCLA (1967–73) to win consecutive titles.

Through 2006 the Blue Devils had played in 30 NCAAs, reached 14 Final Fours, and owned the best winning percentage of any school in tournament history at 75.9, with a record of 85–27. Duke played in the championship game nine times and won three (1991, 1992, 2001). Duke's 85 tournament wins trailed only Kentucky, North Carolina, and UCLA, while the 14 Final Fours trailed only UNC (16) and UCLA (15, plus one vacated). ACC schools had won 10 NCAA Tournaments, with Duke joined by North Carolina (four times), N.C. State (two), and Maryland (one).

Here are all of the NBA early entrant candidates who played at Duke:

Player	Duke Years	Duke Games	Draft Pick
Elton Brand	1998–99	60	1
Corey Maggette	1999	39	13
William Avery	1998–99	74	14
Jason Williams	2000–02	108	2
Mike Dunleavy	2000–02	104	3
Carlos Boozer	2000–02	101	35
Luol Deng	2004	37	7
Shavlik Randolph	2003–05	92	—

During the 2005 tournament coach Mike Krzyzewski won his 66th game in the event to pass former UNC coach Dean Smith for the most career coaching victories in the tourney. Krzyzewski, who guided Duke to 10 Final Fours, was one of only four coaches in history to win three or more NCAA titles. John Wooden won 10, Adolph Rupp four, and Bob Knight three. Five of Krzyzewski's Final Fours were consecutive (1988–92), a feat topped only by UCLA's John Wooden (10 from 1967 to 1976).

Former Duke player Christian Laettner has played in more NCAA Tournament games than anyone else in history, 23. He also set the tournament's all-time records for career points (407), free throws made (142), and free throws attempted (167). Other Duke players with NCAA tourney career records included Bobby Hurley with the most assists (145) and most three-pointers made (42), and Grant Hill with the most steals (39).

Six Duke players have led the NCAA Tournament in scoring: Jeff Mullins, 1964, 116 points; Mike Gminski, 1978, 109 points; Johnny Dawkins, 1986, 153 points; Christian Laettner, 1991, 125 points, and 1992, 115 points; and Jason Williams, 2001, 154 points. Four Duke players have been named the most outstanding player at the Final Four: Art Heyman 1963, Christian Laettner 1991, Bobby Hurley 1992, and Shane Battier 2001.

Duke graduate Bob Bender was the first player to appear in the NCAA final game for two schools. He played in Indiana's national championship victory over Michigan in 1976, transferred to Duke, and played for the Blue Devils in their loss to Kentucky in the NCAA final in 1978. He later coached in the Final Four as an assistant to Krzyzewski.

Vic Bubas was one of six people to play in the Final Four (N.C. State, 1950) and serve as a head coach for a Final Four team (Duke, 1963, 1964, 1966). In 1985, when he was commissioner of the Sun Belt Conference, Bubas was chair of the NCAA Men's Basketball Committee, which administers the tournament. Duke athletics director Tom Butters held that post in 1993 and 1994.

Cameron Indoor Stadium has played host to one men's NCAA Tournament game. In 1954 N.C. State defeated George Washington in a first-round game at Duke's gym (not yet named for Eddie Cameron) to advance to the regionals in Philadelphia. The NCAA had one slot for the southern champion in the regional, and normally that would have gone to the Southern Conference champion. But that was the year the ACC was created from seven former Southern Conference schools, so the NCAA brought the two league champions together for a playoff to decide the spot in Philadelphia. The game was scheduled for Reynolds Coliseum in Raleigh. But after State won the ACC Tournament, Southern Conference and GWU officials rejected the notion of playing on the Wolfpack's home floor, so the game was switched to Duke. A crowd of 4,000 saw State win by two on a tip-in in the final minute. From then on the NCAA reserved spots for the Southern and ACC champs.

The NCAA began conducting a championship tournament for women's basketball in 1982. The ACC had three representatives in the 32-field and hasn't had fewer since. Duke's first appearance was in 1987, when the Blue Devils won a first-round game at home before losing at Rutgers in the second round. Duke did not receive another invitation until 1995, coach Gail Goestenkors's third season. That began a streak of 12 straight bids through 2006, with trips to the Final Four in 1999, 2002, 2003, and 2006. The Duke women appeared in the national championship game for the first time in 1999, falling to top-ranked Purdue. In 2006 they lost to Maryland in the NCAA final. The title was the second for an ACC member, following UNC's of 1994.

Goestenkors's 34 – 12 tournament record through 2006 gave her the third-best winning percentage of any active coach in the event, 73.9, trailing only Connecticut's Geno Auriemma (83.3) and Tennessee's Pat Summitt (83.2). Duke's winning percentage of 72.9 (35 – 13 record) in the NCAA tournament ranked first among ACC members.

Duke star Alana Beard finished her career as the No. 4 scorer in NCAA women's tourney history, with 352 points·in 19 games. Alumna Katie Meier is one of 13 women to both play and coach in the NCAA tourney; she suited up for the Blue Devils in 1987 and coached UNC Charlotte in 2003.

Nelson, DeMarcus. The highest-scoring player in the history of California high school basketball, DeMarcus De'Juan Nelson went through a solid rookie season in 2005 and was voted to the ACC All-Freshman team. A 6 – 3 guard who was born in Oakland, he played in all 33 games and started two, with 206 points and 150 rebounds.

Versatile, strong, and athletic enough to play at least three positions, Nelson got off to a slow start in the preseason when he tore thumb ligaments during the annual Blue-White game. Still, he scored 10 points in the season opener and hit his season high of 17 in the fifth game, versus Valparaiso in Chicago. His best performance was in the home game against UNC, when he played 29 minutes, scored 16 points, and added four steals plus three assists in a one-point win.

"I've had some ups and downs this season and I tried to keep my head in the game," he said. "Tonight was the night for me to make a difference . . . I think I might have surprised them, because looking at the tapes of our games, you really wouldn't have noticed me."

Nelson was expected to emerge as one of the Devils' most significant players in 2006 and got off to a solid start before suffering a stress fracture in his ankle during the fourth game, versus Drexel at Madison Square Garden. He returned to play 24 games, with seven starts and 171 points.

Nelson played his first three prep seasons at Vallejo High before transferring to Sheldon High for his senior year. He totaled 3,462 career points and had 22 to lead the West team at the McDonald's All-America game in 2004. His verbal commitment to Duke in May of his sophomore year is believed to be the earliest of any recruit in school history.

Nessley, Martin. The first 7-footer in Duke history, Martin Scott Nessley was a career reserve center from 1984 to 1987. He had 224 points, 191 rebounds, and 53 blocked shots in 92 career games. A 7 – 2 product of Whitehall, Ohio, where he blocked 420 shots in his high school career, Nessley saw very little playing time during his first three college seasons. A knee injury that required surgery hampered his sophomore year.

Nessley's best year was as a senior in 1987, when he played in all 33 games, started four, and averaged 11 minutes. Though not a prolific scorer, he was efficient in the paint and blocked 24 shots to share the team lead. He enjoyed his career game on a trip to Harvard, when

Height Advantage

The arrival of 7–1 center Brian Zoubek of Haddonfield, N.J., for the 2006–07 season gave the Blue Devils their third 7-footer in program history. Charting the tallest Duke players all-time—anyone 6–11 or bigger:

Size	Player	Duke Years
7–2	Martin Nessley	1984–87
7–1	Brian Zoubek	2007–
7–0	George Burgin	1987–89
6–11	Mike Gminski	1977–80
6–11	Christian Laettner	1989–92
6–11	Cherokee Parks	1992–95
6–11	Greg Newton	1994–97
6–11	Casey Sanders	2000–03

TALLEST DUKE WOMEN:

6–7	Alison Bales	2004–
6–7	Lello Gebisa	2000–2001

he totaled 25 points and eight rebounds. The Los Angeles Clippers selected Nessley in the sixth round of the NBA draft in 1987. He played in the league for just one year, 1988, for both the Clippers and Sacramento.

Newcome, Jim. Moving into the lineup during his sophomore year, James Henry Newcome developed into a frontcourt fixture during his three varsity seasons, 1956–58. A 6–5 native of Gary, Ind., he played in 75 games with 826 points and 600 rebounds. He led the 1957 and 1958 teams in scoring with marks of 14.9 and 13.2 points, and averaged a double-double in 1957 by also contributing 11.4 rebounds a game, the fourth-best figure in the ACC. Newcome was a second-team All-ACC pick in 1957 and moved up to the first team in 1958, when he was the primary and most consistent frontcourt player in Duke's drive to the regular-season championship.

Newcome posted his career scoring and rebounding highs in 1957, when he had 26 points versus South Carolina and 23 rebounds versus West Virginia. He also had 19 points in the West Virginia game as the Devils almost upset the 13th-ranked Mountaineers in the championship game of a tournament in Birmingham. The next season, when Duke did upset West Virginia, then No. 1, Newcome was the Devils' top scorer with 20 points and added 14 rebounds. Another of his finest efforts that year was in a double-overtime victory against N.C. State, when he scored 18 points with 14 rebounds. He was a co-captain of the 1958 team. Newcome was the 85th pick of the NBA draft but did not play in the league.

Newton, Greg. A Canadian import, Greg Michael Newton generated more questions immediately after his Duke career ended than he had in four years on the team. In one of the most second-guessed coaching decisions in program history, Mike Krzyzewski opted not to use Newton, then a senior, for a single minute of a second-round NCAA game against Providence in 1997. When Duke suffered a 98–87 upset loss, Blue Devil fans everywhere supposed that Newton, who stood 6–10, might have made a difference in a contest in which their team had been outrebounded 43–24.

Coming to Duke from Niagara Falls, Ontario, Newton quickly became a Cameron Indoor favorite with his enthusiastic, high-energy style and flamboyant dunks.

He came off the bench for his first two years, when one of his best moments was a perimeter blocked shot on Jerry Stackhouse to ignite a comeback in the classic home game against UNC in 1995. Newton had to miss the last few games of that season on an academic dishonesty charge. But he started every game of the bounce-back season of 1996 and averaged 12.2 points and 8.2 rebounds a game. Highlights were many, including a six-game run of nonconference games when he connected on 49 of 56 shots from the field while averaging 18 points. Over the last six games of the season he averaged 12 rebounds, with a high of 16 against Florida State.

Newton was named one of the team captains for his senior year and started 21 of the first 22 games. But his play became sporadic, he missed a couple of games with a back injury, and Krzyzewski decided to use a smaller lineup featuring freshman Chris Carrawell. Suddenly Newton was coming off the bench. He started his final home game against Maryland, which Duke won to secure the ACC regular-season crown, and he finished with a 10.4 scoring average for the year. But in his final postseason Newton was mostly a spectator, with just six minutes of playing time in three ACC and NCAA games. He did lead the team in rebounding as a senior with a 6.1 mark.

Newton's career totals included 107 games, 812 points, 550 rebounds, and 101 blocked shots. He hit 56.9 percent of his field-goal attempts. After Duke he played professionally in various foreign leagues and represented Canada at the 2000 Olympics in Sydney.

North Carolina. Jason Williams could picture himself in Carolina Blue. A hotly pursued high school star, he toured the Smith Center, saw the banners and trophies, appreciated the tradition. Then coach Bill Guthridge brought him back to earth, telling him that the Tar Heels weren't going to recruit him anymore.

Williams almost wound up at Rutgers, but his parents insisted that he visit Duke. Once he became a Blue Devil, his experience in Chapel Hill came flooding back.

"Coach Guthridge didn't try to recruit me, so I'm going to murder North Carolina every time I step on the court," Williams said. "It's funny how it takes something as little as that, something as minute as that. I thought about that every time before I stepped on the

Daniel Ewing enjoyed an 8–2 career record versus UNC from 2002 to 2005.

court versus Carolina. Even when he wasn't the coach, even when Matt Doherty was coaching, I thought about that. I had that chip on my shoulder and it carried me all the way through college."

Duke-North Carolina was the ultimate grudge match for Williams, just as it has always been for players, coaches, and fans on both sides of the storied Tobacco Road feud. There is no question regarding its status as the best basketball rivalry in the Atlantic Coast Conference. A survey by the National Association of Basketball Coaches labeled it the best rivalry in college basketball, and there are those who are fond of calling it the best in all of sports.

"Duke and North Carolina's the best because the two programs are outstanding," coach Mike Krzyzewski said. "When you talk about a rivalry, some of it has to do with distance, some of it has to do with the same league, or divisions. A lot of it is location. This takes on a whole other level because of the performance by both teams over the years. It does not know a coach, a player, a specific team; it knows excellence. As a result of that, it gets such a focus and attention from people everywhere because chances are, it's going to be a great game. And you know year in and year out, both teams are going to be good, the schools are great. There's really not a downside to this rivalry."

Here's how the rivalry knows excellence: the two schools play each other at least twice every year, sometimes three or four times, and in every one of their contests since 1960, at least one of the two has been nationally ranked in the Associated Press poll. The last time a Duke-UNC game pitted two unranked (AP) clubs was February 27, 1960, when the Tar Heels swamped the Devils in Durham. That was one of those years when they met four times, and UNC was ranked for the other three. But even though the Heels were prohibitive favorites, Duke rose up and pulled an upset in the ACC Tournament en route to its first championship. That could have marked the origin of the cliché about throwing the records out the window when Duke and Carolina play.

Duke and UNC are among the four winningest schools in college basketball history, with seven NCAA championships and 30 Final Fours between them. In the first 53 years of the ACC, they combined to win the tournament 31 times — and played each other in the final 10 times. One or the other either shared or won outright the regular-season crown 40 times during that span. A panel of ESPN officials voted the double-overtime Duke-Carolina game in 1995 the top moment in the first 25 years of the network's association with college basketball, and on ESPN2 the three most-watched games ever have been Duke-UNC contests. Of the 50 players named to the ACC's golden anniversary team, 23 were from Duke or Carolina, and there could have been more. Of the top 101 all-time Duke games highlighted in the preceding section of this encyclopedia, 27 are Carolina contests, and again, there could have been more.

When North Carolina saw four members of its 2005 NCAA championship team selected within the first 14 picks of the NBA draft, it marked just the second time that a draft had been so top-heavy with picks from one school; Duke previously had four of the first 14 in 1999.

"I think both programs, whether we would like to admit it or not, have helped one another," said Krzyzewski. "And certainly it's helped the ACC. Sometimes you hear complaining about it and the reason is because more people want to watch it; it's just at a different level. That doesn't mean that other teams aren't better than either one of us, it's just that over the years, people have been drawn to that. That's helped our conference immensely, this rivalry. There's no question about that."

Along with consistent excellence, the proximity of the two schools has kept the rivalry's cauldron bubbling from the outset. The 10 miles of asphalt that separate their basketball arenas would be only the starting point in an illustration of the Triangle region's sports dynamic. When Grant Hill expressed astonishment one year about the number of mixed marriages in the area, he wasn't talking about race but about the number of families with affiliations to both universities. Fans of both live and work alongside each other, attend the

The Game He'll Never Forget

Mark Alarie, 1984 versus North Carolina

Top-ranked UNC seemed destined for another Final Four and national championship run in 1984 when it stopped by the Greensboro Coliseum for the ACC Tournament. The Tar Heels had gone undefeated in the league, claimed first place by five games, and had dropped just one non-conference contest all year. But a Duke team that was 7–7 in the league knocked off the Heels in the ACC semifinals, 77–75, handing Michael Jordan a defeat in his last league game. The Heels were then eliminated from the NCAA in the Sweet 16.

According to Alarie, then a sophomore with a team-high 21 points, Duke's ACC upset served notice that the rebuilding Blue Devils were ready to battle on even footing with their archrivals once again after a three-year dry spell.

"To me, that was the coming of age for all of us," Alarie recalled 20 years later. "We all truly felt we could do it, although I know a lot of people following us didn't think we could. But Coach K gave us a ton of confidence going into every game that we could compete against Carolina, and when we finally beat them it really felt like the mantle was being handed over to the Duke program.

"Even though the programs have battled back and forth since then, that was a huge monkey off our backs and off of Coach K's back.

"I remember that game vividly. Of all the games that many of us played in that four-year span, that was the biggest one for all of us."

same churches and schools, and share shopping malls, daily newspapers, and television stations. Toss in the allegiances of N.C. State supporters and the result is a unique community blend unseen anywhere else in college athletics.

Duke and North Carolina have frequently recruited the same high school players, and the battles for some prospects elevated the rivalry to new heights. Art Heyman's switch from UNC to Duke polarized local hostilities to a previously unseen level of acrimony and jumpstarted Vic Bubas's mastery of the ACC. Larry Miller's decision to pick the Heels over the Blue Devils did the same for Dean Smith later in the 1960s.

Both schools really wanted point guard Dick DeVenzio, but Bubas prevailed. Duke thought it had the New Jersey sensation Mike O'Koren all set to join his prep teammate Jim Spanarkel in Durham, but the Tar Heels eventually won out. Eight of the 11 players whose jerseys are retired at Duke were also Carolina recruiting targets at some point. Kinston's Jerry Stackhouse was a regular visitor behind the Duke bench as a prep standout, before opting for UNC. Perhaps no recruiting battle between the two schools enjoyed more scrutiny than when Danny Ferry chose the Devils over the Heels in 1985, marking the first major recruiting victory for Krzyzewski over his counterpart Dean Smith. Duke went to three Final Fours with Ferry.

Ferry described the ACC Tournament championship game with UNC in Atlanta in his senior year, 1989, as one of the most physical and intense basketball games he had ever played in. The Heels pulled it out, but only after Ferry's half-court desperation heave bounced off the back of the rim. There is just something different about a Duke-Carolina game. For years, Krzyzewski used the UNC game to illustrate a lesson on desire. He'd roll a ball across the floor and dive on it, passionately pointing out that it had his name on it, that it belonged to him, just as it had to belong to each of his players when they hit the floor versus the Tar Heels.

For Jason Williams, the unique nature of the game hit home in his very first encounter, when his jersey was so drenched with sweat at halftime that he had to change into a fresh one.

"That never happens," he said. "But it's so hot in there and every play is so intense. People are diving here and diving there, people are talking, people are fighting. Everybody wants to win. There are cuts, everything. It's that perfect picture of basketball that you imagine it to be, two teams battling down to the end giving everything they have to win it, just to show who's the best."

Dick Groat's Senior Day, Art Heyman's swan song, Fred Lind in triple overtime, Robby West's shot heard 'round the world, Gene Banks at the buzzer, Jeff Capel's stunner, Chris Duhon's reverse layup — all are among the many treasured Duke moments from the rivalry, and the Tar Heels have a list just as long. UNC has won about 30 more times than Duke, led by Hall of Fame coaches Frank McGuire (winner in eight of his last 10

versus Duke) and Dean Smith (winner in 16 of 17 during the mid-1970s). Duke's senior class of 1954, featuring Blue Devil Hall of Famer Bernie Janicki and the future ACC coach Lefty Driesell, never lost to the Tar Heels, nor did the class of 1964 featuring Jeff Mullins. Duke's most prominent string of success followed Smith's retirement, when Krzyzewski guided his team to victory in 15 of 20 games against the Heels.

In terms of career achievement, North Carolina guard Phil Ford performed better against Duke than perhaps any other Tar Heel. Operating the Four Corners attack to perfection, Ford had a 9–2 mark versus the Devils and averaged almost 23 points a game. His Senior Day contest against Duke in 1978 would be one of the first to archive in a time capsule of great Tar Heel efforts. Likewise, Jason Williams was one of the Duke players who consistently came up big against UNC across an entire career. With that recruiting chip on his shoulder, he spurred his team to a 7–1 mark, and only two of the games were even close. He was undefeated in the Smith Center, beat the Heels twice in the ACC Tournament, and dropped 37 points on them in his final home game. During his sophomore season of 2001, an NCAA title year, he scored 32 in the home game, which Duke lost on a pair of free throws, and 33 in the road game, which everyone thought Duke would lose because Carlos Boozer was injured.

"Being at Duke, I was never in a position where I was an underdog before. That was the first time," Williams said. "It was just an amazing win. That game was so special. I couldn't tell you how many points I scored or how many Shane [Battier] scored. All I could tell you is that we won by about 20 [95–81] when Carolina was a 15- to 20-point favorite."

One of the telling characteristics of the rivalry is that it has transcended all the legendary figures who have competed in it — amazing when you consider the pantheon of names involved.

"We have a great national image and so does North Carolina. I think the two programs probably have as high [an image] as any other programs in the country," Krzyzewski said. "That's another thing that helps the rivalry, and I'm sure the rivalry helps that. People from different parts of the country tune in, and have for years, to watch the two programs. They'll fall in love with a coaching style, a kid on the team, for either one, because they've had great kids and so have we. So we have a great national image.

"There are a lot of people out there who are Duke fans, or there are a lot of people out there who don't like us and want us to lose. But you know, it's the same thing I think with North Carolina. Because you're dealing with excellence, you might not like it, but you respect it. You have to respect it at both programs because it's been there. And I think it's been there because both programs have had high standards on and off the court, and people like that. People should like it. To me, this game over the years has been a showcase for college basketball, and for the student-athletes playing college basketball."

North Carolina women. While the men's rivalry between Duke and North Carolina commands national attention, competition between the two women's programs also has boiled for years. Entering 2006, the Tar Heels held the all-time series lead, 39 – 28, mostly because they won 15 of the first 16 meetings during the Blue Devils' formative years. In the mid-1980s Duke progressed to the point where it could realistically challenge UNC, and for about a decade the two put on some dramatic displays, with 10 games from 1984 to 1996 being decided by three points or fewer and several others going down to the closing possessions.

The Blue Devils enjoyed season sweeps of UNC in 1986, 1991, 1996, and 1999, then dominated from 2000 to 2004 with 12 consecutive victories, the longest winning streak by either team in the series. Four of the dozen were in the ACC Tournament championship game. But the Tar Heels ended their drought emphatically in 2005 by sweeping three games, including the ACC final.

Among the more memorable moments for the Blue Devils were three home games decided on last-second shots: by Carolyn Sonzogni in 1986, 79 – 78; Leigh Morgan in 1990, 90 – 88; and Ali Day in 1995, 74 – 72. The last ended a streak of 32 consecutive Tar Heel wins dating back to the school's 1994 NCAA championship season.

Duke posted the most lopsided triumph in the series, 101 – 58 in 2000, but there was little joy in Cameron Indoor Stadium. As the Devils were leading 70 – 37 with 11 minutes left, senior standout Peppi Browne was trying to finish a fast break when she injured her knee and

was lost for the rest of the season. That was the first of just two occasions when a team scored 100 points in the rivalry; the other was in 2002, when the Devils cruised to victory by a score of 102 – 82 behind 31 points from Beard, 23 from Monique Currie, and steady inside play from Michele Matyasovsky. Currie came back with another great effort against UNC during the postseason in 2002, pouring in 30 points with 12 rebounds to lead the Devils in the ACC championship game. She hit 8 of 12 field goals and 14 of 14 free throws in claiming MVP honors.

Another of Duke's most explosive individual displays against UNC was in 2001 in Chapel Hill. With the Devils' scoring leader Beard out of action because of injury, guard Sheana Mosch stepped up with 29 points to spark a 92 – 85 overtime decision. Mosch missed a point-blank shot late in regulation that probably would have meant victory, but she made sure of it later by scoring 13 consecutive points in overtime.

Duke won a classic on ESPN2 at a sold-out Carmichael Auditorium on Martin Luther King Day in 2003, when it came from seven points behind at the end of regulation and prevailed 78 – 67 in overtime. Duke was undefeated and ranked No. 1 while the Heels were riding a 12-game winning streak. UNC's Leah Metcalf tied the score on a leaning three-point bank shot with 24 seconds left, and the Heels were poised for the upset when a whistle blew on a last-second attempt by the Heels. After reviewing the play, the officials ruled that the shot and a Duke foul had both come after the final buzzer, so the teams went to overtime. Behind 26 points from Beard and 22 from Iciss Tillis, the Devils claimed their 30th straight ACC win.

Four of the best-attended games in ACC women's history have been between Duke and UNC. Contests in Chapel Hill during the 1999, 2003, and 2004 seasons drew 10,000 or more fans, and the one in 2003 at Cameron Indoor Stadium was a sellout at 9,314. Since Duke's rise to prominence under Gail Goestenkors, the game has frequently been shown on national television.

North Carolina Sports Hall of Fame. Inductees in the North Carolina Sports Hall of Fame with ties to the Duke basketball program include coaches Vic Bubas, Eddie Cameron, and Mike Krzyzewski; players Mike Gminski, Jack Marin, and Jeff Mullins; multisport representatives Gordon Carver, Whit Cobb, Bob Gantt, and Ace Parker; media figures Bob Harris, Dick Herbert, Ted Mann, and Add Penfield; and administrator Carl James.

North Carolina State. One of the unfortunate casualties of ACC expansion in 2004–05 was the league's inability to preserve some of the rivalries upon which it had been founded. Triangle neighbors Duke and N.C. State first started playing each other in 1912 when both schools were known by different names. Except for 1925, they had met at least twice every year through the 2004 season, with each always making a visit to the other's home arena every winter. But with the elimination of the ACC's traditional round-robin schedule in 2005, Duke and State were slated to play just once during the regular season for at least the first two unbalanced conference schedules. No doubt that arrangement would have had the legendary Everett Case turning over in his grave. Case, the former State coach, had asked to be buried on Highway 70 between Raleigh and Durham so that he could oversee his Wolfpack on its annual visit to Duke. That's how ingrained the series was.

Duke dominated the Pack before Case arrived on the scene from Indiana in 1947. When the Blue Devils beat State in their first battle against him, it gave them a 15-game winning streak in the series. But Case completely changed basketball in the Triangle and the escalation of the rivalry with Duke was only one example. After that first defeat, Case's teams knocked off the Devils in 12 of their next 13 meetings.

Duke-State games from the early 1950s remain among the series' classic bests, and some viewed the State game in the same light as the UNC game on the Devils' home schedule. In 1951 Duke junior Dick Groat and State senior Sammy Ranzino attracted the headlines for their scoring exploits. When the two met in early January in Durham, they were coming off scintillating performances at the old Dixie Classic, a three-day extravaganza in Raleigh. Groat had won the event's scoring title by a 71–65 margin over Ranzino, but Ranzino had been named tourney MVP because his team had won. When the two went head to head in Durham, Groat poured in 36 points to Ranzino's 32, but the Pack won in overtime. At the rematch in Raleigh, Groat took scoring honors

J. J. Redick had several of his best scoring games against N.C. State, twice in the ACC Tournament.

again, 27–20, but Ranzino's team won again, much to the delight of a raucous, sold-out audience.

Ranzino was gone in 1952, when senior Groat almost sparked another upset of a nationally ranked Wolfpack squad. With time running out, Groat forced a turnover, came up with the ball, and got it to Bernie Janicki, who hit a shot from near midcourt to tie the score. The Wolfpack went on to win in double overtime, but later in the season the Devils won in Raleigh for the first time in five years.

Case unknowingly developed the man who would turn the tables on the Duke-State series. One of his early backcourt aces was Vic Bubas, who later became his assistant coach before taking over the Duke program for the 1960s. Bubas went 17–8 against his alma mater and won 15 of 16 games from 1963 through 1968. That protracted run ended when the Wolfpack held the ball on the Devils in the ACC semifinals in 1968 and won 12 – 10. When Bubas retired the next year, a second straight State alum, Bucky Waters, was named to succeed him.

Under the direction of Norm Sloan, State dominated Duke in the 1970s — and just about everybody else in the ACC, for that matter. Waters's 1972 team knocked State out of the ACC tourney in the first round, but that was the Wolfpack's last loss for close to two years, as it enjoyed an undefeated record in 1973 and won the national title in 1974 with a 30 – 1 mark. The Duke-State feud took a new twist when Sloan and Bill Foster left their schools after the 1980 campaign, to be replaced by a pair of young coaches from the Northeast: Mike Krzyzewski and Jim Valvano. Their rivalry during the 10 years that Valvano coached the Wolfpack was one of the more ardent in the ACC. Valvano grabbed the early leg up by winning the NCAA title in his third season, as Duke struggled. But Krzyzewski went to the Final Four in four of Valvano's last five years and got his first national title the year after Valvano left the Pack.

Post-Valvano, Krzyzewski's team completely dominated N.C. State by winning 32 of 38 games from 1991 through 2006. That included three ACC Tournament victories of note after the turn of the century: 2002, when Carlos Boozer hit 11 of 12 shots in a 30-point rout at the final; 2003, when J. J. Redick scored 30 points to key a late rally in the final; and 2005, when Redick exploded for 35 points in the semifinals to lead his team into its eighth straight championship game.

Northrop, Geoff. A 6 – 6 forward from La Jolla, Calif., Geoffrey Mason Northrop transferred to Duke from California Pomona and played one season for the Blue Devil varsity. In 1977 he appeared in 12 games and scored 17 points while grabbing eight rebounds.

Notre Dame. Though not very balanced over the long term, the Duke-Notre Dame series provided several competitive and interesting installments from its genesis in 1965 through the 2002 NCAA Tournament. The Blue Devils won 19 of 21 meetings, including all six played at Cameron Indoor Stadium and all nine played on neutral courts. The Fighting Irish won two of six played in South Bend.

A four-game series from 1965 to 1968 saw Duke win twice in Chicago as well as at Greensboro and Charlotte. The opener was played at Chicago Stadium in 1965, the second game of a doubleheader with Loyola and Dayton, with almost 9,000 fans in attendance. Jack Marin had 35 points, Steve Vacendak 32, and Bob Verga 21 in a lopsided win. Marin hit 11 of 17 shots for 24 points the following year, when Duke won in Greensboro, while Verga had three straight outside jumpers during crunch time and finished with 23 points in the win at Charlotte in 1967. Only the meeting back in Chicago in 1968 was decided by single figures.

A two-game set in 1973 and 1974 saw each team win on its home floor. Notre Dame was ranked No. 3 in the nation for the second of these and rolled over Duke behind 27 points from freshman Adrian Dantley and 25 from John Shumate. A few weeks prior, Notre Dame had ended UCLA's record 88-game winning streak.

The biggest game in the series was in the Final Four in 1978, when Duke edged the Fighting Irish 90 – 86 to advance to the NCAA championship game. Duke was ranked seventh and Notre Dame sixth in the final Associated Press poll that year. Jim Spanarkel, Gene Banks, and Mike Gminski each scored at least 20 points in that contest.

Duke-Notre Dame then became an non-conference staple of the college schedule in 1985, when the schools began a series that lasted 11 consecutive seasons. The first game was played at the Meadowlands in New Jersey, then at alternating home courts through 1995. Three of the contests went down to the wire: Duke won at home in 1986 when Johnny Dawkins blocked David Rivers's final shot attempt; Notre Dame won the following year in overtime at South Bend; and the Blue Devils pulled out a 74 – 72 decision in 1994 when Marty Clark's tip with three seconds left helped his team overcome a 34-point night by the Irish's Monte Williams.

During that 11-year run, the two schools also met in a Preseason NIT consolation game at New York. After the home-and-home series ended, the teams did not face each other again until November 1998, when they were matched in the opener of the Great Alaska Shootout. The Blue Devils hit 15 three-pointers and got 20-point nights from Trajan Langdon, William Avery, and Corey Maggette to win in an avalanche.

Duke and Notre Dame squared off in the second

round of the NCAA Tournament in 2002 at Greenville, S.C., in a head-to-head between Mike Krzyzewski and his former assistant Mike Brey. Duke advanced with an 84–77 decision thanks to superb free-throw shooting. Notre Dame led by seven points with six minutes left, and the score was tied with 1:29 to go, but Duke hit nine of its last 10 free throws to win.

Novick, Tom. A 6–7 walk-on from Charlotte, Tom Novick played briefly in two games for the 2005 team during his sophomore year. He contributed in practice most of the year but missed about a month of the season because of mononucleosis.

Number One. Duke's first appearance as the No. 1 team in an Associated Press college basketball poll was on December 14, 1965, after the Blue Devils had blitzed previously top-ranked UCLA on consecutive nights. Duke held the ranking for eight weeks. The Blue Devils were ranked No. 1 in the preseason poll for the first time in November 1978 and held the ranking for six weeks, until they were upset in a holiday tournament at New York. The 1986 season marked the first time Duke was ranked No. 1 in the final AP poll of the year. Duke was also ranked No. 1 in the final polls of 1992, 1999, 2000, 2001, 2002, and 2006.

The Duke women were ranked No. 1 by the Associated Press for the first time in the 2003 preseason poll and held the ranking for 12 weeks. They were also ranked No. 1 for five weeks in 2004, when they made their only appearance as the top team in the final poll. The Blue Devils spent three weeks at No. 1 in 2005 and five in 2006, including in the preseason poll.

The Duke men and women were ranked No. 1 during the same week seven times in the AP poll: January 6 and 13 in 2003, January 19 in 2004, and in the preseason poll plus three other weeks of 2006.

The Duke women have been involved in these matchups of AP No. 1 versus No. 2:

November 24, 2002
  Duke (1) versus Tennessee (2)   W, 76–55
February 1, 2003
  Connecticut (2) at Duke (1)   L, 77–65
January 24, 2004
  Tennessee (2) at Duke (1)   L, 72–69
January 23, 2006
  Tennessee (1) at Duke (2)   W, 75–53
February 25, 2006
  Duke (1) at North Carolina (2)   L, 77–65

See also Associated Press Poll.

Duke has been involved in the following games matching the No. 1 versus No. 2 teams in the country:

March 18, 1966	Duke (2) versus Kentucky (1)	L, 83–79
March 29, 1986	Duke (1) versus Kansas (2)	W, 71–67
February 3, 1994	Duke (1) at North Carolina (2)	L, 89–78
February 5, 1998	Duke (1) at North Carolina (2)	L, 97–73
March 27, 1999	Duke (1) versus Michigan State (2)	W, 68–62
December 10, 2005	Duke (1) versus Texas (2)	W, 97–66

Duke has beaten the No. 1 team on these occasions:

January 27, 1958	West Virginia at Duke (1)	W, 72–68
December 10, 1965	UCLA (1) at Duke (6)	W, 82–66
December 11, 1965	Duke (6) versus UCLA (1)	W, 94–75
March 10, 1984	Duke (16) versus North Carolina (1)	W, 77–75
March 26, 1988	Duke (5) versus Temple (1)	W, 63–53
March 30, 1991	Duke (6) versus UNLV (1)	W, 79–77
December 5, 1992	Michigan (1) at Duke (4)	W, 79–68
November 26, 1997	Duke (3) versus Arizona (1)	W, 95–87

O'Connell, Dave. Plagued by a knee injury that cost him an entire season, David Eugene O'Connell, a 6 – 4 guard from Cincinnati, saw reserve action in 64 games, with 183 points and 78 rebounds. He appeared in the 1973 and 1974 campaigns, missed all of 1975, and returned in 1976. But even during 1974 and 1976 he was hampered by injury. O'Connell scored in double figures in a handful of games, topped by back-to-back contests in 1976 when he had 15 points versus Western Kentucky and 16 versus Vermont. His rebounding high of 11 was in his freshman year against Wake Forest.

O'Connor, Richie. After averaging over 20 points a game for an undefeated freshman team, Richard Michael O'Connor, a 6 – 4 forward from Union City, N.J., became an instant point producer for the varsity in 1971. But by the middle of the 1972 campaign, O'Connor was not happy at Duke and abruptly left the team, eventually to transfer to Fairfield. He was the Blue Devils' leading scorer at the time of his departure. O'Connor played in 47 games, with 644 points and 236 rebounds. He averaged 19.5 points in Duke's four NIT contests of 1971, with a career best of 30 in an NIT consolation game loss to St. Bonaventure.

O'Neal, Shaquille. He was named to the NBA's 50th anniversary team in 1996 even though it was just his fourth season in the league. As a collegian at Louisiana State, Shaquille O'Neal twice battled Duke and came up short both times, during the Blue Devils' national championship seasons of 1991 and 1992. Pitted against Christian Laettner, O'Neal had 15 points and 10 rebounds in a loss at Duke in 1991, while Laettner had 24 points with 11 boards. The next year, on a frenzied day in Baton Rouge, O'Neal scored 12 points with 12 rebounds while senior Laettner again sparkled with 22 points and 10 boards. After that season Laettner was the only collegian named to the Olympic team, while O'Neal was the top NBA draft pick, with Laettner going third. O'Neal helped the United States win gold medals at the World Championship in 1994 and the Olympics in 1996.

Olympics. Basketball became an official medal sport at the XI Olympiad in Berlin in 1936. The United States won the first of seven straight gold medals and launched

Grant Hill captured a gold medal at the 1996 Summer Olympics in Atlanta.

a 63-game winning streak that did not end until its controversial loss to the Soviets in 1972. Early U.S. Olympic team rosters included a combination of college and AAU players. In some years, the Olympic Trials consisted of a playoff game between the NCAA championship team and the AAU national championship team, with the best players from each named to the U.S. team. The 1976 team was the first made up entirely of collegians. In 1992 a new era began when USA Basketball turned to NBA stars to represent America in the Summer Games.

Duke's first basketball Olympian was Jeff Mullins in 1964. The 1992 Dream Team featured a former Duke assistant coach, Chuck Daly, as the head coach, with Mike Krzyzewski on his staff and the recently graduated Blue Devil Christian Laettner as the only player with no NBA experience. Krzyzewski has been named USA Senior National Team coach for 2006 – 08, so he will coach the 2008 Olympic Team if it qualifies for the Games in Beijing.

Here is a look at all former Duke players to appear in Olympic basketball competition:

1964	Tokyo	Jeff Mullins	USA	gold
1976	Montreal	Tate Armstrong	USA	gold
1976	Montreal	Cameron Hall	Canada	4th place
1984	Los Angeles	Dan Meagher	Canada	4th place
1992	Barcelona	Christian Laettner	USA	gold
1996	Atlanta	Grant Hill	USA	gold
2000	Sydney	Crawford Palmer	France	silver
2000	Sydney	Greg Newton	Canada	7th place
2004	Athens	Carlos Boozer	USA	bronze

Duke women's coach Gail Goestenkors was an assistant for the USA women's team that won gold at the 2004 Games in Athens.

O'Mara, Bob. His claim to fame in the annals of Duke athletics was his role as the starting fullback and leading scorer for the 1938 Iron Dukes, the most famous football team in school history. Robert James O'Mara was a mainstay of the club that went undefeated and unscored upon during the regular season while earning a trip to the Rose Bowl under Wallace Wade.

But before starring for Duke's first bowl team, O'Mara started at center for the school's first conference championship basketball team in 1938. He lettered for three years in each sport, scoring 233 points on the hardcourt from 1937 through 1939, and five touchdowns on the gridiron for the Iron Dukes as a first-team all-conference performer and 703-yard rusher. He had his best basketball scoring campaign of 105 points for the "never a dull moment boys" that won the Southern Conference Tournament in 1938.

O'Mara, from Ashland, Ky., was a starter and defensive stalwart for the bulk of his cage career and co-captained the 1939 squad as a senior, even though he joined it late because of the Rose Bowl.

Orr, Kira. The recruiting pitch came as prospect and coach sat on the floor of an empty office. Coach Gail Goestenkors outlined her vision for the future of Duke women's basketball, and high school standout Kira Orr believed. Instead of joining a national powerhouse at Stanford, Orr, a 5–6 point guard from Poolesville, Md.,

decided to help Goestenkors redecorate the Blue Devil program and became its first pivotal recruit of a new era.

Orr played in 119 games from 1994 to 1997 and started 91 times, averaging 30 minutes a night as Goestenkors's extension on the floor. She totaled 1,388 points and rewrote the record books for assists. Her 170 assists in 1996 set the Duke season record, and she graduated with 445 as the career leader, a mark that has since been topped twice.

But more importantly, Orr helped guide the Blue Devils to the verge of national prominence. The team had a 16–11 record in her freshman year, then reeled off marks of 22–9, 26–7, and 19–11, with three NCAA Tournament appearances.

Orr earned second-team All-ACC honors in 1997 but might best be remembered for her series of clutch shots. The two most dramatic were in the ACC Tournament semifinals in 1995 against top-seeded Virginia, when she tied the game with a buzzer-beater at the end of regulation, then won it with a 16-footer as the clock expired in overtime. Virginia had gone undefeated during the ACC regular season and had a 20-point lead on the Blue Devils, but Orr's 24 points in the second half and overtime carried the Devils to their first berth in a conference final.

That was not an isolated incident. Earlier in her sophomore season — just 10 days after undergoing exploratory surgery for an irregular heart beat — Orr hit a three-pointer with four seconds left to beat St. Joseph's. As a junior she hit a three with 2:17 remaining to put Duke ahead of Virginia, and then clinched her school's first-ever win in Charlottesville on two free throws with

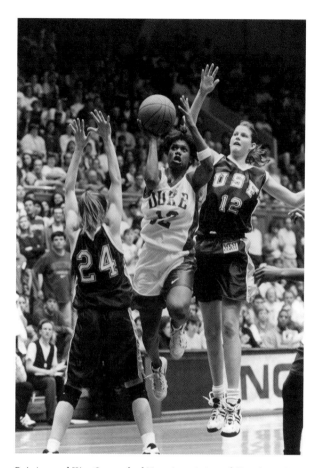

Point guard Kira Orr ranked No. 4 in points and No. 1 in assists when she completed her career for the Duke women in 1997.

12 seconds left. She also scored four points in the last 44 seconds to secure a 61 – 58 victory over UNC in 1996.

During her senior year Orr added another chapter to her last-second textbook in a pulsating 96 – 95 home win over N.C. State. Duke trailed by five points with 30 seconds to play, but Orr hit a jumper in the lane and then tied the score with 2.1 seconds left on a high, arching 25-footer over the outstretched fingers of two taller defenders. The Blue Devils won in overtime and Orr finished with a career high of 32 points. She finished her senior season with a team-best scoring average of 17.5.

Orr closed her career ranked first in assists, second in three-pointers, third in steals, and fourth in scoring in the Duke books. She was drafted by Seattle of the American Basketball League and eventually returned to her high school alma mater, the Bullis School, as a coach and athletics director.

O'Toole, Tim. Intense and enthusiastic, Tim O'Toole spent two years at Duke as an assistant coach for Mike Krzyzewski. After a four-year stint at Syracuse, O'Toole joined the Blue Devil staff for the 1996 season, remained through 1997, and then left to become a member of Tommy Amaker's first staff at Seton Hall. After one year there he was named head coach at his alma mater, Fairfield University, where he had been a standout performer in the 1980s. The Stags' opening game of the 1999 season was in a familiar location for O'Toole, Cameron Indoor Stadium, where the top-ranked Blue Devils administered a 32-point beating. O'Toole also brought his team back to Cameron in 2003 and 2004, losing both times. After eight years as a head coach, 1999 – 2006, O'Toole stepped down with a record of 112 – 120, one conference coach of the year plaque, and one NIT bid.

Packer, Billy. During the heyday of ACC basketball on Saturday afternoon regional television, a TV announcer would typically stand at center court with his microphone and deliver a live introduction of the starting lineups. That practice was curtailed shortly after the color analyst Billy Packer was serenaded by an obscene chant from Duke students while he was on stage at Cameron Indoor Stadium.

But Packer's stage and audience only grew larger as he became one of the top analysts in the history of college basketball broadcasting. After teaming with Jim Thacker to cover ACC games, he worked with Curt Gowdy to cover the NCAA Tournament for NBC and then with Dick Enberg for the network's national broadcasts. In 1978 NBC put together one of the most entertaining and informative trios of all time with the addition of the former Marquette coach Al McGuire. The three came to Cameron Indoor Stadium in 1979, at the height of their popularity, for a nationally televised showdown of top 20 teams, Duke and Marquette. Packer moved on to CBS Sports and in 2006 celebrated his 25th season as the network's lead analyst, as well as his 32nd consecutive year of covering the Final Four and his 34th year of working ACC games for the league's regional package.

Long before his broadcasting career began, Packer was a top player at Wake Forest from 1960 through 1962. He helped the Deacons to a pair of ACC titles and a trip to the Final Four in his senior year. He went up against Duke nine times, with a 5 – 4 record, and averaged 15.6 points a game, better than the 14.8 that he averaged for the 89 college contests in his career. In 1961 he and Duke standout Art Heyman matched 31-point performances in a 100 – 90 win by the Blue Devils in Durham. Five days later they met again in Winston-Salem, with Wake claiming a 103 – 89 decision; Heyman had 31 points again while Packer had 25 and teammate Len Chappell added 38. Packer's team faced Duke in the ACC tourney in all three years, twice for the title (they split) and once in the semis (Wake won en route to the title).

Pagliuca, Joe. A 6 – 2 walk-on guard from Weston, Mass., Joseph Case Pagliuca played in 11 games during his first three seasons, 2004 – 06, with no points and one rebound. His main contribution was as a member of the Blue team in practice. He missed the majority of the 2006 season with a back injury and surgery. In 2005 and 2006 he won the Dr. Deryl Hart award as the top scholar on the team. Pagliuca's father Stephen, the co-owner of the Boston Celtics, was on the Duke junior varsity team in 1973 – 74.

Palmer, Crawford. A diligent inside power man, Henry Crawford Palmer enjoyed three seasons as a solid reserve on the Duke front line, appearing in 82 games and logging 669 minutes during the 1989 through 1991 seasons. He even started nine games and played over 400 minutes for the 1991 national championship team. Palmer averaged 3.6 points and 2.0 rebounds while shooting 65 percent from the floor and blocking 19 shots that year.

A 6 – 9 forward from Arlington, Va., Palmer spent numerous hours in the gym working on his game with associate coach Pete Gaudet, and that paid off in 1991. Playing solid defense, coming up with key rebounds, and providing a physical inside presence were his main objectives, and those skills earned him a place in the regular rotation. Highlights included a career-high 14 points in his first starting assignment, against East Carolina; a brief but effective five minutes (four points, three rebounds) against Shaquille O'Neal when LSU visited Cameron Indoor Stadium; and a key charging foul drawn in the NCAA semis against UNLV.

Palmer's career totals included 195 points, 152 re-

bounds, and 32 blocked shots. He won the Dr. Deryl Hart academic award as the top student athlete on the team in 1990 and 1991.

Palmer did not return to Duke for his senior season. He opted to follow his older brother Walter's footsteps and transferred to Dartmouth, where he sat out the 1992 campaign and completed his college career in 1993. He then launched a professional career that landed him overseas. He married a French woman, gained dual citizenship, and in 2000 landed a spot on the French Olympic team, which won the silver medal. In the Olympic final against a USA team loaded with NBA stars, Palmer played 21 minutes and scored 10 points in a 10-point loss.

Parker, Ace. Perhaps the greatest athlete in Duke history, Clarence McKay "Ace" Parker is best remembered for his exploits on the football field. But in 1936 he earned a letter under Eddie Cameron in basketball. Parker scored 51 points as one of the alternate guards for a team that posted a record of 20 – 6. He was also on the roster for part of the 1937 season, scoring two points in three games; he arrived late after playing in football's East-West Shrine Game in January and left early to sign with the Philadelphia Athletics of major league baseball.

Parker, from Portsmouth, Va., enjoyed a professional career in both football and baseball. At Duke he did everything on the gridiron — running, passing, punting, kicking, defending. His 105-yard kickoff return versus UNC and his 70-yard punt return versus N.C. State rank as two of the most memorable plays in school history. As a pro he earned NFL player of the year honors and a spot in the Hall of Fame. His two seasons of major league baseball began on the best of notes as he hit a home run in his first at-bat, fresh from the Duke campus.

Parker returned to Duke as a football assistant coach from 1947 to 1965 and as baseball head coach from 1953 to 1966. He was a charter inductee in the Duke Sports Hall of Fame in 1975.

Parks, Cherokee. In the starting lineup for the first game of his Duke career, center Cherokee Parks, 6 – 11, scored 16 points and had eight rebounds to aid a runaway against East Carolina. After two games he owned 31 points, 14 rebounds, seven blocked shots, and a perfect shooting mark from the field, 11 of 11. But Parks, a consensus prep All-America from Huntington Beach, Calif., saw mostly reserve action for the rest of his rookie year of 1992, playing behind a coterie of frontline players headed by Christian Laettner for a team that was ranked No. 1 all season and won the national title. It was an injury to Laettner that gave Parks the opportunity to start the opener, and then an ankle sprain of his own that limited him to backup work.

Parks missed only one start over the next three years, however, filling the middle for two more NCAA teams as a solid double-figures scorer, steady rebounder, and shot blocker. In four years, 1992–95, Cherokee Bryan Parks totaled 131 games with 99 starts and had 1,643 points, 874 rebounds, and 231 blocked shots. He also shot 55.1 percent from the field. Parks led the ACC and ranked third nationally in field-goal shooting at 65.2 percent in his sophomore year, and he led Duke as a senior in scoring (19.0) and rebounding (9.3).

Nicknamed "Chief" for his American Indian heritage, Parks was a second-team All-ACC pick in his last two years, shared team MVP honors with fellow big man Erik Meek in 1995, and was a co-captain along with Meek and Kenny Blakeney. Though he projected a laid-back, West Coast image, he recorded several impressive achievements. His 20 rebounds against Xavier in 1994 marked the most by a Duke player since Randy Denton in 1971, and he set the school record for blocked shots in a game with 10 versus Clemson in the 1994 ACC Tournament. When he graduated, Parks ranked as the second-best shot blocker in school history, behind Mike Gminski.

Parks hit his career scoring high twice in his senior year, scoring 29 points against both George Washington and Notre Dame. There was an interesting twist to the performance against GW. It came on a December night, when Duke retired the jersey No. 44 of the 1960s star Jeff Mullins. Parks, who also wore 44, marked the occasion by draining 12 of 15 shots. Parks went 3 for 3 on three-point field goals against the Colonials, an early indication that he would be taking his game away from the basket. For the season he connected on 31 three-point shots after making only three previously in his career. "He's the man on this team, there's no question about it," coach Mike Krzyzewski said after Parks's quick start.

The coach had to leave the team for health reasons in January, and the team's record plummeted to 13–18. It was not the senior year that Parks had envisioned, but

Three-year starting center Cherokee Parks was strong around the basket and once blocked 10 shots in a game.

he still put a positive spin on his career. "I've been to two Final Fours and won a national championship," he said. "There are great players who never ever get to do things like that and I've done it twice. I've done a lot and I've got a lot of good memories. This definitely couldn't damper any of that."

An NBA lottery pick in 1995, Parks spent nine seasons in the NBA with seven teams, mostly as a reserve. One thing that grew bigger than his scoring average was his collection of body art. By the time he left the league, he sported numerous tattoos.

Parsons, Bill. William Parsons, a 5–10 forward from Altoona, Pa., captained the 1940 team that opened Duke's new Indoor Stadium. He played from 1938 through 1940, with a total of 226 points. He scored four points in the arena-opening win versus Princeton.

Paulus, Greg. Considered one of the top high school athletes in two sports, Gregory Russell Paulus was a key member of the Blue Devils' recruiting class of 2005, ranked No. 1 in the nation, and a prominent Duke freshman for the 2006 campaign. A 6 – 1 product of Syracuse, N.Y., he starred at quarterback for Christian Brothers Academy and led it to the state title as a senior, when he was named national player of the year by Gatorade. He was also ranked one of the top point guards by the basketball recruiting services and won the ESPY Award in 2005 as the national high school athlete of the year for all sports.

Paulus orally committed to play basketball at Duke while he was still a junior in high school, but speculation persisted for the next year that he might opt for another university to play football. That speculation increased late in his senior football season when no announcement was made about his college decision during the November signing period. Paulus actually signed his letter of intent during the early week and sent it to Duke, but kept it a secret at the suggestion of Mike Krzyzewski so that he could concentrate on the football playoffs. Soon after his team won the championship, Paulus revealed that he had signed and would follow a long-held passion to play point guard for Krzyzewski.

Paulus was a Parade and McDonald's All-America as a prep senior. He played for USA Basketball in the Nike Hoop Summit in 2005 and set an event record with 10 assists. As a freshman in 2006, Paulus started all but three games, led the team in assists with 187, and averaged 6.7 points. His 15 assists versus Valparaiso were one shy of Bobby Hurley's school record.

Penfield, Add. A North Carolina Sports Hall of Famer, Addison Pierce Penfield was the original radio voice of the Blue Devils. He totaled 21 years across five decades as the play-by-play announcer for Duke basketball and football, served as the school's sports information director when publicist Ted Mann was in the service during the Second World War, and was one of North Carolina's radio pioneers.

A resident of Asheboro, N.C., for over 40 years, Penfield broke into broadcasting as a Duke junior in 1938, when at the insistence of football coach Wallace Wade he joined the Atlantic Refining radio crew that covered the Duke games. It was a noteworthy début season, as the "Iron Dukes" went undefeated and unscored against until their loss in the Rose Bowl.

Also during his undergraduate years, Penfield joined Woody Woodhouse and Gerry Gerard (who was on the Duke athletics staff and later became head coach) for broadcasts of Durham High School's powerhouse basketball teams on WDNC. He graduated in 1940 and took a job with WPTF in Raleigh, returned to Duke in 1941 as a publicist in Mann's absence, moved to Atlanta, then entered the military and worked with U.S. Army Radio in Germany during the Nuremberg war crimes trial.

After the war Penfield helped open a new radio station in Rochester, N.Y., before returning to North Carolina in 1952 when Duke athletics director Eddie Cameron asked him to organize a Duke radio network. He was the Blue Devils' play-by-play man for most of the 1950s and 1960s, covered Wake Forest in the early 1970s, and returned for his final two seasons of Duke football and basketball in 1974 – 75 and 1975 – 76.

When Penfield worked at WPTF in the 1940s his basketball broadcast schedule covered all of the Big Four schools. WPTF ran national NBC programming every evening from 8 to 11 p.m., so most of Penfield's broadcasts were not live. He would call the second half of games over a telephone line from the gym to the station, where the broadcast was recorded and aired after the 11 p.m. news report.

Penfield worked for WBIG in Greensboro when he returned to the state in 1952 and again worked a composite schedule of Big Four games while running the Duke network. On one occasion in the 1960s, his broadcast of a Duke-UNC contest aired simultaneously on both schools' networks. UNC's announcer, Bill Currie, worked at a station in Charlotte and could not get to Durham because of a snowstorm, so UNC got permission to use Penfield's call.

Although he was a Duke grad and quarterbacked the university's network, Penfield was known for his objectivity and professionalism, earning respect that crossed school lines. N.C. State's Everett Case, for example, used to have him narrate his highlight films. UNC's announcer Woody Durham, a member of Penfield's N.C. Sports Hall of Fame class, said, "I learned more being in the broadcast booth with Add Penfield than I think I learned from anybody else as I was coming along in this business."

Tom Connelly, a former Duke player and later a jeweler in Durham, worked as Penfield's color man for several years. Others in that role for Duke broadcasts included Woodhouse, Willard Dean, Phil Ellis, Leo

Morris, Ed Higgins, and Bob Harris. Penfield liked to tell the story of his broadcast of the Southern Conference Tournament in 1941 with Ellis at Memorial Auditorium in Raleigh. Both men were recent grads — Penfield from Duke, Ellis from UNC — and were still friends with many of the players from their respective schools. It made for an interesting broadcast when Duke and UNC met in the first round of the tourney, especially with the wives of both broadcasters sitting right behind them cheering for opposite schools. Duke won by one point and went on to claim the championship.

Bob Harris took over for Penfield during the 1976 basketball season.

Pep band. Duke's first Final Four season of 1963 marked the début of the school's pep band at home basketball games. Coach Vic Bubas called marching band director Jim Henry in 1962 and suggested starting a group to add some pep to the home contests. The result was an energetic group of musicians in distinctive striped jackets and straw hats with a style all their own. The band first appeared in 1962 – 63 and went on the road for trips to the Final Four in 1963, 1964, and 1966 as well as to neutral-site regular-season games in Greensboro and Charlotte. Even in its early days, students' interest in performing in the band was so keen that Henry had to form two bands and have them alternate.

Pergrem, Ernest. Guard Ernest Pergrem, of Ashland, Ky., lettered for the 1949 team and scored 24 points in 16 games.

Perkins, Ross. The son of one of Duke's greatest distance runners, Matthew Ross Perkins, a 6 – 4 guard from Greensboro, N.C., played in 11 games as a walk-on member of the 2005 and 2006 teams. He had three points and only two rebounds but was an invaluable member of the Blue team in practice. In fact, on the heels of a two-game losing streak in 2005, Mike Krzyzewski planned to start Perkins for the home game against Wake Forest because of his commitment and total effort. But Perkins met with the coach and gave up the spot, saying that the team would have a better chance to win with one of the veterans on the floor.

Perkins worked as a student manager for the Blue

Devils during his freshman and sophomore years, along with his older brother Max. Their father Robbie Perkins was a 1976 Duke grad who starred in cross-country and track and was named to the ACC's 50th anniversary team. Ross's mother, two grandparents, and three aunts also went to Duke. He was elected student justice by the Duke Student Government in 2004 – 05.

Perry, Baker. With its active roster reduced to just seven recruited players, Duke loaded up on walk-on contributors during the 1996 campaign. One of the last to join the fold was Baker Perry, a 6 – 5 senior forward added to the roster in mid-January after reserve freshman Matt Christensen fractured his wrist. Perry had played high school basketball in Lake Junaluska, N.C., and club basketball while studying abroad in Bolivia during the fall semesters of 1994 and 1995. The basketball staff had become aware of him when he took former coach Pete Gaudet's basketball coaching class.

Perry played five minutes in five games during the 1996 campaign and scored six points with one rebound. He was a perfect shooter, hitting his only two-point field goal, his only three-point field goal, and his only free throw. He had three points against UCLA, and hit his three-pointer with 22 seconds left on Senior Day against North Carolina. Mike Krzyzewski had emptied his bench in the closing minutes with UNC up by 15 points, but Perry's shot capped an inspired run by the subs that made it a five-point game, prompting Krzyzewski to send his starters back to the floor. The Heels held on and won by six.

Pocius, Martynas. Duke's first Lithuanian-born player, Martynas Pocius, a 6 – 4 shooting guard, was a member of the Blue Devils' top-rated recruiting class of 2005. He played scholastically at Holderness in Plymouth, N.H., before matriculating as a freshman for the 2006 team. Pocius averaged 18 points a game while playing in the European Under 18 Championship in 2004, and he starred for an international team at the annual Nike Hoop Summit in April 2005. He scored 20 points for the World Select team in a 106 – 98 loss to USA Basketball's Junior Select squad, which included Pocius's future Duke teammate Greg Paulus. Pocius scored 42 points as a freshman reserve in 2006.

Podger, Ken. Coach Eddie Cameron tinkered with countless lineups during the mid-1930s, but there was one constant from 1935 through 1937: Kenneth Podger in the backcourt. A 5–9 guard from Kenmore, N.Y., Podger scored 450 points during three seasons as a letterman. He was the leading scorer for the 1936 and 1937 teams and was captain in 1937. Despite Duke's loss in the first round of the Southern Conference Tournament in 1937, Podger made the all-tourney second team. He missed the first team by one vote.

Polack, Bunn. A varsity player from 1933 through 1935, Ernest H. "Bunn" Polack, of York, Pa., played little and did not score in his first two seasons. As a 5–11 senior guard in 1935, Polack appeared in all but two games and scored 105 points. Polack teamed with Ken Podger in the backcourt for one of two primary lineups used by Eddie Cameron in that year. Polack earned a letter in 1934 and 1935.

Posen, John. Three-year reserve John Franklin Posen, a 6–2 guard from Cicero, Ill., played in 29 games from 1968 through 1970. He scored 75 points with 35 rebounds. He had his career best of 11 points versus Virginia in 1970. Posen also played on the baseball team.

Preseason NIT. See National Invitation Tournament.

Price, Glenn. The first points scored in Duke's historic basketball arena came from Glenn F. Price, a 5–10 junior from Beaver Falls, Pa., on the 1940 team. Price had the initial five points in the stadium opener against Princeton on January 6, 1940, and sparked a game-closing spurt as well, to finish with a team-high 13 points in the Duke win.

Price lettered for three years, 1939–41, playing forward and guard, and finished with 401 points. A starter in all three years, he was the second-leading scorer as a sophomore and helped Duke to reach the conference championship game in his next two years. He was a second-team all-conference pick in 1940 and co-captain of the 1941 team that won the league.

Price, Ricky. Had every season played out individually like his sophomore year, Richard P. Price would be re-

Anatomy of a Game-Winning Shot

Ricky Price, 1996 versus Maryland

Down by one point with 6.5 seconds left at North Carolina, Duke point guard Steve Wojciechowski penetrated a gap in the defense and got the ball to senior Price, whose 15-footer from the right wing hit the front of the rim. The Blue Devils lost 73–72, after which Wojo noted, "Great players don't make that shot the first time around. They make it the last time around. Just ask Christian Laettner."

Price's second time around came a few weeks later when Duke was trailing Maryland in College Park. After a timeout with 3.6 seconds left, Wojo got the ball in the left corner to Price for the three-pointer at the buzzer. The Devils won 77–75 for their fifth straight victory, securing at least a .500 finish in the ACC.

"That shot sent us to the NCAA Tournament that year," Price said. "It was a great game, a great win, and the shot was my greatest ever as a Duke player. I just couldn't believe I was so open. The way we played, we spread the court, it was a pressure situation and anybody could have shot it. Wojo was able to find me in the corner, I had my feet set ready to shoot, and I was fortunate."

"Ricky was already faster than everybody and I just remember him running away and we were chasing him trying to grab him and hug him," said teammate Jeff Capel.

garded as one of the greats in Duke history. A 6–6 forward from Carson, Calif., he was a key offensive weapon during that 1996 campaign, averaging 14.2 points while earning third-team All-ACC honors. Price went on to finish with 1,026 career points in 112 games, but was never as productive as in his sophomore year.

After starting 14 times as a rookie during the nightmare year of 1995, Price took off in 1996 with 29 starts in 31 games. He made the all-tournament team at the Great Alaska Shootout, hit a three-pointer to send the Georgia Tech game into overtime, and beat Maryland in College Park with a three at the buzzer. In the best game of his career, against Virginia, he erupted for 28 points.

Price missed much of the 1997 preseason with a broken finger and had trouble hitting his outside shot consistently, but still he played in every game and started 11 while averaging 9.4 points. When Duke ended a seven-game losing streak to its archrival North Carolina, Price contributed one of the most spectacular plays. With the Heels up by six points, he soared in from the wing to claim a one-handed rebound on a missed three-pointer, then launched back up to the basket to score while taking a forearm to the head. That ignited an 8 – 0 run to give the Blue Devils the lead.

Unfortunately for Price, his school work was just as inconsistent as his shot during 1997 and he was declared academically ineligible after the season. He had to sit out the fall semester of his senior year. On the first day that he regained eligibility, December 21, Mike Krzyzewski inserted him into a game with Mercer even though he had not yet practiced. Price scored 10 points in 15 minutes and delighted the crowd with a 360-degree dunk on a fast break. But Price saw limited minutes off the bench the rest of the year, getting just one start in his Senior Day game against UNC, and averaged only 2.7 points. He went on to play professionally overseas.

Princeton. Duke christened its new Indoor Stadium on January 6, 1940, with a victory over Princeton. The Blue Devils revived memories of that event with a "throwback" game on January 6, 2005, as part of their celebration for the 100th year of Duke basketball. The Devils entered that contest having dominated the series, with 14 wins in 15 meetings scattered from 1936 to 2001.

Aside from the stadium opener, the most historically significant battle with Princeton was in the NCAA Tournament in 1960, which the Devils won 84 – 60 for their first-ever March Madness triumph. Princeton's trip to Durham in December 1962 featured the Tiger sophomore star Bill Bradley, who had committed to Duke before changing his mind. Blue Devil veterans Art Heyman and Jeff Mullins outplayed him to key a Duke win. Princeton's only victory in the series was in a regular-season game in December 1981, in one of the Blue Devils' poorest performances in a 17-loss season.

Duke's 2001 NCAA champs opened their season by hammering Princeton in the first game of the Preseason NIT. The Tigers, headed to the NCAAs themselves that year, were in their opening contest under their new coach John Thompson. The Blue Devils drowned them

with outside shooting, as Shane Battier broke the school record with nine three-point shots en route to a 29-point effort. The 87 – 50 decision was Princeton's worst defeat since 1946.

Purdue. Duke's four games with Purdue have been played on neutral courts, beginning with the Las Vegas Classic in 1973. The next three took place in March, each time ending the season for the losing team. In 1980 the Boilermakers beat Duke 68 – 60 in coach Bill Foster's final game, denying the Blue Devils a trip to the Final Four. A year later, Purdue ended Mike Krzyzewski's first season with an 81 – 69 decision in the third round of the NIT. Duke's only win over Purdue was in Knoxville, in 1994, when the sixth-ranked Devils topped the third-ranked Boilermakers 69 – 60 in an NCAA regional final, claiming a spot in the Final Four.

The Duke women met Purdue in their first appearance in an NCAA championship game, falling 62 – 45 to the top-ranked Boilermakers at San Jose in 1999. Ironically, two of Duke's top players that year, seniors Nicole Erickson and Michele VanGorp, had transferred to the Blue Devils after veteran Purdue coach Lin Dunn was dismissed in 1996. Duke coach Gail Goestenkors had been one of Dunn's assistants for six years before moving to Durham for the 1992 – 93 campaign.

Quotations. College basketball games don't end when the final buzzer sounds. Before coaches and players can unwind, recuperate, reflect, and move on to the next play in their lives, they are typically faced with a locker-room invasion and the accompanying barrage of questions from the news media. As a courtesy to reporters who are deadline-pressed to cover both teams' locker rooms, sports information staffs usually distribute a page or two of quotes about the game from each locker room.

Here is an assortment of coaches' quotes, from a variety of sources, covering a wide range of topics relative to Duke basketball. View it as a historical press conference or set of responses to FAQs, presented in chronological order according to the coaches' dates of service.

Eddie Cameron

On the value of having a successful athletics program:

"Sports at Duke University, or for that matter any-where in a similar academic atmosphere, provide a healthy outlet for the pent-up energies of the students. It exists as a rallying point and a point of identification for both students and alumni. A healthy sports program is a morale factor. It serves as an incentive and pace-setter not only in athletic endeavors but in other areas of interest as well.

"For example, do you think that all available basket-ball courts every afternoon would be crammed with stu-dents or that we would have such active participation in intramurals if we had not had a winning program in the past? I am not saying we must win at every varsity sport we compete in. We are proud of the fact that so many nonscholarship athletes succeed in varsity competition at Duke. But in order to continue to offer these sports at the varsity level, we need funds. A winning program in the major sports will eventually be self-sufficient.

"But in order to return to this level, we need money to upgrade our sports program. If these scholarships are granted and more funds obtained, Duke will not have to face a de-emphasis problem." — *Chronicle*, 1967

On conference tournaments:

"I was named chairman of the tourney in 1935 back when we were in the new Southern Conference. They gave me $250 to start the treasury. Last year [1970] the ACC tourney in Charlotte grossed $244,000 and netted $202,000. The basketball tourney is one of the bread-and-butter situations of the conference.

"If we didn't have a tournament, interest in basket-ball would die in February. The tournament enables all teams to generate new hopes. The basketball is good and competitive and the fans like it. It has become a social thing, too. The women who accompany their husbands get all dolled up. I am guessing, but I imagine the tour-ney will mean about a million dollars, or more, to the city of Greensboro [in 1971].

"You could call the tournament the 'late winter hys-teria' or the 'early spring hysteria.'" — *Durham Morning Herald*, 1971

On changes in the game:

"Basketball was fun when I coached it . . . We all know basketball is getting too big. I'm not speaking from the standpoint of competition. I'm looking at the profes-sional infringement, the constant pressure of winning, the strain placed upon a coach even during recruiting season." — *Charlotte Observer*, 1972

Vic Bubas

On the Final Four loss to No. 1 Kentucky in 1966:

"You'll never know for sure, but I think we could have won it with a healthy [Bob] Verga. We all felt like we could have won it all. But it's just speculation. You have to be ready on the right day." — *Blue Devil Weekly*, 1996

On his retirement from coaching after 10 years at Duke:

"Tired of coaching? Yes, I wanted to do something else. I wanted to win every game, went after it as hard as I could. People say, 'You only coached 10 years'; I coached 18 years: those eight under Everett Case count for some-thing. I also thought I could do a lot of other things. If we hadn't had the success we did, I probably would have wanted to stay in it to prove we could do it. One thing I had made up my mind about—I wasn't going to stay on the bench until we won a national championship. I didn't want to do that; maybe I would have been there until I was 65 and maybe still not win it." — *On Tobacco Road*, 1983

His fondest Duke memory:

"You know, people who ask me that question are gen-erally surprised by my response because they remember me best as a basketball coach. However, when I was in the administration, Terry Sanford asked me to head up the task force that would be responsible for building the new student union [the Bryan Center]. It took four years and over $20 million, but we got it built.

"I think that center is like a campus living room, a place where people can just go and be. It was great to see the project go from an idea to a reality, and it's great for me now to go over and sit in the Bryan Center and watch the students enjoy themselves in there.

"People may forget that the teams I coached won some games and did pretty well, but that building is going to be there for a long, long time, and it affects the lives of almost everybody who goes to Duke. That's why my greatest joy in all the years I spent at Duke was my role in building the Bryan Center." — *Blue Devil Weekly*, 1993

On NCAA Tournament expansion during his tenure on the Division I Basketball Committee:

"During the time I was a member of the Basketball Committee and ultimately the chairman, the field was increased from 48 teams to 52, to 53, and then to 64. At that point, all conferences were assured of one automatic bid and there were many more at-large bids. What it did was allow the sport of intercollegiate basketball to capture and dominate the sports pages, television, and radio for the whole month of March.

"It now owns the month of March on TV, and it keeps every fan in every corner of the United States on the edge of his seat because they all have a chance as they head toward their respective conference tournaments. College basketball blew everything else out of the way on the tube during March and now it is like the Super Bowl, Masters, and World Series as a major, major event. I'm glad I had a part in the decision to go to 64." — *Basketball Weekly*, 1990

His vision of basketball in the twenty-first century:

"I hope we will go toward more international and pro rules. We need a wider lane desperately, plus a longer three-point distance and a 30-second shot clock. All of these rules have been tested for years in international ball. They work and work well. There is no doubt in my mind that all three rules will be a part of our game some day. It's just a matter of time." — *Basketball Weekly*, 1990

Bucky Waters

On the victory over UNC the day Duke's stadium was dedicated to Eddie Cameron:

"We were struggling. I led the world in transfers. I didn't adjust very well to that era. But because of the gravity of the day, that was a huge win. The way we all felt about Mr. Cameron, we were staked out there. This was the day, the big dedication. When I think about it now, sometimes people will come up to me and say, 'Were you the coach when Duke was up eight points with 17

seconds left?' No, I was not the coach, but this would have been a similar thing. 'Were you the coach the day they named it Cameron Indoor Stadium and they lost to Carolina?' Thank goodness." — Interview, 2004

Other memorable moments from the early 1970s:

"The Maryland game here [in February 1973] where we spread the floor and Gary Melchionni scored 30-something. The whole front row was guys in the skin-caps, looking like Lefty [Driesell]. That was one of the neatest games for us, and of course he was frustrated, and those guys had a field day. It was very funny . . . I also remember when we went to Michigan when Rudy Tomjanovich was their star player and Hubie Brown was my assistant and we won in Ann Arbor [in December 1969].

"Another good one was when we beat Digger [Phelps] and Notre Dame in Cameron [in February 1973]. But that was also the night I knew I wasn't going to coach any more. Digger had three pros, Shumate, Brokaw, and Clay, but we were really good that night. It was a big win, a dozen points I think. Yes! Then I went in the locker room before I met with the press, we had a couple of young players on that team, and I'm looking at them, and there's no joy. And I said, 'Is anything wrong?' And they said something like, 'Coach, the way we're playing and where we are in the offense, we're just not sure it's really helping us for the next level.'

"When I walked out to go to the press conference, it was still up there on the scoreboard: Duke 86–74. I looked up there and thought, 'That took all the joy out of it.' With all the stuff you put up with, these are the nights you have to enjoy. It just took my heart out. If I can't feel this as a reward, I'm not going to do this any more . . . So I knew at that point. Vic [Bubas] had always said not to stay on that merry-go-round too long. 'You're a young man, do something else.' I feel blessed now that I've been able to stay in basketball so long. This is my 30th year of broadcasting." — Interview, 2004

Neill McGeachy

On a last-second loss at home to North Carolina in 1974:

"I think I made the comment that my whole life flashed across my mind. All the pieces of the puzzle, from when I was a little kid shooting until I really began to analyze basketball and be able to play collegiately, all the things that had brought me to this point in time, went phfft, right across my mind. It was unbelievable." — *Chanticleer*, 1974

Bill Foster

On his decision to leave a winning team at Utah for a losing one at Duke:

"The decision was not involved so much with Duke, because I knew from my Rutgers experience that Duke has a fine academic and athletic tradition. Leaving Utah was the difficult thing. We were judged the second-most improved team in the country, yet we ended one spot ahead of the 'most improved' team [Pittsburgh] in the final polls.

"However, when we came to the NIT, it was the first time I had been back east in three years. It reminded me of the excitement back here, the emphasis on basketball, the proximity to recruiting areas with which I'm familiar. It all dawned on me during that week. Had we not gotten the NIT bid, I'm fairly certain I'd still be at Utah." — *Chapel Hill Newspaper*, 1974

On the aftermath of reaching the Final Four in 1978:

"I think a lot of the pressure on us is self-imposed. We want to get back to being No. 1 and get back to the Final Four.

"The whole thing has changed my life because the demands for my time are tremendous. Now it's not just handling ACC publicity because when you're No. 1, you're national.

"We want to try to win the national championship like 300-and-some other schools. Of course, with the 15-scholarship limit, the country has become much more balanced. That balance and all the upsets is a fan's delight and a coach's dilemma." — Press interview, 1979

On his departure from Duke for South Carolina in 1980:

"South Carolina did a great job of recruiting me. They presented a very vivid idea of where they thought I could take them. I guess I was always looking for a chance to rebuild. I probably was a little bit vulnerable when they approached me. Recruiting wasn't going well. I was disappointed in the way the season had gone. I thought we should have had a better year.

"I wouldn't think much of myself if I left Duke over something as trivial as [a squabble over an unpaved parking lot]. I just thought it was time for a change." — *Blue Devil Weekly*, 2004

Mike Krzyzewski

On Bob Knight's influence over his coaching style:

"Coach Knight is a tremendous influence on me, and he's a great teacher of the game. I think very highly of Coach Knight. But I'm not Bobby Knight . . . I'm a different person. I admire his principles, but I fit them to my own personality.

"I think you make a mistake by being somebody else. I was influenced by a number of coaches, Knight being the biggest influence." — Introductory press conference, 1980

On comparisons with John Wooden after back-to-back NCAA crowns:

"I believe that you learn from your players and that they learn from you. That's why I try to keep a very open line of communication. I learned a lot about courage from David Henderson, a lot about man-to-man defense from watching Tommy Amaker play. Basically I've gotten better each year as a result of working with top-quality players and kids. You've got to create an atmosphere where it's a two-way street. I'm better right now than I was in '86. My goal is to be better in '96 than I am today. That's where you've got to keep up your motivation and hunger. As far as being compared to anybody, that's not my goal. People in Chapel Hill compare me to a rat. I just think you have to keep it all in perspective. I guess I'm somewhere between a rat and John Wooden, maybe a balance of both." — Press conference, 1992

His perspective after a health scare in 1995:

"It's made me appreciate how lucky I am to be able to coach. When you are always achieving and doing, you don't have time to reflect on the good things. That's why talking to some of the former players and having the players come over has been good. One of the really good things was after the Maryland game, when our kids played their hearts out and lost on that last-second tip-in. About 25 or 30 minutes after the game I got a call from Jeff Capel. He said, 'Coach. I feel down.' I told him to come over. He picked up some food, came over and we had a nice talk.

"I enjoy that. It's not about winning and losing, it's about developing relationships and getting closer. I miss that. But you know what? I was getting away from that a little bit in the past couple of years, I think. But for the kids who are in our program now and who will be in the future, that will never happen again. That doesn't mean I didn't coach them real hard on the court, but we can give more. My family loves to do that, too. I just need to do that a little bit better." — Press conference, 1995

Changes in college basketball during his first 25 years at Duke:

"I feel very fortunate. I think I came here just when college basketball was getting ready to explode, especially in the media, television. It's all timing. Not that you know it ahead of time, I certainly didn't notice it my first few years. About the time we started going to the Final Four as much as we did, 1986, TV just boomed. In that market, it seemed so expanding as opposed to today where it's somewhat restrictive. You have a great product that was only shown in so many movie theaters. And only so many movies were shown. So if you were good, they saw you a lot. Since then everybody's seen a lot. There are more movies, more theaters, more games on TV. I'm not sure that's helped the game. We have gotten too much out there and you can see basketball a lot.

"Money-wise, the amount of money that basketball earns, that's one of the biggest things I've seen. It is truly amazing, just what it does for the NCAA. I think over 95 percent of their budget it funded by the men's basketball tournament. To me, that's incredible.

"The biggest disappointment I have is I see over the last four to five years that we are losing our brand. We don't have anybody who just watches this on a day-to-day basis that says we need to switch strategies, have a business plan or marketing plan. It was going so well, maybe you think you don't need it, and I think we need it. That's what [NCAA] president [Myles] Brand is doing.

"I think [the game] is a little more individualistic. I think that kids don't see a big picture, you know, the old forest and the trees, where you see one and not the other. Kids used to be able to see their individual stuff being coordinated with a group effort. Now I think they look at their individual stuff and hope it becomes part of the

group effort . . . It'll be interesting to see how we now as coaches continue to develop the team aspect of playing basketball. I think that we've become a little bit more of an individualistic sport. I think that's the biggest change I've seen." — Press conferences, 2004

His view of Atlantic Coast Conference expansion:

"Obviously we haven't distinguished ourselves in how we've gone about this. That's sad. There's a business part of everything that we do, there's no question about it. But also, we're still a university and we're still a conference that has great universities. We have to be sensitive to our brethren in other conferences. This isn't about big business swooping in and getting another company. And if that's what it's about, the hidden cost there is the destruction of, in essence, what intercollegiate sports should be about. The ACC has done a great job, and a lot of conferences have done a great job, of keeping the spirit of the game. There are some things you just have to do. I think we've gone really overboard with this other side of it, even in the analysis of it . . .

"You also have to look at principles, values, tradition. You're part of a bigger sphere out there than just the ACC. You're part of intercollegiate sports. To me, there's a reason why the United States doesn't have a state in France or Venezuela. We don't belong there. That doesn't mean we don't deal with them. If all of a sudden Georgia is in Venezuela, the people in South America are saying, 'What the heck are these guys doing in here?' And I think we kind of did that. I think there is a lot to be said about your geographic area and that landscape. You don't go in and just say, 'We're going to take you and you and you' and not have sensitivity. I think we haven't distinguished ourselves in doing that . . .

"It's kind of like the mix here in Cameron. I would never want to change venues. I want to update things. But to say that we would be able to take the spirit of Cameron and place it in a 16,000-seat arena across the street, I'm not sure that that's done. That's kind of how I looked at this expansion. To take the spirit, the intangibles that you have in this league, it's incredible. Before you do any of those changes, you better have an unbelievable analysis. That's why I've been against it from the beginning. I'm proud of what our school has done [in opposing expansion]. I think Joe Alleva and Nan Keohane have been unbelievable leaders in this. I'm proud to be on their team. They've represented this conference about as well as you can throughout this whole thing.

"I hope we also mend fences . . . The people who have represented the schools in this conference over time have been great people and that's what we should expect to happen right now." — Press conference, 2004

On his appearance in a heavily aired television commercial for American Express:

"The reaction that we have gotten nationally has been unbelievably good. First of all, have you ever seen me in a commercial locally? I've never done one locally in my 25 years. There are a lot of coaches who do that and I have never said a negative thing about them when they did that. That's their decision to do that.

"To do one nationally like this, I thought, was great for college basketball. A number of people have said that it is good for coaching and good for the college game. For us, it is good because we are in a relationship with a great company. They made a huge contribution to [the Emily Krzyzewski Family Life] Center, they're sponsoring our leadership conference here at Duke for the next three years. Everything we do is approved by Duke, including the content. If Duke doesn't like it, then I won't do it." — Press conference, 2005

Gail Goestenkors

On her involvement with national programs as USA Basketball's coach of the year for 2005:

"I love everything involved with USA Basketball. I feel like every summer that I've been with USA Basketball, I've learned something and I've grown. It forces me to stretch myself as a person going to foreign countries and as a coach scouting other teams and learning new systems and different ways to do things. I think it's been very beneficial for me as a person, as a coach and for my team as well.

"I always feel revitalized when I work with USA Basketball because I do learn so much." — Press conference, 2005

On the impact of Title IX, federal gender equity legislation, in her life:

"When I was in 10th grade, that was the first year one of the seniors on our high school team got a scholarship to go to college. I didn't even know that existed. That was right when they first started giving college scholarships. That made going to college to play basketball a possibility, and that became my goal, that became my dream. One thing led to another and I was able to go and play basketball, then that's where I decided I wanted to become a coach.

"I feel like because of Title IX, I was able to have some dreams I wouldn't have had otherwise and opportunities that I wouldn't have had otherwise. It really changed the course of where I've gone." — Interview, 2002

Raksnis, Charlie. Forward Charlie Raksnis played in two games for the 1961 Blue Devils and scored three points.

Randolph, Shavlik. A grandson of the rebounding machine Ronnie Shavlik, who wore jersey No. 84 when he starred for N.C. State in the mid-1950s, Ronald Shavlik Randolph picked 42 as his number at Duke with hopes of being half the player his grandfather was. Randolph, a 6–10 product of Raleigh, played at Duke for three seasons, 2003–05, but a variety of injuries and illness derailed his all-star possibilities. After his junior year of 2005, he left school early to launch a professional career.

Randolph played in 92 games with 36 starts. He scored 580 points for a 6.3 average and had 394 rebounds while blocking 129 shots. More was envisioned for Randolph during his All-America career at Broughton High School, when he was the centerpiece of an intense recruiting showdown between Duke, N.C. State, and North Carolina. But pain left over from high school injuries limited his growth as a freshman, and off-season hip surgery slowed his strength and conditioning for his sophomore year. Then as a junior he contracted mononucleosis and missed the start of the ACC season.

A two-time state player of the year in high school, Randolph got off to a quick start at Duke with 23 points against Army in the 2003 opener, followed by 17 points and 12 rebounds against Davidson. But like many freshman performances his were up and down, inconsistency combined with foul trouble. He had a career high of 24 points against Butler on 11-of-13 shooting and posted 17 points against Virginia, but his time dwindled at the end of the year and he didn't get off the bench for any of the postseason games because of injury.

Randolph gradually worked back into shape from hip surgery in 2004 and had the best month of his career to close the season. In five NCAA games he hit 20 of 26 shots and scored 51 points as the Blue Devils reached the Final Four. Playing under the shadow of his grandfather's retired jersey at the RBC Center in Raleigh, he scored 20 points in Duke's NCAA opener, and he had 13 points on 6-of-6 shooting against UConn in the Final Four.

After his junior year, when he averaged a career low of 4.5 points, Randolph declared for the NBA draft, saying that he wanted to work out for pro teams while still intending to return for his senior season. But a week before the draft he signaled the end of his college days by opting not to pull his name out. "This is something I prayed a lot about. That's all the decision-making I need," he explained. Randolph was not drafted but signed a free-agent contract with the Philadelphia 76ers. He made the 15-man roster and earned some playing time after recovering from a preseason stress fracture suffered during the team's training camp at Cameron Indoor Stadium.

Recruiting. The head coach of Wake Forest was visiting the head coach of Duke one day in the late 1950s and asked to borrow a telephone to call his mother. Ever gracious, Hal Bradley invited his guest, Durham native Bones McKinney, to use his office and help himself. "When I closed his office door," McKinney wrote in his autobiography, "there on the blackboard was a list of 25 high school players Duke was trying to recruit. So I did what Hal asked me to do. I helped myself. Two of the names on that list were Billy Packer and Len Chappell." McKinney landed both, and they carried his Deacons to two ACC championships plus a Final Four.

While Bones was known to liven up a tale or two, it's no exaggeration to note that recruiting college athletes has evolved drastically since the 1950s. A year after McKinney signed Packer and Chappell, Duke hired Vic Bubas to replace Bradley. His first order of business was to convince the New York prep hot shot Art Heyman to change his allegiance from UNC to Duke. A couple of years later, Bubas was the victim of a similar switch when Bill Bradley opted out of a commitment to Duke so that he could attend Princeton. Neither of those events caused even a ripple compared with what they would have generated 40 years later. In fact, no one including Bubas even knew that Bradley had changed his mind until a couple of days before school started for his freshman year.

A protégé of the N.C. State legend Everett Case, Bubas was one of the coaches who revolutionized recruiting during his 10-year tenure at Duke. He brought a strategic, businesslike approach to the process, delegating specific territories to his assistant coaches and organizing every tactic from mailings and questionnaires to scouting, contacts, and visits. "We were called the IBM of recruiting at that time," recalled Bucky Waters, his ace recruiter and eventual successor. "We were very organized and thought nationally. One of the good things about him was that he empowered you as a coach. He'd tell you, 'This is your territory, get the best out of it.'"

The efforts of Bubas, Waters, and the rest of the staff typically brought at least one of the nation's top players to Duke each year, with talents such as Heyman, Jeff Mullins, Jack Marin, Steve Vacendak, Bob Verga, and Mike Lewis headlining his freshman classes of 1960 through 1965 (with a hole for Bradley in 1962). Consequently, Duke played in the ACC championship game during eight of Bubas's 10 years and visited three Final Fours. But the recruiting battle that helped UNC catch up with Duke late in the decade was telling. Both schools fiercely pursued Larry Miller. He picked Dean Smith over Bubas, and his decision came back to haunt the Blue Devils. In the ACC final in 1967, Miller's 13-of-14 shooting for 32 points made the difference in a Tar Heel victory over Duke. A couple of weeks later, Smith was in his first Final Four.

Waters had a blue-chip class of his own in his first year as Duke's head coach, with Jeff Dawson, Gary Melchionni, Richie O'Connor, and Alan Shaw combining forces for an undefeated freshman season before moving on to the varsity. Soon afterward, however, recruiting changed significantly when freshmen became eligible to play on the varsity. That was also a period during which Duke was in transition, at one time employing three head coaches in less than a year (Waters, Neill McGeachy, Bill Foster).

Foster, well-connected on the eastern seaboard and long affiliated with a basketball camp in the Poconos, recruited several key players to get Duke back on the map in the late 1970s. He made his biggest splash nationally with the signing of the Philadelphia sensation Gene Banks in the spring of 1977. Banks was one of the top two prospects in the country, along with Albert King. When he picked Duke over a host of suitors, it was headline news. The Blue Devils had a charismatic court presence that translated into three NCAA bids and two ACC crowns.

Banks came along in the first year of the McDonald's high school All-America program. Foster got a second McDonald's recruit in 1978 with the signing of Vince Taylor. But the Blue Devils came up dry on the McDonald's list until Johnny Dawkins in 1982 committed to a youthful Mike Krzyzewski, whose recruiting efforts would become the most closely scrutinized of any Duke coach. His ascension as the top recruiter in college basketball coincided with the proliferation of interest in the entire recruiting process, from the mainstream media as well as a subculture of specialists on the subject.

Krzyzewski struck out famously in his early efforts, pursuing a large pool of prospects and finishing second to more established head coaches. In one year he was beat out for Chris Mullin and Bill Wennington (St. John's), Uwe Blab (Indiana), and Jimmy Miller (Virginia). But he immediately adjusted his approach to target fewer players, going after only the prospects he wanted the most and whom he considered signable. The change paid off with his first blockbuster class of Dawkins, Mark Alarie, David Henderson, Jay Bilas, Weldon Williams, and Bill Jackman. That provided the foundation of his program, as four of the recruits started as freshmen and became the senior leaders of Krzyzewski's first Final Four team in 1986.

Dawkins clearly was Krzyzewski's first pivotal recruit. The next was Danny Ferry, whose recruitment in the spring of 1985 surpassed that of Banks as a national story. Ferry was the top prep player in the country, and two other ACC rivals wanted him as much as Duke did. The Blue Devils scouted virtually every one of Ferry's games in his senior year at DeMatha, and when he finally committed, Krzyzewski had made a mark by beating UNC's Dean Smith plus Maryland's Lefty Driesell

for a most coveted player. Ferry's recruitment was the talk of the Triangle for months leading up to his press conference in April 1985, for which several members of the North Carolina media made the drive to his native Maryland. Ferry played in three Final Fours for the Devils and opened the door to many future recruiting successes.

Since then, Duke has won many more recruiting battles than it has lost, with its closest rivals as well as nationally. Landing Christian Laettner, Bobby Hurley, and Grant Hill in successive years provided the base for two national title teams. All were also UNC targets and Hill was an unabashed Tar Heel fan who visited UNC unofficially in high school. But his first official recruiting trip was to Duke, and he found a perfect fit.

In the 1990s, with Duke on top of the polls, on television all the time, and seemingly always in the Final Four, Krzyzewski began landing a succession of recruiting classes considered the best in the nation. The prep senior class of 1997 — Shane Battier, Elton Brand, Chris Burgess, William Avery — matriculated with much acclaim. The class of 1999 included four McDonald's All-Americas in Jason Williams, Mike Dunleavy, Carlos Boozer, and Casey Sanders. Three of those talents had to play early after a stunning mass exodus of the recruits from 1997 and 1998 (Corey Maggette).

The top-rated 2002 class again had four McDonald's All-Americas in J. J. Redick, Shavlik Randolph, Sean Dockery, and Michael Thompson, not to mention Shelden Williams. The 2005 class, which arrived at Duke to join Redick, Williams, and their classmates for their senior year, also was rated No. 1, with Greg Paulus, Josh McRoberts, Eric Boateng, and Jamal Boykin all making the Parade All-America team. With the addition of Martynas Pocius, the 2005 group included two guards, two forwards, and a center.

Some observers have pointed out that Duke recruits with a rifle instead of a shotgun. Besides Krzyzewski's personable and honest manner and his Hall of Fame status, the essential ingredients to making that selective approach work have been the staff's ability to identify its prime targets early and to adjust to the changing climate within the sport.

Before 1982 the basketball signing period always took place in the spring and prospects would be courted throughout their senior seasons. Beginning in the fall of 1982, the NCAA opened up a one-week window every November in which prep seniors could sign letters of intent before the start of their last seasons. Duke secured the services of Tommy Amaker that fall and was one of the first schools to gear its entire strategy toward fall commitments. From 1982 to 2005 Duke signed 54 of its 71 scholarship recruits in November. The most prominent spring signees since 1995 have been Brand, Boozer, and Lance Thomas. Brand committed in the fall but decided to wait until spring to sign, as protection against any unforeseen developments. When Brand decided to leave early for the pros in 1999, Boozer was a spring signee who replaced him on the roster and in the lineup.

Early identification has also resulted in earlier oral commitments than ever before. At first, oral commitments at the end of a prospect's junior season were uncommon, as when Jeff Capel committed to Duke at that point in his prep career. Redick pushed back that time to just before the start of his junior season, and DeMarcus Nelson became the earliest commitment in school history when he announced for Duke in May 2002, at the end of his sophomore year.

Duke has also had to adjust its recruiting efforts to the increased migration of teenage talents to the NBA. As one of the premier programs, the Blue Devils are usually involved with the top players in the country, but they are not known for wasting a lot of effort on prospects who have no interest in college or who declare their intentions of playing just one season. Duke has lost several players early to the pros, but none planned at the outset to use the school as a one-year stepping stone.

After 2000 Duke invested much recruiting effort in securing commitments from Luol Deng, Kris Humphries, and Shaun Livingston. But Humphries switched to another school where he could play one year and leave for the NBA, Deng surprisingly departed from Duke after his freshman season, and Livingston opted for the preps-to-pros route. That meant that Krzyzewski got just one year out of a possible 12 from those players, one reason why his 2005 team was so lacking in depth. While they were being recruited, however, all those players and their families expressed interest in college and education, a prerequisite for Duke's involvement.

"I would never recruit a kid who said, 'I'm just coming for a year.' I never have," Krzyzewski pointed out. "First of all, I would ask the kid, 'How do you know?' If the kid says, 'I want to be a pro player and I value education,' then you go in a year, that is a different starting point. If the kid flat out says, 'I'm going to come here for a year and then I'm gone,' how do you coach that kid? He already knows more than you do.

"That doesn't mean we wouldn't have kids that would go after one year, like Luol Deng. He didn't know he was going to go in one year. It just clicked. Also, for our school, we can't do that. A kid says, 'I'm going to come and use you for a year,' that's not what we should do. That doesn't mean we won't recruit top kids who might go after a year or two years, because we have done that."

Krzyzewski followed up the 2004 losses with his five-player class of 2005 and had already attracted verbal pledges from three highly touted rising seniors before the 2005 crop arrived on campus. It seemed that regardless of national trends or local circumstances, Krzyzewski and his assistants were able to capitalize on their unique stature and the university's renowned excellence to keep talented players pointed toward Duke.

Unquestionably, it's been a recruiting asset for the head coach to populate his full-time staff with former players such as Amaker, Dawkins, Henderson, Quin Snyder, Chris Collins, and Steve Wojciechowski. They helped him to recruit and sign nearly 50 high school All-America players during his first 25 years. Yet when Krzyzewski appeared in a television commercial for American Express in 2005, some media figures and opposing coaches were critical, claiming that it gave the Blue Devils a recruiting advantage.

"I was surprised when I heard that it was going to produce all these unfair advantages, like we had never been good before," Krzyzewski said of the spot, which received heavy airplay during the NCAA Tournament and NBA playoffs. "We are going to recruit good players whether I do a commercial or not. To me that's kind of like a little-kid thing to say. I would hope more coaches do those things because it sells our brand, as long as it is in good taste."

With Duke's growth from a regional to a national university, most of the program's recruiting scope has extended beyond state lines. But a handful of North Carolina's top prep players were recruited successfully by Duke during the Krzyzewski era, most notably David Henderson (Warren County), Kevin Strickland (Mt. Airy), Robert Brickey (Fayetteville), Jeff Capel (Fayetteville), and Shavlik Randolph (Raleigh).

Duke's emergence as a national power in women's basketball also was founded on the recruitment of top talent. Coach Gail Goestenkors cut her recruiting teeth at Purdue, helping to stock one of the Big Ten's top programs before taking over the Blue Devils in the summer of 1992. Her 1993 recruiting class was rated ninth nationally by *Blue Star Report*, the highest mark in program history at that point. The class produced a pair of 1,000-point scorers in Kira Orr and Tyish Hall, who had the Devils in the NCAA Tournament in their sophomore year.

Goestenkors's 1999 recruiting class, featuring Sheana Mosch and Michele Matyasovsky, was ranked fourth by Blue Star. The next year, Duke's incoming freshman crop of Alana Beard, Rometra Craig, Vicki Krapohl, Iciss Tillis, and Crystal White was ranked No. 1 nationally. Subsequent recruiting classes for 2002 and 2003 also topped the charts, while the 2005 group was ranked second. It featured the McDonald's and Gatorade national high school player of the year in Abby Waner.

From the beginning, Goestenkors tried to lure recruits with her vision of developing a championship program at Duke. She has often pointed to the nationally televised victory over the three-time defending champ Tennessee in the 1999 NCAA Tournament as one of the turning points in moving her from the living rooms of good players to great ones.

"When we were doing home visits her very first year, she would go into these recruits' homes and talk about winning a national championship," her long-time assistant Gale Valley once said. "The first couple of visits I let it go, then I had to remind her that we were going to finish last in the ACC that next year and she was talking about national championships.

"That was a lesson for me, to not only dream big but don't be afraid to tell people about it. You can have a secret dream, but when you tell people about it, it becomes real and you have to back up what you say. She was selling the vision of what she had for Duke basketball. It was 10 years ago but it sticks with me like it was yesterday because it was such a great lesson."

See also Freshman basketball; High School All-Americas; Violations.

Redding, Chris. A three-year starter from 1972 through 1974, James Christopher Redding was one of the bright spots at a time when Duke was struggling to win. The Blue Devils' record was just 36 – 42 during his tenure, but Redding played in all 78 games and was first or second on the scoring list for all three years. He consistently delivered double-figures scoring, with 59 such games in his career and a three-year average of 14.6. Redding totaled 1,138 points and 473 rebounds. He ranked as one of the ACC's top 10 scorers and top 10 free-throw shooters in each of his first two years.

Redding overcame an off-season bout with mononucleosis to sparkle as a sophomore in 1972. He had a high of 25 points against Dayton and 24 points with 11 boards in a win over Wake Forest. When Duke edged UNC on dedication day at Cameron Indoor Stadium, Redding contributed 24 points and hit 14 of 15 free throws. He made the All-ACC second team in 1973, when he averaged 16.9 points and turned in an impressive midseason streak, averaging 27 points over a span of six games against Virginia (26), Wake Forest (29), N.C. State (31), Clemson (21), Davidson (28), and North Carolina (27). He set a new Duke record by hitting 84.4 percent of his free throws, a mark subsequently surpassed only by J. J. Redick, Trajan Langdon, and Jim Spanarkel. Redding topped the ACC individually, and his efforts helped Duke to lead the country in free-throw shooting in 1973.

Redding finished behind sophomore Bob Fleischer for the team scoring and rebounding lead in 1974, scoring 26 points versus Davidson, 25 points versus Pittsburgh, and 23 points with 11 rebounds in a win over Virginia that gave the school its 1,000th all-time basketball victory.

Redick, J. J. He decided he was going to play for Mike Krzyzewski and Duke when he was a seven-year-old, while watching the Blue Devils play in the 1992 NCAA Tournament. He learned how to shoot with both hands as an eighth grader because he had to — he broke each wrist that year. Unhappy with the bottom line on his college transcript halfway through college, he buckled down and took aim at a better grade point average. And realizing as a rising junior that he would be The Man for America's most scrutinized basketball program, he changed his lifestyle, amplified his self-discipline, and re-shaped his physique to better handle the responsibility.

Jonathan Clay "J. J." Redick was one of the better players in the Atlantic Coast Conference for his first two seasons, but he reached a higher level as a junior in 2005 before entering another realm in 2006. A 6–4 guard from Roanoke, Va., he stamped himself as one of the top players in the nation and one of the best ever in the conference. From the opening tipoff of his junior year through a frustrating defeat in the Sweet 16 as a senior, Redick was the driving force for a program that won consecutive ACC championships and earned back-to-back No. 1 seeds in the NCAA. And there was nothing subtle about his contributions toward those ends: he was the focal point of every defense and every opposing fan, and the one player whom his own team had to have on the court as much as possible. His heart, resolve, and dedication to purpose were impossible to measure, to say nothing of his renowned ability to shoot a basketball like few others in Duke history.

Redick delivered more than his share of dazzling offensive displays in his first two years — 34 points against Virginia (a freshman record), a lights-out finish for 30 points against N.C. State in the ACC final, a flurry of 20-point games for the 2004 Final Four team. But each of those years ended with Redick feeling as though he was running on empty. His response was to drop 25 pounds so that he could radically improve his stamina and develop every phase of his game to become a more complete player. It was a mission accomplished, as he elevated his playing time to over 37 minutes a game over his final two years while increasing his value. His work and movement without the ball improved, as did his drive, medium-range jumper, and use of screens, all of which made his long-range shot still more deadly. He got to the free-throw line even more frequently than he had in the past, and his court leadership and defense reached new heights as well.

Thus Redick was a unanimous selection to the All-ACC first team, a consensus first-team All-America, ACC player of the year, and MVP of the ACC Tournament in each of his last two seasons. Only three other players in ACC history won the tourney MVP award twice: Len

Known initially for his outside shooting touch, J. J. Redick developed into a multifaceted offensive performer as well as a solid defender.

Chappell of Wake Forest, Larry Miller of UNC, and Tom Burleson of N.C. State. Redick also won one national player of the year award as a junior and several more as a senior.

Redick led the ACC in scoring with a 21.8 average in 2005, but that was merely a prelude to a senior season that ranks as one of the best in school and conference history. His scoring average of 26.8 not only topped the league but was the best mark in Duke history and ranked second nationally, behind Adam Morrison of Gonzaga. He scored at least 20 points in all but eight games, had 30 points on 14 occasions, and averaged over 29 in ACC regular-season games. Three times he reached the 40-point mark, with career highs of 41 against Texas and Georgetown and 40 against Virginia. The game against

Texas may have been the most noteworthy, because in one two-hour window at the Meadowlands in New Jersey, Redick became the ninth 2,000-point man in Duke history, tied Shane Battier's school record for most three-pointers in a game (nine), and passed Trajan Langdon to become the all-time Blue Devil leader in three-pointers. And those efforts sparked a 31-point wipeout of the No. 2 team in the country. The Virginia game a month later, though, may have been his best shooting display: 11 of 13 from the field, 8 of 10 from three-point range, and 10 of 11 from the free-throw stripe.

Among his many highlights, Redick established three major records late in the 2006 season. Against Wake Forest on Valentine's Day, he broke the NCAA record for career three-pointers that had been held by Curtis Staples of Virginia, who attended the game and presented Redick with a ball afterward. In Duke's next game, against Miami, Redick became the Blue Devils' all-time scoring leader, breaking the mark held by his associate head coach, Johnny Dawkins. Two games after that, he became the ACC's career scoring leader, hitting a pair of free throws late in a game at Temple to pass former Wake Forest star Dickie Hemric, who had been recognized as the league's top scorer for over 50 years. In the semifinals of the ACC Tournament, against Wake Forest again, Redick broke the NCAA three-pointer record for a second time; he had been passed on the national list by Keydren Clark of St. Peters. Redick had 225 points in his 12 ACC tourney games, more than any other player in the history of the event.

Redick finished his career with 2,769 points, the 16th-best total in NCAA history, and had a 19.9 average. He hit 457 three-pointers and connected on over 40 percent of his career threes, even though every opponent was geared to disrupt his reception of the ball and textbook stroke. From the free-throw line he made 662 of 726 shots for a mark of 91.2 percent, by far the best in Duke and ACC history and the best in NCAA history for players who made at least 600 shots. Redick once hit 54 free throws in a row, the longest streak in ACC history. Redick played in 139 games, starting all but five, and scored in double figures 122 times. Duke won 116 games during his career, with three ACC titles and a trip to the Final Four.

Krzyzewski called Redick the best pure shooter he had ever coached. But Redick hoped to be remembered for more than his offensive talents. "I think the first thing I'd like people to remember me as is a winner," he said at the end of his career. "But also, as someone who played hard every play. 'J. J. played hard every play. He didn't take any plays off. He was a hard worker.' Those things are important to me."

Redick learned much about basketball from his older twin sisters, Alyssa and Catie, who played collegiately at Campbell. They're also responsible for his nickname, J. J., which dates back to their pronunciation of his first initial long before he could shoot a jump shot. His middle name, Clay, reflects his parents' background as stoneware potters. But it may be the most incongruous aspect of his public identity, because bricks are nowhere to be found in his basketball lexicon.

Best Finishes by Duke Players in NCAA Single-Season Scoring Statistics

J. J. Redick	2006	2nd	26.8
Dick Groat	1952	2nd	26.0
Dick Groat	1951	4th	25.2
Bob Verga	1967	9th	26.1
Art Heyman	1961	9th	25.2
Art Heyman	1963	9th	24.9
J. J. Redick	2005	9th	21.8

Reigel, Bill. His was one of the great one-year careers in school history. William Ernest Reigel suited up for Duke in just one campaign, 1953, but had a profound impact during the Blue Devils' final season in the Southern Conference.

A transfer from Duquesne, where he played freshman ball, Reigel sat out his first year at Duke in 1952 and played intramurals, where he was the unanimous choice as the center on the all-IM team. A 6–4 lefthander from Monaca, Pa., he wowed the varsity with averages of 16.3 points and 7.3 rebounds a game in 1953. His most electrifying performance was against Wake Forest, when he hit 11 of 18 field goals and 16 of 19 free throws for 38 points, with two foul shots in the final minute of regulation forcing overtime in a game that Duke eventually won.

But that was not Reigel's only great game, or even

his only 30-point game. He dropped 31 points on West Virginia to key a narrow win, 27 in the next game in a close victory over NYU, and 29 in a win at 12th-ranked N.C. State just two days after that overtime decision at Wake.

Reigel was expected to provide an anchor point for the 1954 team, but he dropped out of school during the summer of 1953, intending to enlist in the service. His one-year record: 26 games, 425 points, and 189 rebounds for an 18 – 8 team.

Reynolds Coliseum. Apart from their own home floor, the Duke Blue Devils played more games in Reynolds Coliseum than any other arena during their first century of basketball. Located in the heart of N.C. State's campus in Raleigh, the venerable facility has several interesting connections to Duke. It was modeled after the Blue Devils' home stadium, is named for a former Trinity College student, and was the training ground for one of Duke's greatest coaches.

The tobacco manufacturer and philanthropist William Neal Reynolds attended Trinity, Duke's predecessor, in 1882 and 1883 before joining his brother, R. J. Reynolds, in business. The coliseum that bears his name was designed with Duke Indoor Stadium in mind and was supposed to include a like number of seats, around 9,000. Construction began a couple of years after Duke's facility opened in 1940 but was interrupted by the war. After the war, N.C. State imported Everett Case to run its basketball program, and his vision included a bigger arena. With most of the steel framing already in place, the only practical way to enlarge the building was to increase its length. Construction resumed in 1948 and when it was completed, Case had a facility that would hold 12,000 spectators, with unusually deep end-zone seating.

The first game in Reynolds was in December 1949, a 20-point State victory over Washington & Lee. The first basket was scored by Wolfpack floor leader Vic Bubas. He took the first two shots, missed, got the two rebounds, and scored on his third attempt. Bubas was one of Case's top players and later was his assistant coach for most of the 1950s before accepting the head coaching position at Duke in the spring of 1959.

Duke's first game at Reynolds was on Valentine's Day

in 1950. The eighth-ranked Wolfpack pounded the Blue Devils. By the time Duke crushed N.C. State at Reynolds in January 1999, the Blue Devils had played 143 games in the "Big Barn." Fifty of those had been against the home team, but the Devils had also played in three NCAA Tournaments, three Southern Conference Tournaments, 13 ACC Tournaments, 13 Dixie Classics, and five holiday doubleheaders at Reynolds, with an overall record of 82 – 61.

Reynolds arrived at a time when basketball interest was exploding along Tobacco Road, and as the largest arena in the region it was the logical place to hold many of the premier events and tournaments. That lent the Wolfpack tremendous home-court and recruiting advantages, which lasted into the mid-1960s before new coliseums in Charlotte and Greensboro offered more neutral settings for major events. Of course, it should also be noted that State didn't limit its victories to the friendly confines of home during the Case era. When Duke hosted the Southern Conference tourney from 1947 through 1950, the Wolfpack won all four times.

With deafening acoustics exploited by State's zealous fans, Reynolds was one of the nation's most intimidating environments during its heyday. Several Duke-State games there would fall into the category of instant classics, such as the Blue Devils' back-to-back nail-biting wins over nationally ranked State teams in 1953 and 1954, and a pair of ACC Tournament games in the 1960s. The Wolfpack edged Duke in the final in 1965 and then brought the team's ailing, retired coach on to the floor to help clip the nets, a tradition that Case had brought to the area. The next year, in the last ACC at Reynolds, Duke nipped the Wolfpack for the title and Steve Vacendak received the Everett Case award as tournament MVP.

One of Duke's best and one of its worst NCAA Tournament performances were both delivered at Reynolds. Jeff Mullins's 43-point outburst against Villanova in the opener in 1964 triggered the Blue Devils' run to the Final Four, while in 1979 both Duke and UNC were upset in an NCAA doubleheader at Reynolds that came to be known locally as Black Sunday.

During the Mike Krzyzewski era, one of the best games in Reynolds was a two-point Duke victory in 1986 in which Johnny Dawkins hit a pair of free throws after being fouled on a last-second field-goal attempt. In 1984 an overtime win in Reynolds assured a rebuilding Duke club of a .500 ACC record in a season when 12 of its 14 league games were decided by six points or fewer. In 1996 Chris Collins's late jumper gave Duke a critical one-point win in Raleigh to end an 0–4 ACC start.

N.C. State's last men's game at Reynolds was an NIT loss to Princeton in 1999. The school's women's team continued to call it home after the men moved off-campus to the RBC Center, a stadium in Raleigh seating 19,722.

Richardson, Oscar. Nicknamed "Long Rich" by his fellow students, Oscar L. Richardson was the Trinity starting center for three years, 1920–22. A native of Monroe, N.C., he held the position of team captain in 1922, when he was a first-year law student.

Riedy, Bob. After contributing as a sophomore sixth man in 1965, Robert Frederick Riedy emerged as a stalwart in the frontcourt for the team in 1966, when it reached the Final Four, and 1967, when it was an ACC finalist. A 6–6 native of Allentown, Pa., he played in 79 of 82 games, scoring 741 points with 535 rebounds.

Riedy frequently delivered double-digit scoring during his last two years as a regular while battling inside as one of the team's most effective rebounders. He had 23 points against Wake Forest in the opening game of the ACC tourney in 1966 and scored 11 in the championship game win over N.C. State to make the all-tourney second team. He was invaluable on the drive to the Final Four and had 12 points in the regional championship win against Syracuse.

Riedy exploded for his career high of 30 points versus Southwest Louisiana in 1967 but had several other impressive performances as well, including two for 20 points each against Wake Forest and one for 24 against Virginia.

After Duke, Riedy played in the ABA for one year, appearing in 23 games.

Righter, Ron. A 6–7 forward from Chalfont, Pa., Ronald Leslie Righter played in 25 games as a sophomore for the 1972 team, with 162 points and 78 rebounds. He was best known for hitting a 30-foot shot to give the Blue Devils a 74–73 victory in overtime against N.C. State. Four days earlier he had 17 points in an upset of sixth-ranked Virginia. His season high was a 19-point effort versus Virginia Tech. Righter decided to transfer after the 1972 campaign.

Riley, Joe. A 6–1 forward from Collingsdale, Pa., Joe "Lion" Riley subbed as a freshman in 1934, then lettered for three years, 1935–37. Known for his shooting stroke, Riley totaled 249 points during his last three years, which featured records of 18–8, 20–6, and 15–8.

Robb, Spencer. Spencer Robb scored 18 points for Duke's Southern Conference championship team of 1938, the only season he earned a letter.

Robertshaw, Don. A backcourt whiz for Duke's 1930 undefeated freshman team, Don Robertshaw lettered in one year for the varsity, 1931, and scored 66 points.

Robertson, Jerry. Known for his hustle, desire, and rebounding instincts, Jerry Ray Robertson, a dependable 6–6 forward from Burlington, N.C., lettered for three seasons, 1957–59. He appeared in 68 games with 270 points and 255 rebounds. His sophomore season of 1957 was his best statistically, as he averaged 6.7 points and 5.5 boards. He scored 13 points in his first varsity game to help Duke win at Georgia Tech — also the opening game for Tech's Alexander Memorial Coliseum. Robertson had eight double-digit efforts that year, with a high of 16 against North Carolina in the Dixie Classic. He teamed with Marty Joyce as a co-captain of the 1959 squad.

Robinson, David. The only man to play for three U.S. Olympic basketball teams, David Robinson faced Duke twice during his career at Navy. He was on the court for just 10 minutes as a freshman in December 1983, scoring six points with one rebound when the Devils beat Navy in the Rainbow Classic. By the time the teams met again in 1986, he was a junior in the midst of a seven-inch college growth spurt. The Duke-Navy game at the Meadowlands in New Jersey came with a trip to the Final Four on the line, and Duke won again behind some inspired play from two frontcourt seniors, Jay Bilas and Mark Alarie. Robinson had 23 points and

10 rebounds. "The Admiral" went on to an exceptional NBA career that saw him land a spot on the league's 50th anniversary team.

Robinson, Jack. In his only year as a letterman, 1946, guard Jack Robinson of Philadelphia appeared in 20 games and scored 37 points for the Blue Devils, that year's Southern Conference champions.

Roellke, Bob. A 6–1 freshman swing man from Maplewood, N.J., Bob Roellke was one of the more potent offensive weapons on the 1945 Duke team. He scored 164 points, the third-highest total on the club. Roellke posted his high of 22 against Virginia. He added 37 points in 22 games in 1946.

Rogers, George. George H. Rogers, a three-year letterman from Asheville, N.C., scored 372 points over his career, 1929–31, and was co-captain in 1931. When Duke opened its new gym on West Campus, later to be named Card Gym, Rogers hit the first basket in the initial game against Villanova (December 1930). He also played varsity tennis for three seasons, captaining the team and performing at the No. 1 position in the singles lineup. He followed his older brother Stewart to Duke.

Rogers, Jimmy. A 6–0 guard from Athens, W.Va., James Therin Rogers played in six games as a sophomore for the 1955 Blue Devils. He scored three points and had four rebounds.

Rogers, Stewart. A talented student athlete during the mid-1920s, William Stewart Rogers, of Asheville, N.C., played on the varsity basketball team for three years, 1926–28. He saw his most extensive action early in his career. By the time he was a senior, he was coming off the bench behind a promising core of sophomore standouts led by All-America Bill Werber. Rogers was also an exceptional tennis player, serving as team captain twice and winning the state singles title in 1926. His younger brother George was a Duke freshman in 1928, Stewart's senior year.

Rogers, Tom. Known to most in Duke basketball circles as the Colonel, Tom Rogers came to the school with Mike Krzyzewski as a coach and served as one of his full-time assistants for seven years, 1981–87. He handled numerous administrative and other responsibilities, including film exchange. Then he was named a special assistant to the athletics director and continued to serve as a dedicated member and trusted friend on Krzyzewski's support team even after retiring to Pinehurst, N.C.

The relationship between Rogers and Krzyzewski began at the U.S. Military Academy, where Krzyzewski played and coached. Rogers graduated from there in 1947 and served in the Army until 1977, when he retired as a colonel. He was a freshman coach under Bob Knight in the 1960s and served West Point athletics in several other capacities, including officer representative and basketball advisor as well as recruiting coordinator for all sports.

Rosenthal, Richard. A 6–5 forward from Durham, Richard Watkins Rosenthal played in 23 games as a reserve for the 1955 and 1956 teams. He scored 49 points with 23 rebounds. He had 10 points in a game against South Carolina in 1955. Before Duke, Rosenthal played at Durham High and was named most valuable player of the state's annual summer all-star game in Greensboro. Then he went to prep school in Manlius, N.Y., where he was also the team's most valuable player.

Rothbaum, Sammy. The oldest player on the 1947 Blue Devils, Samuel Wilf Rothbaum began his career as a forward for the 1941 and 1942 conference championship teams and was elected captain in 1943. But Rothbaum entered the Army before the 1943 season began, and he served 44 months with the aviation engineers. A 5–11 native of Palmyra, N.Y., Rothbaum began 1941 as a reserve but earned some starts when veteran Glenn Price was injured. He remained as a starter in 1942 and then was a reserve upon his return in 1947, when he was 27 years old. He totaled 289 points for his career.

Rothensies, Walter. Trinity's coach for the 1920 basketball season was Walter J. "Shorty" Rothensies, who produced a 10–4 record in his only year at the helm. Rothensies was no stranger to campus when he was hired in the fall of 1919, since he had attended Trinity as a student in 1916–17 before the call to arms for the First

World War. He served as a first lieutenant in France during the war and also coached service teams. He returned to the United States in the summer of 1919 and was hired on short notice that fall after another coach unexpectedly had to leave because of his wife's illness. According to the *Trinity Chronicle*, Rothensies also had to take some classes in the fall of 1919 to complete his degree. Before his original matriculation to Duke, he had been a student athlete at Hamilton College and then at Princeton.

Rowe, Sam. Samuel Vann Rowe, of Franklinton, N.C., lettered as a sophomore in 1927. He was captain of the freshman team in 1926 after the previous captain, F.H. Wood, had to leave school early.

Russell, Cazzie. One of the great college stars of the 1960s, Cazzie Russell of Michigan averaged 25.8 points in four meetings against Duke. The schools played in the regular season in 1964, 1965, and 1966, and in the Final Four in 1964. Russell scored 21 points with 15 rebounds to lead a regular-season win in 1964, and had 31 when Duke avenged that result in the Final Four. Russell's Wolverines were ranked No. 1 when they came to Duke in the 1965 season, and he had 21 points in their victory, after which coach Vic Bubas compared him to Oscar Robertson. Duke was ranked No. 1 and Michigan No. 3 when the two teams met during the 1966 season in Detroit. The Blue Devils picked up an overtime win despite Russell's 30 points.

Salisbury, Steve. Backup forward Stephen Robert Salisbury, a 6–3 native of Collingswood, N.J., played two games for the 1962 team and scored two points.

Sampson, Ralph. A three-time ACC and consensus national player of the year, Ralph Sampson of Virginia disposed of the Blue Devils all nine times he faced them from 1980 through 1983. Sampson, a dominant center, averaged 19.8 points and 12.8 rebounds against Duke. As a freshman, Sampson totaled 43 points and 23 rebounds in a pair of head-to-heads with senior Mike Gminski, who countered with 44 points and 23 rebounds. But he was rarely challenged in the paint during his last three years. Sampson scored 30 points with 17 rebounds against Duke in 1981 and 36 points with 14 rebounds as a senior.

Sampson's last battle with Duke was in the ACC Tournament in 1983, when he scored 18 points while playing just 14 minutes in handing the Devils the most lopsided defeat in tournament history. But the freshmen who were humiliated that day vowed never to forget it, and the following season they started Duke on a string of 16 straight victories over the Cavaliers.

Sanders, Casey. Since he was Mr. Basketball in Florida, earned McDonald's All-America honors, and stood 6–11, Casey Derrick Sanders was the object of inflated expectations within Blue Devil Nation when he arrived as a freshman in the fall of 1999. He was part of a star-studded, six-player recruiting class that would have to contribute immediately, so many fans just assumed that there was no limit to what he would accomplish.

Sanders did not bring the same basketball pedigree, though, as his classmates Jason Williams, Carlos Boozer, and Mike Dunleavy, who grew up around the game. He didn't spend his youth shooting on a goal in his backyard or in the playground; he came home from school every day and helped his mother in her arts-and-crafts store. Organized basketball wasn't a part of his life until the eighth grade, when he played all of six games. During his first year in college, he could not understand why his roommate Dunleavy watched NBA basketball on television all the time. Dunleavy explained that you had to study good players to become good yourself. Sanders still preferred watching the History Channel and *The Iron Chef*, but he also started taking notes on a young pro superstar who was about his size, Kevin Garnett.

Sanders was the ideal example of a player who ran his own race in college regardless of what fans and critics opined. He played in 124 games from 2000 to 2003, at a time when Duke won the ACC every year, finished first three times in the national poll, and claimed an NCAA crown. He started just 34 times in four years and averaged only 11 minutes a game, with 336 points and 316 rebounds. But he developed physically about as much as his lanky frame would permit, and totally committed himself to the team concept. He was a much better player when he graduated than when he arrived.

Sanders earned his greatest notoriety as a sophomore in 2001 after starter Boozer broke a foot late in the year. When Mike Krzyzewski altered Duke's style of play to a more up-tempo attack, Sanders was inserted in the starting lineup for the last 10 games and played his role to near-perfection on the Blue Devils' championship trek. He ran the floor to tire the opposing center, played solid defense, and was a primary screener for Shane Battier. When upon his début in the new role he blocked two shots on UNC center Brendan Haywood, his confidence began to increase. He followed with an excellent postseason, including perhaps his top effort against Maryland in the ACC semifinals, when he played a strong 26 minutes against the Terps' Lonny Baxter.

With Boozer back in form for 2002, Sanders logged few minutes off the bench. But as a senior in 2003, with most of his classmates off to the NBA, he enjoyed his best year, starting 21 times while averaging 4.6 points and 5.2 rebounds. He had his career high of 13 points against Dayton and his top rebounding game of 14 in a victory over Clemson. At the ACC Tournament he saw the other side of a late-season lineup change when he was moved to the bench in favor of a more guard-oriented lineup. But he continued to support the team with strong defense and energy as a reserve.

One thing that Sanders always did well at Duke was block shots. He had nearly 500 rejections in high school at Tampa Prep, including 19 in one contest. Using his long arms, leaping ability, and increased knowledge of the game, Sanders swatted away 120 shots in college, just about one a game, which was solid production considering his limited minutes on the court. He led Duke with 54 blocks as a senior, two more than freshman Shelden Williams. His career high of five blocks in a game was achieved twice in his last three appearances, in NCAA tourney play.

One of Sanders's favorite games was at Georgia Tech in his senior year. He scored eight points in 17 minutes, but that's not what made the game memorable. It was the one and only time his father was able to watch him play in person for the Blue Devils. Because her health prevented travel, his mother never attended one of his games. As a musician who always worked at night, his father could never make it to Durham but was able to drive the 100 miles from the family's home in Columbus, Ga., for Casey's last Tech stop.

Sapp, Bill. The leading scorer for Duke's 1945 team was Bill Sapp, a 6-1 forward and Navy V-12 trainee from Augusta, Kan. Sapp totaled 221 points and had one of his best-scoring games against Wake Forest with 17 points.

Sapp, Carl. A 6-4 forward from Raleigh who had been an all-state high school player, Carl F. Sapp came to Duke as a 23-year-old freshman after serving as a lieutenant in Naval Aviation in the Pacific. He lettered for three years, 1947-49, and scored 239 points in 74 appearances. His 14 points off the bench helped the Devils edge George Washington in the Southern Conference quarterfinals in 1948, held at Duke.

Saunders, Larry. One of the top high school players in Illinois, Lawrence Craig Saunders began his college career at Northwestern, where he scored 73 points in 19 games as a sophomore. Saunders then transferred to Duke for his last two years and played in every game during the 1970 and 1971 seasons. A 6-9 forward from Elmhurst, Ill., he provided a physical presence, with 505 points and 406 rebounds in 56 contests.

After sitting out 1969 under NCAA transfer regulations, Saunders stepped into the Duke lineup in 1970 as the No. 3 scorer and No. 2 rebounder with averages of 10.0 points and 7.7 boards. He hit 63.6 percent of his shots to set a new Duke and ACC record for field-goal percentage, a mark that stood in the school record books for almost 20 years. Saunders's top scoring output was 29 points against Wake Forest in the ACC Tournament. Among his double-doubles was a 23-point, 14-rebound performance against West Virginia.

After one year on the court Saunders was voted captain for the 1971 season, when he averaged 8.2 points and 6.8 rebounds to help the Devils post a 20-10 record. He captured his career rebounding high of 17 in wins over Virginia Tech and Dayton and again ranked among the ACC leaders in field-goal percentage at 56.4. Duke played in the NIT in both of Saunders's varsity seasons. He hit 59.9 percent of his career field goals, 191 of 319, but is not listed among the school's all-time leaders because he did not make a minimum of 300. Saunders was the 177th pick of the NBA draft but did not play in the league.

Scanlon, Jennifer. An offensive-minded perimeter player from Ballston Lake, N.Y., Jennifer Scanlon was part of the nucleus of key players who helped shape the growth of the women's program during the early years of coach Gail Goestenkors. A 5–10 guard, she was recruited by Debbie Leonard but played her entire career under Goestenkors. She appeared in all 118 games of Goestenkors's first four seasons, 1993–96, and started 93 times.

Scanlon compiled a double-figures scoring average every season and finished with a career mark of 11.7 on 1,377 points. She also had 390 rebounds and 259 assists. Scanlon was one of the Blue Devils' first noteworthy three-point shooters. When she hit 51 threes as a junior in 1995, it marked a school record that has been surpassed several times since. She finished her career with 159 threes, the all-time Duke record until Georgia Schweitzer eclipsed it six years later.

Scanlon was a central figure in Duke's return to the NCAA Tournament after a seven-year absence. The team had a 12–15 record in her freshman year but improved each season, going 26–7 in her senior year. The Blue Devils made the March Madness field in each of her final two years and reached the second round both times. When Duke was ousted by Alabama, playing on its home court, in a four-overtime classic in 1995, Scanlon was the only player on either side to go the entire 60 minutes.

Scarborough, Dave. A 6–3 forward from Philadelphia, David Scarborough played four varsity years, 1947–50, lettering for the last two. He played briefly off the bench as a freshman and sophomore, then moved into the starting lineup for his junior and senior campaigns. He scored 396 points in 70 games. Scarborough was considered solid as a rebounder and dangerous with his set shot from the sidecourt.

Schalow, Jack. Head coach Bucky Waters imported a successful West Coast product when he added John V. Schalow to his staff for the 1970 and 1971 seasons. A former Army paratrooper and team captain at Pacific University, Schalow saw his freshman teams win 81 of 92 games over four years at Pacific and Seattle before he came to Duke. His 1970 Duke freshman team posted a 16–0 record while his 1971 team went 13–3.

Schalow continued with a long basketball coaching career after his brief Duke days. In 1976 he was the Ohio Valley coach of the year at Morehead State. He spent several years in the NBA with the Jazz and Trail Blazers, including a decade in Portland as an assistant and scout. He also served on the coaching staff at the United States Basketball Academy.

Schayes, Dolph. Hall of Famer Dolph Schayes, a 12-time pro all-star who once went over a decade without missing an NBA game, played against Duke twice during his college career at New York University. His squad won both games, at Madison Square Garden in 1947 and 1948, but he was not a major scorer in either. He had three points in one game and 11 in the other.

Schmidt, Fred. Ineligible in 1960 and sidelined by a broken hand for half of 1961, Frederick Karl Schmidt eventually developed into a starter for 1962 and 1963, teaming with Buzzy Harrison in the backcourt. A 6–4 native of Philadelphia, Schmidt played in 64 games in the 1961–63 seasons, scoring 413 points with 106 rebounds. He saved his best for last, averaging 8.3 points on 52.5 percent shooting for the Blue Devils' first Final Four team. While Art Heyman and Jeff Mullins paced the offensive attack, publicist Ted Mann described Schmidt as "a crack shot who pulled the Blue Devils through many a tough one." One of those was the NCAA East Regional final in 1963 against St. Joseph's, when he scored 20 points on 9-of-16 shooting to help propel the Devils to their first Final Four. Duke played in two ACC finals and won one during his career. Schmidt was also president of his fraternity.

Schmidt, Paul. A spirited 6–5 forward from Johnstown, Pa., Francis Paul Schmidt started for the better part of two seasons and lettered for three under coach Harold Bradley, 1956–58. He appeared in 67 games with 559 points and 409 rebounds. His senior year was his best, with averages of 11.9 points and 7.9 rebounds for a club that won the ACC regular season. His best games in 1957 were against the eventual national champ, UNC, with 17 points, and nationally ranked West Virginia, with 15. As a senior he again had a fine performance versus West Virginia with 12 points when the Mountaineers, then top-ranked, were knocked off by the Blue Devils. He also had the team's top rebounding performance of the year with 24 against Wake Forest, in a game in which he added 17 points. Schmidt scored in double figures in the last 14 games of his career, including a high of 20 against Virginia. He was a second-team All-ACC pick as well as the most valuable player of a Duke team that finished No. 10 in the final national poll. He led the ACC in field-goal shooting with a mark of 52.3 percent in 1958.

Schweitzer, Georgia. Coming out of high school, Georgia Schweitzer wasn't featured on many top 50 lists of college prospects. But a year after her graduation from Duke, Schweitzer made a pair of impressive top 50 compilations—the 50 best women athletes and 50 best women basketball players in ACC history.

A 6–0 guard from Columbus, Ohio, Schweitzer constructed a marvelous career from solid raw materials and intense desire. Despite numerous injuries, she never missed a game and led Duke to either an ACC regular-season or tournament championship—or both—in each of her seasons. She played an integral role on the first Duke team to reach the Final Four, the first to win a conference title and the first to achieve a No. 1 seed in the NCAA Tournament.

Duke compiled a record of 111–25 during Schweitzer's run from 1998 to 2001, including a 53–11 mark in ACC play. Schweitzer was on the court for every one of those efforts, with 115 starts. She scored 1,620 points for an 11.9 average, had 533 rebounds, dealt 428 assists, and set the school record for career three-pointers with 202.

Schweitzer had plenty of numbers, but numbers hardly defined her. Most valuable was her selfless devotion to the team and her leadership, which was most evident in her senior year when she guided a squad of young players to 30 wins, an ACC title, and a trip to the Sweet 16 of the NCAA Tournament.

Schweitzer's personal breakout performance came late in her sophomore year, when she scored a team high of 22 points to help the Blue Devils slay three-time NCAA champ Tennessee in the 1999 East Regional, earning the first Final Four berth in school history. Schweitzer was named most valuable player of the regional. The following season she was named ACC player of the year after averaging 15.6 points for the first Blue Devil team to win the ACC tourney. As a senior she repeated as player of

In 2001 Georgia Schweitzer was the ACC player of the year, ACC Tournament MVP, and a Kodak All-America for the Duke women.

the year and added tournament MVP honors to her list of credentials when Duke won its second straight league title. A two-time All-ACC selection, she also became an All-America as a senior, making the Kodak team as well as the U.S. Basketball Writers first team and the Associated Press third team.

Although most observers regarded her as a crafty, cerebral player, Schweitzer turned herself into perhaps the best athlete on the team with a rigorous off-season regimen leading into her senior year. Designed to eliminate some of the nagging injuries that had plagued her, the conditioning program left her with the team's best vertical jump and weight-lifting stats.

Along with her basketball prowess, Schweitzer was the epitome of a student athlete. She undertook a pre-med curriculum, shadowed Dr. Henry Friedman in the Duke Brain Tumor Center, and spoke to several youth groups. Her summer of harsh conditioning came after she had spent several weeks taking a class in invertebrate zoology at the Duke Marine Lab while also preparing for the MCAT.

Schweitzer was accepted at Duke Medical School but deferred her enrollment to play in the WNBA. She spent three summers with the Minnesota Lynx, 2001–03, appearing in 70 games with 17 starts. She totaled 226 points, 78 assists, and 119 rebounds. During her 2002 off-season, Gail Goestenkors asked her to join the Duke coaching staff when assistant Joanne Boyle had to undergo emergency brain surgery. Schweitzer stayed for three years and helped the Devils reach back-to-back Final Fours in 2002–03. She decided to retire from the WNBA before the summer of 2004 and also ended her coaching tenure to begin medical school.

Secret game. North Carolina Central University shares the city of Durham with Duke University, but the two institutions never shared the basketball court for an official game until November 2004, when they met in a preseason exhibition at Cameron Indoor Stadium. But over 60 years earlier, on March 12, 1944, representatives of the two colleges met in an unofficial, unsanctioned contest believed to be the first racially integrated college-level basketball game in the South.

Duke graduate, historian, and writer Scott Ellsworth brought this secret game to light in 1996, when he wrote an account of it for the *New York Times* Sunday magazine. According to Ellsworth, an oral-history specialist who interviewed several of the participants, the game was held on a Sunday morning while most of the Durham populace was in church. It took place on the N.C. Central campus, in a locked gym with a referee and scoreboard but no audience, and was kept a secret from the local police as well as the news media. Durham, like all southern towns, was completely segregated at the time, and the color line was enforced by law. During that same year, a black soldier who did not move to the rear of a city bus quickly enough was shot and killed by the bus driver.

Central at that time was known as the North Carolina College for Negroes and was coached by John McLendon, an eventual Hall of Fame inductee who was the first African American to coach in the professional

ranks and the first to win a national championship at the college level. His 1944 team was one of the best black college teams in the country, with a fast-paced attack that produced victories in all but one game. The NCAA and the NIT, however, did not include black schools in their national tournaments.

Duke won the Southern Conference title in 1944, but that was not the team that McLendon's squad faced. The opponent was a Duke intramural team from the medical center that was stocked with former college players from around the country who were on campus as part of service training programs. One was a former Duke varsity player, David Hubbell. According to Ellsworth, the game probably came about when members of the Duke and North Carolina College YMCA chapters, who had occasional secret meetings, wanted to find out who had the best team in town, and McLendon endorsed the idea.

After a nervous start by both sides, the Eagles got their game in gear and crushed the medical school team 88–44. After the game ended, the guys decided to pick racially mixed teams and played again, shirts versus skins. "Just God's children, horsing around with a basketball," one of the Eagles told Ellsworth. And when that contest came to a close, all the players went to one of the dormitories to talk and relax together for a couple of hours before the Duke students headed back across town. Their activities that day remained a secret for over 50 years.

Secret scrimmage. One of the great high school teams in North Carolina prep history was the Durham High School contingent that won 69 straight games under coach Paul Sykes from 1938 through 1940. Three of the 1940 senior starters—Cedric Loftis, Garland Loftis, and Bob Gantt—went on to star at Duke, along with underclassman Gordon Carver. Many of their home games were played at the Duke Gym (later named Card Gym) because their high school auditorium would hold only about 700 fans. They were wildly popular and their games were usually blowouts.

The center for the team was Bones McKinney, who later went on to play for N.C. State and UNC and coached Wake Forest to a Final Four. In his book *Bones: Honk Your Horn If You Love Basketball* (1988), McKinney said

Art Heyman was honored at halftime of his final home game in 1963.

Selvy, Frank. Frank Selvy of Furman, the only Division I player to score 100 points in a game, lit up the Blue Devils in two career meetings. As a sophomore in 1952 he scored 36 points, almost half the Paladins' total in their 73 – 72 upset of Duke at Shelby, N.C. Duke senior Dick Groat had 15 in that contest, which Furman won on a free throw with 38 seconds left to stun the 12th-ranked Devils in their conference opener. Groat went on to finish second in the nation in scoring while Selvy was fifth. As a senior in 1954, the year of his 100-point game against Newberry, Selvy scored 40 points against Duke in its season opener, but the Devils won by 34. Selvy led the country in scoring in 1953 and 1954.

Senior Day. The practice of honoring outgoing senior players at their final home game has become an emotional ritual in many college basketball programs. Duke traditionally recognizes its seniors before the game and allows them to return to the court to address the fans after the game.

Duke's star players have habitually been at their best for their Senior Day games, beginning in 1952 when Dick Groat set the Indoor Stadium scoring record in his final home appearance.

Memorable Senior Games

1952: Dick Groat scores 48 points, a stadium record, to beat UNC.

1956: Ronnie Mayer knocks out George Washington with 25 points, while classmates Junior Morgan and Joe Belmont also star.

1958: Five seniors start, go the distance, and score in double figures as the Devils clinch the ACC regular season in a showdown with UNC.

1963: Art Heyman has 40 points and 24 rebounds in a rout of UNC.

1966: Steve Vacendak has 20 points and Jack Marin 17 in a win over UNC.

1967: Bob Verga decks Wake Forest with 30 points.

1968: Mike Lewis is at his best with 18 points and 18 rebounds, then fouls out and watches junior understudy Fred Lind spark a triple-overtime win against UNC.

that everyone in town wondered what would happen if the 1940 Durham High squad played the Duke varsity, which won 19 games and reached the Southern Conference championship contest. He reported that a closed-door scrimmage between the two took place after the prepsters won the state title, and that they beat the Blue Devils by 15 points.

The Bulldogs used to play a very public game against the Duke freshman team every season, and came out on the winning side all three years during their long streak. When they were invited to compete for the mythical national championship at a tourney in New York in 1940, Sykes and Eddie Cameron set up a benefit game between DHS and a squad of Wake Forest all-stars at the Duke Gym to help raise funds for the trip. The Bulldogs won and made more than enough money. They returned to town with the trophy and a 69-game winning streak.

1969: Steve Vandenberg leads five seniors with 33 points in an upset of UNC, also coach Vic Bubas's last home tilt.

1971: Randy Denton paces five seniors with 24 points and 10 rebounds in a win over UNC.

1979: Jim Spanarkel's 17 points help beat UNC's slowdown.

1980: Mike Gminski marks the retirement of his jersey with 29 points and 19 rebounds in an overtime win versus Clemson.

1981: Kenny Dennard passes to Gene Banks for a dramatic shot to force overtime, then Duke tops UNC on another Banks basket.

1982: Vince Taylor pours in 35 points in a triple-overtime win versus Clemson.

1986: Johnny Dawkins and his landmark senior class celebrate an emotional win over UNC to clinch the ACC regular season.

1988: Billy King and Kevin Strickland help Duke to end a three-game losing streak by getting a series sweep of UNC.

1989: Danny Ferry rolls to 26 points as Duke rolls over N.C. State.

1992: Christian Laettner has five three-pointers and 26 points for top-ranked Duke in a big win over UNC.

1993: Bobby Hurley breaks the NCAA career assists record in a victory over Maryland.

1998: Steve Wojciechowski and Roshown McLeod key a mammoth comeback win versus UNC.

2000: Chris Carrawell has 21 points in a rout of UNC as Duke clinches its fourth straight outright ACC regular-season title.

2002: Jason Williams, not listed as a senior but about to graduate in three years, pops UNC with 37 points in his home swan song.

2005: Daniel Ewing has the first double-double of his career when Duke storms past Miami.

The 2004 pregame senior ceremonies were particularly moving when three of the departing players — Chris Duhon, Andy Borman, and Andy Means — pulled off their warmup tops to reveal popular Sixth Man, Our House, and Cameron Crazie T-shirts celebrating their fans' support. "I started crying thinking how lucky I am to be coaching these kids," Krzyzewski said.

A Night He'll Never Forget

Jim Spanarkel, 1979 Senior Game

Spanarkel could never have dreamed that the halftime score of his last game in Cameron Indoor Stadium, versus archrival UNC, would be 7–0. Years later he contended that it would have been very irritating to lose on a night when the opposition held the ball for most of 20 minutes. That didn't become an issue, because the second half was played at a normal pace and Duke won 47–40, with Spanarkel scoring 17 points.

But the unusual nature of the game is only one of Spanarkel's memories. Thinking of that evening also evokes feelings of how Spanarkel felt about his whole career and his many experiences in Cameron, from teammate Rob Hardy's traditional words of encouragement just before introductions to the support that he always felt from the fans.

"It's difficult to describe that last game so that you can understand the way it felt to me. Unless you go through it, it's hard to explain," he noted. "I always felt very fortunate at Duke. I came in as a recruited prospect but wasn't looked at as someone who was going to turn into a great college player. I saw the other day that Duke has the most 2,000-point scorers in NCAA history, and when I think that I was the first one to do that in school history, I just feel very fortunate.

"The very high majority of people don't have that kind of experience to even think about or to remember, let alone go through it. So for me, that last game was like the culmination of a decent college career and also a reminder of all the good friends and the great support system I had at Duke. For some reason, the people there got attached to my style of play and I was always very appreciative of that."

Seward, John. He was captured by German troops and held in a prisoner of war camp for 71 days during the winter of 1945, far away from college and basketball. But both before and after his Army service in the European Theater during the Second World War, John Evans "Bubber" Seward was one of the Blue Devils' top basketball players.

Seward, a 6–1 forward from Newport News, Va., was a key member of the "flaming sophomore" platoon that helped Duke win the Southern Conference title in 1942,

Eddie Cameron's last year as coach. In 1943 he was a starter and No. 3 scorer with 10.2 points a game, earning first-team all-conference honors.

After his liberation from the Germans and discharge from the Army in December 1945, Seward soon returned to Duke and joined the basketball team in time to help spark an upset of North Carolina in Chapel Hill. He went on to finish as the second-leading scorer on the team and earned all-tournament honors as Duke won the Southern Conference again. Then, as a 24-year-old senior co-captain of the 1947 team, he was a starting forward and No. 2 scorer.

Seward finished his career with 898 points in four seasons, 1942, 1943, 1946, and 1947. He held Duke's career scoring record for about a month during his last year, until he was overtaken by his teammate Ed Koffenberger. Seward was also regarded as a fine rebounder and inspirational leader.

Shabel, Fred. A 6-0 guard from Union City, N.J., and a member of the Duke basketball program for 10 years, Fred Alan Shabel started his Blue Devil career as a player in the 1950s and finished it as an assistant coach in the 1960s. After spending the 1951 season on the freshman team, Shabel played for three years on the varsity, completing his career in 1954. He saw action in 61 games, scoring 214 points and 76 rebounds. His best year statistically was 1953, when he earned some starting assignments and averaged 4.8 points a game, with a career high of 13 against McCrary.

Shabel went into the Air Force after graduation, coached some service teams, and worked with the 1956 Olympic team during its training before it departed for Australia. He was working as a salesman for Esso Standard Oil when Duke hired him in September 1957 to join Harold Bradley's coaching staff and teach physical education. Shabel was on hand for Bradley's final two years and remained during the first four years of Vic Bubas's tenure, through the Final Four season of 1963.

Shabel left Duke to become the head coach at Connecticut. He had the chance to coach against Bubas and the Blue Devils during his first year with the Huskies, when the two schools met in the NCAA Tournament. Duke claimed a 101 – 54 decision in the Eastern Regional final to earn a second straight Final Four berth.

Shabel later moved on to the position of athletics director at Pennsylvania, where he eventually hired as his head basketball coach Chuck Daly, the former assistant to Bubas who had joined the Duke staff when Shabel left for UConn.

Remaining in Philadelphia, Shabel in 1980 joined Comcast-Spectator, the sports and entertainment firm that operates several pro franchises and arenas, including the Philadelphia 76ers and their Wachovia Center. He became one of its top executives as company vice-chairman.

Shaw, Alan. After a year of support work behind All-America Randy Denton, Alan Richard Shaw, 6-10, from Millville, N.J., performed as a solid, all-around pivotman for the 1972 and 1973 seasons. He was one of the team captains both years and was named team MVP as well as All-ACC second team in 1972. His career totals included 82 games, 744 points, and 673 rebounds.

Shaw received the Ted Mann Jr. award as the reserve contributing most to team morale in 1971, when he shot 60 percent from the floor and 77.8 percent from the line. He then averaged a double-double as a junior, with 12.4 points and 11.8 rebounds, frequently going up against bigger or more heralded opposing centers. He had one of his best outings with 19 points and 17 rebounds against N.C. State's 7 – 4 star Tom Burleson. He also held UNC star Robert McAdoo to a 1-of-12 shooting performance. Shaw reached double figures in rebounding 17 times in 26 games, with a high of 19 against both Dayton and William & Mary. His scoring high of 27 was against Syracuse in the Holiday Festival at New York. Shaw's rebounding average ranked second in the ACC to Burleson's in 1972, and his field-goal percentage of 60.1 was third-best in the league. Perhaps most impressively, Shaw showed the stamina and discipline to play nearly 39 minutes a game that year. He went the distance at least 10 times and twice played all 45 minutes of overtime contests.

Shaw, who did not miss a game in three years, couldn't match his 1972 stats as a senior but still averaged 8.8 points and 7.6 boards while posting several strong games. He had 17 rebounds against Richmond and 20 points against Clemson. For his career he had 15 double-doubles and recorded at least 10 rebounds in

25 games. He was the first player in school history to win both the team MVP and the Ted Mann Jr. reserve award in a career, joined later by only three others: Steve Wojciechowski, Dahntay Jones, and Daniel Ewing.

Shaw, John. After toiling as a backcourt reserve for the 1930 team that won 18 of 20 games, John Dickerson Shaw emerged as a starter in 1931 and again in 1932, when he was team captain. A product of Meriden, Conn., he scored 269 points in three years.

Shoe deals. It's become standard procedure for major college basketball programs to receive footwear as part of endorsement arrangements between shoe manufacturers and coaches. But that hasn't always been the case. Shoe deals for coaches first cropped up in the late 1970s, and Duke was one of the first universities to benefit.

For years Duke purchased Converse basketball shoes for its players to wear in games, and as recently as 1978 each of the Big Four schools was buying its shoes from Converse. After the Blue Devils played in the Final Four in 1978, coach Bill Foster was approached by Nike with an endorsement proposition under which the company would provide Duke with shoes and Foster with a stipend in exchange for the coach's appearance at some clinics and consulting.

The *Washington Post* broke a story in the fall of 1978, suggesting an impending shoe war, with Nike aggressively attacking the college market by signing Foster, Lefty Driesell of Maryland, and 15 other coaches to similar deals worth about $8,000 apiece. Foster reported that the free shoes benefited the school's budget because it had spent $3,000 on basketball footwear the previous year. "People don't realize that some players can go through a half-dozen pairs of shoes in one season," Foster told the *Durham Morning Herald*. Coaches at UNC and N.C. State declined Nike's initial blitz and chose to remain with Converse.

Foster left Duke two seasons later, but shoe contracts continued to propagate. Mike Krzyzewski's initial footwear deal in 1981 was with adidas for shoes and equipment only, but it grew with the program and eventually the coach received handsome compensation. Adidas outfitted the Devils' NCAA championship teams in 1991 and 1992.

When Krzyzewski's adidas contract was up for renewal after the 1993 season — with Duke's visibility at an all-time high — he considered other pitches and settled on a lucrative deal with Nike that reportedly made him the coach paid the most by any of the major shoe companies. Nike had pursued him during a previous renewal period but Krzyzewski had elected to remain with adidas. Duke was a third party to the new Nike contract, with president Keith Brodie and athletics director Tom Butters approving and supporting the arrangement.

The financial terms were not confirmed publicly, but Krzyzewski was pilloried in the media for the financial windfall — even though provisions in the contract included benefits for the entire school. One of the most obvious was an immediate announcement of a $250,000 donation by Krzyzewski toward the construction of a badly needed campus recreation facility for the students, the building that is now known as the Wilson Center. The relationship with Nike extended well beyond shoes to encompass uniforms, product merchandising, clinics, videos, consulting, and a variety of services.

Shokes, Eddie. Guard Edward Christopher Shokes, of Charleston, S.C., spent three years on the varsity, 1939 – 41, lettered for the last two, and started as a senior in 1941. He scored 146 points, getting 111 in 1941 as the No. 3 scorer for the Blue Devils' Southern Conference championship team. Shokes, a 6-footer, also played baseball at Duke and later appeared in the major leagues for the Cincinnati Reds, getting 10 hits in 32 games. In 1944 Shokes was on a Norfolk Air Station service basketball team that visited Durham and routed the Blue Devils. The manager of that team was another player with a baseball background, Pee Wee Reese, of Brooklyn Dodgers fame.

Silar, Jacki. When Title IX became law in 1972, Jacki Silar was a three-sport athlete at High Point (N.C.) College. She remembers well the formative years of intercollegiate athletics for women, when players often had to drive their own vehicles and pay their own expenses for road games. Silar worked the concession stand at men's basketball games at High Point to help raise funds for the women's team; one year she and several teammates grabbed a bed sheet and walked around the floor at halftime, asking fans to throw money into the sheet so that their team could afford to travel to a regional tournament in Kentucky.

Silar was one of the influential figures in the growth of women's athletics at Duke, as a coach and administrator. A native of Pottstown, Pa., she was the school's first full-time women's basketball assistant coach and served in that capacity from the 1980 season through 1992. She was also Duke's head field hockey coach for 15 years, from 1981 to 1995, compiling a record of 162 – 116 – 10. In 1995 Silar became the school's first senior women's administrator, and in 2000 she was promoted to associate athletics director, with involvement in several Olympic sports.

Silar teamed with head coach Debbie Leonard, another High Point alumna, to establish the foundation of Duke women's basketball. Both graduated from High Point in 1974. Silar worked as a part-time volunteer assistant for Leonard during the 1979 campaign — Leonard's second year as head coach — and then joined the department full time after earning a master's degree from UNC. Building from scratch, the two guided the program to its first 20-win campaigns, postseason appearances, and national rankings, usually with fewer scholarships than most of their competitors.

Siler, Beal. Described as being in a "class by himself" on the basketball court, Beal Hendrix Siler started at forward for Trinity for three seasons, 1913 – 15, and captained the club as a junior in 1914. He was from Waynesville, N.C.

Simpson, J. D. A non-scholarship member of Duke's renowned recruiting class of 1997, John David "J. D." Simpson contributed as a reserve guard to four Blue Devil teams, appearing in 80 games before graduating in 2001 with a national championship ring and three ACC titles. He scored 41 points while adding 27 rebounds and 12 assists.

A 6 – 4 product of Woodside, Calif., Simpson never logged extensive minutes, mostly because of the high caliber of talent on the roster. But he grew to become a valuable member of the program. His basketball skills and IQ played an important role in practice, while his leadership qualities were most obvious during his final

two years. And he could play if the opportunity arose. When Duke tied a school record with 18 three-point shots in an NCAA game versus Monmouth in 2001, it was Simpson who hit No. 18.

During his senior season Simpson was named one of the captains of the team that would go on to win the national crown. He also joined the red-shirt transfer Dahntay Jones as the reserve contributing most to team morale that year.

Simpson, Jimmy. A constant in the lineup for the last four Trinity teams, 1921 – 24, James Robert Simpson, of Winston-Salem, N.C., was one of the school's most noted athletes. He played varsity football and varsity basketball for all four years, serving as the basketball captain during the winter of 1923 and the football captain during the fall of 1923. In fact, Simpson is the only player in institutional history to be officially listed as captain of both the basketball and football teams. In Trinity's 15 basketball contests against intercollegiate teams in 1923, Simpson scored 214 of the club's 503 points. He was a prime offensive weapon again in 1924 with 205 points.

Singleton, Todd. Painting a portrait of achievement and persistence during his four years, Todd Michael Singleton, a 6 – 4 forward from Severn, Md., developed from walk-on to scholarship player before graduating in 1998. Singleton joined the 1995 team as a walk-on in January of his freshman year and played in just two games. The following year Singleton saw a little more action on the court and also picked up a partial academic scholarship from Procter & Gamble for minorities in engineering. Singleton's dedication to the basketball program was rewarded in his senior year, when he was given an athletic scholarship. Over four years he appeared in 42 games, with 36 points and 15 rebounds. In 1997 he shared the Ted Mann Jr. award as the reserve contributing most to team morale with his fellow walk-ons Justin Caldbeck and Jay Heaps, and he won it outright as a senior.

Skibsted, Wes. A 6 – 2 player from Miami, Wesley Skibsted worked as a backup center for four years, 1947 – 50, but never lettered. He played in 32 games and scored 74 points.

Smiley, Glen. A 6 – 6 forward from Bozeman, Mont., Richard Glen Smiley saw limited reserve work in his three varsity years, 1968 – 70. He played in eight games, with 14 points and six rebounds. His career high of six points was against Alabama in 1969. Smiley's father owned a radio station, and Glen worked as a disc jockey for WDNC in Durham during summer vacation. Later he did color commentary on Duke radio network broadcasts in the 1970s. A fund-raising specialist, he became president of St. John Health Foundation in the Detroit area.

Smith Center. North Carolina played host to Duke in the first official varsity basketball game at the Dean E. Smith Center in Chapel Hill on January 18, 1986. The Blue Devils' forward Mark Alarie scored the first field goal, but the Tar Heels won 95 – 92. It was the first of just three defeats for Duke that year. At tipoff time, UNC was ranked No. 1 in the nation and Duke No. 3.

During the first 21 years of the Smith Center's existence, Duke had an 11 – 12 record on the Tar Heels' home floor. That included two wins in the opening rounds of the NCAA Tournament in 1988 and a 9 – 12 mark against UNC. Seven of the 12 losses, and six of the nine wins, were decided by six points or fewer, reflecting the two teams' well-chronicled rivalry and stature as national powers. In all 21 of those games, at least one of the teams was ranked within the top 10 of the national poll. The 1994 contest marked the first time that Duke and Carolina ever met as the No. 1 and No. 2 teams in the country. (UNC won by 11.) The 2002 game marked UNC's most lopsided loss at the Smith Center, with Duke prevailing by 29 points.

Smith, Dean. No one coached more games against Duke, or beat the Blue Devils more times, than Hall of Famer Dean E. Smith of North Carolina. When Smith retired in 1997 after 36 years in charge of the Tar Heels, his 879 career victories were more than those of any other Division I coach in history. Fifty-nine of those wins (and 35 losses) were against the archrival Blue Devils.

Smith's ledger commanded respect from friend and foe alike. He departed with 13 ACC championships, 27 NCAA Tournament appearances, 11 Final Fours, and a pair of national titles. His 65 victories in the NCAA tourney led all coaches until Mike Krzyzewski broke the mark in 2005. Smith's record of 23 consecutive NCAA bids, though, might never be topped.

"Whatever is written about him in a positive sense he justly deserves," Krzyzewski said after Smith passed Adolph Rupp on the all-time victory list. "I know he'll give credit, as we all would, to the players who have played for us. But in this situation, the praise for him should rise well above that for the players who played for him."

After replacing Frank McGuire on the UNC bench in 1962, Smith lost his first seven meetings with Duke's kingpin Vic Bubas. He turned the corner after winning a recruiting war with the Blue Devils for the Pennsylvania prep standout Larry Miller, who led UNC to the Final Four in 1967 and 1968.

The Blue Devils continued to hold serve against UNC on the home front for a few years, but after Robby West's buzzer-beater upset the Heels in 1972, Smith directed his team to 16 wins in the next 17 matchups against Duke. The Blue Devils didn't catch up until Bill Foster's 1978 team pulled off a victory at Cameron that got the program back in the national polls. Smith also won eight of his last nine career contests versus Duke.

As the leader of Duke's fiercest rival for over three decades, Smith no doubt was vilified by Blue Devils fans more than any other opponent, on the court or sideline. Assorted episodes involving Smith are intricately woven into the fabric of Duke basketball history, with 1966 as a convenient starting point. That was the year when he unveiled his famed Four Corners offense and nearly upset third-ranked Duke in the ACC semis, before the Devils pulled out a 21 – 20 decision.

"They did so many things," said Bucky Waters, Duke's coach from 1970 to 1973. "When you started to prepare, you had to get ready for Four Corners, the run-and-jump, they had three or four defenses, just the multiplicity of things. He was so organized. I give Dean a lot of credit for that. They executed so well. There's that old joke about who can hold Michael Jordan under 20, but it was because they did so much and were so controlled. But in terms of preparing for all their various techniques, it was hard. You ended up spending 10 minutes on everything, then he would play an arpeggio early and see what 10 minutes wasn't effective."

In 1974 Smith's team trailed an outmanned Duke

contingent by eight points with 17 seconds left on Senior Day, when he gathered his players during a timeout and reportedly said, with a smile, "Wouldn't it be neat if we could win this game?" They did, with a comeback that stamped another mark of genius on Smith's résumé.

Smith always seemed to be a step ahead of most of his colleagues. His total commitment to team play led to the practice of having players point to teammates who would feed them a pass that led to a basket. He customarily had his team's statistics sheet listed in alphabetical order rather than by scoring average, and he never wanted the number of minutes played to be included. He was considered a master at working officials as well as reporters, with uncanny recall of minute details to help him make a point or an impression.

As the ACC's preeminent figure for many years, Smith was a target everywhere but in Chapel Hill. Foster alluded to Smith's exalted stature in the media one time when he remarked that he thought James Naismith invented basketball, not Dean Smith. There are some who will believe that Smith's considerable shadow was among the reasons why Foster eventually left Duke for South Carolina.

Sarcastic quips such as Foster's were not uncommon, but the gloves came off in earnest at Duke one Saturday in 1984 after a narrow loss to UNC in Cameron. On a day when his much-criticized student fans were at their creative best in extending "a hearty welcome to Dean Smith," Krzyzewski spoke very forcefully about a perceived "double standard" within the conference—one set of rules for Smith and another for the rest of the league. The catalyst was an incident in which Smith tried to get the game officials' attention, with the ball in play, by slapping the scorer's table and hitting the buttons that controlled the scoreboard, with no technical foul assessed.

"There was not a person on our bench who was pointing a finger at the officials or banging on the scorer's table," said Krzyzewski in standing up for his program. "You can not allow people to go around pointing at officials and yelling at them without technicals being called. That is just not allowed. So let's get some things straight around here and quit the double standard that exists in this league, all right?" From then on, there were plenty of subplots involving Krzyzewski and Smith to parallel their on-the-court gamesmanship.

Spotting signs at Cameron that declared "J. R. Can't Reid," a reference to UNC player J. R. Reid, Smith shocked most Duke observers by revealing that the combined SAT scores of his front-line players Reid and Scott Williams, who were African American, were better than those of Duke's Danny Ferry and Christian Laettner, who had been Tar Heel recruiting targets. In Ferry's last ACC Tournament of 1989, a particularly contentious title bout between Duke and UNC, Krzyzewski and Smith started yelling at each other during the game. When NCAA Tournament bids came out afterward, Smith complained that his ACC champion team had been sent out of its "natural region" by a committee that included Duke's athletics director, Tom Butters.

After the finale between Duke and UNC in Cameron in 1996, Smith made some outspoken comments about how the Duke fans were chanting vulgarities at his guard, Jeff McInnis. "The esteemed Duke faculty has to be embarrassed," he said. Krzyzewski retorted: "I take offense to that. Our fans have been terrific this year. If there is a problem, it is out there on the court, not in the stands . . . I'm speaking up for the fans. They have been great. I am going to stick up for them. I have nothing against Dean, and Dean and I are pretty good friends. But when I don't like some of the things people in my family do, I tell them about it."

Three of Smith's most admired traits were his class, his competitiveness, and his loyalty. He went after every one of those 879 victories with uncommon vigor, always played by the rules, and was renowned for helping his players long after graduation. While respectful, many opponents also viewed him as one who could manipulate any situation to Carolina's advantage. That thought crossed the mind of Duke forward Fred Lind when he was warming up for his final home game against UNC and one of the Carolina managers told him that Smith wanted to talk to him about something. Lind dismissed the comment as a mind game but later found out that Smith wanted to invite him to play in a postseason all-star game in Hawaii. Lind worked Smith's summer camp after law school and was at the camp when he got the call that he'd been hired for his first full-time job in Greensboro. Former Duke player Kenny Dennard has credited Smith's contacts with helping him get another season in the NBA after he recovered from testicular cancer.

UNC opened its home arena named for Smith in 1986. Duke was the first team the coach faced there, and the last. He won both games, and both were wars. The final one, in 1997, meant little in the standings, since the Devils had wrapped up the regular-season ACC crown in their previous contest. But it was played with typical Duke-Carolina intensity. Antawn Jamison had 33 points and the Heels outrebounded Duke 49 – 18, but the Devils stayed in it to the end thanks in large part to guard Steve Wojciechowski, who hit six three-pointers. "What a game Wojciechowski had," Smith said admiringly afterward.

Smith, John. Front-court reserve, inside scoring threat, starter, key man off the bench — John Franklin Smith accepted a variety of roles and committed himself to all of them during a solid four-year career. Smith, a 6 – 7 forward from Fort Washington, Md., played from 1986 through 1989 with 120 appearances, 49 starts, 945 points, and 358 rebounds.

Smith's freshman minutes were few in 1986, when the Devils were NCAA runners-up, though he did make an impression with an emphatic dunk in the closing seconds of a nationally televised victory over Georgia Tech. Smith then surprised most observers by moving into the starting lineup as a sophomore and emerging as one of the top scorers with an 11.9 average. His career game of 28 points at Clemson marked one of six times that he led Duke in scoring in an ACC game. His 10-of-10 free-throw shooting performance against the Tigers helped him finish seventh in the league in that category with a 79.9 percentage.

Smith continued to start at the beginning of his junior year and then was moved into a role off the bench. He continued to contribute scoring, rebounding, and a veteran presence. After helping Duke win the ACC Tournament, he was playing well in the NCAA with 12 points against Rhode Island when he suffered a broken hand. That kept him out of action until the Final Four. He was presented with the Ted Mann Jr. award as the reserve contributing most to team morale.

Smith came back to play in every game as a senior, with 10 starts. He averaged 20 minutes a night and had a high of 17 points at Washington. Spending more time away from the basket, he hit 25 three-pointers. He finished his career with a field-goal percentage of 54.6.

Duke went to three Final Fours and won two ACC tourneys during his career.

Snyder, Quin. One of the most decorated high school players ever from the state of Washington, Quin Price Snyder brought the skills of a natural shooting guard to Durham and developed instead into one of the school's better point guards. A 6 – 3 native of Mercer Island, he progressively evolved under Mike Krzyzewski from backcourt reserve to part-time starter to full-fledged leader and co-captain during the years when the coach's championship legacy was being established.

A spot reserve as a freshman for Krzyzewski's first Final Four team in 1986, Snyder brought a disposable camera to Greensboro Coliseum for the ACC Tournament and was snapping photos as Duke celebrated its first conference title under Coach K. Snyder moved into

Quin Snyder finished his career by playing in the Final Four in his hometown of Seattle.

a more prominent role in 1987 playing with senior point man Tommy Amaker. When Amaker graduated, Snyder became the prime ball handler and floor leader for the next two Duke teams, both of which reached the Final Four. He started all but one game during those two years, became the No. 2 assists man in school history, and was recognized as the best defender on the club in his senior year. Though occasionally afflicted by migraine headaches, he could also hit a three-point shot and kept errors to a minimum as his responsibilities grew, with an assists-to-turnovers ratio of better than two-to-one his final two seasons.

Snyder played in 136 games with 84 starts. He scored 848 points, with 575 assists, 260 rebounds, and 108 three-point shots. As a setup man for his roommate and classmate, All-America Danny Ferry, Snyder posted the third-best assists season in school history at the time with 223 in 1989. His career best was 12 assists, set twice in his junior year, against Georgia Tech and SMU.

Snyder's most productive string of offensive performances came over the last five games of the regular season in 1988, starting with a career best of 21 points in an overtime win at Kansas. He added 11 points and 12 assists versus Tech, 20 points versus Clemson, and 21 points and 11 assists in a rout of UNC. He also made several heady clutch plays versus the Tar Heels one week later to help the Blue Devils win their second ACC title of his career and earn a three-game season sweep of their archrival. In the closing moments of the final, Krzyzewski broke the tension in a huddle by telling his players how much fun he was having. Snyder promptly returned to the floor and drained a couple of decisive foul shots.

Duke scheduled a homecoming game against Washington in Seattle early in Snyder's senior year, and he delivered 10 assists to help Duke win convincingly. But the bigger prize was a postseason return to Seattle for the Final Four, the culmination of a long-held goal for Snyder. Duke fell to Seton Hall in the semis and Snyder's college career was over. Along with serving as a co-captain for that squad, Snyder was selected Academic All-America and won the team's Dr. Deryl Hart academic award for the third time in his career.

One of Duke's most intelligent and creative players, Snyder eventually turned his attention to coaching. He began in the NBA in 1993 when he worked on the staff of

the Los Angeles Clippers and Larry Brown. Along with work as a bench coach, he handled advance scouting for Western Conference opponents, assisted the player personnel staff, and helped to develop playbook software. He returned to Duke after one year to complete a dual postgraduate degree in law and business while working as an administrative assistant in the basketball office. Snyder then worked as a full-time member of Krzyzewski's staff for four years, 1996–99, the last two as associate head coach, and he applied the same creative touches to recruiting and scouting as he had earlier to floor leadership.

Snyder was hired as head coach at Missouri shortly after helping Duke to the Final Four in 1999. In his first six years he guided the Tigers to a record of 116–80, with four trips to the NCAA and two to the NIT. His 2001 team was eliminated in the second round of the NCAA by Duke, in an emotional game with his alma mater and former boss. "I used to wear that jersey," he said before the game. He had also helped recruit nearly everyone on the Duke roster and worked closely in the early development of seniors Shane Battier and Nate James. "He was a person I could always talk to," James said before the game. "The best way for me to give him respect would be to go out there and play up to the best level I can. That would be my tribute to him."

Snyder's Missouri squad won three games in the tourney in 2002 before being eliminated by Oklahoma in the Elite Eight, becoming the first No. 12 seed in event history to reach the regional final. Snyder came under fire in 2004–05 after the Tigers missed March Madness, endured a wave of bad publicity for the off-court behavior of a transfer player, and were the subject of an NCAA probe that uncovered some minor infractions. He stepped down during the 2006 season with a record of 126–91.

South Carolina. Their series history dates to 1914 and includes competition in two conferences, a total of 76 meetings. But Duke and the University of South Carolina have played basketball just once more since the Gamecocks withdrew from the ACC in 1971, and that was for an unscheduled semifinal date in the Maui Invitational in November 2001.

Duke has dominated the series, winning 57 of the 76

games. During the two schools' long association in the Southern Conference, the most significant matchup was the tournament championship game in 1941, won by the Blue Devils. After both schools became charter members of the ACC, Duke enjoyed prolonged success against the Gamecocks by winning 29 of their first 31 meetings in the league, 1953 – 65. Coach Frank McGuire led South Carolina into the upper division of the ACC late in the 1960s, and the school was 8 – 4 versus Duke in its final six years, although not without controversy.

In 1966 there were two close contests, with third-ranked Duke falling 73 – 71 in Columbia, before later winning 41 – 38 in Durham. Scoring star Bob Verga was held out of that game for disciplinary reasons and the Gamecocks held the ball to increase their upset hopes. But two late jumpers by Steve Vacendak and clutch free-throw shooting by Jack Marin won the game, after which McGuire claimed that he had been hit by an apple thrown from the crowd.

Off the court, bitter feelings brewed between McGuire and Duke officials over some of his recruiting practices. The coach insinuated publicly that Duke's athletics director, Eddie Cameron, controlled the ACC. McGuire's rivalry with the Blue Devils, it should be noted, had deep roots, extending back to when he coached at North Carolina and lost recruit Art Heyman to Duke. After a defeat in Durham one year, he kept his team huddled on the bench for several minutes while students celebrated on the court, a move that was not appreciated by the Duke brass.

There was so much acrimony between McGuire and Duke leading up to the 1967 season that the ACC permitted the schools to cancel their two regularly scheduled games as a cooling-off measure. So Duke and South Carolina played only 12 league games that year while their counterparts had 14. The two met in the semifinals of the tournament, and Duke scraped by to reach the championship game for the fifth straight year.

The Blue Devils and Gamecocks met in an odd ACC semifinal contest in 1969. Both schools used only five players the entire game, with Duke claiming a 68 – 59 decision to make the final in coach Vic Bubas's last season.

In South Carolina's last ACC season, the Gamecocks were a legitimate national power and brought a No. 10 ranking into their contest at Duke. The Blue Devils used a stall for several minutes in an attempt to pull the Gamecocks out of a zone and overall played spectacularly, riding the defense and clutch free-throw shooting of Gary Melchionni to an 11-point upset victory. That after losing to the Gamecocks, then ranked No. 2, by 20 points early in the year at Columbia. South Carolina went on to claim the ACC title in 1971 before withdrawing from the ACC.

There were other Duke-South Carolina connections after that move. Coach Bill Foster left the Blue Devils for the Gamecocks after the 1980 season, and former Duke football star Mike McGee was South Carolina's athletics director from 1993 to 2005, during which time he hired former Duke football coach Steve Spurrier.

Southern Conference. Duke's first conference affiliation was with the Southern Conference, the fourth-oldest Division I league in the country. It was formed with 14 members on February 25, 1921, in Atlanta. Duke was officially admitted as the 23rd member on December 15, 1928, and immediately began competing in basketball during the 1928 – 29 season. The Devils reached the championship game in their first season, which was also Eddie Cameron's first as the head coach. Thirteen members left the Southern to form the Southeastern Conference in 1932. Duke was among the seven members to withdraw in 1953 to form the Atlantic Coast Conference.

Men's basketball was the first sport in which the Southern Conference determined a champion. Its postseason tournament is the oldest in the nation, having launched in 1922. In 25 seasons of Southern Conference basketball competition, Duke played in the tournament final 16 times and won five titles (1938, 1941, 1942, 1944, 1946). The Blue Devils played in seven straight championship games from 1940 through 1946. Duke hosted the tournament the next four years, 1947 – 50, but did not win a title on its home floor. N.C. State claimed all four, twice defeating the host in the final. Duke did not finish high enough in the standings to qualify for the 1949 event. In regular-season play Duke finished first in the basketball standings three times (1940, 1942, 1943).

The first commissioner of the Southern Conference had a direct Duke connection. After completing his football coaching career, Blue Devil legend Wallace Wade was named the league's first commissioner in 1950 and moved the conference headquarters to Durham. Wade held the post until 1960, long after his former school had left the league.

When the Southern Conference celebrated its 75th year in 1995–96, former Duke star Dick Groat was named to the five-player 75th anniversary team. Groat was the player of the year in 1951 and 1952 and the MVP of the tournament in both years even though Duke lost in the finals.

Spanarkel, Jim. The walking definition of a team captain, James Gerard Spanarkel was the leader of a Duke program that recaptured lost glory during the late 1970s. A 6–5 guard from Jersey City, he played in 114 games over four seasons, 1976–79, and became the first 2,000-point scorer in school history. He totaled 2,012 points, 454 rebounds, and 399 assists while shooting 52.7 percent from the field and 80.6 percent from the free-throw stripe. When he graduated, Spanarkel was Duke's all-time leader in points, assists, and steals; had shared the team most valuable player award three times; had been captain twice; and had been recognized as an All-America as well as an Academic All-America.

One of the most complete players in Duke history, Spanarkel could defend and rebound as effectively as he could score and run the fast break. Perhaps his most impressive feat was shooting the ball better than 50 percent every year, with his unique blend of drives and perimeter looks. One journalist opined that his basketball IQ was 200, while a well-known talent guru insisted that Spanarkel didn't just handle the ball, he "seduced" it. He averaged scoring in double figures for all four years and presided over the school's first championship team in more than a decade. Duke had a record of 49–15 over his last two years, with two NCAA bids and a pair of trips to the ACC finals. The previous six years, the Devils had been mediocre at best. Spanarkel was one of the driving forces in bringing them back to prominence, with not only his talent but his blue-collar work ethic.

Spanarkel missed the last three games of his freshman season with an ankle injury but was named the ACC rookie of the year for 1976. In 1977 he and Tate Armstrong appeared to be one of the better guard tandems

Two-time captain Jim Spanarkel was the first player in school history to score at least 2,000 points.

in the ACC before Armstrong went down with an injury. Spanarkel immediately assumed the leadership role and scored at a 19.2 clip while the team suffered several heartbreaking defeats.

By 1978, however, coach Bill Foster had rebuilt the talent base and Spanarkel thrived with a 20.8 scoring average in guiding the young Blue Devils to their first ACC Tournament crown and first Final Four appearance since 1966. One of his best games was at Maryland, where he had a career high of 33 points, but he also had three other 30-point efforts that year and was below double figures just once. He was named to the All-ACC first team and was most valuable player at the ACC Tournament. On Duke's drive through the NCAA Tournament he was named the most outstanding player at the East Regional and made the All-Final Four squad.

With everyone back for 1979, senior Spanarkel piloted his troops to a first-place tie in the ACC standings and again made the All-ACC first team. Spanarkel had 38 points to key two narrow wins in the ACC tourney that put Duke in the championship game opposite North Carolina, but the Tar Heels prevailed. A week later, Spanarkel's career ended with an upset loss to St. John's in the NCAA tourney, as an odd assortment of injuries and illnesses left him and Gene Banks as the only healthy starters.

"Spanarkel was the best leader I've ever encountered," Banks said years later. "He gave me space but knew which buttons to push to bring me back to earth."

"He had a great sense of what we needed and when we needed it," Mike Gminski added. "No question it was his team."

Drafted in the first round by Philadephia, Spanarkel played five years in the NBA. He later became a successful radio and television analyst at the pro and college levels. He has worked as an analyst for New Jersey Nets TV broadcasts and college games on CBS, ESPN Plus, and SportsChannel America. Since 1998 Spanarkel has been one of the analysts for CBS Sports in its coverage of the NCAA Tournament. He is also a vice-president and financial planner for Merrill Lynch. Spanarkel was enshrined in the Duke Sports Hall of Fame in 1990 and was a charter inductee in the Duke Basketball Hall of Honor in 2001.

Spikes, Everett. Lewis Everett Spikes of Durham played varsity basketball and baseball for four years for Trinity, 1921–24. He captained the last Trinity contingent of 1924 and led it in scoring with 291 points, nearly 35 percent of the school's total of 837. On the baseball diamond he batted .532 as a senior, and Cap Card, astute observer of the sport, once wrote in a feature article for a magazine that Spikes was the best hitter he'd ever seen. Spikes became superintendent of city schools in Burlington, N.C.

Sports Illustrated. Duke basketball appeared on the cover of *Sports Illustrated*, one of America's top sports magazines, 25 times in the publication's first 53 years (1954–2006). The first appearance was on March 30, 1964, when Jeff Mullins was pictured playing in the NCAA championship game against UCLA. The 23rd appearance was by Jason Williams on March 18, 2002, the

24th on November 21, 2005, when the Blue Devils were picked No. 1 in the publication's college basketball preview. J. J. Redick joined Adam Morrison of Gonzaga on the cover of *SI* on March 6, 2006. Additionally, a feature on the Duke-Carolina rivalry was highlighted with a special cover flap on March 8, 2004. The first Blue Devil from any sport to grace the cover of *SI* was track star Dave Sime on July 2, 1956. Former Duke All-America Dick Groat was featured three times on the cover, each time as a professional baseball player.

Spuhler, Ray. When Duke gave Eddie Cameron a Southern Conference championship in his final season as basketball coach, guard Raymond "Hap" Spuhler had much to do with the accomplishment. A 5–11 forward from Johnstown, Pa., Spuhler scored 25 points in the conference tournament in 1942 and was a first-team all-tourney selection as Duke won its second straight crown and finished with a 22–2 record. He was also captain of that final Cameron team.

Spuhler totaled 225 points in three seasons, 1940–42, and helped the Devils to a 55–17 record with a pair of league titles. He starred in a 35–33 win over UNC in 1941 with 14 points, and did so again the next year when his basket in overtime accounted for the winning points of a 41–40 regular-season finale with the Tar Heels. Spuhler also played for the baseball team and batted .313 as a senior in 1942.

Stadium dedications. When Duke named its old gymnasium in memory of basketball founder Cap Card in 1958, Card Gym became the first athletic facility on West Campus to bear an individual's name. Hugo Germino, sports editor of the *Durham Sun*, wrote in a column on the same day that the school should name all of its facilities for prominent figures in Blue Devil history. His suggestions included Coombs Park for baseball in honor of former coach Jack Coombs; Wade Gym for the basketball stadium in honor of Wallace Wade, whose football program provided much of the funding through its trip to the Rose Bowl; DeHart Stadium for football to recognize Jimmy DeHart, the coach and athletics director who orchestrated its construction; and Cameron Golf Course to honor Eddie Cameron's efforts in raising the funds and getting the Duke layout built.

Duke eventually named its baseball stadium for Coombs but obviously went in other directions, at much later dates, for its two main stadiums. The football facility was named Wallace Wade Stadium in 1967 and the basketball arena for Cameron in 1972.

Dedication Dates for Basketball Facilities

January 6, 1940. A new, 8,800-seat basketball arena was dedicated as Duke Gymnasium before a win over Princeton. A crowd of about 8,000 attended. Robert House, a dean at UNC, delivered the feature remarks. The gym was plunged into darkness just before the start of the ceremonies but power was restored a few minutes later.

February 15, 1958. Duke's previous home court, adjacent to the new building, was named Card Gym to memorialize W. W. "Cap" Card, who organized the school's first basketball team. Card had died 10 years earlier.

January 22, 1972. The school's home arena was renamed Cameron Indoor Stadium in recognition of former coach and retiring athletics director Eddie Cameron. Duke upset North Carolina on a last-second shot by Robby West, who later presented an autographed game ball to Cameron.

November 17, 2000. The floor at Cameron Indoor was named Coach K Court in honor of coach Mike Krzyzewski, who posted his 500th Duke win that night when the Devils defeated Villanova.

February 4, 2001. The concourse at Cameron was named the Vic Bubas Concourse to recognize the achievements of the former Duke coach. Duke rolled to a win over Florida State that day.

December 2, 2001. Duke established its Basketball Hall of Honor at Cameron to recognize former great players. Top-ranked, the Blue Devils opened their ACC schedule with a win over Clemson that day.

Stark, Bill. A 5–11 guard from Lititz, Pa., William Stark experienced a long gap between the start and finish of his college career. He played for the freshman team in 1940, was a varsity reserve in 1941, and started in the backcourt in 1942 for the team that won the Southern Conference title. Then the war interrupted, and Stark finally made it back to finish up in 1948, when he played in 12 games. He totaled 73 points during his career.

Steele, John. A 6–0 guard from Broadway, Ohio, John Steele lettered for the 1945 team while in Duke's Navy V-12 program. He scored 39 points as a reserve.

Steinwedel, Steve. Joining head coach Bill Foster's staff in April 1978, Steve Steinwedel was a Duke assistant coach for two seasons, 1979 and 1980. A former varsity player at Mississippi State, Steinwedel was an assistant at West Virginia before coming to Duke. After his stint with the Blue Devils he followed Foster to South Carolina and later enjoyed a 10-year tenure as the head coach at Delaware, 1986–95, with a record of 163–121.

Stem, Thad. Chosen the captain of Trinity's first two teams, 1906 and 1907, Thaddeus Garland Stem, of Stem, N.C., started at center and went the distance in the first intercollegiate basketball contest in school history. He scored four of Trinity's 10 points in the loss to Wake Forest. He then started at guard in the second game that season, also against Wake, and went scoreless. Stem graduated in 1906 and played as a law student in 1907. He was president of the Trinity Athletic Association during his student days and later practiced law in Oxford, N.C.

Strickland, Kevin. After two years as a reserve, Kevin Victor Strickland developed into a key point producer for the 1987 and 1988 teams. A 6–5 guard from Mt. Airy, N.C., he played barely seven minutes a game as a sophomore before logging major time with 26.0 minutes as a junior and 29.6 as a senior. Strickland participated in 125 games with 53 starts, scoring 1,095 points for an 8.8 average with 374 rebounds. Known for a smooth outside shot, he totaled 91 three-pointers in his last two years; the three-point shot was not in effect during his first two seasons.

Though he was bothered by a shoulder injury and missed a few games with an infection, Strickland was one of the consistent scorers for a 1987 team on which virtually every player had to develop a new role in the wake of heavy graduation losses. Strickland gave an early indication of his enhanced role when Duke won a 105–103 overtime game at Clemson. During the final 12 minutes of regulation he helped the Devils wipe out a 13-point deficit with a trio of three-pointers, a layup, and a foul shot. Even better during the postseason, Strickland played a major part in NCAA subregional wins versus

Texas A&M and Xavier. He had 20 points against A&M, scored 12 of Duke's last 20, and hit four free throws in the final 66 seconds. Against Xavier he just missed a triple-double with 12 points, nine rebounds, and nine assists. His four foul shots in the last 20 seconds sealed that triumph.

A co-captain with his classmate Billy King in 1988, Strickland averaged 16.1 points a game, second on the team only to All-America Danny Ferry. He was one of the best players at the Fiesta Bowl Classic, pouring in 21 and 25 points in games against nationally ranked Florida and Arizona to make the all-tournament team. Twice he was named ACC player of the week, and he had games of 22 and 24 points against rival North Carolina, the latter on his Senior Day. He fired in his career best of 31 points against SMU in the NCAA tourney and made the All–East Regional team when he helped the Blue Devils advance to their second Final Four of the Krzyzewski era with an upset of Temple. While King's defense headlined that contest, Strickland was the leading scorer with 21 points.

After Duke, Strickland enjoyed a long pro career in Europe.

Student managers. When Duke takes the court for pregame warm-ups, the players are followed from the locker room by a train of suits. Along with the coaches and other professional support personnel, a dozen or so undergraduate student managers accompany the Blue Devils into the arena to help the game operation run smoothly.

Managers typically devote at least 40 hours a week to the Duke program, so there is a lot more involved than wiping perspiration off the floor and providing water to the players when they come to the bench. Managers arrive early and stay late for every practice session, setting up the gym, providing security, chasing down loose balls, keeping statistics, videotaping, and cleaning up. They are responsible for packing all the equipment needed on road trips and for helping the coaching staff to organize and break down videotape for scouting purposes. Many work year-round, spending part of their summer vacation assisting at Duke's basketball camp and the K Academy. They are supervised by the director of basketball operations, a position held since 2002 by Mike Schrage, a former manager at Indiana University.

"The constant in the equation is all the effort and detail," Schrage said of this team within the team. "The amount of detail means there must be a willingness to do anything and everything."

Duke has had student managers involved with the basketball team since the inception of the program at Trinity College in 1905–06, but the size of the staff and the duties have changed drastically. In the early days the team manager was often responsible for setting up preseason tryouts and training and usually put the schedule together. In 1916–17, manager R. L. Smith lined up all of Trinity's opponents and executed the contracts for every game, some of which are still on file in the Duke archives. Financial compensation for schools at the time ranged from $20 to $60 a game, plus "entertainment for 10 men for one day." When Trinity and UNC met for the first time in 1920, the contract agreed upon by the team managers called for a guarantee of $20 to the visiting team, or 50 percent of the net gate receipts. In 1919 student manager Frank Wannamaker ran the Trinity team and assisted captain Henry Cole with the coaching and training, because the school had no head coach on the heels of the First World War.

For many years Duke had just one student manager. Staff size increased slightly in the 1970s and more in the 1980s. The 2005 Duke team had 16 managers, the 2006 team 10. Most bring previous basketball experience to college. On occasion, a student manager has been elevated to the playing roster, such as Ryan Caldbeck in 1999 and Ross Perkins in 2005. In 1993 Kenney Brown made the men's team as a walk-on after working as a manager for the women's team the year before, and in 2004 the women's team put Kalita Marsh on the roster after she'd spent three years as one of its managers. Some managers have used their student experience to launch coaching careers, including George Dorfman (class of 1985) and Jeff La Mere (class of 1995).

Suddath, Jim. Soft-spoken and sweet-shooting, James Edward Suddath was the third member of the recruiting class that helped coach Bill Foster revive the Duke program in the late 1970s. He joined the more celebrated Gene Banks and Kenny Dennard as a four-year player from 1978 through 1981, seeing action in 113 games with 267 points and 148 rebounds. A 6–6 forward from East Point, Ga., he was a reserve for most of his career but had some important moments playing for three NCAA Tournament teams.

As a junior in 1980 Suddath logged over 400 minutes. One of his best games was the season opener against Kentucky at the Tipoff Classic, when he scored 11 points in relief of Dennard, who had foul trouble. He also had five steals in that game as Duke's defense wilted the Wildcats. Suddath later had nine points and five rebounds to help the Devils hold on to an overtime win against Boston College.

Suddath might have been ticketed for more playing time as a senior, but off-season knee surgery delayed his indoctrination into new coach Mike Krzyzewski's system. He eventually became one of the key reserves in 1981, and in his Senior Day game he deflected an offensive rebound to Banks, who hit the winning shot with nine seconds left to beat UNC in overtime. Suddath started the last four games of the season, in the ACC tourney and NIT, and had 16 points, his career high, to help the Banks-less Devils defeat Alabama in the NIT. He received the Ted Mann Jr. award as the reserve contributing most to team morale, as well as the Dr. Deryl Hart award as the top scholar athlete.

After Duke, Suddath coached at his old high school and then entered the seminary and became an ordained minister.

Suk, Bill. A 6–5 spot starter from Midlothian, Ill., William Paul Suk played in 70 games over three years, 1973–75. He scored 193 points with 134 rebounds. Noted mostly for his defensive prowess, he scored in double figures in a handful of games, with career bests of 12 versus Wake Forest and 11 versus Cornell in his senior year. One of his biggest rebounds was off a shot by UNC's Walter Davis with six seconds left in a tie game in 1974. But Duke lost the opportunity to win or go into overtime when Carolina's Bobby Jones stole an inbounds pass after a timeout and scored at the buzzer.

Sullivan, Sarah. A 6–3 center from Wynnewood, Pa., Sarah Sullivan was the first true shot blocker and the first five-year player in the history of the Duke women's program. Sullivan blocked 11 shots, an ACC record, against Richmond in her freshman season of 1983 and set a Duke mark with 68 blocks for the season. She

missed the 1984 campaign with an injury but returned for three more seasons and finished with 212 blocks, the most in school history at the time. Alison Bales broke Sullivan's season record with 134 in 2005 and her career record in 2006.

Sullivan played in 113 games with 104 starts from 1983 to 1987. She finished with 683 points and 671 rebounds. As a senior in 1987 she was the second-best rebounder on Duke's first NCAA Tournament team.

Super Sunday. The most watched sporting event on television in the United States is the NFL's annual Super Bowl championship game. In 1973 someone decided to take advantage of all the TV sets in use on that day by broadcasting a college basketball game nationally before the football kickoff. Two ACC powers, N.C. State and Maryland, were ranked among the top three teams in the country, and they put on a show, with David Thompson's tip-in in the closing seconds winning it for the Wolfpack. Since then, college basketball telecasts have consistently been a part of the Super Bowl prelude. (See page 327.)

Sweet, Andre. Recruited out of Brother Rice High School in Manhattan, Andre Sweet, a 6–6 forward, had a short stay with the Duke program. One of two freshmen on the 2001 NCAA championship team along with his roommate Chris Duhon, Sweet played in seven early-season games. Then he was suspended from game action by coach Mike Krzyzewski, permitted to practice but not to play or travel with the team while he focused on academics. After the season ended, Sweet transferred back to his home area to play for Seton Hall, where he developed into a starter. In the 2004 NCAA Tournament, Sweet led the Pirates against Duke and hit a three-pointer on the first possession of the game. He played 30 minutes and finished with seven points, but the Blue Devils won handily. During his brief Duke career, Sweet had 29 points and 18 rebounds.

Swenson, Chuck. When Mike Krzyzewski took over the Duke basketball program in the spring of 1980, one of the commodities he needed most was players. Among the key figures in helping him obtain the necessary talent was assistant coach John Charles Swenson. After working on Krzyzewski's last three Army staffs,

Duke has played in four Super Bowl Sunday games:

Date	Opponent	Result	Duke Leader	Super Bowl
January 21, 1979	N.C. State	W, 75 – 69	Gminski 31	Pittsburgh d. Dallas
January 28, 1990	Georgia Tech	W, 88 – 86	Laettner 19	San Francisco d. Denver
January 28, 1996	Maryland	W, 83 – 73	Capel 18	Dallas d. Pittsburgh
January 26, 1997	Maryland	L, 74 – 70	McLeod 22	Green Bay d. New England

Swenson accompanied his boss to Durham and stayed through seven seasons, 1981–87, before getting a head coaching job of his own.

An Indiana grad and student manager for the Hoosiers when they were NCAA champs in 1976, Swenson recruited like there was no tomorrow for the Blue Devils. He seemingly was always on the road searching for, evaluating, or contacting potential Duke players. Perhaps his most important contribution was made during the 1981–82 season, when he did much of the legwork in building a class that turned Krzyzewski's program around. He made several extended road trips west, where he could observe Mark Alarie in Arizona, Jay Bilas in California, Weldon Williams in Chicago, Bill Jackman in Nebraska, and JoJo Buchanan in Seattle. During one stretch he was on the road for 33 out of 48 days, but it was worth it when Duke signed four of those five prospects, who became the backbone of an NCAA finalist team in 1986.

Swenson left Duke after the 1987 season to become head coach at William & Mary, where he stayed for seven years. After his release, Krzyzewski brought him back to Duke as director of basketball operations for the 1995 and 1996 seasons. He then went to Penn State, where he was an assistant to Jerry Dunn for five years before heading to Michigan as an assistant to Tommy Amaker beginning with the 2002 season. Swenson had helped recruit Amaker to Duke back in the early 1980s.

Swett-Baylin Award. The official name of the annual most valuable player award for the Duke basketball program is the Swett-Baylin Award. It was established by Dr. George Baylin in memory of Dr. and Mrs. Francis Swett, who were ardent basketball fans. Dr. Swett and his wife Elizabeth came to Duke from Baltimore in 1930

as original faculty members of the newly opened Duke Medical Center. Dr. Swett was the first professor and chairman of the anatomy department. Baylin came to Duke in 1932 as a member of the second class of Duke medical students and later returned as a long-time member of its faculty. Dr. Swett died in 1943, his wife in 1955, and Baylin in 1988. The first winner of the Swett-Baylin Award was Dick Groat in 1952.

Swindell, Ed. Two weeks apart in January 1937, sophomore Duke forward Edmund Swindell delivered a double dose of poison to the Maryland Terps. He sank the game-winning shot in the closing moments of a 34–31 victory at College Park, then hit two baskets in the last two minutes to make sure that the Blue Devils won 34–30 in Durham.

Swindell, a versatile player from Durham, was a thorn in the side of most opponents for his three varsity seasons, 1937–39. He scored at least 100 points every year, finishing with a career total of 497. He was a fixture in the starting lineup for 1938 and 1939, leading the team in scoring in both years. He was the top scorer in the Southern Conference final in 1938, with 14 points to carry Duke to its first title over Clemson. And as a senior in 1939, he was Duke's co-captain as well as a first-team all-league pick, even though the Devils finished with a losing record.

Taylor, Vince. Coach Bill Foster received some subtle criticism for signing just one high school recruit on the heels of his team's 1978 march to the Final Four. But that one player was a pretty good one: Vincent Caldwell Taylor, a 6–5 guard from Lexington, Ky. Taylor made a

Three-year starter Vince Taylor led the ACC in scoring during his senior year of 1982.

favorable impression as a freshman in 1979, coming off the bench for a team that returned all its starters. Then he emerged as a three-year starter who captained the Blue Devils as a senior in 1982, when he was named the club's most valuable player and led the ACC in scoring with a 20.3 average.

Taylor played for two years under Foster and two under Mike Krzyzewski, a total of 120 games. He scored 1,455 points with 343 rebounds and 212 assists, and shot over 50 percent from the floor. Taylor was a first-team All-ACC pick in 1982 despite his team's 10 – 17 record. He registered his career scoring high of 35 points in his final home game, when he simply would not let the Blue Devils lose to Clemson in a three-overtime marathon.

Taylor's switch from wing guard to point guard during the 1981 season played a major role in the Blue Devils' strong finish and invitation to the NIT, and his 25-point night on 12-of-19 shooting against Purdue to close

the season was one of his best games. His persistent determination was one of the few bright spots during the transitional year of 1982, when he was the lone senior.

But the highlight of Taylor's career came during his sophomore year of 1980, when Duke ventured to his home town to play Kentucky in the NCAA Tournament. He grew up only five minutes from Rupp Arena and was Mr. Kentucky Basketball as a prep senior before heading to Duke. The Blue Devils silenced a partisan audience of 23,380 with a one-point win to advance to the regional final, and Taylor starred with 15 points on 7-of-9 shooting.

"Boy, was I ever fired up to play those guys," he recalled. "When I was growing up I always thought about playing against Kentucky. They might have had more talent than we did, but we were in control. We were a much more cohesive unit. We played like a team."

Taylor was selected in the second round of the NBA draft in 1982 and played one season with the New York Knicks. He then enjoyed a lengthy professional tenure overseas before returning to the United States to begin a career in coaching that eventually landed him back in his home state at Louisville for several years. He moved to the NBA sidelines in 2006 with the Minnesota Timberwolves.

Teer, Tim. A product of nearby Orange High School in Hillsborough, N.C., Seymour Eugene "Tim" Teer came to Duke on a baseball scholarship and played three varsity seasons as a basketball reserve, 1968 – 70. A 6 – 3 forward, he appeared in 40 games, with 119 points and 54 rebounds. He scored his career high of 11 points in a slowdown game with Wake Forest in 1968 and proved instrumental in Duke's victory. In baseball Teer was a consistent .300 hitter.

Television. College basketball first appeared on television in 1940 from New York, in the form of a doubleheader at Madison Square Garden. Just over a decade later, on February 17, 1951, Duke made what is believed to be its television début when national scoring leader Dick Groat led the Blue Devils into a Saturday game at Navy that was presented across the country. Weary from playing their fifth contest in a week, the Devils were court-martial victims, losing by 15 points.

Duke versus Michigan at the 1992 Final Four ranks as the most watched college basketball game ever.

Seven years later, during the 1958 season, Castleman D. Chesley began broadcasting weekly ACC contests, the start of a Saturday afternoon tradition that made ACC hoops a regional TV staple long before any other conference followed suit. The ACC Tournament championship game made its first appearance on national TV in 1978, when ABC showed Duke defeating Wake Forest for its first crown in 12 seasons. The next year, on January 28, 1979, NBC aired the Duke-Marquette game in what is generally considered the first nationally televised contest from Cameron Indoor Stadium.

Those are the pioneer landmarks, to be contrasted with seasons such as 2005, Duke's 100th year of basketball, when all 33 Blue Devil games were televised. Twenty-four of those appearances were on nationwide cable — ESPN, ESPN2, or Fox Sports Net — while seven were on either CBS or ABC.

Duke played in the most-watched college basketball telecast of all time. When the Blue Devils beat Michigan in the NCAA final in 1992, 20.9 million homes tuned in to the coverage on CBS. Duke's battle with Arkansas for the 1994 title ranks as the third-most-watched game, with 20.3 million homes. (See page 330.)

On cable, Duke games are ranked in the top two spots on ESPN's most-watched list and in the top three on ESPN2. Duke's home game with Maryland on January 17, 2002, in which the Devils were ranked No. 1 and the Terps No. 3, is the most-watched game in ESPN history, with three million viewers. Duke versus Kentucky at the Jimmy V Classic on December 22, 1998, ranks second. Duke games represent six of the top 10 on the network's most-viewed chart.

On ESPN2, three Duke-UNC games top the most-viewed list: February 5, 1998, at Chapel Hill; February 1, 2001, in Durham; and February 5, 2004, in Chapel Hill. That seems appropriate given that the network known as "the deuce" launched its college basketball coverage in 1994 with a Duke-Carolina game in which the two schools met for the first time as the No. 1 and No. 2 teams in the country. Seven of ESPN2's most-watched college games have featured Duke.

In women's basketball, the Duke-Purdue game for the NCAA championship of 1999 was viewed in 3.2 million homes and drew a 4.3 rating to tie Tennessee-Connecticut in 2004 as the top-rated tournament game televised by ESPN.

Tennessee. Long recognized as the gold standard in women's college basketball, the Tennessee Lady Vols under Hall of Fame coach Pat Summitt annually challenge for the national championship and have won it six times, including three times in a row from 1996 through 1998. Duke's drive toward élite status in the sport has necessarily required periodic challenges with the Vols, eight of which had taken place through the 2006 regular season. Tennessee was ranked among the top four teams in the Associated Press poll for each encounter, and Duke was in the top 10 for all but the first.

The first five games were held on neutral floors, beginning with a 14-point victory by Tennessee in a holiday classic at Orlando in December 1998. Later that season in Greensboro, the Blue Devils posted one of the top victories in school history when they knocked off the Vols

Here are the most-watched Duke basketball games of all time, all from the NCAA Tournament, with each game's ranking on the list of the most-watched college contests in history. The winner of each game is listed first.

Date	Game	Network	Rank	Homes
April 6, 1992	Duke-Michigan	CBS	1	20,910,000
April 4, 1994	Arkansas-Duke	CBS	3	20,350,000
April 2, 1990	UNLV-Duke	CBS	7	18,420,000
April 1, 1991	Duke-Kansas	CBS	10	18,060,000
March 31, 1986	Louisville-Duke	CBS	12	17,780,000
March 29, 1999	Connecticut-Duke	CBS	16	17,139,000
April 2, 2001	Duke-Arizona	CBS	21	15,992,000
April 4, 1992	Duke-Indiana	CBS	23	15,473,000

in the East Region championship game, 69 – 63, to earn their first trip to the Final Four.

Tennessee routed Duke at the ACC-SEC Challenge in Atlanta during the 2002 season, and Duke returned the favor the next year at the Jimmy V Women's Classic in Raleigh with an authoritative 76 – 55 decision. Duke was ranked No. 1 and Tennessee No. 2 at the time. The two teams met for a second time at the end of the 2003 season, when the Vols topped Duke 66 – 56 in the NCAA semifinals at Atlanta.

The two schools began a home-and-home series in 2004. The first battle was at sold-out Cameron Indoor Stadium, again pitting the top two teams in the polls. Duke used the occasion to retire the jersey of standout Alana Beard, but Tennessee pulled off the win, 72 – 69. Duke made its first visit to Knoxville during the 2005 season and claimed a 59 – 57 victory, handing the Lady Vols just their 14th loss at Thompson-Boling Arena since it opened in 1987. In 2006 the two met as the top two teams in the polls, with the Blue Devils registering an impressive 75 – 53 victory sparked by overwhelming defense.

Thomas, James. Playing everywhere from guard to center, James Thomas was a key substitute for three Duke varsity teams, 1937 – 39. After starring for the 1937 freshman squad, he contributed 122 points in varsity action while lettering in his last two seasons, 1938 – 39. Thomas had 85 points, the sixth-best figure on the team, for the Blue Devils when they were conference champions in 1938.

Thompson, David. Considered by many the ACC's greatest basketball player, David Thompson starred for N.C. State in the early 1970s. During the ACC's 50th anniversary gala in 2003 he was named the No. 2 male athlete in the history of the conference. He was inducted into the Basketball Hall of Fame in 1996.

Thompson scored 38 and 31 points against Duke in a pair of freshman games in 1972, then averaged 26.5 points and 10.2 rebounds in his six varsity appearances versus the Blue Devils from 1973 to 1975. The Wolfpack won all six games, by an average margin of 18 points. Thompson turned in one of the all-time best games by a Duke opponent when he scored 40 points and had 14 rebounds against the Blue Devils at Reynolds Coliseum during the Wolfpack's NCAA championship season of 1974.

Thompson, Herb. Coach Eddie Cameron enjoyed the luxury of competent backcourt play during the Blue Devils' formative years in the Southern Conference. Herbert Thompson, a 6 – 0 guard from Washington, D.C., started for three straight years, 1932 – 34, and scored 237 points. His running mate as a sophomore was veteran John Shaw, while his classmate Phil Weaver joined him as a starter for their junior and senior seasons. Thompson had to deal with ankle injuries during his first two years on the varsity and had his best scoring season as a healthier senior co-captain with 114 points. He was a second-team Southern Conference All-Tournament pick in 1933, and in 1934 he joined his brother and teammate Jim Thompson on the first team. Duke played for the championship in both years, losing to South Carolina and Washington & Lee. The Thompsons combined for over half their team's points in each final. In their last win together, a 21–18 victory over UNC in the 1934 Southern Conference semifinal, Herb confounded the Tar Heels' stalling tactics in the closing moments with a steal and a basket to give Duke the lead, 19–18, while Jim followed with another basket shortly thereafter to secure the victory.

Thompson, Jim. One of Duke's legitimate stars of the 1930s, James Thompson, a 6–1 inside player from Washington, D.C., led the Blue Devils in scoring for three straight years, 1932–34. He totaled 619 points in 70 games, breaking Joe Croson's Duke career scoring mark. Thompson's record stood until 1945, when it was overtaken by Gordon Carver.

One of Thompson's top moments was when he scored 24 points against Davidson in 1933, a total believed to be the single-game school scoring record at the time. But Thompson was always at his best for the Southern Conference Tournament, leading the Blue Devils to one semifinal and two championship games. He was a second-team all-tourney pick in 1932 and made the first team in each of his subsequent years. He co-captained the 1934 team.

A natural forward, Thompson had to spend time at center because of the program's search for an effective big man. The presence of Connie Mack Jr. in the pivot in 1934 enabled Thompson to settle in at forward and he had his best year, capped off by unanimous selection to the all-tournament team. He was joined in the lineup all three years by his brother Herb, an all-conference backcourt performer.

Thompson, Michael. One of four high school All-Americas to sign with Duke in 2002, Michael David Thompson spent just a year and a half in the program before transferring to Northwestern after the fall 2003 semester. A 6-foot-10 center from Joliet, Ill., he played in 16 games as a reserve during the 2002–03 season, scoring 20 points with eight rebounds in a total of 59 minutes. He appeared in the first three games of the 2003–04 season, scoring seven points with one rebound in 11 minutes. After the Blue Devils returned from the Great Alaska Shootout, Thompson left the team and announced his plans to transfer.

Thorne, Robert. As the backup to star center Joe Croson, Robert Thorne saw little action during his two seasons as a letterman, 1929–30. A native of Littleton, N.C., he scored 19 points in 1929 and two in 1930.

Thorne, Shag. Three-year starting guard William Alfred "Shag" Thorne came to Trinity from Airlee, N.C., and Warrenton High School and was a team leader from 1913 through 1915, serving as captain in his last year. He also played on the baseball team.

Three-pointers. The three-point field goal was installed in college basketball beginning with the 1987 season and Duke was one of the many schools that only gradually warmed to its possibilities. Just 19 percent of Duke's field goal attempts were from three-point range in 1987, on par with the ACC's 18 percent. Duke led the conference in scoring the following year yet only took 20 percent of its shots from beyond the arc. During the back-to-back NCAA title years, Duke's opponents tried more threes than the Blue Devils did.

But by the mid-1990s, with shooters such as Trajan Langdon and Chris Collins in the fold, Duke's reliance on the three increased. The Final Four team of 1994 took one-fourth of its shots from three-point land, and that ratio increased to one-third in the following year. It hasn't dropped below 30 percent since, and in 2001 the national title team took 42 percent of its shots from beyond the arc.

The most important three-pointer in school history was delivered relatively early in the history of the shot — Bobby Hurley's bomb versus UNLV late in the 1991 NCAA semifinals. Hurley was the school's first fearless, big-time three-point shooter, taking and making over 40 percent of the team's threes in his last three years.

Duke set national records in 2001, when it attempted 1,057 three-pointers and made 407. It also set an NCAA record in 1988 for the best three-point accuracy in a game when it hit 10 of 11 against Clemson for 90.9 percent. The Duke record for most threes made in one game was 17 entering the 2001 season. The Devils matched it at Temple that year, a game that saw Jason Williams hit 8 of 10 threes. Duke broke the mark a few weeks later when it hit 18 against North Carolina A&T, and matched that in the NCAA Tournament with 18 threes against Monmouth.

Family Ties

You could count on one hand the number of times a Blue Devil player quit the team on the eve of the Duke-North Carolina game. In fact, you might need only one finger. In 1933 the Devils and Tar Heels were meeting at the start of the spring semester, and guard Fred Lewis, of Brooklyn, dropped off the team the day before the game. He didn't want to, but it was his only option. He and his brother Henry were both on the team, but their family could only afford the tuition for one of them during those financially challenging times. Fred made the sacrifice to leave so that his younger brother Henry could remain.

The Lewis brothers are among several immediate family combinations to dot Duke rosters over the years.

Other prominent brothers to play for the Devils:

Brinn: Joseph and Claude, often referred to as Big Jennie and Little Jennie, played during the Trinity College era. Natives of Hertford, N.C., Joseph was a starter for the 1910 and 1911 teams, while Claude started from 1911 through 1913. Joseph returned to coach the program in 1913 while his younger brother Claude was team captain.

Caldbeck: Justin and Ryan were 6–3 walk-on reserve guards from Shelburne, Vermont. Their careers overlapped for the Final Four team of 1999, when Justin was a senior and Ryan a sophomore. Ryan returned to the Final Four as a senior in 2001.

Crowder: John and Dick, from High Point, N.C., played several years apart. John was known more as a football player and was the center for Duke's Sugar Bowl team, but he also lettered for one year in basketball, 1945. His younger brother Dick was in the same freshman class as Dick Groat and was a regular in the lineup for three varsity campaigns, 1950–52.

Davidson: Patrick and Jordan were walk-on reserve guards from Melbourne, Ark., by way of Blair Academy in New Jersey. Patrick, 6–0, was at Duke for two years before Jordan, 6–1, arrived as a freshman for the 2006 season.

Gantt: Bob and his brother Sammy, from Durham High, both played center for the Devils in the early 1940s. Bob excelled in basketball and football and wound up in the Duke Sports Hall of Fame. Sammy, a year younger and an inch taller than Bob at 6–4, was a reserve who never lettered. Their father Bob Sr. had been a star baseball pitcher for Trinity College.

Hendrickson: Horace starred at quarterback in football and lettered as a senior reserve for the 1934 basketball team. Evan was a reserve letterman for the 1938 team, Duke's first conference champion. The Hendrickson brothers were from Beaver Falls, Pa.

Loftis: The Loftis family of Durham had six boys, with Cedric and Garland emerging as basketball stars first for Durham High and then for the Blue Devils in the early 1940s. They came to Duke together, helped anchor the 1941 freshman team, and started in the backcourt as juniors in 1943, when Cedric was recognized as one of the top offensive guards in the Southern Conference. Cedric only had two complete fingers on his right hand. Parts of the others had been cut off by an axe in a backyard accident. But he could still handle the ball and shoot with either hand. Cedric played two years for Duke before the war. Garland did the same, then returned after the war and played for the 1947 team.

Duke's record for most three-pointers in a game was established by Shane Battier with nine versus Princeton in 2001. That mark was tied by J. J. Redick versus Texas in December 2005. Redick had the most three-pointers in one season in 2006 with 139. Entering the 2006 season, Langdon led Duke in career three-pointers with 342, but Redick overtook him for the all-time lead in the Texas game and went on to set the NCAA mark with 457.

The ACC experimented with a three-point line in 1983 that was just 17 feet 9 inches from the basket. From that distance, sharpshooter Chip Engelland led the Blue Devils by hitting 55 percent of his threes. When the three-point line was permanently incorporated into the game, it was placed at 19 feet 9 inches from the center of the basket.

Georgia Schweitzer ranked as the top three-point shooter in Duke women's basketball history, with 202 career makes. Guard Vicki Krapohl (171) didn't hit quite as many as Schweitzer but was slightly more accurate (42.4 percent to 40.1). Guard Nicole Erickson was one of the program's best while playing just two seasons after transferring: she led the Devils in threes in both of her years and once hit seven in a game. Jessica Foley tied

Thompson: Herb and Jim, of Washington, D.C., had perhaps the biggest impact of any brother combo. They started together on the varsity for three straight years, 1932–34. Jim, a natural forward who sometimes had to play out of position at center, led the Devils in scoring every year, while Herb lined up in the backcourt every season as he battled injuries. Both were named to the Southern Conference all-tournament team as juniors and seniors.

Weaver: Charles and Phil, from Winston-Salem, each played three seasons on the basketball team as well as in other sports, but none together. Charles lettered from 1926 to 1928, while Phil starred from 1932 to 1934 and captained both the basketball and baseball teams in his senior year. Their older brother Jim was at Trinity College for one year, 1921–22, but did not play basketball. He transferred to Centenary and later became a famous figure in North Carolina sports circles as the athletics director at Wake Forest and the first commissioner of the ACC.

Father-son connections:

Buckley: Jay started at center for most of his three varsity seasons, 1962–64, and was a major factor for two Final Four teams. Son Clay was a reserve center for four years, 1988–91, and a member of four Final Four teams. He was a co-captain of the team that won the 1991 NCAA title. Both players stood 6–10.

Carver: Gordon Sr. played on the Trinity team in 1915, while Gordon Jr. was one of Duke's best all-around athletes from 1941 to 1945, with three seasons on the basketball team. He was later named to the Duke Sports Hall of Fame. Both went to medical school and became surgeons.

Melchionni: Gary was Duke's playmaker in the early 1970s, serving as captain of the 1972 and 1973 teams and earning first-team All-ACC honors in his final year. Son Lee was a sharpshooting wing player who broke into prominence as a junior in 2005 and concluded his career as a co-captain in 2006.

Father-daughter:

Laurie Koffenberger of Delaware earned a varsity letter in 1976, the first year that letters were awarded in women's basketball. Her father Ed had been a basketball and lacrosse All-America in the mid-1940s. Heather McKaig of Charlotte was a reserve letterwinner from 1991 to 1993, while her father Stuart was a backcourt reserve under Vic Bubas from 1965 to 1967.

Sister-sister:

Waner: The Duke women's program has had one pair of sisters play together. Emily and Abby Waner, of Highlands Ranch, Colo., began their Blue Devil careers in 2006. Emily, a 5–8 point guard two years older than Abby, started her college career at Colorado in 2004, transferred to Duke and sat out the 2005 season, and then had three years of eligibility beginning with the 2006 season. Abby, a 5–10 wing guard and the national high school player of the year in 2005, enrolled as a true freshman in 2006. The two learned the game together at an early age and played on one state championship team together at Thunder Ridge High School. Emily was known for her playmaking and three-point shooting, while Abby was regarded as a top all-around player and scorer. She once had a state record of 61 points in a prep game.

Erickson's game mark and set the single-season Duke record with 68 threes in 2005. She also delivered the biggest three in school history with a buzzer-beater to defeat Connecticut in her sophomore year.

Thuemmel, Bob. A 6–0 reserve guard from Englewood, N.J., Robert William Thuemmel played in 18 games as a sophomore for the 1955 team and scored 13 points with five rebounds.

Ticket prices. When basketball made its début at Trinity College, the typical cost of admission for home games at Angier Duke Gymnasium (the Ark) was five or 10 cents, with special occasions at 15 cents. One of those special occasions arose in 1917, when a game against N.C. State for the southern championship was billed at 25 cents, with local newspaper advertisements offering plenty of hype: "Game promises to be the fastest game ever staged on Trinity's court. A game that will give thrills to all lovers of fast, clean sport." Unfortunately, N.C. State did not show up and the contest was forfeited.

Ticket prices were up to $1 by 1940, when Duke opened the Indoor Stadium, although there was one home game that year that cost only 75 cents. When demand exceeded supply later in the century, the school adopted the practice of requiring contributions to the scholarship coffers in exchange for the right to buy season tickets. The 1970 season marked the first time that Duke asked its supporters for a donation ($100) for the right to buy tickets to the ACC Tournament.

Here's a sampling of the cost for one ticket at home games throughout the years.

1940	$1.00	First season in the Indoor Stadium
1952	$1.50	Dick Groat's senior year
1960	$2.50	Vic Bubas's first season
1966	$3.00	Vic Bubas's third Final Four season
1978	$6.00	Bill Foster's Final Four year
1986	$10.00	Mike Krzyzewski's first Final Four year
1996	$20.00	Price doubled after seven Final Fours in a decade
2004	$50.00	Duke scaled the house, with top seats at a premium

Tillis, Iciss. A key member of the program's most highly rated recruiting class ever, Iciss Tillis was inextricably connected to the most successful four-year period in the history of Duke women's basketball. From 2001 to 2004, with Tillis playing in 137 of the team's 140 games, Duke won four consecutive ACC regular-season championships and four ACC Tournaments, played in two Final Fours, posted at least 30 wins every season and 126 overall, and enjoyed four finishes in the top 5. Tillis appeared in 124 of those wins, tying her with Sheana Mosch as the winningest player in Duke history at the time. Tillis's record of 59 wins in the ACC regular season is unmatched in the school record book.

A 6–4 post player from Tulsa, Tillis combined with her classmate Alana Beard to form the most potent one-two punch in ACC history. Tillis finished fifth in career scoring at Duke with 1,712 points and second in career rebounding with 946. She also had 301 assists, 270 steals, and 151 blocked shots. While she was labeled an inside player, she frequently stepped outside on the offensive end and hit 128 three-pointers. And she led the ACC in free-throw percentage in her senior year at 86.5.

Iciss Tillis was the MVP of the ACC women's tourney her last two years and helped Duke to four straight championships, 2001–04.

After making the ACC All-Freshman team in 2001, Tillis was voted to the All-ACC first team in each of her last three years, one of only eight players in league history to earn that distinction. She was at her best in the conference tournament, earning most valuable player honors in 2003 and 2004. She had 21 points and 10 rebounds in the 2003 final, then 17 points and nine boards in the 2004 final as Duke twice crunched UNC. She was on the league's all-defensive team in 2002.

Tillis joined Beard on the Kodak All-America team in 2003 and made the Associated Press All-America team in 2004.

Known for her quick wit, fashion sense, and distinctive dreadlocks, Tillis stood out in the crowd off the court as well. She often confessed to being homesick for her mother and grandmother back in Oklahoma; her mother and her natural father, the boxer James "Quick" Tillis, divorced when Iciss was six years old. "My mother having a child that goes to Duke University says a lot," Tillis noted. "She is such a hard worker. That is why I have so much respect for my mother. She's sacrificed to do things for me. When I think about stuff like that, it's like God has blessed me so much."

Tillis was a first-round WNBA draft pick in 2004 and played in 31 games with one start for the Detroit Shock. She averaged 9.3 minutes and scored 83 points. She was traded to Washington for the 2005 campaign but did not play in the league.

Tison, Hack. During Duke's early glory years under coach Vic Bubas, the inside presence of R. Haskell "Hack" Tison played an instrumental role. A 6–10 center from Geneva, Ill., Tison supplied support for starter Jay Buckley in his sophomore year, teamed with Buckley in a double-post arrangement as a junior, and started in the middle as a senior. During his three seasons, 1963–65, Tison scored 799 points with 583 rebounds while appearing in 85 of the team's 86 games. He also made at least half his shots every year, with a career field-goal percentage of 51.1. Duke won two ACC titles and played in two Final Fours during his tenure in the post.

Tison's breakout games were against West Virginia and Wake Forest in his sophomore year. He had 27 points against top-ranked Kentucky in a narrow last-second loss at the Sugar Bowl Classic early in his junior year. Against Clemson and N.C. State he led Duke in scoring, and later in the season he scored 15 points in a rout of Wake for the ACC title, making second-team all-tournament. Tison was one of five starters in double figures in the NCAA semis versus Michigan in 1964, with 12 points and 13 rebounds to help the Devils reach their first national title game.

Tison led Duke with 24 points in the opening game of his senior year, against Virginia Tech. But possibly his best night ever was in February, when he helped the Devils overcome an eight-point deficit and defeat N.C. State in overtime. He scored 21 points, had 12 rebounds, played brilliant defense, and logged 42 minutes. After Duke he was drafted by the Boston Celtics but did not play in the NBA.

Tissaw, Mike. A member of coach Bill Foster's final recruiting class, Michael Allan Tissaw, a 6–8 forward from Fairfax, Va., saw his most extensive time on the court during Mike Krzyzewski's first two seasons. After coming off the bench for Foster's 1980 club, Tissaw was a regular starter in the front court during 1981 and 1982. Then it was back to a reserve role as a senior in 1983 after Krzyzewski restocked the roster with a highly regarded group of six freshmen. Tissaw handled that change well, as he won the Ted Mann Jr. award for being the reserve who contributed most to team morale. Tissaw played in 94 games, with 235 points and 244 rebounds. His career high of 13 points was against UNC and his top rebounding game of 12 against Vanderbilt.

Tobin, Don. Like a relief pitcher who comes on to get the final out, Donald K. Tobin had a signature moment in Duke basketball that required very little time in the lineup. As a 6–5 sophomore, Tobin played only three minutes when the Blue Devils visited N.C. State in 1954 for a matchup of top 20 teams. But as the clock wound down, Tobin rebounded a missed hook shot by his teammate Rudy Lacy and connected on a one-hander in the lane with 13 seconds remaining to lift Duke to a 90–89 comeback victory. It was his only basket of the game, but it enabled his team to pull off its third straight win over State legend Everett Case.

Known for his fancy ball handling and defensive prowess, Tobin played in 36 games during the 1954 and 1955 seasons. He scored 180 points with 121 rebounds. From Avalon, Pa., he had played high school ball with his Duke teammate Ronnie Mayer and helped the school to an undefeated season. Upon arrival at Duke he led the 1953 JV team in scoring.

Tobin was considered a starter as a junior in 1955 and had good scoring games in the opening two contests. But he was injured against Pitt and missed 16 straight games in the middle of the 1955 campaign. He returned for a strong finish that included 22 points in a narrow loss to Villanova in Duke's first NCAA Tournament contest. He was elected captain for his senior year but decided not to return to school.

Trainers. Throughout history, the trainer of the Duke basketball team has served an invaluable role in the operation of the program. Along with attending to the medical and therapeutic needs of the players, Duke's trainers typically have also been involved in a myriad of duties from arranging team meals and schedules to making travel plans for road trips to providing counsel to athletes and coaches.

The position has been one of remarkable stability. Duke employed eight head coaches and 38 assistant coaches from 1941 through 2006 but had just five team trainers during that 65-season period:

— **Robert Montfort,** a New York City native, was the basketball trainer from 1941 through 1960. A 1940 Duke graduate who had participated in track, cross country, and gymnastics as a student, he was captain of the track team in 1940 and specialized in the pole vault. His track coach, Bob Chambers, also served as Duke's head trainer for all sports, from 1933 to 1965, working 313 consecutive football games. When Montfort graduated he went to work as Chambers's assistant, covered the basketball team's needs, and also taught physical education.

— **Jim Cunningham,** a native of Lexington, Ky., 1960 graduate of South Carolina, and former Gamecock football player, took over for Montfort for the 1961 season but departed early during the 1962 season to become the head trainer at Florida.

— The legendary **Howard "Max" Crowder,** a product of Cherryville, N.C., joined Chambers's training staff as a student in 1960 after transferring to Duke from Gardner-Webb. When Cunningham left for Florida, Crowder, still a student, assumed his duties for a game at Clemson on January 11, 1962. Crowder graduated in 1962 and remained on the training staff, ultimately working 899 consecutive basketball contests, through the Canisius game of December 7, 1991.

Crowder was a Duke institution in addition to being a fixture on the bench. He lived in a small apartment at Card Gym, was unfailingly devoted to his coaches and players, and had the kind of colorful personality that made him both the subject and instigator of countless jokes and pranks. When Duke won its first national title in 1991, no one was happier about it than Crowder, who had been to all nine of the school's Final Fours at that point.

In the book *A Season Is a Lifetime* (1993), former point guard Quin Snyder summed up Crowder as the program's base: "It's kind of a constant in your life," he said.

"Coaches have changed, players have changed, uniforms have changed, but Max is always there."

Crowder became Duke's head trainer of athletics in 1978 and remained in that capacity until retiring from all but his basketball duties in 1989. That was the year when about 150 former Duke athletes contributed $125,000 to create an endowed scholarship in Crowder's name.

Crowder was diagnosed with lung cancer in December 1991 and died on May 28, 1992, at the age of 62. Before his passing he was inducted into the Duke Sports Hall of Fame on April 25, 1992.

— **Dave Engelhardt,** a native of Chaska, Minn., and 1973 graduate of Mankato State, came to Duke in 1981 as a football trainer and was named head trainer in 1989. He began working with the basketball team when Crowder became ill in December 1991. Duke won two NCAA titles while Engelhardt was a trainer, with both championship games taking place in his home state at the Metrodome in Minneapolis. Engelhardt stepped away from his basketball duties after the 2004 campaign, his 13th, but remained the Blue Devils' head trainer, overseeing a staff of nine trainers who take care of medical needs for 26 Duke sports teams.

— **Jose Fonseco,** a native of El Salvador and a 1997 graduate of Penn State, was named basketball trainer beginning with the 2005 season. He previously worked at Nebraska and East Tennessee State.

Transfers. Here is a look at recruited scholarship players to transfer into or out of the Duke basketball program since the 1950s. Before that time the historical record is not complete enough to provide accurate listings, particularly during the war years when there was much player movement in and out of service programs. The following listings are chronological, with the players' other schools in parentheses.

Transferred to Duke: Bill Reigel (Duquesne), Marty Doherty (Colgate), Bob Vernon (Campbell), Larry Saunders (Northwestern), George Moses (junior college), Geoff Northrup (Cal-Pomona), John Harrell (N.C. Central), Bob Bender (Indiana), Roshown McLeod (St. John's), Dahntay Jones (Rutgers).

Women: Barb Krause (Bowdoin), Marcy Peterson (juco), Celeste Lavoie (Stanford), Nicole Erickson (Purdue), Michele VanGorp (Purdue), Emily Waner (Colorado).

Transferred from Duke: Jim Fitzsimmons (Harvard),

Don Blackman (Rhode Island), Sam May (Puget Sound), Jeff Dawson (Illinois), Dave Elmer (Miami of Ohio), Richie O'Connor (Fairfield), Ron Righter, Greg Wendt (Detroit), Kenny Young (Bucknell), Bill Jackman (Nebraska), Crawford Palmer (Dartmouth), Bill McCaffrey (Vanderbilt), Christian Ast (American), Joey Beard (Boston), Mike Chappell (Michigan State), Chris Burgess (Utah), Andre Sweet (Seton Hall), Michael Thompson (Northwestern), Eric Boateng (Arizona State).

Women: Mary Ann Puckett (Belmont), Jennifer McGinnis, LaNedra Brown (Seton Hall), Lello Gebisa (Wisconsin), Rometra Craig (Southern Cal), Crystal White (LSU), Brooke Smith (Stanford), Brittany Hunter (Connecticut), Laura Kurz (Villanova).

Trinity College. Before Duke University was founded and named in honor of the Duke family in December 1924, the institution was known as Trinity College. The first 19 seasons of the school's intercollegiate basketball program were played under the Trinity banner, beginning with the first game in March 1906 through the completion of the 1923–24 campaign. Trinity's varsity record included 167 victories and 103 defeats, under the direction of 10 head coaches. Its best season was in 1917, with a record of 20–4 and the state championship. The origin of Trinity College can be traced to 1859, when Normal College in Randolph County changed its name to Trinity upon its affiliation with the Methodist Church. Trinity relocated to Durham in 1892 at the site now known as Duke's East Campus.

Triple-double. The achievement by a player of double figures in three major categories in one game, usually points, rebounds, and assists. There have been three verifiable triple-doubles in Duke men's basketball history. The first was recorded by Art Heyman against Virginia on February 28, 1963, when he had 21 points, 18 rebounds, and 10 assists in an ACC Tournament game. Gene Banks posted Duke's second triple-double when he had 13 points, 12 rebounds, and 11 assists against Lehigh on January 9, 1978. Shelden Williams had the third on January 11, 2006, versus Maryland, with 19 points, 11 rebounds, and 10 blocked shots.

Katie Meier registered the first triple-double in Duke women's basketball history when she had 16 points, 11 rebounds, and 10 assists against Manhattan in the Devils' first-ever NCAA Tournament game on March 11, 1987. Monique Currie had the second on January 5, 2006, with 21 points, 12 rebounds, and 11 assists against Florida State.

Trumbauer, Horace. Legend has it that the initial design of Duke Indoor Stadium was conceived by Eddie Cameron and Wallace Wade on a matchbook cover in 1935. The actual blueprints, though, were prepared by the Philadelphia firm of Horace Trumbauer, Architect. The tobacco magnate and university benefactor James B. Duke had commissioned Trumbauer to design his townhouse in New York early in the twentieth century. After founding Duke University with the creation of the Duke Endowment in 1924, he turned to Trumbauer to redesign the original campus (now East Campus) and design the new West Campus. Historians believe that Trumbauer had his chief designer, Julian Abele, develop the plans for Duke's initial campus buildings as well as later structures including the Indoor Stadium. Abele's signature appears for the first time at Duke on drawings of the Indoor Stadium. He was one of the nation's first black architects of renown.

Turner, Hal. Called up from the junior varsity early in his sophomore season, Harold Edmond Turner played in 58 games during his three-year career, 1953–55. He scored 258 points with 52 rebounds. A 5–10 guard from Englewood, N.J., he saw his most extensive action as a senior, when he averaged 7.4 points. He had at least 10 points in a dozen games, with highs of 21 versus Davidson and 20 versus N.C. State.

Turner, Kenny. A 6–1 forward from Durham, Kenneth M. Turner came off the bench for the 1943 team and lettered in 1944. He scored 38 points in 28 games.

UCLA. The most remarkable run of championships in college basketball history — UCLA's string of 10 titles in 12 years — got its start in 1964 when the Bruins whipped Duke 98–83 in Kansas City. That was the Blue Devils' first appearance in the national final.

Powerhouses on opposite coasts, the two programs met four more times in the mid-1960s, under unique circumstances. John Wooden brought the Bruins, then two-time defending NCAA champs, to North Carolina in December 1965, where they were summarily routed by Duke in Durham and Charlotte on consecutive nights. The twin killings knocked UCLA from the top of the polls and made Vic Bubas's Blue Devils No. 1. The following December, seventh-ranked Duke headed west for two return games at Pauley Pavilion. The top-ranked Bruins, led by sophomore Lew Alcindor, won both those affairs by lopsided margins to knock Duke out of the polls.

The famed programs did not meet again until matched up in the NCAA Tournament in 1990, with Duke winning. After that, they embarked on a six-game regular-season series, every year from 1992 through 1998 with the exception of 1994. Duke won all three games at Cameron and UCLA won two of the three at Pauley. Duke won at UCLA on its way to the NCAA title in 1992, while the Bruins rolled over Duke in 1995 on the way to their own title. In 1998 Duke handed UCLA one of the worst losses in its history, 120 – 84. Trajan Langdon had a 34-point day and Elton Brand returned to action after missing two months with a broken foot.

UCLA opted not to renew the regular-season series, but the schools met in the Sweet 16 of the 2001 NCAA tourney at Philadelphia. Like Brand a few years before, Carlos Boozer returned to action after a broken foot to play 22 minutes against the Bruins. But the key to a Duke win was Jason Williams's second-half mix of drives and three-pointers. He broke open a three-point game by scoring 19 consecutive Duke points on his way to a 34-point total.

Duke and UCLA also squared off at the Wooden Tradition at Conseco Fieldhouse in Indianapolis early in the 2003 season, with freshman J. J. Redick's first career 20-point game leading the charge. That result gave Duke nine wins in 15 all-time meetings with UCLA.

Ulrich, Bill. A 5 – 10 guard from Audubon, N.J., William Paul Ulrich showed promise after playing on the freshman team in 1961 and made the varsity as a sophomore in 1962, when he appeared in 21 games and scored 78 points. He enjoyed a few starts in 1962, including the West Virginia game, when coach Vic Bubas never made a substitution. The five starters went 40 minutes and the Devils won by four on the road. Ulrich scored 12 points

in a blowout of Arizona, provided a spark off the bench in the season finale at UNC, and was noted for his defense against Maryland in the ACC Tournament.

Ulrich was expected to contend for more starting assignments in 1963, but an injury limited his career to just one season. After his playing days were over, he helped coach the freshman team as a student assistant.

Uniforms. To commemorate the 100th year of Duke basketball and the 65th season of Cameron Indoor Stadium, the Blue Devils wore "throwback" uniforms for their game with Princeton on January 5, 2005. The special uniforms weren't that much different from the team's current attire, because the Duke uniform hadn't changed much in over 40 years.

When the program started under the Trinity College banner, the uniform consisted of a jersey with a large T on the front and baggy, knee-length pants. After the founding of Duke, the front of the jersey featured DUKE in arched, uppercase lettering with a shadow outline, while the pants changed to brief shorts. Kneepads were included in the standard outfit, but there were no numbers on the front of the jerseys until the 1930s.

By the 1950s the shadow effect on the DUKE lettering was replaced by simple uppercase arched type. Some trimming and side stripes were added in the early 1960s and the basic design hasn't changed much since. One of the primary enhancements from 1962 was coach Vic Bubas's move to add players' names to the back of the jerseys; he was the first in the region to make that addition.

During the late 1970s, under coach Bill Foster, the side stripes were removed from the jersey and shorts, and a Duke basketball logo was added to the shorts. When Mike Krzyzewski arrived in 1981, a wide panel was added on each side of the shorts to better showcase the logo, and the rounded neckline on the jersey was changed to a V-cut. The side stripes on the jersey returned in 1988, and the shorts began to lengthen and get baggier in the early 1990s.

Two design changes were made in the mid-1990s. For the 1995 season shoulder panels were added to the jersey, a radical departure from its basic design. That turned out to be a forgettable year, with a 13 – 18 record, and the traditional look was back the following season.

UNIFORMS – USA BASKETBALL 339

But Duke made a major break with tradition in 1996–97 when it added a black uniform as an alternative to the standard royal blue attire normally worn on the road.

Duke introduced its black uniforms on November 20, 1996, for a home game with St. Joseph's. The new uniforms were kept a secret until the team took the floor for warm-ups. The team poster for the year, titled "Back in Black," also was unveiled that night: Krzyzewski wanted Duke's home fans to see the new style in person rather than on television. The Devils went back to their customary white home uniforms with blue trim after that, and have since rotated between blue and black on the road.

"The school heritage, history and philosophy are all considered, and we also work to reflect what the coach and the school really want. We don't design anything without working with the school," said Stan Clark of Nike, which produced the new look after extensive consultation with Krzyzewski and staff. "What we found was that the black uniform exhibits the toughness and competitiveness of the Duke basketball team." Nike began providing Duke uniforms for the 1994 season. Champion had been the manufacturer before that.

UNLV. Duke has faced the University of Nevada, Las Vegas, three times. The first meeting, a loss to the Rebels in their Las Vegas Classic in 1973, barely ranks as a footnote. The other two games, at the Final Four in 1990 and 1991, rank among the more memorable in school history.

In 1990 UNLV crushed Duke 103–73 in the national championship game. Anderson Hunt scored 29 points and Larry Johnson added 22, while nothing went right for the Blue Devils at McNichols Arena in Denver. A second-half explosion by the Rebels enabled them to become the only team in NCAA history to reach the 100-point mark in the NCAA final.

The following year the two programs met in the semifinals at Indianapolis, with the top-ranked and undefeated Rebels expected to roll onward toward a second straight national crown. Anderson Hunt again scored 29 points and UNLV led at the half, but Duke refused to back down and pulled off one of the biggest upsets in tournament history. Bobby Hurley hit a three-point shot late in the game and Christian Laettner scored 28 points

The Shot He'll Never Forget

Bobby Hurley, 1991 versus UNLV

Facing undefeated and seemingly invincible UNLV in the NCAA semifinals in 1991, the Blue Devils found themselves down 76–71 with 2:30 to play after George Ackles converted a tip-in for the Rebels. Next time down the floor, sophomore Hurley nailed the biggest three-pointer in school history to cut UNLV's lead to 76–74 with 2:14 to go. It changed the momentum of the game and Duke went on to win 79–77 to reach the championship contest.

"That's a shot I'll always remember," Hurley said. "That's probably the best shot I made here. It was the right time and I was able to knock down a shot in a game that meant so much for us. I always played not being afraid to take the shot. That was the case where things were going the wrong way for the team at that time, we'd lost the momentum and I was thinking that whole possession that if I got an open look, I was going to try to take it."

with a couple of crucial free throws to pace a 79–77 victory. Duke went on to top Kansas for the NCAA crown two days later.

USA Basketball. Headquartered in Colorado Springs, USA Basketball is the governing body that selects, administers, and funds all teams that officially represent the United States in international competition, from the Olympics and World Championships to the World University Games and Jones Cup. There is also a youth development program and a junior national program.

Duke coach Mike Krzyzewski began an intimate relationship with USA Basketball early in his career. He served the organization as a practice coach, assistant coach, head coach, and member of the player selection committee and games committee. In the fall of 2005 he accepted a three-year assignment as head coach of the Senior National Team, with the responsibility for directing it in the World Championship in 2006 and the Olympics in 2008 (provided that the team qualified). Previously, his highest-profile assignment was as assistant coach of the Olympic "Dream Team" in 1992. He was

During the summer of 1998 Trajan Langdon played for USA Basketball in the World Championship and Elton Brand played in the Goodwill Games.

also the head coach for teams at the World University Games (1987), World Championship (1990), and Goodwill Games (1990). Several of his former players went on to serve in various capacities and on administrative committees, including Billy King, Tommy Amaker, and Steve Wojciechowski. A few received high honors for their play in international competition, including four who were selected as USA Basketball's male athlete of the year: Christian Laettner (1991), Elton Brand (1998), Chris Duhon (2001), and Shelden Williams (2005). The Blue Devils' Brand, Shane Battier, and J. J. Redick were invited to join the 2006 – 08 national team program.

Duke women's coach Gail Goestenkors has also enjoyed a long-term relationship with USA Basketball. She was an assistant coach for teams that won gold medals in the 2002 World Championship and 2004 Olympics, and in July 2005 she was head coach of the team that dominated the Women's Under-19 World Championship event. Her U19 squad was named USA Basketball's team of the year and she was named USA Basketball coach of the year.

Here is a list of Duke players to compete for USA Basketball in major competitions:

Olympics: Jeff Mullins 1964, Tate Armstrong 1976, Christian Laettner 1992, Grant Hill 1996, Carlos Boozer 2004.

World Championship: Tommy Amaker 1986, Christian Laettner 1990, Trajan Langdon 1998, Elton Brand 2002, Jason Williams 2002.

Pan American Games: Christian Laettner 1991, Grant Hill 1991, Thomas Hill 1991, Brian Davis 1995. Women: Iciss Tillis 2003.

Goodwill Games: Tommy Amaker 1986, Bobby Hurley 1990, Christian Laettner 1990, Cherokee Parks 1994, Elton Brand 1998, Shane Battier 2001.

World University Games: Johnny Dawkins 1983, Danny Ferry 1987, Billy King 1987, Bobby Hurley 1991, Tony Lang 1993, Chris Carrawell 1999, Shelden Williams 2005. Women: Monique Currie 2005.

Under 21 World Championship: Cherokee Parks 1993, Carlos Boozer 2001, Chris Duhon 2001, Dahntay Jones 2001, J. J. Redick 2005. Women: Alana Beard 2003.

Under 19 Junior World Championship: Robert Brickey 1987, Tony Lang 1991, Cherokee Parks 1991, Taymon Domzalski 1995, Trajan Langdon 1995, Steve Wojciechowski 1995, J. J. Redick 2003. Women: Monique Currie 2001, Wynter Whitley 2001, Alana Beard 2001, Abby Waner 2005.

Americas Olympic Qualifying Teams: Christian Laettner 1992, Elton Brand 1993 and 1999.

Under 21 Qualifying Teams: Cherokee Parks 1993, Mike Dunleavy 2000, Jason Williams 2000.

Under 19 Qualifying Teams: Grant Hill 1990, Trajan Langdon 1994, Steve Wojciechowski 1994. Women: Alana Beard 2000, Abby Waner 2004.

Vacendak, Steve. A member of the Duke Sports Hall of Fame, Stephen T. Vacendak occupies a unique niche in ACC basketball history. A 6 – 1 guard from Scranton, Pa., he is the only person to be named ACC player of the year after not making the all-conference first team.

That peculiar circumstance arose in 1966, his senior year, when he was selected for the All-ACC second team and then delivered such an outstanding performance in the ACC Tournament that he was voted both player of the year and tournament MVP, with all the honors announced after the tournament. The Atlantic Coast Sports Writers Association changed its procedures after 1966 and began announcing the All-ACC team before the tourney while still accepting votes for player of the year afterward.

Frequently praised by coach Vic Bubas as the best competitor he ever coached, Vacendak played in 84 games over his three varsity seasons, 1964–66, scoring 953 points with 358 rebounds. Known for relishing the so-called dirty work, such as hustling for loose balls and playing scrappy defense, he was also a legitimate offensive factor with scoring averages of 16.2 as a junior and 13.2 as a senior — even though he was surrounded by such prolific point producers as Jack Marin, Bob Verga, and Mike Lewis. His highest-scoring game was a 32-point outing against Wake Forest in his junior year, and he added a 28-point game versus Clemson as a senior.

But no doubt the most important thing that Vacendak did was contribute to victories, lots of them. Duke had a 72–14 record overall and 36–6 in the ACC during Vacendak's three years, with two trips to the Final Four. He was inducted into the Duke Sports Hall of Fame in 1986 and was a charter inductee in the Duke Basketball Hall of Honor in 2001.

A fourth-round NBA selection by San Francisco, Vacendak played in the ABA until 1970. Then he turned to sales, coaching, athletic administration, and private business. During a stint at Duke as assistant athletics director for Tom Butters, he made a significant behind-the-scenes contribution to many future victories for his alma mater through his supportive role in the hiring of coach Mike Krzyzewski.

Vacendak's high school coach, Jack Gallagher, was a close associate and scout for Bob Knight, Krzyzewski's college coach. During the late 1970s Gallagher introduced Vacendak to Krzyzewski, who was preparing to coach an Army-Navy game. Vacendak sat in on the scouting report and was impressed with the young defensive-minded leader of the Cadets. When Duke had a coaching vacancy in the spring of 1980, Gallagher called Vacendak to recommend Krzyzewski, and Vacendak expressed similar sentiments to Butters.

"Let me get this straight," Butters said privately to Va-

A Shot He'll Never Forget

Steve Vacendak, 1966 versus Clemson

Top-ranked Duke was all tied up at Clemson and called a timeout with 50 seconds remaining to set up a winning shot. Senior captain Vacendak controlled the ball for most of that time, and then started to drive with 10 seconds left. His scoop shot went in with four seconds remaining, and Duke won 87–85.

"I had to flip it in underhand from the head of the key because Randy Mahaffey had switched on a pick Mike Lewis had set," Vacendak recalled. "He came up and swarmed over me, and I just reached under his arms and flicked it in the basket."

Vacendak finished the day with 28 points on 10-of-16 shooting. He had 19 of his points in the second half and scored 11 of Duke's last 17 points in the game. Interestingly, he had scored Duke's last 11 points in the Blue Devils' win at Clemson the previous season.

cendak during the interview process. "You're pushing me to hire a man whose name I can't pronounce and certainly can't spell, and who has a losing record?"

"Yes sir," Vacendak replied.

After an interview in Durham, Butters had Vacendak drive Krzyzewski to the airport. Then he paged the two before the flight left and told them to go to dinner instead. While they were eating at the Angus Barn, Butters called and had Vacendak bring Krzyzewski back so that he could hire him.

"I think Tom Butters displayed the epitome of instinctive leadership by recognizing that here was a man who exemplified everything you could possibly want in a coach, despite the appearance to the contrary in the form of a record," Vacendak said several years later. "It was almost a courageous decision for Tom to make. It flew in the face of pressure to hire someone who came in with a national winning record. That's a wonderful tribute to Tom. Mike just needed the opportunity, and Tom had the courage to make that decision."

It didn't hurt that Vacendak was around to facilitate.

Valasek, Cy. A three-year letterman from 1939 through 1941, Cyril John Valasek, a 5 – 10 guard, was a key figure for an unlikely Southern Conference championship team.

During Valasek's senior year of 1941, the Blue Devils had a 7 – 8 record in mid-February but got hot and never lost again. In the regular-season finale they upset North Carolina, which was 14 – 0 in the league, then repeated the feat seven days later in the first round of the conference tournament. An important factor in the second win was Duke's defense on UNC's All-America center George Glamack, one of the nation's premier scorers. Chuck Holley had the primary assignment but enjoyed help from Valasek, his old high school teammate from Ford City, Pa. After knocking off UNC, the Blue Devils won twice more to claim the crown, and Valasek and Holley were the top vote getters for the all-tournament team.

Known for his "looping set shots," Valasek finished his senior year with 152 points, second-best on the team, and made the All-Southern Conference squad. He scored 129 as a junior in 1940, when he was in the starting lineup for the first game at Duke's new Indoor Stadium. Before his two years as a starter, Valasek came off the bench to score 56 points in 1939.

Valley, Gale. The 2006 season was Gale Valley's 17th as an assistant women's basketball coach for the Blue Devils. Her tenure began with the 1990 season under former head coach Debbie Leonard. When Gail Goestenkors replaced Leonard before the 1993 season, she retained Valley, and the two have been together ever since, joining forces to develop Duke into a national power.

A product of Lapeer, Mich., and two-time captain at Michigan State, Valley first met Goestenkors, also from Michigan, when they worked the Spartans' summer camp in the early 1980s. Goestenkors played at Saginaw Valley State at the time. Valley worked as an assistant at Delaware, Vermont, and San Jose State before heading to Duke. She has been intricately involved in every facet of the program, with her tireless efforts contributing to several highly ranked recruiting classes as well as five ACC championship and four Final Four teams.

Valley coached the guards during her first nine years at Duke, worked with the post players her next five, and then returned to the backcourt. She has aided in the development of numerous star players over 17 years and consequently has had opportunities to interview for head coaching vacancies at other schools.

"Why would I leave?" she asked Steve Barnes, columnist for the *Blue Devil Weekly*, in 2005. "I like what we have here. I really believe that Duke is the best school in the country. We have everything here. I also like watching the players come in as teenagers and leave as young women. Working with the players is the most fun for me. I haven't found another situation that matches this one yet."

Valley's career has spanned more seasons than that of any other head or assistant basketball coach in Duke history, men or women, except Mike Krzyzewski.

Valvano, Jim. The head coach at N.C. State from 1981 through 1990, Jim Valvano enjoyed first a heated rivalry and later a special friendship with Duke coach Mike Krzyzewski.

Valvano began his career with the Wolfpack in the same season that Krzyzewski started at Duke. Both were 33 years old and energetic, and arrived from the Northeast transfusing new blood into Triangle and ACC basketball. Valvano played at Rutgers and coached at Iona at the same time that Krzyzewski was playing and coaching at Army. Valvano's personal flamboyance proved infectious in the state capital and he made a quicker impact, guiding his "Cardiac Pack" to an improbable NCAA title in 1983 while Krzyzewski was enduring a second straight season of 17 losses.

Valvano's record over 10 years at State was 209 – 114. He was barely above .500 in the ACC at 71 – 69, but he demonstrated a knack for coaxing passionate play during postseason competition. In addition to the national title, his teams won a pair of ACC tourneys and had a 14 – 6 record in seven NCAA appearances.

Many of the Duke-State games that pitted the coaching genius of Krzyzewski versus that of Valvano were just as tense as the more celebrated ones between Duke and Carolina and between State and Carolina. Valvano posted a 14 – 9 record against the Blue Devils, despite entering many of those contests as an underdog. Six of the wins were against Duke teams that were ranked in the national top 10, including Valvano's last win, by a 76 – 71 score, when Duke was ranked No. 3 in 1990. While many teams had problems with Krzyzewski's pressure man-to-man defense, Valvano delighted in the challenge and was frequently able to exploit Duke's strengths by relying on his quick, athletic perimeter players to break down that defense with a freelance offensive attack.

Duke did savor its share of sweet moments against Valvano's teams, however, including a 73 – 70 win in overtime at Reynolds Coliseum in 1984 and a pair of showcase efforts in 1986. The January game in Cameron that year was a showcase for Duke senior Mark Alarie, who hit 11 of 16 shots and scored 24 points to confound State's defense and give the Devils their first home win in the series since 1982. The next month, in Raleigh, senior Johnny Dawkins's composure under pressure was spotlighted as he hit two free throws with two seconds left to provide the margin for a 72 – 70 victory.

After Valvano's forced departure from N.C. State, he emerged as an engaging college basketball television analyst, among his many endeavors, but was tragically stricken by bone cancer, which claimed his life. He and Krzyzewski became especially close during Valvano's last year, with Krzyzewski making frequent visits to see his old rival during treatments at Duke Medical Center and inviting him to observe his team's practice sessions. Coach K later became a board member for the V Foundation to fund cancer research, which raised over $27 million in its first decade. "Jim was a dreamer, motivator and a fighter. He did all those things to the last day," Krzyzewski said after Valvano's passing in April 1993.

Duke was N.C. State's opponent on February 21, 1993, when the Wolfpack staged a 10th-year reunion for its national championship team. Valvano, hobbled by cancer but still working the game for ABC Sports, made his first appearance at Reynolds Coliseum since his ouster and delivered an emotional pre-game address to a spellbound audience, invoking phrases such as "Don't ever give up," which became a motto for his foundation.

Duke won the game that day, 91 – 82, behind one of guard Bobby Hurley's best efforts. He tied the school record with 15 assists and went over the 1,000-assists mark for his career. The only other player in NCAA history who'd done that previously was former Wolfpack player Chris Corchiani. N.C. State officials gave Duke the game ball afterward so that it could be presented to Hurley in honor of the accomplishment.

Vandenberg, Steve. A three-year letterman from 1967 through 1969, Jan Stephen Vandenberg played in 76 games with 638 points and 458 rebounds. His best season statistically was his junior year, when he averaged 11.9 points and 8.1 rebounds and ranked sixth in the ACC in both field-goal percentage (53.4) and free-throw percentage (76.6).

A physical 6 – 7 forward from Crespatown, Md., Vandenberg averaged a double-double of 15.6 points and 12.0 rebounds for the freshman team in 1966 and was a reserve in his sophomore year. As a junior he came off the bench to score 18 points in a season-opening win against Virginia Tech, a performance that propelled him into the starting lineup for the rest of the year. In the regular-season finale he hit the clinching basket in a triple-overtime victory over third-ranked North Carolina.

Vandenberg was a team co-captain in his senior year. Though no longer a full-time starter, he finished strong by scoring a career high of 33 points in his final home game to key an 87 – 81 upset of second-ranked North Carolina. Then, in the ACC Tournament, he totaled 53 points and 23 rebounds to earn a spot on the all-tournament first team. One of those contests was a semifinal against South Carolina in which the starting five for each team played the entire game with no substitutions. Vandenberg received the team's Ted Mann Jr. Award as the reserve who contributed most to team morale.

Vandenberg was chosen by Detroit in the seventh round of the NBA draft in 1969 but did not play in the league.

VanGorp, Michele. She once described her transfer to Duke as the defining point of her basketball career. Michele VanGorp's arrival in Durham also proved definitive for the Blue Devils. VanGorp gave the school a legitimate, big-time post presence that helped the women's program reach its first Final Four.

A 6 – 6 center and high school All-America from Macomb, Mich., VanGorp began her college career at Purdue and played there for two seasons. She decided to

A transfer from Purdue, center Michele VanGorp was the leading scorer for the first Duke women's team to make the Final Four in 1999.

leave when the Boilermakers dismissed veteran coach Lin Dunn in 1996. She and her Purdue classmate Nicole Erickson both landed at Duke, and after sitting out the 1997 season under the NCAA transfer rule both began influencing the direction of Gail Goestenkors's program.

VanGorp got off to a slower start. Suffering from a career-threatening foot injury, she spent her transfer year going through surgery, 14 weeks on crutches, and extensive rehabilitation so that she'd be ready to play in 1998. But because she had not played or practiced for over a year, she was inconsistent and struggled with adversity on the court. "If she got a bad call she would show too much emotion and I would take her out and sit her down," Goestenkors recalled. "She would get frustrated very quickly and would have to sit down. She would get injured every single game. She spent a lot of time sitting on the bench."

Consequently, VanGorp was a part-time starter who played less than 20 minutes a game and was only the No. 4 scorer on her own team.

But VanGorp turned her career around during the summer before her final year, when she spent all her time in the weight room getting physically and mentally stronger. She was a much more mature player in 1999 and led the program to its breakthrough season: a record of 15 – 1 in the ACC and 29 – 7 overall, and for the first time a trip to the Final Four. VanGorp was the leading scorer at 16.9 points a game with 5.5 rebounds, while hitting 62.0 percent of her shots (best in the ACC). The player who had never made all-conference not only found a spot on the All-ACC first team but was also named Kodak All-America, the first Blue Devil ever so honored. She was also selected to the Associated Press All-America third team, the NCAA East Region team, and the All-Final Four team.

VanGorp nearly reached the 1,000-point mark in two seasons. She scored 943 in 68 games while adding 327 rebounds and hit 59.9 percent of her shots, the third-best figure in ACC history. During the ACC's golden anniversary celebration, VanGorp was named to the list of the top 50 players in league history, and she was a charter inductee in the Duke Basketball Hall of Honor.

After Duke, VanGorp played in the WNBA for six seasons, a year apiece in New York and Portland and four for the Minnesota Lynx. She totaled 427 points and 277 rebounds in 140 games, with 23 starts.

VanSchoik, Dick. A 6 – 0 product of Columbus, Ohio, Dick VanSchoik played and lettered for one season for the Blue Devils, as a guard and forward on the 1945 team, when he was a 19-year-old Naval student. Beginning the year as a reserve, he moved into the starting lineup for several contests during the second half. He saw action in 20 of the team's 22 games and scored 78 points, with a top output of 11 versus Laurinburg-Maxton Army Air Base.

Veal incident. Known for both creative and obnoxious behavior, Duke's student fans stepped well over the line of good taste with the Herman Veal incident in 1984. Veal, senior co-captain of the Maryland basketball team, had been accused of improper sexual conduct by a female student the year before. Though not convicted

Coach Vic Bubas turned Bob Verga loose to the tune of a 26.1 scoring average in 1967, then a school record.

of anything, he was suspended by his university for the last few games of the 1983 season. When Veal was introduced at Duke as part of the Maryland starting lineup on January 14, 1984, several students threw panties and contraceptives on the floor. He was also the target of numerous obscenities, vulgar chants, and signs.

Veal responded to the abuse by scoring 12 points and grabbing 10 rebounds in a close victory by the fifth-ranked Terps. In the days that followed, Duke's fans were scorned nationally for their conduct, prompting university president Terry Sanford to mail all undergraduates a letter asking them to clean up their act. He signed it "Uncle Terry."

Student reaction to the maelstrom was an appropriate and welcome display of renewed creativity. For Duke's next home game, on January 21 against top-ranked North Carolina, many of the undergrads wore halos made from aluminum foil. One student displayed a sign that read, "A Hearty Welcome to Dean Smith," while another held up a "Please Miss!" sign when Tar Heel players shot free throws. Instead of yelling vulgarities at the officials on questionable calls, the students chanted, "We beg to differ."

Verga, Bob. One of the greatest scorers in ACC history, Robert Bruce Verga starred for Duke from 1965 through 1967. He made the All-ACC first team in all three of those years, one of only five players in Duke history to achieve that feat, and was recognized as an All-America after his junior and senior years.

Verga totaled 1,758 points in his 80 career games for an average of 22.0, making him one of just four Duke players with a career average of 20 or more points. Verga's scoring average of 26.1 points in his senior year not only led the ACC but also ranked as the best single-season mark ever at Duke before J. J. Redick topped it in 2006.

A 6–0 native of Sea Girt, N.J., Verga was known for his long-range jump shot. He set his first Duke scoring record before ever donning a varsity uniform. Playing for the freshman team in 1964 — well before the three-point field goal was introduced — he poured in 51 points against the Virginia Tech junior varsity for the highest-scoring individual game ever in Cameron Indoor Stadium. He averaged 32.2 points for the Blue Imps before going on to post averages of 21.4, 18.5, and 26.1 for the varsity. Verga's highest varsity output was 41 points against Ohio State, an exhibition that set the Greensboro Coliseum scoring mark. He almost matched that with a 39-point effort against Wake Forest in his senior year.

One of Verga's most memorable performances was in the NCAA East Regional final against Syracuse in 1966, when he hit 10 of 13 shots for 21 points to help coach Vic Bubas's best team reach the Final Four. He was voted most valuable player of the regional. The next week, though, Verga became the subject of one of the biggest "what ifs?" in Duke basketball lore. A few days before the No. 2 Blue Devils took on No. 1 Kentucky in the NCAA semifinals at College Park, Md., Verga came down with a high fever and illness that sent him to Duke Hospital. He was released in time to make the trip and played in the game, but he was not at full strength. He scored a career low of four points in 28 minutes as Duke lost to the Wildcats 83–79. What if Verga had been healthy?

Many veteran observers of Duke basketball felt that the 1966 team had a legitimate chance to win the school's first NCAA crown.

Early in his junior season, Verga was featured in an eight-page color layout in *Sports Illustrated* entitled "Lonely and Lively Hours of a Star." The spread included photographs of Verga alone in a classroom studying Latin and alone in the gym working on his game, but there was much more emphasis on his lively hours. He drove a burgundy Corvette convertible and dated an attractive blonde model who lived in New York. He garnered the reputation of a party boy, and the only two games he sat out during his career were the result of suspensions for missing curfew. As a senior captain, though, he took his leadership responsibilities more seriously. When Bubas had to suspend nine players from the Penn State game in 1967 for breaking team rules (by attending a New Year's Eve party), Verga was not on the list. With all the other starters grounded, Verga teamed with five subs and scored 38 points in an 89 – 84 triumph that he called one of the best wins of his career.

After Duke, Verga was a third-round selection by St. Louis in the NBA draft in 1967. He opted instead for the start-up ABA, where he was Kentucky's first pick. Kentucky promptly traded him to Dallas for its top pick, Pat Riley. That was the first of four franchises that Verga played for in his first two years in the ABA. Overall he played professionally for six seasons, earning all-pro with the Carolina Cougars and closing his career with one NBA season at Portland in 1974.

After leaving pro basketball Verga became a tennis pro. He was named to the ACC's Silver Anniversary team in 1978 as one of the top 15 players in the league's first 25 years. In 1984 he was inducted into the Duke Sports Hall of Fame, and in 2001 he was one of the 18 charter inductees in Duke's Hall of Honor.

Vernon, Bob. A transfer from Campbell College, where he was the team's most valuable player, Robert Louis Vernon was a fixture in the Duke lineup for the 1957 and 1958 seasons. A 6 – 0 product of Riverside, N.J., he played in 49 games during his two Duke campaigns, scoring 538 points and grabbing 156 rebounds. As a junior he made the all-tournament team at the Birmingham Classic when he scored 24 points against Alabama and 18 against West Virginia. He also added 24 points against N.C. State in the Dixie Classic that year. As a senior Vernon scored in double figures 14 times and had Duke's highest-scoring game of the season when he poured in 28 points against Wake Forest in the Dixie Classic. He developed a reputation as a clutch shooter that year when he hit two free throws to send the Pitt game into overtime and later canned a pair of foul shots with just six seconds left in a one-point double-overtime victory versus N.C. State. He closed his career by earning second-team ACC all-tournament honors in 1958.

Victory list. One of the most successful college basketball teams in history, Duke ranked fourth on the NCAA's all-time victory list with 1,796 wins after the completion of the 2006 season.

Villanova. Duke and Villanova have faced each other just 10 times on the basketball floor, hardly enough to

The national leaders in all-time victories through 2006:

School	Years	Wins	NCAA Titles
1. Kentucky	103	1,926	7
2. North Carolina	96	1,883	4
3. Kansas	109	1,873	2
4. Duke	101	1,796	3
5. St. John's	99	1,689	0
6. Syracuse	105	1,680	1
7. Temple	110	1,656	0

constitute a classic rivalry. But a handful of those meetings proved to be milestone events for the Blue Devils:

— In 1955 Duke met Villanova in its first-ever NCAA Tournament game, falling 74 – 73 in New York.

— In 1964 the two met again in the NCAA East Regional at Raleigh, the first stop on Duke's road to the Final Four. Duke prevailed 87 – 73 with Jeff Mullins pacing the win by scoring 43 points, the most points ever by a Duke player in an NCAA tourney contest.

— In 1978 a cinderella Duke contingent defeated Villanova 90 – 72 in an NCAA regional title game at Providence behind 23 points from Jim Spanarkel to earn a trip to the Final Four in St. Louis.

— In December 1996 a rebuilding Duke club upset fourth-ranked Villanova 87 – 79 before a crowd of 19,214 that at the time ranked as the largest ever to see a college basketball game in Philadelphia. It was the first college game played in the Philadelphia 76ers' new arena (then known as the CoreStates Center, later the Wachovia Center). This also marked the first game in which Duke wore black uniforms on the road.

— On November 17, 2000, the Blue Devils defeated Villanova 98 – 85 in a second-round Preseason NIT game in Durham, giving coach Mike Krzyzewski his 500th victory at Duke. In a special ceremony after the game, university president Nan Keohane and director of athletics Joe Alleva surprised Krzyzewski by naming the Cameron Indoor Stadium floor Coach K Court.

Virginia. Duke's first official ACC game and first ACC Tournament game were both against the University of Virginia in the league's inaugural 1953 – 54 season. The Blue Devils won both, emblematic of their protracted dominance over the Cavaliers. With nine consecutive victories from 2003 through 2006, Duke improved its all-time mark versus Virginia to 107 wins against 47 defeats.

The rivalry predates the ACC, as the two schools met for the first time in 1911 and frequently during the 1930s and 1940s, before and after Virginia dropped out of the Southern Conference in 1936. But Duke built up its imposing .695 winning percentage against the Cavaliers mostly during the ACC era, riding a 22-game winning streak that lasted from 1959 to 1968 and later adding two lengthy streaks under coach Mike Krzyzewski.

The highest-scoring game in Duke history, a 136 – 72 victory, was at the expense of Virginia in 1965, as was the school's 1,000th all-time basketball win in 1974. The Devils saw a 28-game ACC road losing streak that had lasted five years come to an end in Charlottesville with a gutty overtime victory in 1977, but they also ended a long winning streak there: they had won 24 consecutive conference road games (an ACC record) before their two-point loss at University Hall on Valentine's Day in 2001.

The first known triple-double in Duke history was against Virginia in 1963, when Art Heyman had 21 points, 18 rebounds, and 10 assists in a win over the Cavaliers. J. J. Redick, a native Virginian, set Duke's scoring record for a freshman in varsity competition when he dropped 34 points on the Cavs in 2003. Two of Duke's two best individual scoring games in ACC Tournament history were fired against Virginia — Bob Verga's 35 points in the quarterfinals in 1967 and Ronnie Mayer's 34 in the semifinals in 1955.

Duke's largest victory margin in an ACC Tournament game, 37 points in 1999, was against Virginia, as was the largest margin of defeat in an ACC tourney game, 43 points in 1983.

That 1983 shellacking, by a score of 109 – 66, took place in the opening round of the tournament in Atlanta, after which the Cavaliers insinuated that a freshman-dominated Duke team had played "dirty." It was the ninth consecutive win by Virginia over Duke, a streak that coincided precisely with the four-year career of national player of the year Ralph Sampson. Krzyzewski and his players vowed never to forget that moment, and they answered Virginia's longest winning streak in the series by claiming their next 16 games against the Cavaliers. Virginia finally ended the nightmare with a home win in 1990 during veteran coach Terry Holland's last season.

A lackluster performance at Virginia in 1991 provoked Krzyzewski to hold a practice session with his team immediately upon its return to campus, during which freshman star Grant Hill suffered a broken nose that required him to wear a protective mask for several games. In hindsight, the practice was viewed as one of the pivotal events of a season in which Duke won its first national title.

The next year, Duke's home game with Virginia was one of the more noteworthy occasions for a team that would win the school's second NCAA crown. Two days before announcing his own retirement from the school's presidency, Dr. Keith Brodie retired star Christian Laettner's No. 32 jersey before the game with the Cavs. Laettner responded by missing his first six shots, then calmed down to pour in 32 points with 13 rebounds in a 76 – 67 victory. The night was an important one for the Blue Devils, who were top-ranked and coming off just their second defeat of the season and yet had to deal with the loss of Grant Hill to a sprained ankle as well as the return of Bobby Hurley from a broken foot. "It's been kind of a wacko three days," Krzyzewski said afterward.

After that meeting, Virginia won six of its next eight games with Duke, including a 91 – 88 decision in double overtime in Cameron in 1995. Settling into life without Coach K, who was out of action for the majority of that season for health reasons, the Blue Devils squandered a 23-point second-half lead in a nationally televised meltdown. It was a rare UVa win in Durham, as the Cavaliers dropped 45 of their first 53 trips to Cameron Indoor.

The following season, however, Duke launched another long winning streak against Virginia, claiming 12 straight before the Cavs' last-second Valentine's Day triumph in 2001.

Virginia Tech. A beneficiary of the ACC's controversial expansion movement in 2003, Virginia Tech brought a 34-game basketball series history with Duke into its new league. The Hokies were trounced by the Devils 100 – 65 in their first meeting as conference foes in 2005, but dealt Duke a surprising 67 – 65 defeat in the return game at Blacksburg. A Duke sweep of the Hokies in 2006 included a 77 – 75 home victory in which Sean Dockery hit a 45-foot shot as time expired.

Before beginning ACC play in 2005, the Hokies hadn't faced the Blue Devils since 1978, when Mike Gminski's 33 points led Duke to victory over an undefeated Tech team at the Roanoke Civic Center. Duke won 29 of the 34 games on a sporadic ledger that dated back to 1912. Virginia Tech was the opening opponent for six straight Duke seasons, 1965 through 1970, all at neutral sites. Five of those were in Greensboro, where Duke

won each time. The other was in Charlotte, where Tech prevailed.

Violations. The Duke basketball program has been placed on probation for NCAA rules violations one time in school history.

The violations were in the spring of 1971, when a Duke supporter took high school recruit David Thompson to the ACC Tournament in Greensboro, paying for his tickets, room, board, and incidental expenses. A month later, the same supporter drove Thompson to Charlotte and purchased for him a sport coat, a pair of slacks, a shirt, and a tie.

Though the violations took place reportedly without the knowledge of anyone at the university, the NCAA censured the basketball program with one year of probation beginning August 17, 1972, and banned it from any postseason games for the 1972 – 73 season. Thompson enrolled at N.C. State, which also was placed on probation for its recruitment of the player many consider the best in ACC history.

Duke was investigated for possible violations in the recruiting of Corey Maggette, who played for the Blue Devils in 1999 before going to the NBA. Maggette admitted receiving payments from a summer coach while in high school. After a lengthy investigation, the NCAA notified Duke during the fall of 2003 that no action would be taken against the school, citing insufficient evidence that anyone from Duke had been aware of the payments.

Vitale, Dick. As the top college basketball television analyst for ESPN and ABC Sports, Dick Vitale witnessed firsthand the development of Duke basketball into a premier program during the 1980s and 1990s. With Duke ranked No. 1 in the country in 11 seasons from 1986 through 2003, Blue Devil games became national news and Vitale, as the lead commentator for his network, frequently drew the assignment of covering the best. Duke averaged over 16 appearances a year on ESPN from the 1996 through 2006 seasons, many with Vitale on hand.

A native of East Rutherford, N.J., and a graduate of Seton Hall University, Vitale coached at the high school, college, and professional levels before entering the broadcasting field. He had a 78 – 30 record as the head coach at the University of Detroit (1973 – 77) and coached the NBA's Detroit Pistons in 1978 – 79. He was hired by ESPN when it launched in September 1979 and called the network's first college basketball game, Wisconsin versus DePaul, on December 5, 1979.

Vitale's energetic, passionate style as well as his knowledge of the game and his personal connection with its participants helped him to gradually become the best-known figure on the network, while many of his colorful phrases became part of the college basketball vernacular. He embraced his celebrity much as he embraced the game, developing a special rapport with fans. It was not uncommon at Duke games to see him preside over a Vitale look-alike contest for charity, shoot free throws with the students, or allow himself to be held aloft and passed through the bleachers by the Cameron Crazies.

With his rising popularity, Vitale successfully extended his reach beyond the broadcast booth through studio commentary, radio analysis, regular columns on ESPN's web site, and forecasts in various magazines, including ESPN's and his own. He also wrote six books, developed into a sought-after motivational speaker, and committed himself to several philanthropic efforts, including the V Foundation for cancer research in tribute to his former broadcasting and coaching colleague Jim Valvano.

Wagner. Duke and Wagner have met on the basketball court just one time, and the game provided one of the most stunning outcomes in school history. The Seahawks, from Staten Island, N.Y., visited Cameron Indoor Stadium on January 5, 1983, and claimed an 84 – 77 victory before a sparse crowd of 5,500. Duke owned a 5 – 4 record and a three-game home winning streak before being stung by an underdog Wagner team that was 2 – 7 and coming off a 50-point loss to UNLV. The Wagner game came to symbolize a low point in coach Mike Krzyzewski's rebuilding efforts, as a Duke team dominated by freshmen went on to post a second-straight season of 17 losses.

Wake Forest. Duke played and defeated Wake Forest more times than any other institution in the first century of program history, with 229 games and 154 wins

through 2006. Wake provided the opposition for the school's first two basketball games ever, back in March 1906 when Duke was still Trinity College and Wake was still in Wake Forest, N.C. The Baptists were the state's early standard bearers in hoops, but the Methodists eventually caught up. From 1928 to 1948 the Blue Devils posted a remarkable record of 40 – 2 against the Demon Deacons.

Some of the fiercest Duke-Wake action was reserved for the ACC Tournament in the early 1960s. The two schools met in the league championship game in 1960, 1961, 1963, and 1964, showcasing talents such as Art Heyman in blue and Len Chappell and Billy Packer in gold and black. Duke won three of those games and went to the Final Four after the last two. Wake won in 1961 and beat Clemson in the 1962 final on the way to its only Final Four. Wake was the only ACC team to defeat Duke in the 1964 regular season, by one point. Payback was sweet in the tourney, when the Devils coasted to an 80 – 59 victory behind MVP Jeff Mullins and the twin towers Jay Buckley and Hack Tison.

Coach Bill Foster's first Duke team in 1975 reached the century mark against Wake Forest with 109 points. Unfortunately for the Blue Devils, Wake won the game by scoring 122, the most points ever yielded by Duke. A more significant Duke-Wake game from the Foster years was played in 1978 at the ACC tourney. The Deacs made their first final since 1964 and Duke won its first since 1966, in the first ACC title game ever broadcast on national television.

Duke held the upper hand against Wake in the late 1980s, but the 1990s belonged to the Deacons. The Blue Devils' 1991, 1992, and 1994 Final Four teams all lost in Winston-Salem, and the Deacs demonstrated a knack for taming the Cameron Crazies with four straight wins in Durham in the mid-1990s. In 1996 local high school product Rodney Rogers led the way with a 35-point performance on 14-of-16 shooting — "as good a performance as I've seen in Cameron in my 13 years," Krzyzewski said.

The next two years, Randolph Childress hit game-winning shots to provide one-point Wake wins in Cameron. In 1994 his old AAU pal from the Washington, D.C., area, Grant Hill, had him blanketed and was chirping, "It's just you and me, Randolph, it's just you and me," as the clock wound down. Childress stepped behind the three-point line and nestled in the winner with 11 seconds left, 69–68. In 1995 Duke defender Kenny Blakeney told Childress with 20 seconds left that he knew he would take the last shot. With eight seconds remaining Childress obliged, scoring over Blakeney for a 62–61 victory.

Then in the 1995 ACC Tournament, a beleaguered Duke team looked to be making a resurrection when it hit 12 of its first 15 shots to take a 31–13 lead on the Deacons. But Childress hit eight straight field goals, had 27 points by halftime, and finished with 40 for the game. Wake won the quarterfinal contest and the tournament. Childress had 107 points in three days, the most in event history, and hit the game-winning shot against UNC as the Deacs won the league for the first time since 1962.

Tim Duncan teamed with Childress to win his first few Duke games and stretched his mark against the Devils to 8–0 before Duke pulled off an upset in Winston-Salem in 1997. That result started a string of 14 consecutive Duke victories in the series, most by comfortable margins. The 2001 road skirmish, though, was decided on the last possession when freshman Chris Duhon connected on a buzzer-beater. In the next few years the Devils habitually blasted the Deacons in Durham while engaging in close, contentious games at Lawrence Joel Coliseum, where the fans were always primed for Duke's annual invasion.

In 2003, for example, Duke and Wake were the only undefeated teams remaining in the nation when they met in a Sunday night game at Cameron. Duhon found his three-point stroke and everyone played defense as the Devils built up a 64–37 lead in the second half to win going away. When the teams met in Winston-Salem, the game went into double overtime before the Deacs prevailed, setting off a siege of the court by Wake students. The results in 2005 were similar, with Wake surviving a ferocious flurry of threes by J. J. Redick (33 points) to win 92–89 in Winston. In Durham the Deacs led at halftime before Duke took total command after intermission for a 102–92 victory, paced by Redick's 38 points, then a career high.

Wallace, Carmen. One of the most popular Blue Devils of the mid-1990s, Carmen Maurice Wallace used his hustle and athleticism to delight his fellow students at Cameron Indoor Stadium, often eliciting rhythmic chants of his name. Wallace, a 6–5 forward from Wilmington, Del., played in 81 games from 1994 to 1997, scoring 280 points with 138 rebounds. An excellent leaper and solid defender, Wallace also showed that he could hit the three-point shot during his junior and senior years.

After seeing limited minutes in his first two years, Wallace earned more playing time and eight starts as a junior, when he averaged 6.0 points a game. Unfortunately, he suffered a knee sprain that kept him out of the last nine games of the season. As a senior he was chosen a team captain and played in 30 games with three starts, helping the program return to the top of the ACC with a regular-season championship. One of Wallace's best games was the ACC opener of his senior year, when he played 27 minutes and had 13 points with 11 rebounds in an overtime win over Florida State.

Wallace moved on to the business side of sports after Duke, becoming an agent for professional athletes. Former Duke football player Joby Branion, working for the superagent Leigh Steinberg, arranged for his boss to interview Wallace, who was soon a part of the representation team, headquartered in Newport Beach, Calif. In 2001 Steinberg's partner David Dunn left the firm with about 50 clients and a few employees, including Wallace and Branion. They formed a rival agency, Athletes First, and built a client list featuring several football names such as Drew Bledsoe and Steve Young, and Missouri basketball coach Quin Snyder. Steinberg sued Dunn for breach of contract and won a $44.7 million jury settlement, but the verdict was overturned in 2005 by a federal appeals court.

Wallace, Grady. During his senior year at South Carolina, Grady Wallace set the individual scoring record for an opponent at Duke Indoor Stadium. Wallace, who led the ACC in scoring and rebounding in 1957, totaled 43 points in his Gamecocks' loss in Durham on February 23, 1957. Wallace hit 11 field goals and 21 free throws. Two weeks later he had a 41-point game versus Duke in the ACC Tournament.

Wallingford, Tom. Backup center Tom Wallingford never lettered but served the Blue Devils in a reserve role, 1947 – 49. A 6 – 4 product of Maysville, Ky., he appeared in 30 games and scored 35 points.

Ward, Charlie. In Florida State's second year as a member of the ACC, the Seminoles won their first national football title behind the exploits of Heisman Trophy quarterback Charlie Ward. Ward also played point guard for the basketball team and faced Duke five times in his career. In 1993, just three weeks after beating Nebraska in the Orange Bowl, Ward scored 11 points to help the Seminoles upset Duke in overtime at Tallahassee. The next year, after his Heisman campaign, Ward had a 19-point game against the Blue Devils in a losing effort. He averaged nine points and four assists against Duke, with a 1 – 4 record.

Warren, Dick. A 5 – 11 guard from Charlotte, Richard Paul Warren played in five games as a sophomore for the team that went to the Final Four in 1966, scoring one point.

Waters, Bucky. When Vic Bubas decided to resign from his post as Duke basketball coach, he called West Virginia coach Raymond C. "Bucky" Waters and asked for a meeting. The two got together at a motel in Pittsburgh, where Bubas broke the news and warned Waters to be prepared for speculation that he would be the next coach of the Blue Devils.

Bubas and Waters had a long history. Bubas had been an assistant coach at N.C. State and helped Everett Case recruit Waters out of Camden, N.J., in the 1950s. Bubas was Waters's freshman coach with the Wolfpack and moved up to the varsity with him. When Duke hired Bubas as its head coach in the spring of 1959, Bubas got Waters, then 23, to join him as an assistant a few months later. Waters, a 1958 State grad, remained on Bubas's staff for six years, until West Virginia picked Waters to run its program beginning with the 1966 season.

When the Blue Devils asked Waters to return as Bubas's replacement, Waters thought about it long and hard and said no. He didn't think it was the best move professionally to give up a thriving situation in Morgantown to replace a legend in Durham. But as he was

Former N.C. State player and Vic Bubas assistant Bucky Waters coached the Blue Devils for four years, 1970 – 73.

preparing for his press conference to announce that decision, Waters received a call and a telegram from Duke president Doug Knight asking him to reconsider. This time he went with his heart over his head.

Waters had been the nation's youngest head coach when he left for West Virginia, and he registered one of the biggest victories in that school's history in his first year when the Mountaineers upset Bubas and Duke, then ranked No. 1. He knocked off his mentor again in 1969 and owned a 70 – 41 record when he returned to Duke at the age of 33. He'd beaten 12 nationally ranked teams, taken his school to the NCAA and NIT one time each, and helped spearhead the construction of a new arena at WVU.

Waters spent four years as the Duke coach, with records of 17 – 9, 20 – 10, 14 – 12, and 12 – 14 for a total of 63 – 45. His teams were 27 – 25 in the ACC. His first two teams played in the NIT, reaching the semifinals in 1971 before falling to UNC, the fourth meeting of the year between those rivals. Waters's team beat the Tar Heels in Cameron three of four times, once spectacularly so on a last-second shot by Robby West the day the arena was named for Cameron. He posted wins over nationally ranked Davidson, N.C. State, and UNC in the last month of his first season, knocked South Carolina out of the top 10 in his second year, and upset nationally ranked Maryland teams in two straight years, the second in 1973 when Gary Melchionni ran Waters's spread offense, the mongoose, to perfection. But the Devils did not do well under Waters in the ACC tourney, losing in the first round in three of four years. They were ranked in the national polls for just five weeks during his tenure.

Waters was an ace recruiter for Bubas during his years as an assistant, helping to stock some of Duke's best teams of the 1960s, and he continued to perform well on the recruiting trail as a head coach. But he had trouble retaining many of his top prospects. Waters held true to his disciplinarian roots during a time when college students were protesting the Vietnam War and resisting old school standards. He readily admitted in later years that he did not adapt enough to the changing times. "A lot of guys really rolled with that punch, and I coached like I was coached, and that made it difficult," he said.

Thus there were numerous player transfers during his years, and eventually unrest among the fan base. Five player transfers over a two-year span culminated in December 1971 with a "Fire Bucky" movement on campus, led by a group that billed itself Concerned Students for Duke Basketball.

In September 1973, a month away from the start of what would have been his fifth preseason training camp, Waters abruptly resigned. But he didn't leave the university. He took a post in the Duke Medical Center, became one of its chief fund raisers and ambassadors, and was instrumental in the rise of the Duke Children's Classic, a celebrity charity event. Waters remained a part of the health affairs team until his retirement in 2004. He also maintained an active schedule as a basketball television analyst for NBC, the ACC's regional network, and Madison Square Garden.

Watson, Bill. After doubling as a reserve quarterback on the freshman football team and a reserve guard on the freshman basketball team, William Thomas Watson spent three seasons as a backcourt reserve for the varsity

basketball squad. A 6 – 2 product of Huntington, W.Va., he appeared in 32 games over his three seasons, 1957 – 59, scoring 74 points with 34 rebounds. His best season was his senior year of 1959, when he played in 19 games and averaged 2.9 points. He enjoyed his career high of 11 points in a home win over Maryland and added a 10-point game in a loss at sixth-ranked N.C. State a month later.

Wayand, Bob. After appearing as a regular with the freshman team in 1957, Robert F. Wayand sat out the 1958 season and returned to action with the varsity in 1959 as a 23-year-old sophomore. A 6 – 6 forward from Scotia, N.Y., he saw action in one game, against West Virginia, when he scored one point and had two rebounds. He was a couple of years older than most of his classmates because he took an apprentice program given by General Electric before enrolling at Duke engineering school. During that time he played for company teams in a commercial league.

Weaver brothers. The sons of a prominent Methodist minister who had graduated from Trinity College in 1895, both Charles Clinton Weaver Jr. and Philip Johnson Weaver, from Winston-Salem, enjoyed active athletic careers during the early years of Duke University. The brothers each played three seasons of varsity basketball as well as other sports.

Charles lettered in basketball for three years, 1926 – 28, seeing most of his game action early in his career. During his senior year of 1928 the Blue Devils went with a core of strong sophomores that included future Duke Hall of Famers Bill Werber, Harry Councilor, and Boley Farley. Charles continued to contribute off the bench. He also played football and baseball, served on the Athletic Council, and was president of the student government.

Phil, a 6 – 0 guard, lettered in basketball and baseball for three seasons, 1932 – 34. After a sophomore basketball season of playing behind captain John Shaw, he stepped into the starting lineup and was a prominent player for the next two years. He scored 249 points during his three campaigns and helped Duke to a record of 35 – 11 over his two years as a starter, with a pair of trips to the championship game of the Southern Conference Tournament. As a senior in 1934 he was a captain of the basketball team that posted an 18–6 record, as well as a captain of the baseball team that had one of the best seasons in early program history at 20–4.

Charles and Philip Weaver had a third brother who attended the university briefly but went on to more athletic notoriety. James H. Weaver started his collegiate career at Emory & Henry while his father was president of the institution, then transferred to Trinity College in the fall of 1921. He left after the spring of 1922, reportedly because of a hazing incident, and became a standout football lineman at Centenary. Jim Weaver was hired as the head football coach at Wake Forest, while brother Phil was a Duke athlete, stayed on as the Deacons' director of athletics for 17 years, and was selected in 1954 as the first commissioner of the Atlantic Coast Conference, a position he held until his death in 1970.

Weingart, Jon. A sophomore walk-on for the 1981 team, Jon David Weingart played in six varsity games and scored two points with one rebound. He was a 6–5 product of Bath, Ohio.

Wendelin, Ron. After providing a steady scoring punch with 15.4 points a game for the freshman team, Ronald Lee Wendelin went on to a productive varsity career in the Duke backcourt. A 6–1 native of Peoria, Ill., he played in 81 games from 1966 to 1968, scoring 295 points with 154 rebounds. He was a starter for most of those games. Statistically his best year was his last, when he averaged 4.4 points and 2.9 rebounds. His career scoring high of 15 points was against Virginia Tech in the season opener that year. He enjoyed an 11-point game against UNC in his junior year. Wendelin once said that the biggest thrill of his career was the first time he took the court in a Duke uniform.

Wendt, Greg. A member of Mike Krzyzewski's second recruiting class, Gregory Mark Wendt, a 6–6 forward from Livonia, Mich., enjoyed extensive playing time as a freshman in 1982, when he averaged 3.6 points and 2.4 rebounds while picking up four starting assignments in 23 games. His best contest was against Wake Forest, when he had 11 points and 14 rebounds to earn ACC rookie of the week honors.

But Krzyzewski restocked the Duke cupboard with a higher level of talent in 1983 and Wendt saw minimal time, playing only 86 minutes. As a player who was in love with the game and craved to be on the court rather than the bench, he decided to transfer back to his home area. He moved to the University of Detroit, where he enjoyed a productive career.

Wentz, Willard. Playing in all but two games, Willard Wentz scored 31 points in his lone season as a Blue Devil letterman, 1935. He and Herbie Cheek were the guards for one of Eddie Cameron's two primary lineups. Wentz also lettered for the baseball team.

Wenzel, Bob. Former Rutgers player Bob Wenzel worked as a Duke assistant coach for all six seasons that the Devils were guided by head coach Bill Foster, 1975–80. Wenzel played collegiately at Rutgers, where Jim Valvano was his freshman coach and Foster his varsity coach. He was the Scarlet Knights' most valuable player as a junior and senior, 1970–71, then followed Foster to Utah as a graduate assistant coach for two years. Wenzel was an assistant at Yale for one year before Foster named him to his first Duke staff in the spring of 1974. Wenzel's recruiting efforts helped Foster put together the core of a team that went to three NCAA tourneys, won two ACC titles, and appeared in the Final Four in 1978.

Duke interviewed Wenzel to replace Foster in March 1980 but opted to hire Mike Krzyzewski instead. So Wenzel joined Foster's staff at South Carolina and stayed for one season. He then got his opportunity to be a head coach at Jacksonville University for six years (1982–87) and ultimately guided his program to the NCAA Tournament. He spent one year as an NBA assistant with the New Jersey Nets before returning to his alma mater Rutgers for a nine-year run as head coach (1989–97). In 1993 his Rutgers team faced Duke at the Meadowlands complex and lost.

In 1986 Wenzel received the U.S. Basketball Writers Association's most courageous award for returning to the sideline after suffering a life-threatening cerebral aneurysm and undergoing brain surgery. When his head coaching career ended, Wenzel began working as a television and radio analyst for college basketball broadcasts.

Werber, Bill. Long after he coached his last game, long after he retired from a full life of putting Duke athletics on the map, legendary Blue Devil Eddie Cameron recalled that the best player he ever coached was a member of his first team, back in 1929. William Murray Werber, from Berwyn, Md., was a 5 – 10 starting guard who directed Cameron's first two Duke contingents to the Southern Conference championship game, and his exploits stood the test of time, making him one of the great athletes in school history.

Werber starred in the backcourt for the 1928, 1929, and 1930 teams, along with his classmates and future Duke Hall of Famers Boley Farley and Chalky Councilor. Those three were joined by center Joe Croson in 1929 and 1930 to form a quartet that played almost every significant minute during the school's first two Southern Conference seasons. Werber was the No. 2 scorer behind Croson on both teams, with 277 points overall, and was named All-Southern both years. His reputation skyrocketed in 1929 when journalists at the conference tournament in Atlanta proclaimed him one of the best players in the history of the event. As a senior in 1930 he was even better for a team that posted a record of 18 – 2, enjoyed a 15-game winning streak, and upset national power Loyola of Chicago. He was named Duke's first basketball All-America selection that year.

Werber was also an exceptional baseball player, starring for the varsity at shortstop from 1928 to 1930 before launching an 11-year career in the major leagues with five teams, including the World Champion Cincinnati Reds in 1940. In his book *Memories of a Ballplayer* (2001), Werber detailed his under-the-table signing with the New York Yankees after his freshman year at Duke. A handshake agreement between one of the team's scouts and Werber's father provided the funding for the last three years of Werber's college education, with the stipulation that he would sign with the Yankees after graduation in 1930, which he did. He played in 1,295 major league games, most at third base, and batted .271.

Werber was a charter inductee in the Duke Sports Hall of Fame in 1975 and a charter member of the Duke Basketball Hall of Honor in 2001.

West, Jerry. An NBA Hall of Famer and one of the best basketball executives of all time, Jerry West played in two memorable games for West Virginia against Duke during his college career. He scored 20 points and had 14 rebounds in 1958 when the Blue Devils handed his top-ranked Mountaineers their only regular-season defeat. The following year, when the teams played in Morgantown, West had 29 points to lead his fourth-ranked club to a 101 – 63 win. At the time it was the worst defeat in Duke history (and exceeded by only one bigger deficit from the Trinity College days). The game had been postponed by a day because the Blue Devils were trapped in a snowstorm while trying to get to West Virginia. Coach Harold Bradley called it the most antagonistic atmosphere he'd ever experienced, with West Virginia students jeering his team and chanting "pour it on" as the game got out of hand.

West, Robby. A single shot cemented Robert Samuel West's position in the rich heritage of Duke basketball. On January 22, 1972, the day Duke's home arena was named for retiring legend Eddie Cameron, West fired in the game-winning basket as the Blue Devils upset third-ranked North Carolina 76 – 74. Described as the "shot heard round the world," West's 18-footer came after UNC's Bill Chamberlain had hit an amazing bucket to tie the score. Coach Bucky Waters called a timeout with eight seconds remaining to set up a play. Gary Melchionni got the ball across halfcourt to West, who buried his shot with three seconds left. Fans rushed the floor to celebrate but had to be cleared off so that UNC could inbound the ball. After the Tar Heels came up short, the students stormed the floor a second time.

"It was such an adrenaline rush to beat Carolina because they were so highly ranked in the country at that point," recalled West, who had 10 points on 4-of-8 shooting. "You don't remember a lot until you're in the locker room, then all of a sudden the net is around my neck and I'm going, 'Wow, we won this game.' It was a pretty exciting moment for me, for the team and for Duke."

A 6 – 2 guard from South Orange, N.J., West had played in only 12 games off the bench in his first two varsity years, 1970 and 1971. As a senior in 1972 he gained a starting berth early in the year and had seven games in double figures, with a high of 13 against Maryland and

N.C. State. His career totals: 37 games, 142 points, 49 rebounds, and 40 assists.

West Virginia. Duke and West Virginia met regularly in the early 1950s when both were members of the Southern Conference, and West Virginia was considered for membership when the ACC was formed. The two schools continued their relationship through the late 1950s and 1960s and met three times during the 1970s, but their only meeting after 1977 was in the NCAA Tournament in 1989. Duke's record versus the Mountaineers stands at 17 – 6.

In 1958 Duke defeated West Virginia 72 – 68 to mark the Blue Devils' first-ever victory over a nationally top-ranked team. The Mountaineers gained their revenge a year later by routing Duke 101 – 63.

Three games in the series — 1966, 1967, and 1969 — pitted the Blue Devils against a Mountaineer team coached by Bucky Waters, who had been a Duke assistant before taking the West Virginia job. Waters's team knocked off his mentor Vic Bubas's team in 1966 when the Blue Devils were ranked No. 1 in the country, and again late in 1969 during Bubas's final month on the sideline. After taking over for Bubas at Duke, Waters then beat his old West Virginia team by 12 points during his first season back in Durham, but he never faced his former school again after that.

Whitted, Gordon. A partial scholarship player for coach Mike Krzyzewski's first team, Gordon Seeley Whitted played in 11 games during the 1981 season, with no points, two rebounds, and three steals on his ledger. He was a 6 – 2 freshman guard from Winston-Salem.

Whiting, Dick. In his only year as a letterman, Richard Whiting, of Wynnewood, Pa., started at guard and helped the Blue Devils to the Southern Conference championship in 1946. He played in all 27 games and scored 215 points as the Blue Devils posted a 21 – 6 record and reached the Southern Conference final for a seventh straight year. Whiting, a Navy ROTC transfer from Muhlenburg, was a first-team selection at the tournament, where he was Duke's No. 2 scorer behind Ed Koffenberger. One of his biggest games was Duke's upset of the nation's best amateur team, the Wright Field Kitty-

hawks. Whiting scored 14 points and had several clutch plays down the stretch.

Williams, Allen. During his first start for the Blue Devils, Edward Allen Williams injured his ankle on the jump ball and missed the next five games. He earned 10 more starts over the next two years but spent the majority of his career as a frontcourt reserve. A 6 – 8 center from Princeton, W.Va., he played in 73 games from 1980 to 1982, with 217 points and 128 rebounds. His best career scoring game came in 1982, when he had 20 points against LaSalle. He had several other productive games early that year but also spent long stretches on the bench, as coach Mike Krzyzewski employed 19 starting lineups in search of a winning combination. Despite limited minutes, including no action at all over the last six games, Williams led the 1982 team in blocked shots (11) and dunks (7). He did not return to the team for his senior year.

Williams, Gary. Of the 59 men to serve as ACC head coaches in the league's first 53 seasons, Gary Williams of Maryland trailed only Dean Smith and Mike Krzyzewski in ACC and NCAA Tournament wins. In 2002 he joined those two in the more select circle of seven conference coaches to win an NCAA championship.

A three-year point guard and former captain for the Terps, 1965 – 67, Williams was on the opposing sideline in 1985 for Duke's third NCAA game under Krzyzewski. Williams coached Boston College at the time and guided his team to a one-point victory over the Blue Devils. He also coached Ohio State to an NCAA bid and then took over his alma mater's program in 1990. Williams directed it out of turmoil and into regular contention in the conference race as well as to its first two Final Fours, in successive years (2001 – 02).

Once at Maryland, Williams lost his first 12 games to the Blue Devils and 19 of 23 during the decade of the 1990s. But Duke's knack for frustrating Williams's teams abated somewhat after the turn of the century, when Maryland returned to the forefront of the ACC and became perhaps the Blue Devils' most pointed rival aside from UNC. From 2000 through 2005 Williams coached his Terps to at least one win over Duke in each season, including three of six in Cameron Indoor Stadium. While Duke students were busy chanting "Sweat, Gary, sweat" at the vigorous coach, his teams were responsible for ending the Devils' 31-game conference winning streak in 2000 (an ACC record), ruining Senior Day for All-America Shane Battier in 2001, and handing the 2005 Devils their first loss after a 15–0 start.

Williams won his first ACC title at Duke's expense in 2004, when the Terps overcame a 12-point deficit in the final five minutes and prevailed in overtime. The Blue Devils were attempting to win a sixth straight ACC tourney. Williams called the title one of his most satisfying moments, partly because of the level of competition.

"It means a lot, especially today, beating a team as good as Duke," he said. "I was thinking about that right after the game. To win five straight ACC Tournament championships is incredible. I don't think you will ever see that again in the ACC. That is one of those things that is looked over sometimes because of the importance of the NCAA Tournament. I don't think there have ever been many programs that pulled that off."

The next year the Terps got their first season sweep of the Blue Devils since 1995 when they coupled the win in Cameron with an overtime triumph in College Park, during which five Duke regulars fouled out. "I thought I was very fortunate to be on the sideline tonight to watch two teams play that hard," Williams said. "The competitive level for both teams was just incredible. That's college basketball. It's not perfect, it's not supposed to be. It's supposed to be played like that. At both ends of the court, nobody gives you an inch. We're fortunate to win. Nobody respects their program more than me."

Through the 2006 season, Duke's record against Williams was 30–12 overall, 11–7 since 2000. The most noteworthy sequence of games was in 2001, when the two schools played four times, including in the ACC tourney and the Final Four. Duke won three of the games, twice after making improbable comebacks.

As a player, Williams faced Duke six times and lost five. Known more for his ball handling than his scoring, he totaled 30 points against the Devils. The one win came in 1965, when he was a sophomore starter and the Terps knocked off the fifth-ranked Devils before a packed house. The fans were chanting, "We beat Duke" and the *Washington Post* called the game Maryland's "most thrilling victory in years." The Terps had double-

digit leads against Duke at Cole Field House in the next two years, but the Devils rallied to win. Senior Williams scored 12 points in the 1967 contest but had to leave the game in the last minute of overtime with a pulled muscle. The Devils won 72–69.

Williams, Jason. Among the moments forever etched in Jason Williams's mind is an encounter with his college coach, Mike Krzyzewski, when his life had come perilously close to ending in a motorcycle accident in 2003 after his rookie season in the NBA.

"The room was dark at the time and I was in the hospital bed. It was kind of like a soap opera," Williams recalled. "I'm laying there, my leg is casted up in the air, I have pins in my hip, they have me on all this medication, and I see this figure walking toward me. I know that walk, and it was him. And he looked at me with those eyes and said I would be okay, and that he believed in me. Then he gave me a pendant that I pray to every morning and told me to give it back to him when I come back and play."

Several surgeries later, Williams, a gifted point guard, still faced an uncertain professional future as a result of the tragic off-season mishap. But at Duke he has an enduring legacy as one of the school's most talented, successful, and distinctive players. In only three seasons he accomplished nearly all of his athletic as well as academic goals while being a catalyst for three ACC championships and one NCAA title.

A 6–2 product of Plainfield, N.J., Jason David Williams stepped into the starting backcourt from the opening of his freshman year and remained there through all 108 games of his college career, 2000–02. Duke posted records of 29–5, 35–4, and 31–4 in those years, with an aggregate mark of 41–7 against ACC foes. The Blue Devils were 9–0 in the conference tournament and 10–2 in the NCAA while finishing No. 1 in the AP poll in each of Williams's three campaigns.

Much was expected of Williams as one of the nation's top recruits, but more was delivered. With three underclassmen departing for the NBA just before he arrived, Williams had more responsibility than might have been expected when he signed his letter of intent. And his opening bell clanked with the cacophony of 12 turnovers and 8-of-34 shooting in back-to-back losses at

Jason Williams won one national player of the year award as a sophomore and was the consensus pick in 2002.

Madison Square Garden. But by the end of his rookie year, 2000, Williams was teaming with veterans Shane Battier and Chris Carrawell to lead the Blue Devils to the ACC championship with a regular-season record of 15 – 1 and a sweep of the tournament. He made the transition so well from his anticipated shooting guard role to the point that he was chosen the MVP of the ACC tourney, only the fourth freshman ever so honored. His 23 points versus Maryland in the final marked his high of the year.

Williams was even better in his last two seasons, when he led the ACC in scoring with marks of 21.6 and 21.3 points a game. Perhaps the incident that best typified his ability to take over any game was at College Park, Md., in 2001, when the Terps were having their way with the Devils in a Saturday night showdown of top 10 teams. Late in the game the crowd started chanting "Over-rated" at second-ranked Duke, and the cheer got under Williams's skin. No question that he was having a bad game, but suddenly he came alive with eight points in 14 seconds to cut a 10-point deficit to two in the closing minute. The Devils forced overtime and won 98 – 96.

That was not Williams's only eye-opening effort in his sophomore year. Early in the season Duke played Temple twice in eight days. In the first meeting, for the Preseason NIT title, Williams drove into the Owls' defense and dished 10 assists, many of them to Carlos Boozer, as the Devils won a close one. In the next contest, Williams notched his first 30-point game with a deadly shooting display that included an 8-of-10 effort from three-point range. He topped the 30-point mark five more times that year, with 32 and 33 in a pair of games against UNC and 31 and 34 in successive NCAA games. The 33-pointer versus the Tar Heels was noteworthy because it featured seven three-point shots and nine assists in a reworked scheme as the team responded to Boozer's injury. The 34-pointer versus UCLA in the NCAA included one run in the second half in which Williams had 19 consecutive Duke points.

Williams averaged 25.7 points in the NCAA to spark the Blue Devils' national championship finish. His shooting was off at the Final Four, but still he never hesitated in taking, and making, the biggest shot of the national championship game, a three with 1:44 to play against Arizona. His 154 tournament points were the most in the event that year, his 132 three-pointers set a new season record at Duke, and his 841 total points for the year broke one of the oldest marks on the books. The previous record of 831 had been held by Dick Groat since 1951. The National Association of Basketball Coaches made Williams its national player of the year.

Williams could easily have gone pro after that season, but he was committed to getting his sociology degree. With a specially crafted academic plan, he could graduate in three years plus one summer, so he returned for the 2002 campaign and not only captained the Blue Devils but also negotiated a long year with a heavy load of coursework. All he did was repeat as a consensus first team All-America, claim every national player of the year honor, become the first Duke player to pass 2,000 career points in three years, and lead the Devils to another No. 1 finish.

Williams lit up Tommy Amaker's Michigan team for 35 points early in the year, had his career high of 38 against Kentucky in a pulsating overtime win at the Jimmy V Classic, and pinned 34 on Maryland in a display that included just one three-pointer. To close his Cameron career he hit eight three-pointers in a 37-point outburst against North Carolina.

Williams finished with 2,079 points in 108 games for a 19.3 average. He also had 644 assists and 395 rebounds. His scoring total tied Gene Banks for sixth-best in Duke history and in assists he trailed only Bobby Hurley and Amaker, though his teammate Chris Duhon eventually passed him. His 313 three-pointers trailed only Trajan Langdon in the Duke books, before J. J. Redick passed him in 2005.

Williams graduated as planned after three seasons and was the No. 2 pick in the NBA draft, behind Yao Ming. He was named to the ACC's 50th anniversary team just a couple of months after his graduation. He made a visit to Duke during a break in his rookie year with the Chicago Bulls so that his alma mater could retire his jersey No. 22 at halftime of the annual home game with North Carolina.

"When I first walked in that gym, the first thing that I did when I came here on my unofficial visit, I looked up at the rafters," he recalled during that trip. "I saw Johnny Dawkins. I saw Dick Groat. I saw Christian Laettner, Grant Hill, all these great names. And I just sat there and I stared at them. The light was kind of gleaming on them in a different way, and I was like, 'This is what this is about.'

"I saw pictures of Coach and his guys hugging and them winning national championships and going through hard times, growing up together, and I was like, 'I want to be part of that. I want to be part of something bigger than myself.' And that's what it is. It's not just me getting my jersey retired. I'm becoming part of something that is bigger than myself, becoming part of a family."

Williams, Mistie. Regarded as one of the top post players in the ACC, Mistie Williams was a four-year starter for the Duke women from 2003 to 2006. She became the school's 19th 1,000-point scorer during the NCAA Tournament in 2005 and completed her career year with 1,409 points and 800 rebounds in 142 games. She played in more games and participated in more victories (127) than any other player in program history.

A 6–3 forward from Janesville, Wis., Williams began her Duke career as Mistie Bass, a decorated prep All-America and three-time state player of the year. After averaging 6.9 points as a part-time freshman starter, she became a consistent double-figures scorer in her last three years and improved every facet of her game. She made the All-ACC third team as a sophomore and junior while helping Duke to NCAA quarterfinal showings each year. She was a second-team All-ACC pick for the 2006 Final Four team.

Mistie Bass became Mistie Williams on August 7, 2004, when she married Kenneth Williams. She is the daughter of singer Chubby Checker, who performed the national anthem at Cameron Indoor Stadium before a game in 2005.

Williams, Roy. The first college campus that North Carolina coach Roy Williams ever visited was Duke's. But it was not a basketball visit. "I don't want everyone to start giggling too much," he said several weeks before accepting the Tar Heel post, "but my first activity on a college campus in the entire nation was when I was on a square dance team at a Duke folk festival, so I go back a long way with those guys."

As a native North Carolinian and a 10-year assistant to Dean Smith, Williams was certainly familiar with the Duke program when he had to face the Blue Devils in his first year as a head coach. His 1989 Kansas team was the only one during his 15 years in Lawrence not to compete in the NCAA tourney, and it was hammered by the Blue Devils 102–77 on the day that Danny Ferry's jersey was retired.

Williams coached against the Devils three more times as a Jayhawk, all in the NCAA. Duke won its first national title in 1991 by topping Kansas in Indianapolis (Williams beat his mentor Smith to reach the final), and the Devils advanced to the Sweet 16 in 2000 by surviving a brutal confrontation with KU in Winston-Salem, a trip during which Williams had to spend an inordinate amount of time answering questions about whether he would follow Bill Guthridge as the next UNC coach. He didn't, but he was faced with similar interrogations during the 2003 tourney about the possibility of succeeding Matt Doherty in Chapel Hill. His team beat Duke in the Sweet 16 on its way to the Final Four; shortly thereafter he was headed back to UNC.

Williams's first two games against Duke as the Tar Heels' coach were even more hyped than usual for the storied rivalry: Roy versus K and UNC's thirst to end a five-year famine in which the Devils had won 12 of 13 in the series. But Duke prevailed in both nail-biters in 2004 by making key plays in the closing seconds, and won again at Cameron in 2005 before Williams finally delivered a win. In the regular-season finale, before the largest crowd ever at the Smith Center (22,125), his Heels finished the game on an 11 – 0 run to win by two, marking the fourth straight time that Williams saw the Duke game decided in the last seconds. Duke had a nine-point lead with 2:40 to play, and the Devils also had two shots to pull it out after Marvin Williams put UNC ahead with 17 seconds left.

"I love the competitiveness of our team when we were down nine inside three minutes," Williams said. "I told them that if they were to make a total commitment to every possession on the defensive end and every possession on the offensive end, that we would have a chance still at the end. I think that's what they did.

"I can't say enough positive things about Duke," he added. "They have had some problems this year with injuries, but those guys that stayed on the court for them are 100 percent heart. I have total respect for them and the job that Mike does. I feel very lucky, and very fortunate to have won."

A month later, Williams made his fifth career appearance in the Final Four and coached the Heels to their fourth NCAA title. Through 2006 his record against Duke was 3 – 7.

Williams, Shelden. When he was in the ninth grade, Shelden Williams blocked 16 shots in a high school varsity game that happened to be on local television. The commentators gushed that Williams owned the lane and all the other players were his tenants. The local newspaper picked up on the nickname "the Landlord," and he's had it ever since.

A strapping 6 – 9 inside force from Forest Park, Okla., Williams changed neighborhoods and time zones when

Shelden Williams became the first player coached by Mike Krzyzewski to lead the ACC in rebounding and average a double-double.

he relocated to Duke, but he continued to collect the rent from his opponents. By the time he graduated in 2006, he ranked as the school's all-time leader in blocked shots and rebounds, eclipsing records that had stood for over a quarter-century. Mike Gminski previously held both, with 1,242 rebounds and 345 blocks.

Shelden DeMar Williams played in all 139 games during his four seasons, 2003 – 06, and started 128 times. He scored 1,928 points for a 13.9 average and grabbed 1,262 rebounds for a 9.1 average. He hit 57.2 percent of his field goals and totaled 422 blocks. Duke won the ACC championship in three of his seasons, made one Final Four appearance, and won 116 games, an average of 29 a year.

The son of a former college player from Oklahoma Christian University, Williams turned to basketball after he'd tried several other sports as a youth. His father coached high school and junior high teams and instructed Shelden as he learned the game. Williams's education also included countless games at the goal in his front yard.

"All the neighborhood kids would come out, there would be a boom box out there, and we'd have tournaments from noon 'til night, all the time," he said. "It got to the point where we got dirt spots in the grass from playing so much and my dad got mad that we were messing up the lawn. Our whole neighborhood and kids from other neighborhoods would come and try to run games with us. Sometimes we had to write down who got next."

Williams's high school team won the state championship in 2001, and his AAU team won a national title. As a college freshman he was the most effective post player for a perimeter-oriented squad. He became a valuable offensive option as a sophomore in 2004 and blossomed in 2005, when he became the first player under Krzyzewski to average a double-double, with 15.5 points and 11.2 rebounds. He repeated the double-double in 2006, with 18.8 points and 10.7 rebounds. For his career, Williams registered double figures in points and rebounds in 59 games, more than any other Blue Devil except Gminski (63).

Williams also became the first of Krzyzewski's players to lead the ACC in rebounding, which he accomplished in back-to-back years with averages of 11.2 in 2005 and 10.7 in 2006. He was the first Duke player in almost three decades — and just the third ever — to post a triple-double, when against Maryland in 2006 he had 19 points, 11 rebounds, and 10 blocks (matching the school record for the most in one game). His 137 blocks in 2006 set the single-season Duke mark; no other Duke player has ever blocked as many as 100 shots in a season.

Williams posted his career high of 30 points in 2005, when he hit 11 of 12 field goals and 8 of 8 free throws at Miami. He equaled that point total against Memphis early in his senior year in a performance that earned him MVP honors at the NIT Season Tip-Off. He established a career rebounding high a week later with 19 boards in the ACC opener against Virginia Tech. Another of his most impressive games was near the end of his last campaign, when he had 29 points and 18 rebounds in an NCAA Tournament victory over Southern.

With Duke's defense often geared to deny three-point shots and funnel drivers to Williams, it was imperative that he stay on the court. Thus he fulfilled a critical objective in his last two years by avoiding excessive foul trouble; he was disqualified from just three contests in 2005 and two in 2006 after fouling out 11 times during his first two years. That was a benefit of having experience on the court and learning from assistant coach Steve Wojciechowski to understand game situations and make the smart play. "A lot of times people try to make statements by throwing the ball way back into the stands," Williams noted. "I used to do that when I first started blocking shots, but my dad always told me that while it's cool and gets the crowd going, it doesn't do any good for your team. So a lot of times I try to tip it where I can get it or a teammate can get it, so we can start a fast break."

Williams's dad also used to tell him that any time he wasn't working to improve, there was someone else out there who was. Consequently, after resisting the temptation to turn pro a year early, Williams put together a list of the main goals for his senior season and kept it on his desk as a constant reminder. "Almost every day I look at it and see if I'm actually doing things that will help me achieve those goals," he said. "I don't want to have a day where I'm not doing something to help me achieve those goals."

Williams achieved plenty. He earned ACC and national defensive player of the year honors for both his junior and senior seasons. He also made the All-ACC first team in both years, as well as several All-America teams. He was on the short list of finalists for several national player of the year awards in 2006.

"He's great, in every sense of the word," Krzyzewski said. "We're so lucky to have him. He's going to go down as one of the great players in this conference, and at Duke. He's broken all of these records, and he's scored over 1,900 points, too. He's such a team guy. Someone at the next level's going to be really lucky, because he'll play for 12 years, be a starter, and bring his lunch pail every time, and be a double-double guy."

A co-captain at Duke, Williams was named a captain of the USA Basketball team that won the gold medal at the 2005 World University Games in Turkey. He paced the squad in scoring and rebounding as it claimed its eight contests by an average margin of nearly 30 points.

USA Basketball named Williams its male athlete of the year for 2005.

Williams, Weldon. Often overlooked because of his reserve role, Weldon Herschel Williams II was a member of the landmark recruiting class that helped rebuild Duke basketball under Mike Krzyzewski. A 6–6 forward from Park Forest, Ill., he played in 73 games from 1983 to 1986 and enjoyed his most extensive minutes as a senior reserve for the team that reached the Final Four in 1986. He played 189 minutes in 31 games that year. Williams totaled 126 points and 81 rebounds for his career, while hitting 54 percent of his shots. A biomedical engineering major, Williams missed one semester of his sophomore year because of academic difficulties but still graduated with his class. He later became a Methodist minister.

Williamson, Paul. A two-year member of the Duke basketball staff, Paul Williamson worked under Gerry Gerard in 1948–49. He was the head coach for the freshman team in both years. In 1949 his high-scoring freshman team sometimes overshadowed the varsity as it posted a 15–2 record and featured future All-America Dick Groat.

Williamson, Scott. The son of a former Duke football player, Monroe Scott Williamson was a 6–5 forward from Sanford, N.C., whose career was truncated by injury. He came to Duke on an academic scholarship and played for the freshman team in 1960, but a preseason injury kept him out of action in 1961. He was able to play briefly in 1962 and 1963, totaling 18 games with 11 points and 15 rebounds.

Winkin, John. Though he is not listed in the scoring statistics for the 1941 Southern Conference championship team, John W. Winkin Jr. was one of the senior lettermen for that team. He appeared in one game in 1940 and one in 1941. He went on to greater fame as a college baseball coach. Winkin guided the University of Maine Black Bears from 1975 through 1996 and compiled a record of 642–430–3 in 22 seasons. His teams reached the College World Series six times, once finishing third and once fourth.

Winning streaks. Duke's longest winning streak was achieved during the 1999 season, when the Blue Devils won 32 consecutive games before falling to Connecticut in the national championship contest. Three other Duke winning streaks established ACC records for the longest in conference history: 31 in ACC games, over portions of the 1998, 1999, and 2000 seasons; 24 in ACC road games, beginning with a win at N.C. State in February 1998 and concluding with a loss at Virginia in February 2001; and 46 in home games from the 1997 season to the 2000 season.

Duke also owned, at one point, a 95-game home court winning streak over non-ACC teams. That mark ended when Illinois won in Durham in December 1995.

Duke's longest overall winning streaks:

Started	Ended	Games
December 1998	March 1999	32
February 1992	January 1993	23
March 1991	February 1992	23
January 1986	March 1986	21
December 1962	March 1963	20

The longest winning streak in Duke women's basketball history lasted 22 games, covering the bulk of the 2002 season. It ended when Oklahoma stopped the Blue Devils at the Final Four. The Duke women won 42 consecutive regular-season ACC games from February 2001 to February 2004 and had an overall ACC winning streak of 51 games including conference tournament play. Florida State snapped that string when it handed the Devils their only league defeat of the 2004 campaign.

WNBA draft. The Women's National Basketball Association opened for business in the summer of 1997. Through the 2006 season, five Blue Devils had been drafted to play in the league. One, Peppi Browne, proved unable to compete because of a knee injury. Another, Georgia Schweitzer, was traded on draft day from Miami to Minnesota.

The first Duke women's player drafted by an American professional league was Kira Orr, who was chosen by the Seattle Reign in the fourth round of the American Basketball League draft in 1997. The ABL folded during its third season in 1998–99.

Here are Duke's WNBA draft picks:

Date	Player	Round	Pick	Team
May 4, 1999	Michele VanGorp	2	18	New York
April 25, 2000	Peppi Browne	4	43	Charlotte
April 20, 2001	Georgia Schweitzer	2	21	Miami
April 17, 2004	Alana Beard	1	2	Washington
April 17, 2004	Iciss Tillis	1	11	Detroit
April 5, 2006	Monique Currie	1	3	Charlotte
April 5, 2006	Mistie Williams	2	21	Phoenix
April 5, 2006	Jessica Foley	3	38	Indiana

Wojciechowski, Steve. It might have been the longest incident of "icing" a shooter in college basketball history. The scene was University Hall in Charlottesville, Va., in February 1997. The hometown Cavaliers had just made a free throw to take a 61–60 lead against the Duke Blue Devils with five seconds remaining. UVa coach Jeff Jones had sent a substitute to the scorer's table to check in for the free-throw shooter, as a strategic move to give his team time to set up on defense for Duke's final shot. But the game officials did not signal the sub into the game, instead motioning for Duke to inbound the ball. So Jeff Capel threw the ball in to his backcourt mate Steve Wojciechowski, who motored toward the other end of the court to make something happen. He was fouled with 2.2 seconds to go. The clock operator had not started the clock on time, though, because he was still blowing the horn trying to get the sub into the game. So needless to say, the atmosphere in U-Hall was tense, chaotic, and pressure-packed while the game officials spent seven minutes trying to sort things out.

The result was that Wojciechowski would have a chance to shoot free throws with 0.7 seconds left. The antagonistic crowd of over 8,000 fans began chanting "Wojo, Wojo" to try to intimidate him, and even Virginia forward Jamal Robinson stood on the lane and joined the chorus as Wojo waited to shoot. But just as he had practiced and dreamed many years before in his backyard, Wojo knocked down both shots to give Duke the win. The Cavaliers may have deserved better treatment from the officials, who were reprimanded a few days later, but the fact remained that Wojo had to make

Sparkplug Steve Wojciechowski was named the national defensive player of the year in 1998.

a play in the most difficult of circumstances and came through. "No matter what happens, after all that delay going up to the line and sinking those two free throws, it takes a lot of guts to do that," Krzyzewski said.

Steven Michael Wojciechowski used his toughness

Christian Laettner received the 1992 Wooden Award from former UCLA coach John Wooden.

and gut instincts to carve out a special career. A 5 – 11 sparkplug from Severna Park, Md., he played in 128 of Duke's 131 games during his four years, 1995 – 98, with 88 starts. He scored 687 points, with 505 assists, 291 rebounds, and 203 steals. Of the 198 field goals made in his career, 141 were from three-point range. But numbers rarely evaluated his impact. He may have been one of the most valuable 5-points-a-game scorers in program history.

Wojo's freshman year got off to a rocky start when his coach had to leave the team for health reasons after 12 games. He missed the guidance that Krzyzewski would have provided, but still split starting duties with Kenny Blakeney. He came off the bench for most of his sophomore season and then started every game as a junior and senior, when it was impossible to keep him off the court. He came through with more than his share of timely big shots, ran the offense, set up his teammates, and played defense with the tenacity of a bulldog. He scored in double figures just 19 times in his career, but he had a hand in most of what Duke did on both ends of the floor. And one of the best things he did was help lead the Devils from a losing record in 1995 to a No. 1 national ranking in 1998.

One of Wojo's best games was his final home contest of 1998, when as a co-captain he helped the Blue Devils to rally from a 17-point deficit to defeat UNC 77 – 75. He scored only one point but motivated the rally with his defense and playmaking, which included 11 assists to match his career high (he also had 11 versus Chaminade in the Maui Invitational). Wojo's career scoring high was 18 points against UNC in his junior year, but there were several games in which he came up with a critical basket at the right time, such as a decisive three-pointer to help Duke beat Iowa for the Great Alaska Shootout title.

Wojo was voted the Duke MVP by his teammates in 1997, when he quarterbacked the club to a regular-season conference title. He led the ACC in steals, made the All-ACC second team, and set a new standard in efficiency by committing just 58 turnovers in 33 starts. Wojo made the All-ACC third team in 1998 and capped his playing career by earning national defensive player of the year honors from the National Association of Basketball Coaches.

After a brief fling with pro basketball in Poland, Wojciechowski spent part of the 1999 season working with the Duke Radio Network and then was named a member of Krzyzewski's coaching staff in 2000. Working mostly with the inside players, he brought the same passion and intensity to that post as he did to his point guard duties on the floor. The Blue Devils won the national championship in his second year on the staff and made another trip to the Final Four in his fifth year.

Wojciechowski was a charter inductee in the Duke Basketball Hall of Honor in 2001.

Wood, Bob. Robert Wood, a 5 – 11 forward from Harrisburg, Pa., was a Duke reserve from 1936 to 1938 and lettered as a senior in 1938 for the team that won the Southern Conference championship.

Wooden, John. UCLA legend John Wooden coached against Duke six times during his 29-year Hall of Fame career. In 1953 – 54 his Bruins topped the Blue Devils in the consolation game of the Kentucky Invitational. The other five meetings were in the 1960s, beginning with the national championship game in Kansas City in 1964 that started Wooden's run of 10 NCAA crowns in 12 years. UCLA and Duke met twice in 1966, with Wooden's team losing twice in North Carolina on back-to-back nights. In 1967 he gained revenge with two home wins on consecutive nights.

Wooden made another trip to Duke in 2001 for the McDonald's High School All-America game. During his stay he visited the locker room of the Duke team and sat in on a video session as the Blue Devils were preparing for the Final Four. Wooden's collegiate record of 664 wins and 162 defeats included a 4–2 record against Duke. The Blue Devils also played in two events named for Wooden, the Wooden Classic in Anaheim during the 2000 season and the Wooden Tradition in Indianapolis in 2003.

Woodhouse, Woody. Generations of Duke fans in Durham and around the state experienced Blue Devil sports through the eyes of Charles James "Woody" Woodhouse, one of North Carolina's radio pioneers. Aside from his stint in the Navy during the Second World War, Woodhouse worked at Durham station WDNC from its inception in 1935 through 1958. He was the color commentator on Duke football network broadcasts during most of that period, working with another broadcasting legend, Add Penfield. Woodhouse also maintained an active basketball schedule in and out of Duke sports. He and former Duke coach Gerry Gerard broadcast many of the games played by Durham High School's powerhouse teams in the late 1930s and early 1940s, including a trip to a national tournament in 1940 that extended the school's winning streak to 69 games. That team featured four future Duke players. In December 1951 his call of Duke's season opener with Temple was boomed nationwide by Liberty Broadcasting. Known for his old-school style, flowery descriptions, and scripted pregame comments, Woodhouse also worked early in his career for the sports department at the *Durham Sun*, the local evening newspaper. His work at WDNC included serving as sales manager, and he helped maintain strong relationships with top broadcast sponsors such as Chesterfield cigarettes by doing their commercials himself.

Worthy, James. Hall of Fame forward James Worthy averaged 15 points against Duke during his three-year career at North Carolina, 1980–82. There were nine Duke-Carolina games during his run, but Worthy missed three of them because of injury. The Tar Heels won five of the six games he did play in. But Duke defeated the Worthy-less Heels in the ACC semifinals in 1980 while en route to the title, and again in 1981 on Gene Banks's memorable Senior Day. Worthy's best games against Duke were in the Big Four tourney, when he had 26 points, and in his last home game, when he had 20. As a pro, Worthy made the NBA's 50th anniversary team.

Wright, Bill. William H. Wright, from Knoxville, had one of the great single seasons in early Duke history when he arrived in 1944 from Tennessee during the Second World War. Wright played inside at forward and center and saw action in all 26 games, scoring 296 points to help the Devils win the Southern Conference title despite a record of only 13–13. A starter, Wright finished one point behind Gordon Carver for the team scoring lead. He had a team high of 15 points in the tournament championship game win over UNC and was named to the all-tourney first team. Earlier in the year, Wright's free throw with 30 seconds left enabled Duke to upset UNC in Chapel Hill, 41–40.

Yarbrough, Stu. Under the guidance of former Duke standout Doug Kistler, Stuart Johnson Yarbrough led Durham's Jordan High School to a pair of trips to the state finals, with a 26–0 record and a title in 1967. Then he brought his act to Duke for a collegiate career in which he lettered for three years, 1970–72, and started for one. Yarbrough appeared in 51 games, with 277 points and 116 rebounds. As a sophomore, his season high of 14 points helped spark a rally that left the Blue Devils just short of an upset at North Carolina. He also had a pair of second-half baskets to key a comeback against Virginia. Yarbrough played in only six games as a junior, missing a good portion of the season with a broken thumb. He was pegged for reserve duty again as a senior in 1972, but after Duke's leading scorer Richie O'Connor left the team at midseason Yarbrough stepped into the starting lineup and enjoyed a strong finish to his career. A 6–5 forward, he scored in double figures in seven of Duke's last nine games, averaging 13 points during the stretch, with a career high of 17 against William & Mary and back-to-back 16-point games in wins over Virginia and N.C. State. Yarbrough also got married during his college career, to Sandy Bubas, the daughter of former head coach Vic Bubas.

York, Scotty. A 6 – 0 guard from Cleveland Heights, Ohio, Scott York played on the varsity for four seasons, 1948 – 51, and lettered for the last three. He totaled 411 points in 98 games and was most valuable in setting up teammates for baskets. York and Bill Fleming moved into the starting backcourt in 1950 after leaders Dick Groat and Tommy Hughes were suspended at midseason for academic violations. As a senior York started alongside Groat and averaged 7.8 points while also serving as team captain. One of his biggest feeds that year was to Dayton Allen for the winning points in a victory over Tulane in the Dixie Classic. The Blue Devils had rallied from 32 points down to tie the score entering the final minute.

Youmans, Ceep. A four-year player, rare for his era, Corren P. "Ceep" Youmans saw action as a true freshman in 1947 and graduated in 1950 as the school's career scoring leader. In between he earned first-team all-conference honors three times — the first Duke player ever to do so — and also starred on the football field.

Youmans, a 6 – 1 forward from Miami, played in 99 games and scored 973 points, which broke Ed Koffenberger's Duke career scoring mark. Youmans's record lasted until Dick Groat became the school's first 1,000-point scorer in 1951, the season following Youmans's departure. Youmans scored 38 points in 20 appearances as a freshman, then posted averages of 12.1, 11.5, and 11.8 as a fixture in the next three seasons, when he made the All-Southern Conference team. His 329 points in 1948 were the second-highest in school history at the time, until he surpassed his own total with 352 in 1950.

As a sophomore Youmans led Duke to the conference championship game and scored 63 points in the tournament, setting a new individual scoring record for the event. He also led the Blue Devils back to the tourney final in 1950, when he was a co-captain.

Youmans didn't confine his records to the basketball court. He lettered at end for the 1949 and 1950 football teams, and in his last season he caught a school record

of 40 passes for 446 yards. The previous mark of 26 by Steve Lach had stood since 1940, and no one came close to topping Youmans's total for another 10 years, until Tee Moorman had 54 catches in 1960. Youmans had 47 career catches for 617 yards and three scores.

Youmans was a charter inductee in the Duke Basketball Hall of Honor in 2001.

Young, Kenny. Erratic play and erratic behavior contributed to a short Duke career for Kenneth Lloyd Young, a 5 – 10 guard from Orange, N.J. As a freshman in 1975 he played in 23 games and averaged 6.2 points, showing promise with his speed and quickness. In extended minutes at the end of the year, with standout Tate Armstrong hobbled by an injury, Young put together games of 16, 12, and 10 points to close the season.

But Young also missed a team bus to Clemson and, as a result, two games. As a sophomore his shot disappeared and his playing time diminished while Armstrong and Jim Spanarkel logged most of the backcourt minutes. When Spanarkel was injured at the end of the year, senior Paul Fox got the call instead of Young. Then Young was arrested for allegedly breaking into a soft-drink machine after the season. During preseason practice for the 1977 campaign he decided to leave school and went to Bucknell. Young's final Duke totals included 43 games, 190 points, 24 rebounds, and 45 assists.

Youngkin, Carroll. A three-year starting big man, Carroll Wayne Youngkin was one of the ACC's best performers during his era. He played in all 81 Duke games from 1959 through 1961 and led the conference in field-goal percentage for all three years, with a career mark of 54.0 percent. He scored 1,154 points and had 829 rebounds, annually ranking among the ACC's top board men as well. He averaged a double-double for his career, with 14.2 points and 10.2 rebounds.

A 6 – 6 native of Winston-Salem, N.C., Youngkin burst into prominence as a sophomore after being held out of the 1958 campaign by coach Harold Bradley. Since he was not eligible in the first semester, Bradley wanted him to wait a year so that he could play a whole season when he returned. Youngkin had Duke's top-scoring game of the 1959 season with 35 points and 18 rebounds in a televised showdown against Pitt, and one of the best stat lines in school history with 30 points and 20 rebounds in a win over Wake Forest. He was named first-team All-ACC that year.

Youngkin's best game of 1960 was a 33-point outing versus South Carolina, but his most important effort was in the ACC semifinals against UNC, when he rammed home 30 points on 12-of-19 shooting to send the Devils to the final. During two previous losses to the Heels, he had scored just eight and five points. Youngkin also had 22 points in the NCAA tourney to beat St. Joseph's as his team advanced to the Elite Eight.

Youngkin maintained his consistent production as a senior on a front line with Doug Kistler and sophomore Art Heyman, and had his best shooting year at 57.7 percent. He again glittered in the ACC semis with 23 points and 19 rebounds against South Carolina to get Duke into the final.

Zimmer, Bill. Perhaps no one could appreciate the talents of all-star guards Bob Verga and Steve Vacendak as much as William Allen Zimmer, a backcourt reserve who had to contend with those standouts every day in practice during the height of their careers. A 6-0 product of Poland, Ohio, Zimmer played in nine career games and scored 14 points, all during his junior and senior seasons of 1965 and 1966. After playing freshman basketball in 1963, Zimmer opted to focus on golf as a sophomore before returning to basketball for his last two years, lettering in 1965. When Duke scored 136 points against Virginia in 1965, it was Zimmer's layup that pushed his team past the school's previous single-game scoring record.

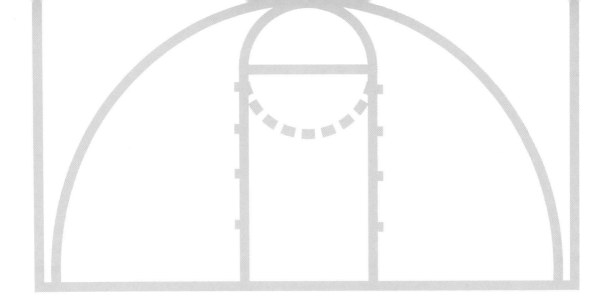

Record Book

Duke Basketball Year by Year

This section includes summaries of every season in the first century of Duke basketball history. For its first 19 years of intercollegiate basketball competition, the school was known as Trinity College. Information from that time period is limited, especially regarding individual statistics. For individual scoring leaders, total points scored are used through 1945, after which the available statistical records make it possible to list scoring averages.

The lineups listed in most cases are by position, following the traditional box score format: forward, forward, center, guard, guard. During most seasons several lineups were used; typical late-season lineups are presented here, based on the premise that a team generally aims to be playing its best by the end of the season and would have established its most effective lineup by that time. Key injuries and personnel changes may or may not be reflected in these lineups. Examples: In 1950 Dick Groat and Tommy Hughes made up the starting backcourt until withdrawing from school in February, so they are not listed as the starters. In 1977 Tate Armstrong was the team captain, leading scorer, and co-MVP, but he missed the last 13 games of the year with an injury and is not listed as a starter. Grant Hill had more starts than Antonio Lang in 1992, but Hill came off the bench at the end of the season after suffering an injury while Lang started the last 13 games, so Lang is listed as the starter. Elton Brand in 1998 missed 15 games because of an injury in the middle of the year but returned to the lineup late in the season, so he is listed as a starter here. The aim here is to list the lineup that was in use near the end of each season, not the year's most common lineup or a projection of what the best lineup would have been had everyone been healthy.

Duke joined the Southern Conference (SC) beginning with the 1928–29 season and became a charter member of the Atlantic Coast Conference (ACC) for the 1953–54 season. All-Southern Conference honors listed here refer to the all-tournament team until the mid-1940s, to the official all-conference team thereafter. All-ACC honors refer only to official all-conference teams, not all-tournament teams. Duke first began recognizing a team most valuable player (MVP) with the 1951–52 season. The MVPs listed here are the players officially listed as such by the university, not selections made by the author.

The postseason category lists Duke's won-lost record and how far the Blue Devils advanced in tournament play in their conference (SC or ACC) and nationally (NCAA or NIT). The 1975 season marked the first time that the NCAA Tournament invited multiple teams from any conference.

1905–06
Record: 2–3
Team scoring: Trinity 15.6, opponents 17.8
Coach: W. W. "Cap" Card
Captain: Thad G. Stem
Lineup: Greever, Claywell, Stem, Pugh, White

1906–07
Record: 4–2
Team scoring: Trinity 25.8, opponents 6.5
Coach: W. W. "Cap" Card
Captain: Thad G. Stem
Lineup: Puryear, Lilly, Kiker, Stem, White

1907–08
Record: 2–3
Team scoring: Trinity 19.6, opponents 14.2
Coach: W. W. "Cap" Card
Captain: Bill Lilly
Lineup: P. Kiker, Tuttle, Armfield, W. Kiker, Lilly

1908–09
Record: 8–1
Team scoring: Trinity 26.7, opponents 11.7
Coach: W. W. "Cap" Card
Captain: Emsley Armfield
Lineup: Stewart, Baxter, Armfield, W. Kiker, Hedrick

1909–10
Record: 4–4
Team scoring: Trinity 26.3, opponents 18.3
Coach: W. W. "Cap" Card
Captain: Paul Kiker
Lineup: Stewart, Jones, P. Kiker, Hedrick, J. Brinn

1910–11
Record: 4–3
Team scoring: Trinity 37.4, opponents 21.6
Coach: W. W. "Cap" Card
Captain: Bull Hedrick
Lineup: C. Brinn, Jones, P. Kiker, Hedrick, J. Brinn

1911–12
Record: 6–1
Team scoring: Trinity 37.6, opponents 19.3
Coach: W. W. "Cap" Card
Captain: Claude Brinn
Lineup: Jones, Crowell, Cherry, Hedrick, C. Brinn

1912–13
Record: 11–8
Team scoring: Trinity 24.5, opponents 25.7
Coach: Joseph E. Brinn
Captain: Claude Brinn
Lineup: Siler, White, Cherry, Thorne, C. Brinn

1913–14
Record: 12–8
Team scoring: Trinity 30.0, opponents 24.9
Coach: Noble L. Clay
Captain: Beal Siler
Lineup: Siler, McKinnon, Neal, Cherry, Thorne

1914–15
Record: 10–10
Team scoring: Trinity 29.2, opponents 27.3
Coach: Noble L. Clay
Captain: Shag Thorne
Lineup: Siler, Anderson, Neal, Wooten, Thorne

1915–16
Record: 9–11
Team scoring: Trinity 31.4, opponents 29.2
Coach: Bob Doak
Captain: Hip Martin
Lineup: Ferrell, Anderson, Bunting, Lilly, Martin

1916–17
Record: 20–4
Team scoring: Trinity 36.3, opponents 22.7
Coach: Chick Doak
Captain: Hip Martin
Lineup: Ferrell, Swan, Groome, Patton, Martin

1917–18
Record: 10–5
Team scoring: Trinity 31.4, opponents 25.5
Coach: Chick Doak
Captain: Earl Long
Lineup: Cole, Starling, Douglas, Long, Hathaway

1918–19
Record: 6–5
Team scoring: Trinity 25.2, opponents 25.5
Coach: Henry P. Cole
Captain: Henry P. Cole
Lineup: Cole, Starling, Page, Aldridge, Hathaway

1919–20
Record: 10–4
Team scoring: Records incomplete
Coach: Walter J. Rothensies
Captain: Loyd B. Hathaway
Lineup: Ferrell, Starling, Richardson,
    Hathaway, Martin

1920–21
Record: 9–6
Team scoring: Records incomplete
Coach: Floyd Egan
Captain: Loyd B. Hathaway
Lineup: Simpson, Moore, Richardson,
    Hathaway, Crute

1921–22
Record: 6–12
Team scoring: Trinity 25.4, opponents 27.6
Coach: James Baldwin
Captain: Oscar L. Richardson
Lineup: Simpson, Spikes, Richardson, Neal, Crute

1922–23
Record: 15–7
Team scoring: Trinity 32.8, opponents 26.5
Coach: Jesse S. Burbage

Captain: Jim Simpson
Lineup: Simpson, Spikes, Bullock, Neal, Crute

1923–24
Record: 19 – 6
Team scoring: Trinity 33.5, opponents 26.4
Coach: Jesse S. Burbage
Captain: Everett Spikes
Lineup: Simpson, Spikes, Richardson, Bullock, Crute

1924–25
Record: 4 – 9
Team scoring: Duke 24.2, opponents 29.1
Coach: George Buckheit
Captain: Ed Bullock
Lineup: Bullock, Burkheimer, Kimball, Graham,
    Moss

1925–26
Record: 8 – 12
Team scoring: Duke 29.4, opponents 31.2
Coach: George Buckheit
Captain: Pete Moss
Lineup: Bullock, Hartness, Moss, Bennett, Butler

1926–27
Record: 4 – 10
Team scoring: Duke 27.2, opponents 32.3
Coach: George Buckheit
Captain: Marshall Butler
Lineup: Kelley, Rogers, Rowe, Bennett, Butler

1927–28
Record: 9 – 5
Team scoring: Duke 37.4, opponents 34.5
Coach: George Buckheit
Captain: Doug Kelley
Lineup: Councilor, Werber, Jankoski, Candler, Farley

Duke was admitted to the Southern Conference
    on December 15, 1928

1928–29
Record: 12 – 8 overall, 5 – 4 sc (10th)
Postseason: Reached Southern Conference final (3 – 1)
Top scorers: Joe Croson 173, Bill Werber 131
Team scoring: Duke 35.8, opponents 33.3
Coach: Eddie Cameron

Captain: Coke Candler
Lineup: Councilor, Jankoski, Croson, Werber, Farley
Honors
    All-Southern Conference: Werber 1st, Croson 1st

1929–30
Record: 18 – 2 overall, 9 – 1 sc (tie 2nd)
Postseason: Reached Southern Conference final (3 – 1)
Top scorers: Joe Croson 189, Bill Werber 146
Team scoring: Duke 37.7, opponents 28.1
Coach: Eddie Cameron
Captains: Boley Farley, Harry Councilor
Lineup: Councilor, Rogers, Croson, Werber, Farley
Honors
    All-Southern Conference: Councilor 1st, Werber 1st,
        Croson 2nd
    All-America: Werber

1930–31
Record: 14 – 7 overall, 5 – 4 sc (7th)
Postseason: Reached Southern Conference
    quarterfinal (1 – 1)
Top scorers: Joe Croson 196, John Shaw 146
Team scoring: Duke 34.5, opponents 26.3
Coach: Eddie Cameron
Captains: Joe Croson, George Rogers
Lineup: Rogers, Capelli, Croson, Robertshaw, Shaw
Honors
    All-Southern Conference: Croson 2nd

1931–32
Record: 14 – 11 overall, 6 – 5 sc (11th)
Postseason: Reached Southern Conference
    semifinal (2 – 1)
Top scorers: Jim Thompson 180, Roy Alpert 159
Team scoring: Duke 28.8, opponents 28.8
Coach: Eddie Cameron
Captain: John Shaw
Lineup: Carter, Jim Thompson, Alpert,
    Herb Thompson, Shaw
Honors
    All-Southern Conference: Jim Thompson 2nd

1932–33
Record: 17 – 5 overall, 7 – 3 sc (tie 2nd)
Postseason: Reached Southern Conference final (2 – 1)
Top scorer: Jim Thompson 208

Team scoring: Duke 34.7, opponents 29.0
Coach: Eddie Cameron
Captain: By games
Lineup: Hayes, Horne, Jim Thompson,
    Herb Thompson, Weaver
Honors
    All-Southern Conference: Jim Thompson 1st,
        Herb Thompson 2nd

1933–34

Record: 18–6 overall, 9–4 sc (4th)
Postseason: Reached Southern Conference final (2–1)
Top scorers: Jim Thompson 231, Phil Weaver 150
Team scoring: Duke 34.5, opponents 26.4
Coach: Eddie Cameron
Captains: Jim Thompson, Herb Thompson,
    Phil Weaver
Lineup: Bell, Jim Thompson, Mack, Herb Thompson,
    Weaver
Honors
    All-Southern Conference: Herb Thompson 1st,
        Jim Thompson 1st

1934–35

Record: 18–8 overall, 10–4 sc (3rd)
Postseason: Reached Southern Conference
    semifinal (1–1)
Top scorers: Charles Kunkle 124, Sam Bell 107
Team scoring: Duke 33.3, opponents 29.2
Coach: Eddie Cameron
Captain: Sam Bell
Lineup: Bell, Kunkle, Naktenis, Podger, Polack

1935–36

Record: 20–6 overall, 4–5 sc (6th)
Postseason: Lost Southern Conference
    quarterfinal (0–1)
Top scorers: Ken Podger 168, Charles Kunkle 128
Team scoring: Duke 41.5, opponents 29.9
Coach: Eddie Cameron
Captain: Charles Kunkle
Lineup: Huiskamp, Kunkle, Herrick, Podger, Cheek

1936–37

Record: 15–8 overall, 11–6 sc (5th)
Postseason: Lost Southern Conference
    quarterfinal (0–1)
Top scorers: Ken Podger 196, Herbert Cheek 123

Team scoring: Duke 35.3, opponents 32.1
Coach: Eddie Cameron
Captain: Ken Podger
Lineup: Bergman, O'Mara, Herrick, Podger, Cheek
Honors
    All-Southern Conference: Podger 2nd

1937–38

Record: 15–9 overall, 9–5 sc (5th)
Postseason: Won Southern Conference
    championship (3–0)
Top scorers: Ed Swindell 206, Russell Bergman 125
Team scoring: Duke 35.6, opponents 34.4
Coach: Eddie Cameron
Captains: Fred Edwards, John Hoffman
Lineup: Edwards, Swindell, O'Mara, Bergman,
    Hoffman
Honors
    All-Southern Conference: Bergman 2nd,
        Edwards 2nd

1938–39

Record: 10–12 overall, 8–8 sc (8th)
Postseason: Lost Southern Conference
    quarterfinal (0–1)
Top scorers: Ed Swindell 190, Glenn Price 148
Team scoring: Duke 40.3, opponents 39.4
Coach: Eddie Cameron
Captains: Ed Swindell, Bob O'Mara
Lineup: O'Mara, Bergman, Holley, Swindell, Price
Honors
    All-Southern Conference: Swindell 1st,
        Bergman 2nd

1939–40

Record: 19–7 overall, 13–2 sc (1st)
Postseason: Reached Southern Conference final (2–1)
Top scorers: Bill Mock 184, Clyde Allen 182
Team scoring: Duke 41.3, opponents 35.5
Coach: Eddie Cameron
Captain: Bill Parsons
Lineup: Parsons, Price/Mock, Holley, Valasek, Connelly
Honors
    All-Southern Conference: Mock 1st, Allen 2nd,
        Price 2nd
    All-America: Mock 3rd

1940–41

Record: 14–8 overall, 8–4 sc (5th)

Postseason: Won Southern Conference
championship (3–0)

Top scorers: Chuck Holley 203, Cy Valasek 152

Team scoring: Duke 42.4, opponents 36.4

Coach: Eddie Cameron

Captains: Tom Connelly, Glenn Price

Lineup: Price, Mock, Holley, Valasek, Shokes

Honors

All-Southern Conference: Holley 1st, Valasek 1st,
Spuhler 2nd

1941–42

Record: 22–2 overall, 15–1 sc (1st)

Postseason: Won Southern Conference
championship (3–0)

Top scorers: Cedric Loftis 200, Clyde Allen 169

Team scoring: Duke 52.6, opponents 40.3

Coach: Eddie Cameron

Captain: Ray Spuhler

Lineup: Spuhler, Rothbaum, Allen, McCahan, Stark

Honors

All-Southern Conference: McCahan 1st, Spuhler 1st,
Cedric Loftis 2nd

1942–43

Record: 20–6 overall, 12–1 sc (1st)

Postseason: Reached Southern Conference final (2–1)

Top scorers: Cedric Loftis 293, Gordon Carver 292,
John Seward 268

Team scoring: Duke 54.0, opponents 46.2

Coach: Gerry Gerard

Captain: Not available

Lineup: Seward, Carver, Gantt, Garland Loftis,
Cedric Loftis

Honors

All-Southern Conference: Gantt 1st, Seward 1st,
Cedric Loftis 1st, Carver 2nd

1943–44

Record: 13–13 overall, 4–2 sc (3rd)

Postseason: Won Southern Conference
championship (3–0)

Top scorers: Gordon Carver 297, Bill Wright 296

Team scoring: Duke 46.7, opponents 43.1

Coach: Gerry Gerard

Captain: Not available

Lineup: Carver, Gilbert, Wright, Harner, Bailey

Honors

All-Southern Conference: Carver 1st, Wright 1st,
Harner 2nd

1944–45

Record: 13–9 overall, 6–1 sc (3rd)

Postseason: Reached Southern Conference final (2–1)

Top scorers: Bill Sapp 221, Ed Koffenberger 190

Team scoring: Duke 48.0, opponents 42.4

Coach: Gerry Gerard

Captain: Not available

Lineup: Carver, Roellke, Koffenberger, Sapp, Buckley

Honors

All-Southern Conference: Buckley 1st, Carver 1st,
Koffenberger 2nd

1945–46

Record: 21–6 overall, 12–2 sc (2nd)

Postseason: Won Southern Conference
championship (3–0)

Top scorer: Ed Koffenberger 11.7

Team scoring: Duke 47.7, opponents 38.4

Coach: Gerry Gerard

Captain: Ed Koffenberger

Lineup: Seward, Cheek, Koffenberger, Whiting,
Gordon

Honors

All-Southern Conference: Koffenberger 1st,
Seward 1st, Whiting 1st

All-America: Koffenberger 2nd

1946–47

Record: 19–8 overall, 10–4 sc (3rd)

Postseason: Lost Southern Conference
quarterfinal (0–1)

Duke hosted Southern Conference Tournament

Top scorer: Ed Koffenberger 15.4

Team scoring: Duke 54.1, opponents 48.2

Coach: Gerry Gerard

Captains: Ed Koffenberger, John Seward

Lineup: Koffenberger, Seward, Collins, Loftis, Gordon

Honors

All-Southern Conference: Koffenberger 1st,
Collins 2nd

All-America: Koffenberger 2nd

1947–48

Record: 17–12 overall, 8–6 SC (7th)

Postseason: Reached Southern Conference final (3–1)

Duke hosted Southern Conference Tournament

Top scorer: Corren Youmans 12.1

Team scoring: Duke 52.8, opponents 50.4

Coach: Gerry Gerard

Captain: Doug Ausbon

Lineup: Youmans, Ausbon, Collins, Hughes, Martin

Honors

    All-Southern Conference: Youmans 1st, Hughes 2nd

1948–49

Record: 13–9 overall, 5–7 SC (10th)

Postseason: Duke hosted the Southern Conference
    Tournament but did not finish high enough in the
    standings to qualify to compete in it.

Top scorers: Corren Youmans 11.5, Ben Collins 9.8

Team scoring: Duke 53.7, opponents 49.4

Coach: Gerry Gerard

Captains: Ben Collins, Dick Gordon

Lineup: Youmans, Scarborough, Collins, Hughes,
    Gordon

Honors

    All-Southern Conference: Youmans 1st, Hughes 2nd

1949–50

Record: 15–15 overall, 9–7 SC (8th)

Postseason: Reached Southern Conference final (2–1)

Duke hosted Southern Conference Tournament

Top scorers: Dick Groat 14.5, Corren Youmans 11.8

Team scoring: Duke 58.8, opponents 58.0

Coach: Gerry Gerard

Captains: Corren Youmans, Tommy Hughes

Lineup: Youmans, Scarborough, Allen, Fleming, York

Honors

    All-Southern Conference: Youmans 1st, Groat 2nd

1950–51

Record: 20–13 overall, 13–6 SC (4th)

Postseason: Reached Southern Conference final (2–1)

Top scorer: Dick Groat 25.2

Team scoring: Duke 71.7, opponents 70.2

Coach: Harold Bradley

Captain: Scotty York

Lineup: Crowder, Fleming, Deimling, York, Groat

Honors

    All-Southern Conference: Groat 1st

    Southern Conference Tournament MVP: Groat

    All-America: Groat 2nd

1951–52

Record: 24–6 overall, 13–3 SC (3rd)

Final ranking: No. 12 AP poll

Postseason: Reached Southern Conference final (2–1)

Top scorers: Dick Groat 26.0, Bernie Janicki 14.9

Team scoring: Duke 77.3, opponents 67.3

Coach: Harold Bradley

Captain: Dick Groat

Lineup: Janicki, Fleming, Crowder, D'Emilio, Groat

Honors

    Team Most Valuable Player: Dick Groat

    All-Southern Conference: Groat 1st

    Southern Conference Tournament MVP: Groat

    All-America: Groat 1st

    National Player of the Year: Groat (UPI, Helms)

1952–53

Record: 18–8 overall, 12–4 SC (6th)

Postseason: Lost Southern Conference
    quarterfinal (0–1)

Top scorers: Bernie Janicki 16.8, Bill Reigel 16.3,
    Rudy D'Emilio 14.6

Team scoring: Duke 83.8, opponents 78.4

Coach: Harold Bradley

Captains: Bernie Janicki, Rudy D'Emilio, Rudy Lacy

Lineup: Janicki, Reigel, Decker, D'Emilio, Shabel

Honors

    MVP: Rudy D'Emilio

Duke became a charter member of the Atlantic Coast
    Conference on May 8, 1953

1953–54

Record: 22–6 overall, 9–1 ACC (1st)

Final ranking: No. 15 AP poll

Postseason: Reached ACC semifinal (1–1)

Top scorers: Bernie Janicki 13.5, Rudy D'Emilio 13.2,
    Ronnie Mayer 12.9, Joe Belmont 12.4

Team scoring: Duke 83.2, opponents 72.7

Coach: Harold Bradley

Captains: Bernie Janicki, Rudy D'Emilio

Lineup: Janicki, Mayer, Morgan, D'Emilio, Belmont

Honors

MVP: Bernie Janicki

All-ACC: D'Emilio 1st, Belmont 2nd, Mayer 2nd

1954-55

Record: 20 - 8 overall, 11 - 3 ACC (2nd)

Postseason: Reached ACC final (2 - 1), lost NCAA first round (0 - 1)

Top scorers: Ronnie Mayer 21.7, Joe Belmont 15.7

Team scoring: Duke 85.2, opponents 72.7

Coach: Harold Bradley

Captains: Joe Belmont, Ronnie Mayer

Lineup: Mayer, Lakata, Morgan, Tobin, Belmont

Honors

MVP: Ronnie Mayer

All-ACC: Mayer 1st, Belmont 2nd

1955-56

Record: 19 - 7 overall, 10 - 4 ACC (tie 3rd)

Final ranking: No. 17 AP poll

Postseason: Reached ACC semifinal (1 - 1)

Top scorers: Ronnie Mayer 22.1, Joe Belmont 17.0

Team scoring: Duke 80.6, opponents 69.8

Coach: Harold Bradley

Captain: Joe Belmont

Lineup: Mayer, Lakata, Morgan, Harris, Belmont

Honors

MVP: Joe Belmont

All-ACC: Belmont 1st, Mayer 2nd

1956-57

Record: 13 - 11 overall, 8 - 6 ACC (3rd)

Postseason: Lost ACC quarterfinal (0 - 1)

Top scorers: Jim Newcome 14.9, Bucky Allen 13.3

Team scoring: Duke 78.4, opponents 77.0

Coach: Harold Bradley

Captain: None

Lineup: Newcome, Schmidt, Clement, Allen, Harris

Honors

MVP: Bobby Joe Harris

All-ACC: Newcome 2nd

1957-58

Record: 18 - 7 overall, 11 - 3 ACC (1st)

Final ranking: No. 10 AP poll

Postseason: Reached ACC semifinal (1 - 1)

Top scorers: Jim Newcome 13.2, Bucky Allen 12.4, Bob Vernon 12.2, Paul Schmidt 11.9

Team scoring: Duke 69.2, opponents 65.2

Coach: Harold Bradley

Captains: Bobby Joe Harris, Jim Newcome

Lineup: Newcome, Schmidt, Vernon, Allen, Harris

Honors

MVP: Paul Schmidt

All-ACC: Newcome 1st, Allen 2nd, Schmidt 2nd

1958-59

Record: 13 - 12 overall, 7 - 7 ACC (tie 3rd)

Postseason: Reached ACC semifinal (1 - 1)

Top scorers: Carroll Youngkin 15.9, Howard Hurt 15.7

Team scoring: Duke 65.4, opponents 68.7

Coach: Harold Bradley

Captains: Jerry Robertson, Marty Joyce

Lineup: Kistler, Youngkin, Kast, Hurt, Frye

Honors

MVP: Howard Hurt

All-ACC: Youngkin 1st, Hurt 2nd

1959-60

Record: 17 - 11 overall, 7 - 7 ACC (4th)

Final ranking: No. 18 AP poll

Postseason: Won ACC championship (3 - 0), reached NCAA regional final (2 - 1)

Top scorers: Howard Hurt 13.4, Carroll Youngkin 13.4, Doug Kistler 12.3

Team scoring: Duke 64.4, opponents 63.2

Coach: Vic Bubas

Captain: Howard Hurt

Lineup: Hurt, Kistler, Youngkin, Mullen, Frye

Honors

MVP: Doug Kistler

All-ACC: Hurt 2nd

ACC Tournament MVP: Kistler

1960-61

Record: 22 - 6 overall, 10 - 4 ACC (3rd)

Final ranking: No. 10 AP poll

Postseason: Reached ACC final (2 - 1)

Top scorers: Art Heyman 25.2, Carroll Youngkin 13.6

Team scoring: Duke 81.5, opponents 71.2

Coach: Vic Bubas

Captain: Howard Hurt

Lineup: Heyman, Kistler, Youngkin, Hurt, Frye
Honors
    MVP: Art Heyman
    All-ACC: Heyman 1st, Hurt 2nd
    All-America: Heyman

1961–62

Record: 20–5 overall, 11–3 ACC (2nd)
Final ranking: No. 10 AP poll
Postseason: Reached ACC semifinal (1–1)
Top scorers: Art Heyman 25.3, Jeff Mullins 21.2
Team scoring: Duke 82.0, opponents 67.9
Coach: Vic Bubas
Captains: Buzz Mewhort, Art Heyman
Lineup: Heyman, Mullins, Buckley, Schmidt, Harrison
Honors
    MVP: Art Heyman
    All-ACC: Heyman 1st, Mullins 1st
    All-America: Heyman 2nd

1962–63 Final Four

Record: 27–3 overall, 14–0 ACC (1st)
Final ranking: No. 2 AP poll
Postseason: Won ACC championship (3–0), finished
    third in NCAA (3–1)
Top scorers: Art Heyman 24.9, Jeff Mullins 20.3
Team scoring: Duke 83.3, opponents 68.9
Coach: Vic Bubas
Captain: Art Heyman
Lineup: Heyman, Mullins, Buckley, Schmidt,
    Harrison
Honors
    MVP: Art Heyman
    All-ACC: Heyman 1st, Mullins 1st
    ACC Player of the Year: Heyman
    ACC Tournament MVP: Heyman
    All-America: Heyman 1st, Mullins
    National Player of the Year: Heyman (AP, UPI,
        Helms, USBWA)
    Final Four MVP: Heyman

1963–64 Final Four

Record: 26–5 overall, 13–1 ACC (1st)
Final ranking: No. 3 AP poll
Postseason: Won ACC championship (3–0), reached
    NCAA championship game (3–1)

Top scorers: Jeff Mullins 24.2, Jay Buckley 13.8
Team scoring: Duke 84.2, opponents 69.3
Coach: Vic Bubas
Captain: Jeff Mullins
Lineup: Mullins, Tison, Buckley, Ferguson, Harrison
Honors
    MVP: Jeff Mullins
    All-ACC: Mullins 1st, Buckley 2nd, Harrison 2nd,
        Tison 2nd
    ACC Player of the Year: Mullins
    ACC Tournament MVP: Mullins
    All-America: Mullins 2nd

1964–65

Record: 20–5 overall, 11–3 ACC (1st)
Final ranking: No. 10 AP poll
Postseason: Reached ACC final (2–1)
Top scorers: Bob Verga 21.4, Jack Marin 19.1,
    Steve Vacendak 16.2
Team scoring: Duke 92.4, opponents 77.8
Coach: Vic Bubas
Captain: Denny Ferguson
Lineup: Marin, Vacendak, Tison, Ferguson, Verga
Honors
    MVP: Denny Ferguson
    All-ACC: Marin 1st, Verga 1st, Vacendak 2nd

1965–66 Final Four

Record: 26–4 overall, 12–2 ACC (1st)
Final ranking: No. 2 AP poll
Postseason: Won ACC championship (3–0), finished
    third in NCAA (3–1)
Top scorers: Jack Marin 18.9, Bob Verga 18.5
Team scoring: Duke 82.8, opponents 71.6
Coach: Vic Bubas
Captain: Steve Vacendak
Lineup: Marin, Riedy, Lewis, Vacendak, Verga
Honors
    MVP: Jack Marin, Steve Vacendak
    All-ACC: Marin 1st, Verga 1st, Vacendak 2nd
    ACC Player of the Year: Vacendak
    ACC Tournament MVP: Vacendak
    All-America: Marin 2nd, Verga 2nd

1966–67

Record: 18–9 overall, 9–3 ACC (2nd)
Final ranking: No. 19 UPI poll

Postseason: Reached ACC final (2–1), lost NIT first
round (0–1)
Top scorers: Bob Verga 26.1, Mike Lewis 15.5
Team scoring: Duke 82.8, opponents 76.2
Coach: Vic Bubas
Captain: Bob Verga
Lineup: Riedy, Kolodziej, Lewis, Wendelin, Verga
Honors
    MVP: Bob Verga
    All-ACC: Verga 1st, Lewis 2nd
    All-America: Verga 1st

1967–68

Record: 22–6 overall, 11–3 ACC (2nd)
Final ranking: No. 10 AP poll
Postseason: Reached ACC semifinal (1–1), reached
NIT quarterfinal (1–1)
Top scorers: Mike Lewis 21.7, Dave Golden 13.1
Team scoring: Duke 78.9, opponents 67.5
Coach: Vic Bubas
Captain: Mike Lewis
Lineup: Kennedy, Vandenberg, Lewis, Wendelin,
Golden
Honors
    MVP: Mike Lewis
    All-ACC: Lewis 1st
    All-America: Lewis

1968–69

Record: 15–13 overall, 8–6 ACC (tie 3rd)
Postseason: Reached ACC final (2–1)
Top scorers: Randy Denton 17.4, Rick Katherman 13.7
Team scoring: Duke 82.0, opponents 79.4
Coach: Vic Bubas
Captains: Dave Golden, Steve Vandenberg
Lineup: Lind, Katherman, Denton, Golden,
DeVenzio
Honors
    MVP: Fred Lind
    All-ACC: Denton 2nd

1969–70

Record: 17–9 overall, 8–6 ACC (4th)
Postseason: Lost ACC quarterfinal (0–1), lost NIT first
round (0–1)
Top scorers: Randy Denton 21.5, Rick Katherman 13.1

Team scoring: Duke 75.6, opponents 72.1
Coach: Bucky Waters
Captain: Larry Saunders
Lineup: Saunders, Katherman, Denton, Evans,
DeVenzio
Honors
    MVP: Randy Denton
    All-ACC: Denton 2nd

1970–71

Record: 20–10 overall, 9–5 ACC (3rd)
Postseason: Lost ACC quarterfinal (0–1), finished
fourth in NIT (2–2)
Top scorers: Randy Denton 20.4, Richie O'Connor 12.7
Team scoring: Duke 79.6, opponents 73.7
Coach: Bucky Waters
Captain: Larry Saunders
Lineup: Saunders, O'Connor, Denton, Melchionni,
DeVenzio
Honors
    MVP: Randy Denton
    All-ACC: Denton 1st
    All-America: Denton

1971–72

Record: 14–12 overall, 6–6 ACC (tie 4th)
Postseason: Reached ACC semifinal (1–1)
Top scorers: Richie O'Connor 15.4, Chris Redding 14.8
Team scoring: Duke 68.4, opponents 68.1
Coach: Bucky Waters
Captains: Pat Doughty, Gary Melchionni, Alan Shaw
Lineup: Redding, Yarbrough, Shaw, Melchionni,
West
Honors
    MVP: Alan Shaw
    All-ACC: Melchionni 2nd, Shaw 2nd

1972–73

Record: 12–14 overall, 4–8 ACC (tie 4th)
Postseason: Lost ACC quarterfinal (0–1)
Top scorers: Chris Redding 16.9, Gary Melchionni 15.8
Team scoring: Duke 78.1, opponents 76.6
Coach: Bucky Waters
Captains: Gary Melchionni, Alan Shaw
Lineup: Redding, Fleischer, Shaw, Melchionni,
Billerman

Honors

    MVP: Gary Melchionni

    All-ACC: Melchionni 1st, Redding 2nd

1973–74

Record: 10–16 overall, 2–10 ACC (7th)

Postseason: Lost ACC quarterfinal (0–1)

Top scorers: Bob Fleischer 15.7, Chris Redding 12.2

Team scoring: Duke 75.3, opponents 77.6

Coach: Neill McGeachy

Captain: Kevin Billerman

Lineup: Redding, Kramer, Fleischer, Burch, Billerman

Honors

    MVP: Bob Fleischer

1974–75

Record: 13–13 overall, 2–10 ACC (tie 6th)

Postseason: Lost ACC quarterfinal (0–1)

Top scorers: Bob Fleischer 17.2, Pete Kramer 15.1

Team scoring: Duke 82.9, opponents 81.5

Coach: Bill Foster

Captains: Kevin Billerman, Bob Fleischer

Lineup: Kramer, Fleischer, Hodge, Armstrong, Billerman

Honors

    MVP: Bob Fleischer

    All-ACC: Fleischer 2nd

1975–76

Record: 13–14 overall, 3–9 ACC (7th)

Postseason: Lost ACC quarterfinal (0–1)

Top scorers: Tate Armstrong 24.2, Willie Hodge 16.9

Team scoring: Duke 88.3, opponents 85.0

Coach: Bill Foster

Captains: Terry Chili, Willie Hodge

Lineup: Crow, Moses, Hodge, Spanarkel, Armstrong

Honors

    MVP: Tate Armstrong

    All-ACC: Armstrong 1st

    ACC Rookie of the Year: Spanarkel

1976–77

Record: 14–13 overall, 2–10 ACC (tie 6th)

Postseason: Lost ACC quarterfinal (0–1)

Top scorers: Tate Armstrong 22.7, Jim Spanarkel 19.2

Team scoring: Duke 76.4, opponents 72.9

Coach: Bill Foster

Captains: Tate Armstrong, Mark Crow

Lineup: Crow, Morrison, Gminski, Spanarkel, Gray

Honors

    MVP: Tate Armstrong, Jim Spanarkel

    All-ACC: Spanarkel 2nd

    ACC Rookie of the Year: Gminski

1977–78 Final Four

Record: 27–7 overall, 8–4 ACC (2nd)

Final ranking: No. 7 AP poll

Postseason: Won ACC championship (3–0), reached NCAA championship game (4–1)

Top scorers: Jim Spanarkel 20.8, Mike Gminski 20.0, Gene Banks 17.1

Team scoring: Duke 85.6, opponents 74.4

Coach: Bill Foster

Captain: Jim Spanarkel

Lineup: Banks, Dennard, Gminski, Spanarkel, Harrell

Honors

    MVP: Gene Banks, Mike Gminski, Jim Spanarkel

    All-ACC: Gminski 1st, Spanarkel 1st, Banks 2nd

    ACC Tournament MVP: Spanarkel

    ACC Rookie of the Year: Banks

    All-America: Gminski, Spanarkel

1978–79

Record: 22–8 overall, 9–3 ACC (tie 1st)

Final ranking: No. 11 AP poll

Postseason: Reached ACC final (2–1), lost NCAA second round (0–1)

Top scorers: Mike Gminski 18.8, Jim Spanarkel 15.9

Team scoring: Duke 71.9, opponents 65.5

Coach: Bill Foster

Captain: Jim Spanarkel

Lineup: Banks, Dennard, Gminski, Spanarkel, Bender

Honors

    MVP: Mike Gminski, Jim Spanarkel

    All-ACC: Gminski 1st, Spanarkel 1st, Banks 2nd

    ACC Player of the Year: Gminski

    All-America: Gminski 1st, Spanarkel 2nd, Banks

1979–80

Record: 24–9 overall, 7–7 ACC (tie 5th)

Final ranking: No. 14 AP poll

Postseason: Won ACC championship (3–0), reached NCAA regional final (2–1)

Top scorers: Mike Gminski 21.3, Gene Banks 17.3

Team scoring: Duke 73.3, opponents 68.3
Coach: Bill Foster
Captains: Bob Bender, Mike Gminski
Lineup: Banks, Dennard, Gminski, Taylor, Bender
Honors
  MVP: Gene Banks, Mike Gminski
  All-ACC: Gminski 1st, Banks 2nd
  All-America: Gminski 2nd

1980–81
Record: 17–13 overall, 6–8 ACC (tie 5th)
Postseason: Lost ACC quarterfinal (0–1), reached NIT
  third round (2–1)
Top scorers: Gene Banks 18.5, Vince Taylor 14.7
Team scoring: Duke 69.9, opponents 66.9
Coach: Mike Krzyzewski
Captains: Gene Banks, Kenny Dennard
Lineup: Banks, Dennard, Tissaw, Emma, Taylor
Honors
  MVP: Gene Banks, Kenny Dennard
  All-ACC: Banks 1st
  All-America: Banks

1981–82
Record: 10–17 overall, 4–10 ACC (tie 6th)
Postseason: Lost ACC quarterfinal (0–1)
Top scorers: Vince Taylor 20.3, Chip Engelland 15.2
Team scoring: Duke 64.0, opponents 70.0
Coach: Mike Krzyzewski
Captain: Vince Taylor
Lineup: Meagher, Tissaw, Engelland, Emma, Taylor
Honors
  MVP: Vince Taylor
  All-ACC: Taylor 1st

1982–83
Record: 11–17 overall, 3–11 ACC (7th)
Postseason: Lost ACC quarterfinal (0–1)
Top scorers: Johnny Dawkins 18.1, Mark Alarie 13.0
Team scoring: Duke 80.2, opponents 83.7
Coach: Mike Krzyzewski
Captains: Tom Emma, Chip Engelland
Lineup: Bilas, Henderson, Alarie, Emma, Dawkins
Honors
  MVP: Johnny Dawkins
  All-ACC: Dawkins 2nd

1983–84
Record: 24–10 overall, 7–7 ACC (tie 3rd)
Final ranking: No. 14 AP poll
Postseason: Reached ACC final (2–1), lost NCAA second
  round (0–1)
Top scorers: Johnny Dawkins 19.4, Mark Alarie 17.5
Team scoring: Duke 77.2, opponents 72.3
Coach: Mike Krzyzewski
Captains: Richard Ford, Doug McNeely
Lineup: Alarie, Meagher, Bilas, Dawkins, Amaker
Honors
  MVP: Mark Alarie, Johnny Dawkins
  All-ACC: Alarie 1st, Dawkins 2nd

1984–85
Record: 23–8 overall, 8–6 ACC (tie 4th)
Final ranking: No. 10 AP poll
Postseason: Reached ACC semifinal (1–1), reached
  NCAA second round (1–1)
Top scorers: Johnny Dawkins 18.8, Mark Alarie 15.9
Team scoring: Duke 78.9, opponents 67.9
Coach: Mike Krzyzewski
Captains: Jay Bryan, Dan Meagher
Lineup: Alarie, Meagher, Bilas, Dawkins, Amaker
Honors
  MVP: Johnny Dawkins
  All-ACC: Dawkins 1st, Alarie 2nd
  All-America: Dawkins 1st

1985–86 Final Four
Record: 37–3 overall, 12–2 ACC (1st)
Final ranking: No. 1 AP poll
Postseason: Won ACC championship (3–0), reached
  NCAA championship game (5–1)
Top scorers: Johnny Dawkins 20.2, Mark Alarie 17.2
Team scoring: Duke 79.9, opponents 67.2
Coach: Mike Krzyzewski
Captains: Johnny Dawkins, David Henderson
Lineup: Alarie, Henderson, Bilas, Dawkins, Amaker
Honors
  MVP: Johnny Dawkins
  All-ACC: Alarie 1st, Dawkins 1st
  ACC Tournament MVP: Dawkins
  All-America: Dawkins 1st, Alarie
  National Player of the Year: Dawkins (Naismith)

1986–87

Record: 24–9 overall, 9–5 ACC (3rd)

Final ranking: No. 17 AP poll

Postseason: Lost ACC quarterfinal (0–1), reached
NCAA regional semifinal (2–1)

Top scorers: Danny Ferry 14.0, Tommy Amaker 12.3

Team scoring: Duke 77.2, opponents 67.3

Coach: Mike Krzyzewski

Captain: Tommy Amaker

Lineup: Ferry, King, Smith, Strickland, Amaker

Honors

MVP: Tommy Amaker, Danny Ferry

All-ACC: Amaker 2nd, Ferry 2nd

All-America: Amaker

National Defensive Player of the Year: Amaker

1987–88 Final Four

Record: 28–7 overall, 9–5 ACC (3rd)

Final ranking: No. 5 AP poll

Postseason: Won ACC championship (3–0), reached
NCAA national semifinal (4–1)

Top scorers: Danny Ferry 19.1, Kevin Strickland 16.1

Team scoring: Duke 83.8, opponents 68.8

Coach: Mike Krzyzewski

Captains: Billy King, Kevin Strickland

Lineup: Ferry, King, Brickey, Strickland,
Snyder

Honors

MVP: Danny Ferry

All-ACC: Ferry 1st

ACC Player of the Year: Ferry

ACC Tournament MVP: Ferry

All-America: Ferry 2nd

National Defensive Player of the Year: King

1988–89 Final Four

Record: 28–8 overall, 9–5 ACC (tie 2nd)

Final ranking: No. 9 AP poll

Postseason: Reached ACC final (2–1), reached NCAA
national semifinal (4–1)

Top scorers: Danny Ferry 22.6, Phil Henderson 12.7

Team scoring: Duke 86.5, opponents 69.8

Coach: Mike Krzyzewski

Captains: Danny Ferry, Quin Snyder

Lineup: Ferry, Brickey, Laettner, Henderson,
Snyder

Honors

MVP: Danny Ferry

All-ACC: Ferry 1st

ACC Player of the Year: Ferry

All-America: Ferry 1st

National Player of the Year: Ferry (Naismith, UPI,
USBWA)

1989–90 Final Four

Record: 29–9 overall, 9–5 ACC (2nd)

Final ranking: No. 15 in AP poll

Postseason: Reached ACC semifinal (1–1), reached
NCAA championship game (5–1)

Top scorers: Phil Henderson 18.5,
Christian Laettner 16.3

Team scoring: Duke 89.1, opponents 76.6

Coach: Mike Krzyzewski

Captain: Robert Brickey

Lineup: Brickey, Laettner, Abdelnaby, Henderson,
Hurley

Honors

MVP: Phil Henderson, Christian Laettner

All-ACC: Henderson 2nd, Laettner 2nd,
Abdelnaby 3rd

All-America: Laettner

1990–91 Final Four

Record: 32–7 overall, 11–3 ACC (1st)

Final ranking: No. 6 in AP poll

Postseason: Reached ACC final (2–1), won NCAA
championship (6–0)

Top scorer: Christian Laettner 19.8

Team scoring: Duke 87.7, opponents 73.4

Coach: Mike Krzyzewski

Captains: Clay Buckley, Greg Koubek

Lineup: Grant Hill, Koubek, Laettner, Thomas Hill,
Hurley

Honors

MVP: Bobby Hurley, Christian Laettner

All-ACC: Laettner 1st, Thomas Hill 3rd,
Hurley 3rd

All-America: Laettner 2nd

Final Four MVP: Laettner

1991–92 Final Four

Record: 34–2 overall, 14–2 ACC (1st)

Final ranking: No. 1 in AP poll

Postseason: Won ACC championship (3 – 0), won NCAA championship (6 – 0)

Top scorers: Christian Laettner 21.5, Thomas Hill 14.6

Team scoring: Duke 88.0, opponents 72.6

Coach: Mike Krzyzewski

Captains: Brian Davis, Christian Laettner

Lineup: Davis, Lang, Laettner, Thomas Hill, Hurley

Honors

> MVP: Bobby Hurley, Christian Laettner
>
> All-ACC: Laettner 1st, Grant Hill 2nd, Hurley 2nd, Thomas Hill 3rd
>
> ACC Player of the Year: Laettner
>
> ACC Tournament MVP: Laettner
>
> All-America: Laettner 1st, Grant Hill, Hurley
>
> National Player of the Year: Laettner (AP, Naismith, Wooden, NABC, USBWA)
>
> Final Four MVP: Hurley

1992 – 93

Record: 24 – 8 overall, 10 – 6 ACC (tie 3rd)

Final ranking: No. 10 in AP poll

Postseason: Lost ACC quarterfinal (0 – 1), reached NCAA second round (1 – 1)

Top scorers: Grant Hill 18.0, Bobby Hurley 17.0

Team scoring: Duke 86.4, opponents 71.2

Coach: Mike Krzyzewski

Captains: Thomas Hill, Bobby Hurley

Lineup: Grant Hill, Lang, Parks, Thomas Hill, Hurley

Honors

> MVP: Bobby Hurley
>
> All-ACC: Grant Hill 1st, Hurley 1st, Thomas Hill 3rd
>
> All-America: Hurley 1st, Grant Hill 2nd
>
> National Defensive Player of the Year: Grant Hill

1993 – 94 Final Four

Record: 28 – 6 overall, 12 – 4 ACC (1st)

Final ranking: No. 6 in AP poll

Postseason: Reached ACC semifinal (1 – 1), reached NCAA championship game (5 – 1)

Top scorers: Grant Hill 17.4, Cherokee Parks 14.4

Team scoring: Duke 77.6, opponents 67.3

Coach: Mike Krzyzewski

Captains: Marty Clark, Grant Hill, Antonio Lang

Lineup: Hill, Lang, Parks, Capel, Collins

Honors

> MVP: Grant Hill
>
> All-ACC: Hill 1st, Parks 2nd, Lang 3rd

ACC Player of the Year: Hill

All-America: Hill 1st

1994 – 95

Record: 13 – 18 overall, 2 – 14 ACC (9th)

Postseason: Reached ACC quarterfinal (1 – 1)

Top scorers: Cherokee Parks 19.0, Jeff Capel 12.5

Team scoring: Duke 77.7, opponents 73.7

Coach: Mike Krzyzewski (9 – 3 record), Pete Gaudet (4 – 15 record)

Captains: Kenny Blakeney, Erik Meek, Cherokee Parks

Lineup: Parks, Price, Meek, Capel, Langdon

Honors

> MVP: Erik Meek, Cherokee Parks
>
> All-ACC: Parks 2nd

1995 – 96

Record: 18 – 13 overall, 8 – 8 ACC (tie 4th)

Postseason: Lost ACC quarterfinal (0 – 1), lost NCAA first round (0 – 1)

Top scorers: Jeff Capel 16.6, Chris Collins 16.3

Team scoring: Duke 75.4, opponents 69.8

Coach: Mike Krzyzewski

Captains: Jeff Capel, Chris Collins

Lineup: Domzalski, Price, Newton, Capel, Collins

Honors

> MVP: Chris Collins
>
> All-ACC: Collins 2nd, Capel 3rd, Price 3rd

1996 – 97

Record: 24 – 9 overall, 12 – 4 ACC (1st)

Final ranking: No. 8 AP poll

Postseason: Lost ACC quarterfinal (0 – 1), reached NCAA second round (1 – 1)

Top scorers: Trajan Langdon 14.3, Jeff Capel 12.4

Team scoring: Duke 79.7, opponents 66.2

Coach: Mike Krzyzewski

Captains: Jeff Capel, Greg Newton, Carmen Wallace

Lineup: Carrawell, McLeod, Capel, Langdon, Wojciechowski

Honors

> MVP: Steve Wojciechowski
>
> All-ACC: Langdon 1st, Wojciechowski 2nd

1997 – 98

Record: 32 – 4 overall, 15 – 1 ACC (1st)

Final ranking: No. 3 AP poll

Postseason: Reached ACC final (2–1), reached NCAA regional final (3–1)

Top scorers: Roshown McLeod 15.3, Trajan Langdon 14.7

Team scoring: Duke 85.6, opponents 64.1

Coach: Mike Krzyzewski

Captains: Trajan Langdon, Roshown McLeod, Steve Wojciechowski

Lineup: McLeod, Battier, Brand, Langdon, Wojciechowski

Honors

    MVP: Roshown McLeod

    All-ACC: Langdon 1st, McLeod 1st, Wojciechowski 3rd

    All-America: Langdon, McLeod

    National Defensive Player of the Year: Wojciechowski

1998–99 Final Four

Record: 37–2 overall, 16–0 ACC (1st)

Final ranking: No. 1 AP poll

Postseason: Won ACC championship (3–0), reached NCAA championship game (5–1)

Top scorers: Elton Brand 17.7, Trajan Langdon 17.3

Team scoring: Duke 91.8, opponents 67.2

Coach: Mike Krzyzewski

Captain: Trajan Langdon

Lineup: Carrawell, Battier, Brand, Langdon, Avery

Honors

    MVP: Elton Brand, Trajan Langdon

    All-ACC: Brand 1st, Langdon 1st, Avery 2nd, Battier 3rd, Carrawell 3rd

    ACC Player of the Year: Brand

    ACC Tournament MVP: Brand

    All-America: Brand 1st, Langdon 2nd

    National Player of the Year: Brand (AP, Naismith, Wooden, NABC, USBWA)

    National Defensive Player of the Year: Battier

1999–2000

Record: 29–5 overall, 15–1 ACC (1st)

Final ranking: No. 1 AP poll

Postseason: Won ACC championship (3–0), reached NCAA regional semifinal (2–1)

Top scorers: Shane Battier 17.4, Chris Carrawell 16.9

Team scoring: Duke 88.0, opponents 71.3

Coach: Mike Krzyzewski

Captains: Shane Battier, Chris Carrawell, Nate James

Lineup: Battier, Carrawell, Boozer, James, Williams

Honors

    MVP: Shane Battier, Chris Carrawell

    All-ACC: Battier 1st, Carrawell 1st, Williams 3rd

    ACC Player of the Year: Carrawell

    ACC Tournament MVP: Williams

    All-America: Carrawell 1st, Battier 2nd

    National Defensive Player of the Year: Battier

2000–01 Final Four

Record: 35–4 overall, 13–3 ACC (tie 1st)

Final ranking: No. 1 AP poll

Postseason: Won ACC championship (3–0), won NCAA championship (6–0)

Top scorers: Jason Williams 21.6, Shane Battier 19.9

Team scoring: Duke 90.7, opponents 70.5

Coach: Mike Krzyzewski

Captains: Shane Battier, Nate James, J. D. Simpson

Lineup: Battier, Dunleavy, Sanders, Duhon, Williams

Honors

    MVP: Shane Battier, Jason Williams

    All-ACC: Battier 1st, Williams 1st, James 3rd

    ACC Player of the Year: Battier

    ACC Tournament MVP: Battier

    ACC Rookie of the Year: Duhon

    All-America: Battier 1st, Williams 1st

    National Player of the Year: Battier (AP, Naismith, Wooden, USBWA), Williams (NABC)

    National Defensive Player of the Year: Battier

    Final Four MVP: Battier

2001–02

Record: 31–4 overall, 13–3 ACC (2nd)

Final ranking: No. 1 AP poll

Postseason: Won ACC championship (3–0), reached NCAA regional semifinal (2–1)

Top scorers: Jason Williams 21.3, Carlos Boozer 18.2, Mike Dunleavy 17.3

Team scoring: Duke 88.9, opponents 69.2

Coach: Mike Krzyzewski

Captains: Carlos Boozer, Mike Dunleavy, Jason Williams

Lineup: Jones, Dunleavy, Boozer, Williams, Duhon

Honors

    MVP: Mike Dunleavy, Jason Williams

    All-ACC: Williams 1st, Boozer 1st, Dunleavy 1st

    ACC Tournament MVP: Boozer

    All-America: Williams 1st, Dunleavy 2nd, Boozer

    National Player of the Year: Williams (AP, Naismith, Wooden, NABC, USBWA)

2002–03

Record: 26–7 overall, 11–5 ACC (tie 2nd)

Final ranking: No. 7 in AP poll

Postseason: Won ACC championship (3–0), reached NCAA regional semifinal (2–1)

Top scorers: Dahntay Jones 17.7, J. J. Redick 15.0

Team scoring: Duke 81.1, opponents 69.6

Coach: Mike Krzyzewski

Captains: Chris Duhon, Nick Horvath, Dahntay Jones

Lineup: Jones, Williams, Redick, Ewing, Duhon

Honors

    MVP: Dahntay Jones

    All-ACC: Jones 1st, Duhon 3rd, Redick 3rd

    ACC Tournament MVP: Ewing

2003–04 Final Four

Record: 31–6 overall, 13–3 ACC (1st)

Final ranking: No. 6 AP poll

Postseason: Reached ACC final (2–1), reached NCAA national semifinal (4–1)

Top scorers: J. J. Redick 15.9, Luol Deng 15.1

Team scoring: Duke 79.8, opponents 65.0

Coach: Mike Krzyzewski

Captains: Chris Duhon, Daniel Ewing, Nick Horvath

Lineup: Deng, Williams, Redick, Ewing, Duhon

Honors

    MVP: Chris Duhon

    All-ACC: Duhon 1st, Redick 2nd, Williams 2nd, Deng 3rd

    All-America: Duhon, Redick, Williams

2004–05 | 100th Season

Record: 27–6 overall, 11–5 ACC (3rd)

Final ranking: No. 3 AP poll

Postseason: Won ACC championship (3–0), reached NCAA regional semifinal (2–1)

Top scorers: J. J. Redick 21.8, Shelden Williams 15.5, Daniel Ewing 15.3

Team scoring: Duke 78.2, opponents 65.2

Coach: Mike Krzyzewski

Captains: Daniel Ewing, Reggie Love, J. J. Redick

Lineup: Randolph, Williams, Redick, Ewing, Dockery

Honors

    MVP: Daniel Ewing, J. J. Redick, Shelden Williams

    All-ACC: Redick 1st, Williams 1st, Ewing 3rd

    ACC Player of the Year: Redick

    ACC Defensive Player of the Year: Williams

    ACC Tournament MVP: Redick

    All-America: Redick 1st, Williams 3rd

    National Player of the Year: Redick (Rupp)

    National Defensive Player of the Year: Williams

2005–06

Record: 32–4 overall, 14–2 ACC (1st)

Final ranking: No. 1 AP poll

Postseason: Won ACC championship (3–0), reached NCAA regional semifinal (2–1)

Top scorers: J. J. Redick 26.8, Shelden Williams 18.8

Team scoring: Duke 81.1, Opponents 68.1

Coach: Mike Krzyzewski

Captains: Sean Dockery, Lee Melchionni, J. J. Redick, Shelden Williams

Lineup: McRoberts, Williams, Redick, Dockery, Paulus

Honors

    MVP: J. J. Redick, Shelden Williams

    All-ACC: Redick 1st, Williams 1st

    ACC Player of the Year: Redick

    ACC Defensive Player of the Year: Williams

    ACC Tournament MVP: Redick

    All-America: Redick 1st, Williams 1st

    National Player of the Year: Redick (AP, Naismith, Wooden, Rupp, co-NABC, co-USBWA)

    National Defensive Player of the Year: Williams

Duke Women Year by Year

Season	Overall	ACC	Place	ACC Tourney	Rank	Postseason	Top Scorer
Coach Emma Jean Howard							
1975 – 76	0 – 14						
1976 – 77	2 – 12						
Coach Debbie Leonard							
1977 – 78	1 – 19	0 – 8	7th	0 – 1			Tara McCarthy 16.6
1978 – 79	11 – 11	3 – 6	5th	0 – 1			Barb Krause 14.5
1979 – 80	14 – 13	5 – 5	4th	0 – 1			Barb Krause 13.1
1980 – 81	12 – 13	3 – 6	6th	0 – 1			Stacy Hurd 13.0
1981 – 82	14 – 15	3 – 8	6th	0 – 1			Stacy Hurd 13.6
1982 – 83	15 – 10	6 – 7	4th	0 – 1			Jennifer Chestnut 14.0
1983 – 84	13 – 14	5 – 9	6th	0 – 1			Candy Mikels 14.3
1984 – 85	19 – 8	7 – 7	5th	1 – 1, reached semis			Chris Moreland 17.6
1985 – 86	21 – 9	9 – 5	3rd	0 – 1		WNIT 1 – 2	Chris Moreland 23.0
1986 – 87	19 – 10	7 – 7	4th	0 – 1		NCAA 1 – 1	Chris Moreland 20.9
1987 – 88	17 – 11	5 – 9	5th	0 – 1			Chris Moreland 18.4
1988 – 89	12 – 16	2 – 12	7th	0 – 1			Sue Harnett 19.5
1989 – 90	15 – 13	4 – 10	6th	0 – 1			Katie Meier 18.9
1990 – 91	16 – 12	6 – 8	5th	0 – 1			Sue Harnett 17.5
1991 – 92	14 – 15	4 – 12	8th	1 – 1, reached quarters			Celeste Lavoie 12.8
Coach Gail Goestenkors							
1992 – 93	12 – 15	3 – 13	9th	0 – 1			Carey Kauffman 12.1
1993 – 94	16 – 11	7 – 9	5th	0 – 1			Carey Kauffman 12.7
1994 – 95	22 – 9	10 – 6	4th	2 – 1, reached final	20	NCAA 1 – 1	Ali Day 16.1
1995 – 96	26 – 7	12 – 4	2nd	2 – 1, reached final	13	NCAA 1 – 1	Tyish Hall 15.1
1996 – 97	19 – 11	9 – 7	5th	1 – 1, reached semis		NCAA 1 – 1	Kira Orr 17.5
1997 – 98	24 – 8	13 – 3	1st	1 – 1, reached semis	8	NCAA 3 – 1	Nicole Erickson 12.8
1998 – 99	29 – 7	15 – 1	1st	1 – 1, reached semis	t10	NCAA 5 – 1, Final Four	Michele VanGorp 16.9
1999 – 2000	28 – 6	12 – 4	2nd	3 – 0, won title	10	NCAA 2 – 1	Georgia Schweitzer 15.6
2000 – 01	30 – 4	13 – 3	1st	3 – 0, won title	5	NCAA 2 – 1	Alana Beard 17.0
2001 – 02	31 – 4	16 – 0	1st	3 – 0, won title	3	NCAA 4 – 1, Final Four	Alana Beard 19.8
2002 – 03	35 – 2	16 – 0	1st	3 – 0, won title	2	NCAA 4 – 1, Final Four	Alana Beard 22.0
2003 – 04	30 – 4	15 – 1	1st	3 – 0, won title	1	NCAA 3 – 1	Alana Beard 19.7
2004 – 05	31 – 5	12 – 2	t1st	2 – 1, reached final	7	NCAA 3 – 1	Monique Currie 17.5
2005 – 06	31 – 4	12 – 2	2nd	1 – 1, reached semis	4	NCAA 5 – 1, Final Four	Monique Currie 16.4

All-Americas: Chris Moreland 1988, Sue Harnett 1991, Michele VanGorp 1999, Georgia Schweitzer 2001, Alana Beard 2002, 2003, 2004, Iciss Tillis 2003, 2004, Monique Currie 2005, 2006

National Player of the Year: Alana Beard 2004 (AP, USBWA, Wade, Wooden)

ACC Athlete of the Year (Mary Garber Award): Alana Beard 2003, 2004

ACC Player of the Year: Chris Moreland 1987, Georgia Schweitzer 2000, 2001, Alana Beard 2002, 2003, 2004, Monique Currie 2005

ACC Rookie of the Year: Chris Moreland 1985, Katie Meier 1986, Alana Beard 2001

ACC Coach of the Year: Debbie Leonard 1986, Gail Goestenkors 1996, 1998, 1999, 2002, 2003, 2004

ACC Tournament MVP: Georgia Schweitzer 2001, Monique Currie 2002, Iciss Tillis 2003, 2004

Center Alison Bales held the school shot-blocking record entering her senior year of 2007.

Individual Records

Scoring and rebounding statistics at Duke date back over 50 years, but other statistics such as assists, steals, blocked shots, and minutes played were not compiled until the 1970s or later. The three-point field goal was used as an experiment in 1983 and added permanently to the game in 1987.

(A = ACC record, N = NCAA record)

Most Points Scored

Game

58	Danny Ferry	versus Miami December 10, 1988
48	Dick Groat	versus North Carolina February 29, 1952
46	Dick Groat	versus George Washington February 2, 1952
43	Jeff Mullins	versus Villanova March 13, 1964
42	Tate Armstrong	versus Clemson February 25, 1976
41	J. J. Redick	versus Georgetown, January 21, 2006
41	J. J. Redick	versus Texas, December 10, 2005
41	Bob Verga	versus Ohio State, December 29, 1966
40	Tate Armstrong	versus N.C. State, February 18, 1976
40	Art Heyman	versus North Carolina, February 23, 1963
40	Dick Groat	versus South Carolina, February 23, 1952

Season

964	J. J. Redick	2006
841	Jason Williams	2001
831	Dick Groat	1951
809	Johnny Dawkins	1986
791	Danny Ferry	1989

Career

2,769	J. J. Redick	2003 – 06
2,556	Johnny Dawkins	1983 – 86
2,460	Christian Laettner	1989 – 92
2,323	Mike Gminski	1977 – 80
2,155	Danny Ferry	1986 – 89

Best Scoring Average

Season

26.8	J. J. Redick (A)	2006
26.1	Bob Verga	1967
26.0	Dick Groat	1952
25.3	Art Heyman	1962
25.2	Dick Groat	1951
25.2	Art Heyman	1961

Career

25.1	Art Heyman	1961 – 63
23.0	Dick Groat	1950 – 52
22.0	Bob Verga	1965 – 67
21.9	Jeff Mullins	1962 – 64
19.9	J. J. Redick	2003 – 06

Most Rebounds

Game

31	Bernie Janicki	versus North Carolina, February 29, 1952
25	Randy Denton	versus Northwestern, December 29, 1970
24	Mike Lewis	versus Wake Forest, February 21, 1967
24	Art Heyman	versus North Carolina, February 23, 1963
24	Paul Schmidt	versus Wake Forest, February 15, 1958

Season

476	Bernie Janicki	1952
402	Mike Lewis	1968
385	Randy Denton	1971
384	Shelden Williams	2006
382	Elton Brand	1999

Career

1,262	Shelden Williams	2003 – 06
1,242	Mike Gminski	1977 – 80
1,149	Christian Laettner	1989 – 92
1,067	Randy Denton	1969 – 71
1,051	Mike Lewis	1966 – 68

Best Rebounding Average

Season

15.9	Bernie Janicki	1952
14.4	Mike Lewis	1968
12.8	Randy Denton	1971
12.8	Randy Denton	1969
12.5	Randy Denton	1970

Career

12.7	Randy Denton	1969 – 71
12.5	Mike Lewis	1966 – 68
11.1	Bernie Janicki	1952 – 54
10.9	Art Heyman	1961 – 63
10.5	Bob Fleischer	1973 – 75

Most Assists (since 1969)

Game

16	Bobby Hurley	versus Florida State, February 24, 1993
15	Greg Paulus	versus Valparaiso, December 18, 2005
15	Bobby Hurley	versus UCLA, February 28, 1993
15	Bobby Hurley	versus N.C. State, February 21, 1993
15	Bobby Hurley	versus Oklahoma, January 4, 1993

Season

289	Bobby Hurley	1991
288	Bobby Hurley	1990
262	Bobby Hurley	1993
241	Tommy Amaker	1986
237	Jason Williams	2001
237	Bobby Hurley	1992

Career

1,076	Bobby Hurley (N)	1990 – 93
819	Chris Duhon	2001 – 04
708	Tommy Amaker	1984 – 87
644	Jason Williams	2000 – 02
575	Quin Snyder	1986 – 89

Most Steals (since 1976)

Game

11	Kenny Dennard (A)	versus Maryland, February 3, 1979
8	Steve Wojciechowski	versus Vanderbilt, November 22, 1996
8	Grant Hill	versus California, March 20, 1993

Season

93	Jim Spanarkel	1978
82	Shane Battier	2001
82	Steve Wojciechowski	1997
81	Chris Duhon	2002
81	Jason Williams	2000
81	Tommy Amaker	1986

Career

300	Chris Duhon	2001 – 04
266	Shane Battier	1998 – 2001
259	Tommy Amaker	1984 – 87
253	Jim Spanarkel	1976 – 79
243	Christian Laettner	1989 – 92

Most Blocked Shots (since 1976)

Game

10	Shelden Williams	versus Maryland, January 11, 2006
10	Cherokee Parks	versus Clemson, March 11, 1994
9	Shelden Williams	versus Davidson, November 19, 2005

9	Shelden Williams	versus Virginia, January 16, 2005
9	Mike Gminski	versus Wake Forest, November 30, 1979
9	Mike Gminski	versus Davidson, January 2, 1979
9	Mike Gminski	versus N.C. State, February 15, 1978
9	Mike Gminski	versus Davidson, January 5, 1977

Season

137	Shelden Williams	2006
122	Shelden Williams	2005
111	Shelden Williams	2004
97	Mike Gminski	1980
92	Mike Gminski	1978

Career

422	Shelden Williams	2003 – 06
345	Mike Gminski	1977 – 80
254	Shane Battier	1998 – 2001
231	Cherokee Parks	1992 – 95
145	Christian Laettner	1989 – 92

Most Field Goals Made

Game

23	Danny Ferry	versus Miami, December 10, 1988
19	Jeff Mullins	versus Villanova, March 13, 1964
19	Dick Groat	versus North Carolina, February 29, 1952
18	Tate Armstrong	versus Clemson, February 25, 1976
18	Jack Marin	versus Wake Forest, January 15, 1966

Season

331	Johnny Dawkins (A)	1986
302	J. J. Redick	2006
300	Danny Ferry	1989
300	Jeff Mullins	1964
288	Dick Groat	1952

Career

1,026	Johnny Dawkins (A)	1983 – 86
901	Mike Gminski	1977 – 80
834	Christian Laettner	1989 – 92
828	Mark Alarie	1983 – 86
827	Gene Banks	1978 – 81

Best Field-Goal Percentage

Game

100.0	Carlos Boozer	11 – 11 versus Portland, December 19, 2000
100.0	Christian Laettner	10 – 10 versus Kentucky, March 28, 1992
100.0	Mike Gminski	10 – 10 versus Johns Hopkins, November 30, 1976

Season (min. 100 FGs made)

72.3	Christian Laettner	115 – 159 in 1989
66.5	Carlos Boozer	230 – 346 in 2002
65.2	Cherokee Parks	161 – 247 in 1993
63.4	Alaa Abdelnaby	123 – 194 in 1989
62.1	Erik Meek	118 – 190 in 1995

Career (min. 300 FGs made)

63.1	Carlos Boozer	2000 – 02
61.2	Elton Brand	1998 – 99
59.9	Alaa Abdelnaby	1987 – 90
57.4	Christian Laettner	1989 – 92
57.2	Shelden Williams	2003 – 06

Most Free Throws Made

Game

20	Bucky Allen	versus N.C. State, January 5, 1957
19	Joe Belmont	versus Pennsylvania, December 16, 1955
18	Jim Spanarkel	versus N.C. State, February 15, 1978
18	Jim Spanarkel	versus North Carolina, December 2, 1977

17	Mike Gminski	versus N.C. State, January 21, 1979
17	Dick Groat	versus Davidson, January 29, 1951

Season

261	Dick Groat	1951
225	Christian Laettner	1990
221	J. J. Redick	2006
220	Jim Spanarkel	1978
217	Art Heyman	1963

Career

713	Christian Laettner	1989 – 92
662	J. J. Redick	2003 – 06
564	Jim Spanarkel	1976 – 79
558	Art Heyman	1961 – 63
550	Shelden Williams	2003 – 06

Best Free-Throw Percentage

Game

100.0	Dick Groat	17 – 17 versus Davidson, January 29, 1951
100.0	J. J. Redick	14 – 14 versus Princeton, January 5, 2005
100.0	Gene Banks	14 – 14 versus N.C. State, February 28, 1980
100.0	Elton Brand	13 – 13 versus N.C. A&T, December 20, 1998
100.0	Christian Laettner	13 – 13 versus St. John's, December 5, 1991
100.0	Christian Laettner	13 – 13 versus Maryland, January 13, 1990
100.0	Steve Vandenberg	13 – 13 versus North Carolina, March 1, 1969
100.0	Mike Lewis	13 – 13 versus Vanderbilt, December 13, 1966

Season (min. 100 FTs made)

95.3	J. J. Redick (A)	143 – 150 in 2004
93.8	J. J. Redick	196 – 209 in 2005
91.9	J. J. Redick	102 – 111 in 2003
89.7	Trajan Langdon	113 – 126 in 1997
88.6	Trajan Langdon	101 – 114 in 1998

Career (min. 200 FTs made)

91.2	J. J. Redick (A)	2003 – 06
86.2	Trajan Langdon	1995 – 99
84.3	Tom Emma	1980 – 83
80.7	Chris Redding	1972 – 74
80.6	Christian Laettner	1989 – 92
80.6	Jim Spanarkel	1976 – 79

Most Three-Pointers Made

Game

9	J. J. Redick	versus Texas, December 10, 2005
9	Shane Battier	versus Princeton, November 14, 2000
8	J. J. Redick	versus Virginia, January 26, 2006
8	J. J. Redick	versus Florida State, January 22, 2005
8	Jason Williams	versus North Carolina, March 3, 2002
8	Jason Williams	versus Florida State, January 6, 2002
8	Jason Williams	versus Temple, December 2, 2000
8	William Avery	versus Florida, December 9, 1998

Season

139	J. J. Redick (A)	2006
132	Jason Williams	2001
124	Shane Battier	2001
121	J. J. Redick	2005
112	Trajan Langdon	1999

Career

457	J. J. Redick (N)	2003 – 06
342	Trajan Langdon	1995 – 99

313	Jason Williams	2000 – 02
264	Bobby Hurley	1990 – 93
246	Shane Battier	1998 – 2001

[Note: The three-point shot was used experimentally in 1983 and permanently beginning in 1987.]

Best Three-Point Percentage

Game (min. 5 attempted)

85.7	J. J. Redick	6 – 7 versus Georgia Tech, February 26, 2003
85.7	Trajan Langdon	6 – 7 versus St. Joseph's, November 20, 1996
85.7	Bobby Hurley	6 – 7 versus Southern Illinois, March 18, 1993

Season (min. 35 made)

55.7	Christian Laettner (A)	54 – 97 in 1992
55.4	Chip Engelland	41 – 74 in 1983
46.0	Jeff Capel	63 – 137 in 1995
44.6	Quin Snyder	41 – 92 in 1988
44.4	Shane Battier	79 – 178 in 2000

Career (min. 75 made)

48.5	Christian Laettner	1989 – 92
42.6	Trajan Langdon	1995 – 99
41.6	Shane Battier	1998 – 2001
40.6	J. J. Redick	2003 – 06
40.5	Bobby Hurley	1990 – 93

Most Shots Attempted

Field Goals, Game

| 37 | Dick Groat | versus North Carolina, February 29, 1952 |

Free Throws, Game

| 24 | Art Heyman | versus Navy, February 18, 1961 |
| 24 | Joe Belmont | versus Pennsylvania, December 16, 1955 |

Three-Pointers, Game

| 18 | Bobby Hurley | versus California, March 20, 1993 |

Field Goals, Season

| 713 | Dick Groat | 1951 |

Free Throws, Season

| 331 | Dick Groat | 1951 |

Three-Pointers, Season

| 330 | J. J. Redick | 2006 |

Field Goals, Career

| 2,019 | Johnny Dawkins (A) | 1983 – 86 |

Free Throws, Career

| 885 | Christian Laettner | 1989 – 92 |

Three-Pointers, Career

| 1,126 | J. J. Redick (A) | 2003 – 06 |

Most Games Played

Season

40	Mark Alarie (N)	1986
40	Tommy Amaker (N)	1986
40	Johnny Dawkins (N)	1986
40	Danny Ferry (N)	1986
40	Billy King (N)	1986

Career

148	Christian Laettner (A)	1989 – 92
147	Greg Koubek	1988 – 91
146	Shane Battier	1998 – 2001
144	Chris Duhon	2001 – 04
143	Danny Ferry	1986 – 89

Most Minutes Played

Game

53	Chip Engelland	versus Clemson, February 24, 1982
51	Vince Taylor	versus Clemson, February 24, 1982
50	Ed Koffenberger	versus NYU, January 9, 1947

| 49 | Christian Laettner | versus Arizona, February 24, 1991 |
| 48 | Cherokee Parks | versus North Carolina, February 2, 1995 |

Season

1,363	Shane Battier	2001
1,353	Bobby Hurley	1991
1,336	J. J. Redick	2006
1,324	Johnny Dawkins	1986
1,311	Chris Duhon	2004

Career

4,813	Chris Duhon (A)	2001 – 04
4,802	Bobby Hurley	1990 – 93
4,749	Johnny Dawkins	1983 – 86
4,732	J. J. Redick	2003 – 06
4,666	Tommy Amaker	1984 – 87

Most Wins Participated In

Career

131	Shane Battier (A)	1998 – 2001
123	Chris Duhon	2001 – 04
122	Christian Laettner	1989 – 92
117	Nate James	1997 – 2001
117	Danny Ferry	1986 – 89

Most Double-Figures Scoring Games, Career

129	Johnny Dawkins (A)	1983 – 86
122	J. J. Redick	2003 – 06
118	Christian Laettner	1989 – 92
118	Mark Alarie	1983 – 86
111	Grant Hill	1991 – 94
111	Mike Gminski	1977 – 80

Most Consecutive Games Played

| 144 | Chris Duhon | 2001 – 04 |

Most Consecutive Games Started

| 138 | Tommy Amaker | 1984 – 87 |

Most Consecutive Games Scoring in Double Figures

| 86 | Jeff Mullins (A) | 1962 – 64 |

Most Consecutive Field Goals Made

| 20 | Alaa Abdelnaby (A) 4 games, November 19 – December 3, 1988 |

Most Consecutive Free Throws Made

| 54 | J. J. Redick (A) 17 games, March 20, 2003 – January 15, 2004 |

Team Records

(A = ACC record, N = NCAA record)

Season

Most Games Played: 40 in 1986 (N)

Most Wins: 37 in 1999 and in 1986 (N)

Most Losses: 18 in 1995

Most ACC Wins: 16 in 1999 (A)

Most ACC Losses: 14 in 1995

Best Winning Percentage: 94.9 in 1999 (37 – 2)

Most Wins to Open Season: 17 in 1992 and 2006

Longest Winning Streak: 32 games (December 2, 1998 – March 29, 1999)

Longest ACC Winning Streak: 31 games (February 8, 1998 – February 9, 2000)

Longest Home Winning Streak: 46 games (January 13, 1997 – February 9, 2000)

Longest Non-conference Home Winning Streak: 95 games (February 2, 1983 – December 2, 1995)

Longest Losing Streak: 8 games in 1922

Longest ACC Losing Streak: 9 games in 1995

Highest Scoring Average: 92.4 in 1965

Highest Average Scoring Margin: 24.6 in 1999 (A)

Highest Scoring Average by Opponents: 85.0 in 1976

Lowest Scoring Average by Opponents (since 1951): 63.2 in 1960

Best Field-Goal Percentage: 53.7 in 1989

Lowest Field-Goal Percentage by Opponents: 33.1 in 1952

Best Three-Point Field-Goal Percentage: 43.4 in 1992

Best Free-Throw Percentage: 79.1 in 1978

Highest Rebounding Average: 58.6 in 1952

Highest Rebounding Margin: 12.7 in 1966

Most Three-Pointers Made: 407 in 2001 (N)

Most Assists: 701 in 2001

Most Blocked Shots: 245 in 1999 (A)

Most Steals: 411 in 2001

Most Overtime Games: 5 in 2000, 1980, and 1958

Highest Attendance: 650,550 for 39 games of 2001 season (16,681 average)

Game

Most Points Scored: 136 versus Virginia, February 11, 1965

Most Points Scored by Opponent: 122 by Wake Forest, January 22, 1975

Fewest Points Scored (since 1955): 10 versus N.C. State, March 8, 1968 (A)

Fewest Points by Opponent (since 1955): 12 by N.C. State, March 8, 1968

Largest Victory Margin: 80 versus Furman, 1910 (85 – 5)

Largest Victory Margin versus ACC Opponent: 64 versus Virginia, February 11, 1965 (136 – 72)

Largest Defeat Margin: 75 versus Washington & Lee, 1913 (15 – 90)

Largest Defeat Margin versus ACC Opponent: 43 versus Virginia, March 11, 1983 (66 – 109)

Largest Combined Score: 231 versus Wake Forest, January 22, 1975 (109 – 122)

Largest Halftime Margin: 42 versus Clemson, January 29, 2000 (58 – 16), and versus Harvard, November 25, 1989 (72 – 30)

Largest Halftime Deficit: 29 versus Tulane, December 30, 1950 (27 – 56)

Most Points in One Half: 72 versus Harvard, November 25, 1989, and versus Virginia, February 11, 1965

Fewest Points in One Half (since 1955): 4 versus N.C. State, March 8, 1968

Most Opponent Points in One Half: 66 by Wake Forest, January 22, 1975, and by George Washington, December 22, 1952

Fewest Points by Opponent in One Half (since 1955): 0 by North Carolina, February 24, 1979

Most Field Goals Made: 55 versus Virginia, February 11, 1965

Most Field Goals Attempted: 102 versus N.C. State, March 5, 1955

Best Field-Goal Percentage: 74.5 versus Johns Hopkins, November 26, 1977 (41 – 55)

Most Three-Point Field Goals Made: 18 versus Monmouth, March 15, 2001, and versus N.C. A&T, December 30, 2000

Most Three-Point Field Goals Attempted: 38 versus Monmouth, March 15, 2001, versus North Carolina, March 4, 2001, and versus N.C. A&T, December 30, 2000

Best Three-Point Field-Goal Percentage: 90.9 versus Clemson, February 1, 1988 (10 – 11) (A)

Most Free Throws Made: 42 versus Fairfield, November 14, 1998, and versus Pennsylvania, December 22, 1980

Most Free Throws Attempted: 61 versus Davidson, December 16, 1952, and versus Vanderbilt, December 1, 1952

Best Free-Throw Percentage: 100.0 several times — most attempts, 29 – 29 versus Virginia Tech, December 2, 1966

Most Rebounds: 76 versus Wake Forest, February 14, 1968, and versus Virginia, February 9, 1956

Most Assists: 33 versus Miami, February 19, 1986

Most Blocked Shots: 18 versus Illinois-Chicago, December 14, 2004 (A)

Most Steals: 22 versus Davidson, November 20, 1997

Largest Deficit Overcome to Win Game: 32 points versus Tulane, December 30, 1950 (trailed 54 – 22 in first half) (N)

Most Overtimes: 3 versus Clemson, February 24, 1982, versus North Carolina, March 2, 1968, and versus Virginia, February 25, 1958

Largest Attendance: 50,379 versus Michigan, April 6, 1992, and versus Indiana, April 4, 1992, at NCAA Final Four in Minneapolis

Women's Individual Records

(A = ACC record, N = NCAA record)

Most Points Scored

Game	43	Monique Currie	versus Miami, February 19, 2006 (2 OT)
	41	Alana Beard	versus Virginia, January 9, 2003 (regulation)
Season	813	Alana Beard	2003
Career	2,687	Alana Beard	2001–04

Best Scoring Average

Season	23.0	Chris Moreland	1986
Career	20.1	Chris Moreland	1985–88

Most Rebounds

Game	24	Barb Krause	versus Catawba, January 10, 1979
Season	354	Chris Moreland	1986
Career	1,229	Chris Moreland	1985–88

Best Rebounding Average

Season	12.3	Chris Moreland	1988
Career	11.1	Chris Moreland (A)	1985–88

Most Assists

Game

12	Monique Currie	versus Georgia Tech, February 7, 2004
12	Katie Meier	versus N.C. State, January 10, 1990
12	Leigh Morgan	versus California, December 27, 1988

Season

170	Kira Orr	1996

Career

533	Hilary Howard	1996–99

Most Steals

Game

9	Missy Anderson	versus Drake, December 28, 1992
9	Kim Matthews	versus Davidson, February 12, 1979

Season

114	Alana Beard	2002

Career

404	Alana Beard	2001–04

Most Blocked Shots

Game

11	Sarah Sullivan (A)	versus Richmond, January 22, 1983

Season

134	Alison Bales (A)	2005

Career

283	Alison Bales	2004–06 (active)

Most Field Goals Made

Game

16	Alana Beard	versus Virginia, January 9, 2003
16	Sue Harnett	versus VCU, December 10, 1988

Season

294	Alana Beard	2003

Career

1,005	Alana Beard	2001–04

Best Field-Goal Percentage

Game

100.0	Sheana Mosch (A)	12 – 12 versus Clemson, January 28, 2001
100.0	Tyish Hall	9 – 9 versus Oklahoma State, March 16, 1995
100.0	Kathy Friend	9 – 9 versus North Carolina, February 24, 1978

Season

65.5	Tyish Hall (A)	216 – 330 in 1996

Career

63.0	Tyish Hall (A)	1994 – 97

Most Free Throws Made

Game

15	Monique Currie	versus Miami, February 19, 2006 (2 OT)
15	Nicole Johnson	versus Wake Forest, February 26, 1992

Season

201	Alana Beard	2003

Career

582	Alana Beard (A)	2001 – 04

Best Free-Throw Percentage

Game

100.0	Monique Currie	14 – 14 versus North Carolina, March 4, 2002

Season

90.0	Jenni Kraft	90 – 100 in 1989

Career

88.0	Nicole Erickson (A)	1998 – 99

Most Three-Pointers Made

Game

7	Jessica Foley	versus Georgia Tech, January 17, 2005
7	Nicole Erickson	versus Clemson, January 14, 1999

Season

68	Jessica Foley	2005

Career

202	Georgia Schweitzer	1998 – 2001

Best Three-Point Percentage

Game

100.0	Nicole Erickson	6 – 6 versus Notre Dame, November 22, 1997

Season

53.9	Jenni Kraft (A)	41 – 76 in 1989

Career

42.9	Ali Day	1993 – 96

Most Shots Attempted

Field Goals, Game

30	Alana Beard	versus Virginia, January 9, 2003

Field Goals, Season

558	Alana Beard	2003

Field Goals, Career

1,906	Alana Beard	2001 – 04

Free Throws, Game

22	Tara McCarthy	versus North Carolina, February 24, 1978

Free Throws, Season

267	Chris Moreland (A)	1986

Free Throws, Career

868	Chris Moreland (A)	1985 – 88

Three-Pointers, Game

13	Kira Orr	versus Illinois, March 16, 1997

Three-Pointers, Season

191   Jessica Foley   2005

Three-Pointers, Career

504   Georgia Schweitzer   1998 – 2001

Most Games Played

Season

37   Alana Beard (A)   2003
     Lindsey Harding
     Sheana Mosch
     Iciss Tillis
     Wynter Whitley
     Mistie Williams

Career

142   Mistie Williams   2003 – 06

Most Minutes Played

Game

60   Jennifer Scanlon   versus Alabama,
                        March 18, 1995

Season

1,164   Alana Beard   2002

Career

4,285   Alana Beard   2001 – 04

Most Wins Participated In

Career

125   Mistie Williams   2003 – 06

Most Games Scoring in Double Figures

Season

36   Alana Beard   2003

Career

127   Alana Beard   2001 – 04

Most Consecutive Games Played

142   Mistie Williams   2003 – 06

Most Consecutive Games Started

118   Alana Beard   2001 – 04

Most Consecutive Free Throws Made

32   Nicole Erickson
     14 games, January 22 – March 20, 1999

Most Consecutive Games Scoring in Double Figures

67   Chris Moreland   1986 – 88

Most Consecutive Games Scoring at Least 20 Points

11   Chris Moreland   1986

Top Ten Scoring Games

43   Monique Currie   versus Miami,
                       February 19, 2006
41   Alana Beard   versus Virginia,
                       January 9, 2003
37   Ali Day   versus Alabama,
                       March 18, 1995
37   Sue Harnett   versus VCU,
                       December 10, 1988
36   Katie Meier   versus N.C. State,
                       February 3, 1987
35   Alana Beard   versus Maryland,
                       January 2, 2002
35   Michele VanGorp   versus Clemson,
                       February 14, 1999
35   Carey Kauffman   versus UNC Asheville,
                       November 30, 1994
34   Chris Moreland   versus Northwestern State,
                       March 21, 1986
34   Chris Moreland   versus Radford,
                       January 4, 1986
34   Chris Moreland   versus Indiana State,
                       December 30, 1985

Women's Team Records

(A = ACC record, N = NCAA record)

Season

Most Games Played: 37 in 2003 (A)

Most Wins: 35 in 2003 (A)

Most Losses: 19 in 1978

Most ACC Wins: 16 in 2002 and 2003 (A)

Most ACC Losses: 13 in 1993

Best Winning Percentage: 94.6 in 2003 (35–2) (A)

Most Wins to Open Season: 20 in 2003 and 2006

Longest Winning Streak: 22 games (December 30, 2001–March 29, 2002)

Longest ACC Winning Streak: 42 games (February 22, 2001–February 4, 2004, regular season only; 51 games including tournaments) (A)

Longest Home Winning Streak: 21 games (December 16, 2001–February 1, 2003)

Longest Losing Streak: 16 games (December 3, 1975–January 29, 1977)

Longest ACC Losing Streak: 11 games (twice, over the 1988–89 and 1992–93 seasons)

Highest Scoring Average: 86.0 in 2006

Highest Average Scoring Margin: 27.8 in 2006

Best Field-Goal Percentage: 49.8 in 2006

Best Three-Point Field-Goal Percentage: 40.6 in 1989

Best Free-Throw Percentage: 76.0 in 2002 (A)

Highest Rebounding Average: 45.2 in 1986

Most Three-Pointers Made: 213 in 1999

Most Assists: 717 in 2006

Most Blocked Shots: 267 in 2005 and 2006 (N)

Most Steals: 462 in 2003

Most Overtime Games: 2 (several times)

Top Home Attendance: 93,553 in 2004 for 15 games (6,237 average)

Game

Most Points Scored: 128 versus Howard, December 6, 2002

Fewest Points Scored: 31 versus East Carolina, January 20, 1976

Most Points Scored by Opponent: 125 by N.C. State, January 19, 1978

Fewest Points Scored by Opponent: 24 by Ball State, December 19, 2005

Largest Victory Margin: 86 points versus Ball State, December 19, 2005 (110–24)

Largest Defeat Margin: 82 points versus N.C. State, January 19, 1978 (125–43)

Largest Combined Score: 241 versus Alabama, March 18, 1995 (121–120), 4 OT

Most Points in One Half: 70 versus Stephen F. Austin, November 29, 2003

Fewest Points in One Half: 12 versus Virginia, January 30, 2000

Most Points by Opponent in One Half: 63 by Clemson, January 9, 1980

Fewest Points by Opponent in One Half: 6 by Catawba, January 10, 1979

Most Field Goals Made: 51 versus Howard, December 6, 2002

Most Field Goals Attempted: 97 versus Morgan State, November 26, 1993

Best Field-Goal Percentage: 68.2 versus Arkansas State, November 25, 2005

Most Three-Point Field Goals Made: 13 versus San Diego, December 30, 2005; versus St. John's, December 28, 2005; versus Georgia Tech, January 17, 2005

Most Three-Point Field Goals Attempted: 30 versus Illinois, March 16, 1997, and versus Georgia Tech, January 17, 2005

Best Three-Point Field-Goal Percentage: 100.0 versus New Hampshire, December 1, 1989 (4–4)

Most Free Throws Made: 40 versus Cheyney State, December 28, 1985 (A)

Most Free Throws Attempted: 49 versus Cheyney State, December 28, 1985

Best Free-Throw Percentage: 94.1 versus Drake, December 27, 1992 (16–17)

Most Rebounds: 68 versus Catawba, January 10, 1979

Most Assists: 36 versus San Diego, December 30, 2006

Most Blocked Shots: 16 versus Ball State, December 20, 2004 (A)

Most Steals: 25, three times, last versus Tulsa, December 21, 2002

Most Overtimes: 4 versus Alabama, March 18, 1995

Top Attendance: 29,619 versus Oklahoma, March 29, 2002 at NCAA Final Four in San Antonio

Top Attendance for ACC Game: 17,243 for Duke at Maryland, February 13, 2005

Progression of Records

This section charts the progression of Duke single-game and career records in points, rebounds, and assists. Each list begins with the earliest known record holder in the category and notes who subsequently tied or broke that record, culminating with the current mark (through 2006). Of the records listed, the longest-held is Bernie Janicki's single-game rebounding mark, on the books for over 50 years. It was set in 1952, the first year that Duke began compiling rebounding statistics. Duke compiled assists totals during the 1952 season, but then not again until 1969.

Scoring, Game

30	Ed Koffenberger	versus Washington & Lee, February 4, 1947
31	Dick Groat	versus Hanes Hosiery, December 2, 1950
34	Dick Groat	versus Washington & Lee, December 16, 1950
36	Dick Groat	versus N.C. State, January 6, 1951
37	Dick Groat	versus Davidson, January 29, 1951
46	Dick Groat	versus George Washington, February 2, 1952
48	Dick Groat	versus North Carolina, February 29, 1952
58	Danny Ferry	versus Miami, December 10, 1988

Rebounds, Game

31	Bernie Janicki	versus North Carolina, February 29, 1952

Assists, Game

11	Dick DeVenzio	versus Clemson, December 28, 1968
12	Dick DeVenzio	versus N.C. State, January 25, 1969
12	Gary Melchionni	versus Virginia, February 13, 1973
14	Kevin Billerman	versus North Carolina, March 2, 1974
14	Tommy Amaker	versus Miami, February 19, 1986
14	Bobby Hurley	versus LSU, February 10, 1991
15	Bobby Hurley	versus Oklahoma, January 4, 1993
15	Bobby Hurley	versus N.C. State, February 21, 1993
16	Bobby Hurley	versus Florida State, February 24, 1993

Scoring, Career

558	Joe Croson	1931
619	Jim Thompson	1934
683	Gordon Carver	1945
791	John Seward	1947
923	Ed Koffenberger	1947
973	Corren Youmans	1950
1,886	Dick Groat	1952
1,984	Art Heyman	1963
2,012	Jim Spanarkel	1979
2,323	Mike Gminski	1980
2,556	Johnny Dawkins	1986
2,769	J. J. Redick	2006

In 1947 Seward passed Carver to take possession of the record for about a month, until he was passed by Koffenberger.

Groat became the first 1,000-point scorer on February 23, 1951, with a 29-point game versus North Carolina.

Spanarkel became the first 2,000-point scorer on March 11, 1979, with a 16-point game versus St. John's.

Dawkins passed Gminski on March 2, 1986, during his final home game versus North Carolina.

Redick broke Dawkins's mark with a three-pointer against Miami on February 19, 2006.

Rebounds, Career

923	Bernie Janicki	1954
954	Ronnie Mayer	1956
1,051	Mike Lewis	1968
1,067	Randy Denton	1971
1,242	Mike Gminski	1980
1,262	Shelden Williams	2006

Lewis became the first to reach 1,000 rebounds on February 28, 1968, with 18 rebounds versus N.C. State.

Williams passed Gminski with 14 rebounds versus George Washington on March 18, 2006.

Assists, Career

229	Dick Groat	1952
388	Dick DeVenzio	1971
399	Jim Spanarkel	1979
426	Johnny Dawkins	1985
516	Johnny Dawkins*	1986
588	Tommy Amaker*	1986
708	Tommy Amaker	1987
1,076	Bobby Hurley	1993

Hurley became the first player to reach 1,000 assists on February 21, 1993, with 15 assists at N.C. State. He became the NCAA career assists leader on March 3, 1993, against Maryland, on a basket scored by Erik Meek.

*Dawkins was the career leader with 426 assists entering the 1986 season. He became the first to reach 500 assists on February 6, 1986, versus Virginia. Amaker reached 500 assists two games later, versus Stetson on February 11, 1986. Dawkins held the career record at 516 entering the Miami game on February 19, 1986, when he was caught and passed by Amaker, who had 14 assists against the Hurricanes. Amaker finished the 1986 season with 588 career assists (to Dawkins's 555) and extended his record to 708 by the end of the 1987 season.

Coaching Records

This section lists the won-lost records of every head coach in Duke basketball history, arranged in order of the number of games coached. Conference records refer to regular-season conference games, while conference titles reflect the number of tournament champion- ships won. Mike Krzyzewski and Pete Gaudet are each credited for one season for the 1995 campaign, in which Gaudet was named to replace Krzyzewski for reasons of health at midyear.

Coach	Years	Seasons	Games	Overall Record	Winning Percentage	Conference Record	Titles
Mike Krzyzewski	1981–2006	26	871	680–191	78.1	264–115	10
Eddie Cameron	1929–42	14	325	226–99	69.5	119–56	3
Vic Bubas	1960–69	10	280	213–67	76.1	106–32	4
Harold Bradley	1951–59	9	245	167–78	68.2	94–37	
Gerry Gerard	1943–50	8	209	131–78	62.7	66–30	2
Bill Foster	1975–80	6	177	113–64	63.8	31–43	2
Bucky Waters	1970–73	4	108	63–45	58.3	27–25	
George Buckheit	1925–28	4	61	25–36	41.0		
W. W. "Cap" Card	1906–12	7	47	30–17	63.8		
Jesse S. Burbage	1923–24	2	47	34–13	72.3		
Noble L. Clay	1914–15	2	40	22–18	55.0		
Chick Doak	1917–18	2	39	30–9	76.9		
Neill McGeachy	1974	1	26	10–16	38.5	2–10	
Bob Doak	1916	1	20	9–11	45.0		
Joseph E. Brinn	1913	1	19	11–8	57.9		
Pete Gaudet	1995	1	19	4–15	21.1	2–13	
James Baldwin	1922	1	18	6–12	33.3		
Floyd Egan	1921	1	15	9–6	60.0		
Walter Rothensies	1920	1	14	10–4	71.4		
Henry P. Cole	1919	1	11	6–5	54.5		
Duke Women Coaches							
Gail Goestenkors	1993–2006	14	461	364–97	79.0	165–55	5
Debbie Leonard	1978–92	15	402	213–189	53.0	69–119	
Emma Jean Howard	1976–77	2	28	2–26	7.1		

Standout Opponent Marks

Top Scoring Games versus Duke

47   Ernie Beck, Penn
December 30, 1952

45   Don Hennon, Pittsburgh
December 21, 1957

45   Kenny Carr, N.C. State
January 2, 1976

44   Dickie Hemric, Wake Forest
February 12, 1953

44   Kenny Higgs, LSU
December 20, 1974

44   Kenny Carr, N.C. State
January 24, 1976

43   Grady Wallace, South Carolina
February 23, 1957

42   Buzz Wilkinson, Virginia
March 4, 1954

41   Grady Wallace, South Carolina
March 7, 1957

41   Jack Givens, Kentucky
March 27, 1978

41   Len Bias, Maryland
January 25, 1986

40   Marvis Thornton, St. John's
January 24, 1999 (most recent of several times)

Top All-Time Points Scored versus Duke

270   Dickie Hemric, Wake Forest, 1953 – 55 (9 games)
255   Len Chappell, Wake Forest, 1960 – 62 (10 games)
251   Lennie Rosenbluth, North Carolina, 1955 – 57 (9 games)
251   Phil Ford, North Carolina, 1975 – 78 (11 games)
240   Bob Leonard, Wake Forest, 1964 – 66 (10 games)
237   Len Bias, Maryland, 1983 – 86 (10 games)
228   Rod Griffin, Wake Forest, 1975 – 78 (13 games)
222   Al Wood, North Carolina, 1978 – 81 (14 games)
217   Kenny Carr, N.C. State, 1975 – 77 (8 games)

Top Rebounding Games versus Duke

26   Clyde Lee, Vanderbilt
December 11, 1963

24   Sean May, North Carolina
March 6, 2005

23   Len Chappell, Wake Forest
February 3, 1960

22   Len Chappell, Wake Forest
February 15, 1962

22   Lew Alcindor, UCLA
December 10, 1966

21   Ronnie Shavlik, N.C. State
March 5, 1955

21   Tom Owens, South Carolina
February 1, 1969

21   Bobby Jones, North Carolina
January 20, 1973

21   Sean May, North Carolina
February 5, 2004

20   Horace Grant, Clemson
February 26, 1986 (most recent of several times)

Top Assists Games versus Duke

19   Jerry Kroll, Davidson
February 19, 1969

19   Anthony Jenkins, Clemson
February 26, 1986

19   Craig Neal, Georgia Tech
February 28, 1988

14   Jason Kidd, California
March 20, 1993 (most recent of several times)

Duke's All-Time Record versus Every ACC Opponent, 1906–2006

School	Overall W-L	At Cameron
Boston College	6 – 1	2 – 0
Clemson	97 – 27	52 – 4
Florida State	25 – 5	15 – 0
Georgia Tech	57 – 21	27 – 5
Maryland	101 – 58	47 – 13
Miami	8 – 1	4 – 0
North Carolina	96 – 125	38 – 31
N.C. State	131 – 95	43 – 23
South Carolina	57 – 19	19 – 3
Virginia	107 – 47	45 – 8
Virginia Tech	32 – 6	13 – 0
Wake Forest	154 – 75	52 – 16

Duke Women versus Every ACC Opponent, through 2006

School	Overall W-L	At Cameron
Boston College	4 – 1	1 – 1
Clemson	28 – 32	15 – 10
Florida State	25 – 7	12 – 3
Georgia Tech	48 – 7	24 – 2
Maryland	29 – 33	15 – 12
Miami	3 – 0	1 – 0
North Carolina	28 – 41	16 – 13
N.C. State	25 – 38	13 – 16
Virginia	23 – 32	13 – 14
Virginia Tech	7 – 2	4 – 1
Wake Forest	47 – 18	21 – 7

Duke's 1,000-Point Scorers

This section includes season-by-season career statistics for Duke players with at least 1,000 points, 500 rebounds, or 500 assists. Players are listed in order of total career points scored. Blank spaces in the line-by-line data indicate that the statistic was not maintained by Duke at the time in question or did not exist. For example, the three-point shot was used experimentally in 1983 and then adopted permanently beginning in 1987; for all other seasons, the three-point columns are blank. Rebounding statistics were compiled by Duke beginning in 1952 and assists beginning in 1952, then resuming in 1969.

Year	GP	FG	FGA	Pct	3P	3PA	Pct	FT	FTA	Pct	Reb	Avg	Ast	Pts	Avg
J. J. Redick															
2003	33	149	361	41.3	95	238	39.9	102	111	91.9	81	2.5	67	495	15.0
2004	37	172	407	42.3	102	258	39.5	143	150	95.3	115	3.1	58	589	15.9
2005	33	202	495	40.8	121	300	40.3	196	209	93.8	108	3.3	86	721	21.8
2006	36	302	643	47.0	139	330	42.1	221	256	86.3	71	2.0	95	964	26.8
Totals	139	825	1,906	43.3	457	1,126	40.6	662	726	91.2	375	2.7	306	2,769	19.9
Johnny Dawkins															
1983	28	207	414	50.0	19	54	35.2	73	107	68.2	115	4.1	134	506	18.1
1984	34	263	547	48.1				133	160	83.1	138	4.1	138	659	19.4
1985	31	225	455	49.5				132	166	79.5	141	4.5	154	582	18.8
1986	40	331	603	54.9				147	181	81.2	142	3.6	129	809	20.2
Total	133	1,026	2,019	50.8	19	54	35.2	485	614	79.0	536	4.0	555	2,556	19.2
Christian Laettner															
1989	36	115	159	72.3	1	1	100.0	88	121	72.7	170	4.7	44	319	8.9
1990	38	194	380	51.1	6	12	50.0	225	269	83.6	364	9.6	84	619	16.3
1991	39	271	471	57.5	18	53	34.0	211	263	80.2	340	8.7	76	771	19.8
1992	35	254	442	57.5	54	97	55.7	189	232	81.5	275	7.9	69	751	21.5
Totals	148	834	1,452	57.4	79	163	48.5	713	885	80.6	1,149	7.8	273	2,460	16.6
Mike Gminski															
1977	27	175	340	51.5				64	91	70.3	289	10.7	20	414	15.3
1978	32	246	450	54.7				148	176	84.1	319	10.0	50	640	20.0
1979	30	218	420	51.9				129	177	72.9	275	9.2	23	565	18.8
1980	33	262	487	53.8				180	214	84.1	359	10.9	35	704	21.3
Totals	122	901	1,697	53.1				521	658	79.2	1,242	10.2	128	2,323	19.0

Year	GP	FG	FGA	Pct	3P	3PA	Pct	FT	FTA	Pct	Reb	Avg	Ast	Pts	Avg
Danny Ferry															
1986	40	91	198	46.0				54	86	62.8	221	5.5	60	236	5.9
1987	33	172	383	44.9	25	63	39.7	92	109	84.4	256	7.8	141	461	14.0
1988	35	247	519	47.6	38	109	34.9	135	163	82.8	266	7.6	139	667	19.1
1989	35	300	575	52.2	45	106	42.5	146	193	75.6	260	7.4	166	791	22.6
Totals	143	810	1,675	48.4	108	278	38.8	427	551	77.5	1,003	7.0	506	2,155	15.1
Mark Alarie															
1983	28	130	263	49.4	0	2	0.0	104	128	81.3	181	6.5	30	364	13.0
1984	34	230	400	57.5				134	176	76.1	245	7.2	47	594	17.5
1985	31	206	352	58.5				80	101	79.2	158	5.1	49	492	15.9
1986	40	262	490	53.5				162	197	82.2	249	6.2	26	686	17.2
Total	133	828	1,505	55.0	0	2	0.0	480	602	79.7	833	6.3	152	2,136	16.1
Jason Williams															
2000	34	179	427	41.9	73	206	35.4	61	89	68.5	143	4.2	220	492	14.5
2001	39	285	603	47.3	132	309	42.7	139	211	65.9	128	3.3	237	841	21.6
2002	35	249	545	45.7	108	282	38.3	140	207	67.6	124	3.5	187	746	21.3
Totals	108	713	1,575	45.3	313	797	39.3	340	507	67.1	395	3.7	644	2,079	19.3
Gene Banks															
1978	34	238	451	52.8				105	146	71.9	292	8.6	120	581	17.1
1979	30	175	353	49.6				79	126	62.7	255	8.5	89	429	14.3
1980	33	212	404	52.5				146	183	79.8	254	7.7	103	570	17.3
1981	27	202	350	57.7				95	134	70.9	184	6.8	48	499	18.5
Totals	124	827	1,558	53.1				425	589	72.2	985	7.9	360	2,079	16.8
Jim Spanarkel															
1976	23	120	219	54.8				67	97	69.1	101	4.4	65	307	13.3
1977	27	172	331	52.0				175	209	83.7	147	5.4	96	519	19.2
1978	34	244	460	53.0				220	255	86.3	116	3.4	126	708	20.8
1979	30	188	364	51.6				102	139	73.4	90	3.0	112	478	15.9
Totals	114	724	1,374	52.7				564	700	80.6	454	4.0	399	2,012	17.6
Shane Battier															
1998	36	96	178	53.9	4	24	16.7	79	108	73.1	230	6.4	40	275	7.6
1999	37	114	209	54.5	39	94	41.5	71	98	72.4	180	4.9	55	338	9.1
2000	34	190	383	49.6	79	178	44.4	134	164	81.7	192	5.6	72	593	17.4
2001	39	251	533	47.1	124	296	41.9	152	191	79.6	285	7.3	72	778	19.9
Totals	146	651	1,303	50.0	246	592	41.6	436	561	77.7	887	6.1	239	1,984	13.6
Art Heyman															
1961	25	229	488	46.9				171	263	65.0	272	10.9		629	25.2
1962	24	219	506	43.3				170	276	61.6	269	11.2		608	25.3
1963	30	265	586	45.2				217	314	69.1	324	10.8		747	24.9
Totals	79	713	1,580	45.1				558	853	65.4	865	10.9		1,984	25.1

Year	GP	FG	FGA	Pct	3P	3PA	Pct	FT	FTA	Pct	Reb	Avg	Ast	Pts	Avg
Trajan Langdon															
1995	31	124	274	45.3	59	138	42.8	44	56	78.6	65	2.1	48	351	11.3
1997	33	137	308	44.5	86	195	44.1	113	126	89.7	97	2.9	68	473	14.3
1998	36	171	385	44.4	85	215	39.5	101	114	88.6	104	2.9	70	528	14.7
1999	36	191	413	46.2	112	254	44.1	128	152	84.2	123	3.4	69	622	17.3
Totals	136	623	1,380	45.1	342	802	42.6	386	448	86.2	389	2.9	255	1,974	14.5
Shelden Williams															
2003	33	95	184	51.6	0	1	0.0	80	128	62.5	195	5.9	15	270	8.2
2004	37	164	280	58.6	2	5	40.0	138	200	69.0	314	8.5	34	468	12.6
2005	33	191	328	58.2	0	0	0.0	131	198	66.2	369	11.2	31	513	15.5
2006	36	237	410	57.8	2	6	33.3	201	270	74.4	384	10.7	39	677	18.8
Totals	139	687	1,202	57.2	4	12	33.3	550	796	69.1	1,262	9.1	119	1,928	13.9
Grant Hill															
1991	36	160	310	51.6	1	2	50.0	81	133	60.9	183	5.1	79	402	11.2
1992	33	182	298	61.1	0	1	0.0	99	135	73.3	187	5.7	134	463	14.0
1993	26	185	320	57.8	4	14	28.6	94	126	74.6	166	6.4	72	468	18.0
1994	34	218	472	46.2	39	100	39.0	116	165	70.3	233	6.9	176	591	17.4
Totals	129	745	1,400	53.2	44	117	37.6	390	559	69.8	769	6.0	461	1,924	14.9
Dick Groat															
1950	19	109	256	42.6				57	98	58.2				275	14.5
1951	33	285	713	40.0				261	331	78.9				831	25.2
1952	30	288	700	41.1				204	281	72.6	229	7.6	229	780	26.0
Totals	82	682	1,669	40.9				522	710	73.5				1,886	23.0
Jeff Mullins															
1962	25	214	416	51.4				98	138	71.0	259	10.4		526	21.0
1963	30	256	466	54.9				96	131	73.3	241	8.0		608	20.3
1964	31	300	613	48.9				150	183	82.0	276	8.9		750	24.2
Totals	86	770	1,495	51.5				344	452	76.1	776	9.0		1,884	21.9
Bob Verga															
1965	25	229	431	53.1				76	116	65.5	84	3.4		534	21.4
1966	28	216	441	49.0				87	119	73.1	113	4.0		519	18.5
1967	27	283	614	46.1				139	179	77.7	102	3.8		705	26.1
Totals	80	728	1,486	49.0				302	414	72.9	299	3.7		1,758	22.0
Bobby Hurley															
1990	38	92	262	35.1	41	115	35.7	110	143	76.9	68	1.8	288	335	8.8
1991	39	141	333	42.3	76	188	40.4	83	114	72.8	93	2.4	289	441	11.3
1992	31	123	284	43.3	59	140	42.1	105	133	78.9	61	2.0	237	410	13.2
1993	32	157	373	42.1	88	209	42.1	143	178	80.3	84	2.6	262	545	17.0
Totals	140	513	1,252	41.0	264	652	40.5	441	568	77.6	306	2.2	1,076	1,731	12.4

Year	GP	FG	FGA	Pct	3P	3PA	Pct	FT	FTA	Pct	Reb	Avg	Ast	Pts	Avg
Randy Denton															
1969	28	212	425	49.9				62	102	60.8	358	12.8	18	486	17.4
1970	26	237	437	54.2				86	132	65.2	324	12.5	15	560	21.5
1971	30	244	433	56.4				124	166	74.7	385	12.8	23	612	20.4
Totals	84	693	1,295	53.5				272	400	68.0	1,067	12.7	56	1,658	19.7
Ronnie Mayer															
1953	25	40	101	39.6				58	83	69.9	121	4.8		138	5.5
1954	27	114	280	40.7				121	153	79.1	265	9.8		349	12.9
1955	28	217	509	42.6				173	229	75.5	348	12.4		607	21.7
1956	25	195	452	43.1				163	208	78.4	220	8.8		553	22.1
Totals	105	566	1,342	42.2				515	673	76.5	954	9.1		1,647	15.7
Cherokee Parks															
1992	34	60	105	57.1	0	0	0.0	50	69	72.5	81	2.4	13	170	5.0
1993	32	161	247	65.2	0	0	0.0	72	100	72.0	220	6.9	14	394	12.3
1994	34	186	347	53.6	3	17	17.6	115	149	77.2	284	8.4	31	490	14.4
1995	31	222	443	50.1	31	85	36.5	114	147	77.6	289	9.3	45	589	19.0
Totals	131	629	1,142	55.1	34	102	33.3	351	465	75.5	874	6.7	103	1,643	12.5
Jeff Capel															
1994	34	109	238	45.8	32	76	42.1	42	64	65.6	93	2.7	108	292	8.6
1995	31	144	323	44.6	63	137	46.0	36	56	64.3	84	2.7	126	387	12.5
1996	31	185	492	37.6	73	221	33.0	71	93	76.3	122	3.9	114	514	16.6
1997	33	142	309	46.0	52	119	43.7	72	116	62.1	91	2.8	85	408	12.4
Totals	129	580	1,362	42.6	220	553	39.8	221	329	67.2	390	3.0	433	1,601	12.4
Daniel Ewing															
2002	35	80	167	47.9	32	70	45.7	35	51	68.6	78	2.2	47	227	6.5
2003	33	126	293	43.0	42	105	40.0	101	123	82.1	104	3.2	45	395	12.0
2004	37	151	362	41.7	74	180	41.1	92	124	74.2	96	2.6	69	468	12.6
2005	33	181	424	42.7	69	199	34.7	74	107	69.2	104	3.2	132	505	15.3
Totals	138	538	1,246	43.2	217	554	39.2	302	405	74.6	382	2.8	293	1,595	11.6
Thomas Hill															
1990	34	46	89	51.7	3	7	42.9	22	35	62.9	74	2.2	25	117	3.4
1991	39	164	297	55.2	21	52	40.4	101	136	74.3	142	3.6	51	450	11.5
1992	36	196	367	53.4	37	91	40.7	96	125	76.8	121	3.4	54	525	14.6
1993	32	184	384	47.9	34	96	35.4	100	147	68.0	151	4.7	47	502	15.7
Totals	141	590	1,137	51.9	95	246	38.6	319	443	72.0	488	3.5	177	1,594	11.3

Year	GP	FG	FGA	Pct	3P	3PA	Pct	FT	FTA	Pct	Reb	Avg	Ast	Pts	Avg
David Henderson															
1983	28	100	238	42.0	9	33	27.3	45	64	70.3	120	4.3	44	254	9.1
1984	33	153	318	48.1				140	193	72.5	109	3.3	76	446	13.5
1985	28	116	233	49.8				85	137	62.0	98	3.5	51	317	11.3
1986	39	217	419	51.8				119	160	74.4	186	4.8	92	553	14.2
Totals	128	586	1,208	48.5	9	33	27.3	389	554	70.2	513	4.0	263	1,570	12.3
Carlos Boozer															
2000	34	164	267	61.4	0	0	0.0	115	155	74.2	213	6.3	37	443	13.0
2001	32	160	265	60.4	0	0	0.0	105	146	71.9	208	6.5	40	425	13.3
2002	35	230	346	66.5	0	1	0.0	178	236	75.4	303	8.7	38	638	18.2
Totals	101	554	878	63.1	0	1	0.0	398	537	74.1	724	7.2	115	1,506	14.9
Chris Carrawell															
1997	31	72	125	57.6	0	2	0.0	27	47	57.4	97	3.1	34	171	5.5
1998	32	121	251	48.2	14	38	36.8	66	103	64.1	117	3.7	35	322	10.1
1999	39	144	317	45.4	19	55	34.5	79	137	57.7	188	4.9	130	386	9.9
2000	34	205	422	48.6	29	77	37.7	137	176	77.8	206	6.1	110	576	16.9
Totals	136	542	1,115	48.6	62	172	36.0	309	463	66.7	608	4.5	309	1,455	10.7
Vince Taylor															
1979	30	49	90	54.4				17	31	54.8	31	1.0	17	115	3.8
1980	33	138	289	47.8				73	108	67.6	69	2.1	82	349	10.6
1981	30	169	341	49.6				104	169	61.5	110	3.7	63	442	14.7
1982	27	217	419	51.8				115	171	67.3	133	4.9	50	549	20.3
Totals	120	573	1,139	50.3				309	479	64.5	343	2.9	212	1,455	12.1
Mike Lewis															
1966	30	161	271	59.4				84	112	75.0	329	11.0		406	13.5
1967	26	152	285	53.3				99	126	78.6	320	12.3		403	15.5
1968	28	230	418	55.0				148	197	75.1	402	14.4		608	21.7
Total	84	543	974	55.7				331	435	76.1	1,051	12.5		1,417	16.9
Phil Henderson															
1987	8	20	36	55.6	9	13	69.2	9	15	60.0	6	0.8	9	58	7.2
1988	34	72	168	42.9	11	41	26.8	44	60	73.3	59	1.7	30	199	5.9
1989	36	167	318	52.5	29	75	38.7	94	123	76.4	124	3.4	93	457	12.7
1990	37	251	531	47.3	79	191	41.4	102	122	83.6	141	3.8	85	683	18.5
Total	115	510	1,053	48.4	128	320	40.0	249	320	77.8	330	2.9	217	1,397	12.1
Mike Dunleavy															
2000	30	97	211	46.0	34	97	35.1	45	61	73.8	128	4.3	50	273	9.1
2001	39	184	388	47.4	57	153	37.3	68	98	69.4	222	5.7	103	493	12.6
2002	35	218	451	48.3	88	233	37.8	81	119	68.1	251	7.2	72	605	17.3
Totals	104	499	1,050	47.5	179	483	37.1	194	278	69.8	601	5.8	225	1,371	13.2

Year	GP	FG	FGA	Pct	3P	3PA	Pct	FT	FTA	Pct	Reb	Avg	Ast	Pts	Avg
Joe Belmont															
1953	22	42	120	35.0				39	62	62.9	54	2.4		123	5.6
1954	27	129	322	40.1				77	107	72.0	106	3.9		335	12.4
1955	28	160	436	36.7				120	168	71.4	137	4.9		440	15.7
1956	26	140	381	36.7				160	210	76.2	123	4.7		440	16.9
Total	103	471	1,259	37.4				396	547	72.4	420	4.1		1,338	13.0
Tate Armstrong															
1974	22	55	114	48.2				28	35	80.0	18	0.8	9	138	6.3
1975	20	73	154	47.4				48	57	84.2	46	2.3	33	194	9.7
1976	27	265	507	52.3				124	155	80.0	77	2.9	120	654	24.2
1977	14	136	245	55.5				46	59	78.0	41	2.9	55	318	22.7
Total	83	529	1,020	51.9				246	306	80.4	182	2.2	217	1,304	15.7
Robert Brickey															
1987	33	79	135	58.5	0	0	0.0	30	62	48.4	99	3.0	14	188	5.7
1988	35	126	234	53.8	0	1	0.0	114	167	68.3	180	5.1	24	366	10.5
1989	36	150	263	57.0	2	6	33.3	93	165	56.4	207	5.8	48	395	11.0
1990	30	129	252	51.2	0	2	0.0	92	137	67.2	163	5.4	60	350	11.7
Total	134	484	884	54.8	2	9	22.2	329	531	62.0	649	4.8	146	1,299	9.7
Jack Marin															
1964	31	97	219	44.3				46	65	70.8	146	4.7		240	7.7
1965	25	195	357	54.6				87	123	70.7	257	10.3		477	19.1
1966	30	221	451	49.0				116	148	78.4	292	9.7		558	18.6
Total	86	513	1,027	50.0				249	336	74.1	695	8.1		1,275	14.9
Chris Duhon															
2001	39	92	217	42.4	44	122	36.1	52	80	65.0	124	3.2	174	280	7.2
2002	35	100	244	41.0	54	159	34.0	59	83	71.1	109	3.1	208	313	8.9
2003	33	102	264	38.6	35	128	27.3	66	96	68.8	106	3.2	212	305	9.2
2004	37	138	308	44.8	29	96	30.2	65	90	72.2	150	4.1	225	370	10.0
Total	144	432	1,033	41.8	162	505	32.1	242	349	69.3	489	3.4	819	1,268	8.8
Bernie Janicki															
1952	30	185	487	38.0				77	126	61.1	476	15.9	42	447	14.9
1953	26	155	411	37.7				126	181	69.6	272	10.5		436	16.8
1954	27	140	385	36.4				84	122	68.9	175	6.5		364	13.5
Totals	83	480	1,283	37.4				287	429	66.9	923	11.1		1,247	15.0
Tommy Amaker															
1984	34	103	203	50.7				48	57	84.2	82	2.4	163	254	7.5
1985	31	96	214	44.9				61	79	77.2	69	2.2	184	253	8.2
1986	40	101	225	44.9				53	70	75.7	80	2.0	241	255	6.4
1987	33	156	348	44.8	44	103	42.7	50	62	80.6	77	2.3	120	406	12.3
Totals	138	456	990	46.1	44	103	42.7	212	268	79.1	308	2.2	708	1,168	8.5

Year	GP	FG	FGA	Pct	3P	3PA	Pct	FT	FTA	Pct	Reb	Avg	Ast	Pts	Avg
Carroll Youngkin															
1959	25	136	266	51.1				127	212	59.9	277	11.1		399	16.0
1960	28	131	246	53.3				113	208	54.3	278	9.9		375	13.4
1961	28	146	253	57.7				88	152	57.9	274	9.8		380	13.6
Totals	81	413	765	54.0				328	572	57.3	829	10.2		1,154	14.2
Bob Fleischer															
1973	26	100	190	52.6				85	108	78.7	221	8.5	27	285	11.0
1974	26	163	312	52.2				81	107	75.7	323	12.4	51	407	15.7
1975	26	178	287	62.0				91	118	77.1	273	10.5	47	447	17.2
Totals	78	441	789	55.9				257	333	77.2	817	10.5	125	1,139	14.6
Chris Redding															
1972	26	124	265	46.8				134	172	77.9	165	6.3	12	382	14.7
1973	26	158	296	53.4				124	147	84.4	167	6.4	13	440	16.9
1974	26	117	252	46.4				82	105	78.1	141	5.4	19	316	12.2
Totals	78	399	813	49.1				340	424	80.2	473	6.1	44	1,138	14.6
Alaa Abdelnaby															
1987	29	47	81	58.0	0	0	0.0	12	23	52.2	50	1.7	6	106	3.7
1988	34	61	123	49.6	0	0	0.0	44	63	69.8	67	2.0	3	166	4.9
1989	33	123	194	63.4	0	0	0.0	47	67	70.1	125	3.8	11	293	8.9
1990	38	217	350	62.0	0	0	0.0	138	178	77.5	252	6.6	27	572	15.1
Totals	134	448	748	59.9	0	0	0.0	241	331	72.8	494	3.7	47	1,137	8.5
Willie Hodge															
1973	23	47	87	52.9				31	40	77.5	79	3.4	10	125	5.3
1974	26	101	212	47.6				38	60	63.3	131	5.0	18	240	9.2
1975	26	126	243	51.9				44	61	72.1	185	7.1	24	296	11.4
1976	27	189	364	51.9				78	102	76.5	210	7.8	48	456	16.9
Totals	102	463	906	51.1				191	263	72.6	605	5.9	100	1,117	11.0
Nate James															
1997	17	15	36	41.7	5	16	31.3	11	20	55.0	34	2.0	8	46	2.7
1998	6	6	14	42.9	2	4	50.0	7	9	77.8	9	1.5	0	21	3.5
1999	39	69	152	45.4	15	52	28.8	43	65	66.2	102	2.6	34	196	5.0
2000	34	136	290	46.9	46	122	37.7	55	77	71.4	153	4.5	63	373	11.0
2001	39	161	326	49.4	43	137	31.4	115	144	79.9	202	5.2	42	480	12.3
Totals	135	387	818	47.3	111	331	33.5	231	315	73.3	500	3.7	147	1,116	8.3
Kevin Strickland															
1985	27	49	84	58.3				10	17	58.8	36	1.3	15	108	4.0
1986	32	29	78	37.2				9	13	69.2	37	1.2	19	67	2.1
1987	31	120	261	46.0	36	92	39.1	79	97	81.4	143	4.6	41	355	11.5
1988	35	213	404	52.7	55	149	36.9	84	104	80.8	158	4.5	44	565	16.1
Totals	125	411	827	49.7	91	241	37.8	182	231	78.8	374	3.0	119	1,095	8.8

Year	GP	FG	FGA	Pct	3P	3PA	Pct	FT	FTA	Pct	Reb	Avg	Ast	Pts	Avg
Howard Hurt															
1959	24	134	379	35.4				108	140	77.1	197	8.9		376	15.7
1960	28	146	355	41.1				84	104	80.8	238	8.5		376	13.4
1961	28	140	336	41.7				63	97	64.9	140	5.0		343	12.3
Totals	80	420	1,070	39.3				255	341	74.8	575	7.2		1,095	13.7
Chris Collins															
1993	29	56	139	40.3	37	85	43.5	20	32	62.5	33	1.1	34	169	5.8
1994	34	110	275	40.0	76	202	37.6	45	63	71.4	68	2.0	77	341	10.0
1995	28	36	121	29.8	17	73	23.3	20	26	76.9	31	1.1	48	109	3.9
1996	29	155	332	46.7	79	179	44.1	83	115	72.2	111	3.8	132	472	16.3
Totals	120	357	867	41.2	209	539	38.8	168	236	71.2	243	2.0	291	1,091	9.1
Jay Bilas															
1983	28	88	159	55.3	0	0	0.0	69	103	67.0	159	5.7	15	245	8.8
1984	34	95	191	49.7				84	130	64.6	181	5.3	19	274	8.1
1985	31	106	177	59.9				100	144	69.4	186	6.0	14	312	10.1
1986	34	76	128	59.4				79	134	59.0	166	4.9	8	231	6.8
Totals	127	365	655	55.7	0	0	0.0	332	511	65.0	692	5.4	56	1,062	8.4
Kenny Dennard															
1978	34	140	254	55.1				51	76	67.1	215	6.3	72	331	9.7
1979	29	81	168	48.2				25	46	54.3	124	4.2	54	187	6.4
1980	24	93	169	55.0				35	60	58.3	126	5.3	43	221	9.2
1981	30	138	290	47.6				42	78	53.8	206	6.9	63	318	10.6
Totals	117	452	881	51.3				153	260	58.8	671	5.7	232	1,057	9.0
Rudy D'Emilio															
1952	30	135	382	35.3				65	102	63.7	121	4.0	100	335	11.2
1953	23	120	363	33.1				96	138	69.6	105	4.6		336	14.6
1954	27	138	380	36.3				81	123	65.9	104	3.9		357	13.2
Totals	80	393	1,125	34.9				242	363	66.7	330	4.1		1,028	12.8
Ricky Price															
1995	27	90	190	47.4	13	41	31.7	27	40	67.5	90	3.3	26	220	8.1
1996	31	164	374	43.9	44	112	39.3	69	97	71.1	107	3.5	46	441	14.2
1997	33	106	269	39.4	32	108	29.6	65	98	66.3	90	2.7	28	309	9.4
1998	21	22	62	35.5	1	12	8.3	11	17	64.7	23	1.1	12	56	2.7
Totals	112	382	895	42.7	90	273	33.0	172	252	68.3	310	2.8	112	1,026	9.2
Chip Engelland															
1980	32	56	121	46.3				15	23	65.2	12	0.4	19	127	4.0
1981	30	83	149	55.7				29	34	85.3	29	1.0	30	195	6.5
1982	27	167	315	53.0				77	88	87.5	75	2.8	68	411	15.2
1983	24	105	208	50.5	41	74	55.4	41	46	89.1	32	1.3	51	292	12.2
Totals	113	411	793	51.8	41	74	55.4	162	191	84.8	148	1.3	168	1,025	9.1

Year	GP	FG	FGA	Pct	3P	3PA	Pct	FT	FTA	Pct	Reb	Avg	Ast	Pts	Avg
Antonio Lang															
1991	36	57	94	60.6	0	0	0.0	40	76	52.6	92	2.6	7	154	4.3
1992	34	77	137	56.2	0	0	0.0	65	99	65.7	139	4.1	23	219	6.4
1993	31	80	153	52.3	0	1	0.0	55	84	65.5	171	5.5	25	215	6.9
1994	34	153	260	58.8	0	2	0.0	118	163	72.4	184	5.4	35	424	12.5
Totals	135	367	644	57.0	0	3	0.0	278	422	65.9	586	4.3	90	1,012	7.5
Rick Katherman															
1969	26	165	352	46.9				27	42	64.3	122	4.7	17	357	13.7
1970	26	143	322	44.4				54	68	79.4	121	4.7	27	340	13.1
1971	30	139	291	47.8				30	34	88.2	119	4.0	21	308	10.3
Totals	82	447	965	46.3				111	144	77.1	362	4.4	65	1,005	12.3

Other Players with at Least 500 Rebounds or 500 Assists

Assist statistics at Duke available for 1952, then every season beginning with 1969.

Year	GP	FG	FGA	Pct	3P	3PA	Pct	FT	FTA	Pct	Reb	Avg	Ast	Pts	Avg
Elton Brand															
1998	21	100	169	59.2	0	0	0.0	81	134	60.4	154	7.3	10	281	13.4
1999	39	255	411	62.0	0	0	0.0	181	256	70.7	382	9.8	41	691	17.7
Total	60	355	580	61.2	0	0	0.0	262	390	67.2	536	8.9	51	972	16.2
Doug Kistler															
1959	25	109	273	40.0				32	48	66.8	225	9.0		250	10.0
1960	28	136	300	45.3				71	104	68.3	262	9.4		343	12.3
1961	28	143	291	49.1				53	88	60.2	269	9.6		339	12.1
Total	81	388	864	44.9				156	240	65.0	756	9.3		932	11.5
Jay Buckley															
1962	24	62	129	48.1				37	80	46.3	138	5.8		161	6.7
1963	30	130	217	59.9				76	145	52.4	298	9.9		336	11.2
1964	31	160	271	59.0				109	166	65.7	278	9.0		429	13.8
Total	85	352	617	57.1				222	391	56.8	714	8.4		926	10.9
Quin Snyder															
1986	32	29	62	46.8				16	22	72.7	36	1.1	41	74	2.3
1987	33	72	190	37.9	33	92	35.9	45	60	75.0	62	1.9	113	222	6.7
1988	35	95	198	48.0	41	92	44.6	61	78	78.2	86	2.5	198	292	8.3
1989	36	96	232	41.4	34	119	28.6	34	63	54.0	76	2.1	223	260	7.2
Total	136	292	682	42.8	108	303	35.6	156	223	70.0	260	1.9	575	848	6.2

Year	GP	FG	FGA	Pct	3P	3PA	Pct	FT	FTA	Pct	Reb	Avg	Ast	Pts	Avg
Jim Newcome															
1956	26	58	155	37.4				22	37	59.4	90	3.4		138	5.3
1957	24	143	360	39.7				61	103	59.2	273	11.4		347	14.5
1958	25	129	321	40.2				73	116	62.9	237	9.5		331	13.2
Total	75	330	836	39.5				156	256	60.9	600	8.0		816	10.9
Greg Newton															
1994	21	8	22	36.4	0	0	0.0	7	13	53.8	27	1.3	9	23	1.1
1995	25	41	62	66.1	0	0	0.0	17	36	47.2	84	3.4	6	99	4.0
1996	31	150	264	56.8	0	0	0.0	79	134	59.0	255	8.2	15	379	12.2
1997	30	111	197	56.3	0	0	0.0	89	132	67.4	184	6.1	18	311	10.4
Total	107	310	545	56.9	0	0	0.0	192	315	61.0	550	5.1	48	812	7.6
Hack Tison															
1963	30	61	112	54.5				25	41	61.0	133	4.4		147	4.9
1964	30	130	260	50.0				93	136	68.4	229	7.6		353	11.8
1965	25	124	245	50.6				51	81	63.0	221	8.9		299	11.7
Total	85	315	617	51.1				169	258	65.5	583	6.9		799	9.4
Alan Shaw															
1971	30	57	95	60.0				77	99	77.8	168	5.6	20	191	6.4
1972	26	119	198	60.1				85	127	66.9	308	11.8	49	323	12.4
1973	26	87	187	46.5				56	74	75.7	197	7.6	35	230	8.8
Total	82	263	480	54.8				218	300	72.7	673	8.2	104	744	9.1
Bob Riedy															
1965	25	59	133	44.4				32	50	64.0	132	5.3		150	6.0
1966	29	105	228	46.1				61	89	68.6	224	7.7		271	9.4
1967	25	124	266	46.6				72	94	76.6	179	7.2		320	12.8
Total	79	288	627	45.9				165	233	70.8	535	6.8		741	9.4
Junior Morgan															
1954	25	46	109	42.2				36	59	61.0	132	5.3		128	5.1
1955	28	107	248	44.0				78	134	58.0	255	9.1		292	10.4
1956	26	96	254	37.7				101	137	73.7	256	9.8		293	11.2
Total	79	249	611	40.8				215	330	65.2	643	8.1		713	9.0
Steve Wojciechowski															
1995	28	35	102	34.3	27	76	35.5	15	26	57.7	40	1.4	81	112	4.0
1996	31	27	85	31.8	19	68	27.9	32	42	76.2	64	2.1	84	105	3.4
1997	33	66	149	44.3	41	104	39.4	56	73	76.7	100	3.0	176	229	6.9
1998	36	70	181	38.7	54	139	38.8	47	64	73.4	87	2.4	164	241	6.7
Total	128	198	517	38.3	141	387	36.4	150	205	73.2	291	2.3	505	687	5.4

Year	GP	FG	FGA	Pct	3P	3PA	Pct	FT	FTA	Pct	Reb	Avg	Ast	Pts	Avg

Erik Meek

Year	GP	FG	FGA	Pct	3P	3PA	Pct	FT	FTA	Pct	Reb	Avg	Ast	Pts	Avg
1992	25	22	38	57.9	0	0	0.0	18	36	50.0	30	1.2	5	62	2.5
1993	32	38	64	59.4	0	0	0.0	36	63	57.1	92	2.9	5	112	3.5
1994	34	36	66	54.5	0	0	0.0	48	80	60.0	142	4.2	13	120	3.5
1995	31	118	190	62.1	0	0	0.0	83	143	58.0	256	8.3	26	319	10.3
Total	122	214	358	59.8	0	0	0.0	185	322	57.5	520	4.3	49	613	5.0

Women's 1,000-Point Scorers

Year	GP	FG	FGA	Pct	3P	3PA	Pct	FT	FTA	Pct	Reb	Avg	Ast	Pts	Avg

Alana Beard

Year	GP	FG	FGA	Pct	3P	3PA	Pct	FT	FTA	Pct	Reb	Avg	Ast	Pts	Avg
2001–2004	136	1,005	1,906	52.7	95	317	30.0	582	752	77.4	789	5.8	509	2,687	19.8

Chris Moreland

| 1985–1988 | 111 | 828 | 1,448 | 57.2 | 0 | 0 | 0.0 | 576 | 868 | 66.4 | 1,229 | 11.1 | 119 | 2,232 | 20.1 |

Monique Currie

| 2002–2006 | 140 | 749 | 1,592 | 47.0 | 86 | 258 | 33.3 | 538 | 688 | 78.2 | 874 | 6.2 | 413 | 2,122 | 15.2 |

Sue Harnett

| 1987–1991 | 117 | 727 | 1,385 | 52.5 | 0 | 1 | 0.0 | 331 | 484 | 68.4 | 899 | 7.7 | 164 | 1,785 | 15.3 |

Katie Meier

| 1986–1990 | 109 | 653 | 1,374 | 47.5 | 8 | 32 | 25.0 | 447 | 624 | 71.6 | 670 | 6.1 | 409 | 1,761 | 16.2 |

Iciss Tillis

| 2001–2004 | 137 | 673 | 1,537 | 43.8 | 128 | 367 | 34.9 | 238 | 307 | 77.5 | 946 | 6.9 | 301 | 1,712 | 12.5 |

Georgia Schweitzer

| 1998–2001 | 136 | 579 | 1,248 | 46.4 | 202 | 504 | 40.1 | 260 | 358 | 72.6 | 533 | 3.9 | 428 | 1,620 | 11.9 |

Mistie Williams

| 2003–2006 | 142 | 557 | 983 | 56.7 | 0 | 1 | 0.0 | 295 | 459 | 64.2 | 800 | 5.6 | 175 | 1,409 | 9.9 |

Kira Orr

| 1994–1997 | 119 | 500 | 1,235 | 40.5 | 133 | 416 | 32.0 | 255 | 349 | 73.1 | 505 | 4.2 | 445 | 1,388 | 11.7 |

Year	GP	FG	FGA	Pct	3P	3PA	Pct	FT	FTA	Pct	Reb	Avg	Ast	Pts	Avg
Jennifer Scanlon															
1993–1996	118	502	1,206	41.6	159	420	37.9	214	315	67.9	390	3.3	259	1,377	11.7
Payton Black															
1996–1999	127	510	936	54.5	0	1	0.0	292	443	65.9	541	4.3	104	1,312	10.3
Tyish Hall															
1994–1997	109	543	862	63.0	0	0	0.0	200	290	69.0	632	5.8	135	1,286	11.8
Sheana Mosch															
2000–2003	140	448	1,008	44.4	41	123	33.3	346	436	79.4	500	3.6	271	1,283	9.2
Stacy Hurd															
1981–1984	104	541	1,169	46.3				159	226	70.4	595	5.7	97	1,241	11.9
Ali Day															
1993–1996	115	473	881	53.7	60	140	42.9	229	287	79.8	617	5.4	156	1,235	10.7
Carey Kauffman															
1992–1995	111	506	1,055	48.0	2	5	40.0	214	287	74.6	726	6.5	140	1,228	11.1
Connie Goins															
1983–1986	101	428	906	47.2				284	374	75.9	461	4.6	297	1,140	11.3
Peppi Browne															
1997–2000	117	417	865	48.2	11	48	22.9	287	399	71.9	677	5.8	234	1,132	9.7
Jennifer Chestnut															
1981–1984	100	423	884	47.9				177	342	51.8	737	7.4	82	1,023	10.2

Duke in the NCAA Tournament

Year	Date	Region	Opponent	Result	Score	Top Duke Scorer
1955		East				
First round	March 8	at New York	Villanova	L	73–74	22 Tobin
1960		East				
First round	March 8	at New York	Princeton	W	84–60	26 Kistler
Regional semis	March 11	at Charlotte	St. Joseph's	W	58–56	22 Youngkin
Regional final	March 12	at Charlotte	NYU	L	59–74	20 Kistler
1963		East				
Regional semis	March 15	at College Park, Md.	NYU	W	81–76	25 Mullins
Regional final	March 16	at College Park, Md.	St. Joseph's	W	73–59	24 Mullins
National semis	March 22	at Louisville	Loyola, Ill.	L	75–94	29 Heyman
Nat'l consolation	March 23	at Louisville	Oregon State	W	85–63	22 Heyman
1964		East				
Regional semis	March 13	at Raleigh	Villanova	W	87–73	43 Mullins
Regional final	March 14	at Raleigh	Connecticut	W	101–54	30 Mullins
National semis	March 20	at Kansas City	Michigan	W	91–80	25 Buckley
National final	March 21	at Kansas City	UCLA	L	83–98	22 Mullins
1966		East				
Regional semis	March 11	at Raleigh	St. Joseph's	W	76–74	22 Verga
Regional final	March 12	at Raleigh	Syracuse	W	91–81	22 Marin
National semis	March 18	at College Park, Md.	Kentucky	L	79–83	29 Marin
Nat'l consolation	March 19	at College Park, Md.	Utah	W	79–77	23 Marin
1978		East				
First round	March 12	at Charlotte	Rhode Island	W	63–62	25 Gminski
Regional semis	March 17	at Providence	Pennsylvania	W	84–80	21 Banks, Spanarkel
Regional final	March 19	at Providence	Villanova	W	90–72	23 Spanarkel
National semis	March 25	at St. Louis	Notre Dame	W	90–86	29 Gminski
National final	March 27	at St. Louis	Kentucky	L	88–94	22 Banks
1979		East—2 seed				
Second round	March 11	at Raleigh	St. John's	L	78–80	24 Banks
1980		Mideast—4 seed				
Second round	March 8	at West Lafayette, Ind.	Pennsylvania	W	52–42	19 Gminski
Regional semis	March 13	at Lexington, Ky.	Kentucky	W	55–54	17 Gminski
Regional final	March 15	at Lexington, Ky.	Purdue	L	60–68	17 Gminski

Year	Date	Region	Opponent	Result	Score	Top Duke Scorer
1984		West —3 seed				
Second round	March 18	at Pullman, Wash.	Washington	L	78 – 80	22 Dawkins
1985		Midwest —3 seed				
First round	March 15	at Houston	Pepperdine	W	75 – 62	22 Henderson
Second round	March 17	at Houston	Boston College	L	73 – 74	18 Dawkins
1986		East —1 seed				
First round	March 13	at Greensboro	Miss. Valley St.	W	85 – 78	27 Dawkins
Second round	March 15	at Greensboro	Old Dominion	W	89 – 61	25 Dawkins
Regional semis	March 21	at E. Rutherford, N.J.	DePaul	W	74 – 67	25 Dawkins
Regional final	March 23	at E. Rutherford, N.J.	Navy	W	71 – 50	28 Dawkins
National semis	March 29	at Dallas	Kansas	W	71 – 67	24 Dawkins
National final	March 31	at Dallas	Louisville	L	69 – 72	24 Dawkins
1987		Midwest — 5 seed				
First round	March 12	at Indianapolis	Texas A&M	W	58 – 51	20 Strickland
Second round	March 14	at Indianapolis	Xavier	W	65 – 60	20 Amaker
Regional semis	March 20	at Cincinnati	Indiana	L	82 – 88	23 Amaker
1988		East — 2 seed				
First round	March 17	at Chapel Hill	Boston Univ.	W	85 – 69	21 Ferry
Second round	March 19	at Chapel Hill	SMU	W	94 – 79	31 Strickland
Regional semis	March 24	at E. Rutherford, N.J.	Rhode Island	W	73 – 72	17 Ferry
Regional final	March 26	at E. Rutherford, N.J.	Temple	W	63 – 53	21 Strickland
National semis	April 2	at Kansas City	Kansas	L	59 – 66	19 Ferry
1989		East — 2 seed				
First round	March 16	at Greensboro	South Carolina St.	W	90 – 69	22 Henderson
Second round	March 18	at Greensboro	West Virginia	W	70 – 63	20 Ferry
Regional semis	March 24	at E. Rutherford, N.J.	Minnesota	W	87 – 70	21 Brickey, Henderson
Regional final	March 26	at E. Rutherford, N.J.	Georgetown	W	85 – 77	24 Laettner
National semis	April 1	at Seattle	Seton Hall	L	78 – 95	34 Ferry
1990		East — 3 seed				
First round	March 16	at Atlanta	Richmond	W	81 – 46	22 Abdelnaby
Second round	March 18	at Atlanta	St. John's	W	76 – 72	22 Brickey
Regional semis	March 22	at E. Rutherford, N.J.	UCLA	W	90 – 81	28 Henderson
Regional final	March 24	at E. Rutherford, N.J.	Connecticut (OT)	W	79 – 78	27 Abdelnaby
National semis	March 31	at Denver	Arkansas	W	97 – 83	28 Henderson
National final	April 2	at Denver	UNLV	L	73 – 103	21 Henderson

Year	Date	Region	Opponent	Result	Score	Top Duke Scorer
1991		Midwest — 2 seed				
First round	March 14	at Minneapolis	NE Louisiana	W	102 – 73	22 Laettner
Second round	March 16	at Minneapolis	Iowa	W	85 – 70	19 Laettner
Regional semis	March 22	at Pontiac, Mich.	Connecticut	W	81 – 67	19 Laettner
Regional final	March 24	at Pontiac, Mich.	St. John's	W	78 – 61	20 Hurley
National semis	March 30	at Indianapolis	UNLV	W	79 – 77	28 Laettner
National final	April 1	at Indianapolis	Kansas	W	72 – 65	18 Laettner
1992		East — 1 seed				
First round	March 19	at Greensboro	Campbell	W	82 – 56	22 Laettner
Second round	March 21	at Greensboro	Iowa	W	75 – 62	21 Davis
Regional semis	March 26	at Philadelphia	Seton Hall	W	81 – 69	16 Laettner, Lang
Regional final	March 28	at Philadelphia	Kentucky (OT)	W	104 – 103	31 Laettner
National semis	April 4	at Minneapolis	Indiana	W	81 – 78	26 Hurley
National final	April 6	at Minneapolis	Michigan	W	71 – 51	19 Laettner
1993		Midwest — 3 seed				
First round	March 18	at Chicago	Southern Illinois	W	105 – 70	25 Hurley
Second round	March 20	at Chicago	California	L	77 – 82	32 Hurley
1994		Southeast — 2 seed				
First round	March 18	at St. Petersburg	Texas Southern	W	82 – 70	20 Collins
Second round	March 20	at St. Petersburg	Michigan State	W	85 – 74	25 Hill
Regional semis	March 24	at Knoxville	Marquette	W	59 – 49	22 Hill
Regional final	March 26	at Knoxville	Purdue	W	69 – 60	19 Lang, Capel
National semis	April 2	at Charlotte	Florida	W	70 – 65	25 Hill
National final	April 4	at Charlotte	Arkansas	L	72 – 76	15 Lang
1996		Southeast — 8 seed				
First round	March 14	at Indianapolis	Eastern Michigan	L	60 – 75	15 Capel, Newton
1997		Southeast — 2 seed				
First round	March 14	at Charlotte	Murray State	W	71 – 68	25 Capel
Second round	March 16	at Charlotte	Providence	L	87 – 98	26 Capel
1998		South — 1 seed				
First round	March 13	at Lexington, Ky.	Radford	W	99 – 63	23 McLeod
Second round	March 15	at Lexington, Ky.	Oklahoma State	W	79 – 73	22 McLeod
Regional semis	March 20	at St. Petersburg	Syracuse	W	80 – 67	20 Brand
Regional final	March 22	at St. Petersburg	Kentucky	L	84 – 86	19 McLeod

Year	Date	Region	Opponent	Result	Score	Top Duke Scorer
1999		East — 1 seed				
First round	March 12	at Charlotte	Florida A&M	W	99 – 58	17 Brand
Second round	March 14	at Charlotte	Tulsa	W	97 – 56	19 Avery
Regional semis	March 19	at East Rutherford, N.J.	SW Missouri State	W	78 – 61	24 Langdon
Regional final	March 21	at East Rutherford, N.J.	Temple	W	85 – 64	23 Langdon
National semis	March 27	at St. Petersburg	Michigan State	W	68 – 62	18 Brand
National final	March 29	at St. Petersburg	Connecticut	L	74 – 77	25 Langdon
2000		East — 1 seed				
First round	March 17	at Winston-Salem	Lamar	W	82 – 55	18 Williams
Second round	March 19	at Winston-Salem	Kansas	W	69 – 64	21 Battier
Regional semis	March 24	at Syracuse	Florida	L	78 – 87	20 Battier
2001		East — 1 seed				
First round	March 15	at Greensboro	Monmouth	W	95 – 52	22 Williams
Second round	March 17	at Greensboro	Missouri	W	94 – 81	31 Williams
Regional semis	March 22	at Philadelphia	UCLA	W	76 – 63	34 Williams
Regional final	March 24	at Philadelphia	Southern Cal	W	79 – 69	28 Williams
National semis	March 31	at Minneapolis	Maryland	W	95 – 84	25 Battier
National final	April 2	at Minneapolis	Arizona	W	82 – 72	21 Dunleavy
2002		South — 1 seed				
First round	March 14	at Greenville, S.C.	Winthrop	W	84 – 37	19 Dunleavy, Boozer
Second round	March 16	at Greenville, S.C.	Notre Dame	W	84 – 77	18 Williams, Ewing
Regional semis	March 21	at Lexington, Ky.	Indiana	L	73 – 74	19 Boozer
2003		West — 3 seed				
First round	March 20	at Salt Lake City	Colorado State	W	67 – 57	23 Jones
Second round	March 22	at Salt Lake City	Central Michigan	W	86 – 60	28 Jones
Regional semis	March 27	at Anaheim	Kansas	L	65 – 69	23 Jones
2004		Atlanta — 1 seed				
First round	March 18	at Raleigh	Alabama State	W	96 – 61	20 Randolph
Second round	March 20	at Raleigh	Seton Hall	W	90 – 62	21 Redick
Regional semis	March 26	at Atlanta	Illinois	W	72 – 62	18 Deng
Regional final	March 28	at Atlanta	Xavier	W	66 – 63	19 Deng
National semis	April 3	at San Antonio	Connecticut	L	78 – 79	16 Deng

Year	Date	Region	Opponent	Result	Score	Top Duke Scorer
2005		Austin — 1 seed				
First round	March 18	at Charlotte	Delaware State	W	57 – 46	14 Williams
Second round	March 20	at Charlotte	Mississippi State	W	63 – 55	22 Ewing
Regional semis	March 25	at Austin	Michigan State	L	68 – 78	19 Williams
2006		Atlanta — 1 seed				
First round	March 16	at Greensboro	Southern	W	70 – 54	29 Williams, Redick
Second round	March 18	at Greensboro	Geo. Washington	W	74 – 61	20 Redick
Regional semis	March 23	at Atlanta	LSU	L	54 – 62	23 Williams

Duke Women in the NCAA Tournament

Year	Date	Region	Opponent	Result	Score	Top Duke Scorer
1987		East — 7 seed				
First round	March 11	Durham	Manhattan	W	70 – 55	25 Moreland
Second round	March 14	Piscataway, N.J.	Rutgers	L	64 – 78	22 Moreland
1995		East — 5 seed				
First round	March 16	Tuscaloosa, Ala.	Oklahoma State	W	76 – 64	22 Hall
Second round	March 18	Tuscaloosa, Ala.	Alabama (4 OT)	L	120 – 121	37 Day
1996		Mideast — 4 seed				
First round	March 16	Durham	James Madison	W	85 – 53	18 Black, Scanlon
Second round	March 18	Durham	San Francisco	L	60 – 64	24 Black
1997		Midwest — 5 seed				
First round	March 14	Champaign, Ill.	DePaul	W	70 – 56	20 Orr
Second round	March 16	Champaign, Ill.	Illinois	L	67 – 85	22 Orr
1998		West — 2 seed				
First round	March 14	Durham	Middle Tenn. St.	W	92 – 67	19 VanGorp
Second round	March 16	Durham	Louisville	W	69 – 53	21 Erickson
Regional semis	March 21	Oakland	Florida	W	71 – 58	20 Erickson
Regional final	March 23	Oakland	Arkansas	L	72 – 77	20 Browne
1999		East — 3 seed				
First round	March 13	Durham	Holy Cross	W	79 – 51	19 VanGorp
Second round	March 15	Durham	St. Joseph's	W	66 – 60	20 VanGorp
Regional semis	March 20	Greensboro	Old Dominion	W	76 – 63	24 Erickson
Regional final	March 22	Greensboro	Tennessee	W	69 – 63	22 Schweitzer
National semis	March 26	San Jose	Georgia	W	81 – 69	22 Erickson
National final	March 28	San Jose	Purdue	L	45 – 62	15 VanGorp

Year	Date	Region	Opponent	Result	Score	Top Duke Scorer
2000		East — 2 seed				
First round	March 18	Durham	Campbell	W	71–42	15 West
Second round	March 20	Durham	Western Kentucky	W	90–70	25 Mosch
Regional semis	March 25	Richmond	LSU	L	66–79	17 Rice
2001		West — 1 seed				
First round	March 17	Durham	Wisc.-Milwaukee	W	96–63	22 Beard
Second round	March 19	Durham	Arkansas	W	75–54	14 Beard
Regional semis	March 24	Spokane	SW Missouri State	L	71–81	27 Beard
2002		East — 1 seed				
First round	March 15	Durham	Norfolk State	W	95–48	29 Beard
Second round	March 17	Durham	TCU	W	76–66	26 Beard
Regional semis	March 23	Raleigh	Texas	W	62–46	15 Beard
Regional final	March 25	Raleigh	South Carolina	W	77–68	24 Beard
National semis	March 29	San Antonio	Oklahoma	L	71–86	19 Tillis
2003		Midwest — 1 seed				
First round	March 23	Raleigh	Georgia State	W	66–48	19 Beard
Second round	March 25	Raleigh	Utah	W	65–54	27 Beard
Regional semis	March 29	Albuquerque	Georgia	W	66–63	21 Tillis
Regional final	March 31	Albuquerque	Texas Tech	W	57–51	28 Beard
National semis	April 6	Atlanta	Tennessee	L	56–66	29 Beard
2004		Mideast — 1 seed				
First round	March 21	Durham	Northwestern State	W	103–51	18 Foley
Second round	March 23	Durham	Marquette	W	76–67	30 Beard
Regional semis	March 28	Norfolk	Louisiana Tech	W	63–49	18 Currie
Regional final	March 30	Norfolk	Minnesota	L	75–82	19 Currie
2005		Chattanooga — 2 seed				
First round	March 20	Chapel Hill	Canisius	W	80–48	21 Williams
Second round	March 22	Chapel Hill	Boston College	W	70–65	21 Currie
Regional semis	March 26	Chattanooga	Georgia	W	63–57	16 Currie
Regional final	March 28	Chattanooga	LSU	L	49–59	15 Williams
2006		Bridgeport — 1 seed				
First round	March 19	Norfolk	Southern	W	96–27	19 Currie
Second round	March 21	Norfolk	Southern Cal	W	85–51	22 Bales
Regional semis	March 26	Bridgeport	Michigan State	W	86–61	17 Currie
Regional final	March 28	Bridgeport	Connecticut (OT)	W	63–61	15 Bales
National semis	April 2	Boston	LSU	W	64–45	14 Williams
National final	April 4	Boston	Maryland (OT)	L	75–78	22 Currie

Conference Results Year by Year

Southern Conference

Year	Regular Season Champion	Tournament Champion	Player of Year	Tournament MVP	Coach of Year
1929	Washington & Lee	N.C. State			
1930	Alabama	Alabama			
1931	Georgia	Maryland			
1932	Kentucky, Maryland	Georgia			
1933	South Carolina	South Carolina			
1934	South Carolina	Washington & Lee			
1935	North Carolina	North Carolina			
1936	Washington & Lee	North Carolina			
1937	Washington & Lee	Washington & Lee			
1938	North Carolina	Duke			
1939	Wake Forest	Clemson			
1940	Duke	North Carolina			
1941	North Carolina	Duke			
1942	Duke	Duke			
1943	Duke	George Washington			
1944	North Carolina	Duke			
1945	South Carolina	North Carolina			
1946	North Carolina	Duke			
1947	N.C. State	N.C. State			Case, N.C. State
1948	N.C. State	N.C. State		Bunting, W&M	Gerard, Duke
1949	N.C. State	N.C. State		Giermak, W&M	Case, N.C. State
1950	N.C. State	N.C. State		Ranzino, N.C. State	Gerard, Duke
1951	N.C. State	N.C. State	Groat, Duke	Groat, Duke	Case, N.C. State
1952	West Virginia	N.C. State	Groat, Duke	Groat, Duke	Brown, W.Va.
1953	N.C. State	Wake Forest	Selvy, Furman	Shue, Md.	Greason, Wake

Atlantic Coast Conference

Year	Regular-Season Champion	Duke Seeding	Tournament Champion	Player of Year	Tournament MVP	Coach of Year
1954	Duke	1	N.C. State	Hemric, Wake	Hemric, Wake	Case, N.C. State
1955	N.C. State	2	N.C. State	Hemric, Wake	Shavlik, N.C. State	Case, N.C. State
1956	N.C. State & UNC	4	N.C. State	Shavlik, N.C. State	Molodet, N.C. State	Greason, Wake

Year	Regular-Season Champion	Duke Seeding	Tournament Champion	Player of Year	Tournament MVP	Coach of Year
1957	North Carolina	3	N. Carolina	Rosenbluth, UNC	Rosenbluth, UNC	McGuire, UNC
1958	Duke	1	Maryland	Brennan, UNC	Davis, Md.	Case, N.C. State
1959	N.C. State & UNC	3	N.C. State	Pucillo, N.C. State	Pucillo, N.C. State	Bradley, Duke
1960	UNC & Wake	4	Duke	Shaffer, UNC	Kistler, Duke	McKinney, Wake
1961	North Carolina	2	Wake Forest	Chappell, Wake	Chappell, Wake	McKinney, Wake
1962	Wake Forest	2	Wake Forest	Chappell, Wake	Chappell, Wake	Stevens, S.C.
1963	Duke	1	Duke	Heyman, Duke	Heyman, Duke	Bubas, Duke
1964	Duke	1	Duke	Mullins, Duke	Mullins, Duke	Bubas, Duke
1965	Duke	1	N.C. State	Cunningham, UNC	Worsley, N.C. State	Maravich, N.C. State
1966	Duke	1	Duke	Vacendak, Duke	Vacendak, Duke	Bubas, Duke
1967	North Carolina	2	N. Carolina	Miller, UNC	Miller, UNC	Smith, UNC
1968	North Carolina	2	N. Carolina	Miller, UNC	Miller, UNC	Smith, UNC
1969	North Carolina	3	N. Carolina	Roche, S.C.	Scott, UNC	McGuire, S.C.
1970	South Carolina	4	N.C. State	Roche, S.C.	Williford, N.C. State	Sloan, N.C. State
1971	North Carolina	3	South Carolina	Davis, Wake	Dedmon & Roche	Smith, UNC
1972	North Carolina	4	N. Carolina	Parkhill, UVa	McAdoo, UNC	Gibson, UVa
1973	N.C. State	4	N.C. State	Thompson, N.C. State	Burleson, N.C. State	Sloan, N.C. State
1974	N.C. State	7	N.C. State	Thompson, N.C. State	Burleson, N.C. State	Sloan, N.C. State
1975	Maryland	6	N. Carolina	Thompson, N.C. State	Ford, UNC	Driesell, Md.
1976	North Carolina	7	Virginia	Kupchak, UNC	Walker, UVa	Smith, UNC
1977	North Carolina	6	N. Carolina	Griffin, Wake	Kuester, UNC	Smith, UNC
1978	North Carolina	2	Duke	Ford, UNC	Spanarkel, Duke	Foster, Duke
1979	Duke & UNC	2	N. Carolina	Gminski, Duke	Bradley, UNC	Smith, UNC
1980	Maryland	6	Duke	King, Md.	King, Md.	Driesell, Md.
1981	Virginia	5	N. Carolina	Sampson, UVa	Perkins, UNC	Holland, UVa
1982	Virginia & UNC	6	N. Carolina	Sampson, UVa	Worthy, UNC	Holland, UVa
1983	Virginia & UNC	7	N.C. State	Sampson, UVa	Lowe, N.C. State	Cremins, Ga. Tech
1984	North Carolina	4	Maryland	Jordan, UNC	Bias, Md.	Krzyzewski, Duke

Year	Regular-Season Champion	Duke Seeding	Tournament Champion	Player of Year	Tournament MVP	Coach of Year
1985	Ga. Tech, N.C. State, UNC	4	Ga. Tech	Bias, Md.	Price, Ga. Tech	Cremins, Ga. Tech
1986	Duke	1	Duke	Bias, Md.	Dawkins, Duke	Krzyzewski, Duke
1987	North Carolina	3	N.C. State	Grant, Clemson	Del Negro, N.C. State	Ellis, Clemson
1988	North Carolina	3	Duke	Ferry, Duke	Ferry, Duke	Smith, UNC
1989	N.C. State	2	N. Carolina	Ferry, Duke	Reid, UNC	Valvano, N.C. State
1990	Clemson	2	Ga. Tech	Scott, Ga. Tech	Oliver, Ga. Tech	Ellis, Clemson
1991	Duke	1	N. Carolina	Monroe, N.C. State	Fox, UNC	Odom, Wake
1992	Duke	1	Duke	Laettner, Duke	Laettner, Duke	Kennedy, Fla. State
1993	North Carolina	3	Ga. Tech	Rogers, Wake	Forrest, Ga. Tech	Smith, UNC
1994	Duke	1	N. Carolina	Hill, Duke	Stackhouse, UNC	Odom, Wake
1995	Md., UNC, UVa, Wake	9	Wake Forest	Smith, Md.	Childress, Wake	Odom, Wake
1996	Ga. Tech	4	Wake Forest	Duncan, Wake	Duncan, Wake	Cremins, Ga. Tech
1997	Duke	1	N. Carolina	Duncan, Wake	Williams, UNC	Krzyzewski, Duke
1998	Duke	1	N. Carolina	Jamison, UNC	Jamison, UNC	Guthridge, UNC
1999	Duke	1	Duke	Brand, Duke	Brand, Duke	Krzyzewski, Duke
2000	Duke	1	Duke	Carrawell, Duke	Williams, Duke	Krzyzewski, Duke
2001	Duke & UNC	2	Duke	Battier & Forte	Battier, Duke	Hewitt, Ga. Tech
2002	Maryland	2	Duke	Dixon, Md.	Boozer, Duke	Williams, Md.
2003	Wake Forest	3	Duke	Howard, Wake	Ewing, Duke	Prosser, Wake
2004	Duke	1	Maryland	Hodge, N.C. State	Gilchrist, Md.	Sendek, N.C. State
2005	North Carolina	3	Duke	Redick, Duke	Redick, Duke	Greenberg, Va. Tech
2006	Duke	1	Duke	Redick, Duke	Redick, Duke	Williams, UNC

Duke in Conference Tournament Championship Games

Southern Conference (5 – 11 in 16 finals)

Year	Champion	Runner-up	Final Score	Site		Top Duke Scorer
1929	N.C. State	Duke	44 – 35	Atlanta	12	Croson
1930	Alabama	Duke	31 – 24	Atlanta	10	Werber
1933	South Carolina	Duke	33 – 21	Raleigh	9	J. Thompson, Holbrook
1934	Washington & Lee	Duke	30 – 29	Raleigh	10	J. Thompson
1938	Duke	Clemson	40 – 30	Raleigh	14	Swindell
1940	North Carolina	Duke	39 – 23	Raleigh	6	Price
1941	Duke	South Carolina	53 – 30	Raleigh	16	Holley
1942	Duke	N.C. State	45 – 34	Raleigh	10	Allen
1943	George Washington	Duke	56 – 40	Raleigh	13	C. Loftis
1944	Duke	North Carolina	44 – 27	Raleigh	15	Wright
1945	North Carolina	Duke	49 – 38	Raleigh	13	Carver
1946	Duke	Wake Forest	49 – 30	Raleigh	11	Ausbon, Koffenberger
1948	N.C. State	Duke	58 – 50	Durham	16	Youmans
1950	N.C. State	Duke	67 – 47	Durham	11	Youmans, York
1951	N.C. State	Duke	67 – 63	Raleigh	31	Groat
1952	N.C. State	Duke	77 – 68	Raleigh	27	Groat

Atlantic Coast Conference (16 – 11 in 27 finals)

Year	Champion	Runner-up	Final Score	Site		Top Duke Scorer
1955	No. 1 N.C. State	No. 2 Duke	87 – 77	Raleigh	19	Belmont
1960	No. 4 Duke	No. 2 Wake Forest	63 – 59	Raleigh	22	Kistler
1961	No. 1 Wake Forest	No. 2 Duke	96 – 81	Raleigh	26	Heyman
1963	No. 1 Duke	No. 2 Wake Forest	68 – 57	Raleigh	24	Heyman
1964	No. 1 Duke	No. 2 Wake Forest	80 – 59	Raleigh	24	Mullins
1965	No. 2 N.C. State	No. 1 Duke	91 – 85	Raleigh	25	Verga
1966	No. 1 Duke	No. 2 N.C. State	71 – 66	Raleigh	18	Vacendak
1967	No. 1 North Carolina	No. 2 Duke	82 – 73	Greensboro	20	Verga
1969	No. 1 North Carolina	No. 3 Duke	85 – 74	Charlotte	19	Denton
1978	No. 2 Duke	No. 5 Wake Forest	85 – 77	Greensboro	25	Gminski
1979	No. 1 North Carolina	No. 2 Duke	71 – 63	Greensboro	19	Gminski
1980	No. 6 Duke	No. 1 Maryland	73 – 72	Greensboro	21	Banks
1984	No. 2 Maryland	No. 4 Duke	74 – 62	Greensboro	22	Dawkins
1986	No. 1 Duke	No. 2 Georgia Tech	68 – 67	Greensboro	20	Dawkins
1988	No. 3 Duke	No. 1 North Carolina	65 – 61	Greensboro	19	Ferry

Year	Champion	Runner-up	Final Score	Site		Top Duke Scorer
1989	No. 4 North Carolina	No. 2 Duke	77 – 74	Atlanta	16	Henderson
1991	No. 2 North Carolina	No. 1 Duke	96 – 74	Charlotte	22	Laettner
1992	No. 1 Duke	No. 3 North Carolina	94 – 74	Charlotte	25	Laettner
1998	No. 2 North Carolina	No. 1 Duke	83 – 68	Greensboro	24	McLeod
1999	No. 1 Duke	No. 3 North Carolina	96 – 73	Charlotte	29	Avery
2000	No. 1 Duke	No. 2 Maryland	81 – 68	Charlotte	23	Williams
2001	No. 2 Duke	No. 1 North Carolina	79 – 53	Atlanta	24	Dunleavy
2002	No. 2 Duke	No. 4 N.C. State	91 – 61	Charlotte	26	Boozer
2003	No. 3 Duke	No. 4 N.C. State	84 – 77	Greensboro	30	Redick
2004	No. 6 Maryland	No. 1 Duke	95 – 87 (OT)	Greensboro	21	Duhon
2005	No. 3 Duke	No. 5 Ga. Tech	69 – 64	Washington	26	Redick
2006	No. 1 Duke	No. 3 Boston College	78 – 76	Greensboro	26	Redick

Duke Women in ACC Tournament Championship Games

Atlantic Coast Conference (5 – 3 in 8 finals)

Year	Champion	Runner-up	Final Score	Site	Top Duke Scorer
1995	No. 2 North Carolina	No. 4 Duke	95 – 70	Rock Hill, S.C.	19 Orr
1996	No. 4 Clemson	No. 2 Duke	71 – 54	Rock Hill, S.C.	10 Orr
2000	No. 2 Duke	No. 5 North Carolina	79 – 76	Greensboro	16 Schweitzer, Rice
2001	No. 1 Duke	No. 3 N.C. State	57 – 45	Greensboro	18 Beard
2002	No. 1 Duke	No. 2 North Carolina	87 – 80	Greensboro	30 Currie
2003	No. 1 Duke	No. 2 North Carolina	77 – 59	Greensboro	21 Tillis
2004	No. 1 Duke	No. 2 North Carolina	63 – 47	Greensboro	17 Tillis
2005	No. 1 North Carolina	No. 2 Duke	88 – 67	Greensboro	26 Currie

ACC Women Results Year by Year

Year	Regular Season Champion	Tournament Champion	Player of Year	Tournament MVP	Coach of Year
1978	N.C. State	Maryland		Heiss, Md.	
1979	Maryland	Maryland		Kirchner, Md.	
1980	N.C. State	N.C. State		Beasley, N.C. State	
1981	Clemson	Maryland		Kennedy, Clemson	
1982	Maryland	Maryland		Kennedy & Richardson	
1983	N.C. State	Maryland		Page & Perazic	
1984	Virginia	North Carolina	Brown, UNC	Brown, UNC	Ryan, UVa
1985	N.C. State	N.C. State	Leake, UNC	Royster, UNC	Ryan, UVa
1986	Virginia	Maryland	Leake, UNC	Tate, Md.	Leonard, Duke
1987	Virginia	N.C. State	Moreland, Duke	Holt, UVa	Ryan, UVa
1988	Maryland & Virginia	Maryland	Holt, UVa	Tate, Md.	Sanchez, Wake
1989	Maryland	Maryland	Bullett, Md.	Bullett, Md.	Weller, Md.
1990	N.C. State	Virginia	Stinson, N.C. State	Stinson, N.C. State	Davis, Clemson
1991	Virginia	N.C. State	Staley, UVa	Manning, N.C. State	Ryan, UVa
1992	Virginia	Virginia	Staley, UVa	Staley, UVa	Weller, Md.
1993	Virginia	Virginia	Burge, UVa	Evans, UVa	Ryan, UVa
1994	Virginia	North Carolina	Barr, Clemson	Smith, UNC	Davis, Clemson
1995	Virginia	North Carolina	Palmer, UVa	Smith, UNC	Ryan, UVa
1996	Virginia	Clemson	Palmer, UVa	Cottrell, Clemson	Goestenkors, Duke
1997	North Carolina	North Carolina	Reid, UNC	Jones, UNC	Hatchell, UNC

Year	Regular Season Champion	Tournament Champion	Player of Year	Tournament MVP	Coach of Year
1998	Duke	North Carolina	Reid, UNC	Reid, UNC	Goestenkors, Duke
1999	Duke	Clemson	Erb, N.C. State	Umoh, Clemson	Goestenkors, Duke
2000	Virginia	Duke	Schweitzer, Duke	Teasley, UNC	Ryan, UVa
2001	Duke	Duke	Schweitzer, Duke	Schweitzer, Duke	Semrau, Fla. State
2002	Duke	Duke	Beard, Duke	Currie, Duke	Goestenkors, Duke
2003	Duke	Duke	Beard, Duke	Tillis, Duke	Goestenkors, Duke
2004	Duke	Duke	Beard, Duke	Tillis, Duke	Goestenkors, Duke
2005	Duke & North Carolina	North Carolina	Currie, Duke	Latta, UNC	Semrau Fla. State
2006	North Carolina	North Carolina	Latta, UNC	Latta, UNC	Hatchell, UNC

Statistics for Duke Players in Professional Basketball

This section includes statistics for former Duke players who moved on to professional basketball in the National Basketball Association (NBA) or the American Basketball Association (ABA), with the number of seasons played in each league (through 2006).

Years	Games	FG	FGA	Pct	FT	FTA	Pct	Reb	Ast	Pts	Avg
Alaa Abdelnaby 1991 – 95											
NBA 5	256	620	1,236	50.2	225	321	70.1	846	85	1,465	5.7
Mark Alarie 1987 – 91											
NBA 5	325	1,037	2,184	47.5	324	418	77.5	1,120	363	2,432	7.5
Tate Armstrong 1978, 1979											
NBA 2	92	159	350	45.4	32	40	80.0	88	105	350	3.8
William Avery 2000 – 02											
NBA 3	142	137	415	33.0	65	91	71.4	199	125	379	2.7
Gene Banks 1982 – 87											
NBA 6	468	2,134	3,961	53.9	1,035	1,418	73.0	2,718	1,335	5,305	11.3
Shane Battier 2002 – 06											
NBA 5	396	1,503	3,307	45.4	765	1,028	74.4	1,908	684	4,160	10.5
Carlos Boozer 2003 – 06											
NBA 4	240	1,382	2,610	53.0	653	882	74.0	2,208	486	3,418	14.2
Elton Brand 2000 – 06											
NBA 7	526	4,060	8,098	50.1	2,549	3,472	73.4	5,458	1,386	10,670	20.3
Mark Crow 1978											
NBA 1	15	35	80	43.8	14	20	70.0	27	8	84	5.6
Brian Davis 1994											
NBA 1	68	40	126	31.7	50	68	73.5	55	22	131	1.9
Johnny Dawkins 1987 – 95											
NBA 9	541	2,361	5,175	45.6	1,082	1,262	85.7	1,336	2,997	5,984	11.1
Luol Deng 2005 – 06											
NBA 2	139	722	1,599	45.2	327	438	74.7	838	282	1,823	13.1
Kenny Dennard 1982 – 84											
NBA 3	95	109	254	42.9	47	73	64.4	286	93	268	2.8

Years	Games	FG	FGA	Pct	FT	FTA	Pct	Reb	Ast	Pts	Avg
Randy Denton 1972–77											
ABA 5	368	1,932	4,047	47.7	643	821	78.3	3,329	495	4,510	12.3
NBA 1	45	103	256	40.2	33	47	70.2	218	33	239	5.3
Chris Duhon 2005–06											
NBA 2	156	387	1,026	37.7	166	210	79.0	433	771	1,134	7.3
Mike Dunleavy 2003–06											
NBA 4	317	1,230	2,858	43.0	545	709	76.9	1,490	766	3,332	10.5
Daniel Ewing 2006											
NBA 1	66	97	255	38.0	36	46	78.3	85	84	252	3.8
Danny Ferry 1991–2003											
NBA 13	917	2,505	5,615	44.6	752	895	84.0	2,550	1,185	6,439	7.0
Bob Gantt 1947											
NBA 1	23	29	89	32.6	13	28	46.4		5	71	3.1
Mike Gminski 1981–94											
NBA 14	938	4,208	9,047	46.5	2,531	3,002	84.3	6,480	1,203	10,953	11.7
Dick Groat 1953											
NBA 1	26	100	272	36.8	109	138	79.0	86	69	309	11.9
David Henderson 1988											
NBA 1	22	47	116	40.5	32	47	68.1	35	34	126	5.7
Art Heyman 1964–70											
ABA 3	163	854	1,996	42.8	731	1,021	71.6	1,047	513	2,511	15.4
NBA 3	147	564	1,322	42.7	391	576	67.9	414	346	1,519	10.3
Grant Hill 1995–2005											
NBA 10	570	4,281	8,932	47.9	3,114	4,113	75.7	4,171	3,199	11,739	20.6
Bobby Hurley 1994–98											
NBA 5	269	361	1,023	35.3	246	320	76.9	283	880	1,032	3.8
Dahntay Jones 2004–06											
NBA 3	143	207	506	40.9	109	168	64.9	196	72	550	3.8
Joe Kennedy 1969–71											
ABA 1	82	189	498	38.0	130	160	81.3	341	73	508	6.2
NBA 2	86	177	475	37.3	100	126	79.4	261	67	454	5.3
Doug Kistler 1962											
NBA 1	5	3	6	50.0	2	4	50.0	1	0	8	1.6
Christian Laettner 1993–2005											
NBA 12	868	4,036	8,045	48.0	2,957	3,604	82.0	5,806	2,224	11,121	12.8

Years	Games	FG	FGA	Pct	FT	FTA	Pct	Reb	Ast	Pts	Avg
Antonio Lang 1995–2000											
NBA 6	143	121	266	45.5	87	121	71.9	210	50	329	2.3
Trajan Langdon 2000–2002											
NBA 3	119	220	529	41.6	121	133	91.0	159	152	647	5.4
Mike Lewis 1969–74											
ABA 6	337	1,613	3,239	49.8	855	1,164	73.5	4,022	1,000	4,081	12.1
Corey Maggette 2000–06											
NBA 7	444	2,072	4,633	44.7	2,246	2,738	82.0	2,140	893	6,668	15.0
Jack Marin 1967–77											
NBA 11	849	5,068	10,890	46.5	2,405	2,852	84.3	4,405	1,813	12,541	14.8
Roshown McLeod 1999–2001											
NBA 3	113	338	827	40.9	136	166	81.9	308	124	817	7.2
Gary Melchionni 1974, 1975											
NBA 2	137	434	978	44.4	206	248	83.1	329	298	1,074	7.8
Jeff Mullins 1965–76											
NBA 12	804	5,383	11,631	46.3	2,251	2,764	81.4	3,427	3,023	13,017	16.2
Martin Nessley 1988											
NBA 1	44	20	52	38.5	8	18	44.4	82	16	48	1.1
Cherokee Parks 1996–2004											
NBA 9	472	868	1,848	47.0	312	495	63.0	1,703	265	2,056	4.4
Shavlik Randolph 2006											
NBA 1	57	44	97	45.4	43	71	60.6	133	19	131	2.3
Bob Riedy 1968											
ABA 1	23	45	129	34.9	41	67	61.2	68	5	131	5.7
Jim Spanarkel 1980–84											
NBA 5	259	844	1,796	47.0	805	941	85.5	652	572	2,505	9.7
Vince Taylor 1983											
NBA 1	31	37	102	36.3	21	32	65.6	36	41	95	3.1
Steve Vacendak 1968–70											
ABA 3	83	316	810	39.0	190	252	75.4	238	194	824	9.9
Bob Verga 1968–74											
ABA 5	321	2,572	5,871	43.8	1,543	2,054	75.1	1,318	987	6,814	21.2
NBA 1	21	42	93	45.2	20	32	62.5	18	17	104	5.0
Jason Williams 2003											
NBA 1	75	273	685	39.9	103	161	64.0	195	350	714	9.5

Jersey Numbers of Duke Men

The following is a list of jersey numbers used by Duke men's basketball players since 1947; a few earlier players are included as well.

Under current NCAA rules, a player's number must include only digits between 0 and 5.

2 Josh McRoberts
Luol Deng
Andre Buckner

3 Greg Paulus
Nick Horvath
Justin Caldbeck
Ricky Price
Marty Clark
Phil Henderson

4 J. J. Redick
Carlos Boozer
Roshown McLeod
Kenny Blakeney
Tommy Amaker
Bernard Pergrem

5 Martynas Pocius
Daniel Ewing
Ryan Caldbeck
William Avery
Jeff Capel
Ron Burt
Billy McCaffrey
Larry Ashley
Bob Duff

10 Dick Groat
(number retired)
Doug Ausbon

11 Bobby Hurley
(number retired)
Doug McNeely
Jim Corrigan
Rick Gomez
Edgar Burch
Zeno Edwards
Bob Verga
Fred Schmidt
Johnny Morris
Bob Vernon
Don Cashman
Dick Brewer
Tom Peters
Bill Downing
Dave Scarborough

12 Jordan Davidson
Andre Sweet
Steve Wojciechowski
Thomas Hill
David Henderson
Vince Taylor
Tate Armstrong
Richie O'Connor
Tony Barone
Frank Harscher
Jack Boyd
Bob Thuemmel
Don Cashman
Bill Martin
Scotty York

13 Lee Melchionni
Andy Means
J. D. Simpson

Taymon Domzalski
Joe Cook
Brent Kitching
Don Miller
Tony Buhowsky
Herky Lamley

14 David McClure
Nate James
Kenney Brown
Quin Snyder
Vince Crump
Chip Engelland
Rob Hardy
Willie Hodge
Bill Zimmer
Scott Williamson
Jerry Robertson
Don Tobin
Kes Deimling
Ceep Youmans

15 Sean Dockery
Andre Buckner
Ryan Caldbeck
Todd Singleton
Bruce Bell
Pat Doughty
Bob Riedy
Burton Fitts
Fred Kast
Paul Schmidt
Jim Rogers
Rudy D'Emilio
John Engberg
Bill Armour

20 Casey Sanders
D. Bryant
Mike Chappell

Chris Collins
Gene Banks
Dave O'Connell
Larry Saunders
Dave Golden
Denny Ferguson
Jack Mullen
Larry Bateman
Dick Rosenthal
Bernie Janicki
Jim Kulpan
Buck Cheek
Bill Fleming
Pat Lyons

21 DeMarcus Nelson
Chris Duhon
Trajan Langdon
Antonio Lang
Robert Brickey
Jay Bilas
Gordon Whitted
Bob Bender
Kenny Young
Jeff Burdette
Dick DeVenzio
Stuart McKaig
Roger Hamilton
Howard Hurt
Ed Bryson
Rudy Lacy
John Engberg
Harold Hibbitts
Wes Skibsted

22 Jason Williams
(number retired)
Jay Heaps
Greg Koubek
Andy Berndt

Tom Emma

John Harrell

Paul Fox

Rick Katherman

Rob Wendelin

Bob Riedy

Jay Buckley

Bill Watson

Bobby Joe Harris

Tom Blackburn

Marv Decker

Dayton Allen

Scotty York

23 Shelden Williams

Chris Carrawell

Brian Davis

Richard Ford

Larry Linney

Steve Gray

Bill Suk

C. B. Claiborne

Dick Warren

Elliott McBride

Ray Cox

Carroll Youngkin

Don Miller

Marty Doherty

Dick Latimer

Buck Simmons

24 Johnny Dawkins

(number retired)

Harold Morrison

Kevin Billerman

Jeff Dawson

Jack Marin

John Cantwell

Marty Joyce

Jim Newcome

Tom Blackburn

Don Cashman

Dick Johnson

Peter Johnson

Wes Skibsted

25 Thomas Hill

Greg Wendt

Mark Crow

Gary Melchionni

Art Heyman

(number retired)

Bob Wayand

Joe Marcovechio

Don Sims

Jake Tarr

Charlie Driesell

C. B. Johnson

Bob Strauss

30 Joe Pagliuca

Reggie Love

Dahntay Jones

Andy Borman

J. D. Simpson

Tony Moore

Alaa Abdelnaby

Jim Suddath

Rob Hardy

Rick Mainwaring

William Hannon

Robby West

Buzzy Harrison

John Frye

Bobby Joe Harris

Joe Belmont

31 Shane Battier

(number retired)

Justin Caldbeck

Stan Brunson

Kevin Strickland

Mike Tissaw

Randy Denton

Tim Kolodziej

Hack Tison

Doug Albright

Hayes Clement

Bill Reigel

Bill Fleming

Jack Lasseter

32 Christian Laettner

(number retired)

Mark Alarie

Geoff Northrup

Ron Righter

Brad Evans

Jim Liccardo

Merrill Morgan

Bob Lakata

Charlie Driesell

Carl Glasow

Lloyd Caudle

33 Grant Hill

(number retired)

John Smith

Jay Bryan

Kenny Dennard

Randy Abernathy

Doug Jackson

Steve Vacendak

Bob Jamieson

Larry Bateman

Jim Newcome

Junior Morgan

Dick Crowder

34 Jamal Boykin

Mike Dunleavy

Chris Burgess

Carmen Wallace

Crawford Palmer

Dave Colonna

Bill Jackman

Loel Payne

Jim Spanarkel

Bob Cook

Judge Carr

Tim Teer

Buzzy Harrison

Fred Cox

Doug Kistler

Jack Kalbfus

Fred Shabel

Rod Boyce

35 Danny Ferry

(number retired)

Cameron Hall

Phil McLeod

Stu Yarbrough

Phil Allen

Buzz Mewhort

George Barrett

Ronnie Mayer

40 Ross Perkins

Andy Borman

Taymon Domzalski

Weldon Williams

Neil Chinault

Steve Litz

Joe Kennedy

Tom Gebbie

Jay Beal

Bucky Allen

Sammy Rothbaum

Wright

Hollingsworth

Cedric Loftis

John Heath

41 Patrick Davidson

Matt Christensen

Jon Goodman

Allen Williams

Ray Kuhlmeier

Doug Kistler

Tom Peters

Irving Gray

Kenny Turner

Bill Parsons

42 Shavlik Randolph

Reggie Love

Elton Brand

Joey Beard

George Burgin

Ned Franke

Bob Fleischer

Don Blackman

Mike Lewis
Fred Cox
Hal Turner
Garland Loftis
Bill Flentye
Billy Huiskamp

43 Mike Gminski
(number retired)
Terry Chili
John Posen
Bill Ulrich
Ed Koffenberger
Harry Harner
Bill Mock

44 Cherokee Parks
Phil Henderson
Todd Anderson
Scott Goetsch
Pete Kramer

Jeff Mullins
(number retired)
Doug Ausbon
Richard Gilbert
Ray Spuhler

45 Eric Boateng
Joe Pagliuca
Mark Causey
Clay Buckley
Dan Meagher
Ted Mann Jr.
Sammy Rothbaum
Eddie Shokes
Charles Kunkle

50 Tom Novick
Michael Thompson
Corey Maggette
Rey Essex
Alan Shaw

Glen Smiley
Wes Skibsted
Bob Gantt
Jim Bowman
Albert Herrick

51 Patrick Johnson
Martin Nessley
Dave Elmer
Cy Valasek
Ken Podger

52 Erik Meek
Steve Vandenberg
Terry Murray
Bob Moyer
Tom Wallingford
Eugene Bledsoe
Bob Wood

53 Andy Means
George Moses
Chris Redding
Fred Lind
Glenn Price
Ace Parker

54 Christian Ast
Warren Chapman
Clyde Allen
Fred Edwards

55 Greg Newton
Billy King
Allen Williams
Ron Herbster
Chuck Holley

All-Time Letter Winners, Duke Women

Paula Andersen 1985, 1986, 1987, 1988
Missy Anderson 1991, 1992, 1993, 94

Robin Baker 1989, 1990, 1991, 1992
Alison Bales 2004, 2005, 2006
Alana Beard 2001, 2002, 2003, 2004
Betsy Bergeron 1976, 1977, 1978, 1979
Chante Black 2005, 2006
Payton Black 1996, 1997, 1998, 1999
Zeki Blanding 1992, 1993, 1994, 1995
Joanne Boyle 1982, 1983, 1984, 1985
Susan Brandau 1992, 1993, 1994, 1995
Katie Brodnik 1996, 1997
LaNedra Brown 2000, 2001
Shaeeta Brown 1994, 1995, 1997, 1998
Peppi Browne 1997, 1998, 1999, 2000
Liz Bulger 1977, 1978, 1979

Tracy Carter 1989
Jennifer Chestnut 1981, 1982, 1983, 1984
Tracey Christopher 1986, 1987, 1988, 1989
Windsor Coggeshall 1994, 1995, 1996, 1997
Heather Conway 1981
Jennifer Copeland 1982
Rometra Craig 2001
Monique Currie 2002, 2004, 2005, 2006

Ali Day 1993, 1994, 1995, 1996

Leslie Earnhardt 1979, 1980
Ruth Ellis 1978
Nicole Erickson 1998, 1999
Valerie Evans 1991, 1992, 1993, 1994

Jessica Foley 2003, 2004, 2005, 2006
Jennifer Forte 1997, 1998, 1999
Kathy Friend 1978

Carrem Gay 2006
Lello Gebisa 2000, 2001
Krista Gingrich 1999, 2000, 2001, 2002
Carol Giordano 1978
Connie Goins 1983 1984, 1985, 1986
Jeanne Griffin 1979
Olga Gvozdenovic 2000, 2001

Tyish Hall 1994, 1995, 1996, 1997
Lynne Hanrahan 1986
Lindsey Harding 2003, 2004, 2006
Jo Harlow 1981, 1982, 1983, 1984
Sue Harnett 1987, 1988, 1989, 1991
Allison Hart 1983, 1984, 1985
Maureen Hathorn 1978
Janee Hayes 1999, 2000, 2001
Ada Healey 1981
Juanita Hepburn 1996, 1997, 1998
Maura Hertzog 1982, 1983, 1984, 1985
Hilary Howard 1996, 1997, 1998, 1999
Caitlin Howe 2004
Brittany Hunter 2004
Kim Hunter 1984, 1985, 1986, 1987
Stacy Hurd 1981, 1982, 1983, 1984

Keturah Jackson 2006

Brittany James 1989
Joy James 1976
Nicole Johnson 1991, 1992, 1993, 1994
Takisha Jones 1996, 1997, 1998, 1999

Rita Kalinowski 1985, 1986, 1987
Carey Kauffman 1992, 1993, 1994, 1995
Laurie Koffenberger 1976, 1977
Monika Kost 1988, 1990, 1991, 1992
Jenni Kraft 1989
Vicki Krapohl 2001, 2002, 2003, 2004
Barb Krause 1979, 1980, 1981
Laura Kurz 2005, 2006

Ellen Langhi 1986, 1987, 1988, 1989
Celeste Lavoie 1991, 1992
Laurie Layman 1976
Sue Leonard 1979
Mary Lockey 1977, 1978

Pam Markiewicz 1979, 1980
Kalita Marsh 2004
Kim Matthews 1979, 1980, 1981, 1982
Michele Matyasovsky 2000, 2001, 2002, 2003
Tara McCarthy 1978, 1979, 1980
Dana McDonald 1990, 1991, 1992, 1993
Pam McFarland 1989, 1990, 1991, 1992
Jennifer McGinnis 1995
Heather McKaig 1991, 1992, 1993
Jackie McKisson 1990
Nazrawit Medhanie 1996, 1997, 1998, 1999

Katie Meier 1986, 1987, 1988, 1990

Kristina Meiman 1992, 1993, 1994, 1995

Candy Mikels 1982, 1983, 1984, 1985

Brittany Mitch 2006

Sue Monroe 1979, 1980

Chris Moreland 1985, 1986, 1987, 1988

Dana Morgan 2004

Leigh Morgan 1987, 1988, 1989, 1990

Sheana Mosch 2000, 2001, 2002, 2003

Kira Orr 1994, 1995, 1996, 1997

Rochelle Parent 1998, 1999, 2000, 2001

Marcy Peterson 1989, 1990

Mary Ann Puckett 1994

Kathy Radabaugh 1986

Holly Reid 1980, 1981

Lauren Rice 1997, 1998, 1999, 2000

Teri Rodgers 1988, 1989, 1990

Jennifer Rokus 1980

Claire Rose 1980, 1981, 1982, 1983

Jennifer Scanlon 1993, 1994, 1995, 1996

Georgia Schweitzer 1998, 1999, 2000, 2001

Brooke Smith 2003

Wanisha Smith 2005, 2006

Carolyn Sonzogni 1984, 1985, 1986, 1987

Alice Steuby 1990

Sarah Sullivan 1983, 1985, 1986, 1987

Sigrid Taylor 1977

Kathy Tenney 1981

Patti Thomasson 1980, 1981

Iciss Tillis 2001, 2002, 2003, 2004

Michele VanGorp 1998, 1999

Margo Walsh 1980, 1981, 1982, 1983

Patty Walsh 1976, 1977

Abby Waner 2006

Emily Waner 2006

Lisa Warren 1977, 1978, 1979, 1980

Susan Weeks 1985

Missy West 1997, 1999, 2000, 2001

Crystal White 2001

Wynter Whitley 2002, 2003, 2004, 2005

Mistie (Bass) Williams 2003, 2004, 2005, 2006

Traci Williams 1988, 1989, 1990, 1991

Shannon Wills 1990, 1991, 1992

Bibliography

Research Sources

Barrier, Smith. *On Tobacco Road: Basketball in North Carolina*. New York: Leisure Press, 1983.

Brill, Bill. *Duke Basketball: An Illustrated History*. Dallas: Taylor Publishing, 1986.

Brill, Bill. *One Hundred Seasons: Duke Basketball, A Legacy of Achievement*. Champaign, Ill.: Sports Publishing, 2004.

Brill, Bill, and Mike Krzyzewski. *A Season Is a Lifetime: The Inside Story of the Duke Blue Devils and Their Championship Seasons*. New York: Simon and Schuster, 1993.

Cragg, Mike. *Back to Back: The Story of Duke's 1992 NCAA Basketball Championship*. Durham: Duke University, 1992.

Cragg, Mike, and Mike Sobb. *Crowning Glory: The Story of Duke's 1991 NCAA Championship Season*. Durham: Duke University, 1991.

DeCourcy, Mike. *The Sporting News Selects Legends of College Basketball*. New York: McGraw-Hill, 2002.

Feinstein, John. *Forever's Team*. New York: Villard, 1989.

Fulks, Matt. *The Sportscaster's Dozen: Off the Air with Southeastern Legends*. Lincolnwood, Ill.: Masters, 1998.

Jackson, Jon. *Championship Dance: A Celebration of Duke Basketball's Title Season*. Durham: Duke University, 2001.

Jacobs, Barry. *Coach K's Little Blue Book: Lessons from College Basketball's Best Coach*. Kingston, N.Y.: Total Sports Publishing, 2000.

Jacobs, Barry. *Golden Glory: The First 50 Years of the ACC*. Greensboro: Mann Media, 2002.

Johnson, Gary, Sean Straziscar, and J. D. Hamilton. *NCAA Men's Basketball Record Book*. Indianapolis: National Collegiate Athletic Association, 2005.

King, William E. *If Gargoyles Could Talk: Sketches of Duke University*. Durham: Carolina Academic Press, 1997.

Krzyzewski, Mike, with Donald T. Phillips. *Five-Point Play: Duke's Journey to the 2001 National Championship*. New York: Warner, 2001.

Krzyzewski, Mike, with Donald T. Phillips. *Leading with the Heart: Coach K's Successful Strategies for Basketball, Business, and Life*. New York: Warner, 2000.

Landwehr, Hazel. *Home Court: Fifty Years of Cameron Indoor Stadium*. Durham: Phoenix Communications, 1989.

McKinney, Bones, with Garland Atkins. *Bones: Honk Your Horn If You Love Basketball*. New York: Garland, 1988.

Moore, Johnny, John Roth, Bill Brill, and Jim Sumner. *Blue Devil Weekly*, vols. 1–15. Durham: Moore Productions, 1991–2006.

Powell, William S., ed. *Dictionary of North Carolina Biography*, vols. 1–6. Chapel Hill: University of North Carolina Press, 1979–96.

Prouty, John C., ed. *The ACC Basketball Stat Book*. Huntingtown, Md.: Willow Oak, 1993, 1999.

Shouler, Ken, Bob Ryan, Sam Smith, Leonard Koppett, and Bob Bellotti. *Total Basketball: The Ultimate Basketball Encyclopedia*. Wilmington, Del.: Sport Media, 2003.

Werber, Bill, and C. Paul Rogers III. *Memories of a Ballplayer*. Cleveland: Society for American Baseball Research, 2001.

Other Reference Materials

Alumni Register of Duke University
Chanticleer (Duke yearbook)
Chronicle (Duke student newspaper)
Durham Morning Herald
Durham Sun
News & Observer (Raleigh)

Other Books about Duke Basketball

Barrier, Smith. *The ACC Basketball Tournament Classic*. Greensboro: Greensboro Publications, 1981.

Blythe, Will. *To Hate like This Is to Be Happy Forever: A Thoroughly Obsessive, Intermittently Uplifting, and Occasionally Unbiased Account of the Duke-North Carolina Basketball Rivalry*. New York: Harper Collins, 2006.

Chansky, Art. *Blue Blood: Duke-Carolina: Inside the Most Storied Rivalry in College Hoops*. New York: St. Martin's, 2005.

Corrie, Bruce. *The Atlantic Coast Conference, 1953–1978*. Durham: Carolina Academic Press, 1978.

Dinin, Aaron. *The Krzyzewskiville Tales*. Durham: Duke University Press, 2005.

Doyel, Gregg. *Coach K: Building the Duke Dynasty*. Lenexa, Kan.: Addax, 1999.

Feinstein, John. *A March to Madness: The View from the Floor in the Atlantic Coast Conference*. Boston: Little, Brown, 1998.

Jacobs, Barry. *Three Paths to Glory: A Season on the Hardwood with Duke, N.C. State and North Carolina*. New York: Macmillan, 1993.

Menzer, Joe. *Four Corners: How UNC, N.C. State, Duke and Wake Forest Made North Carolina the Crossroads of the Basketball Universe.* New York: Simon and Schuster, 1999.

Morris, Ron. *ACC Basketball: An Illustrated History.* Chapel Hill: Four Corners, 1998.

Sumner, Jim. *Tales from the Duke Blue Devils Hardwood.* Champaign, Ill.: Sports Publishing, 2005.

Weiss, Dick. *True Blue: A Tribute to Mike Krzyzewski's Career at Duke.* Champaign, Ill.: Sports Publishing, 2005.

John Roth is vice-president of Moore Productions, editor of *Blue Devil Weekly*, sports announcer for the Duke Radio Network, and a basketball columnist. A native of Cincinnati, he graduated from Duke in 1980 with a degree in anthropology and worked in the school's sports information office from 1982 through 1990, the last five years as director.

Library of Congress Cataloging-in-Publication Data

Roth, John, 1957 –

The encyclopedia of Duke basketball / John Roth ; with photographs by Ned Hinshaw.

p. cm.

Includes bibliographical references.

ISBN-13: 978-0-8223-3904-5 (cloth : alk. paper)

ISBN-10: 0-8223-3904-8 (cloth : alk. paper)

1. Duke University — Basketball — History — 20th century. 2. Duke Blue Devils (Basketball team) — History — 20th century. 3. Basketball teams — North Carolina — History — 20th century. 4. Sports rivalries — North Carolina — History — 20th century. 5. NCAA Basketball Tournament. I. Title.

GV885.43.D85R68 2006

796.323'6309756563 — dc22   2006014256